The New York Times reviews
"the ultimate inside story"
on
The New York Times . . .

"This is a different kind of book. It is done in the
novelistic style of Truman Capote, William Manchester, and Theodore White, moving real contemporary men through real contemporary events
. . . But this is not just another book about organization men scheming to reach the top . . . It is a
fascinating book, compelling for those addicted to
newspapers, and for anyone else who lets himself
get caught up in the interplay of the characters,
whether or not he recognizes the bylines . . .
[Talese's] writing is lively, aided by an eye for irreverent detail that reminds you constantly that
this is not an official biography . . . Seldom has
anyone been so successful in making a newspaper
come alive as a human institution."
—The New York Times Book Review

THE KINGDOM AND THE POWER
"combines the documentary quality of Arthur Hailey's institutional epics *Airport* and *Hotel* with the ambitious maneuvering of Cameron Hawley's *Executive Suite*."

—**Time**

"Reads like the most exciting novel of the year."
—**Cosmopolitan**

"Far and away the best book about an American newspaper ever published and possibly the best ever written about any newspaper . . ."
—John Barkham, **Saturday Review Syndicate**

"An epic work . . . Rich in anecdote, intimate in detail, the book puts on parade a fascinating parade of personalities . . . a superb study of people and power . . ."
—**Women's Wear Daily**

"An amazing amalgam of gossip, fact, history, and inside stuff made eminently entertaining . . ."
—**Saturday Review**

GAY TALESE has written
"the *Peyton Place* of
journalism"*

"If Mr. Talese is not overly flattering to his subjects, he is only following the best traditions of journalism taught him at the *Times*...Refreshing."
—Wall Street Journal

"Talese is a romantic who can find glamour in that drab factory on 43rd Street and excitement in dissecting its cautious managers."
—The New Republic

"He has done something for his subjects which they could not do for themselves and done it superlatively well."
—Murray Kempton, **Life**

*Chicago Daily News

THE KINGDOM AND THE POWER
by Gay Talese

A NATIONAL GENERAL COMPANY

*This low-priced Bantam Book
has been completely reset in a type face
designed for easy reading, and was printed
from new plates. It contains the complete
text of the original hard-cover edition.*
NOT ONE WORD HAS BEEN OMITTED.

THE KINGDOM AND THE POWER

PRINTING HISTORY

World Publishing Company edition published June 1969
2nd printing....September 1969   4th printing......October 1969
3rd printing......October 1969   5th printing....November 1969

Book-of-the-Month Club edition published 1969

Some of the material in this book appeared originally in a different
form, some in exactly the same form—between 1966 and 1969—in
ESQUIRE *and* HARPER'S *magazines, to whose editors the author is very
grateful. A fuller explanation about the book and how it was researched will be found in the Author's Note that follows the final
chapter.*

Bantam edition published May 1970
2nd printing

*Bantam Books are published by Bantam Books, Inc., a National
General company. Its trade-mark, consisting of the words "Bantam
Books" and the portrayal of a bantam, is registered in the United
States Patent Office and in other countries. Marca Registrada.
Bantam Books, Inc., 666 Fifth Avenue, New York, N.Y. 10019*

for NAN

THE KINGDOM
AND THE POWER

1

MOST journalists are restless voyeurs who see the warts on the world, the imperfections in people and places. The sane scene that is much of life, the great portion of the planet unmarked by madness, does not lure them like riots and raids, crumbling countries and sinking ships, bankers banished to Rio and burning Buddhist nuns—gloom is their game, the spectacle their passion, normality their nemesis.

Journalists travel in packs with transferable tension and they can only guess to what extent their presence in large numbers ignites an incident, turns people on. For press conferences and cameras and microphones have become such an integral part of the happenings of our time that nobody today knows whether people make news or news makes people—General Ky in Vietnam, feeling no doubt more potent after his sixth magazine-cover story, challenges Red China; after police in New York raided the headquarters of young hoodlums, it was discovered that some gang leaders keep scrapbooks; in Baltimore, a day after the Huntley-Brinkley Report mentioned that the city had survived the summer without a race riot, there was a race riot. When the press is absent, politicians have been known to cancel their speeches, civil rights marchers to postpone their parades, alarmists to withhold their dire predictions. The troops at the Berlin Wall, largely ignored since Vietnam stole the headlines, coexist casually, watching the girls go by.

News, if unreported, has no impact. It might as well have not happened at all. Thus the journalist is the im-

portant ally of the ambitious, he is a lamplighter for
stars. He is invited to parties, is courted and complimented, has easy access to unlisted telephone numbers
and to many levels of life. He may send to America a
provocative story of poverty in Africa, of tribal threats
and turmoil—and then he may go for a swim in the
ambassador's pool. A journalist will sometimes mistakenly assume that it is his charm, not his usefulness,
that gains such privilege; but most journalists are realistic men not fooled by the game. They use as well as
they are used. Still they are restless. Their work, instantly published, is almost instantly forgotten, and
they must endlessly search for something new, must
stay alive with by-lines and not be scooped, must nur-
ture the insatiable appetites of newspapers and networks, the commercial cravings for new faces, fashions,
fads, feuds; they must not worry when news seems to
be happening *because* they are there, nor must they
ponder the possibility that everything they have witnessed and written in their lifetime may someday occupy only a few lines in the plastic textbooks of the
twenty-first century.

And so each day, unhaunted by history, plugged into
the *instant*, journalists of every creed, quality, and
quirk report the news of the world as they see it, hear
it, believe it, understand it. Then much of it is relayed
through America, millions of words a minute, some
thousands of which penetrate a large fourteen-floor fact
factory on Forty-third Street off Broadway, *The New
York Times* building, where each weekday afternoon at
four o'clock—before it is fit to print, before it can influence the State Department and perplex the President
and irritate David Merrick and get the ball rolling on
Wall Street and heads rolling in the Congo—it is presented by *Times* editors seated around a conference
table to one man, the managing editor, Clifton Daniel.

He is a most interesting-looking man but difficult to
describe because the words that quickly catch him best,
initially, seem entirely inappropriate for any man who
is a man. But the impression persists. Clifton Daniel
is almost lovely. It is his face, which is long and pale

and soft and dominated by large dark eyes and very long lashes, and his exquisitely groomed, wavy gray hair that makes him seem almost lovely. His suits are very Savile Row, his hands and nails immaculate, his voice a soft, smooth blend of North Carolina, where he was born in a tiny tobacco town, and England, where he came of age as a journalist and squire of fashionable women and was sometimes referred to as the Sheik of Fleet Street. London in those days, during and just after World War II, was a great city for young American journalists. There was a feeling of warmth and common purpose with the British, a romantic bond built during the blackout and bombing raids; British society was democratic at every level, and if an American journalist, particularly a well-tailored bachelor, also possessed, as did Clifton Daniel, a certain formality and reserve and understated charm—Tory manners that in Daniel's case were partly cultivated out of a small-town Southern boy's shyness—then London could be an even more responsive city, and for Daniel it was. He was sought out by London hostesses, was often seen escorting distinguished women to the theater and ballet, and he generally avoided the men's clubs for the drawing-room scene where, sometimes in the company of Bea Lillie and Noel Coward, Margot Fonteyn and Clarissa Spencer-Churchill, who later married Anthony Eden, he could listen to the latest gossip about politics and people as he had many years before when he worked behind the fountain of his father's drugstore in Zebulon, North Carolina.

Today it is difficult to imagine Clifton Daniel, even as a boy, in a drugstore setting. His style of cool elegance, the courtly way in which he conducts corporate matters at *The New York Times*, the ease with which he occasionally rejects a bottle of vintage wine at the Oak Room of the Plaza, all suggest that he is a man bred from the very beginning into a world of privilege and power. And this impression, this outer layer of Daniel, his London layer, is all that is seen by most of his subordinate editors and colleagues on *The New York Times*. They rarely socialize with him outside the of-

fice, and so their closest personal contact with him is
the news conference held in his office each weekday
afternoon at four o'clock, and not a moment later.

It is now 3:40. It is a sunny afternoon in early summer and Daniel sits in his large office off the busy newsroom on the third floor of the *Times* building. He had
arrived at *The Times* in the morning feeling relaxed and
looking well, the beginnings of a deep suntan obscuring
the circles under his eyes and accentuating the silver in
his long wavy hair. He and his wife, the former Margaret Truman, had rented a summer home with a pool
near Bedford Village, a somewhat exclusive and quiet
community in New York State with plenty of trees and
space and unpaved country roads for horsemen and
with none of the frantic entertaining that Margaret and
Clifton Daniel try to avoid in Manhattan but not always can. They had married relatively late—she was
thirty-two, he forty-three—and by that time they had
both enjoyed the full fling of freedom and were ready
to settle down. Margaret especially wanted privacy,
having had little of it as a girl in Washington, and later
she had to contend with rumors of her engagement to
almost every man she dated more than a few times.
The report that she had been a summer houseguest in
1955 of the bachelor Governor of New Jersey, Robert
Meyner, was news that even *The Times* could not resist, but later that year she met Clifton Daniel.

She had been out to a dinner party, and afterward
at the urging of her escort they stopped in at another
party at the home of Mrs. George Backer, a friend of
Daniel's from the war years in London. Daniel had
recently returned from a foreign assignment in Moscow,
but at this point in 1955 he had given up reporting
and had begun to move up the executive ladder of *The
Times*. He had been introduced to Margaret by Mrs.
Backer that night, and to this day he can remember
very sharply the smallest details. He can remember the
way Margaret wore her hair, her shoes, her wonderful
complexion, never suggested in her photographs, and
the dark blue Fontana dress with the plunging neckline,

he not resisting the temptation of looking downward and being impressed with what he saw. They conversed in the corner for a good while that night, Daniel telling Margaret that if she, the daughter of a prominent political figure, had been reared in Russia she would be practically unknown because the politicians there shun publicity for their families. This interested her, and he continued to talk in his worldly way, and before she left he had made a date for lunch. Five months later, in the spring of 1956, in an Episcopal church in Independence, Missouri, where Margaret had once sung in the choir, they were married.

Now, ten years and four sons later, Margaret and Clifton Daniel were enjoying the summer in Bedford, and Daniel was enjoying a new sense of being somebody other than Harry Truman's son-in-law. Daniel was finally getting singular recognition as an important figure in journalism. Magazine articles had recently featured him, he had just made the new edition of *Current Biography*, and a speech he had delivered a month ago to the World Press Institute, a speech about a tense scene within the *Times* building prior to the Bay of Pigs invasion of Cuba, received nearly a full page of coverage in *The Times* itself. It had been a remarkable speech. It told of *Times* editors fuming and disagreeing with one another over how the preinvasion story should be played on the front page on that particular evening in 1961. Originally, Daniel recalled, the story had been scheduled for the lead position on page one. But then the publisher of *The Times*, Orvil Dryfoos, following the advice of his close friend James Reston, ordered the story toned down, moved to a less prominent place on the page, its headline minimized, and any reference to the imminence of the invasion eliminated. It was in the national interest to withhold certain vital facts from the American people, including the CIA involvement, Dryfoos and Reston felt, but other *Times* editors strongly disagreed. One of them, according to Daniel's speech, became so infuriated that he quivered with emotion and turned "dead white" and demanded that Dryfoos himself come down from the publisher's office and personally order *The Times'* self-censorship. Dryfoos did, justifying it on grounds of national security and concern for the safety of the men preparing to offer their lives on the beaches of Cuba. But after the invasion had failed, Daniel said in his speech, even President Kennedy conceded that perhaps *The Times* had been overly protective of American interests; if *The Times* had printed all it knew about the Cuban venture beforehand, Kennedy suggested, the invasion might have been canceled and the bloody fiasco avoided.

What was most interesting about Daniel's speech was not the presumption that the mere printing of words in *The Times* could stop a military invasion, a notion acceptable to many people who respect *The Times'* persuasive power in Washington; rather it was that *The Times*, in publishing the full text of Daniel's speech, had inadvertently given new insight into itself. It had thus admitted for the first time the existence of discord among its editors, of fuming and fretting in the newsroom, and this undoubtedly was a startling revelation to many readers who had never before conceived of *The New York Times'* offices in quite this way. They had probably imagined the interior of *The Times* to be closer to its prevailing image, a cathedral of quiet dignity, the home of the Good Gray Lady, and perhaps years ago *The Times* was more like this. But now, in the Nineteen-sixties, it was not.

On the surface things seemed fine—circulation was higher than ever, advertising linage was up, money was pouring in, the newspaper was expanding in prestige and power. But as the paper had grown it had become less manageable, office empires had flourished, and during the last few years a quiet revolution had been going on within *The Times*, a revolution distinguished for its tactics and intrigue, and Daniel's speech had hinted at only part of it. It was more than diversity of opinion, the vanity and taste of men at the top; there were also philosophical differences dividing older *Times*-men who feared that the paper was losing touch with its tradition and younger men who felt trapped by tradition, and there was reappraisal and doubt even among members of the family that owned *The Times*, the heirs of the great patriarch, Adolph Ochs, who had come up to New York from Chattanooga before the turn of the century and had purchased the declining *Times* and revived it. When Ochs bought the paper in 1896 its daily paid circulation was down to 9,000, less than *The Times* had when it was ten days old in 1851. At Ochs's death, in 1935, the daily circulation was 465,000. This figure now has nearly doubled, and there have been several changes for the better since the death of Adolph Ochs. But in many ways *The Times* remains Ochs's paper, his shrine, his words of wisdom being reechoed by old sages still under his influence.

A photograph of Ochs, white-haired and imperious, hangs on Daniel's office wall, as it does in the offices of all other top editors. A bronze statue of Ochs stands in the lobby and also up on the fourteenth floor where the stockholders and directors meet, and Ochs's credo—"To Give the News Impartially, Without Fear or Favor"—is on display in various places around the building and in *Times* bureaus around the nation and world. Until relatively recent years the editors who had risen within the institution had been those most reverential toward Ochs fundamentalism, and the highest-paid reporters were those who were the most objective and accurate, aware of the weight of each word in *The Times*. This awareness often stifled their writing style. They might have written with lucidity and freedom on other publications but on *The Times* they felt the weight and became overly cautious, rigid, and dull. Dullness had been no sin during the Ochs era. Better to be a little dull than to dazzle and distort, the thinking went, and as long as they remained faithful to the principles of Ochs, a sense of responsibility and caution, the old morality, they need not worry. They were secure on *The Times*. They were paid well, treated fairly, protected from the sham and uncertainties of the outside world. Economic recessions and depressions did not cut off their income, and threats to world survival seemed not to disturb the inner peace of the *Times* building.

The Times stood apart, solid and unshakable. If it sometimes seemed a bit crusty and out of touch with popular trends, this was not so bad. It was, like Ochs, never frivolous. It was almost never caught out on a limb. *The New York Times* was a timeless blend of past and present, a medieval modern kingdom within the nation with its own private laws and values and with leaders who felt responsibility for the nation's welfare but were less likely to lie than the nation's statesmen and generals. *The Times* was the bible, émerging each morning with a view of life that thousands of readers accepted as reality. They accepted it on the simple theory that what appeared in *The Times* must be true, and this blind faith made monks of many men on *The Times*. Many. Not all. There had been *Times*men who were less than truthful, or truthful in their fashion, or not truthful in the journalistic sense, which is a truth that is limited but verifiable. Or they had perhaps been *too* truthful, so controversial as not to be in the national interest or the newspaper's interest, which was often the same thing. *The New York Times*, after all, grew with the nation during the two great wars, prospered with it, and *The Times* and the nation were equally committed to capitalism and democracy, and what was bad for the nation was often just as bad for *The Times*.

And it was this thinking, Ochs's ghost of caution, that had come filtering into the newsroom on that night in 1961 when *The Times* decided not to publish all it knew about the Bay of Pigs invasion. The decision had been debated, accepted in one corner of the newsroom, damned in another, but it had finally prevailed. Orvil Dryfoos, *The Times'* publisher and husband of Ochs's first and prettiest granddaughter, and James Reston, *The Times'* bureau chief in Washington and star of the staff, had teamed up to tone down the story, and in so doing they had reaffirmed once again the bond between them, a personal and philosophical compatibility that was Reston's main source of power in the New York office.

It was not surprising that Dryfoos would be so fond of Reston personally and so respectful of Reston's judgment. Even before he had known Reston well he had admired Reston's writing style, which was bright and informal, different from *The Times'* and yet complementary to it. And not long after Dryfoos had left Wall Street in 1942, six months after his fortunate marriage, to begin his career on *The Times*, Reston had left reporting temporarily to serve as an executive assistant to Dryfoos' father-in-law, Arthur Hays Sulzberger, the handsome man who in 1917 had married Ochs's daughter and only child—and upon Ochs's death in 1935 Sulzberger had assumed command of *The Times*, ruling it for the next twenty-six years, until stepping aside for Dryfoos in 1961, with a particular modesty and self-consciousness that comes from marrying into the Ochs dynasty and moving among senior *Times*men who had made it the hard way. But *The Times* prospered under Sulzberger, as it would under Dryfoos, because both men had the wisdom to guide *The Times* gently and the money to resist impropriety, and both men maintained enough of the Ochsian atmosphere to attract and keep employees who were dedicated and talented, and none was more dedicated and talented than James Reston.

A short, dark-haired man with a spry step and an air of self-assurance that was never graceless, Reston had been born in 1909 to poor and pious parents in Clydebank, Scotland. When he was eleven his parents immigrated to the United States, settling in Ohio, and Reston attended public schools but was undistinguished as a student, neglecting his books for the golf course. Soon he was scoring in the seventies and winning tournaments and he could have become a professional; but his mother, who greatly influenced him, was opposed—"Make something of yourself!" she cried—and with some financial assistance from a rich man for whom he had caddied, Reston got through the University of Illinois. Though he was a slow starter, his dream unfocused, he possessed tremendous energy and ambition, and when he finally concentrated on journalism he shot up through the system more swiftly and smoothly than any young man of his generation. But despite the success that would enable him to meet the great thinkers of his time, and would eventually make them as eager to meet him, Reston never forgot his impoverished past and the circumstances that allowed him to be where he was. He was a poor boy to whom America had indeed been a land of opportunity, and out of this grew a gratitude, a patriotism that made him a better convert than a critic. He was clearly an American advocate and, even as he matured, he would never achieve the universal scope of a Walter Lippmann. Columns by Reston on national or foreign affairs often reflected the pardonable prejudice of the sportswriter he had once been. He was reluctant to condemn the home side, even when it made the errors, or to concede that the local heroes also played dirty sometimes when they had to win. Occasionally he seemed almost naive, seeing only righteousness and never greed in American ambition, and somehow suggesting that there were probably more good guys in the CIA than in the spy ranks of the enemy. But he was at least never cynical and always readable, and this made him just right for *The New York Times*, where cynicism would not be tolerated, Ochs having detested it, and where readability was often rare. And there was finally in Reston's style an element far more significant than his writing skill or wit, and this was his persuasive tone of moralism and idealism that brought to his readers the inner elevation of a good Sunday sermon— James Reston was something of a preacher. His strict Scotch Presbyterian mother had wanted him to become a preacher, and as a *Times*man he had become one, his column being the podium from which he could spread his Calvinist view of life throughout the land, thrilling thousands with his sound logic and clarity, influencing students, educators, and politicians, sometimes infuriating such presidents as Eisenhower, who once asked, "Who the hell does Reston think he is, telling me how to run the country?" Reston expected great things from the mighty, not only muscle and heart but also some piety and nobility of spirit; and yet when they failed him, as they most often did, he did not damn them but rather foresaw signs of redemption and hope. This was Reston's special appeal. He communicated hope. The front-page headlines were overcast with gloom and doom, but turning to Reston's column made the world seem brighter. Or, if not brighter, at least less confused. He could somehow cut through all the complex facts and figures, the allegations and lies and illusions of daily life and put his finger on a central point that suddenly brought everything into sharp focus, making it clear and understandable. There was little negativism or doubt in his vision, and thus his America was a positive place of right-thinking people, and God was on our side—it was as it had been during World War II.

In those days, twenty-five years ago, Reston had been a young political reporter in Washington, and before that a war correspondent in London during the Blitz, living with his Midwestern wife and baby son on the edge of destruction and rubble, working among a generation of American journalists profoundly influenced by the spirit of that time and place. There was then a purity about the Allied purpose, and the characters in the war drama were well defined, it was the Virtuous versus the Huns; and there was great adventure, danger, and commitment to being a newsman then, and London left a lasting mark on many of these men, giving to Edward R. Murrow a voice, giving to Clifton Daniel a style in manner and dress, and giving to Reston such a deep conviction about the war as a holy crusade that he wrote a book about it, and this book was his first big step to fame. Entitled *Prelude to Victory*, and published in the summer of 1942, it introduced for the first time the spark and patriotism of Reston's prose. The theme of the book was that "we cannot win this War until it ceases to be a struggle for personal aims and material things and becomes a national crusade for America and the American Dream," and the voice of Reston from the pulpit could almost be heard in such passages as: "We must defy the danger and welcome the opportunity. We must strengthen the things that unite us and remove the things that divide us. We must look forward to the future with faith in each other and in the rightness of the American Dream. For that is the Prelude to Victory." Rave reviews greeted the book's publication both in America and in England, and the movie producer Walter Wanger was so inspired by it that he arranged for a Hollywood bookshop to refund the money to any reader who did not share his view of the book's importance. The book also expressed great loyalty to *The Times*, and this fact, together with Reston's general philosophy and the acclaim it received, did him no harm with *The Times'* publisher, Arthur Hays Sulzberger.

Sulzberger was then, in 1942, in the prime of his life—fifty years old, a lean and well-tailored man with gray hair, alert blue eyes, wrinkles in the right places, and finally in a position to make big decisions without having to first clear everything with his father-in-law. Ochs had now been dead for seven years, and Sulzberger was the boss, although he could never be the boss that Ochs had been. Nor would he wish to be. Sulzberger was by nature a modest man, not a monument builder, and he preferred making decisions quietly, taking into account the counsel of his colleagues, and then remaining in the background with the other shrine-keepers and paying homage to the memory of the departed patriarch. Except for the fact that Sulzberger was of Jewish ancestry, as Ochs had been, the two men had little in common. Adolph Ochs's climb had been a continuous struggle against great odds, he quitting school at fifteen to begin at the bottom—a printer's apprentice and floor-sweeper in the composing room of a small newspaper in Tennessee. Sulzberger had been privileged from the start. He had been born of a prominent New York family that had settled in Colonial America in 1695—one of his mother's relatives, Jacob Hays, had been New York's first police chief—and Sulzberger had been educated in good schools, and had been permitted to indulge a taste for expensive things. He wrote verse, had some talent as a painter, and he thought seriously of someday becoming an architect. But after graduation from college he became, like his father, a textile importer, and was on a buying trip in Peking, China, when the United States entered World War I. He quickly returned for training as an artillery officer, and while in the army he met again some of his New York friends, one being a nephew of Ochs's. And it was through the latter that Sulzberger became reacquainted with Ochs's daughter, Iphigene, whom he had known casually a few years before when they both had attended classes on the campus of Columbia University.

When the courtship began, Ochs had been displeased. Ochs had fashioned his daughter to his Victorian taste, and thought there was no great need for her to marry, all her needs being satisfied at home; but if she were ever to seriously contemplate marriage, as she obviously was with Sulzberger, Ochs had hoped that she would at least select someone with a journalistic background who could make a useful contribution to *The Times* and perhaps one day help run it. But his daughter was set on Sulzberger, and Ochs finally consented on the condition that the young man, after his discharge from the army, join *The Times* and learn the newspaper business. If he had any ability, he would rise within the hierarchy—meanwhile, Ochs could keep an eye on him.

In 1918, a year after the wedding, Arthur Hays Sulzberger appeared at *The Times*. He was given an office and a secretary and very little to do. His presence naturally caused curiosity throughout the building, particularly among some of the women who found him extremely attractive, and few details about him eluded their gossip. He loved flowers in his office and was fond of miniature animals, there being some samples on his desk and atop the bookshelves. He was forever moving furniture around the room, and emptying the ash trays, and rolling a stand that held a large atlas globe back and forth along the floor until finding a spot where the north light hit it at an interesting angle. He was absorbed by music and poetry, color and fabric, and could properly have worked in some cultural department on the newspaper, which he would have preferred. But Ochs kept him away from the more glamorous aspects of the business. After he had been assigned to work for a while on *The Times'* annual charity drive, The Hundred Neediest Cases, he was sent for half of each day to *The Times'* paper mill in the Bush Terminal building in Brooklyn, where he was to familiarize himself with the logistics of newsprint. Soon he became more knowledgeable about this than anybody on *The Times,* and within a few years it was obvious that Sulzberger possessed a great willingness for work and was learning fast. He seemed constantly busy, remaining late at his office studying the complicated tabulated reports of the various departments within the building, always appearing at *The Times* on Sundays and holidays if for no other reason than to walk around the place, to talk to people, and, as he once put it, "to register the fact that I wasn't playing polo with the boss's money."

By the late Twenties, with Adolph Ochs slowing down as he approached seventy, Sulzberger's authority increased, although never to a point of presumption. Once when Sulzberger went a bit far Ochs reminded him, "I'm not dead yet." And Ochs became irritated on another occasion when he learned that Sulzberger, whose taxicab had been delayed by Macy's Thanksgiving Day parade, had suggested to an editor that *The Times* might print a paragraph or two about the congestion. While Ochs would never alter news to accommodate advertisers, he was nonetheless a practical man, and he saw no reason to risk offending Macy's just because his son-in-law had gotten into a traffic jam. There were other things about Sulzberger, too, that grated on Ochs in the beginning, small things that were not the result of any disaffection but were inspired rather by their difference in style and by Ochs's desire to have *The Times* run as he wished not only until his death, but long after it.

This was one reason why, in his final years, Ochs became almost obsessed by his last will and testament, consulting endlessly with his lawyer lest there be confusion about his ultimate dream: *The New York Times* must, upon his death, be controlled only by his immediate family, and in turn by their families, and it would be the responsibility of them all to govern during their lifetime with the same dedication that he had during his. But he knew also that this was the predictable dying wish of many men who had established dynasties, it having possibly been the same with Joseph Pulitzer, the great publisher of the *World*, who died in 1911. But by 1931 Pulitzer's heirs had sold the *World* to Scripps-Howard. This fact, occurring so shortly before Ochs's own death, had caused him particular despondency. For the *World* had been a remarkable combination of writing and reporting, urbanity and intelligence, and what hurt it was not so much an editorial decline as the mismanagement of its business side. Ochs knew that a talented and idealistic staff alone could not guide *The Times* through future decades. The paper also had to make money. Ochs's genius had been not only in the type of newspaper he created but in the fact that he had made such a newspaper pay. Of course Ochs had worked hard, being an indomitable little man with no interests outside his newspaper and with no doubt that news, as he presented it, was a durable and salable commodity. But with his business acumen Ochs had an instinct for avoiding the temptations of business, and he hoped his heirs would also inherit some of this. During Ochs's earliest days in New York, for example, he was so short of money that, to save a few pennies, he would sometimes wander through *The Times* shutting off the lights over desks not in use —and *yet*, when a prominent New Yorker, a trusted friend, offered him a contract for $150,000 worth of municipal advertising with no strings attached, Ochs refused. He did so on the theory that he needed the revenue so desperately that he might adjust his operation to the windfall and he was unwilling to trust himself as to what he might do if, after that had happened, he was threatened with a cancellation of the contract. Ochs was a very human man with his share of human frailties and, knowing this, he was wary of the slightest twitch of temptation in himself. As for his heirs, he could only hope that they too would possess the wisdom to resist, and would run *The Times* not merely for profit but somewhat along the business lines of a great church, gilding the wealth with virtue, and in such a place Adolph Ochs, after death, could live long in the liturgy.

How long he could live, of course, depended largely on how well his heirs got along in the decades ahead. Nothing would crumble his foundation faster than family squabbles, selfish ambition, or shortsighted goals. His successors would have to make money but not be enticed by it, would have to keep up with trends but not be carried away by them, would have to hire talented people but not people so talented or egocentric that they could become too special as writers or indispensable as editors. Nobody could be indispensable on *The New York Times*, including Ochs. *The Times* would go on indefinitely, he hoped, towering over all individuals and groups in its employ, and his family would work together, repressing any personal animosity for the greater good, and, if possible, choose mates in marriage who would also be wed to *The Times*.

This was part of Ochs's dream, and when he died in 1935 during a nostalgic visit to the place in Tennessee where it all began, the fulfillment of his wishes became the responsibility of Sulzberger, the son-in-law, and of Ochs's daughter, Iphigene.

Iphigene Sulzberger was a serious, somber-eyed brunette, no great beauty but pleasant to look at, and, beneath a seemingly soft surface, of very firm fiber. As a girl she had been Ochs's little princess, and as a young woman at Barnard, from which she graduated in 1914, she had been alert and bright, making her father, who had always been impressed by education and envious of it, extremely proud. Her mother, the unconventional member of the family, was a marvelously strange tiny woman with raven hair who wore long dark dresses and walked around the house alone at night, sleeping by day, and who seemed more charmed by the animals around the Ochs household, including the mice, for which she sometimes left bread crumbs in the fireplace, than by the important men who so often came to dinner. She was the daughter of the distinguished Rabbi Isaac Wise of Cincinnati, founder of Hebrew Union College, and Adolph Ochs had met her while visiting the rabbi's home one day in 1882. They were married a year later, spending their honeymoon in Washington, where they had tea with President Chester Arthur, and Ochs then returned with his bride to Chattanooga, where he was the precocious publisher of the *Chattanooga Times*, gaining experience for his future venture in New York. His wife's interest in journalism was limited almost entirely to the literary supplement, for which she wrote book reviews, and she had little inclination for cooking or running a home. But this was no problem in Chattanooga because Adolph Ochs's female relatives there, including his mother, happily occupied and helped run the big house, thus remaining close to Adolph, their pride and joy, and the young Mrs. Ochs, a guest in her own home, was free for such things as riding the new horse that her husband had bought for her soon after their marriage. Far from being displeased with her ethereal quality, Ochs was actually attracted by it, finding it a congenial contrast with his more bourgeois background. The only thing lacking in the early years of their marriage was children, two having died, but nine years after their marriage, in 1892, a baby girl was born and survived, and the ecstatic Ochs named her Iphigene in honor of his wife.

Young Iphigene shared her mother's great interest in literature but little of her mother's romantic detachment. She was her father's child. Had he permitted it she might have become a journalist, a crusading sort urging reform. As a schoolgirl she had been keenly aware of the slums of New York, and during her family's many trips to Europe she saw more of the same. At Barnard College, where she majored in economics, she developed what was then considered a social point of view. She joined with other students in advocating a better welfare program in New York and also worked as a volunteer in some of the city's settlement houses. Her father admired her idealism but he was sometimes startled by the assertive manner in which she expressed her opinions. One day he introduced her to a passage in Benjamin Franklin's autobiography in which Poor Richard, discussing the futility of trying to win arguments by dogmatic force alone, advocated instead the use of such softer phrases as "it appears to me at present" or "I imagine" or "I apprehend"—and this approach in conversation, reinforce by Ochs's own example of never raising his voice and his tolerant way in correcting Iphigene ("perhaps you had better look into that a little more"), gradually influenced her girlhood and it grew as she got older to a point where people were impressed by her reasonable nature, mistaking it sometimes for timidity.

No perceptive editor on *The Times*, however, made this mistake, particularly after Ochs's death. It was not that Iphigene Sulzberger was ever intrusive. In fact she was hardly ever seen in the newsroom and her visits to the *Times* building were usually limited to social calls to her husband's office or to meetings of *The Times'* board of directors. And yet the impression was shared by nearly all senior *Times*men that Iphigene, in her gentle way, her friendly hints and reminders, in her very existence as Ochs's only offspring and the direct heir to his fortune, exerted a tremendous influence on the character of *The Times* and on the three men who had followed her father to the top—her husband Arthur Hays Sulzberger, her son-in-law Orvil Dryfoos, and finally, in 1964, her son Arthur Ochs Sulzberger. She was the living link in their lives with the spirit of Ochs, and during the century she had grown from Ochs's little princess into the grande dame of *The Times*, its good gray lady, and the editors and executives were courtly in her presence and mindful in her absence, and some of them would quote from her favorite stories or observations when they made speeches in public. One of her favorite stories that they used was the medieval tale about a traveler who meets three stonecutters along a road one day and asks each of them what he is doing. The first stonecutter says, "I am cutting stone." The second stonecutter, when the question is repeated, replies, "I am making a corner stone." But when the question is asked of the third stonecutter, he answers, "I am building a cathedral." The strength of *The New York Times*, Iphigene Sulzberger always said, lies in the fact that most of its staff are cathedral-builders, not stonecutters. And of all the cathedral-builders to join *The Times* in the last twenty-five years, perhaps her favorite was James Reston.

She admired his idealism, his devotion to *The Times* and the nation, his solid middle-class values that were not unlike those of her father. Reston and Ochs had never met, their generations separated by a half-century, but both had made their own way from the smaller cities to the Eastern seaboard, and both had been guided by many of the same principles and inspirations. Much of what Ochs had understood and admired in America, but could never put into words, would later be written by Reston, and if Adolph Ochs had lived long enough to read Reston and know him personally he would have undoubtedly shared Iphigene's enthusiasm for him. Reston was just right for *The Times*. His writing expressed faith in the nation's future, was gentle with the Establishment—he did not rock the boat. He wrote interestingly, often humorously without being excessively cutting or clever. Reston, like Ochs, saw the spirit of America not in the large cities with their teeming tenements, their angry demonstrators and tough labor unions, but rather in the smaller towns with their God-fearing families, their sandlots and Rotary clubs. Having emerged from this America, and having accepted it, James Reston reflected much of its mood in his writing, and thus his America was a land in which the citizens seemed not so disenchanted, the police not so brutal, the United States' bombing of Vietnam not entirely unjustified, the politicians in Washington not so self-serving, the age of Jefferson not so long ago or lost in essence. The fraternity houses on college campuses, as Reston saw them, were not perpetuators of prejudice but were places where poor young men such as he had been could learn to use the

proper fork, and his attitude toward women was, like
Ochs's, both romantic and puritanical. Reston thought
that a woman's place was in the home, and when one
of the best reporters in the country, Mary McGrory,
appeared for a job on his Washington staff he said she
could have it if she would work part time on the telephone switchboard, which she refused to do. The
heroines in Reston's world did not work in offices—
they were mothers and wives who excelled in their
roles, who inspired their husbands as his wife had
always inspired him, and he was deeply saddened when,
as he first began to work in Washington, it occurred to
him that the women of that city, the wives of newly
arrived Congressmen, would now have to lie to protect
their husbands. He could not condemn them for it,
this was their duty as wives, but he was saddened by
the thought.

There was much in Reston's lofty outlook that quietly
piqued some of his fellow journalists, but both Iphigene
Sulzberger and her husband were very proud of him
and that was what mattered. Arthur Hays Sulzberger,
to be sure, liked Reston in a somewhat different way
than his wife. He was awed by Reston's talent and
admired him personally, having gotten to know him
quite well in the Nineteen-forties during Reston's days
as his young administrative assistant and occasional
traveling companion, although there *were* times when
Reston's early-to-bed habits and rigidly moral character
palled on Sulzberger a bit, the latter being an extremely
sophisticated man who drank well and had an eye for
an ankle, and who, away from his work, knew the art
of relaxation. But Reston's shortcomings, such as they
were, could not detract from his overwhelming assets.
Sulzberger recognized that he had a preacher on the
payroll who could pack the church, and he also knew
that Reston was much harder on himself than he was on
others. For example, during Reston's first year on *The
Times*, in 1939, he and a fellow *Times*man in the London office committed an indiscretion that most journalists
would have soon forgotten, or would have laughed off

or bragged about, but the incident remained on Reston's conscience for the next twenty-five years.

It happened in the late fall of 1939 when, after a Nazi submarine had penetrated the British sea defense around the Firth of Forth and damaged a British cruiser, Reston and a colleague contrived a way to get the news past British censorship. They accomplished this by cabling a series of seemingly harmless sentences to *The Times'* editors in New York after having first sent a message instructing the editors to regard only the last word of each sentence. Thus they were able to convey enough words to spell out the story. The fact that the news of the submarine attack was printed in New York before it had appeared in the British press sparked a big controversy that led to an investigation by Scotland Yard and the British Military Intelligence. But it took the investigators eight weeks to decipher *The Times'* reporters' code, an embarrassingly slow bit of detective work, and when it was finally solved the incident had died and little was done about it. *The Times'* editors in New York, though they had given the story very prominent play, later expressed dismay that the reporters had risked so much for so little; and the incident left Reston deeply distressed. It was so out of character for him to become involved in such a thing. The tactics were questionable and, though the United States was not yet in the war, Britain was already established as America's close ally and breaking Britain's censorship seemed both an irresponsible and unpatriotic thing to do. A more mature Reston, such as the one who in 1961 opposed the publication of *The Times'* Bay of Pigs story, would never have indulged in such journalism.

As far as anybody on *The Times'* staff knew, this incident in 1939 was Reston's last and only claim to fallibility, for not long after that, particularly after the publication of *Prelude to Victory* in 1942, Reston's career took a sharp turn upward and his fellow reporters would never again get a level look at him. Following the book, which the critic Clifton Fadiman said established Reston as a "valuable propagandist," Reston left *The New York Times* temporarily to help the United States government reorganize the London bureau of the Office of War Information. While there he greatly impressed the United States Ambassador John Winant, who later praised him to Sulzberger, and not long after that Reston had come to New York as Sulzberger's assistant. It was during this period that Reston met Orvil Dryfoos, the future publisher, then just beginning his career on *The Times*, a somewhat shy thirty-year-old son-in-law of *the* son-in-law. By 1944 Reston was working again as a reporter, this time in the Washington bureau under the durable Arthur Krock, soon becoming the young star of Krock's staff and winning a Pulitzer Prize and receiving impressive offers from other publications, one being the editorship of the *Washington Post's* editorial page. Reston found this very tempting in 1953 and he told Krock about it. Krock did not want *The Times* to lose Reston, but Krock suspected that the only job that could keep Reston was Krock's own. Krock was then sixty-six years old, having been the bureau chief in Washington for twenty-one years. During this time he had achieved much of the social and professional status he had dreamed about during his younger days in his native Kentucky. He had first come up to Washington for the *Louisville Times* during the administration of President Taft in 1910, and in 1927, on the recommendation of Bernard Baruch, Krock had been hired by Adolph Ochs, who in 1932 asked Krock to reorganize *The New York Times'* bureau in Washington. Krock did so with reluctance, preferring at that time to remain in New York, but for his willingness he received almost *carte blanche* treatment from Ochs. Since things change very slowly at *The Times*, Krock was still running his twenty-four-man bureau with autonomy long after Ochs's death, taking very little advice and certainly no nonsense from the editors in New York, even those who outranked him. Outranking Mr. Krock was of dubious value so long as Krock was unwilling to be outranked; to oppose him would cause a scene, and nobody likes scenes on *The New York Times*. And so Arthur Krock year after year ran the bureau as his private principality, establishing a relationship with the New York office that continued until the Nineteen-sixties, at which point it became one of the most dramatic and bitter issues in *The Times'* interoffice power struggle. But in 1953 things were going as Krock wished and, having reached that age when important men so often become magnanimous, or if not magnanimous, realistic, he voluntarily relinquished his title to Reston, though continuing to write his column and to occupy a revered position within the bureau as its *éminence grise.* In James Reston, then forty-three, Krock believed he had a successor who had enough stature as a journalist and more than enough stature with the Sulzberger family to stave off any attempt by the New York editors to encroach upon the Washington bureau; and Krock was right.

Smoothly, discreetly, rarely ruffling feathers, Reston not only preserved the bureau's autonomy but also increased its prestige within a very few years. To Krock's staff he added many new men and, as was soon obvious, a special breed of man, an almost Restonian species: they were lean and tweedy journalists, usually quite tall, educated at better universities and brighter than they first seemed to be. They were deceptively aware and low-pressured, slow nodders and ponderous puffers of pipes, very polite and altogether disarming. Most of them had been reared in the Midwest or South, or at least they affected the easy manner of small-town America, contrasting noticeably with the many fast-talking, city-sharp men who had emerged from crowded urban neighborhoods and worked on *The Times'* staff in New York, a city that, as time went on, Reston began to loathe almost as much as did Arthur Krock, who, in later years, saw New York as a city of decadent aggression.

Having hired such men, Reston, unlike the editors in New York, did not let them languish in a large impersonal newsroom waiting for another *Titanic* to sink; with a staff one-twentieth the size of New York's, Reston could and did get to know each man personally, and he assigned each of them to cover an important phase of government activity that would guarantee them ample space and a byline in *The Times*, and this in turn gave them an identity in the newspaper and an entrée to the influential circles of the capital. To work on Reston's staff was to be a member of an elite corps of *Times*-men, and Reston used his considerable influence with top management to see that his men were well paid and appreciated, and he expected nothing in return but loyalty to *The Times*, pride in the bureau, and he also asked that they please call him by his nickname—"Scotty." Even the office boys called him that. Scotty Reston. They idolized him.

To the younger men on the staff, it was *Reston* who personified whatever grandeur *The Times* had, not the high priests in New York, and when one of his reporters was offered a much better job on another paper, he was very slow in accepting it. It meant leaving Scotty. Some reporters were so inspired by Reston's manner and talent that they tried to imitate him, one going so far as to dress like him, switching to bow ties and button-down shirts, to smoke a pipe like him, to walk with his bounce and glitter, to try to mimic the way he spoke, the latter being an impossible undertaking—for there was something in the timbre of Reston's wonderful distant voice, the words he slowly chose, the way he paused, that gave to almost everything he said the ring of instant history.

Many New Yorkers, not unexpectedly, were envious of Reston's staff, and would have loved to become a part of it. On those rare occasions when New York reporters would be working with Reston and some of his men on a special out-of-town assignment—such as a big space shot from Cape Kennedy, Florida—the New Yorkers would become the benefactors of certain little conveniences rendered by Reston's mere presence; for example, in the morning outside of Reston's motel door there would be a fresh bundle of twenty-five copies of *The Times* flown to Florida from New York at Reston's request. Reston understood the journalists' ego—he knew that what most of them miss when working on a remote assignment is the breakfast pleasure of their own words and by-line.

Several New York reporters tried to be transferred to Reston's bureau, but very few made it. Reston did not have to accept any applicants or choices from the New York office, and he usually did not, preferring to make his own discoveries in the smaller towns closer to the heart of America, and Reston could also prevent New York reporters from moving into the Washington area to cover news. In 1959 he even did this to one of New York's specialists, A. H. Raskin, generally regarded as the best labor reporter in the nation. Raskin had then been covering the daily developments of a big steel strike, moving with the story from New York to Pittsburgh, and then he followed it into Washington as a Presidential panel was about to hold hearings on a possible emergency injunction. But when Raskin appeared in the Washington office Reston informed him, politely but unmistakably, that the strike story would now be taken over by one of the Washington reporters. Raskin telephoned New York for instructions. He was told to return home. There later was much fuss in New York about this incident, one editor declaring loudly that *The Times* was being run from New York, not Washington; another editor observing that *The Times* after all, was *one* newspaper and not a cluster of feudal fiefs—but this talk was mostly out of embarrassment or resentment, and none of the editors wished to have a showdown with Reston at this time, all being cognizant of Reston's closeness to the ruling family. As for A. H. Raskin, he was not really surprised by what had happened in Washington; like most veterans on the New York staff, he had previously experienced difficulty with the bureau, finding them slow or reluctant to help him reach sources in Washington to check facts, or quick to dismiss as insignificant almost any news tip he offered—and, if anything, the scene with Reston had been far more cordial than Raskin would have expected had Arthur Krock still been the bureau chief.

Raskin remembered one experience with the Washington bureau back in 1949 that was so awful it was comic. During that year, a period of national economic decline marked by substantial unemployment, Raskin learned from a friend in the Federal Security Agency that President Truman was preparing to send to Congress a special message urging that the Federal government appropriate funds to help the states and cities run emergency work-relief programs for the first time since the WPA in the Great Depression. Suspecting that it would be hopeless to get anybody on Krock's staff to help confirm this tip, Raskin did his own research by telephone and he finally got enough facts together to write the story from New York. This story made page one of *The Times*, appearing at the top of the page under a two-column headline, and when it reached Washington there was fury in Krock's bureau. Krock's deputy, Luther Huston, quickly assigned reporters to prove that Raskin's story was a hoax. Huston even went to the length of having *The Times'* White House correspondent, Anthony Leviero, put a press-conference question to President Truman in a negative enough way to invite, and get, a negative response. Then Huston sent an irate letter to New York listing the names of high-ranking officials in Washington who had told the bureau that there was absolutely nothing to Raskin's story. The letter ended with a strong reiteration of the theme that trying to cover Washington from Times Square was bound to result in disaster and when would New York learn its lesson? (On the same day that Huston's letter arrived in New York, President Truman sent the work-relief message to Capitol Hill, and everything in it corresponded to Raskin's forecast.)

But James Reston would never have condoned such pettiness, nor would he have permitted his bureau to function with such haughty arrogance, which was bound to boomerang sooner or later. Reston presented himself and his staff as team players. And his artistry as an administrator could not be measured simply by the fact that he usually got his own way—what was more interesting was that Reston's way, as he presented it, seemed solely designed for the greater

glory of *The New York Times*. Reston, after all, was a
cathedral-builder, not a stonecutter, and it would have
been highly imprudent of any New York editor to
openly challenge Reston's motives. They might be
angry at him, as when he prevented Raskin from
writing the steel-strike story in Washington, but they
could never catch Reston in an act of arrogance or self-
ishness or power-building. He might have indulged in
such things, but they could never catch him. Everything he did seemed of high purpose and sound principle. In taking the strike story away from A. H. Raskin, Reston did not deprive *The Times'* readers of
knowledgeable coverage; Reston had his *own* labor
specialist.

Reston's whole stance seemed so intertwined with
The Times, his idealism and character so in keeping
with the concepts endorsed by the Sulzbergers, that to
question James Reston would be to question *The Times*
itself. If Reston's hand seemed to be involved in some
tricky office maneuver, as it would from time to time,
particularly during the shake-up of the Nineteen-sixties, his participation would be from such a high moral
position that it would be almost treasonable of any
New York editor to call it office politics. For all they
knew, Reston probably had cleared his moves in advance with the publisher, Arthur Hays Sulzberger,
or after Sulzberger retired because of ill health in
1961, with Orvil Dryfoos. Reston and Dryfoos had
become exceedingly close friends during the Nineteen-
fifties, and when Reston came up to New York he often
stayed at the Dryfoos home, serving as the new publisher's confidant and adviser, and serving within the
institution as part of its national conscience, its legate
to the capital, its poet laureate. He sang the praises of
the paper and the family that owned it in his speeches
and writings, and, when workers struck *The Times*
in 1963, Reston rebuked the labor leaders with an
indignant lament: "Striking *The Times* is like striking
an old lady."

And so it was not surprising then, when the Bay of
Pigs story demanded a big decision in *The Times'*

newsroom on that night in 1961, that Orvil Dryfoos, newly in command, would turn to Reston for advice— and Reston, so sensitive to the national interest and to *The Times*' stake in that interest, would advise that the story be toned down; and it was. It would have been toned down, published, and forgotten, too, along with a hundred other big stories and delicate decisions made since 1961, if Clifton Daniel's speech in St. Paul, Minnesota, in the spring of 1966, had not dredged up the issue once again, and if the New York editors who had been overruled five years before had not played up the story of Daniel's speech as they did in *The Times*' edition of June 2, 1966. They spread the entire four-thousand-word text of the speech across six columns inside the paper and also printed a photograph pertaining to the Cuban invasion and a seven-hundred-word story written by the AP man covering the speech in St. Paul, under a headline: "Kennedy Later Wished Times Had Printed All It Knew." Such extensive coverage of Daniel's speech, which surprised even Daniel when he returned from delivering it, was ostensibly justified on the grounds that it contributed an important footnote to history. But there was little doubt that another reason for its prominent display was that the speech made heroes of the New York editors who had been vetoed in 1961 by Dryfoos and Reston—it actually, in a subtle way, pointed a finger at the Dryfoos-Reston alliance, something that might not have occurred five years before; but now, in 1966, things were different. Orvil Dryfoos was dead.

2

FORTUNATELY for Clifton Daniel, and *The New York Times,* most of what goes on in or around his office does not usually get beyond the thick walls of the *Times* building. If it did, if there were reporters and columnists from other publications each day watching and questioning the editors of *The Times,* following them around and analyzing their acts and recording their errors, if *The Times* were covered as *The Times* covers the world, then Daniel's large office would lose much of the dignity and decorum that it now seems to possess. But Daniel is usually very skillful at concealing his thoughts and sustaining poise under pressure, and his suntan in the early summer of 1966 also helped obscure signs of tension, and only once so far had he lost his composure to a point where it was noticeable to the secretaries and subordinate editors who sit around the newsroom that adjoins his office door.

That incident had been unforgettable for Daniel. He had actually became so enraged at one of his younger editors, Tom Wicker, the new bureau chief in Washington, that he pounded his fists on the desk several times, screaming and shouting, his soft chin trembling. Even if it were true, as charged, that Wicker had not kept in close enough touch with the New York office, and had also been remiss in some of his other duties as a journalist and administrator, there was no justification for this reaction, Daniel knew, and he was sorry that it had happened, was astonished that he had allowed it to happen. This sort of thing is not supposed

to happen at *The New York Times.* It happens in bad
novels about big business, or it happens within some of
the more high-pressure publications around New York
perhaps, but not at *The Times;* not so openly anyway.
And there was much more to the whole thing than
merely the temporary displeasure with Tom Wicker.
Wicker was no doubt paying part of the price for all
those years of autonomy enjoyed by his predecessors,
Reston and Krock. Still, what probably did not help
matters was that Wicker, who can be very impulsive,
had become angry at Daniel's behavior, declaring that
he was unaccustomed to being talked to in this way,
and he added that he was not sure what he was going
to do about it. Then he quickly turned and left
Daniel's office and took the next plane back to Washington.

Three or four days later Daniel was in Washington
having dinner with Wicker, and the whole thing was
officially forgotten, although it will never really be forgotten by either man. If Daniel were to be completely
candid with Wicker, which he would never be, he would
admit that from the beginning he had not been very
fond of Wicker personally nor impressed with him
professionally. When Wicker first applied to *The Times*
for a job in 1958, Daniel had been one of the New
York editors who had turned him down. Wicker was a
tall, raw-boned, ruddy-complexioned Southerner with
thick fingers and alert narrow eyes and a heavy jaw
partially concealed by a reddish beard. He was then
in his early thirties and had not been very experienced
as a journalist, although he did have interesting credentials. He had already written five novels, three under a
pseudonym, that captured some stark scenes of violence
and sex and politics in rural settings, and in 1957 he
had won a Nieman Fellowship in journalism at Harvard after having worked the previous six years on the
staff of the *Winston-Salem Journal* in North Carolina,
his native state. Wicker was the son of a railroad man,
and had been reared in the poverty of the Depression in
a small place called Hamlet. Like Clifton Daniel, he
had gotten his degree in journalism from the Univer-

sity of North Carolina, but this did not result in any preferential treatment for Wicker; it might have had a reverse effect, making Daniel more aware and critical, especially when Wicker came into *The Times'* newsroom with that beard. Nobody on *The Times* reportorial staff then wore a beard except a foreign correspondent recently returned from Turkey, and he was quickly transferred to Jersey City.

Shortly after Wicker had completed his fellowship at Harvard, he joined the staff of the *Nashville Tennessean,* and then in 1960, his beard shaved off, he appeared again at *The Times,* this time in Reston's bureau in Washington, and he was hired. He became one of Reston's boys and four years later, at the age of thirty-eight, Reston's successor as bureau chief. It was an incredibly quick rise made possible by *The Times'* great shift in the Sixties and also by Wicker's talent as a journalist. Wicker was a driven man, sensitive and tough, one who had become resigned without bitterness to the probability that he would never make it as a novelist, although he could never completely understand the success of some of his contemporaries, Updike and Roth and others, men who wrote well but, it seemed to Wicker, knew very little about the world around them.

But Tom Wicker had little time to ponder contemporary American taste in fiction once he joined *The Times.* Suddenly he became caught up in the current of journalism, the daily opiate of the restless. He traveled cross-country with politicians, wrote his stories on airplanes and in the backs of buses. He wrote easily under deadline pressure and liked this life that, through his position on *The Times,* brought him a recognition that would most likely have eluded him had he continued to take the long, solitary gamble of the novelist. As a journalist Wicker could usefully employ other assets, too, among them a disarming country-boy manner that he did not attempt to modify, it being no handicap in Washington, it being almost an asset, in fact, during the early administration of Lyndon Johnson, a fellow southerner, the onetime farmboy and rural schoolteacher: Wicker's coverage of Johnson through 1964 showed a depth of understanding that was not so evident during the Kennedy years.

In addition to Wicker's great interest in politics and people, he possessed a quick mind and an ability to articulate what was on his mind. Like many Southern journalists, Wicker often talked better than he wrote. And he wrote well. He could probably have become a good television commentator, and he was effective when debating on panel shows, making his points with long Faulknerian sentences mixed with regional metaphors and wit, coated in a Carolina accent. One night, after a small dinner party in New York, Wicker became locked in a debate with James Baldwin, a smoldering scene in which Baldwin occasionally jumped to his feet to shriek insults down at Wicker, the white devil from the South, and the evening later became so filled with fury that Wicker's wife left the table angrily in tears. But Wicker remained cool under the barrage of hysteria from Baldwin and another Negro at the table, debating them point for point, and he probably got the better of most exchanges that evening without ever resorting to rage.

But with all his qualities, Tom Wicker's early success on *The Times* owed a great deal to luck, to the fact that he had been at the right place, at the right time. While this may also be generally true of many journalists who succeeded in a big way when young, it was extraordinarily true in Wicker's case: he joined *The Times* just before its revolution, he joined Reston's bureau just in time for the early excitement of the Kennedy era and the drama that followed, and he happened to be the only *Times*man among the Washington press corps who traveled with Kennedy to Dallas. Wicker's story of the assassination took up more than a page in *The Times* of November 23, 1963, and it was a remarkable achievement in reporting and writing, in collecting facts out of confusion, in reconstructing the most deranged day in his life, the despair and bitterness and disbelief, and then getting on a telephone to New York and dictating the story in a voice that only rarely cracked with emotion.

Wicker had chosen that day to be without a note-book, so he scribbled his observations and facts across the back of a mimeographed intinerary of Kennedy's two-day tour of Texas. Today Wicker cannot read many of these notes, but on November 22 they were as clear to him as 60-point type. He wrote his story with other reporters in the pressroom of the Dallas air terminal, having gotten there after a half-mile run while lugging his typewriter and briefcase, jumping a fence along the way without breaking stride, remembering almost everything he saw and heard after Kennedy had been shot, although remembering relatively little of what had happened before that. Wicker had been riding in the Presidential motorcade in one of the press buses, he is not sure which one; and when Kennedy was hit, Wicker heard no shots, although another reporter in the bus noticed that the President's car, which was about ten cars ahead, was speeding away.

The press buses continued to travel at a parade pace. But things quickly began to change. Wicker noticed a motorcycle policeman bump over a curb, dismount, and begin to run. There seemed to be some confusion within the crowds of people who had been lined along the road to get a glimpse of the President. The press buses stopped at the place where Kennedy was to address the crowd. Wicker noticed how the heads of the large crowd of people began to turn as the word was passed back. Wicker was literally *seeing* a rumor travel. It reminded him of wind sweeping over a wheat field. Then a stranger grabbed him by the arm and asked, "Has the President been shot?" "I don't think so," Wicker said, "but something hap-pened."

Wicker and the other reporters, about thirty-five of them, moved to where they were to hear Kennedy speak, and it was there that another reporter came run-ning with the news. Then all the reporters ran. They jumped into the press buses that would take them to

Parkland Hospital. During the next few hours, the details began to pile up—the eyewitness accounts, the medical reports, the words of White House spokesmen, the recollection of one newsman that he *had* heard shots, the description of a Dallas television reporter who had seen a rifle being withdrawn from the corner fifth- or sixth-floor window of the Texas School Book Depository. There were truths, half-truths, errors, illusions, rumors, secondhand accounts, thirdhand accounts—all these were passed freely to the press, were circulated among them, and there was very little time to check these facts or allegations. Wicker and the rest had to go largely on instinct, the totality of their experience so far in life, their insight into others, a special sense that good reporters develop and use in a crisis. And Wicker's instincts in this crisis served him well.

It is probably true that Wicker's reporting from Dallas that day, one afternoon's work, will live longer than any novel, or play, or essay, or piece of reportage that he has ever written or will ever write. It was not that he had produced a classic. He had not. He had previously reported as well, written better. But the test in Dallas was like no other test. It was the sort of assignment that could make or break a *Times*man's whole career in a few hours. Wicker was writing for history that day, and his story dominated the front page, was spread in double measure and set in larger-than-usual type, as was his by-line—this edition of *The Times* would not be thrown away by readers a day later, it was a collector's item. It would be saved by hundreds, perhaps thousands of readers, and they would store it for decades in their attics or closets, and would pass it on as a family heirloom or a relic or a vague testimony to their existence on the day a President was shot.

If there were major errors in Wicker's story, which there were not, they too would survive, degrading Wicker among his colleagues but degrading *The Times* much more among its readers, not only the million or so who would see the story that day, but also those who would read it a half-century from now, the students and historians who would be turning it up again and again on microfilm.

The Times is expected to cover this kind of story, the single spectacular event, as no other newspaper in the world. This expectation is partly based on *The Times*' traditional commitment to being the paper of record, and partly on the fact that *The Times* has the facilities for meeting any emergency—its large reportorial staff with supernumeraries waiting in the wings; its many deskmen, rewrite men, and clerks in the infinite morgue, a combination that permits large volumes of copy to be quickly processed, checked, and fortified by background or sidebar material; its financial wealth that will support any expense in communications and travel; its echelons of editors who, while they sometimes seem to get into one another's way during those days when the news is normal, nevertheless can transform themselves into a remarkably well-coordinated team during a crisis. And finally, mixed in with his mélange, is the unseen force of the ruling family, the ghost of Ochs.

Many years ago, after a task force of *Times*men had acquitted themselves very well on a big story, the editors sat around at conference the following day extending congratulations to one another; but Adolph Ochs, who had been sitting silently among them, then said that he had read in another newspaper a fact that seemed to be missing from *The Times*' coverage. One editor answered that this fact was minor, and added that *The Times* had printed several important facts that had not appeared in the other newspaper. To which Ochs replied, glaring, "I want it *all*."

It is this thinking, rigidly enforced, that has created an odd turn of mind and fear in some *Times*men, and has created odd tasks for others. For several years there were clerks in *The Times*' newsroom assigned each day to scan the paper and count each sports score, each death notice, making sure that *The Times* had them *all*, or at least more than any other newspaper. At night there were *Times* editors in the newsroom pacing the floor waiting for a copyboy to arrive with the latest editions of other newspapers, fearful that these papers might have a story or a few facts not printed in *The Times*. When Tom Wicker's story began to come in from Dallas, two pages at a time, he running down the steps of the Dallas terminal each time across the waiting room into a phone booth, miraculously never having to wait for a booth or a line to New York, the main concern was not with Wicker's prose style—it was with whether he had it *all*, and had it right, even things that would have seemed too trivial on any other day: the names of certain streets in the motorcade route; the fact that the Texas School Book Depository, from which the shots were fired, was a leased state building; the names of the witnesses, and where they stood, during the swearing-in ceremony of Lyndon Johnson in the airplane; the name of the judge who presided at the ceremony, and the date of judgeship; the names of the two priests who administered the last rites to Kennedy; the identity of witnesses who claimed to have seen this or that, and the precise time of each happening—and of all that happened during that long afternoon in Dallas, Wicker saw almost none of it. He was writing blind. He was feeling the facts and was guided by instinct. There were 106 paragraphs in his story in *The Times* the next day, and yet only slightly more than one of these paragraphs described what Wicker had seen with his own eyes. That occurred while Wicker stood with other reporters near the emergency entrance in the hospital as Mrs. Kennedy walked out, and Wicker later wrote: "Her face was sorrowful. She looked steadily at the floor. She still wore the raspberry-colored suit in which she had greeted welcoming crowds in Fort Worth and Dallas. But she had taken off the matching pillbox hat she wore earlier in the day, and her dark hair was wind-blown and tangled. Her hand rested lightly on her husband's coffin as it was taken to a waiting hearse."

After the assassination story that day, and the re-lated stories that followed, Wicker's stock rose sharply at *The New York Times*. He was then thirty-seven, having been on Reston's staff only three years, and he had undoubtedly been lucky at being at the right place, at the right time; but in Dallas on that particular afternoon he had also been the right man. He had made the most of things as they exist in his somewhat bizarre profession, one that often bestows the greatest fame on chroniclers of the greatest chaos, and it was not surprising a year later when Reston selected Wicker to succeed him as the Washington bureau chief, although there were members of the bureau who were not enchanted by the choice. They believed that Wicker has been moved up too fast. And one of Reston's bright young men, Anthony Lewis, disappointed that he had not gotten the job, arranged a transfer to the London office, becoming the bureau chief there. Another Reston protégé, Max Frankel, resigned from *The New York Times* altogether, accepting a job with *The Reporter* magazine, although Frankel suddenly had second thoughts about it a few days later, and asked *The Times* to rescind his letter of resignation, which it did. But there was no doubt that the meteoric rise of Tom Wicker, engineered by Reston, who was then also involved in some interesting executive choreography on a higher level, had bruised the egos of a few ambitious *Times*men, and it had also displeased some of the editors in New York, among them Clifton Daniel.

Daniel had not even known of Wicker's appointment until after it had been made, so quick had Reston been in arranging the details. But in the two years that followed, life was not so smooth for Wicker. His scene in Daniel's office was just one of several disagreeable incidents that he had experienced since becoming the bureau chief, and by the spring of 1966 the persistent rumor in the New York office was that Wicker would soon be replaced. Daniel was in favor of this, but he knew it was a very delicate proposition. Regardless of whatever differences exist between *Times*men, they do share a concern for *The Times'* image. Any executive shifting must be executed gracefully. It should not appear to be a hasty decision, for nothing is done hastily at *The Times*, nor should it seem that *The Times* had made an internal mistake and was now trying to correct it. It must all be handled quietly and in a gentlemanly fashion, with no conspicuous bickering or open dissension that might produce office gossip and possibly leak out to one of the news magazines. If this happened, it would be most unfortunate. *The Times* is supposed to report news, not *make* it, particularly not this kind of news. And yet it was the considered opinion of Daniel and his subordinate editors in New York, among them Harrison Salisbury, his close ally, that Wicker was not the right man for the bureau-chief job in Washington and should be moved, gracefully, to some other position.

Precisely *what* position was a bit of a problem for New York. Wicker was a talented man, there was no question of that. He deserved an important place on the paper and he was young enough to be relied upon to carry a large part of *The Times'* burden into the future. If only Arthur Krock would retire, the editors knew, Wicker could take over Krock's column. That would be an ideal spot for Wicker. *If* Krock would retire. Krock was seventy-eight years old, but he seemed as nimble now as when he first joined *The Times* in 1927, and a relatively recent attempt by New York to get him to retire had failed. A letter concerning Krock's retirement had been sent to Krock's home in Washington but, according to the word in New York later, the letter had been intercepted by Mrs. Krock without her husband's knowledge; she had told Reston about it, and Reston had pulled a few strings with the publisher's office, and that took care of that. The durable Arthur Krock, who had survived ten presidents, four wars, countless rebellions, and various awkward events, had done it again.

Still, a place had to be found for Wicker somewhere. And this was one of the things that occupied Daniel's thoughts now, in the early summer of 1966, although not to the exclusion of other more pressing problems, of which there were many, even if they did not show on his face or have a disquieting effect on his manner. Daniel seemed very much in control of things, sure of himself and the position he held. The memory of the outburst with Wicker had represented a rare bad day to him, a wildly distorted picture of the individual he imagined himself to be. He was by nature a man of containment and poise, he felt sure, and a more recognizable picture of himself would be one showing him as he was on this summer afternoon, seated sedately behind his desk in his black leather chair in his office, fifteen minutes before the four-o'clock news conference was to begin, dictating notes to his secretary, Patricia Riffe, an extremely pretty blue-eyed young woman who dresses impeccably. He chose her himself, and one is not surprised.

When Miss Riffe first appeared at *The Times* a few years before, there was hardly a reporter in the newsroom who was not aware of her—feminine beauty not being all that common in the newspaper business, at least not in front of the office door of *The Times'* managing editor. Daniel's predecessor had hired only male secretaries, and the editor before *him* had employed a dogmatic grayhaired woman whose hauteur conveyed the impression that *she* was the managing editor.

This woman had worked for various managing editors of *The Times* between 1928 and 1951, during which time she discovered where most of the bodies were buried and lost whatever awe of her superiors she might have once possessed, and she came to regard the younger executives on *The Times* as office boys, clerks, or worse. But she had made the mistake of including in this category one assistant managing editor who in 1951, upon the death of her boss, became his successor. One of the new editor's first acts was to accept her resignation, replacing her with a series of male secretaries, and this went on until Clifton Daniel moved into the big office in 1964 and brought in Miss Riffe. Many staff members were anxious to date Miss Riffe, and a few did, but her obvious discretion and mildly aloof manner soon discouraged them, all but one forthright young copyreader who worked on the foreign desk. Soon he was talking Miss Riffe to lunch, and later they were exchanging little notes through *The*

Times' housemail, and chatting briefly during the day on office telephones—he sitting at one end of the newsroom behind a post that permitted him to peek at her without seeming too obvious, she sitting at her desk outside Daniel's office looking straight ahead, striking a pose of rigid efficiency.

The Times' newsroom is an odd setting for a courtship: it is an enormous, functional room stretching from Forty-third to Forty-fourth Street through the third floor of the fourteen-story *Times* building, and it is lined with rows and rows of gray metal desks, teletype machines, telephones, and a few hundred men sitting with pencils in their hands, or keyboards under their fingers, writing or editing or reading about the world's latest horror. Every five minutes, it seems, there arrives in this room a late report of another disaster—a riot in Rangoon, turmoil in Tanzania, a *coup d'état*, or an earthquake. But all this seems to make no impression on the people within this room. It is as if so much bad news has punctured the atmosphere of this place for so long that now everybody within is immune to it. The news is just a harmless virus that comes floating into the building, is circulated through the system, in and out of typewriters, under pencils, into spinning molten metal machines, is imprinted on paper, packed in trucks, delivered to newsstands, and sold to worrisome readers, causing reactions and counterreactions around the world—but the inhabitants of *The Times'* newsroom remain unaffected, uninvolved, they think of other things. Love. Or, in the case of Miss Riffe and the young man on the foreign desk, marriage. One day they went off quietly and got married. And then, with Daniel's blessing, they returned, resumed their places behind their desks in the room, and proceeded to conduct their private lives in such a way as not to distract from the larger purpose of this place. Which is as Daniel wishes it.

He is interested in appearances, and this extends not only to an individual's grooming or clothes, but also to the manner in which he conducts his private life. Daniel is not a puritanical man. It matters little to him

if the whole staff of *The New York Times* is engaged
in a vast assortment of pleasurabl pursuits, sexual or
otherwise. But how a thing appears is often as meaningful to him as how it really is, and this attitude has
influenced his life, the things he has done, the way he
has done them, his reaction toward people and places,
his taste in objects, his choice in women, be they wife,
lover, or secretary. Even his office reflects this. Traditional English, thirty-five feet long and eighteen feet
wide, trimmed in draperies of a white linen stripe, it is
lined with a blue-black tweed rug that conceals the inky
footprints of editors who have been up to the composing room. Toward the front of the room is an oval
walnut conference table surrounded by eighteen Bank
of England chairs, modeled after one that belonged to
Adolph Ochs. In the rear of the room, a long walk for
visitors, is Daniel's big desk and his black leather chair
which, according to the decorator, was selected because it produces a minimum of wrinkles in Daniel's
suits.

To the right of the desk is a door leading into a
small, tastefully appointed sitting room, on the walls of
which are hung photographs showing Clifton Daniel
and his wife at White House receptions with the Lyndon Johnsons, the Harry Trumans, the John Kennedys
—these being but a sample of many such photographs
that the Daniels have, a few of which, blurred, were
taken by Jacqueline Kennedy. Behind this little room
is a bathroom and also a small kitchenette and bar.
On the walls of the kitchenette are posters representing
the nations in which Daniel has worked as a *Times*
correspondent—England, Egypt, West Germany, Russia—and there are other personal mementos in this
small room. But there is nothing that is conspicuously
personal in the large room of Daniel's suite. Everything in this room reflects the institution, Daniel's taste
here being infused with subtlety. The framed photographs along one side wall, blown up and changed
periodically, are recent news pictures that appeared
in *The Times* and caught Daniel's eye. Lined along the
shelves behind Daniel's desk are many books written

or edited by *Times*men, and when these men appear in his office their eyes invariably scan the shelves quickly, hoping that their books have survived his latest scrutiny. To the left of the bookshelves are hung the photographs of the publishers who have so far guided the paper through this century, Ochs and his three successors. To the right, overlooking Daniel's left shoulder as he sits at his desk, are photographs of the four men who preceded him as managing editor, men who both presented their era and were representative of it.

In the first picture, Carr Van Anda. He was appointed managing editor by Ochs in 1904, having been hired away from the *New York Sun*, to which he had gone in 1888 after some distinguished years on the *Baltimore Sun* and on smaller papers in his native Ohio. Van Anda poses in this picture with firm lips and cool pale eyes, a formal man with a high forehead, rimless glasses, a high stiff collar, and a pearl stickpin piercing his tie. He appears to be a distant, impersonal man, and he appears as he most often was. One *Times* reporter of that period described Van Anda's look as a "death ray," and when a group of *Times*men petitioned Van Anda to put by-lines on their stories he snapped, *"The Times* is not running a reporters' directory!"* But if he was not a folk hero with his staff he was nonetheless respected as few editors would be, for he was not only a superb newsman but also a scholar, a mathematical genius, and a student of science and logic. It was he who pushed *The Times* toward its expanded coverage of the great feats in polar exploration and aviation, forming the foundation for the paper's portrait of the space age. He was the first editor to publicize Einstein—and once, in checking over a story about one of Einstein's lectures, discovered that the scientist had made an error in an equation. Van Anda, who read hieroglyphics, printed many stories of significant excavations, and one night, after examining under a magnifying glass the inscription of a four-thousand-year-old Egyptian tomb, he discovered a forgery, and this fact, later confirmed by Egyptologists, led to the conclusion that a young Pharaoh, Tutankhamen, had been assassinated by a military chief named Horemheb. It was Van Anda who disputed the new *Titanic*'s claim to being unsinkable and when the ship's radio went silent, after an emergency call for help, he deduced what had happened and drove his staff to get the story of the disaster that would be a world scoop. During World War I, Carr Van Anda, equipping himself with every available military map, charted the course of battle, and he anticipated many future campaigns, getting his reporters there in advance, and *The Times*' coverage during that time was unparalleled.

By 1926 Van Anda had gone into semiretirement devoting more time to his lifelong study of mathematics, astronomy, and cosmogony, and his place at *The Times* was taken by his assistant of many years, Frederick T. Birchall. Birchall was an impulsive, quick, tiny Englishman who, because he chose to remain a British subject, never received the full title of managing editor from Ochs, performing for the next five years as *acting* managing editor. He had been a brilliant deskman under Van Anda in the 1890's on the *New York Sun*, and he had joined *The New York Times* at Van Anda's urging in 1905. In the newsroom Birchall always wore a green eyeshade that partially covered his bald head, and he also had an impressive Vandyke beard that, from the photograph in Daniel's office, appears to be black. Actually it was pink. "Old Pink Whiskers" was Birchall's nickname in the newsroom, and the staff felt a bit more relaxed around him than it had with Van Anda. Birchall was more liberal, a luxury *The Times* could then afford since the staff had been so thoroughly disciplined under Van Anda. Not being a genius, Birchall was more human, but he worked hard to maintain the standards of his mentor. Birchall worked at his desk half the night rereading stories for errors in fact or tone, and he read galley proofs upside down to see if any typos would come popping into his sharp scanning sight. Sometimes he would remain all night at *The Times*, sleeping in a little room down the hall from his office, and occasionally he would be awakened by a copyboy as a big story broke. Then he would reappear in *The Times'* newsroom wearing his pajamas, slippers, and bathrobe; suddenly alert, excited by the news, he would put on his green eyeshade and proceed to pad around the room giving instructions to his reporters and subordinate editors.

Outside the newsroom, Birchall was something else. There seemed to be some romantic fantasy trapped within him, and he was once spotted up in *The Times'* library moving between high shelves of books with his eyes slightly closed, twirling tiptoe in a trance of secret ballet. With his British wife he lived, among other places, near the Hudson River in a large farmhouse around which he kept dozens of monkeys, birds, stray cats and dogs, and a parrot who would greet each of Birchall's arrivals with a cockney call, " 'Allo, dahling," and then make *click-click* noises simulating the sound of the ice cubes that Birchall was dropping into a highball glass. Birchall's eye for women was never a secret at *The Times*, and it was said that a particular woman, a German baroness, was a factor in his decision to vacate the acting managing editor's job in 1931 and go overseas as *The Times'* chief European correspondent. He saw a good deal of her in Europe, and one day while driving in his car with one hand on the steering wheel and the other on the Baroness's leg, and with two American friends in the back seat, Birchall rammed into the rear of a German bus. No one was seriously injured, but shortly afterward Birchall made the observation, "Foreign correspondents should be eunuchs." He was a living refutation of that statement. He was an outstanding correspondent for *The Times* in the early Thirties, reporting perceptively the early rise of Hitler, and in 1933 he won the Pulitzer Prize.

Birchall's place in the managing editor's office had been taken by a flamboyant Virginia dude named Edwin Leland James. Of the four editors whose pictures hang on Daniel's wall, James was undoubtedly the most popular with the staff and they referred to him by a variety of names—"Jimmy James," "King James," "Jesse

James," "Dressy James." A stocky little man with blue-eyes and suits tailored in Paris, where during the Twenties he had been *The Times'* chief correspondent, James continued to live the life of the boulevardier long after he had returned to the New York office as an editor. He would appear each morning wearing one of his brightly colored suits and highly polished pair of shoes, sometimes carrying a cane that he rapped against the elevator when it moved too slowly. In his office, sitting behind an eight ball on his desk, he puffed cigars and talked at length to almost any visitor, and he also found time each morning to study the racing form and place a bet with a bookmaker who doubled as a clerk on one of the news desks.

It was in many ways remarkable that such a man could ever have attained such a demanding editorial position. One possible explanation was that Ochs, Van Anda, and Birchall had been both charmed by his personality and impressed with his reporting during World War I and through the Twenties. And when Ochs wished to escape temporarily from the Victorian citadel he had created, he would go alone to Paris and make the nocturnal rounds with James, then to the racetrack the following day. James was Ochs's tonic.

James could do these things, and still succeed at his job, because he had great physical stamina and incredible speed at a typewriter. He never labored over his writing, and he was no stylist, but he did achieve a high level of readability by packing his stories with interesting details and by coming up with angles that gave his stories a twist. In fact, on his very first assignment as a *Times* reporter on the local staff in 1915, after he had been sent to the Astor Hotel to cover a reception for the new consul-general from Romania—an event attended by New York dignitaries and preceded by an eleven-gun salute from the battleship *Wyoming*—James became suspicious of the consul-general, wondering if he might be a fraud. The consul-general's boots were scuffed and untidy, and his accent seemed artificial, and there were other things, too, that somehow seemed wrong to James. He later reported this to Van Anda, and then began to investigate further—and finally, with cooperation from government officials in Washington, James exposed the consul-general as a psychopathic poseur who had previously served time in the Elmira Reformatory in upstate New York. This story appeared in *The Times* the next morning under the headline, "Bogus Consul General Gives Dinner at Astor," resulting in another jail term for the impostor, and quickly establishing James's identity with Van Anda.

Three years later, when James was twenty-eight, he was getting by-lines regularly from Van Anda for his war reporting from Europe, an assignment that he sometimes covered on horseback, wearing jodhpurs and a hacking jacket under his trench coat. After the war he covered the conferences at Versailles, Locarno, and Geneva, bringing to his reporting a descriptive touch that is not unusual now in *The Times* but was then quite rare: "At the end of a perfect day, just as nightfall descended rapidly from surrounding mountains, two middle-aged figures, both stoop-shouldered, one with flowing hair, the other bald as can be, stood arm in arm framed in a brightly lighted window and looked out together on the lengthening shadows fast reaching across Lake Maggiore. There was Aristide Briand, Foreign Minister of France, and Hans Luther, Chancellor of the German Republic. Behind their backs secretaries were blotting the ink on the signatures of a treaty by which their two countries promised never to fight one another again."

For five years, beginning in 1925, James roved around Europe covering the best stories, and in 1927 he was at the Le Bourget Airdrome as Lindbergh landed ("PARIS, May 21—Lindbergh did it. Twenty minutes after 10 o'clock tonight suddenly and softly there slipped out of the darkness a gray-white airplane as 25,000 pairs of eyes strained toward it. . . ."); and then, in 1930, with his French wife and three children, and with a Legion of Honor ribbon in his lapel, Edwin James returned to New York as Birchall's assistant, and in 1932 he was named managing editor. He held this position until his death in 1951, and during his tenure *The New York*

Times became larger and more prosperous than ever before, expanding its coverage around the nation and the world. But James was easily bored by much of the necessary trivia of his job, and he permitted other men of talent and ambition, men with their *own* ideas of what was best for *The Times*, to move in and assume more responsibility. *The Times*, with Ochs dead, soon became splintered into several small office empires, little dukedoms, with each duke having his loyal followers and special territory to protect. One of the grand dukes of *The Times*, of course, was Arthur Krock. Another was Lester Markel, an autocratic figure who in 1923, at the age of twenty-nine, had been hired by Ochs as the Sunday editor with a staff of five; by 1951, Markel had a staff of eighty-four. This included fifty-eight editors, layout and picture crews, and special correspondents in Paris, London, and Washington. He had converted the Sunday department, which in 1923 had consisted of a slim magazine and a flimsy feature supplement, into a gigantic operation that published a book review, a review of the week's news, a section on entertainment and the arts, and a thick magazine that, while often criticized for its ponderous articles and endless advertisements of ladies' underwear, was nonetheless very influential and profitable. Lester Markel, in effect, had built a major newspaper within the newspaper, and his taste dominated his product and the men who helped produce it, and for forty years his authority within the Sunday department was unquestioned—he was the Sun King.

There were powerful individuals elsewhere within the building, too, men who had carved out their domains in or around the newsroom during World War II as the staff was increased and the workday was expanded so that *The Times* could publish the maximum amount of late-breaking news from around the world. This procedure resulted, among other things, in the staff being divided into "day side" and "night side" factions, each controlled by editors who ruled over a vast pecking order of subeditors, who in turn ruled over platoons of deskmen assigned to one of three competing desks—the foreign desk, the national desk, and the New York desk. Finally, there were dukes who operated with virtual autonomy across the sea, running their bureaus in foreign capitals where they could not be quickly reached or directed by New York due to the delayed pace of communications that then existed.

And so during James's nineteen years as managing editor, a time when the job became much more difficult and complicated than it had been under Van Anda and Birchall, the dukes abounded in New York and Washington, London and Paris, and in other foreign cities. While they paid homage to the memory of Ochs and his principles of selfless dedication, they competed with one another in an amazing variety of ways, often influencing how a news story was covered, who covered it, how much space it was allotted, where it appeared in the paper; and sometimes, instead of conducting their campaigns quietly, the dukes or their henchmen played out their ambitions openly on the very locations where headline news was being made, providing journalistic sideshows that were as lively on occasion as the news happenings reported in the paper.

During the Korean war, for example, there were *Times*men at the front who were attached to Markel's Sunday department, Krock's Washington bureau, and the foreign desk in New York, and the hostility that developed between certain members of these factions was such that even now nearly two decades later, these individuals rarely speak when they meet by chance in the elevators of the *Times* building. There was one incident in Korea during the winter of 1950 in which a *Times*man from Washington, assisted by a colonel who was his frequent drinking companion, schemed to have a *Times*man from New York removed from the theater of operations on the false charge that he was a psychotic who feared the sound of gunfire, a result of a combat wound he had received in the cheek of his buttock during World War II, and consequently he was covering the Korean War from his hotel room. The New York man, disliked by the Washington man for competitive reasons and by the colonel because his reporting of the

war had seemed too pessimistic, was completely unaware of the plot until he received his notice of disaccreditation—and then he protested so loudly that it
came to the attention of General MacArthur. Mac-
Arthur was also very annoyed because he had been kept
uninformed of the disaccreditation order and because
he had recently been called upon to arbitrate a similar
dispute involving the *Herald Tribune's* correspondent
Marguerite Higgins. She had been asked to leave Korea
but, after the protests of *Tribune* executives and other
high-placed individuals, MacArthur had reinstated her,
relieved to have the problem off his back. Now, in *The
Times'* case, MacArthur did not want a feud with the
newspaper that had been giving him editorial support at
a time when he greatly needed it at home; still, he was
infuriated by all the journalistic backbiting of late, and
as he listened to the *Times*man's plea to be reaccredited,
he frowned, drawing on his corncob pipe. Finally Mac-
Arthur granted the correspondent his wish, but then he
angrily waved him out of his office. "For God's sake,"
MacArthur cried, "can't *The New York Times* wash its
dirty laundry in private?"

The managing editor who succeeded Edwin James
was a tall, smiling, dark-eyed charmer from Mississippi
named Turner Catledge. Catledge was a man who liked
to spend evenings with friends drinking whiskey and
telling good stories, and some people misinterpreted
this as a sign of his laxity or indifference to work. Actually, Catledge was probably the shrewdest managing
editor of them all. While lacking Van Anda's brilliance
or the busy-beaver quality of Birchall, Catledge was
their master when it came to handling men and manipu-
lating situations without seeming to be doing so. He
had covered politics in Washington through the Thirties
and Forties, and he was a believer in the political organization, the coordinated team with unchallenged
hard power at the top, and he was appalled by what
had been going on within *The Times* during James's
final years. When James died in December of 1951,
Catledge's main problem was what to do about the
dukes.

Had he been on another publication the solution would have been simpler, but on *The Times* it had never been easy to remove people, particularly people with power, or people who possibly had connections with the publisher or members of the family. *Times*men in key positions like to stay there, they fight to stay there, for employment on *The Times* is very prestigious—doors open elsewhere, favors are for the asking, important people are available, the world seems easier. Also, from the early days of Ochs, there had been a traditional delicacy toward faithful employees, and people with prestige on the staff were rarely humiliated. Many of the dukes, too, were valuable men who had made, and were still making, important contributions to the paper which, in addition, was a very successful enterprise, and many people on *The Times* saw no reason for change. If Catledge wished to stage a revolution and demote the dukes and thus bring the power back to the managing editor's office in New York, he had better do it subtly, he knew, and he had better be lucky. Still, there was no alternative, he thought; the paper could continue with its factionalism for just so long before it would proceed to destroy itself. He had seen firsthand some of the abuses of the dukedom in Washington, having gone there in 1929 shortly after he had been hired by *The Times*. In those days, the Washington chief, Richard V. Oulahan, Krock's predecessor, ran a bureau in which reporters did as they pleased, and if three of them wished to cover the same assignment on a particular day, they did, and sometimes all three versions would be sent to New York and be printed. When Krock took over the bureau in 1932 upon the death of Oulahan, he quickly converted this self-directed staff into a team, *his* team, and the most ambitious young member of the team was Turner Catledge.

Catledge sometimes wrote four to six major stories a day, became an expert on tax law, developed news sources throughout Washington; and all this tremendous energy and ambition could have worked against him if he had not also possessed a quality that redeemed him. Catledge had a wonderful way with men. Particularly older men. Particularly older men with power. This is a quality that perhaps cannot be learned but is inherent in certain rare young men who, partly because they are respectful and not privileged, confident but not *too* confident, attract the attention of older men, selfmade men, and receive from these men much advice and help. The older men probably see something of themselves in these bright young men, something of what they were, or *think* they were, at a similar age. And so they help the younger men up the ladder, feeling no threat because these younger men are also endowed with a fine sense of timing.

Turner Catledge had all this as no other young *Times*man would have it until the arrival in 1939 of James Reston, and it is not surprising that these two would become, in their mannered ways, rivals throughout the Forties and Fifties, and especially during the Sixties.

One of the first important men to help Catledge was Herbert Hoover, who, as Secretary of Commerce in 1927, was on a survey of the Mississippi River flood area; Catledge was there for the *Memphis Commercial Appeal*. Catledge had left his home state of Mississippi for Memphis in 1923, riding the rails with $2.07 in his pocket, and now four years later he had come into prominence as a newsman principally for his vivid reporting on the Missippi flood. Hoover, an orphan who always admired initiative in young men, was so charmed by Catledge that he wrote a letter in his behalf to Adolph Ochs. It was not until 1929, however, after Hoover had been elected President, that *The Times* hired Catledge.

Krock also was much impressed with Catledge and by 1936, when Krock was fifty and Catledge thirty-five, Krock hinted that he did not intend to spend his whole life in Washington and that Catledge had the makings of an ideal successor as bureau chief. Catledge was very pleased but he still continued to call him *Mister* Krock, and was not encouraged to do otherwise, and this formality later stiffened a bit when Krock heard that President Roosevelt was also becoming enchanted with Turner Catledge. Krock disliked Roosevelt, and the feeling was returned, due in part to Krock's turning against the New Deal in 1936, and due also to an episode prior to Roosevelt's inauguration in March of 1933. Roosevelt suspected Krock of attempting to act as an intermediary between the outgoing President, Hoover, and Roosevelt on a future Presidential action Roosevelt was being pressed to make. Roosevelt felt that Hoover did not have to go through Krock but could have come directly to the President-elect, and Roosevelt blamed Krock for agreeing to become a go-between in an effort to establish himself in an important role. So after the Democratic National Convention of 1936, possibly as a way of embarrassing Krock, President Roosevelt told Catledge to feel free to check out stories or acquire information directly from the President; in short, Roosevelt was offering a line of communication that Catledge should use on his own without going through Krock.

Catledge immediately felt uncomfortable and he went to Krock and told him about it, and he also told a very close friend on the United Press, Lyle Wilson. Catledge wanted first to let Krock know that he was not available for such double-dealing and he wanted some intimate friend to know the story, too, and he was lucky that he did. For Krock got the episode mixed up, or at least Catledge felt that he did, and the word got around that Catledge had been intrigued by Roosevelt's proposition. Catledge, backed by Lyle Wilson, was able to counter Krock's suspicion and to reiterate that, far from being intrigued, he was actually offended by Roosevelt's move, even frightened.

Roosevelt's antipathy toward Krock was actually aimed at others on *The Times* as well, including Arthur Hays Sulzberger after the latter became publisher in 1935. Roosevelt thought he had an opportunity to benefit by a less independent *Times* immediately after Ochs's death during the settlement of Ochs's estate tax. Roosevelt expected that the Ochs family would be forced to go into the money market or sell some of its stock in *The Times* in order to raise the necessary funds. But when the family got the money by the sale of some of its preferred stock, not its common stock, Roosevelt became very distressed, and he admitted as much to some of his confidants in the Senate. Some editors on the newspaper felt then, and feel now, that Roosevelt's resentment of *The Times* was based on nothing more complicated than the fact that he could not control it. Few active Presidents actually believe in a free press—Truman did not, nor did Eisenhower nor Kennedy nor Johnson; nor do most newspaper publishers, including those at *The Times*, whenever their own personal stakes are involved, a fact soon discovered by any writer who has ever attempted to do a publisher's biography.

Turner Catledge, at any rate, never became the Washington bureau chief of *The New York Times*. Arthur Krock, who in 1936 was saying that he did not intend to spend his whole life in Washington, was still there thirty years later. In 1938, in fact, a year in which he had condemned the Roosevelt administration for "official favors surreptitiously extended to syndicated columnists who are sympathetic," Krock strangely got an exclusive interview with Roosevelt, for which he received the Pulitzer Prize. Catledge at the same time felt his career had stalled, and in the winter of 1941, at the age of forty, Catledge quit *The New York Times*. He left for Chicago to become chief correspondent and later editor-in-chief of the *Chicago Sun*. But even before he left, Krock telephoned Sulzberger in New York and told the publisher to keep the door open—Catledge would probably be back.

Looking at Catledge's photograph in Clifton Daniel's office today, one is impressed by the serenity of expression, the bright dark eyes and round face that is almost smiling, the neatly combed black hair graying at the temples. The nearby photographs of Van Anda and Birchall and James seem dated, there is a faded quality about their texture, a sense of the past in the faces and clothes of the men. But the picture of Catledge is sharp and contemporary, portraying a man who seems very much alive. And he is. On this summer day in 1966, he was still at *The New York Times*, sixty-

five years old, looking no different from his picture in
Daniel's office, which until 1964 was Catledge's office.
When Daniel moved into it he changed the whole decor,
eradicating all traces of the political-clubhouse atmosphere that Catledge had brought to it during his years
as a benevolent boss. In the late afternoons, after the
four-o'clock news conference, in the little back room,
Catledge and some of his *Times* cronies—a few of
whom, like himself, were having marital difficulties
and were in no rush to get home—would gather around
a bucket of ice and bottle of whiskey and talk for hours
about life at *The Times*. How many important decisions
were made in that little room is impossible to document, just as the character of Catledge himself has remained ill-defined even by those who think they know
him. During his years as managing editor, from 1951
to 1964, it was never possible for them to know exactly
what he was doing—big decisions were being made,
they knew, but they did not know how or by whom.
Catledge's hand seemed to be in everything, but not his
fingerprints. He was a smooth, behind-the-scenes administrator. He moved at oblique angles and shifts,
never hitting things head-on, never making deals that he
could not get out of. He so often seemed to be dragging
his feet, or testing the wind, or leaning and listening;
it would seem at times that nothing was being accomplished. And then it was done.

He rarely made enemies. He was well liked by the
staff mostly because he greeted them warmly, knew all
their first names; and sometimes he would stand outside his office door with a pair of binoculars raised to
his eyes, bringing everybody in the vast newsroom into
close, sharp focus. It was Catledge who initiated the
four-o'clock conference in his office each afternoon, a
maneuver toward bringing a large number of editors
under his direct control, and this was one of his first acts
toward centralization. Though Clifton Daniel removed
Catledge's big table when he became the managing
editor, the conference itself has remained a part of the
procedure, it now being conducted at a more sleek table
of Daniel's choosing.

With the elevation of Clifton Daniel, there was some doubt about Catledge's future. Many members of the staff assumed that Catledge had been kicked upstairs, inheriting an impressive new title, and an opulent new office, signifying nothing. But later, as the subordinate editors watched Catledge watching Daniel at the conference each afternoon, and perceived the effect it was having on Daniel, the impression changed. But they could never be sure. Where Catledge was concerned, there was no certainty.

3

AFTER Clifton Daniel had finished his dictation, Miss Riffe stood up and, with that nice hip motion she has when she walks, left his office. Daniel sat back in his chair, rubbing his eyes momentarily, his horn-rimmed glasses tucked up into his long hair like a tiara. He had almost ten minutes left before the four-o'clock news conference, so he busied himself with some of the papers that Miss Riffe had left on his desk. There were cables sent from the bureaus overseas, and memos sent from within the building. There was a tearsheet of an editorial in *The Nation* praising his Bay of Pigs speech, and there were a few letters from carping readers, one being from Arthur Schlesinger, Jr., that began, "Dear Clif." There was also a letter from a lady in Fort Worth who had known Daniel almost forty years ago when he worked in his father's drugstore in Zebulon, North Carolina. He remembered her, too. Hazel Perkins. She had been one of the belles of Zebulon in the Twenties, and for a town of its size, he had always thought, there had been a remarkably large number of very pretty young women. There had been Melba Chamblee, a blue-eyed redhead whom he had dated in high school and continued to date for a while after he had gone to the University at Chapel Hill. And there had been Sadie Root, who came later, and then had gotten into an automobile accident that had cost her an eye. And there was Betsy Anderson, the prettiest of them all, he thought, and he had often wondered what had ever become of her. She and Hazel Perkins used to sit at the curbside tables and he would serve them, and he re-

membered this as one of the more pleasant parts of his
job at the drugstore—the walking back and forth and
meeting people, and talking to the girls who gathered in
Daniel's drugstore that then, much more than now, was
a center of social life in Zebulon. The deputy sheriff
and the police chief also used to hang out there, as did
the farmers talking about the price of tobacco and cotton, and the visiting politicians would drop in to shake
hands. There was a piano in the front of the place and
when Tad Chavis, a Negro, was not grinding ice for
drinks or delivering things on his bicycle, he was usually
playing ragtime on it, although he was sometimes competing with a loud and scratchy rendition of "In a Little
Spanish Town" blaring from the Edison phonograph
that stood not far from the piano. There was no radio
in the drugstore then, and so young Clifton Daniel
would occasionally slip across the street to the rear of a
feedstore to hear the radio news and baseball scores,
and it was there, too, that he remembers hearing about
Lindbergh's flight. He never stayed away too long, however, for the drugstore was busy, and when he was not
waiting on tables he was inside taking telephone calls
for the doctors, or listening to the deputy sheriff's account of some local brawl, and one night Daniel saw
walking into the drugstore a man whose throat was
cut from ear to ear. Daniel called a doctor. He also
called the *Zebulon Record*.

He had been sending news items into the paper during
the summer months of his high school years, earning
five dollars a week; the drugstore, a great clearing
house for local gossip and news, was a perfect place for
a young reporter. When he returned to high school in
the fall he continued to write for the *Zebulon Record*,
covering student activities and sports. He was never an
athlete himself. From the age of twelve he had been a
little deaf in his left ear, and he also was built along frail
lines, although for a while he did calisthenics in his
bathroom at home. One morning, however, he leaned
over too far and slipped and broke a front tooth against
the bathtub. This ended his physical-culture program
for a while, and he sought to satisfy his ego by describ-

ing the actions of others, by getting his stories published, seeing his name in the paper. Sometimes, when writing a story that was a collection of local news items, he would separate each item with a small design bearing his initials—*ECD*—for Elbert Clifton Daniel—and a few people in Zebulon thought this was a bit much.

There was something a little cute and fancy about young Daniel, they said, those few who were put off by his formality in this so informal town. They saw him developing, too early, a sense of self and a manner that seemed mildly patronizing. But the pretty girls whom he knew liked him very much, liked not only his fine clothes and politeness but also his respect for older people, especially his parents, and they liked the fact that he was the brightest boy in the class and voted the "best looking" in the Wakelon High School yearbook of 1929. But the girls sensed that they did not have a chance with him, not from anything he said or did but from what he did not say or do. He did not get involved. He seemed to have big plans in distant places, a smooth country boy's sense of getting ahead, and many years later, after he had begun his rise at *The New York Times* and had married Margaret Truman, some people back in Zebulon smiled and nodded knowingly.

But Margaret Truman was also a small-town girl, and she and Daniel were more alike in their origin and attitude than most people realized. Margaret had been an only child, as had Daniel, and both had received a surfeit of attention and guidance from their parents, confidence in the values of the community, and little self-doubt, and they grew up in a rather prim setting in a fixed society with an awareness that their families were a bit better off than most of their neighbors. Both of their fathers had begun as small shopkeepers, sharing many provincial notions about life and the Negro, and the elder Daniel was once also active in politics. Twice he served as mayor of Zebulon, getting the city to put in running water in the early Twenties, then to replace the kerosene street lamps with electric lights, and Harry Truman once told him, "Hell, you did just as well as I did—you just stayed down in your little town helping the poor people, and I went up and mixed with those rich bastards."

When Margaret was eleven her father, a newly elected Senator from Missouri, began taking his family to Washington for the first half of each year; but this experience, as well as her later years in the White House and her career in show business, did not remove from her the aura of her region. If anything, her local allegiance might have become even more pronounced as she got older and solidified her views. She moved to New York, but was not moved *by* New York. She occupies it as a kind of permanent tourist. She responds to New York's cultural offerings and challenges but is quick to see signs of New York's coarseness or the gaucherie of its people. She is unimpressed by the sophisticated glitter that encircles her East Side address, and after her marriage and the birth of her children she has rarely invited to her home the social butterflies that her husband has long found so fascinating. A few have resented this, and they have spread unflattering stories— Margaret cannot keep her help, Daniel does most of the cooking—but she continues to do as she wishes and, in a gracious way, to protect her privacy and be very selective of those invitations she accepts: yes, with some hesitation, to the Capote ball; yes, without hesitation, to the supper-dance in New York honoring England's Princess Margaret; no, with regret, to Bennett Cerf's party for Frank Sinatra, the Daniels being otherwise occupied on that occasion. While Margaret Truman Daniel has a closet full of well-designed clothes, her simplicity dominates them. Like her father, she is forthright and opinionated; unlike her husband, she is open and casual, although in recent years her influence, coupled with his own success, may have led Daniel to reveal himself with greater ease.

He still is a formal man, however, and still is fascinated by people who are privileged and rich—a decisive factor in the exhaustive coverage *The New York Times* now gives to news of society—but he is also more at home with himself and his past. Occasionally, when in high spirits, he even refers to himself as a "country boy." He was never really that in its fullest sense, although there is no telling what he might have become had his father, a proud man, not helped clear a path through the rustic tobacco tract of Carolina to the more lush land in the distance.

Elbert Clifton Daniel, Sr., is now in his eighties. His facial features, particularly his eyes, strongly resemble his son's, although his gray wavy hair is shorter and his clothes far less conservative. He will sometimes appear at his drugstore wearing a pair of formal gray-striped morning trousers and over them a brown double-breasted jacket, and under it a blue-striped shirt and pale polka-dot bow tie, and also a brown hat, black shoes, a brown cane; all of which, on him, looks fine. He is thought of as the town's most distinguished living landmark, being the first man in Zebulon to have a telephone, and nearly everyone is very fond of him, although there are a few, very few, who find him somewhat patronizing, a characteristic he may have passed on to his son. In addition to his ventures into politics, he had a brief fling at owning the Vakoo movie theater, and he once merchandised his own brand of liver pills and a diarrhea cure. Had it not been for an attack of appendicitis, however, when he was about eighteen years old, he might never have escaped the rugged farm life of *his* father, his grandfather, and nearly all the other Daniel kin who had sailed during the previous century from England and settled in this area of the South; but the illness enabled him to meet a young doctor from Raleigh who befriended him and later encouraged him to go into the drug business. And in 1905, after borrowing some money from his grandfather, Zachariah G. Daniel, an illiterate but industrious tobacco farmer who sometimes peddled his product by horse wagon through Virginia, and after acquiring a drug "permit" from the doctor friend, Clifton Daniel, Sr., bought an interest in his first drugstore. He practiced pharmacy on his permit until 1911, when he supplemented his training with schooling at Greensboro; in the same year, in the drugstore one day, he saw seated at the counter with other girls, sipping a soda, Miss Elvah Jones. She was the daughter of a tobacco warehouseman, had attended junior college at Raleigh, having once been the May Queen, and she was very pretty. He quickly courted her and in December of that year, at her grandmother's home in the next county, they were married and off to a honeymoon in Richmond and Baltimore, and during the following September was born their son, the future managing editor of *The New York Times*, Elbert Clifton Daniel, Jr.

He was an agreeable child, and he did most of the right things. He had his first tooth at nine months, was walking within a year, but carefully, revealing a caution that would always be with him, and he displayed a premature aversion to dirt. There was nothing of the farmer in him. He was like his mother in his quiet manner, neat about his clothing, clean and precise, and his father later worried about him when he preferred to remain near his mother, indoors, much of the time sprawled on a rug reading a book. But the boy was very bright in school and obedient at home, and after school he helped out in the drugstore and also sold *Grit* and other magazines around town, saving his pennies, and when it came time for college, in the fall of 1929, with money scarce and the *Zebulon Record* offering a year's subscription for a fat hen or a bushel of potatoes, he was able to contribute sixty-five dollars from his side earnings toward his tuition.

Most of what he wanted out of college life, he got; and that which he did not get, he did not miss. He joined Phi Delta Theta fraternity, did well in class, wrote for the *Daily Tar Heel*. He would have liked to become editor of the *Tar Heel* but not long after joining it he was fired for being too haughty with a senior editor, and by the time he was reinstated to the staff he was out of line for the editor's job. He did become editor of the campus literary magazine, *The Carolina*, and, backed by the interfraternity political machine, he was elected vice-president of the student body over the clamorous objections of one independent candidate who went around telling everybody: "I don't care if you don't vote for me, but for *God's* sake don't vote for Clifton Daniel!"

Daniel could also have gotten the nomination for the presidency later but he declined because he had the notion—"somewhat presumptuous," he later conceded —that he was a newspaperman, and he believed that newsmen, in the interest of objectivity, should stay out of party politics and never become irretrievably committed to any one cause or person, a policy shared by nearly all journalists, although at a cost. For this detachment from the world they observe robs them of a deeper experience that springs from involvement, and they sometimes become merely voyeurs who see much, feel little. They take death and disaster as casually as a dock strike, and they take for granted their right to publicize the weakness in others but they never have to lay it on the line themselves. Of course if journalists become identified with a cause or a great figure they may become apologists or propagandists, flunkies for the famous. Clifton Daniel would know some journalists to whom this would happen, but it would never happen to him. He was always too cautious, too sure of what he wanted, and he was possibly assisted by a natural aloofness, perhaps even lack of passion. If he ever made a compromise in his professional or private life, few people would know it, there would be no scandal, he would cover his tracks well.

After graduating from the University of North Carolina in 1933, and after a year on a small newspaper downstate, Daniel joined the *Raleigh News and Observer*. There between 1934 and 1937 he covered politics and crime, a variety of assignments, meeting many interesting people, among them Katharine Cornell, the first famous actress he ever interviewed, and Thomas Wolfe, whose novel *Look Homeward, Angel* had been published a few years before. By 1941, Daniel had left Raleigh and was working for the Associated Press. He had come up to New York in the spring of 1937 but had been turned down by nearly all the dailies, including *The New York Times*. The one paper that offered him a job was the *World-Telegram*, and he turned it down when the offer was only $35 a week, $10 less than he had been making in Raleigh.

His interview at the *New York Times* building had been short. He had visited the newsroom but had not gotten in to see the managing editor's office that he would one day occupy, nor did he meet the man himself, Edwin James. He had seen one of James's subordinates, a night city editor named Bruce Rae, a small, self-possessed man who had been a first-rate crime reporter in the Twenties and now aspired to become in time James's successor, not suspecting that James quietly abhorred him. The exact reasons were vague but easily understood—James was a cocky little man and what James least desired nearby was another cocky little man. Rae would get as high as assistant managing editor but then, as Catledge was brought into the home office as James's assistant, Rae was sent to Guam and put in charge of the Pacific correspondents during World War II. When Daniel succeeded Catledge as the managing editor, Rae was still on *The Times* in a lesser editorial position, mellowed by time and quite pleasant, and if he remembered having not hired Daniel in 1937, he never mentioned it, nor did Daniel, who did remember it. But it had been only a routine meeting, the usual institutional once-over, a mild mixture of politeness and noncommitment, and Daniel was not really disappointed when he was rejected. As a newsman in Carolina, Daniel had been very conscious of *The Times* but not awed by it. His father's drugstore in Zebulon did not sell *The Times*, and it still does not. Daniel had recognized the dignity and importance of being employed by *The Times*, but he did not regard it as a place where he would particularly want to work. The journalists whose work he knew best in those days were either working on the afternoon papers or on the *Herald Tribune*, such writers as H. Allen Smith and Joseph Mitchell, the latter a 1929 graduate of the University of North Carolina who would become the great reporter on *The New Yorker*. *The Times* had, as always, many fine reporters but almost no fine writers. Its one notable exception, Meyer Berger, whose descriptive coverage of Al Capone's tax trial in Chicago in 1932 had quickly established his credentials, had quit *The Times* in 1937 for *The New Yorker*, although he would return a year later, discovering that he worked best when surrounded by noise, distractions, and the constant pressure of a newsroom and a daily deadline.

The New York Times, when Clifton Daniel applied to it in 1937, was a paper in slow transition. Adolph Ochs had been dead for two years, and Arthur Hays Sulzberger, though introducing changes, was making them gradually and quietly, wishing to avoid any impression that *The Times* was shifting from its Ochsian course. The daily edition was selling for two cents a copy in 1937 and was about to go up a penny. Its circulation had gone over 500,000 for the first time in its history, and the Sunday edition was almost 770,000. The appearance of the newspaper, its front-page makeup and design, was not radically different in those days from what it would be when Daniel would become its managing editor twenty-seven years later, although photographs were still a rarity on page one. Ochs had preferred it that way, relenting only when a very special news event seemed to demand a photograph of the principal, such as a two-column front-page photograph of Lindbergh after his flight in 1927; a two-column photograph of Roosevelt after his Presidential victory in 1932 and a one-column photograph of New York's newly elected Governor Herbert H. Lehman; a two-column picture of the German President Paul von Hindenburg upon his death in 1934, and no picture of his successor, Adolf Hitler; a four-column photograph of Adolph Ochs upon his death in 1935.

Sulzberger liked pictures, as future editions of the paper would show, but he infused his taste with such a subtle sense of timing that few readers would notice the transition from the era of Ochs to Sulzberger. One of the more startling moves that Sulzberger did make by 1937, one that would undoubtedly have been rejected by Ochs had he been alive, was the appointment of a woman, Anne O'Hare McCormick, as a foreign-

affairs columnist. Perhaps nothing would have appealed
to Ochs less than the authoritative tone of a lady
columnist in *The Times*. Still, Mrs. McCormick had
been getting articles published in *The Times* on a free-
lance basis from Europe since 1921, and the clarity of
her reporting, the depth of her perception, had impressed not only Sulzberger but also the three editors
who presided during these years, Van Anda and
Birchall and James. They were all aware of the fact
that she had been one of the first journalists in Europe
to note the rise of fascism in Italy and to write about
its new young spokesman, then referred to in *The Times*
as "Professor Mussolini"; and so Sulzberger, with
absolutely no resistance from his advisers or from his
wife, Iphigene, who had politely deplored many of her
father's Victorian reservations about lady pundits, assigned Mrs. McCormick in 1937 to the important job
in Europe—as *The New York Times* continued to build
up its foreign staff for the great war that seemed inevitable.

This was the big news of 1937—not what *had* happened, but what was *going* to happen. And *The Times*
unlike much of the nation, was getting ready. Hanson
Baldwin, then beginning his career as the paper's military specialist, was sent to Europe in 1937 to learn all
he could about European military establishments while
he still could. Herbert Matthews, covering the Spanish
Civil War in 1937, was already writing in *The Times*
and in a book that this was just a warm-up for the
larger conflict to follow, and in one appraisal from
Spain he warned: "You who stroll along the Great
White Way, thinking complacently how far away it all
is from peaceful America—you, too, will feel a tap on
your shoulder one of these days, and will hear the call.
. . . War has a long, long arm and it is reaching out for
all of us."

Matthews was thirty-six years old when he wrote
this. He was a tall, very thin, solemn, and scholarly
man, a student, of Dante, and he had a lean ascetic face
and dark sad eyes and a romantic fatalism about the
world and his place in it. He was both quietly fascinated

by the heroics of war and deeply concerned about its victims, and this concern, together with his sense of history and hypocrisy, brought a dimension and edge to his reporting that was involving and memorable. He was not a reporter's reporter, he was a *writer's* reporter, and during the Spanish Civil War, covering it from the Loyalist side, he was greatly admired by the literary left and others in Europe and America who despised Franco. Hemingway, a friend of Matthews', called him the "straightest, the ablest and the bravest correspondent, a gaunt lighthouse of honesty," but Matthews at the same time was being called a Communist along the Catholic front in New York and elsewhere. A year earlier, in 1936, when Matthews had been the only correspondent to serve throughout the Ethiopian campaign on the Italian side, he had been called a fascist by many *Times* readers. There was something in the chemistry of Herbert Matthews that could activate readers, provoking them to extravagant praise or scorn. Matthews did not, like so many correspondents, play it safe with the official version of things, and perhaps only *The New York Times* could absorb within its ranks for so long such an endlessly controversial figure; but by the Nineteen-sixties, during Clifton Daniel's years as the managing editor, after Matthews' reporting on Castro's Cuba had again hit the raw nerve of the nation, there was some question as to how much even *The Times* could take. It was not that *The Times* hierarchy would ever dismiss Matthews. He was too much a part of them for that. There were other ways. But in 1937 Herbert Matthews was one of the exciting young men on *The Times,* an inspiration to his juniors if a trial to his seniors, and his reporting from Spain was dramatic, his insight into its consequences prophetic.

Also reporting from Europe in those days, though he was sixty-five years old, was the former managing editor, Frederick T. Birchall, crossing and recrossing Europe as energetically as he had ever since replacing Edwin James as the chief correspondent five years before. In the process Birchall became as familiar with

Cracow as Paris, Dublin as Geneva or Berlin, and from these places he cabled stories that at times focused on the visible signs of a tense Europe—such as when German customs officers held him up at an airport and forced him to strip to the skin while searching for a nonexistent supply of money they believed he was trying to smuggle out of the country. At other times Birchall's stories caught the quiet eerie hours of Europe waiting for war. In one story from London Birchall described how, while walking through the park that afternoon, he had suddenly become aware of a strange new change in the city. At first he could not perceive what it was. He knew that it was not the result of the obvious preparations for war that he saw all around him—the sandbag craters, the wheel tracks, the balloon barrages, the shelter trenches. Then, he wrote, it began to occur to him as he walked "that in the whole park, formerly at this hour filled with laughing children playing ball, chasing each other and making merry in all sorts of ways, there was not a child in sight. Thinking back," he went on, "it was also certain that throughout this week one had not seen anywhere a boy or girl below the age of 16. This was a childless city."

Frederick Birchall's reporting in the Thirties, particularly from Paris, was so often denigrating to the Germans that one night a *Times* editor in New York, anticipating the harm that might come to Birchall from the German agents in Paris, did something that *Times*-men are warned never to do. The editor falsified a dateline. He scratched out "Paris" and wrote in "London" at the top of Birchall's story preceding the date, thereby violating what was perhaps Sulzberger's pet rule. A dateline on a *Times* story was sacred, Sulzberger had often said, adding that readers were always entitled to know precisely from where and when a dispatch had originated. Had Sulzberger known of the editor's act, the editor would have been severely reprimanded or fired, which is what had happened, and would happen, to other transgressors. But Sulzberger never learned of it. Nor did the editor, a large and

resolute man named Neil MacNeil, reveal it to his colleagues. This was possible because during the Thirties
MacNeil was a senior editor answerable to few others
in the newsroom; he also worked the night shift, arriving in the newsroom at 6 p.m. just as Edwin James
was leaving, and James, anxious to get out, was
pleased that he had such experienced subordinates as
MacNeil to hold the fort through the night.

MacNeil worked in a section of the newsroom
known, for no apparent reason, as the "bullpen." It
consisted of three or four desks arranged to form a
right angle in the southeast corner of the newsroom,
and these desks were occupied by senior editors who
read the news as it came in and then determined how
much of it would be printed and where it would appear
in the paper. Technically the bullpen editors were
under the managing editor, but during Edwin James's
era their judgment went unquestioned. It was not until
Turner Catledge succeeded James in 1951 and established the daily news conference in the managing
editor's office, on the opposite side of the newsroom,
that the bullpen editors lost their exclusivity as re-
ceivers and appraisers of news, desk dons *sans re-
proche;* and when this happened Neil MacNeil, who
had been on *The New York Times* for thirty-three
years, asked to be retired, and he was.

But during the Thirties the paper was governed at
night by the bullpen editors—men who, through the
years, had slowly and patiently worked their way up
through what was probably the most tedious and unheralded craft in the newsroom. Copyreading. Copyreaders were a special breed of journalists. They were
indoor creatures, retainers of rules, anonymous men.
Many had come to New York from all over America
seeking some greater fulfillment, and when this did not
materialize they ended up, through circuitous and often
bizarre circumstances, on a copydesk at *The New York
Times.* Educated men, well-read travelers, they were
ideally suited for the work, though few would admit it.
They had not planned on becoming copyreaders. *Nobody* planned on that. And they often spoke of quitting

or getting an outside job as a reporter, which a few of them had once been in smaller cities. But most of them remained for years on the copydesk, and secretly they liked the sedentary life, this almost monastic existence of measured words and precise routines and quiet rewards. Here, within the insular atmosphere of *The Times*, they had security and isolation from uncertainty. They spent their nights reading bulletins and editing stories about the world's latest calamity and chaos, threats and failures, but their only contact with this reality was with the point of a pencil. They did not seem to mind working late at night, the most miserable hours in the newspaper business, missing the theater and dinner parties, arriving in the newsroom at a time when most of the staff was preparing to leave, and leaving when the charwomen arrived. The charwomen and the prostitutes in Times Square were usually the only females who crossed their path, but they did not mind this either, seeming perfectly contented within the male circle of deskmen when away from the daytime distractions of wives and children. After work, copyreaders joined other copyreaders for a few drinks in taverns around Times Square or Broadway, savoring a special intimacy about New York at this hour, and mingling with an interesting crowd around the bar, actors and musicians, rogues and hustlers and tipsters, and these people considered it a privilege of sorts to meet *Times*men, and thus the copyreaders felt themselves a part of a rather gamy night scene in New York; but they felt it from a distance. They remained copyreaders, introspective men, careful men, dreamers not doers. Which is not to degrade them. They were more valued on newspapers than most reporters, and they made more money at the start. Many copyreaders were scholarly men, and nearly all possessed a wealth of information and knowledge of law that helped the newspaper avoid errors and libel. Still, the copyreader could not go very far. If he was diligent, he might during a decade move from one end of the curved copydesk, where he began his career, to the middle of the desk, becoming slotman, and this permitted him to distribute stories as they came in to other copyreaders for editing and headlines. If he was diligent and lucky, he might someday be promoted to the head of the desk and be given a title. And if he was *very* diligent and lucky, he might finally end up one night sitting in the bullpen. This is what had happened to Neil MacNeil. And it was understandable, once he had worked his way through the maze and reached the top in the Thirties, that he would appear to be a man of great certainty, pride, and confidence.

MacNeil had been born in Nova Scotia, a big muscular man with none of the bad posture and pallor of so many copyreaders. He had a deep commanding voice, and on his desk in the bullpen he had a little bell that he would ring with his thick forefinger when he wanted a copyboy. The copyboys, in deference to his position, were quick in responding, and because he had a gentle manner and did not address them in the peremptory tone used by some lesser editors of that time, they liked him and tried hard to please him and did not resent it when he occasionally sent them out at midnight to a food shop on Eighth Avenue to buy him a small bag of apples.

As was the case with a high percentage of editors in the newsroom in the Thirties, MacNeil was a Roman Catholic, and it was often said of *The Times* during these years that it was a paper "owned by Jews and edited by Catholics for Protestants." The bullpen was lightly styled the "Catholic bullpen" within the office and, though no one could prove it, Neil MacNeil, Raymond H. McCaw (the senior bullpen editor), and others were said to reflect a Catholic viewpoint when appraising the news, with the results ranging from the playing down of stories about birth control to the playing up of stories expressing alarm over communism. If a *Times* reporter was even rumored as leaning to the left, his stories were vigilantly read and reread by the bullpen editors, and they were no less scrupulous with the controversial dispatches from Spain by Herbert Matthews than with the less noticeable stories from New York by such younger men as A. H. Raskin, the latter having gotten onto the staff after having served, during his undergraduate days, as *The Times'* campus correspondent at the City College of New York, the Berkeley of the Thirties.

In Matthews' case, his difficulty with a large portion of the pro-Franco Catholic readership in America was no secret at *The Times*, there having been several organized campaigns and statements attacking Matthews, and on one occasion the Catholic Press Association made an official protest to *The Times'* publisher. It had "no confidence" in Matthews' reporting from the Loyalist side, it said, and it was particularly annoyed, among other things, by Matthews' repeated suggestions in his stories that the Fascists in Italy and even Germany were participating heavily on the side of Franco. *The New York Times'* correspondent covering the war from Franco's side, William P. Carney, had denied this, and one night a message went out to Matthews from the newsroom reading: "Why do you continue to say Italians are fighting in Spain when Carney claims there are no Italians in Spain?" Matthews' subsequent dispatch repeated the claim—"These troops were Italians and nothing but Italians"—but this sentence in *The Times* was changed to read: "These troops were insurgents and nothing but insurgents."

When A. H. Raskin, who had been an aggressive campus correspondent at City College, was promoted to *The Times'* staff in 1934, an official from the college asked Neil MacNeil why *The Times* would tolerate such a political risk as Raskin. MacNeil said he had no idea Raskin was a risk, and for several years afterwards MacNeil watched Raskin's reporting very carefully, finding no justification for the inference. Still, for whatever reason, it took Abe Raskin a long time to get a by-line in *The New York Times*, even by the slow editorial procedures of that period.

One day in 1936 Raskin had five front-page stories in *The Times*, none of which carried his by-line. Then in 1939 there was a story by Raskin that was particularly well liked by Raymond McCaw in the bullpen, and McCaw walked over to the city desk to ask who had written it.

"Abe Raskin," was the reply.

"Put a by-line on it," McCaw said, and then, as an afterthought, he asked, "What's Abe's middle initial,"

"H."

"Well," McCaw said, "sign it 'A. H. Raskin.'"

McCaw's saying "sign it 'A. H. Raskin,'" and not "sign it 'Abraham Raskin'" or "'Abraham H. Raskin'" was interesting, because it raised quietly a question that would not have been raised aloud in *The New York Times'* newsroom. There was a feeling among some Jewish reporters in the Thirties, however reluctant they were to discuss it openly, that Ochs and Sulzberger, sensitive men, did not want *The Times* to appear "too Jewish" in public, and one small result of this was the tendency of editors to sign stories with initials in place of such names as Abraham; although, again, the reporters could not prove it and they were wise to keep this theory to themselves. To mention it to an editor might expose the reporter as an ungrateful paranoiac, one who was completely ignorant of *The Times'* policy against discrimination of any kind, to say nothing of the fact that there were Christian staff members who used initials, it being quite customary in those days; and further, to make a Jewish issue of this trivial point might put a reporter in the same category with those cranks and special-interest groups who endlessly seek to embarrass *The Times* by doubting its purity, groups who charged consecutively through the Thirties into the Sixties that *The Times* was a tool of Wall Street, was pro-British, pro-German, anti-Labor, pro-Communist, anti-Zionist, an apologist for the American State Department.

In actual fact, a case could have been made against *The Times* on any of these charges, but a weak case, for it could easily be counter-balanced with evidence to offset it—but not always. *The Times* in principle tried to be objective in its news coverage, but in reality it could not always be. It was run by humans, flawed figures, men who saw things as they *could* see them, or sometimes *wished* to see them; interpreting principles to suit contemporary pressures, they wanted it both ways; it was the oldest story of all. Ideally, *The Times* desired no opinions within its news columns, restricting opinion to its editorial page. Realistically, this was not possible. The editors' opinions and tastes were imposed every day within the news—either by the space they allowed for a certain story or the position they assigned to it, or the headline they ordered for it, and also by the stories they did not print, or printed for only one edition, or edited heavily, or held out for a few days and then printed in the back of the thick Sunday edition between girdle advertisements and dozens of Bachrach photographs of pretty girls just engaged. The reporter's ego was also a factor in the news coverage—he wrote what he wrote best, he wrote what he understood, reflecting the total experience of his lifetime, shades of his pride and prejudice; he wrote sometimes to please the editor, at other times to call attention to his own style, reducing stories that did not suit his style, and at still other times he wrote with the hope that he would get a by-line in *The Times*, a testimony to his being alive on that day, alive in *The Times* through that day and all the tomorrows of microfilm.

The Times was a very human institution, large and vulnerable. Even by the Nineteen-thirties it was too big *not* to be vulnerable. Every working day hundreds of decisions were made within the *Times* building, each of which, if singled out, could lead to misconceptions —which was also the inherent problem of news coverage itself—but it was equally true that *The Times* nearly always tried to be fair, and sometimes without reason or design things just happened at *The Times*. There were no villainous editors behind the deeds. No acts of vanity. *Things just happened.* Or the happening was the result of one man acting unofficially—a Neil MacNeil changing a dateline from Paris to London. Or it might be a Raymond McCaw saying, without ulterior motive, "Sign it 'A. H. Raskin' "— as other *Times* editors, years later, would sign the by-line of Abe Weiler, a movie critic, "A. H. Weiler," and of Abe Rosenthal, a foreign correspondent, "A. M. Rosenthal." It was perhaps pure coincidence, too, that since Ochs's paper had become the bible of the American establishment, no Jew had been elevated to the position of managing editor, even as Jewish subordinate editors would begin to outnumber other ethnic and religious groups on the paper. Some *Times*men interpreted these things as more than mere coincidence but no case could be made. Nothing could be proved. There was no policy, there was an almost conspicuous lack of policy on so many things within *The Times*, and this led to assumptions about the paper that were not true, causing some *Times*men to obey rules that did not exist—causing other *Times*men, the less inhibited ones, to operate freely and then suddenly discover rules *did* exist, hundreds of them, thousands. But there was nothing fixed within the institution despite all of its exterior commitment to tradition. Every generation of *Times*men was subject to the changing interpretations of the rules and values of the men at the top. And *The Times* in the Thirties was a paper in transition. There was an atmosphere of vagueness.

Sometimes Ochs seemed to be running the paper from his grave. At other times it seemed that the strings were being pulled by Arthur Hays Sulzberger and, not to be ignored, his wife, Iphigene. The great Van Anda was long retired by 1937, devoting himself to astronomy and cosmogony, living in Manhattan or in the country, spending hours at night squinting up at the sky through his telescope pondering, as he described it, "planetary parentage"; but his influence was still strong in the newsroom, and two of his apostles from the copydesk, now risen to the bullpen, were McCaw and MacNeil. The staff was quickly expanding, and there were more subeditors, specialists, critics. Bosley Crowther, who had joined *The Times* as a reporter in 1928, sharing a desk in the overcrowded newsroom with Hanson Baldwin, had moved into the movie department in 1937. Brooks Atkinson, a tweedy gentleman from New England, a scholar and bird watcher whose one extravagance was a lemon-colored roadster he raced wildly on weekends in the country, was the drama critic. The dour-looking Olin Downes, the world's worst typist, was the music critic. The religious-news editor was a puritanical woman named Rachel McDowell, known within the office as "Lady Bishop." A reporter in the Science department was William L. Laurence, a modest, shaggy-haired little man who would become the paper's expert on the atom and journalism's only witness to the destruction at Nagasaki. *The Times'* ship-news editor was an old English sea captain, Walter "Skipper" Williams, the son of a lawyer who, rather than follow in that profession, had gone to sea, working as a boatman on the Nile, a gold hunter up the Orinoco, a lightning-rod installation man in Central America, a foreman during the Panama Canal digging, and finally a journalist for Hearst. In 1905, with an introduction from an English nobleman who knew Ochs, Williams came to *The Times,* settling down, although on rare occasions he was again led astray by his imagination. One of his stories, a collector's item that somehow slipped past the copydesk, reported the sighting of a huge sea serpent in the Caribbean from the bridge of the liner *Mauretania.* The story was quickly questioned by several newspapers but Mr. Williams stuck to it, producing an excerpt from the ship's log and a drawing of the monster done by the ship's senior first officer.

The Times' sports editor in those days was, like Skipper Williams, a wandering individualist, the sort of man rarely seen at *The Times* today but not uncommon then. His name was Bernard William St. Denis Thomson, and he was an elegant man mildly scented with perfume; he was known in the office as "Colonel" Thomson, even though he had never gotten higher than captain in the United States Army, a rank he attained during World War I in France as a trainer of pack animals. Born in Canada, he had a law degree from Harvard, had ridden burros prospecting for gold in the West, later became a rancher, still later a dabbler in gambling, and he twice broke the bank at

Monte Carlo. Like his father, he finally settled into journalism, and during his twenty-one years as the sports editor of *The Times* he built up his staff from six to fifty, and he insisted, obeying Ochs, that *The Times* print more sports scores than any other newspaper—his clerks obliging on occasion by slipping in the scores of contests between small Negro colleges in the South, infuriating Thomson—and he greatly expanded the coverage of such fashionable minor sports as tennis, sailing, and rowing, *especially* rowing. He loved this sport, it being the only one he had ever mastered, and because of this *The New York Times* gave elaborate treatment to the Poughkeepsie and Thames regattas and other rowing events, establishing a policy that persists even now, decades after Colonel Thomson's death.

Among the more autonomous editors on *The Times* in 1937, of course, were Lester Markel in the Sunday department and Arthur Krock in Washngton, and one member of Krock's staff, thinking big, was Turner Catledge. James Reston was still with the London bureau of the Associated Press in 1937, covering sports events in summer and the Foreign Office in winter, and Tom Wicker in that year was a boy of ten who, with his parents and sister, had recently taken an overnight train from Hamlet, North Carolina, into Washington for a first visit, a thrilling experience he would vividly remember in later years after he had succeeded Reston, remembering the walk from Union Station in the brilliant sunshine toward the Capitol and its dome against the sky, the most beautiful sight he had ever seen, and remembering the rooming house in which he and his family had stayed, the trolleys rolling past the door, and how his mother wept in front of Lincoln Memorial, and the marvelously strange sight of green money flowing from the presses at the Bureau of Engraving, and the sound of the Marine band playing on the very spot where Roosevelt had been sworn in as President; and Wicker remembered having dinner one night at the Occidental Restaurant, a place where the famous men of Washington ate, somebody had said, and many years later, when Wicker was as famous himself, he would sometimes have lunch at the Occidental Restaurant, it being as crowded and noisy in the Sixties as it was in the Thirties, and he would wonder what table he and his sister and parents had been given that night —"those two wide-eyed children, my father, my mother, spending money they could ill afford to make sure our trip was complete. If I thought it was a bad, out-of-the-way table I could never go there again."

Clifton Daniel, unable to get a job on *The New York Times* in 1937, walked crosstown to the Associated Press. He had a friend working there, a rewrite man from North Carolina, and Daniel's reception at the AP was more cordial than elsewhere; before he left that afternoon he had a job offer of $50 a week. He quickly accepted, went back to North Carolina to pack his things and sell his car, and then he returned to New York. He got an apartment off Gramercy Park with another reporter and worked on the AP desk until midnight. After work he explored the town, going to those places that most young people patronize during their early years in New York, and never again, doing more with less money than he ever could again. The parties he went to, the girls he dated were mainly connected somehow with newspaper circles or North Carolina, and one of the persons he got to know during these years was Thomas Wolfe. Daniel and a few others would sometimes go out drinking until dawn with Wolfe at bars in mid-Manhattan, later taking long walks on Broadway listening to the towering novelist sound off on a thousand subjects, monologues that went on and on through the street noise and passing crowds, under the bright theater marquees and tall buildings, and as Daniel strained to listen he realized that Thomas Wolfe talked as he wrote, the words streaming endlessly within a low tone of tension. While never a close friend, Daniel thought he knew Wolfe fairly well at this time, but then one night at a restaurant, after joining Wolfe at a table, Daniel could tell from the way the conversation went that Wolfe had no recollection of ever having seen him before. Wolfe was drinking heavily then, and later that year he was dead.

By 1939 Daniel had transferred to the AP bureau in Washington, meeting journalists who would later be met again, including Turner Catledge; and in November of 1940, at the age of twenty-eight, his dark wavy hair already turning gray, Clifton Daniel sailed to Switzerland for the AP on a ship whose passengers included Lady Jersey, a stunning blue-eyed blonde who had been married to the Earl of Jersey, and before that to a Chicago lawyer and to Cary Grant. She would later, after the war, marry a Polish R.A.F. pilot, but in London during the war—a year or so after meeting Daniel on the ship—she and Daniel would become sufficiently well acquainted to cause their friends to speculate that the two would someday marry. They underrated Daniel's power of resistance. He was fascinated by her, there seemed little doubt of that, but he was fascinated as well by the whole glamorous setting of that time, the excitement of his first foreign assignment, the anticipation of reporting the war, the new situations in strange lands, and it had all begun propitiously on that winter day in 1940 when Daniel and Lady Jersey—née Virginia Cherrill of Carthage, Illinois, a onetime actress who had been Charlie Chaplin's leading lady in *City Lights* —boarded a ship across the river from New York during a dock strike, the garbage piled high along the pier, the champagne flowing on deck and smiling crowds waving good-bye; and weary refugees arriving from Europe on another ship, relieved to be landing in an America free of Nazis; and spies and smugglers moving along the docks in the crowds, one of them even approaching Daniel with a proposition.

Shortly after Daniel had arrived in Switzerland and settled in the AP bureau in Bern, he began getting letters from her, and nine months later he arranged a transfer to London and he saw her again. He had arrived in London after a flight to Bristol with Walter Cronkite, then with the United Press, and at the London terminal Daniel was surprised when a cheerful little cockney woman stopped him and grabbed his luggage, the first lady porter he had ever seen. It was so dark that as he rode through the city he saw virtually nothing except the arch of Hyde Park, then he was through the swinging doors into the Savoy Hotel, and later he had a marvelous dinner in a quiet restaurant nearby that he could never find again.

To be an American journalist and a bachelor in London then was to be a most welcome addition to the city. The British were generally receptive to American contacts on all levels for a great variety of reasons, everything from obtaining PX provisions to pulling strings for friends or relatives in the joint U.S.-British military setup everybody knew was coming; and a presentable and charming American journalist could, through his contacts at the United States Embassy, easily gain entrée into London circles that were clustered with engaging women and short of available men. There was a not very visible British Establishment then, the war having turned everything upside down—parvenu industrialists throughout the country suddenly having become vitally important to the war effort, much of the oldline aristocracy away in the British army or navy, and London society marked by a sort of freeform socializing and some very spicy indiscretion. But Daniel, as always, was not careless in his relationships, and he and Lady Jersey conducted their lives with the utmost in decorum. She worked hard during the day for the Red Cross, and at night in her home she conducted a salon in an unpretentious way, convoking groups of active pleasant people—newsmen, actors, R.A.F. fliers—for no more than conversation and drinks or even tea. She was very intelligent and well informed, conservatively opulent in dress, had straight blonde hair and a sort of Dresden-doll face with a small Cupid's-bow mouth and perfect complexion, excellent wit, and a lilting, trilling, musical-scale laugh. She was one of the very desirable women of London then, and Daniel was much taken by her company; but it was also obvious that he was not to be distracted from his primary purpose, his work. Daniel was an ambitious man, more ambitious than he seemed. And he knew that if he wished to distinguish himself on the AP bureau in London it would require considerable effort on his part because the AP had working for it many talented young men. There was Drew Middleton and Gladwin Hill and William White, to name a few who would be hired away by *The New York Times*, following in the path of James Reston, who had already quit the AP for *The Times*, and Clifton Daniel worked hard and well for the Associated Press. By 1944 he, too, had attracted the attention of *The Times,* and when a job was offered in that winter he took it.

Daniel had been hired on the recommendation of *The Times'* London bureau chief, Raymond Daniell, who is no relation. Raymond Daniell had been an outstanding *Times* reporter since 1928, reporting on the Scottsboro case and Huey Long's rise to power, the sharecropper disputes in Arkansas and coal-miner troubles in Kentucky. He had been in Mexico City in 1939 but, as the European war spread, he was quickly reassigned to London, where in 1940, his quarters at Lincoln's Inn were shattered by bombs and he and his colleagues moved *The Times'* bureau into the Savoy Hotel, where they also lived. Since London time is five hours ahead of New York, the staff usually wrote until dawn while bombs shook the city; they slept through the afternoons, raids or no raids, and then after their customary round of martinis they were back at work on what were called "inraids" and "out-raids"—the "inraids" being the German attacks on Great Britain, the "out-raids" being the retaliation by the R.A.F.

When Raymond Daniell first became aware of the AP reporter with the similar name, he did not particularly like him, especially his looks. A little too smooth and suave. And this first impression was fortified by other reporters' observations about Clifton Daniel: he seemed haughty, he never removed his jacket in the office, he was the only American newspaperman they had ever known who had lapels on his vests— and they made many other points about his clothes and hair, as reporters would continue to do for years, even speculating in 1956 that Clifton Daniel owned more suits than Harry Truman ever sold. But Raymond Daniell dug more deeply into the character of the man. And he learned that Clifton Daniel was not only a very fast and facile writer, but had often been put in charge of running the AP's London bureau during its most hectic hours and had always functioned calmly and efficiently; furthermore Daniel was known for his loyalty to the AP bureau chief and was not the sort who would ever overstep his boundaries or attempt to take over.

So Raymond Daniell offered him a job and Daniel accepted. But first, taking some time off, he visited New York, where a rather unusual thing happened that nearly cost him his job on *The New York Times*. Daniel had been invited to deliver a short speech about wartime London to a luncheon gathering of The Dutch Treat Club and, noticing the servicemen in the audience, he proceeded with anecdotes that he thought the GI's might enjoy. He gave one vivid description of an American colonel falling into a fountain during the blackout, and he also told the servicemen that if they got to London they need not worry about women; there were plenty of girls on the streets, Daniel said, and they were easy to pick up.

Seated in the audience, becoming very indignant and barely suppressing his rage, was General Julius Ochs Adler, a high executive on the business side of *The Times* and a nephew of Adolph Ochs. This profane and irreverent newspaperman was *not Times* material, General Adler declared later at *The Times'* office. And it took a great deal of persuasion on the part of more tolerant *Times*men to get General Adler to withdraw his objection and give Daniel a chance.

Daniel did well for *The Times* in London. Night after night he sat among other *Times*men in the Savoy or in the field, writing stories that would carry his byline the next day on page one. On a single day in November, riding in a jeep behind the advancing First Army, Clifton Daniel visited three countries and filed news stories from each—Eupen, Belgium; Aachen, Germany; and Vaals, the Netherlands. Then, in March of 1945, he was in Paris watching as "the big, dirty, green trucks speed along the Rue La Fayette, their heavy tires singing on the cobblestones and their canvas tops snapping in the winter wind. The men in the back," Daniel wrote, "are tired and cramped after eleven hours on the road. The last wisecrack was made a hundred miles back. But one of them peers out, sees the name on the street and says, 'La Fayette, we're here.' The trucks growl to a halt. . . . The men dismount, a little stiff at first, light up cigarettes and start looking. They inspect the cornices of the Opera House, watch the crowds swirling past the Galeries Lafayette and eye the passing girls—always the girls."

By spring, Daniel was back in London describing the city as the blackout restrictions were lifted, but before he could become adjusted to the light and tranquillity he was sent to North Africa and back to the sound of gunfire and rioting; then from Egypt he went to Iran, arriving in Tabriz with two other journalists hours ahead of the Iranian army that was to take over the city from a collapsing Soviet-backed Azerbaijanian rebel regime. As Daniel and the two others rode into town they were greeted by thousands of villagers lined along the road, and several sheep were sacrificed in their honor. The ceremony, the highest honor that a Persian can pay, consisted of beheading a sheep on one side of the road as the traveler approaches and carrying the head to the other side of the road; the traveler then passes between the body and the head.

The exotic sights and sounds, the headline makers and head-hunters from the Middle East to Great Britain—this was Daniel's world for the next seven years, although now, in 1966, all those events and faces are, if not forgotten, rarely remembered by anyone except those who were there, like Daniel, watching twenty years ago in Dhahran as a fat roasted hump of young camel was set before King Ibn Saud; listening at midnight from his hotel in Jerusalem as the troops below with rifles shuffled through the sloping street near Zion Square; dancing and dining in Cairo at Shepheard's with a pretty English girl when King Farouk arrived and asked Daniel and the girl to join him for a drink and a discussion about things that now mean little. Then Daniel was back in London observing "an elderly cherub with a cigar almost as big as the butt end of a billiard cue"—Winston Churchill, one of the few names that survives the momentary madness that makes headlines; the others quickly die or fade—Naguib, Mossadegh, Klaus Fuchs. Men like Daniel go off to new names, new places, never getting *involved*, although sometimes they worry about the impermanence of their work and wonder where it will lead them.

Daniel would have liked to have become chief of *The Times*' London bureau, but Drew Middleton, suspected by a few New York editors of having a private line of communication with Sulzberger, got the job. Daniel was assigned to replace Middleton in Germany and, as an Anglophile, he could barely abide the Germans. His reporting was uninspired, sometimes noticeably disdainful: "BERLIN—In the cold, dirty slush of last night's snow a few thousand of Berlin's millions stood along Potsdamer Strasse today watching the custodians of Germany's destiny roll by in a fleet of limousines. They were typical Berliners, seedy, cynical and slangy."

In the New York office at this time, 1954, there was the major personnel problem of finding a replacement in Russia for Harrison Salisbury. Salisbury, a tall and remote individualist, had been the *Times*man in Moscow since 1949. He had worked long and hard under the most adverse conditions—the Stalin era, censorship —and yet Turner Catledge had no other qualified *Times*man who wished to go to Moscow. Then Clifton Daniel volunteered.

Catledge was delighted. It confirmed for him many of the things he had come to accept about Daniel: in fact, Catledge had for the last two years been thinking of Clifton Daniel as a future executive, a possible successor, being impressed with Daniel's performance in the London bureau, as both an administrator and newsman, and Catledge also had been pleased with Daniel's attitude in accepting the Bonn assignment. Daniel was eleven years younger than Catledge, was an organization man who could operate within the corporate ego of *The Times*. And—he was a Southerner. Take away all that fancy English tailoring, that long wavy hair and courtly manner, and Daniel was what Catledge was—a country boy who said "sir" to his superiors, and had reverence for the Southern past and big-city dreams for the future.

So Clifton Daniel returned to New York to study Russian at Columbia University. After class he lunched at Sardi's, checking his Russian primer with the blonde in the cloakroom. He also took a trip down to Zebulon to see his parents and friends, and while in the Zebulon Post Office he was approached by the clerk, Whitley Chamblee, who leaned forward and whispered, "Did I hear you're going to *Russia*?"

After Daniel confirmed it, Whitley Chamblee asked, "I wonder, when you're there, if you would buy me one of those cuckoo clocks."

"Whitley, I don't believe they make cuckoo clocks in Russia," Daniel said. "They make them in Germany and Switzerland. But, well, if I find one, I'll send it to you."

A year later Clifton Daniel was in Geneva for the Big Four Conference. He had flown there from Moscow to join a team of *Times*men reporting on the big story. While there he also bought a cuckoo clock and mailed it to the postman in Zebulon.

Clifton Daniel arrived in Moscow in the late summer of 1954, a vintage period in Russian news—Stalin only eighteen months dead, Khrushchev emerging with a new party line that would include vodka toasts and receptions in the Great Kremlin Palace; at one reception, Daniel reported to the readers of *The Times*, "I was as close to Mr. Malenkov as this paper is to your nose." His reporting in *The New York Times* was remarkable in that it captured not only the political rumblings but also the mood of the people: the audience at the Bolshoi and the barber in Kharkov; the athletes preparing for the Olympics, and the fashion models wearing designs of "socialist realism" in this land where "bosoms are still bosoms, a waist is a waist, hips are hips, and there is no doubt about what they are and where they are situated." He reported, too, how tipping—a "relic of the dark bourgeois past"—was a necessary reality despite government disapproval, and he also described the arrival of winter:

> This was Christmas morning in Russia, and a cruel snow-laden wind blowing straight out of the pages of Russian history and literature whipped across roofs and through the frozen streets of Moscow. At midnight the bells in the tower of Yelokhovskaya Cathedral in the northern quarter of the city set up an insistent clangor. The faithful of the Russian Orthodox Church—women tightly wrapped in shawls and men in fur-collared coats and caps—hastened through the churchyard to escape the icy bite of the wind.

Since Daniel was then the only permanent correspondent of a Western non-Communist newspaper in the Russian capital, he was able to pick his themes at will and write them well and not have to contend with the editorial second-guessing that would have come from New York had there been rival papers' men in Moscow focusing on government spokesmen with their endless pronouncements. And not being part of a pack, Daniel had to work harder than he ever had. He developed an ulcer and lost between thirty and forty pounds. In November of 1955, Turner Catledge, acting on orders from Arthur Hays Sulzberger—who had by this time received letters from *Times*men commenting on how Daniel looked at the Big Four Conference in Geneva—ordered Daniel home immediately.

He returned, emaciated, but was not long in recovering, and soon was working in the New York office. He had been named *an* assistant to the foreign-news editor, although nobody in the city room knew precisely what this meant, including possibly *the* foreign-news editor.

But it seemed obvious from the way Daniel moved around the room, and from the way the room moved around him, that he was not going to remain an assistant to the foreign-news editor for very long. Daniel's desk, which normally would have given a clue, was in a nondescript spot. It was on the south side of the room, where all the senior editors sit, but it was partially obscured by a post. It was also up a bit between two lady secretaries, equidistant from the foreign editor and the bullpen. He also rarely remained seated. Usually he walked slowly around the big room, his glasses sometimes tucked into the top of his silver hair. Sometimes he would stop, sit down, and chat with reporters or deskmen in the Science department, or in Sports, or Education, or Financial, or Society. Occasionally he would return to one of these departments for a whole week or two, sitting in various places, and conversing in a very casual, disarming way about *The New York Times*, and asking occasionally what they liked about working there, or did not like. He was living at the Algonquin Hotel then, and was spotted at night also in Sardi's after the theater, and was once seen at the opera with a tall, striking brunette.

After they had gone twice more to the opera they became a "twosome" in Walter Winchell's column. The lady was mildly upset, partly because she felt that Daniel, a *Times* editor in a gossip column, might be very embarrassed, especially when their relationship had been so innocent: a drink, dinner, the opera, another drink perhaps, then home. Directly. A pleasant good-night in front of the doorman. That was it.

She had met Clifton Daniel at a New York party prior to his leaving for Moscow, had received one postcard from him, and was now pleased to be seeing him again. And, hoping that he would not be angered by the Winchell item, she telephoned Daniel at *The Times*.

He could not have been nicer. He only laughed when the Winchell subject was brought up, and hardly seemed sorry about the item appearing—which, she had to admit, surprised her. Shortly after that, in March of 1956, she read in the newspapers the engagement announcement of Margaret Truman and Clifton Daniel. She wrote a note of congratulations to Daniel, and received in turn a note thanking *her* "for being such a fine cover-up for myself and Margaret."

The brunette was devastated by the note, and she neither spoke to nor saw Clifton Daniel again for two years. Now, looking back, she concedes that perhaps she was wrong to have reacted as she did. Perhaps this was his way of being light, she thought, or humorous.

4

THE editors in the newsroom, having heard from their correspondents that the world today was in its usual state of greed and disorder, confusion and apathy, were now preparing to attend the news conference and relay the information to Daniel. Daniel would take it all very calmly, they knew, and within an hour the conference would be over, and within a few hours the news would be printed, and then most *Times*-men would go home and forget about it, knowing that in the morning it would all come out neatly and tidily in *The Times*.

They regarded *The Times* as one of the few predictable things left in modern America and they accepted this fact with degrees of admiration and cyncism, seeing *The Times* with a varying vision: it was a daily miracle, it was a formula factory. But no matter. It was *The Times*. And each day, barring labor strikes or hydrogen bombs, it would appear in 11,464 cities around the nation and in all the capitals of the world, fifty copies going to the White House, thirty-nine copies to Moscow, a few smuggled into Peking, and a thick Sunday edition flown each weekend to a foreign minister in Taiwan, for which he would each time pay $16.40. He would pay this because, with thousands of other isolated men in all corners of the earth, he required *The Times* as necessary proof of the world's existence, a barometer of its pressure, an assessor of its sanity. If the world did indeed still exist, he knew, it would be duly recorded each day in *The Times*—as the world was in the process of being recorded on this particular afternoon in New York, June 23, 1966, at three minutes before four, in *The Times'* massive Gothic gray-stone building off Broadway at Forty-third Street.

At this moment there were approximately four thousand employees working within the fourteen-story building. They were receptionists and telephone operators, printers and photoengravers, map makers, cafeteria cooks, nurses, editorial writers. Most of them had been in the building since 9 or 10 a.m., arriving as big trucks were backed into the curb unloading dozens of huge rolls of paper that went bumping, thumping down into *The Times'* basement and into machines whose paper consumption each year devours more than five million trees.

Of *The Times'* complete roster of 5,307 employees, only seven hundred work within the News department on the third floor. They are editors, reporters, copyreaders, critics, news assistants, and they tend to think of themselves as the totality of *The Times*, its embodiment and only spirit. If they do not completely ignore such other large departments within the building as Production, Promotion, and Advertising, they acknowledge them with a certain condescension. This is particularly true with regard to the Advertising department, which, after all, deals directly and constantly with that most contaminating of commodities, money. It hires hundreds of men to sell what in the News department cannot be bought. It exists as the mundane side of Ochs's sanctuary.

In the beginning Adolph Ochs was fundamentally a businessman. Later he became much more than that, but without his uncanny business sense he could not have taken over the declining *Times* in 1896 and revived it, an achievement accomplished by such expedient if inglorious tactics as price-cutting. Ochs in 1898 reduced the price of *The Times* from three cents a copy, which is what most respectable journals were then charging, to one cent, which was the standard price of the more sensational sheets. Ochs's associates thought that he was making a major mistake, cheapening *The Times'* image without solving its financial problems.

Ochs disagreed. *The New York Times* would not diminish in character, only in price, he said, adding that great numbers of bargain-conscious New Yorkers might switch from the cheaper papers to *The Times* if the price were the same.

That his assumption was correct was apparent within a year, when *The Times'* circulation had tripled, advertising revenue poured in. And by 1915 Ochs's paper was rich and powerful enough to select and reject advertisers and to eliminate certain ads when more space was needed in the paper for late-breaking news. Such prerogatives, which would quite naturally breed pride and pretension within the News department, were highlights in the career of Adolph Ochs, allowing him to satisfy a duality of drives—he could, under one roof, run both a thriving business and a theocracy, but there must be no intermingling, he knew: they must function separately on different floors; the money changers must stay out of his temple. He meanwhile, financially solid and rising socially, responded to the higher call, never succumbing to such circulation gimmicks as comic strips in his newspaper (although comics were tolerated in his first newspaper, the *Chattanooga Times,* and still are); and following his death, history would not place Adolph Ochs with so many of his *landsmen,* those great businessmen, the merchant princes who became bankers—Ochs would be in the more stately company of noble servants.

Still, Ochs never left his store untended, and now in the summer of 1966 the man in charge of making money for *The Times* was an all-business, no-nonsense type named Monroe Green. Green, who is sixty, sits behind a busy desk in his big office on the second floor, directing the 350-man department that brings in more than $100 million a year by selling ads. A full-page advertisement costs roughly $5,500 in the weekday edition, and $7,000 on Sundays, and the revenue derived from advertising is three times what the paper earns from its circulation sale and its other business ventures combined.

Monroe Green is a big, dark, wavy-haired man who wears sharply tailored dark suits, gleaming cufflinks, white or silvery ties. He speaks quickly, forcefully into a red telephone that rings incessantly on his desk, and he keeps a thousand facts at his manicured, tapping fingertips. He has been on *The Times* for twenty-five years as an advertising man, before that was on the advertising staffs of the *Herald Tribune* and the *Journal-American,* and before that was advertising manager of Macy's department store, to which he had gone after working his way through the University of Pennsylvania. The luxurious world that is portrayed each day in the advertisements of *The Times,* the romping happy people off to Europe on holiday, the slim mannequins wearing mink or Tiffany gems, resembles not in the least the world that Green knew most of his life. His father, who ran a small clothing store in South Amboy, New Jersey, died when Green, an only child, was ten years old, and while he can be light-hearted and pleasant, he is more naturally a serious man, a hardened realist, one not easily affected by the airy dreams of his ads.

From his office window he can see the street and a wino sleeping on a stone step behind an old theater. Green can faintly hear the horns of a traffic jam that will inevitably attract a mounted policeman who will inevitably notice press cars or trucks parked illegally but will give out no tickets, knowing that he will park his horse in *The Times'* enclosure behind the loading ramps later in the day. Green can feel the vibrations of the press machinery below and sense the power of *The Times* in ways quite different from Clifton Daniel on the floor above, and his view of life is certainly different from that of the editorial writers on the tenth floor who, within their quiet retreats, write of lofty expectations and ideals that sometimes irritate Green. He remembers one morning when he read a *Times* editorial critical of the new luxury-apartment skyscrapers being built along the Hudson River, on the New Jersey side a mile south of the George Washington Bridge; the buildings as seen by *The Times'* editorial writer were a desecration to the natural beauty of that section of the Jersey cliffs. But Green did not agree—and besides, he had recently sold the builders and owners of the apartments, the Tishman Realty & Construction Company, a $50,000 advertising supplement that had just appeared in *The Times* praising the project. The Tishman family would be most unhappy about *that* editorial, Green knew, sitting at his desk expecting a call from them at any moment. They might even wish to withdraw future advertising, which is not an uncommon reaction among some big-business men when a *Times* article or editorial offends them. A cigarette manufacturer boycotted the Advertising department after a *Times* editorial dealt with smoking and lung cancer, and this cost the paper several thousand dollars. But with the possible exception of Green, no executive at *The Times* really cared. When *The New York Times* cares about what its advertisers think, a few executives have said, it will no longer be *The New York Times*.

While this is true, Green nonetheless quietly resents the cavalier attitude of a few of his *Times* colleagues on the floors above, suspecting that their approach to the business side of the paper might also be a reflection of the way they secretly feel about him. He is as aware as they of *The Times'* magnetic appeal, but he also believes that it is not this magnetism alone that attracts more than $100 million a year in advertising revenue—*Green* had something to do with this, his drive, his determination, and that of his staff. It is *they* who bring in the money that permits piety to reign among the ten wisemen who write editorials on the tenth floor, and it is this money too that permits reporters on the third floor to place a telephone call to Cambodia if necessary to check a single fact. Green also feels that the advertising, though it is paid for by partisans, still provides legitimate news to *Times* readers. It not only tells what is selling and where, but it also gives a daily portrait of the nation's economy, an insight into contemporary taste. The ads offer a second perspective on the day, proof that the world is not entirely preoccupied with poverty and threats, bombs and ashes. The pretty girl in the ad wearing a Peck & Peck dress, the man inhaling a mild luxury-length Pall Mall, both offer *Times* readers an indulgent pause between the gray columns of gravity. And the historians fifty years from now, Green suspects, when they want to know how people lived and dreamed in the Nineteen-sixties, will get as many clues from reading the ads as reading the news. Of course the advertising will stress the positive, the news the negative. The truth will be somewhere in between.

The news of this day in June focused on the "long hot summer," the race riots in Mississippi; the ads highlighted the summer bargains—Macy's mink stoles, regularly $299, were down to $236. The news singled out the vast problem of unemployment; the help-wanted ads were jammed with job offers for the skilled and unskilled. The news stressed the shortage of housing; the ads emphasized the availability of housing at all prices around New York, praising the neighborhoods without hinting at the discrimination that exists in these neighborhoods. The news was concentrated on fame and power, grand success and grand failure; the ads catered to the everyday dreams of Everyman, the attainable sweet life, the gadgets and vehicles of escape.

The ads recorded the average man's tragedies, too, but only in the smallest print in the back of the newspaper, back between the stock-market listings and the bland photographs of executives on the rise—here, buried near the bottom, one could read in tiny type the names of those who had gone bankrupt, those who had been abandoned, those who had lost something including dreams and sought recovery, and they told this to *The Times*. *The Times* would publish this, charging a few dollars a line, within its classified-advertising pages —a special department on the sixth floor of the *Times* building largely staffed by middle-aged women who sit within glass-partitioned cubicles, telephones to their ears, jotting down the forlorn facts of daily life, and then they relay these facts, if they are not too vulgar or vengeful, to the composing room on the fourth floor, where they are methodically set into type for the Public Notices column of the next edition of *The Times*.

Today *The Times* would announce the fact that Jean Pompilio, sales girl, 89-01 Shore Road, Brooklyn, had gone bankrupt, her liabilities being $15,251, her assets $1,275. Today Edward Dougherty, 89-36 207th Street, Queens, would declare in *The Times* that his wife, Florence, "having left my bed and board several months ago," was now completely responsible for her own debts; he would pay no longer. Today the wife of a runaway husband would plead in *The Times*: "Len W. —Elizabeth and I are alone and lost. We know you feel our pain and tears. We have nothing without you. Please hurry home." A Manhattan woman on the East Side, upset because she had misplaced her favorite watch, called *The Times* and announced: "1 Patek Philippe square shaped gold watch, white & yellow gold band. Liberal reward. RH 4-2765."

The watch was never returned, so the East Side lady soon purchased another one, and *not* another Patek Philippe, but this was not news for *The Times*. The whereabouts of Len W. and Florence Dougherty would not be followed up in *The Times* either, nor would *Times* readers ever know the precise circumstances that caused Jean Pompilio, sales girl, to fall $14,000 into debt. If asked to discuss her financial plight she will not do so, it is nobody's business, she will say. It is not news. News, to the *The Times'* editors on the third floor, is composed of *significant* current events that you did not know and should know. News, in the world of Monroe Green, is the drumbeat of business with an emphasis on the upbeat, success, comfort, enchantment. It is news to Green that B. Altman & Co.'s shoe salon has an "exciting op-art pump" for $41, that J. Press Inc. has jackets of weightless Vycron Polyester Cotton Collie Cloth with patch and flap lower pockets, hook vent, washable, dryfast; that Eastern Airlines has nonstop jet service to San Antonio. It is news to Green that "Coppertone gives you a better tan!" and illustrating this point in the ad is a big tawny photograph of Raquel Welch in a bikini, a *Playboy* pose that raised the eyebrows but not the objections of *The Times'* Advertising Acceptability department, which has become more liberal in recent years. These men, who work with Green but not under him, reject advertisements dealing with fortune-telling and horoscopes, miracle medicines, and speculative investments in mines, and they generally tone down the wording in ads to avoid overstatement—"the best buy in town" becomes "one of the best buys," and "the finest coat we have ever seen" "The finest coat we have ever sold." They will not permit advertisements in a foreign language unless the English translation is included, and they are quick to turn down advertising copy that is too sexually suggestive or tasteless. They disallow nudes in ads except in the case of children, but they will permit the scantiest of bikinis in ads for tropical islands and suntan lotions and soap—*The Times*, one executive explained, now accepts the fact that women have navels. Which is good news to Green, and he has since made a fortune for *The Times* from the ads of ladies' panties and bras, particularly in the Sunday *Times Magazine*, which has been called the "*Girdle Gazette.*" It was rare insight on Green's part to recognize the commercial possibilities of selling ladies' clothing within a magazine noted for its weighty content, its articles on the Common Market, famine in India, dilemmas in Washington; but Green knew that the Sunday *Times,* with its circulation of more than 1.4 million, was browsed through by as many women as men, and the improved color process for advertising gave him an added incentive for turning part of the *Magazine* into a flamboyant leaping ladies' locker room which, while it sometimes stole scenes from the foreign ministers photographed on the facing pages, actually gave bounce to the product, a recurring stimulant that seemed to unite within the pages these men who were ideologically different.

Monroe Green and *The New York Times*—the combination can sell almost anything, and it was quite natural that Green, hearing of Tishman's skyscraper apartments along the Hudson, would approach his friend Alan Tishman and suggest that he purchase advertising space that would call attention to the construction and would lure tenants. Tishman agreed, and the $50,000 advertising supplement was put together. Then came *The Times*' editorial condemning the Tishman construction, and now Monroe Green sat in his office awaiting Alan Tishman's call. There was little that Green could do. It had been a most unfortunate editorial but it was too late to do anything about it. Personally, Green did not believe, as the editorial writer did, that the skyscrapers marred the natural beauty of the New Jersey cliffs along the Hudson River. The land used by the Tishmans was not a historical landmark or sanctified preserve, Green reasoned, it was almost the opposite—grim acres of weeds and shanties and untrimmed trees, and the construction of apartment houses there, Green thought, was more an improvement than anything else. But Green had no influence with editorial writers. He was not even sure who had written about the site, each editorial being written anonymously by one of the ten-man Editorial Board, but Green knew who was responsible for having it written. He was John Oakes, the editor of the editorial page, an individual widely known throughout the building and beyond as a zealous conservationist, one almost obsessed with the defense of trees and streams and mountains against the intrusion of land developers. Oakes was a high-minded person with almost an abhorrence of money and the profit motive, and once he even denounced the gold-tinted aluminum telephone booths along Fifth Avenue, declaring in an editorial that "the bogus opulence of golden phone booths and golden trash cans . . . merely detracts from the integrity of the avenue."

Of the men with power on *The Times*, perhaps no two have less in common than Monroe Green and John Oakes. Oakes is a tweedy man in his fifties with tight curly white hair, pale blue eyes, a very youthful but serious face; he is a Princeton graduate who became a Rhodes scholar. Oakes has strong opinions on almost everything and, more important, his opinions dominate the editorial page of the paper. While it is true that he does not expect his editorial writers to espouse causes with which they do not agree, it is also true that he does not expect them to espouse causes with which *he* does not agree. If their views conflict with his, they are not published. If they are consistently in disagreement with him on the major political, social, or economic issues of the day, they are wise to consider transferring to another part of the paper because Oakes insists, as any editorial-page editor must, on a consistent and unified policy harmonious with his own views and with those of the publisher, to whom Oakes is responsible.

The editorial page, Oakes believes, is the "soul" of a newspaper, a reflection of its inner character and philosophy, and since he took over the page at *The Times* in 1961 that character and philosophy has been more vividly revealed than ever before. It has been condemning of the war in Vietnam, staunch in its support of the Civil Rights movement. It has been generally pro-Labor but critical of such leaders as James Hoffa and the late Michael Quill, a supporter of Israel in wars with the Arabs but critical of some Israeli territorial ambitions and actions following the victories. Though endorsing John F. Kennedy for President, it became disenchanted later when Kennedy did not, in Oakes's opinion, fulfill his promise with the Federal Aid to Education Bill, and as the editorial sniping continued on this and other issues during the Kennedy years many family members and friends of the President came to detest John Oakes more and more, charging that the negativism was really a manifestation of a deep personal disaffection that Oakes had cultivated during Kennedy's earlier years in the Senate.

It was Oakes, a few of them suspected, who helped spread the rumor in late 1957 that Kennedy was not the sole author of *Profiles in Courage*. Oakes actually played no part in the spreading of this rumor. The man most responsible was probably Drew Pearson, who made the charge on an ABC television show, causing the network to follow up with an investigation that could not produce sufficient evidence to justify the charge, and ABC later publicly apologized to Kennedy.

All that Oakes did was to inquire of an editor whom he met at a social gathering, a Harper editor who had worked with Kennedy on the book, if there was any substance to the rumor that Theodore Sorensen, or some other Kennedy associate, had helped with the writing. The editor denied it, and that was the end of it as far as Oakes was concerned. But some weeks later, while John Oakes was in Washington on one of his regular visits to various Congressmen, he was greeted in Kennedy's office with a long hard look from the Senator: then Kennedy lifted from his desk a letter and handed it to John Oakes, saying, "I'll give this to you now rather than send it to you." The letter began, "Dear John: It recently came to my attention that you had been quoted as stating that the rumors concerning my authorship of *Profiles in Courage* were true." The letter, 300 words in length, went on to state unequivocally that no other author had collaborated on the work, and after Oakes had finished reading the letter Kennedy wanted to further prove the point by having Oakes examine stacks of notes in Kennedy's own handwriting that formed the book. Oakes assured Kennedy that this was unnecessary and soon they were discussing other things, but Oakes was most impressed with the time and effort that Kennedy was devoting to the refutation of the rumor, and Oakes concluded on this January day in 1958 that Kennedy now had serious plans for the Presidency. Later, in New York, Oakes received a copy of *Profiles in Courage* from Kennedy; it was inscribed: "To John Oakes—with high esteem and very best wishes from his friend—the author—John Kennedy."

The deferential treatment accorded John Oakes by ambitious men outside the *Times* building as well as within is not based entirely on his position as editor of the editorial page, as prestigious as this may be; also involved is the fact that Oakes is a member of *The Times'* ruling family. His father, who altered his surname in 1917, was a brother of Adolph Ochs. The name change by George Ochs to George "Ochs-Oakes," with the stipulation that his sons be known as "Oakes,"

was inspired by an intense anti-German feeling during
World War I and by a belief that a decidedly German
name such as Ochs would be considered repellent
by Americans for many years to come. This opinion
was certainly not shared by other members of the Ochs
family in Chattanooga or New York. They were in
fact insulted by George's presumption, but on second
thought they were not altogether surprised. They had
always looked upon George Ochs as something of a
maverick within the family, an unpredictable and complex person who sought his own identity and fulfillment beyond the pale of indebtedness and yet he could
not or would not permanently leave the guaranteed
grandeur provided by his older brother Adolph.

Adolph Ochs was three years older than George, the
first in a family of three sons and three daughters.
They were a remarkable combination of conflicting
character, of strong dissent nearly always overcome by
a stronger devotion to each other; they were the prog-
eny of German Jews who had met and married in the
American South before the Civil War, parents whose
political allegiances clashed during the war—their
father, Julius Ochs, was a captain in the Union Army;
their mother, Bertha Ochs, was loyal to the South and
was accused, with some justification, of being a Confederate spy. Their family may well have been separated
in later years if Adolph, the child genius, had not at the
age of twenty begun to buy and build newspapers that
would become towering totems of nepotism, elevating
and shaping his family, his grandchildren, nephews,
cousins, and in-laws for almost an entire century, committing them to an orthodoxy stronger than their religion—and establishing Adolph Ochs as their benefactor, a little father-figure even to his own father.

Julius Ochs, who immigrated to America in 1845, was
a wise and well-educated man of many talents, but
making money was not one of them. He was a fine guitar
player, an amateur actor, a classically educated student
of Greek, Latin, and Hebrew and fluent in English,
French, and Italian. He had been born in 1826 in the
Bavarian city of Fürth, in southwest Germany, a cul-

tured and relatively tolerant city with a large Jewish community that, while well respected, was denied certain civil rights and privileges. These restrictions, however, did not apply to Julius Ochs's family, which had lived and prospered in Fürth for several generations. In the old Jewish cemetery in Fürth there were tombstones of Ochses going back to 1493. Julius Ochs's father had been a successful diamond broker, also a linguist and Talmudic scholar, and his mother was a handsome and refined woman who had nine children, Julius being the youngest. During Julius' second year at a military academy in Cologne his father died and Julius' older brother, becoming head of the family, withdrew him and placed him in an apprenticeship with a bookbinding firm. Julius rebelled and in the spring of 1845 he left Fürth with a friend, tramped to Bremen, and sailed on a full-rigged ship across the Atlantic, arriving seven weeks later in New York. He first settled in Louisville, where two of his sisters were living and where a brother-in-law, refusing to subsidize Julius' reentry into college, put him to work as a peddler. He soon quit that and later found a job teaching French at a girls' seminary at Mount Sterling, Kentucky. When war was declared against Mexico in 1848, Julius Ochs enlisted and, because of his military background in Germany, was made a drill sergeant, but the war ended before his unit was sent to the front. He spent the next several years trying to find work that would suit his intellectuality and wistful idealism and curb his restlessness, but he never found it, being neither very determined nor very lucky, and so his life was one of travel and variety between New York and New Orleans. He was a road salesman for a jewelry company, owned and operated dry-goods stores, organized small theatrical clubs; he dabbled in small-town politics and held municipal government jobs; he occasionally served as a rabbi in marriage ceremonies, and during his ventures into Mississippi he played the guitar at plantation parties. In Natchez, Mississippi, where he briefly settled and ran a store, he met an attractive, somewhat dogmatic young woman named Bertha Levy.

Born in Landau, Bavaria, she was then living with an uncle in Natchez, having been sent there by her father so that she could escape prosecution from German authorities following her role, while she was a sixteen-year-old student in Heidelberg, in political demonstrations at the graves of several martyrs of the revolutionary uprisings of 1848. Julius Ochs met her in 1851 but his stay in Mississippi was too brief for any romance to flourish, and three years later, during the yellow-fever epidemic in the Mississippi valley, he read in a newspaper list of the dead the name Bertha Levy of Natchez. Two years later, at a reception in Nashville, Tennessee, he saw her again; yes, she had been very ill, she said, but as a final desperate attempt to save her life the doctors had resorted to ice-packing, and now she was fully recovered and living in Nashville with her parents, recently immigrated from Bavaria. Within a year, Bertha Levy and Julius Ochs were married. Three years later, in March of 1858, in Cincinnati, where Julius Ochs was based as a traveling salesman, was born the future publisher of *The New York Times*, Adolph Ochs.

Julius Ochs joined the Union Army when the Civil War began, becoming a captain in a battalion assigned to guard the railroad between Cincinnati and St. Louis. His wife stayed with him during the war but she remained intensely loyal to the South. On one occasion a warrant for her arrest was issued after she had been caught by Union sentries while attempting to smuggle quinine, hidden in the baby carriage of her infant son George, to Confederate troops positioned on the opposite end of a bridge across the Ohio River. This put Captain Ochs in a most embarrassing and crucial situation, requiring of him a performance far more persuasive than any he had been able to demonstrate during his career as a salesman; but he somehow managed to get a senior officer whom he knew to dismiss the warrant, an act of generosity that inspired no sign of gratitude from Mrs. Ochs. She persisted in her dedication to the Southern cause and way of life, being unappalled even by its system of slavery, and years later when the family settled in Chattanooga she became a charter member of the local chapter of the Daughters of the Confederacy. Before her death, which came in 1908 during her seventy-fifth year, she requested that a Confederate flag be placed on her coffin, and this was done. Next to her grave, on a knoll overlooking the city of Chattanooga, is that of her husband; he died in 1888 in that city and, as he instructed, his funeral was conducted by the Grand Army of the Republic with the Stars and Stripes placed on his coffin.

Such displayed partisanship and commitment to causes, particularly to lost causes, never enticed their son Adolph. He was a hard worker, an unfanciful middle-of-the-road thinker who saw no virtue in offending one faction to please another. He wished to do business with all groups, offending as few people as possible. He was a truly precocious young man who recognized early the aimless, varied course of his father's life, and he set out to concentrate on *one* thing, to stay with it, succeed with it. This vehicle for him was the newspaper business, which promised some of the prestige and excitement that he sought, and an opportunity to follow in the tradition of his boyhood hero, Horace Greeley, who rose from a farm in New Hampshire to the ownership of the *New York Tribune*.

Ochs began at fourteen by sweeping the floors of the *Knoxville Chronicle*. Three years before he had been a newsboy at the *Chronicle* but had left to earn a bit more money as an apprentice in a drugstore, then as an usher in a theater, finally as a clerk in his uncle's grocery in Providence, Rhode Island, attending business school at night. He was bored by these jobs, experiencing none of the exuberance he had felt during his newsboy days at the *Chronicle* office; and so in 1872, when he applied to the *Chronicle* for a full-time job, and was hired as an office boy, he decided that newspapers would be his life's calling and his parents did not attempt to dissuade him. Ochs's nature, combining the idealism of his father and the *chutzpa* of his mother seemed well suited to the running of a newspaper.

It might have led him into politics, where he could have fulfilled some of the social-worker spirit within him, but the spotlight would have distracted him and overemphasized the awkwardness he felt whenever undue attention was focused on him. He was acutely aware of his limitations, both educationally and socially, and he was forced to compensate in an endless variety of ways even after he had achieved greatness at *The New York Times*, or possibly *because* he had achieved this greatness. He would usually smile or grin after delivering a comment or observation to his editors so that, should it seem insane or be in some way wrong, it might appear that his words were not really meant to be taken all that seriously. At times his grammar was faulty, his words poorly chosen, but he balanced this by an enthusiasm for detail and an enormous sympathy and tolerance for subject. His mind was always quietly at work challenging the obvious, and this was true even when he was driving through the countryside and stopped to ask directions; he never accepted the directions without asking if he could not also get to the same place by taking a different route. He was both cautious and optimistic, sentimental and tough, a short, dark-haired, blue-eyed little man who, when someone observed that he resembled Napoleon, replied, "Oh, I am very much taller than Napoleon," and yet he was very humble. He was a modest organizer of grand designs, possessing a sure insight into human nature and into what would sell, and still he was dedicated to the old verities that in another age would mark him as "square." But he truly believed that honesty was the best policy, and he honored his father and mother and was never blasphemous, and he was convinced that hard work would reap rewards.

Shortly after his debut as an office boy on the *Knoxville Chronicle*, Ochs was promoted to printers' apprentice, learning a skill that would become a hallmark on the papers he would own, and this would also make him a printers' hero throughout his later years and even decades after his death—in the Nineteen-sixties, during a newspaper strike in New York, picket lines of printers would respectfully part ranks, forming a path whenever Ochs's white-haired daughter, Iphigene, then in her seventies, would approach the front entrance of the *New York Times* building.

When Adolph Ochs was eighteen, he was setting type for the *Louisville Courier-Journal*, living with cousins and sending his savings to his family in Knoxville, and working during his spare hours as a part-time reporter, proving to be a dull writer but a very reliable gatherer of facts. When he was nineteen he and two older men obtained an interest in a failing newspaper, the *Chattanooga Dispatch*, which they could not revive, but it provided for Ochs an introduction to a new city, one that was on the brink of a building boom, which Ochs sensed, and thus he stayed.

Chattanooga, whose ridges and plateaus had been singed and scarred by the cannons and rifle fire of thousands of battling troops during the Civil War, had a population in 1865 of less than 2,000 but this had grown to 12,000 when Ochs arrived in 1877. There had been rumors of iron ore in the mountains, and now the dirt roads were being covered with planks, and stores and homes were being built; there was an atmosphere of optimism, a promise of prosperity among the new settlers. There were no telephones or information centers in Chattanooga then, and newly arrived strangers seeking information had to ask around—until Adolph Ochs came up with the idea of printing a city directory. In it he listed every store in Chattanooga, its location and the type of merchandise it sold, and in the process of collecting this information he walked back and forth through every block in the city, getting to know the merchants, politicians, bankers—people who would be very helpful and useful when, one year later, in 1878, he needed a loan and advertising support to buy and rebuild the *Chattanooga Times*. The *Times* was then a mismanaged four-page paper so poorly printed as to be almost illegible, with a declining circulation and little hope of recovery. Its owner was so desperate to sell that Ochs was able to buy it with an initial down payment of $250 and a total cost of $5,750. Ochs's father,

Julius, came down to Chattanooga from Knoxville for a ceremony that highlighted the change of ownership—not for purely sentimental reasons, but also to sign the legal papers in his son's behalf. Adolph Ochs was eight months shy of twenty-one.

What he did with the *Chattanooga Times* was what he would later do, on a much grander scale, with *The New York Times*—he made it into a *news*paper and not a gazette of opinion, or showcase for star writers, or a champion of the underdog or topdog, or a crusader for political or social reform. Ochs had something to sell—news—and he hoped to sell it dispassionately and with the guarantee that it was reliable and unsoiled and not deviously inspired. Adolph Ochs wanted to be accepted in Chattanooga, to grow with the town and help it grow, and he knew that one way to do this was not to criticize it but, inoffensively, to boost it. As the building boom continued in Chattanooga, as land speculators and investors moved into the valley and up along Lookout Mountain, chopping down trees and leveling the land that had been a Civil War battleground, Adolph Ochs saw this as progress and he did not, as his nephew John Oakes could afford to do almost a century later, worry about the destruction of trees or desecration of natural beauty.

Ochs worried about, and advocated on his editorial page, the dredging of a deeper channel in the bordering Tennessee River, the construction of an opera house for the increasingly cultured community, the building of better libraries and schools for the young who would one day read and support his newspaper. When the yellow-fever epidemic spread into Chattanooga, stalling the economy temporarily and killing 366 citizens, the *Chattanooga Times* helped conduct an emergency relief fund and Ochs wrote in an editorial: "Will this ruin Chattanooga? No! If this city was born to be ruined, it would have been blotted out years ago."

Ochs's most salient characteristic was optimism, and it was this more than anything else that attracted financial support from bankers and businessmen, although in his first years in Chattanooga Ochs was also a fantastic wheeler and dealer. He printed his own checks on high-quality paper of exquisite design, signing them with a flourishing hand—and then he would just barely get to the bank on time with newly borrowed money to prevent his check from bouncing. He was forever juggling a loan here to repay one there, but he was very honest and punctual, and he demanded that his debtors be equally scrupulous in their dealings with him. Subscribers who had fallen behind in their payments would receive stern notes from Ochs: "The *Times* will be discontinued if not paid for within five days after the presentation of the account. We will not carry a Deadhead list. Everyone must pay." He then needed every nickel he could lay his hands on to help with the purchase of legible type, better machinery, and to expand his staff. And after he achieved these goals he met larger challenges, his horizons ever widening, his success inspiring him toward greater risks rather than toward smugness or quiescence. Within not too many years, without his realization at first, Adolph Ochs began to outgrow his town.

Chattanooga, to be sure, was not fulfilling its promise as the South's leading industrial center. While it had recovered from epidemics and small economic crises, it suffered a serious setback when its ore proved to be too sulfurous to produce the high-quality steel of which Birmingham was capable. This discovery took much of the momentum out of Chattanooga. It made money very tight at a time when Ochs—who had lost considerably in land speculation, a victim of his own optimism—was desperately in need of more loans to continue to improve his newspaper and to complete its new six-story granite building that would be topped by a glittering gold-painted dome.

There was no question in his mind, or in anybody else's, that he was a good business risk. He had demonstrated as a young man in his twenties that he could take a wreck of a newspaper and, within a decade or so, convert it into a large and enterprising journal earning $25,000 annual profit. He also owned a small farmer's weekly that was making money. He had bought a big, rambling brick house in one of the better residential areas of Chattanooga and into it he had moved his parents and brothers and sisters from Knoxville, and then his wife from Cincinnati, and there, too, he entertained many distinguished people when they were visiting Chattanooga. When President Grover Cleveland came to Chattanooga, Ochs was on the greeting committee. Borrowing an elegant gray coat for the occasion, he rode in an open carriage near the President in a parade, and during the festivities he conversed privately with the President, confident he was as impressive to the President as the President was to him—and after Grover Cleveland returned to Washington, Ochs kept in touch. And yet despite Ochs's pluckiness and his profitable management of the *Chattanooga Times*, he was deeply in debt. This was partly the result of the overborrowing he had done to keep improving his growing paper, and partly the result of his land-speculation project across the Tennessee River which had cost Ochs more than $100,000.

He could not recover, he knew, unless he could make more money at a faster rate, and he could not do this in Chattanooga during a recession. He would have to expand elsewhere. He must try to keep his *Chattanooga Times* running at a profit while he traveled through Tennessee and beyond in search of another newspaper that he could buy cheaply and rebuild as he had the *Times*. Any thought of trying to make money in a nonjournalistic way was rejected by Ochs from the start. The real-estate fiasco had taught him his lesson. From that point on he vowed that he would never again invest in anything but newspapers, the only business he really liked.

Newspaper publishers in those days were given free rides by many railroad companies, a forerunner of the "junket," and Ochs made good use of his pass as he traveled back and forth between Nashville, Knoxville, Cincinnati, Louisville, and even New York, familiarizing himself with the larger newspapers and the men who ran them. Much of the responsibility for the running of the *Chattanooga Times* was meanwhile trans-

ferred to his family, whom Ochs had started to employ
shortly after he had acquired the *Chattanooga Times*.
His father, Julius, had been appointed treasurer of the
newspaper. His younger brother, George, and then
his youngest brother, Milton, were trained as reporters. Following the marriage of two of his three sisters,
Ochs brought their husbands into the business; and
then there were cousins, nephews, family friends—
Ochs's dynasty had begun. Those who did not work
for Ochs in Chattanooga might, after he had bought
The New York Times in 1896, work for him in New
York, or, after 1901, work on the newspaper Ochs
would own for more than a decade in Philadelphia.
Everybody at one time or another seemed to be working
for Adolph Ochs, and they blended into his institutional
framework with proper modesty and reverence—all but
one, his brother George.

George Ochs, or George Ochs-Oakes as he wished
to be called after 1917, joined the *Chattanooga Times*
in 1879 as a reporter, earning nine dollars a week. He
had completed three years at East Tennessee University in Knoxville and achieved such high grades that,
though he joined his family in Chattanooga rather
than complete his senior year, the university awarded
him a Bachelor of Arts degree with his class of 1880.
He was a sensitive and an articulate young man, having
been a member of the university's debating society, and
he was very different from his older brother Adolph.
While Adolph sought to avoid controversy, George
seemed to court it. Adolph did not crave personal attention, having had more than he wanted as the family's favorite son; George, three years younger than
Adolph, could never get enough of it. He clung to the
memory of every honor he ever received. He never forgot a compliment, no matter how small. He never tired
of hearing his mother retell the story of how, during
the Civil War, she had concealed supplies for the Confederates in his baby carriage, with him asleep within,
and he would become infuriated and often cry when
ever Adolph would teasingly suggest that it was he,
Adolph, who was actually sleeping in the carriage. But

Adolph did not often try to provoke his younger brother, a thing too easily done; instead Adolph tried to help George as he had helped the entire family, guiding and inspiring as he earned their respect and devotion, maintaining his position as the loving older brother, the imperturbable marvelous manchild who was his mother's favorite. Adolph was her first son to survive— a previous son had died in infancy—and after Adolph had been delivered and lived his mother knew no joy to equal it, except possibly the joy that would come as he delivered her, and her family, from poverty to prominence. Adolph could be counted upon, she knew, as her husband, good man that he was, could not. Adolph always made the right moves. Except for the land-speculation deal, he was shrewd about money. He had married a girl that his mother greatly approved of, Rabbi Wise's gentle Iphigene, and Adolph did not, like his brother Milton, marry outside the faith; nor did he, like George, lose his temper in public and bring embarrassment to the family. George seemed almost driven to prove how different he could be. As a young boy, if told *not* to do something, he would be sure to do it. As a young man, working on his brother's staff at the *Chattanooga Times*, he became embroiled in dramatic situations, controversies, threats—and once he almost killed a man.

George was then a twenty-two-year-old newspaperman on the *Chattanooga Times* and on this particular day, while he was in the county courthouse making notes from a divorce record that involved the name of a prominent county official, the same county official strolled by and noticed what George was doing, became very angry, and warned that if George printed the item he would "shoot him full of holes." George printed it. A few days later, as George was conversing with a friend on the main street, he suddenly felt on his head a sharp blow from behind; turning, he saw the county official holding a cane upraised to strike again. George shouted, "If you strike me again, you'll pay the penalty." As the county official hit him again and also reached into his pocket, possibly for a pistol, George reached into his pocket, pulled out a gun, and shot the man through the lower abdomen and hip. Though staggering, the man continued to raise his cane and attempted to draw the object from his pocket, whereupon George pushed his gun to the man's throat and pulled the trigger. The gun jammed. But the man collapsed to the ground and George did not fire a second shot. A large crowd had now gathered, and the victim was removed to a hospital where, after being in critical condition for several days, he recovered. George surrendered to the sheriff but no warrant was issued. Nor did George cease to carry a gun. When he was approached a week later and was threatened by the brother of the victim, George dissuaded him by pointing *two* guns at him. The aftereffect of this encounter left George emotionally shaken but he soon recouped his sense of daring—and a few months later he was knocked unconscious by a large Negro for publishing the fact that there had been an angry dispute in the train station between the Negro and a railroad official who had refused to let the Negro sit in the parlor car. A posse was instantly organized to capture the man, but he fled to Texas and did not return to Chattanooga for several years, by which time George Ochs had drifted into politics and had been elected mayor of Chattanooga. As mayor he graciously accepted his assailant's apology.

Having entered political life over Adolph's strong but futile objections, George turned out to be a very successful mayor. He won two terms as a Democrat, beginning in 1893 when he was thirty-one years old, and he could have won the party nomination a third time had he wished. His administration was so efficient that it lowered taxes while improving the welfare of the citizens, but George Ochs remained as independent and unpredictable as ever. In 1896 he refused to support the Democratic party's choice for President, William Jennings Bryan, and the local leaders in Chattanooga demanded that Ochs resign as mayor, which he would not do. On another occasion Ochs withheld patronage from one of the local political bosses who had strongly supported him, and this provoked a protest visit to the mayor's office from a delegation of leading Democrats that included George's younger brother, Milton, and one of his in-laws. But George remained implacable. He had made no deals, he said, adding that he would run the city in a manner he thought proper. He fancied himself an incorruptible man, independent and different, and while he occasionally flaunted his integrity, he nevertheless behaved in accordance with his self-image, doing as he wished and saying what he wanted to say even if the subject was controversial, which it often was.

As a Jew, a German Jew, George Ochs shared with some members of his family, and many German Jews around the nation, a feeling of superiority and disaffection toward the more recently arrived Jewish immigrants from Eastern Europe—and, unlike Adolph, George was outspoken on this subject. While he sympathized with their poverty and struggle, George had little tolerance for Jews who adhered to foreign customs after settling in America, Jews who persisted in speaking Yiddish along the street, who read Yiddish newspapers on trains and saw Jewishness in terms of a nation or race rather than in terms of a religion. Such Jews, he felt, encouraged by their clannishness the bigotry that kept them aliens, disqualified them socially, stereotyped them commercially, made life not only more difficult for them but, regrettably, also for the more established Jews who had assimilated themselves and prospered in America. He was equally critical of the get-rich quick Jews who displayed their wealth with ostentation, if not vulgarity.

Throughout his lifetime to the year of his death, which came in 1931 when he was seventy, George Ochs-Oakes overwhelmingly opposed the Zionists and all other advocates of a Jewish state in Palestine, and this view was also endorsed by Adolph Ochs and for years it was part of the editorial policy of *The New York Times*. When Arthur Hays Sulzberger became publisher of *The Times* he made speeches and statements urging Jews not to agitate for a Jewish Palestinian state, and in 1939 Sulzberger was among a group of influential Jews who urged President Roosevelt not to appoint Felix Frankfurter to the Supreme Court because they believed that it would intensify anti-Semitism in America, a notion that Roosevelt resented and ignored. In 1946 *The New York Times* canceled an advertisement submitted by the American League for a Free Palestine, infuriating Zionists and causing Sulzberger to explain at length that while *The New York Times* had in the past often run the ads of organizations that it opposed editorially—it had previously carried many Zionist ads, Sulzberger reminded them, and had even run advertising by the Communist party; had in fact once lent the *Daily Worker* newsprint when the Communist journal was short of it—the decision to cancel the Zionist advertising on this occasion was based, first, on *The Times'* conviction that the American League for a Free Palestine was directly connected with one of the Jewish terrorist groups in the Middle East; and second, the anti-British charges in the ad were not supportable by facts, and thus Sulzberger said he could not be responsible for the ill will that the advertisement in *The Times* would stir between Britain and the United States. "We happen to believe that the British are acting in good faith and not in bad faith," Sulzberger wrote to one of the Zionist leaders. "From our standpoint, therefore, your advertisement is not true; but since there is no yardstick by which truth of this kind can be proved, it means that we are putting our judgment ahead of yours— something of which you will not approve and which we do only with the greatest hesitancy."

By the time that George Ochs-Oakes's son, John Oakes, became influential on *The New York Times*, the state of Israel had become a reality and *The Times'* editorial page has been generally friendly to it in recent years, reaching a high point in 1967 when, during the Israeli-Arab war, *The Times* reminded the United States government of its commitment to defend the sovereignty and independence of Israel and even advocated the intervention of American military forces if the Israeli army needed help, which, as things turned out, it did not. *The New York Times'* News department has also maintained for a number of years, and *still* maintains in the Nineteen-sixties, a full-time reporter who specializes in covering Jewish activities in America, a very sensitive assignment whose aims include, according to one editor, "keeping the New York Zionists off Sulzberger's back." And yet the old German-Jewish attitude that George Ochs-Oakes expressed more than thirty years ago, the disenchantment with American Jews who dwelled on their Jewishness, the desire that Jews blend into the American scene—this thinking on occasion still pervades the hierarchy of *The New York Times*. Veteran reporters in *The Times'* newsroom have long been aware of higher management's sensitivity to things Jewish. The editing and handling of stories that are about Jews or are of special interest to Jews is a bit more delicate and cautious, if such is possible to perceive—and even if it is not, the reporters' mere supposition sustains some of the past consciousness of George Ochs-Oakes. *The New York Times* does not wish to be thought of as a "Jewish newspaper" which indeed it is not, and it will bend over backwards to prove this point, forcing itself at times into unnatural positions, contorted by compromise, balancing both sides, careful not to offend, wishing to be accepted and respected for what it is—a good citizens' newspaper, law-abiding and loyal, solidly in support of the best interests of the nation in peace and war.

That such a formidable institution as *The Times* should be so lacking in arrogance, so weighed down by its sense of responsibility and a fear of going one step too far, may explain in part its survival and strength and it may also hint at a part of its vulnerability—not only the vulnerability of the Jewish family that owns it but also the vulnerability of the nation upon which the family has hitched its star. The anti-Semitic slights and subtleties beneath the surface of America have, in one way or other, touched nearly every member of the family, extending even into the third generation—Sulzberger's son, a Marine on his way to Korea, was turned away from a restricted resort in Hobe Sound, Florida; a Sulzberger daughter in a girls' private school in New

York was assumed to be a friend of the only other Jewish girl in the class (the two girls came to dislike one another rather quickly); George Ochs-Oakes's son, John Oakes, a brilliant student, was accepted within a Jewish quota at the Lawrenceville School. Given these and similar incidents, the fact that even the family that owns *The New York Times* can be subjected to such social scrutiny, it is no wonder that there would be within the institution a sensitivity to Semitism and a fastidiousness about keeping *The Times* above reproach, untouched by the prejudice within the nation.

The prejudice first became apparent to certain members of the Ochs family when they began to move northward shortly after Adolph had purchased *The New York Times* in 1896. In Chattanooga they had sensed no anti-Semitism, a circumstance that may have been the result of the very mobile, loosely structured society that had settled there after the Civil War, turning Chattanooga into a kind of frontier town, and it was also possible, George Ochs-Oakes believed, that this type of Jew was more acceptable to Gentiles than the Eastern European Jews who would immigrate to America in great numbers at the turn of the century. George interpreted his own acceptance in Chattanooga, and that of his family, as evidence to support his theory. His father was for years the lay rabbi of the Jewish community in Chattanooga, and George had sung in the choir, and he would later marry a Jewish woman and bring up his sons in the faith: he saw himself as a "good" Jew insofar as religion was concerned, but otherwise he avoided any ethnic or nationalistic commitment to Jews, and when he was elected mayor of Chattanooga in 1893 he was convinced that he had conducted his life wisely and well.

But when he moved to Philadelphia in 1901, accepting his brother's offer to run a newly acquired Ochs newspaper in that city, George gradually became aware of the fuller meaning of being Jewish. The more tightly entrenched society of Philadelphia was not in the least bit subtle in its discrimination, and George was surprised and appalled, although, uncharacteristically, he did not make an issue of it. He believed that to do so would only further aggravate an unpleasant situation, and he held the Jews partly accountable for the prejudice. If Jews would curtail their desire for their own schools and universities in America, would not seek political power through a Jewish vote, would stop thinking of themselves as primarily Jewish, he felt sure that the wall between Jews and other Americans would be lowered. He conceded that full integration into the American social system might take several years or even decades; the first generation of Jews born in America, and perhaps also the second, might not fully achieve a 100 percent American status. But if they remained patient and set a fine example as outstanding and loyal citizens, then the third and fourth generations would undoubtedly gain acceptance—different from their compatriots in church affiliation, but otherwise typically and totally American. This, at any rate, is what he hoped would happen, and he attempted to live the latter part of his life in such a way that would further this cause and benefit the future of his two sons.

Both sons were born and reared in the Philadelphia area, as had been his wife, the daughter of a merchant and banker whose family had been residents of Philadelphia for nearly three-quarters of a century. George's first son, George, Jr., was born in 1909. He would attend Princeton and Oxford, becoming a skilled collegiate debater; he would work on various journals and write travel books, would serve as an artillery officer during World War II, and later he would spend about five years working for the CIA. In 1965, at the age of fifty-five, he would be killed in an automobile accident in Vermont.

The second son, John, was born in 1913. Approximately one week later, due to complications during the birth, the mother died, and thereafter George's sons were brought up with the help of his unmarried sister, Nannie. Nannie Ochs was the oldest of the three daughters of Julius and Bertha Ochs, a year older than George, two years younger than Adolph. She had attended a girls' college in Bristol, Virginia, but had been

called home to help run the household when her mother
became ill. Nannie had been courted but had never
married, nor had she been encouraged to marry, especially by Adolph, who had a critical eye for suitors.
Nannie was needed at home, and that is where she remained until her mother's death. Her mother died in
1909, at seventy-five, while in New York visiting
Adolph.

Nannie was then forty-eight, and she went to Europe
to live and travel for the next five years, returning to re-
side with her brother George in Philadelphia upon the
death of his wife. The boys adored Nannie, and as
they got older they came to appreciate her keen mind
and her strong social conscience which, in the early
Thirties, transformed her into an ardent supporter of
the New Deal, one who stood up to all the opposition
she received at the large family gatherings of the Ochs
dynasty, particularly from Arthur Hays Sulzberger and
his wife, Iphigene, both of whom could barely tolerate
Roosevelt—and Iphigene could absolutely *not* tolerate
Eleanor Roosevelt, could not *stand* the sound of her
voice. But Nannie was invariably persuasive in her
views, and many years later John Oakes would trace
part of his own political origin as a Liberal Democrat
to his Aunt Nannie, his formal personality warming up
with the mere mention of her name; although the overwhelming influence on his life was his father, George.

Long after most sons have abandoned the final illusion about their fathers, John Oakes remains firmly
convinced that his father was a brilliant man of rare integrity, one who certainly possessed a superior mind
to, if not the gall of, the celebrated Adolph. John has
always admired his father's forthrightness in doing and
saying what he thought, regardless of how unpopular
or awkward the result, and John likes to retell stories
that project his father in the role of an independent
thinker, bold, uncompromising. He tells of how a large
delegation of Philadelphia advertisers once visited his
father's office at the *Philadelphia Public Ledger* to protest the editorial support that George Ochs had been
giving to a Republican reform candidate opposed to

the Democratic machine, and they hinted that the continuance of this policy might be costly to the newspaper's advertising revenue; but George responded with even more support for the reform candidate in the mayoralty race, and this candidate eventually won and, by way of gratitude, asked George if he had any individual whom he wished to recommend for a political job in the new administration, but George declined the offer. He had no favors to ask, no suggestions to make, George told the mayor, wishing only that the city be run with efficiency and honesty. During the mayor's entire term George never entered the mayor's office and he made every effort never to talk to the mayor again.

John Oakes's interest in the protection of trees, rivers, and mountains against the ambitions of land developers was also partially inspired by his father, a devotee of national parks and an enthusiastic hiker, although John Oakes is a much more passionate conservationist than his father ever was—Oakes, in fact, is capable of more emotion and intensity over trees than perhaps any *New York Times*man since Joyce Kilmer, the poet, who at the time of his death, in 1918, while serving in the United States Army, was on military leave from *The Times*' Sunday department. Since Oakes became influential on *The Times*, the changing seasons have been regularly rhapsodized on the editorial page, and one of the major themes on that page has been the endless battle of nature against human greed. Such issues often bring Oakes into disagreement with men of influence, wealth, and self-righteousness, qualities not entirely lacking in John Oakes himself, and it is precisely this delicate balance between Oakes and the world that he weighs, the reflection of himself that he sometimes sees in the people that he criticizes, that has no doubt contributed to his hypersensitivity and soul-searching manner. He seems to be constantly in a state of self-examination, fussing with the words that he writes, agonizing over ideas, worried that he is either too critical or not critical enough, careful to avoid the impression that it is a personal motive that prompts him to do what he is doing, has done, or will do. Thus he may not publish a deserving editorial about a school that he once attended, or an organization to which he belongs; at other times he will condemn something of which he is a part but he will not sever his connection with it because this would be a predictable act, and he does not wish to be predictable. As a student editor at Princeton he was critical of the club system, but was a member of a club; as a *Times* editor with a commitment to the Civil Rights movement, he was personally repulsed by some of the racial policies of the Metropolitan Club in Washington, among other similar organizations, but he did not join the distinguished ranks that quit the club in the early Nineteen-sixties, making headlines: Oakes quit a few years later, quietly, and refused to discuss publicly the reasons for his resignation.

Like most newspaper editors and critics, Oakes does not relish criticism. Should unflattering comments about *The New York Times*, particularly about its editorial page, appear in another journal or magazine, Oakes will quickly send off a letter of reply. His letter will most often attempt to discredit the criticism by dwelling on any errors of fact or interpretation that appeared in the criticism, even if the errors were minor or inconsequential to the larger purpose of the piece. It is not that Oakes is more prissy than other editors are, or must often be; it is rather that he is unable to resist the impulse to lash back whenever there is an attack, however slight, upon something that is very close to his heart. He is thin-skinned and intense, a man whose life was made no less complex by the tragedy associated with his birth, by the strong sentimentality for a father reared in a tight family dominated by an older brother, by his name change that requires regular clarification as to who he is, where he stands, how he got there. Oakes accepts all challenges and his life has been a series of small skirmishes, mostly with himself.

Shortly after returning home from Oxford in 1936, he applied for a job at a Trenton newspaper while wearing an FDR button on his lapel; he got the job, but the editor warned him not to reappear in the office for work until he had removed the button. Oakes was offended by the remark, interpreting it somehow as an affront to his independence, and he waited a few extra days, until after Roosevelt's reelection, before reporting to the *State Gazette and Trenton Times* without his FDR button. Later, at the *Washington Post*, and still later at *The New York Times*, Oakes seemed unable to decide precisely how he wished to sign his articles, and as a result his by-lines have varied through the years from John Oakes to John B. Oakes, J. B. Oakes to John Bertram Oakes—and some of the articles on conservation that he wrote for *The Times* were signed "by John Bertram." After he took over *The Times*' editorial page and began publishing pieces by Tom Wicker, Oakes began to wonder if that by-line was not perhaps too informal, and one day he wrote Wicker inquiring if Thomas Wicker or Thomas G. Wicker might not be more appropriate. Wicker said he liked his name the way it was.

While John Oakes claims to be pleased that his father changed the name, relieving his family branch of some unnecessary Ochsian weight, he is nonetheless disappointed by his father's obscurity and the lack of high regard that some members of the family had for him. In a biography about Adolph Ochs written with the cooperation of Iphigene Sulzberger and other close relatives, George was referred to as a "gun-toting dandy." Adolph himself retained a deep affection for his younger brother throughout his lifetime, but he apparently also sensed in George qualities that were out of harmony with institutionalism, and so he always kept George at a safe distance from the center stage of power. When Ochs began spending more time in New York than in the South, he appointed George to manage the *Chattanooga Times*, and he was well satisfied with things until George decided that he wanted to run for mayor. Unable to discourage him, Adolph neither helped him nor did he vote for him. After George had left political life, Adolph offered him a job in Paris to supervise *The New York Times*' exhibit at the Paris Exposition of 1900, a responsibility that included the publishing of a daily Paris edition of *The Times*; George accepted this challenge and was very successful, both professionally and socially, moving around town with the international set and promoting *The Times* as well. When the Exposition ended George received from the French government the Legion of Honor.

A year later George went to Philadelphia to run the Ochs newspaper there, a profitable venture that ended in 1913 when Adolph Ochs, becoming increasingly involved in *The Times'* expansion in New York and remaining sentimentally attached to his paper in Chattanooga, accepted George's advice and sold the Philadelphia newspaper to Cyrus Curtis for two million dollars, with the stipulation that George be retained as publisher of the Philadelphia paper. But policy differences soon arose between George and Curtis—one of George's complaints had to do with Curtis' installing his son-in-law in the business department—and by 1915 George had resigned and was again working for Adolph, this time in New York. George was put in charge of two auxiliary publications of The New York Times Company, *Current History Magazine* and the *Mid-Week Pictorial*, and he had an office on the tenth floor of the *Times* building, the same floor on which John Oakes now supervises *The Times'* editorial page.

George never did become involved with *The Times'* News department—nor has his son John. And John Oakes prefers it that way, liking the clear line that separates his editorial-page staff from the rest of the newspaper, protecting it from the commercial ambitions of Monroe Green on the second floor and the sprawling bureaucracy of Clifton Daniel on the third floor. Oakes enjoys an independence within the institution that is rare—his opinions, and those of the editorial writers under him, are subject only to the scrutiny of the publisher. Oakes is regularly in touch with the publisher and receives what amounts to total freedom, and as a result the editorial page in recent years has been converted from vapidity to vibrance, attacking issues with an aggressiveness that Adolph Ochs would never have tolerated, and sniping at important people once regarded within *The Times* as "sacred cows," such people as Chiang Kai-shek, Robert Moses, and Francis Cardinal Spellman. When Oakes began writing editorials for *The Times* in 1949, after three years of writing for Lester Markel's "Week in Review" section in the Sunday department, the editorial policy was strongly in support of Chiang Kai-shek. The editorial specialist who produced most of these pieces was an old China hand who had become an admirer of Chiang and expressed few opinions that might offend the Generalissimo, who read *The Times* through translation. After the writer's retirement, and with the increasingly important role played by John Oakes in the Fifties, highlighted by his scathing editorials on McCarthyism, *The Times'* policy on China, among other major issues, noticeably began to change. Oakes weighed the wisdom of having Communist China admitted to the United Nations, and when this thinking started to penetrate *The Times'* editorial page, Chiang Kai-shek was furious. One such editorial appeared a day before a *Times* correspondent on Taiwan was scheduled to have an interview with Chiang, an exclusive story that the correspondent had dutifully arranged weeks in advance. When the correspondent appeared, the Generalissimo, arms flailing, angrily refused to cooperate, being unappeased by the correspondent's explanation that the news staff and the editorial page are run as entirely separate departments within *The New York Times*.

The privileged treatment accorded Robert Moses by *The New York Times* until relatively recent years was remarkable, and it was achieved mainly through Moses' audacity, his skill at using his personal connections, or the presumption of these connections with top people at *The Times*, including the Sulzbergers, to browbeat some *Times* reporters who were assigned to cover aspects of his vast and varied career. As New York's most powerful public servant—during the Nineteen-fifties he was, among other things, the Commissioner of Parks, head of the Mayor's Slum Clearance Committee, chairman of the Triborough Bridge and

Tunnel Authority, chairman of the State Power Authority, a member of the Planning Commission—Moses was undeniably a great and valuable source of news. It was also true that he had definite ideas on how news should be covered, and if he was displeased by a story in the newspaper he would unhesitatingly fire off a telegram to *The Times* denouncing the reporter as incompetent, or he would sometimes call a press conference to castigate the reporter publicly, or sometimes he would write a gentle letter of complaint to Arthur or Iphigene Sulzberger, a note that would be bucked down through channels to the third floor, ending up in the hands of perhaps a second-assistant city editor who might quietly wonder if Robert Moses' low opinion of the reporter was not in some way justified. While Moses never did succeed in getting a *Times* reporter dismissed or even chastised, he was never discouraged from trying, and what he did accomplish was to alert reporters to his possible reaction, making many reporters—the less secure ones, to be sure, but *The Times* always had its quota of these—extraordinarily cautious with every story they wrote about him; they became sensitive to his sensitivity. These reporters knew, or thought they knew, or preferred to believe, that Moses had to be more delicately handled than other important newsmakers in New York. They had heard it rumored about the newsroom that Moses was a friend of the family, that Iphigene Sulzberger particularly liked his manner in responding to her suggestions about city parks; and to what extent this was true was unimportant, truth or rumor being equally persuasive in this context—there *seemed* to be sufficient evidence within the *Times* building to support the theory that Robert Moses required special handling, and so he got it.

For example in 1959 when Moses became angered by a series of articles in *The Times* dealing with the city's Title I slum-clearance program, which he headed, his letters of objection did not appear in the "Letters to the Editor" space, where they belonged; instead they were published on various days within the news columns as *news,* being prefaced by an explanatory paragraph, appearing under a news headline, and being given immediate and serious play. This not only raised readers' doubts about the credibility of the series, but it also took some of the edge off the series, which the reporter had carefully researched for months—and which was accurate and objective, if not totally satisfactory to Moses in all of its detail and interpretation. When Moses wrote magazine articles in *The Times* for his friend Lester Markel, an editor known for the severity of his stylistic standards, there was rarely any tampering with Moses' florid prose, cushioned as it was with barbs and pretension, and these articles were featured in the Sunday *Times Magazine* almost as prominently as those written by Markel himself. During these years, too, there was employed on *The Times* news staff a veteran reporter who was known among his colleagues as a "Moses man," meaning that Moses had him as a confidant and friend, entrusting to him his private telephone numbers and his whereabouts on weekends so that should *The Times* wish to reach Moses to confirm or deny or comment on some news development, *The Times'* editors could do so by contacting Moses' man, who would contact Moses. This particular reporter's status on the staff, his inner confidence and manner, and no doubt his courage in seeking merit raises, was fortified in part by his relationship with Robert Moses; and when Moses went into decline as an important newsmaker in the Nineteen-sixties, so did Moses' man decline in *The New York Times'* newsroom.

Robert Moses' deterioration as a sacred cow on *The Times* was largely attributable to the newspaper's great organizational shift during the Sixties, events prompted by the illness and incapacity of Sulzberger and then the unexpected death of his fifty-year-old successor, Orvil Dryfoos, in 1963. The quick exit of two publishers in three years, together with the reshuffling of the old guard under them, had a disruptive effect on many traditional habits and values at *The Times*. Suddenly there were new editors with new ideas making decisions on the third floor, and there was John

Oakes running the editorial page on the tenth floor, and most of these men had little reverence for the sacred cows. Among the first to feel this change was Robert Moses; another was Francis Cardinal Spellman.

Moses began to feel it during the winter of 1963 when, as president of the forthcoming New York World's Fair, he encountered a chilly press reception to so many of his plans and deeds—the mood of the media seemed against him, tired of him, not only *The Times* but the other newspapers as well, plus radio and television. It was not that they reported the news incompletely or inaccurately. If anything they were *too* complete, *too* accurate, they overlooked nothing. They quoted that one extra word or phrase that was too much, inserted that extra little detail that can subliminally convey skepticism to a reader. They had fun with Moses, this cranky old man trying to ballyhoo the Fair, and they picked it apart before its flimsy construction was complete, and then they continued to downgrade it through the next two summers.

The Times' editorials criticized Moses' financial handling of the Fair, his "penchant for invective," and the reporters seemed to delight in recording his every frustration—his futile attempt to get the A & P to remove its big neon bread sign that peeked over the Fair grounds, his inability to get the Russians to participate in the Fair, his unfulfilled optimism about the number of people who would be visiting the Fair each day. The press, including *The Times*, overdramatized the Fair's opening-day threat of racial disturbances, including an automobile "stall-in" by Negro militants along the highways—a threat that, while it never materialized, did not help attendance. No one seemed particularly interested in helping Moses at this point, and the press would display little of the blithe spirit, the indifference to minor flaws that had characterized its coverage of the previous Fair in Brussels, or would spark the reporting of the later Fair in Canada. Moses, the symbol of the New York Fair, had made too many enemies during his long career. He had written too many letters, pushed too many people. And he got what he deserved, even though, as is often the case, he did not get it when he deserved it. For the New York World's Fair of 1964/65 was not really the ugly, dull, uninspired extravaganza that much of the press coverage indicated. Each day thousands of visitors greatly enjoyed the Fair, found the sights and sounds both marvelous and memorable, but they had no way of expressing this, no voice that could compete with a press that focused on the demonstrators at the gates, the problems of parking, the labor disputes, the flaws that can always be found if one looks for them—as one *Times*-man did when he reported in his column, "At the Fair," that there were no paper towels in the men's room of the Scott Towel Pavilion.

Francis Cardinal Spellman was one of those men who for decades in *The New York Times* was written about constantly, but never deeply. *The Times* from Adolph Ochs's day was hypersensitive in its coverage of religion, ever fearful of offending one group or another, and in Cardinal Spellman's case the editors' job was even more precarious because he was not only an immensely powerful clergyman but he also sometimes said or did things that were controversial, putting the onus on the editors to somehow print the news and yet not offend the Cardinal or his many thousands of followers. The editors managed to do this for many years with great skill, blunting the reportorial edge, softening the headlines, emphasizing whenever possible his personal kindnesses, his charities, his simple manner, and the warm applause he received at parochial school graduations and police communion breakfasts, without ever stressing and sometimes totally ignoring Cardinal Spellman's less glorious moments— his blessing of bombers, his affection for Senator Joseph McCarthy, his involvement in New York politics. And this polite press policy toward him would have undoubtedly continued indefinitely had he not so persistently paraded his patriotism during the Vietnamese war, a time of loosening restraint in America, of growing discord within his own Church—Spellman in the Sixties had, like Robert Moses, gone on too long, and the liberals were now becoming increasingly less liberal, including some on *The New York Times* like John Oakes. One year before Spellman's death an editorial in *The Times* attacked the Cardinal for saying, during his Christmas visit to American troops in Vietnam, that anything "less than victory is inconceivable," a remark not only repulsive to many Catholic liberals in America but also to Pope Paul, who had been carrying on a campaign for a negotiated peace. Even in *The Times'* news columns, in an analysis article by the recently hired religious-news editor, John Cogley, a liberal Catholic formerly of the Catholic magazine *Commonweal*, the Cardinal was chided for his words; Cogley also pointed out that the number of Catholics who traditionally express serious moral reservations about war is proportionately smaller than the number of Protestant and Jewish objectors—a statement that no *Times* journalist would probably have gotten into print a few years before, and a *Times*man with a Jewish by-line might not have gotten into print even on this occasion.

Even more remarkable was the editorial on Cardinal Spellman that appeared in *The Times* on the day after his death, an appraisal that not only shocked many Catholics but surprised many other *Times* readers who had mistakenly assumed that *The Times'* editorial page would now temper its views on the Cardinal and publish a kind of eulogy to him. Instead, describing him as a man of fixed convictions, strongly expressed, the editorial dredged up what it deemed to be his sins: "He backed the late Senator Joseph McCarthy in his demagogic excesses, and he made a dismaying attack on Mrs. Franklin D. Roosevelt when she upheld separation of church and state in education. In political affairs and in public debate he often tended to speak in a commanding tone and to don a mask of authoritarianism which, however appropriate in some other time and some other place, was ill-suited to a pluralist democracy. Whether he was trying to ban the motion picture 'Baby Doll' or block the reform of New York's divorce law, Cardinal Spellman sometimes squandered his own and his church's prestige on trivial issues and lost causes."

Dozens of letters and calls of protest immediately followed, overwhelmingly opposing the editorial. Of the first seventy letters received, sixty-two condemned it, and a few of these were later published in the "Letters to the Editor" space on the editorial page. In the *National Review*, its editor, William F. Buckley, wrote an editorial about the editorial, rebuking *The Times* for not criticizing Spellman's delinquencies at the time he committed them, charging that it had been editorially silent about Spellman when his friendship with McCarthy and his differences with Mrs. Roosevelt were newsworthy. The Cardinal had then terrorized *The Times* into restraint, Buckley wrote, and because of this, Buckley concluded, "We mourn the Cardinal's passing even more."

Buckley was incorrect in his assertion that *The Times* was silent over the Mrs. Roosevelt incident; in two editorials in 1949 it supported Mrs. Roosevelt's position, although its rebuff of the Cardinal was most delicate.

John Oakes remained calm through the clamor following Spellman's death. Oakes had been through this sort of thing many times before, and he would again, and he rather liked the excitement that such editorials can provoke. He had wanted to run a stimulating editorial page on *The Times* and that is what he was now doing, expressing opinions that are not always popular but are at least his own, and the publisher's, and are not influenced by powerful people outside *The Times* nor by the advertisers who buy space in *The Times* from Monroe Green.

Monroe Green sat in his office waiting for the telephone call from Alan Tishman about the new luxury sky-scraper apartments that *The Times'* editorial page that day described as a desecration of the natural beauty of the New Jersey cliffs along the Hudson River. When Green's secretary announced that Mr. Tishman was

on the line, Green was not surprised by Tishman's immediate tone of anger and confusion. It was terrible,
Tishman said—terrible, cruel, stupid, unfair. The apartment buildings did not violate the skyline, as the editorial claimed; instead they brought elegance to that
dreary plot of land, Tishman said. Why had *The
Times* permitted such a diatribe to be published? What
was gained by it? Who had done such a thing?

Monroe Green, who had been listening sympatheti-
cally, told Tishman that he was sorry, and that, while
he agreed with Tishman, he had no control over the
editorials. As to what recourse to take, Green said
that Tishman had two alternatives. He could write a
letter of protest to the editorial page, and it would be
printed and might do some good—or it might do more
harm. It might merely call attention to the editorial
itself. Green strongly advised against sending the letter.
The best thing to do, Green continued, his salesman's
voice becoming more reassuring, was to do nothing.
Forget about it. Pretend it did not happen. The advertising supplement—and future advertising—would
offset whatever damage the editorial had done, and
personally, Green said, he did not think that the editorial had done any damage at all. Nobody reads the
editorials, Green said.

Tishman gave it some thought, and he finally decided to follow Green's advice. And later, after the
luxury apartment houses had opened and were filled
with tenants, Tishman decided that Green had probably been right. Nobody reads the editorials.

5

CLIFTON DANIEL sat at his desk enjoying the final few seconds of silence that remained before his office would be crowded with editors discussing the news. It was perhaps the most pleasant moment of the day. The late-afternoon sunlight streamed down between tall buildings in Times Square and filtered through the Venetian blinds and white draperies of Daniel's office, heightening the many colors in the room and illuminating the faded photographs of Van Anda, Birchall, and James that hung on the wall. The big polished conference table, surrounded by chairs modeled after Adolph Ochs's own chair, stood in the front of the office; beyond it was an open door revealing part of the newsroom. Daniel leaned back, way back, twirling his horn-rimmed glasses in his right hand, and looked out across his long office, through the door, and watched the people moving about within the newsroom. He could see a tall blond copyboy, a tweedy young man who probably felt as equal to his superiors as most copyboys do on *The New York Times*, walking toward the bullpen while reading a set of galley proofs—hoping, no doubt, to find an error. Daniel could see the bent-over heads of copyreaders on the foreign desk, supplicants at the altar of the wire god, pondering and scratching, and he could also see two photo clerks squinting up at the pictures that they had just torn from the telephoto machine. Though Daniel did not have a view of the dozens of reporters who were now assembled behind rows of desks, he could hear the muted tapping of their typewriters, the distant ring of telephones. He knew that the tension of the deadline was building, but he also knew that some reporters, unassigned on this day, were now sitting idly behind their keyboards reading a newspaper or a book, waiting for another *Titanic* to sink, or waiting for the coffee wagon, or waiting for the news conference to begin so that they could dial one of the secretaries and perhaps make a date later for a drink.

It had been a relatively easy day so far, and Daniel looked forward to getting home on time tonight and spending all of tomorrow and Sunday at his summer place in Bedford with Margaret and the children. There was no great international crisis today to keep him late at the office, and the inter-*Times* problems, the personality differences between certain senior editors, the painful personnel changes that were soon to be made, were such that they could not be dealt with this weekend. One of the individuals involved was Daniel's friend Harrison Salisbury. During Salisbury's long and distinguished career as a reporter, and during his more recent role as one of Daniel's four assistant managing editors, he had made invaluable contributions to *The Times* and to Daniel's position on *The Times*. Throughout the executive reorganization of the last few years, Harrison Salisbury, as Daniel's troubleshooter, had performed many of the necessary, if ungracious, functions that were bound to make him unpopular and *did*. But Salisbury did not seem to mind. He saw himself as carrying out his duties and was unaware of the resentment he was causing, the enemies he was making not only in the Washington bureau, which was his primary target, but also in New York among a few of Daniel's other editors. And now, in the summer of 1966, the rumors around the newsroom were that Salisbury was on his way out as an assistant managing editor; he was being kicked upstairs to head *The Times'* Book Division, which was being expanded.

Clifton Daniel did not want to see Salisbury go, but the question was whether Daniel had enough singular power, or even the will, to do anything about it. Salisbury had rendered fine service during the struggle, but

now the publisher and his executive editor, Turner
Catledge, apparently wanted to see harmony restored
at almost any price. Perhaps Salisbury's mere presence
in the newsroom would be a grim reminder of things
best forgotten—Daniel would have to wait and see.
Nothing could be done at this time. Anything done
should appear to have Salisbury's blessing and Salisbury was not even in the country now. He was on a
special assignment traveling around the periphery of
China hoping to get down into Hanoi or up into Peking. So far, he had been unable to get a visa into
either place, and it looked as if he would return to the
office later in the summer without the big story that he
wanted and with only an outside chance of surviving
as the devil's advocate in the newsroom. Already, a
younger man, A. M. Rosenthal, who was forty-four
years old—Salisbury was fifty-seven—was assuming
many of Salisbury's duties, and Rosenthal had been
assigned a desk against the south wall of the newsroom where the assistant managing editors sit. Rosenthal was ostensibly filling in during Salisbury's absence.
But nobody in the newsroom underestimated the significance of where Rosenthal was sitting. Where one sits
in *The Times'* newsroom is never a casual matter. It is
a formal affair on the highest or lowest level. Young
reporters of no special status are generally assigned to
sit near the back of the room, close to the Sports department; and as the years go by and people die and
the young reporter becomes more seasoned and not
so young, he is moved up closer to the front. But he
must never move on his own initiative. There was one
bright reporter who, after being told that he would
help cover the labor beat, cleaned out his desk near
the back of the room and moved up five rows into an
empty desk vacated by one of the labor reporters who
had quit. The recognition of the new occupant a few
days later by an assistant city editor resulted in a reappraisal of the younger reporter's assets, and within
a day he was back at his old desk, and within a year
or so he was out of the newspaper business altogether.
Editors, too, must respect the system, and the story is

told that one day twenty years ago an assistant managing editor, Bruce Rae, made the mistake of sitting in Edwin James's chair when the managing editor was out ill. When James heard about it, he was furious. Bruce Rae, regarded as a possible successor to James, got no further.

But Rosenthal was a very aware young man. Since his appointment as editor of the New York staff in 1963, following a brilliant career as a correspondent in India, Poland, and Japan, Rosenthal had inspired a very large and somewhat lethargic assemblage to compete favorably with Reston's men in Washington and with the traditionally superior foreign staff. Now Rosenthal was obviously being considered for one of the four assistant-managing-editor positions. These jobs, except in Salisbury's case, were held by men who had been on *The Times* for thirty or forty years and had risen from the ranks of copyreaders. The men were still physically sound and mentally alert, and they would no doubt be displeased by any lessening of their responsibilities—but if Rosenthal was to gain experience as a top executive, one of the older men would have to be moved elsewhere. It was the inevitable process by which the institution perpetuated itself— *the old order changeth*. If Harrison Salisbury did not go, then it would have to be one of the other three editors. One of these was a man who had been giving Clifton Daniel much trouble of late—the editor of the bullpen, Theodore Bernstein.

Bernstein, a native New Yorker in his early sixties, was a quick, sharp, didactic editor. He was a chain smoker who had suffered a mild heart attack recently, although outwardly he seemed very calm and contained. Of average height and slight build, with fair complexion and thinning dark hair, he had an alert, thin, friendly face with soft brown eyes, and he was as approachable as any man on *The Times*. But with a pencil in his hand, Theodore Bernstein could become suddenly cold and dogmatic. He had been an outstanding professor of journalism at Columbia University, from which he had graduated in 1925, the year he joined *The Times* as a copyreader; since then he had written several successful books on journalism and the proper use of the English language, and in 1939, though he was only thirty-five, he was put in charge of war copy at *The Times*. He wrote many of the big headlines of World War II and he personally scrutinized the metal matrix of *The Times'* front page at night before it was rolled away to the press machines. Bernstein later edited the Churchill memoirs for the paper, as well as those of Cordell Hull and General Walter Bedell Smith, and when Turner Catledge in the Nineteen-fifties called for a better-written, better-edited *New York Times*, Bernstein was established as the enforcer of standards—he became *The Times'* grammarian or, as *Encounter* magazine later described him, its "governess."

From his tiny enclosed office in the southeast corner of the newsroom, fortified outside his door by subordinate editors who shared most of his opinions on news and grammar, Bernstein also published a little bulletin called *Winners & Sinners* that was distributed to *Times*men in New York and throughout the world; it listed examples of their work, good and bad, that had appeared recently in *The New York Times*, and it also included a recitation of Bernstein's grammatical rules and comments. These were memorized by deskmen throughout the newsroom, who were held accountable by Bernstein for the maintenance of his principles; thus the deskmen, in the interest of a more readable and grammatical newspaper, gained new and rather heady power during the Nineteen-fifties with Bernstein as their mentor, chief of the super-desk. Such a position, of course, made Bernstein a villain with those reporters who had their own ideas about writing. They charged that the deskmen, overreacting to Bernstein's rules, were merely hatchet men who deleted from stories the choicest phrases and gems of originality. Turner Catledge did not become involved in the feud at the time. If Bernstein's men went too far they could always be checked, and the quicker pace of postwar life, the coming of television, the increased cost of news production, among other factors, required that *The Times* become a more tightly edited paper for faster reading. Catledge realized that *somebody* had to worry about the proper uses of *that* or *which, whom* or *who*, and so Catledge left this to Bernstein, who knew best, and Catledge concerned himself with interoffice politics, which *he* knew best.

Bernstein's power as an assistant managing editor begin to diminish after Catledge brought Daniel back to New York from Moscow in 1955 and began to groom him as the next managing editor. While Bernstein knew that he had never been a candidate for Catledge's job, being of Catledge's generation, to say nothing of his being a Jew, he nonetheless quietly resented Catledge's elevating his younger Southern protégé to a point where Daniel, even while Catledge was still the managing editor, outranked Bernstein in the executive pecking order. Bernstein and Daniel saw things in a quite different way, their styles did not blend; Bernstein, a reverse snob, was as conspicuously informal as Daniel was formal. When Daniel was named to succeed Catledge in 1964 and when he redecorated Catledge's old office, ordering a brand-new blue-black tweed rug, Bernstein requested and received for *his* floor a chunk of the old tattered Catledge rug that had been pulled up, possibly to be junked. While Daniel sat in his traditional English office in his wrinkle-proof chair, Bernstein occupied his office across the newsroom with his shirtsleeves rolled up to the elbow, sitting on an old wooden chair behind a scratchy desk, upon which he wrote with flawless grammar on the cheapest memo paper he could find. During Daniel's first two years as managing editor he admitted to having raised his voice in anger only once, presumably at Tom Wicker; but others in the newsroom claimed to have heard Daniel locked in quarrels with Bernstein on at least a half-dozen occasions, usually the result of Bernstein's having passed off an irreverent remark about one of Daniel's pet projects, most likely the women's page.

Though Daniel would prefer to be identified with

several of *The Times'* recent changes for the better—
the expanded coverage of cultural news, the more
literate obituaries, the encouragement of flavor and
mood in "hard-news" stories that formerly would have
been done in a purely routine way, he is more quickly
credited with, or blamed for, the women's page. Bernstein and other critics say that the women's page gets
too much space, and they particularly oppose the publication of lengthy stories by the women's-page editor,
Charlotte Curtis, a five-foot fast-stepping Vassar
alumna, describing the activities of wealthy wastrels
from Palm Beach to New York at a time when most
of America is moving toward the goals of a more
egalitarian society. Although Miss Curtis is rarely
flattering to her subjects, many of them lack the wit
to realize this—but what is more important about Miss
Curtis' work is that Clifton Daniel likes to read it.
Bernstein's deskmen, therefore, rarely trim her stories,
and she is extremely careful with her facts, knowing
that should she make an error it will most likely be
Daniel, and not Bernstein, who will catch her. A few
years ago, in a story on Princess Radziwill, she mentioned the Prince's nickname, "Stash," only to receive
the next day a memo from Daniel noting that while
it was pronounced *Stash*, it was spelled *Stas*. Having
previously checked the spelling with Pamela Turnure,
then secretary to Prince Radziwill's sister-in-law, Jacqueline Kennedy, Miss Curtis telephoned Daniel to inform
him that he was wrong—it was spelled *Stash*.

"On what authority?" he asked

"The White House," she quickly answered.

"Well, when I knew him," Daniel said, "it was
spelled *S-t-a-s*."

Daniel hung up. She thought that was the end of it.
But Daniel tracked the Prince down in Europe, and
some months later Miss Curtis got another memo from
Daniel—it was *Stas*.

But should Bernstein criticize Charlotte Curtis' work,
Daniel is usually quick to defend her, as he did in a
lengthy memo after one of her stories had been
challenged in *Winners & Sinners*. Bernstein, offended by

a Curtis paragraph that read—"The McDonnells are like the Kennedys. They are rich Irish Catholics, and there are lots of them."—reprinted this in *Winners & Sinners* with a warning to the staff: "Omit racial, religious or national designations unless they have some relevance to the news or are part of the biographical aggregate, as in an obit or a Man in the News. Perhaps it is a tribute to the Irish that 'Irish Catholic' does not seem offensive, but would you write 'rich Russian Jews'?"

Bernstein then received a note from Daniel: "I agree with you that it is a tribute to the Irish that 'Irish Catholic' does not seem offensive, and I also agree that 'rich Russian Jew' might be offensive. But it seems to me that the prejudice is more in the mind of the reader than it is in the words of the writer, and that we can certainly say that a family is rich, that it is Russian and that it is Jewish, if those things are relevant to the news. In fact, I myself have written about such families and nobody ever questioned the relevance of doing so. But the trick is not to put these facts together in one bunch so that they have a cumulative, pejorative aroma." In a postscript, Daniel added: "Since this note was dictated, we have published an obituary of Sean O'Casey, calling him a poor Irish Protestant."

Another point of contention between Bernstein and Daniel was centered around Harrison Salisbury, who, with Daniel's strong support, had been elevated from the reporting ranks in 1962 and made an editor; by 1964 he had become an assistant managing editor. One of Salisbury's duties was to read *The Times* each morning and then write a memo for Daniel about the strengths and weaknesses of the edition, not only comparing *The New York Times*' reporting with the *New York Herald Tribune*'s and other newspapers', but also commenting on the general appearance of the paper, its makeup and headlines and pictures and prose style—Salisbury was suddenly encroaching upon Bernstein's *spécialité*, and Bernstein became very uneasy in the newsroom. Bernstein, the watchdog of *The Times* for so long, now felt that *he* was being watched.

One evening, after Salisbury had invited himself into the bullpen to observe Bernstein and two subordinate editors laying out page one, Bernstein could contain himself no longer. He wrote a long memo to Daniel that night. He wrote it in his own hand, the secretary having gone, and it was just as well. It would be embarrassing to dictate this sort of note. In it he emphasized that Salisbury had no business watching the bullpen editors making up the front-page dummy, which is distributed to all the senior editors anyway, and he added that he would interpret a reappearance by Salisbury as a vote of "no confidence" from Daniel. Bernstein then described Salisbury in a way that he would never have done under ordinary circumstances: "It was almost as if he were a spy and we [the bullpen editors] the ones being spied upon." The reply from Daniel the next day dismissed the significance of the incident. There had apparently been a slight misunderstanding on Salisbury's part, Daniel said, and he was sorry if it had caused uneasiness or resentment.

The Harrison Salisbury that Clifton Daniel knew was not the Salisbury that Bernstein knew. Daniel had first met Salisbury in London during World War II while Salisbury was working for the United Press. Salisbury was then a very shy, solitary figure separated from his wife, who was still in the United States, a man uncertain of himself and his future. After Salisbury had joined *The Times*, and particularly after Daniel had taken Salisbury's place in Moscow—Salisbury had been *The Times'* Moscow bureau chief for five very difficult years—the two men discovered that they had a good deal in common and much compatibility. Therefore it did not surprise Salisbury, although it surprised nearly everyone else on *The New York Times'* staff, when Daniel began to pull Salisbury up the executive ladder as Daniel himself started to rise. And Daniel had not regretted it. Salisbury was an indefatigable working executive, possessing a creative mind bursting with new ideas and approaches. He had overcome the shyness that had once so dominated him; and, happily remarried and incredibly well organized, Salisbury was one of the most impressive journalists that Daniel had ever known. He had written many fine books, including a novel, and he was much sought after as a panelist on television shows and speechmaker on campuses; and there was nothing about Harrison Salisbury's manner that was in the least conspiratorial, insofar as Daniel could see. And yet Bernstein was not alone in his feelings about Salisbury. The Washington bureau, not unexpectedly, was quick to condemn him, with one reporter nicknaming Salisbury "Rasputin," and another explaining: "Salisbury spent so many years watching who was standing next to Stalin that now *he's* standing next to Stalin!"

The mere sight of Salisbury, to those who do not know him, conveys a sense of severity, a chilling aloofness. He has an angular face with a slightly drooping gray moustache over thin lips that rarely smile, and his small pale blue eyes peer without expression through steel-rimmed glasses which, worn out of habit, do not appreciably improve his adequate eyesight. Six feet tall, Salisbury seems even taller because he has a lean, lanky body, broad shoulders, and a rather small head; his hair, once blondish, is now a silk-thread gray parted high on the right and combed hard across his forehead, the longer strands usually hanging over his left eye when, head down, he sits at his desk reading or typing. He neither drinks nor smokes. He gave up drinking in 1949 while preparing himself, psychologically and physically, for the *New York Times* assignment in Moscow during the very worst years of the Cold War, days of denial and conspiracy. He gave up smoking a few years later in the interests of his health, and now, instead of cigarettes, he sucks Life-Savers, clicking and cracking them against his teeth as he sits behind his desk in *The Times'* newsroom reading Soviet journals, or jotting tiny notes in his little black book, or looking with a glazed stare out across the rows and rows of heads bent over typewriters.

Though few knew him in the summer of 1966, nearly everyone in the newsroom seemed to have strong opinions about Salisbury, but by no means were they all negative. He was regarded by many as not only a superb reporter and writer, but also a highly effective editor, and his supervision of *The Times'* coverage of the Kennedy assassination was regarded as extraordinary. Salisbury's unpopularity, a few of them said, was undoubtedly the result of his having to carry out orders from Daniel, or from above. And yet Salisbury, others said, carried out orders with excessive enthusiasm. He seemed to *like* playing Rasputin. And fortifying this image, however unjustly, were several small inter-office tales of Salisbury's suspecting schemes within the United States government and then chastising reporters for not detecting them, of his flying down to Washington to encourage the resignation of a veteran *Times*man who had fallen out of favor with the New York office, or of Salisbury's sudden reply to the person who had just returned to him a piece of paper that he had let fall to the floor: "When I drop a piece of paper on the floor, that's where I want it to stay!" One day Salisbury, angry, walked across the room after noting that *The Times* had not, in its late-edition story about Jacqueline Kennedy, included the fact that she had visited her husband's grave unexpectedly the night before.

"Who was the late man last night?" he called out, as a curved desk of copyreaders all looked up.

"I was," one man said, finally.

"Why didn't you put a new lead on that Jackie story?"

"I didn't believe it warranted a new lead."

"Well, you guessed wrong."

"I don't agree with you, Mr. Salisbury. Jackie had done that before. That's why I didn't think the story warranted a new lead."

"Did you check with the bullpen?"

"I did, and they agreed that it didn't warrant a new lead."

Salisbury's lips tightened, and quickly he turned and walked away. A few days later one of the subordinate editors on the national desk showed the copyreader a memo that Salisbury had written charging the copyreader with bad judgment, and accusing him of having made similar errors in the past.

"That's not true," the copyreader said. "I'd like to answer this."

"Oh, *no*," the subordinate editor said, quietly, "don't answer. Just watch your step. He's keeping a dossier on a lot of guys."

The two other assistant managing editors—one was named Robert Garst, the other Emanuel Freedman— were quiet, unprovocative men, and the newsroom gossip had never centered around them in the way that it had around Harrison Salisbury and Theodore Bernstein. Robert Garst was a thin, trimly tailored, sandy-haired, somewhat chilly Virginian. He had a lean, ruddy face and light horn-rimmed eyeglasses that made his cool, pale eyes seem even more distant. A graduate of the Columbia School of Journalism, Garst joined *The Times* in 1925 as a copyreader on the city desk, and was joined on that desk three months later by Theodore Bernstein, whom he had known on the Columbia campus. Shortly after their employment on *The Times*, Garst and Bernstein also got jobs teaching journalism at Columbia during their off hours, and in 1933 they collaborated on a book of instruction for copyreaders. A few years later Garst and Bernstein were promoted to subordinate editorships on the copy-desk, beginning a somewhat parallel climb up through the desk complex that culminated in 1952 with Cat-ledge's announcement that they were now assistant managing editors. But at the same time, privately, Cat-ledge told them that they would go no further. This was to be their final advancement on *The Times*, they would never succeed him. From now on, Catledge said, they should devote themselves to helping him run the expanding staff, blending their personal aims into the larger purpose of the paper, and assisting him in the selection and training of younger *Times*men who would one day be their successors.

Bernstein did this—it had been Bernstein, in fact, who had first alerted Catledge to Rosenthal's possibilities as an editor—and if Bernstein lost any personal incentive as a result of being told at the age of forty-eight that he would climb no higher, it was never perceivable. But in Garst's case it might have been different. Perhaps Bernstein had been much more realistic about his limitations on *The Times* than Garst. If Arthur Hays Sulzberger did not want Felix Frankfurter sitting on the Supreme Court bench, he certainly did not want Theodore Bernstein sitting in the managing editor's chair—a showcase position on *The Times,* one that should offer the ultimate in social mobility, a passport through all the prejudicial barriers of the American democratic system. And Theodore Bernstein, accepting the situation as it was, concentrated on his craft as an editor, gaining his confidence from this; and he was a free man, or at least he *seemed* unintimidated by a fear of going too far: he did as he pleased, said what he thought. It had been Bernstein, together with a bullpen subordinate editor named Lewis Jordan, who led the opposition within the office during that night in 1961 when Orvil Dryfoos ordered *The Times* to tone down Tad Szulc's story about the Bay of Pigs invasion plan. The next day Bernstein was in Dryfoos' office on the fourteenth floor arguing that there was a difference between matters of national interest and national security, and Bernstein said that Dryfoos had confused the two. When matters of national security arise in a war situation or a near-war situation, Bernstein told Dryfoos, there is not the slightest question about what course the press should follow—it should do nothing that would jeopardize the nation's safety. But in matters of national interest, Bernstein went on, the press has not only a proper option but indeed a bounden duty to speak up.

While this might have been regarded as insubordination in another editor, Bernstein could get away with it because he was special: he was *The Times'* technical genius, its supreme authority on grammar and rules, he was not an easily interchangeable part in the big machine. Catledge knew this and he gave Bernstein great latitude; indeed, there were times in the Nine-

teen-fifties, before Daniel's ascension and during Catledge's drinking days before his divorce, when Theodore Bernstein seemed to be running the entire News
department.

But Robert Garst, after being made an assistant
managing editor, did not appear to have authority
comparable to Bernstein's. Garst also seemed increasingly remote as a person. While he had never been
gregarious, he now had even less to say. It was as if he
had been promoted into obscurity, or was deeply
bothered by some private problem. Each morning he
would come walking into the newsroom in his soft,
loping stride, a bit stiff and proud and with a slow
roving eye scanning the rows of reporters' desks as he
headed toward the men's locker room; then, seconds
later, he would be out again walking toward the desk
against the south wall, forcing a smile at the people he
met along the way, and then he would be seated behind
his desk occupying himself for the rest of the day with
tasks that were a mystery to nearly everyone on the
staff. He seemed to be responsible for scrutinizing the
expense accounts of the staff, and he also had something to do with office equipment and with other vague
administrative details. Once, after a high executive
from the publisher's office had complained about the
untidy appearance of the newsroom, singling out the
reporters' habit of piling their coats atop certain desks
and littering the floor with cigarette butts, Garst issued
a staff memorandum requesting that all coats be hung
in the locker room, and he had ash trays placed along
the rows of desks. Within a month or so, nearly every
ash tray had disappeared and the floors were as littered
as ever—a principal offender being the chain-smoking
television critic, Jack Gould.

And yet during the winter of 1956, an uncertain
period during which several *Times* reporters and copyreaders were subpoenaed by a Senate subcommittee investigating Communists or former Communists in the
newspaper business, Robert Garst's integrity and personal kindness toward some subpoenaed *Times*men was
such that they shall never forget it. At a time when

other executives seemed under intense pressure, Garst remained cool. He assured the subpoenaed staff members that, while he had no sympathy for communism, he respected their position of not revealing the names of other past associates in the party, and that their jobs were secure if they had left the Communist party and had been completely honest in the statements that they had signed to this effect and had sent to Sulzberger through Catledge's office. Garst did not seem so righteous and pessimistic as some other editors did toward those being investigated. Garst, they were surprised to discover, had sympathy and compassion for people in trouble. Now, ten years later, Garst was still the quiet man seated against the south wall of the newsroom. Whatever his specific duties were, he must have performed them adequately, for he had retained his position through twelve years of Catledge's managing-editorship and, so far, had survived the first two years of Daniel's tenure.

The other assistant managing editor, Emanuel Freedman, was the youngest of the four. He was a very serious, solidly built man in his middle fifties who never seemed to smile. His broad shoulders and strong facial features, a rather large head and ears with wideset eyes and heavy brows and precisely combed graying brown hair, made him seem when seated to be much taller than he was, which was about five-feet-eight. He wore a gray homburg and conservatively cut suits that were more expensive than they appeared to be. The workmanship of his clothing was on the inside, meticulously done by modest tailors, and this style was in concert with Freedman's personality. He was a meticulous man of no frivolity, and while he was always courteous he was never informal. He never took his jacket off at the office, and reporters liked to say that Freedman did not even take off his jacket when making love. Generally he was well liked by the staff, not only by those who worked under him as foreign correspondents during his many years as the foreign editor—a group that included Daniel, Salisbury, and Rosenthal—but also by those in the New York office who had never

gone overseas and who knew him only by reputation.
He was said to be a very fair man with his subordinates,
modest about himself, and, except when in the company of old friends, extremely shy.

Born in York, Pennsylvania, he had, like Garst and
Bernstein, graduated from the Columbia School of
Journalism. In those days, much more than now,
Columbia was *the* school for *Times*men, having established with *The New York Times* a kind of institutional alliance. Sulzberger was a trustee of Columbia
University, many family members had gone there,
and news releases from the Columbia campus got
special care within *The Times'* newsroom. The Columbia School of Journalism, while endowed by Pulitzer,
seemed to function as a factory for aspiring *Times*men.
Its faculty was festooned with *Times* editors advancing
Ochsian fundamentalism, and the brightest students
were regularly recruited by *The Times*, were moved up
through the system, and many of them would later return to teach journalism at Columbia and perpetuate
the process. Out of this process, in the early Nineteen-
thirties, came Emanuel Freedman.

He had been an outstanding student at Columbia and
had studied under Theodore Bernstein, and in 1934
when a copyreader's job opened up on *The Times'* foreign desk, Bernstein, who was then an assistant foreign
editor, telephoned Freedman and got him hired.
Freedman's entire career on *The Times* would be spent
behind a desk. He ran the desk at *The Times'* London
bureau from 1945 to 1948, and it was during this period that he got to know Clifton Daniel, who had returned to London after a tour of reporting in the Middle
East. The two men, then both bachelors, got along
very well in a quiet, undemanding way. Daniel liked
Freedman's taste in clothes, his reserve, and the precision of his schedule—one could set a watch by Freedman's comings and goings. At precisely the same time
every evening, the office car was waiting to take Freedman to dinner; exactly one hour later, it brought him
back. Once a week Freedman played poker, his expression being no different from what it was when he

was not playing poker. He drank on rare occasions, and when he did he never seemed to enjoy it. Reliable, solid, no bad habits—it was not surprising that such a man would become *The Times'* foreign-news editor, the ringmaster of fifty far-flung correspondents that had to be directed through various time zones, cable routes, political shifts, and upheavals. Nor was it surprising, despite the difficulties of his job, that he made few enemies among his correspondents. His dealings with them were formal, impersonal. He was an arm of *The Times*, an instrument of the institution, a rock in its foundation. But he was also privately pleased when, in 1956, he received an invitation to Clifton Daniel's wedding.

Very few *Times*men had been asked down to Independence, Missouri, to witness the Daniel-Truman marriage. Among them were Turner Catledge; Mr. and Mrs Raymond Daniell (*The Times'* bureau chief in London during the war years); and Mr. and Mrs. Emanuel Freedman. Clifton Daniel's title at the time of his marriage to Margaret Truman was "assistant to the foreign-news editor." This title was used so many times in hundreds of pre-wedding news stories that there suddenly was curiosity as to who *the* foreign-news editor was. *The New Yorker* magazine decided to find out, and a "Talk of the Town" piece was the result. In it Freedman was discovered to be "sedate, intelligent, soft-spoken." And in 1964, thirty years after he had begun on *The Times'* copydesk, and two months after Daniel had been made *The Times'* managing editor, Emanuel Freedman became an assistant managing editor.

Now A. M. Rosenthal was being pushed in the same direction. It seemed a bit premature to some of the other assistant managing editors, although they would never admit this openly. Rosenthal, bright as he was at forty-four, had only been editor of the New York staff for three years, and they could not understand the urgency of bringing Rosenthal into the upper ranks at this time. Neither Salisbury nor Bernstein, Garst nor

Freedman, was approaching the mandatory retirement age, although this was a rather vague thing at *The Times*, subject to all sorts of adjustments, depending on who was being retired. Arthur Krock, still writing his column from Washington, was seventy-eight. Lester Markel was seventy-two. Throughout the fourteen-story *Times* building—in the corners of crowded rooms, in musty little offices along hidden halls, behind the towering shelves of libraries—could be found individuals who, because of some connection with someone, or because they had escaped notice for years, were growing older and older but were kept on by *The Times*. Advanced age seemed to be something to be used if the manipulators wished to use it. And who were the manipulators? Turner Catledge was undoubtedly among them. A harsh description of Catledge's position, perhaps, but perhaps not: *Manipulate—to handle, manage, or use, esp. with skill.* Catledge had unquestionably manipulated, esp. with skill, the lives and destinies of dozens of *Times*men during the last two decades. All those years as a political reporter in Washington, his ringside seat in the Senate, observing the great indoor strategists of his time, had given to Catledge an education in the subtle use of power and timing, the art of illusion. And he had made the most of this later during his years as *The Times'* managing editor, and he was probably still doing so today, although an accurate judgment of Catledge's influence was difficult to assess. Power has almost always been a rather nebulous thing at *The Times*, losing much of its bold line and shape as it achieved height. A sharp, clear display of power by a top *Times* executive was not good form, was in conflict with the Ochsian maxim on modesty, was considered unwise: and so through the years the behavior of *Times*men at the top was not noticeably different from that of those nearer the bottom.

Those *Times*men directly below the top, the scramblers, did on occasion assert themselves, some of them pushing too hard and failing, others of them climbing to the top but then, absorbed into the hierarchy, they lost much of the individuality and drive that had once distinguished them. In any event, the *Times*men below, the reporters and copyreaders, rarely knew who was pulling which string from above. They could only guess, and sometimes they wondered if getting ahead at *The Times* was really worth the effort. Each step up, it seemed, cost the individual a part of himself. With greater power went greater responsibility, more caution, more modesty, less freedom. Those who finally attained great power did not seem to use it, perhaps could not use it. If they could not use it, what was the point in having it? And, more important, how could its existence be confirmed? A politician must win elections, a star actor must make money at the box office, a network-television commentator must maintain ratings, but a titled *Times*man may go on for decades on the momentum of the institution, facing no singular test, gaining no confidence from individual accomplishment; and yet he is personally catered to by statesmen, dictators, bankers, presidents of the United States, people who believe that he possesses persuasive powers within the institution—but they cannot be sure; *he* cannot be sure.

High power at *The Times* is a vaporous element— energy is harnessed, pressure is built, decisions emanate from a corporate collective, but it is difficult to see which man did what, and it often seems that nobody really did anything. Decisions appear to ooze out of a large clutch of executive bodies all jammed together, leaning against one another, shifting, sidling, shrugging, bending backwards, sideways, and finally tending toward some tentative direction; but whose muscles were flexed? whose weight was decisively felt? The reporters in the newsroom do not know. They know a great deal about the clandestine affairs of city government, Wall Street, the United Nations, but they do not know what goes on at the top of *The Times*. They may find out if they probe, but *Times* employees are not expected to probe deeply into the affairs of their superiors. Since the average *Times*man does not regularly sit in on the daily news conference in Daniel's office, he cannot gain clues from observing the editors' mannerisms, their reactions to one another, the little asides often made around the table. Thus the reporters must rely on rumors or be aware of small changes—such as the fact that Rosenthal was sitting at a desk against the south wall on this summer afternoon, that Salisbury and Bernstein were both missing, that Garst and Freedman looked no different than they usually did.

Robert Garst, detached and a bit bored, sat behind his desk reading. Emanuel Freedman, poker-faced, was talking on the telephone. At another desk, barely suppressing his buoyance, sat Rosenthal. In the big office, cool and relaxed, was Clifton Daniel. Daniel had had lunch today with the Secretary of Defense, Robert McNamara. McNamara probably knew more about *The Times'* hierarchy than any reporter in the newsroom, for the highest levels of the United States government and *The New York Times* are constantly in touch. These men often dine together, see one another at receptions, converse regularly on the telephone. They are curious about one another's bureaucracies, the policy shifts and personnel changes, realizing that what transpires in one place might affect the other —a mini-domino theory. And so despite their occasional differences on the slightly lower level, a hard alliance prevails at the top—and in any large showdown, the two forces would undoubtedly close ranks and stand together.

This does not mean that *The Times*, in the winter of 1966, had complied with the government's desire to suppress a series of articles on the Central Intelligence Agency; it did mean, however, that *The Times* felt obliged to have a former head of the CIA, John McCone, visit the *Times* building and read the articles before publication and suggest changes where the facts might imperil national security Some of McCone's suggestions were accepted, others were not. There was a little give and take on both sides, the *entente cordiale* surviving as it had to survive. The two forces were both committed to essentially the same goals, the preservation of the democratic system and the established order, and this kindred spirit at the top often filters down through the ranks toward the bottom: a minor government official immediately accepts all telephone calls from *Times* reporters; the mounted policeman on Forty-third Streets looks after the illegally parked cars of his newspaper friends, and *The Times* looks after his horse; and the clerk in the courthouse can fix what a recalcitrant New York policeman will not. Mayor Lindsay will dance at a *Times* jamboree, and when Governor Nelson Rockefeller spots Clifton Daniel at a large cocktail gathering there is an instant smile, and within seconds they both edge their way to the patio and a very private conversation.

Times reporters wishing to know what goes on within the hierarchy of *The Times* must subtly search for clues in their talks with government officials, ambassadors, Senators, those who move in the same circles as the Sulzbergers and other heirs of Ochsian power. It is remarkable how much the government knows and cares about the inner workings of *The Times*. When Turner Catledge was a reporter in Washington in the late Nineteen-thirties, he had been tipped off by both President Roosevelt and the Speaker of the House, Sam Rayburn, that he would be Arthur Krock's successor, and Catledge undoubtedly would have been, had he chosen to remain in Washington.

For nearly a century, the presidents of the United States have tried to maintain warm personal relationships with members of the Ochs family, and while this has not always guaranteed flattering news coverage of the White House, it has at least enabled the President to know a good deal about the paper and about those executives whom he might one day wish to influence or charm or to whom he might wish to address a letter of complaint.

Lyndon Johnson, three months after he became President, visited the *Times* building and had lunch with eleven senior executives in the publisher's dining room. (Dozens of kings, queens, and national leaders had been there previously, including Winston Churchill, who once paused during the meal to ask Sulzberger: "Do the resources of the great *New York Times* extend to a bit of mustard?") President Johnson was an engaging guest. He ate everything on his plate, was complimentary of the shrimp and the roast beef. He told a few jokes and did not permit the luncheon to be interrupted by his calls even though, less than an hour before he arrived, he had received news of Cuba's decision to cut off the water supply to Guantánamo. He sat between Arthur Hays Sulzberger and Arthur Ochs Sulzberger, father and son, on a special upholstered folding chair that a Secret Service agent had placed there before lunch: the chair was lower than a normal dining chair, and wider. The table was set with gold-rimmed dishes and silverware embossed with *The New York Times'* emblem, the eagle that adorns the masthead each day on the editorial page. The floral arrangements sprouted the national colors—red carnations, white roses, blue delphiniums—and they were set in transparent glass bowls so that the Secret Service men could be certain that they were bomb-free. After lunch, one of Johnson's aides came in with a handful of telephone messages. Johnson excused himself and went out to the foyer and took one telephone call. Then he returned and told the others, some of whom he knew quite well from previous meetings—Catledge, Daniel, Oakes—the latest news about Cuba. Then he shook hands all around and headed for the elevator.

After the visit, Lyndon Johnson kept in touch with *Times* executives in various ways. Sometimes he communicated through intermediaries; at other times, Johnson himself picked up the telephone and called a *Times* editor. One night at a dinner in Manhattan, there was a call for John Oakes. When Oakes answered, he heard Lyndon Johnson's voice, in its most folksy drawl: "*John . . . Ah been thinkin' about you . . .*" Oakes could barely hear because of the noise of the party, and he was thoroughly confused by Johnson's words, and all that Oakes could think of replying was, "*I . . . I've been thinking about you, too, Mister President.*"

Johnson finally got to the point of his call—he was making Thomas Mann, the Latin-American expert, an Assistant Secretary of State. Oakes agreed that Mann was a good choice, and an editorial favorable to Mann later appeared in *The Times*. Shortly afterwards, at another social gathering, Oakes was approached by Arthur Schlesinger, Jr., and was berated for publishing the Mann editorial. Mann's wisdom on Latin-American and Cuban affairs had rarely impressed Schlesinger during the Kennedy years, but the vehemence of Schlesinger's reaction to the editorial both shocked and startled Oakes, and he was very angry as he turned away from Schlesinger. It seemed to Oakes that Schlesinger was resurrecting much of the old hostility that President Kennedy's people in Washington had felt toward Oakes a few years before; now, instead of being labeled anti-Kennedy, Oakes was being damned as pro-Johnson, which was untrue. Still, Kennedy's aides did understand correctly the inner workings of *The New York Times*. They knew that if the editorials were negative, there was one man to blame—Oakes. They knew that the power in *The Times'* News department was much more diffuse, and that it was sometimes more advantageous to gain the good will of a reporter than an editor, and it is possible that the administration of John F. Kennedy had handled the working press with more finesse than had ever been done before.

Kennedy himself was a masterful student of journalism. An omnivorous reader of newspapers since his days at Choate, Kennedy had on two occasions worked as a reporter, and he had often expressed the desire to own a newspaper after retiring from public office. Through his father, he had been introduced at an early age to many prominent journalists, and he developed a keen awareness of their vanity and style, their susceptibility to flattery and sensitivity to criticism, their delight in being on the inside of anything momentous or intimate. As a Senator he had sent notes of thanks to those who had praised him in print; as the President he was particularly adroit in his use of the press, timing his announcements to meet various deadlines, being gracious to friends, cool to critics, bestowing favors like a king.

Those journalists whom he liked and trusted were admitted to his court. They dined with him, played golf with him, were privileged observers of his New

Frontier, were treated with an informality and charm that former presidents had not extended even to most publishers and star columnists. But the Kennedy manner was not comparable with the past. He had altered the social structure of the press establishment, creating his own system of stardom. By merely favoring a journalist in small ways, even a journalist of relatively minor talent, Kennedy could and did elevate the status of that journalist, and in a few instances such men became columnists or featured faces on television.

Kennedy's willingness to give interviews on television, and his use of television for his news conferences, offended some veterans in the press corps. James Reston called the televised news conference "the goofiest idea since the hula hoop," even though Reston's career itself did not suffer during the Kennedy years. Reston, together with other good reporters and writers, was able to compensate for television and for any social absence at Kennedy dinner parties by working harder. Perhaps they also profited by not getting too close to Kennedy: they were able to judge him with more detachment and honesty without the fear of losing such a costly friendship, and they were capable of criticism— as Reston was a week before Kennedy's death:

> There is a vague feeling of doubt and disappointment in the country about Kennedy's first term. . . . He has touched the intellect of the country but not the heart. He has informed but not inspired the nation. He is undoubtedly the most popular political figure of the day, but he has been lucky in his competition. . . . It is not a general reaction, but there is clearly a feeling in the country, often expressed by middle-aged women, that the Kennedys are setting standards that are too fancy, too fast, and as one woman said in Philadelphia, "too European." . . . Not since the days of Franklin Roosevelt have there been so many men's-club stories in circulation against "that man in the White House." . . . [It] is a far cry from the atmosphere he promised when he ran for the Presidency in 1960.

But one *Times* columnist who felt the Kennedy style adversely was Arthur Krock. The recognition accorded Krock by other presidents and their aides did not continue during the Kennedy years, and this both disturbed and disappointed Krock. He had been a friend of the Kennedy family for decades and had been very courteous in his coverage of Joseph P. Kennedy's political career, earning the elder Kennedy's everlasting gratitude. Once, while the Kennedy family was in England, Arthur Krock received the loan of the Kennedy's large villa in Palm Beach for a short winter vacation. When John F. Kennedy was writing his senior thesis at Harvard, he brought it at his father's direction to Arthur Krock to see if the latter had any suggestions to make. Krock, very impressed with the manuscript, said that it could be published as a book. Together they went over the work, Krock's role being that of a copy-editor. Then Krock secured a publisher and suggested the book's title, *Why England Slept*, borrowing from Churchill's earlier book, *While England Slept*. Joseph Kennedy, then the American Ambassador in London, proceeded to promote the book among his powerful friends. He got Henry R. Luce to write the foreword and he sent copies to such potential taste-makers as the Queen of England. The book sold eighty thousand copies in the United States and England, and John Kennedy, who was twenty-three when he wrote it, donated part of his royalties to the English town of Plymouth, which had been partially destroyed during the war, and he also bought for himself a new Buick.

When John Kennedy became President of the United States, Arthur Krock did not seek any preferential treatment, nor did he receive any. Krock was a proud and formal man, a hardened political conservative in a town now dominated by young liberals and the Jet Set, the Beautiful People, and what the writer Midge Decter would later call "Discothèque Radicals." Since first arriving in Washington more than a half-century before, Arthur Krock had witnessed the comings and goings of every conceivable movement and madness, had heard all the new singing jingles created for old political hogwash—Wilson's "New Freedom," Roosevelt's "New Deal," Truman's "Fair Deal," and now it was Kennedy's "New Frontier"—except that Arthur Krock, as a venerable member of the loyal opposition, was not being listened to now as he once had been. While Krock had been critical of the New Deal, Roosevelt had nonetheless given him an exclusive interview, an unprecedented honor, and it had won for Krock the Pulitzer Prize in 1938, his second such award. Although Krock had also been critical of Truman's administration, President Truman, too, had been interviewed exclusively by Krock in 1950, and this would have earned Krock a third Pulitzer had not one member of the voting board objected to it. That objector was Krock himself. Mindful of the gossip that the Pulitzer awards had been influenced by "logrolling," among other factors not entirely noble, Krock believed that if the Pulitzer board awarded the prize to one of its own board members, it would lend substance to the gossip; so he offered a resolution barring any member of the awards group from eligibility, and the resolution was adopted.

But now, in the Sixties, Krock felt that such grand gestures and standards were a thing of the past. Now the social order had been overturned, the traditional Presidential news conference had become an electronic circus, and almost *anybody* could get an exclusive interview with the President—even Krock's colleague Lester Markel.

Markel had merely telephoned Kennedy's press aide, Pierre Salinger, and made an appointment. Markel spent forty-five minutes with Kennedy, during which he apparently did not charm the President. After Markel had left, Kennedy approached Salinger with a frown, asking, "What the hell was *that* all about?"

"What?"

"Markel didn't come down here to interview me," Kennedy said. "He came down to tell me what to do as President."

The next time that Lester Markel called for an interview, Salinger put him off, explaining that there had been several *Times*men in to see the President recently—at which Markel quickly interrupted: "I do not wish to be treated as a *New York Times*man. I wish to be treated as an adviser to Presidents."

Salinger did not back down, and neither Lester Markel nor any other *Times* editor became an "adviser" to the President during Kennedy's tenure; although there was one *Times*man, a reporter, who did develop a close friendship with Kennedy, and this led to situations that were resented within *The New York Times*—and eventually this caused an incident that ended with the reporter's quitting *The Times*.

His name was Bill Lawrence. Lawrence was a big, strong, tough-talking man who looked like an Irish plainclothesman. He was also a drinker, a womanizer, a good golfer, an aggressive reporter who could keep a secret—and John Kennedy was enchanted with him, which said as much about Kennedy as it did about Lawrence. The type of man that Lawrence was would probably not get a job on *The New York Times* today; but when Bill Lawrence was hired by *The Times* in 1941, a brash young bully of twenty-four, journalists were not so uniformly stylized and stamped out by schools of journalism. There was then more freedom and a more romantic notion about the newspaper business, although the reporters of that time were generally less sober and perhaps also less responsible with their facts.

Bill Lawrence, born in Nebraska, had won a scholarship to Swarthmore in 1933 but lacked the money to cover the incidentals and so he took a job on the *Lincoln Star* at night and entered the University of Nebraska. Expelled eleven weeks later for cutting classes, he became a full-time reporter; and in 1936, at the age of nineteen, he was covering local politics for the Associated Press. During one of his first big assignments, a convention of the Young Democrats of Nebraska, Lawrence's passions were suddenly and angrily aroused when the Young Democrats were about to endorse Senator Edward R. Burke, a Democrat who had opposed most of Roosevelt's programs. Shouting from the floor, waving his arms, Lawrence threatened to offer a resolution commending a Republican, George W. Norris, who *was* sympathetic to Roosevelt. Lawrence's challenge was accepted and, though not a delegate, Lawrence offered the resolution—and, to his amazement, it passed. This made a bulletin on the AP wire, which Lawrence wrote, somehow ignoring the name of the resolution's sponsor. A few days later, Lawrence received word from the AP bureau chief in Nebraska that he was through.

Lawrence next got a job in Chicago with the United Press as a labor reporter, and in 1938 he was transferred to the UP bureau in Washington, one of his colleagues there being Harrison Salisbury, who had also come out of the Chicago bureau. Lawrence covered the Presidential campaign of 1940, gaining the attention and friendship of Wendell Willkie, who proceeded to recommend Lawrence to some editors on *The Times,* which had backed Willkie against Roosevelt in 1940. Although Willkie's recommendation did not get Lawrence hired at that time, it was indirectly through Wendell Willkie that Bill Lawrence came to be a *Times*-man.

One night at a gathering of the White House Correspondents Association, after Roosevelt's reelection, Lawrence noticed that as Roosevelt was being wheeled out of the room he had been approached briefly by Willkie and that the two had exchanged a few words. Anxious to know what had been said, Lawrence began to push through the crowd toward Willkie. He did not get there in time, but learning that Willkie was scheduled to be at Arthur Krock's home later in the evening, Lawrence waited and then called him there, announcing over the telephone in his forthright manner, "This is Bill Lawrence of the United Press and I'd like to speak with Wendell Willkie."

"I'm sorry," said a gentle voice on the other end, "but Mr. Willkie is engaged at this moment with guests and cannot be interrupted."

"*Look,*" said Lawrence, "you tell Mr. Willkie that this is Bill Lawrence of the United Press. And if he doesn't have time to talk to me, that's all right. *But deliver that message.*"

There was silence for a few moments. Then Wendell Willkie came to the telephone and told Lawrence what had been said, which, as it turned out, was not all that important.

The next day Lawrence met Turner Catledge, whom he knew casually, and Catledge exclaimed, "Boy, what did you say last night to Mr. Krock?"

"I didn't say anything to Mr. Krock."

"You didn't call him up?"

"I called his home but I spoke to the butler."

"That wasn't any butler," Catledge said. "That was Mr. Krock."

Catledge that afternoon reminded Krock of his recently expressed wish to hire a young, hard-working man for the bureau, and Catledge proposed Lawrence. Krock thought it over for a few moments and agreed.

Bill Lawrence was hired at $80 a week, five dollars more than he had been making at the United Press, and within the next two decades Lawrence became one of the most industrious, highest-paid reporters on the paper. His by-line—"W. H. Lawrence"—appeared over important stories in Washington and Okinawa, London and Moscow. He toured South America and was the correspondent in the Balkans until he was thrown out for reporting them pro-Soviet. He helped to organize *The Times'* United Nations bureau in 1946, rejecting as incompetent some of the veteran correspondents assigned to him; he concentrated instead on developing the talents of younger men that he thought were potentially first rate, particularly one skinny newcomer named Abe Rosenthal.

But no matter where Lawrence worked for *The Times*, whether at the United Nations or Europe or Korea, he remained "on loan" from the Washington bureau, and this was as Lawrence preferred it. He was fearful of the bureaucracy of the New York office, the layers of editors and formality in the big newsroom, and the only time that he lingered there was on the night of national elections when he was writing one of the political leads, or was analyzing the election results with other *Times*men over the newspaper's radio station, WQXR. Inevitably, Lawrence was accompanied to the newsroom on these occasions by a very pretty young woman who dolefully sat in a corner waiting for him to finish so that they could go off to Sardi's or "21." And then he would be back in Washington, another story, another pretty girl, another round of drinks, his manner seeming more reverential toward bartenders or copyboys than Congressmen or editors. One day in Washington, Lawrence called the bureau desk and asked in a loud voice, "Is that little jackass of a Napoleon still there?" to which James Reston, who had picked up the extension, replied with resignation, "Yes, Bill, I'm here."

Reston liked Lawrence for reasons that often escaped both of them. Lawrence *was* hard-working and did have a certain boyish charm. As for Lawrence's other side—the carousing, the two divorces, the impetuosity and apparent lack of guilt—this did grate on Reston's Calvinism, but in every family there was room for an erring son, and in the Washington bureau this role was Lawrence's. And he might have maintained it indefinitely had the knowledge of his growing friendship with Kennedy during the 1960 campaign not magnified his every move, causing the New York editors to scrutinize his stories with heightened intensity, to speculate on whether his reportorial objectivity was being compromised as he covered a Kennedy speech in one town, then played golf with Kennedy in another town, then attended a New Year's Eve party with Kennedy in Palm Beach, then flew back with other reporters in the Kennedy airplane with a very lovely Kennedy aide on his arm.

The romance that developed between the girl and Lawrence along the whistle stops and plane hops of the campaign at first amused John Kennedy, then it seemed to delight him to a point where he tried to encourage it by his attention. At crowded airports, while posing for pictures, Kennedy would sometimes scan the room until he had spotted the couple standing together, and he would smile and remark, "*There* they are."

The full extent of this never reached the editors in New York, but they already had sufficient misgivings about Lawrence. They had felt that Lawrence's coverage of the West Virginia primary had made Kennedy's battle seem much more difficult than it really was, and consequently when Kennedy triumphed his victory seemed all the more spectacular. After Kennedy's election, when Bill Lawrence produced a number of exclusive stories about the new administration, *The Times* published them but within the office there was editorial grumbling about *The Times'* news columns being used for John Kennedy's "trial balloons," and when this comment was made after Lawrence's exclusive that identified Robert Kennedy as possibly the next Attorney General, Lawrence became infuriated. Although Lawrence was unaware of it, even some of his friends in the bureau were now becoming a bit disenchanted with him. One morning after Lawrence's story had named Kennedy's new Secretary of Commerce, but had not beaten the *Washington Post* to Dean Rusk's appointment as the Secretary of State—an exclusive obtained by the *Post's* late publisher, Philip Graham—Arthur Krock walked into the office, paused in the aisle, and said to another reporter, "Well, I'd give three Secretaries of Commerce for one Secretary of State, wouldn't you?"

Reston and his deputy, Wallace Carroll, were also down on Lawrence, but they did not make an issue of it, nor did they have to: there was enough pressure coming from New York, most of it from Clifton Daniel, and when Lawrence learned of this he was resentful, but not really surprised. He had never been impressed with Daniel personally or professionally, and he had assumed that the feeling was mutual. He had first met Daniel twenty years before in Washington when Daniel was working for the Associated Press, and when Daniel began his executive rise on *The New York Times*, Lawrence was not ecstatic. Lawrence felt that Daniel resented, among other things, Lawrence's breezy first-name acquaintanceship with most of the leading politicians, including Daniel's father-in-law, and while Daniel did not openly restrain Lawrence at first, he gave Lawrence the impression that he was watching him closely, waiting for a slip. Then Lawrence was removed from a few important out-of-town political assignments, these being covered by *The Times'* regional correspondents. And finally, in the spring of 1961, came the crushing blow: Lawrence, though he was *The Times'* White House correspondent, was told that he would not accompany President Kennedy and the White House press to Europe for the big visits with de Gaulle in Paris, Krushchev in Vienna, and Macmillan in London. Reston approached Lawrence one day and informed him bluntly, and to his amazement, that he was not going—Reston himself would make the trip. Lawrence at first could not believe it. He had already arranged through Kennedy to be the "pool" reporter on the trip, and he had anticipated the reunion with the girl from the campaign days, she now being employed in one of the American embassies. It was a dream assignment for so many reasons, and to be abruptly cut in this manner was more than Lawrence could tolerate. He urged Reston to reconsider. Reston said he would, and then he left for Europe without saying anything further to Lawrence about it.

Lawrence, who had received job offers from the three major television networks in the past, now called his friend James Hagerty at ABC. Hagerty offered him a position as a news commentator, adding that he could begin by helping to cover the President's European trip. Lawrence pondered the ABC offer for about a half-hour. During this time he received a call from President Kennedy, who had heard what had happened.

"Take it," Kennedy said. "That'll show the bastards."

Lawrence thought about it for a few moments more, then called Wallace Carroll at the bureau and said he was quitting *The Times*. Lawrence said he needed a quick release because his new employers wanted him to leave almost immediately for Europe. Carroll called New York, interrupting Daniel during the daily news conference, which angered Daniel. Carroll was told to call back later, which he did, and Daniel said that Lawrence's resignation was accepted. Catledge was in New Orleans, Dryfoos was unreachable, and so Daniel who was then an assistant managing editor, was making the decision in their absence.

A few days later, Lawrence received a letter forwarded to him from Arthur Hays Sulzberger.

"Dear Bill," it began. "I have just been told that you are leaving and I write to express my very real regret. You and *The Times* just seemed to go together and it won't quite be the same place without you."

Lawrence reread the letter a few times, and then he began to cry.

6

IN a moment it would be 4 p.m. in
New York, 9 p.m. in London, and
11 p.m. in Cairo; 5 a.m. in Saigon,
6 a.m. in Tokyo, and 8 a.m. in the Solomon Islands—
and *Times* correspondents around the world are in
various states of anxiety, sobriety, propriety, and sleep;
and in the New York newsroom the secretaries, untouched by the exotica and erotica of distant lands,
are contemplating a coffee break; and the copyreaders,
sedentary scriveners, are calmly writing headlines:
Chinese-Romanian Rift Indicated in Rally Delay . . .
Mississippi Police Use Gas to Rout Rights Campers.
The editors are about to stand and walk across the
newsroom into Daniel's emporium, and Clifton Daniel
is waiting for them, sitting behind his desk reading
over some notes that he had written earlier to remind
himself that he had not been entirely happy this morning as he rode the train in from Bedford reading *The
New York Times*.

This morning's edition had been up to standard in
most ways, but there nevertheless were things in it that
had appalled him—a lack of clarity, a bit of conjecture,
reportorial sloppiness—and he intended to tell this to
his editors once they assembled in his office. For example, on page seven, there was a story from the London correspondent about Britain's flourishing illegal
radio stations, and a House of Commons bill that would
silence them, that was so badly presented that Daniel
was forced to read the story two or three times in order
to understand it. Also, on page forty-eight, there was
a most unfortunate error in the headline over a politi-

cal story from California: *Reagan Rules Out Help by Goldstein in California Race.* Goldstein? Who was Goldstein? Daniel read the story and discovered that Goldstein was really Goldwater, *Barry Goldwater,* and while this might have been a printer's error, Daniel was astonished that no copyreader had noticed it and corrected it after the first edition.

But what most offended Daniel this morning was the story, on page eleven, of Charles de Gaulle's visit to Siberia. It was actually a well-written piece for the first eight paragraphs, and Daniel was particularly engrossed in it because eleven years ago, in the summer of 1955, Daniel himself had traveled through Siberia, his final fling as a correspondent, and it had been an unforgettable assignment for him. Daniel was then the only permanent correspondent of a Western non-Communist newspaper in the Soviet Union, and his articles throughout 1954–55 had conveyed the thrilling time he was having, an elegant bachelor in his early forties, wandering around Russia visiting museums, attending the ballet, reporting on Soviet fashion shows, enjoying the sudden improvement in East-West relations now that Stalin was dead and Khrushchev was embarking on a new policy of vodka diplomacy. When Daniel arrived in Siberia, wearing his new fur hat, imagining himself a fashionable frontiersman, and privately expecting to be quite bored by Siberian drabness, he was delightfully surprised by what he found there and his reaction to it. He was almost charmed by the place, the sight of hearty factory workers and farmers living an arduous but normal life, attempting to build a better life, and part of this scene strangely evoked for Daniel memories of some stories his father used to tell with such warmth and humor about North Carolina at the turn of the century, how the early Daniels and other settlers had had to hack down trees to carve out the town of Zebulon, the rugged backwoods existence replete with raw challenges and rickety dreams. And Clifton Daniel's article in *The Times* had compared part of the Siberia he saw with the Zebulon he had heard his father describe—except now, in 1966, reading of de Gaulle's visit, reading of how thousands of Siberians had cheered the French leader along the parade route, Daniel suddenly stopped short at a sentence that speculated that it was "curiosity and pleasure that had brought them there—an interruption in an otherwise unexciting existence." *Unexciting existence?* Daniel became irritated. How could the *Times* reporter be so sure that the Siberians' existence was unexciting? The reporter had merely flown into Siberia with the other newsmen covering de Gaulle, Daniel reasoned, and there was absolutely no justification for placing such a value judgment on life in Siberia. Impatiently, Daniel read on. . . .

Now Daniel looked up as the editors began to file into his office. All were dressed in dark summer suits except the assistant sports editor, who was in his shirtsleeves and was wearing a hideous purple tie. Behind him walked the women's-news editor, Charlotte Curtis, wearing a flamboyant slim Pucci-style dress that Daniel seemed to like. Her strawberry-blonde hair was teased atop her head and her thin long face was cooly composed until Daniel smiled at her; quickly, she smiled back. Then she sat next to him on his left, tucking one of her legs up under her right buttock and letting a high-heeled shoe dangle from her tiny toes under the table.

Daniel stood at the head of the table nodding as the others, sixteen in all, walked in. When Rosenthal arrived, Daniel smiled again, waving Rosenthal into the chair on Daniel's right. Rosenthal, dark-haired and boyish, blue-eyed and wearing dark horn-rimmed glasses, blushed ever so slightly. Then, self-consciously, Rosenthal shot a glance toward his close friend Arthur Gelb, seated at the opposite end of the table. Gelb, a tall intense editor who was substituting for Rosenthal as the New York editor while Rosenthal was filling in for the absent Salisbury, had seen it all. Gelb grinned back at Rosenthal.

Among the last to enter the room was Catledge. Large and loose-limbed, with a round ruddy face and graying at the temples, Catledge ambled through the door past the other editors, extending greetings as he passed, but not sitting among them at the conference table. Catledge walked to the back of the room and took a seat almost directly behind Daniel, settling himself comfortably before crossing his legs. Daniel looked back at Catledge, nodded, and then turned back toward the others and waited until they had all assembled.

Daniel knew pretty much what to expect even before the first report on the day's news was delivered to him. He had seen most of the advance summaries earlier in the afternoon, and this assemblage was largely ceremonial, a ritual around a table involving a circle of editors each held accountable by Daniel for a piece of the world, each witnessed and judged by older editors who sat beyond the circle closer to the wall—Catledge, veterans from other departments, executives from the publisher's office, the publisher himself on occasion. And overlooking the proceedings were the wall photographs of Ochs and Van Anda and their successors. This gathering in Daniel's office each day was, among other things, a reaffirmation of *Times* tradition, a blending of past and present. If Adolph Ochs were alive, Daniel felt sure, he would not be displeased by what he might see or read in *The Times* today. Ochs might be surprised by some of the changes, confused perhaps, but on the whole he would not be displeased. *The Times* was still a conservative paper, relatively speaking, and at the top of page one was Ochs's favorite slogan, "All the News That's Fit to Print," which has endured since Ochs bought the paper in 1896. True to its patriarch, *The Times* was still trying to be a *news*paper, not a showcase for feature writers, not a gazette of opinion; and the *Times* edition that Daniel had read this morning, a typical edition that reported no earthshaking calamity, no genius dead, supported Daniel's high opinion of the paper despite the flaws he found. *The Times* that day carried more news than any other paper in the world, more names, more statistics, more reports from more places—the Senate, the garment center, Wall Street, Yankee Stadium, Quantri province, The Hague. Daniel saw *The Times* as a vast banquet table containing something for everybody: tidbits of trivia, roasts of political pork, morsels of mayhem, Pakistani puffs—if it was news, if it was printable in the editors' opinion, it appeared in *The New York Times* and made its bid for history.

This morning the lead story on page one, sedately displayed under a single column of gray type, was the Senate hearing of misconduct charges against Senator Thomas J. Dodd of Connecticut. The off-lead, in the extreme left-hand column of page one, concerned the debate in Washington over escalation of the air war in North Vietnam. There were also other stories about the alleged brutality of the police in New York, an indictment against fifteen suspected Klansmen in Mississippi, a plea by U Thant for peace in Cyprus. The most-discussed story was Mayor Lindsay's cancellation of an official dinner in New York for King Faisal because the Saudi Arabian monarch had said, in reply to a reporter's loaded question at a press conference in Washington, following Faisal's cordial visit with President Johnson, that he considered friends of Israel to be enemies of the Arabs. This was big news? Faisal had said this before, and most Arab leaders had been saying it for years. And yet today this story was spread across four columns in the middle of page one of *The Times*, and as Daniel read it on the train from Bedford he had privately conceded that it was a lot of clamor about very little.

Daniel had met King Faisal years ago, had known him when he was only a prince, in fact; and Daniel was aware, as most journalists were, that if Faisal were publicly asked to comment on the Arab boycott of American firms that trade with Israel, Faisal could certainly not say kind words about the Israelis or condone trade with them—not if he wished to keep his palace and preserve his leadership among the increasing number of restless Nasserites in the Arab world. And so Faisal said what he had to say: friends of Israel were not friends of the Arabs—"Jews support Israel, and we consider those who provide assistance to our enemies as our own enemies." Suddenly, his published statement aroused Jewish groups around America, alerting the New York politicians concerned with the large Jewish vote in New York, and Mayor Lindsay canceled the Faisal banquet, Governor Nelson Rockefeller canceled his appointment with the King; the Arabs in the Middle East were insulted, the White House was embarrassed, the press had a hot story, and Margaret Daniel—discussing it at home with her husband earlier, her small-town Midwestern loyalty proclaiming itself amid new evidence of provincialism along the supposedly sophisticated Eastern seaboard—shook her head and said, "Oh, New Yorkers *really* behaved badly this time, didn't they?" Her husband could only agree.

Still, *The New York Times* could not ignore the news, and it devoted four stories, three photographs, and an inside page to the Faisal incident this morning. John Oakes also published an editorial in which he called the King's comments "shocking," although he cited the "rudeness" of Lindsay and Rockefeller in refusing, despite pleas from the White House and State Department, to perform their "public duty to receive a head of state." (The reporter who had asked the question that sparked the controversy, not a *Times*man, was neither identified nor commented upon.)

Now, seated at the conference table, his editors ready and waiting, Clifton Daniel knew that he had not heard the last of the story. It would undoubtedly be on the front page again tomorrow, maybe also on the following day. Glancing toward the far end of the table, Daniel could see the tall, attentive figure of Arthur Gelb waiting to read from the notes that he held rigidly in his long, thin fingers—presumably more local reaction to the Faisal statement. It appeared that Daniel would call on Gelb first, relieving Gelb of the sense of urgency that seemed to possess him now that he was sitting in for Rosenthal and had a big story to handle; but then Daniel turned away and looked toward the foreign-news editor, Sydney Gruson.

"Sydney," said Daniel, softly.

Sydney Gruson was a small, wiry, dapper man of

forty-nine who looked about ten years younger. He had a preserved, friendly face of florid complexion, wide-set lively eyes that detracted from the bags beneath, and a full head of shiny dark hair slicked back and precisely parted. Daniel had met Gruson in London during the war, liking him well enough to arrange the interview that got Gruson onto *The Times*. Gruson was a good reporter who, like Daniel, was fascinated by wealth and society. But as Gruson gained acceptance into this world by virtue of his elevation on *The Times*, becoming most recently a personal friend of Jacqueline Kennedy and moving within her East Side circle, he managed not to compromise himself professionally. At one Kennedy gathering at a New York restaurant, after Stephen Smith had charged the Sulzbergers with using *The Times* to downgrade the Kennedys, Gruson angrily interrupted and replied: "It is not enough to like the Kennedys 60 percent or 70 percent—*you* demand we love them 110 percent . . . you are all myth makers, and, frankly, you are all lousy at it!" Much more was said on both sides, and Gruson was embarrassed the next morning by his outrage, blaming it on the combination of whiskey and wine; but this behavior was not uncharacteristic of Gruson. He was loyal to the Sulzbergers, was on good terms with the right people within the institution, and his casual manner as an editor reflected the comfort and self-assurance that he felt as a *Times*man. When Daniel had called out his name, Gruson had been reading through a few cables he had received just prior to entering Daniel's office. Now, his head down, still reading, Gruson said, "I'm not ready yet."

Daniel did not seem perturbed. He nodded toward Miss Curtis.

"Charlotte."

Charlotte Curtis, who *was* ready, immediately began to read from a single sheet of paper on which she had typed a summary of what would appear on her page tomorrow.

Since tomorrow was a Saturday, the slight decrease in advertising would limit the edition to sixty-four pages, compared with this morning's seventy-six, and she had only one page to fill. It would not be, as she would readily admit, a very exciting page—certainly not as photogenic as this morning's layout, which was devoted largely to a study of female knees and the miniskirt (*The Knee Is Fancy Free—and Fashionable*); but she did have a good feature story about a chic new neighborhood in Washington, and in her slightly nasal Ohio accent she read: "Although Georgetown still has a corner on being the right address in the capital, a new contender for that status is Watergate East where, according to the ads, it overlooks the Potomac River and offers elegance for as little as sixty-thousand dollars per apartment."

Daniel liked her approach, breezy, informative, a little bite here and there. He was pleased that he had convinced her to take the editor's job a year ago, the reporting and writing of the women's-news staff having greatly improved under her direction, and Daniel did not care what the men in the bullpen thought of such reporting—*he* liked to read it, and he was confident that thousands of other readers did also.

"Arthur," said Daniel, after Miss Curtis had finished.

Arthur Gelb, sitting tall, tight, squinting through thick eyeglasses, began to read the latest on the Faisal incident and other local-news items. Gelb had begun his career as a copyboy on *The Times*, had worked his way up to second-string drama critic under Brooks Atkinson, and had co-authored with his wife, Barbara Gelb, an impressive biography of Eugene O'Neill. When Rosenthal returned from Japan to become the New York editor in 1962, he asked that his close friend Gelb be switched from the Cultural-News department, where Gelb was a subordinate editor, to the New York desk. In the last three and a half years, Rosenthal and Gelb, brimming with ebullience and new ideas, had injected much life into *The Times'* local reporting. Gelb was now aware that if Rosenthal moved up to replace Salisbury, Rosenthal's present position would likely become Gelb's—unless he made some horrible blunder during this summer replacement period. Gelb had been very careful earlier in the day with his assignment sheet, and now he was confident that there was not a major story or news angle in New York that his reporters were ignoring.

"King Faisal visited the UN today, and we have Mickey Carroll following him," Gelb said. "Faisal indicated that he was not really upset by what's happened."

"How did he indicate this?" Daniel asked.

"He actually said it," Gelb quickly replied. "He also posed for photographers, *smiling*."

"He's up for election," Catledge chimed in, grinning.

"What?" asked Daniel, turning around.

Daniel is unable to hear well from his left, an impairment he has borne since he was twelve, and he wished that if Catledge insisted on interrupting, that he would do so from one of the chairs closer to the window, on Daniel's right, and not from the rear, almost directly behind Daniel's left ear. When Daniel looked back, Catledge, large, ruddy, comfortable, casually shrugged, suggesting that the remark was not worth repeating. So Daniel turned toward the front again and continued to listen as Gelb ticked off dozens of assignments that reporters were working on at this moment—a contract dispute between the city and the Doctors' Association, a murder in the Bronx, a move by Senator Robert Kennedy to promote the career of a Buffalo Democrat named Peter Crotty. . . .

Cigarette smoke climbed higher in Daniel's office .The circle of editors listened politely, if not intently. There was nothing very special about today. It was like yesterday, the day before. The summer had begun, and a Friday-afternoon laziness had set in. The highways and bridges around New York City were now beginning to rumble and vibrate with the early waves of weekend traffic, and except for Catledge and two lesser executives, there were no senior *Times*men seated along the outer edge of the room. The publisher was absent. So was the executive vice-president, Harding F. Bancroft, a tall, blond, tweedy pipe smoker who in 1963 had replaced Amory H. Bradford, a tall, blond, tweedy pipe smoker who had resigned. Lester Markel, who had attended yesterday's session, was not here today. John Oakes never attends these meetings, maintaining the clear line of separation that exists between the News and Editorial departments.

Daniel looked around the table. It was 4:31 and, since Gelb, he had heard from four editors—Cultural, Foreign, Finance, Sports—and had learned, among other things, that a Van Gogh painting had sold for $441,000 to Walter Chrysler, Jr.; that the Chinese were streamlining the doctrine of Mao Tse-tung so that it would be more palatable for school students; that Wall Street was unalarmed; that the Yankees were in seventh place, fifteen games behind Baltimore. Daniel nodded toward the national-news editor, Claude Sitton, seated in the far corner of the table to the left of Gelb.

"Claude," Daniel said.

A lean, slightly balding gray-haired man edged forward. Claude Sitton, a native of Atlanta, had joined *The Times* as a reporter ten years before, at the age of thirty. He then had dark hair, a limber gait, a benign expression—he seemed almost too bland for the assignment that would be his specialty: the Civil Rights movement in the South. But between 1957 and 1964, traveling thousands of miles a year, getting to know by heart the schedule of every airline operating in the South, getting to know the black preachers and red-neck sheriffs, the young militants and dreamy blonde coeds who temporarily took leave of their segregated suburbs in the North to denounce the South—Sitton superbly covered the story. He moved with it from town to town, little places that made headlines for a week and were not heard from again—Poplarville, McComb, Sasser—and he infused his reporting with the angry dialogue and grim detail that made it all seem so meaningful, if only for a day. When Medgar Evers, the Negro leader in Mississippi, was shot to death three years ago on a June night in Jackson, Sitton wrote:

. . . the sniper's bullet struck him just below the right shoulder blade. The slug crashed through a front window of the home, penetrated an interior wall, ricocheted off a refrigerator and struck a coffee pot. The battered bullet was found beneath a watermelon on a kitchen cabinet. Evers staggered to the doorway, his keys in his hand, and collapsed near the steps. His wife, Myrlie, and their three children rushed to the door . . .

Now, at the conference table, Claude Sitton, aged forty, showed the wear of all those years on the road. He had been pleased by his promotion to editor and the salary increase, was happy that he could now spend more time with his family in a new home in suburban New York and could avoid the endless air terminals and the grueling routine. But there were also times when the executive pressure and office politics had made him nostalgic for the reporter's life, particularly when the stories were good, as they were today.

Today, Sitton told Daniel, there were dramatic new developments in Mississippi—Dr. Martin Luther King, Jr., leading 2,500 Civil Rights marchers through the state, was having problems with some of his followers, especially such younger ones as Stokely Carmichael. It had begun last night in Canton, Mississippi, Sitton said, remembering the place from his own reporting two years ago, remembering the old white-columned courthouse, the Confederate flag sticker on the glass window of the voter registrar's office inside the building, the long line of Negroes waiting outside and being watched by a sheriff's deputy who wore a black leather jacket, black slacks, black Western boots, and who paced up and down the line with an automatic carbine swinging in his left hand, a wooden club dangling from his belt . . . it had begun last night in Canton as King's marchers, pitching their tents on the grounds of an elementary school for Negroes, were suddenly interrupted by sixty gun-wielding state troopers ordering them to move. Two minutes later, the order ignored, the troopers had donned gas masks and begun to approach the crowd, with King urging his followers, black and white, to remain nonviolent—"There's no point in fighting," he had cried, "don't do it."

Canister after canister of gas was then tossed into the crowd, and within seconds dozens of men, women, and children retreated, running and crying confusedly through the haze, tents tumbling. Other demonstrators persisted, burying their faces deep into the damp grass, but they were soon dragged up by the feet and hands by the troopers and pushed into the street beyond the school grounds. One trooper had grabbed a Catholic priest from Chicago and hit him with the butt of a shotgun. A photographer from Florida had been tackled and knocked into a ditch. Twelve demonstrators had passed out from the gas fumes, including the three-year-old son of a white couple from Toronto.

Today, Sitton continued, many marchers were in no mood for more nonviolence, and Carmichael and other militants were on the verge of mutiny. Sitton did not really know the full extent of it, Carmichael's call for "Black Power" having not yet been shouted through the media of the land, but Claude Sitton seemed to sense the change as he said softly, at the conference table, "It could be very bad for King now."

"What was the great objection to their spending the night on the school grounds?" Daniel asked.

"The troopers said that they were acting on orders from the city and county school officials, who said that the marchers had no permission to put up tents there. It was also in a transitional neighborhood."

"What's a transitional neighborhood?"

Sitton seemed surprised by Daniel's question, the answer seeming obvious, but perhaps this was Daniel's way of hinting that he wanted this to be defined in tomorrow's story.

"That's where Negroes are moving into a white neighborhood," Sitton said.

Sitton went on to say that Homer Bigart, perhaps the best reporter in the newsroom, had arrived in Canton to reinforce the coverage. The news from Mississippi might easily become worse. James Meredith, who had recovered from the gunshot wounds he had suffered in Mississippi three weeks ago when ambushed at the beginning of the march, was now on his way back to join the others. Also, fifteen Mississippi whites identified as Klansmen were indicted yesterday in Biloxi by a Federal grand jury in connection with the firebomb slaying last January of a Hattiesburg, Mississippi, Negro leader; and so the racial climate was now primed for further violence, and the newspaper and television reporting today emphasized this, quoting embittered whites shouting "nigger," and quoting angry blacks damning Mississippi as a "police state," and comparing it with "Hitler's Germany."

Turner Catledge, the Mississippi-born grandson of slave owners, listened. His fingernails drummed against the armrest of his chair a few times but he said nothing, and it was not possible to know whether he was tapping from tension or boredom. His home state had been denigrated regularly in the press for a decade, although some of the little Southern towns that had made the hottest headlines were placid places in Catledge's memory, places where Negroes and whites had once lived in more harmony than Northern liberals could ever imagine, these liberals not having lived so close to Negroes as had Catledge's countrymen, nor ever having understood or shared with the Negro such poverty and deprivation.

Faulkner once said that the rest of the nation knows next to nothing about the South, and Catledge might agree, but quietly, for this was not the time for Southerners to be making excuses. It was a time for atonement in the Deep South. In the wake of such southern atrocities as took place in Selma, Alabama, a year before, the aroused nation demanded, if only briefly, that the Negro be reimbursed for past abuses, and the guilt of white men all over America was now borne by the South, for it was in the South that the white man's sins were more easily seen. Even Faulkner, had he lived, would have experienced difficulty in trying to de-

fend the South after the scene in Selma had been
filmed on television and had been played again and
again on the home screen in millions of living rooms:
the sight of a charging wedge of troopers with billy
clubs and gas grenades crashing into a procession of
Negroes, the odd sound of plastic helmets and wood
beating against flesh, *clop, cluck, clap,* the cries of
Negroes falling to the highway, the cheers of white
locals watching on the other side of the road, the hoof
clicks of nervous horses mounted by a sheriff's posse
anxious to get into the act, the ticking of television
cameras. Soon, from all over America, thousands of
sympathizers, black and white, were bound for Selma
—nuns, newsmen, debutantes, psychiatrists, banjo players, Senators' wives, stock clerks, sculptors, social workers—and for most of the month they lived in Selma's
Negro quarter, shared the Negro's food and misery,
sang his songs, and scorned his oppressors; helped inspire a new guilt, a new social conscience, a new voting
bill in America; helped instill in many illiterate and uninspired Negroes throughout the land a strange new
hope that after Martin Luther King's marchers had
crossed the little bridge and had completed the fifty-
mile journey down the road to the state capital, everything would somehow get better, a kind of miracle
would occur; it would be like Lourdes and the faithful
might toss away their crutches.

Months later, a *Times* reporter revisited Selma. The
town was quiet. The sympathizers from the North had
come and gone—as they had come and gone in Selma
one hundred years before—and now Selma's blacks
and whites were left with the pieces, life was no better,
and the marchers and journalists were making news
elsewhere in the South—and eventually in the North,
where some Northern whites who had so eagerly come
to Selma were not so willing to openly oppose in-
equities closer to home.

Turner Catledge liked the story that reported this,
and he sent the *Times* reporter a congratulatory note,
but it would have been imprudent of Catledge to be

less private about his feelings; he might appear too defensive about the South, too unobjective as an editor, perhaps also foolish—as Faulkner had appeared during his final years, when, in his public statements and letters to various newspapers, he tried to defend the South when national opinion was not very receptive to unrepentant white Southerners. The editors published Faulkner's letters, usually without comment, although the editorial writers around the country did not castigate Faulkner as a racist, as they might have. Faulkner was still a much-admired man, and when such men reach a certain age they are free to make fools of themselves in public and to expect, and receive, from the press the utmost in courtesy. Faulkner was a recipient of this respect. So was former President Truman, who was much bolder than Faulkner on the question of race, and as a result was possibly of concern to his son-in-law at *The New York Times*, or at least some *Times* reporters thought that he was. While *Times* reporters had once looked forward to joining Harry Truman on his traditional morning walks and talkathons during his frequent visits to New York, this assignment began to lose its charm during Truman's later years, as the issue of integration became more intense, and as he began to reveal signs of bigotry that *Times*men had to report, although they imagined the dismay that Truman's revelations in print might cause Clifton Daniel. The *Times*men should not have worried so. Daniel was a hardened newspaperman, after all, and his father in Zebulon had used "nigger" most of his life, and when there had been a student movement at the University of North Carolina in the Thirties to admit Negroes, Clifton Daniel, though a campus leader, did not become involved.

Still, racial remarks by a former President of the United States in the Nineteen-sixties were never treated casually at *The Times*. *The New York Times* wishes to protect all of the Grand Old Men of the Republic whenever it can, and there was a bit of fussing on the copydesk over stories that contained controversial Trumanisms—such as when he said, while a Negro sit-in was making headlines, that if anyone tried to do that in *his* store he'd kick them out; or when he called the Selma protest "silly" and called Martin Luther King a "troublemaker," earning a telegram of thanks from Selma's Sheriff James G. Clark; or when Truman declared that racial intermarriage ran counter to teaching of the Bible. This latter remark, which inspired no editorial retort from *The Times*, was made during a stroll along Park Avenue, when a reporter, *not* a *Times*-man, asked the former President if he thought that racial intermarriages would become widespread in the United States.

"I hope not," Truman said. "I don't believe in it. What's that word about four feet long? Miscegenation?" Truman, still walking, swinging his cane, then turned to the reporter and asked, "Would you want your daughter to marry a Negro?" When the reporter responded that he would want his daughter to marry the man she loved, Truman said, "You haven't answered my question," adding, "Well, she won't love someone who isn't her color. You'll edit the man she goes out with. I did. And mine married the right man."

All of this was published the next morning in *The Times*, on an inside page under a small headline, the story not failing to mention in the second paragraph that Truman had long been "an advocate of integration in other respects," and also mentioning that the "right man" that Margaret Truman had married was Clifton Daniel of *The New York Times*.

When Catledge is asked his views on miscegenation, as he sometimes is during his travels out of town, he replies that this subject is not really his main concern at the moment: *his* concern, he says in a mockingly confidential manner, is that his daughter wants to marry a certain *white* man that he does not like. (She did marry the man, and now is divorced.) But Turner Catledge, who is quick at anticipating a question before it is asked, usually sidesteps such flippancy, regarding all aspects of the Civil Rights movement as too important to be discussed seriously with those who badger him most about it. Even at *The Times*, Catledge manages to keep his private thoughts largely to himself, sometimes parrying a sharp question with humor, at other times remaining aloof—as he was this afternoon, sitting in the conference room listening to the cultivated voices of two younger Southerners, Daniel and Sitton, newbreed city slickers, discussing the latest malefaction in Mississippi; listening until the day's conference had ended and Daniel had said to the departing editors: "Thank you, gentlemen."

Catledge has not lived in Mississippi in almost forty years. Now he is a New Yorker, indulging in the sweet urban life that the most successful of Southerners adapt to so quickly, patronizing the better restaurants, knowing all the head waiters by name, living in a large luxury apartment on the East Side where it is the New York landlords who uphold segregation, having honed it down to a fine and polished art. Catledge's second marriage, to a wealthy and attractive New Orleans widow whom he met nine years ago at an editors' convention in San Francisco, is a happy one. He is now earning about $100,000 a year, has a wide and interesting circle of friends. He is not a big celebrity, nor did he ever wish to become one, preferring to function within the corporate code, but his name is nevertheless known in nearly every newsroom in America, and he is regarded with respect and a certain awe by the most powerful politicians in New York and Washington. He has fulfilled, at sixty-five, and long before attaining that age, the most fanciful dreams of his youth, and he has felt at home in a very tough town that a young transplanted Mississippi friend of his, Willie Morris, calls the Big Cave.

But emotionally, Catledge remains a Southerner. He still speaks with a Southern accent that gets thicker with each drink. He can become sentimental to the point of mawkishness, even dewy-eyed, when reminiscing late at night about his days in the South, memories of the farm, the friends he had, black and white, down in the red-clay hill country of central Mississippi in Neshoba County, named after an Indian tribe, but now better known as the place where, on a lonely country road in 1964, three young Civil Rights workers—Michael Schwerner, Andrew Goodman, James Chaney—were slain one by one in a Ku Klux Klan conspiracy that, according to the FBI, involved Neshoba County's chief deputy sheriff.

There is little resemblance between the South that Catledge knew as a boy and the South that he now reads about in his newspaper—but this is, as he would not care to admit, partly the fault of journalism. Journalists concentrate on isolated incidents, current confrontations, printable news that fits—they leave historical perspective to others, and they leave the pleasanter side of any place to the memory of those who predate disorder and press coverage, people like Catledge whose South no longer exists except when resurrected by an old familiar word that jumps up at him from his newspaper, *Neshoba*, or when there is printed a fact or a name that is otherwise linked to the Mississippi of his mind.

This morning's *Times*, for example, carried a military article by Hanson Baldwin that makes reference to General Nathan Bedford Forrest. Forrest was a Confederate cavalry officer who, among other things, tried to defend Selma in 1865 against the invasion of 9,000 pillaging Union soldiers, including a regiment of Negroes. Though Forrest failed, he remains a revered name in the Deep South, a hero to thousands of young Southern boys, including James G. Clark, who in 1965 was Selma's sheriff and its symbol of segregation.

Turner Catledge's maternal grandfather, James Turner, rode with Forrest's cavalry. To ride with Forrest an aspirant had to have a horse, a saddle, a saber, and had to contribute two sides of bacon. These James Turner possessed and he eagerly joined, fighting with Forrest's troops in Mississippi and Tennessee, battling Union soldiers whose ranks possibly included the paternal grandfather of Harrison Salisbury. If so, it was quite appropriate that these two ancestors of *Times*men should be on opposite sides of the Civil War—for *The New York Times*' staff itself was divided, two *Times*men having quit the paper to join the Confederate Army. The publisher of *The Times*, however, behaving like a publisher of *The Times*, remained equivocal. He was not in favor of slavery, but he was not violently opposed to it, either. His name was Henry Jarvis Raymond, and he had much in common with Adolph Ochs, who would buy *The Times* thirty-five years later—Raymond, like Ochs, wanted to keep all doors open, not to be caught too far out on a limb. As Raymond wrote: "There are very few things in the world which it is worth while to get angry about, and they are just the things that anger will not improve."

Henry Jarvis Raymond, born on a farm in upstate New York in 1820, a graduate of the University of Vermont, was a politician. He had worked as a reporter and editor for Horace Greeley's *Tribune* and other papers, but political life was more enticing, and in 1850 Raymond was a New York State Assemblyman, a Whig representative. But when he learned in 1851 that his former employer, Greeley, had made a $60,000 profit the year before, Raymond quickly reconsidered the virtues of journalism; and with another onetime employee of Greeley's *Tribune*, George Jones, who had become a small but successful banker in Albany, Raymond began to enlist the financial support of people who shared his enthusiasm for a paper that would be politically conservative and temperate in taste. There was a market in New York for such a paper, Raymond thought, the other newspapers being either too socialistic or scandalous, and the city was also greatly expanding in prosperity and population. Though churches still towered over the rooftops of the city, and though New York itself was a town of half-a-million centered mostly in lower Manhattan, being semirural above Fourteenth Street and with animals and farms sprawled not far from what is now Times Square, the harbor was teeming with large sailing vessels unloading cargo and thousands of immigrants from Ireland and Germany, future consumers and cops and parents of Ochs. It was relatively easy for Henry Raymond and George Jones to raise $70,000 to start *The Times*, which began publishing in the fall of 1851, and the paper was almost immediately successful.

Printed and produced by a few dozen staff members in a narrow brownstone in downtown Manhattan, *The Times'* first edition, a four-page paper with small single-column headlines, reported the news with a detachment and calm that would characterize the paper through the next century. Its first edition featured news from Europe, most of it lifted from the more respectable London journals, as well as news from around the nation—such as a fugitive slave riot in Lancaster, Pennsylvania—and several short items of local interest, e.g.:

> At a late hour on Tuesday night, Policeman Coalter of the Fourth Patrol District, found an unknown female, aged 35 years, lying in Madison-st., laboring under the effects of delirium tremens, and apparently lifeless. A dray was procured, and the poor woman was conveyed to the station-house, where she seemed to somewhat revive, but was yet under the influence of strong drink, and was accordingly placed in a cell in the female department, where she was found a corpse in about two hours after. Yesterday morning the Coroner held an inquest on the remains, and the jury rendered a verdict of "Death by an apoplectic fit."

The Times' circulation approached 10,000 within a fortnight, 26,000 within a year, and 40,000 by 1857. The coming of the Civil War, as it did with nearly all newspapers, accelerated the growth of *The Times*, which had reached a circulation of 75,000 by 1861. The war also intensified readers' interest in late-breaking news to a point where it quickened the pace of news gathering and forced such papers as *The Times* to produce an edition not merely six days a week, but also on Sunday. *The Times'* first Sunday edition appeared in the spring of 1861, ten years after the paper began, and ten days after the attack on Fort Sumter.

In many ways, the coverage of the Civil War was a more difficult and dangerous assignment than any to be faced by latter-day war correspondents of *The Times*. In this era before the handout and headquarters briefing —and the credibility gap—correspondents often wrote only what they saw with their own eyes. Of course, these eyewitness accounts usually gave a very limited view of the war, but on occasion they were grandly revealing and it was not uncommon for *Times* readers to get important war news before even President Lincoln had received it officially.

The defeat of the confederates at Franklin, Tennessee, appeared in *The Times* four days before the War Department had received word of it. *The Times* also prematurely disclosed the news of Sherman's march from Atlanta to the sea, an exclusive that might have produced disastrous results for the North had *The Times'* circulation wagons in the South not been slower than Sherman's army. One night when Generals Grant and Meade were conversing privately in a tent, they heard noises in the bushes which, upon inspection, turned out to be a *Times*man lying on his stomach scribbling notes. Raymond himself covered the first battle of Bull Run, with some assistance from *The Times'* Washington bureau, and saw enough of the battle to be convinced that the North would easily triumph and march into Richmond. After filing a dispatch that indicated this, Raymond returned to the battlefield to discover that the Union forces had been beaten back. Quickly, he rewrote his story and had it sent to Washington to be filed, but a Union censor intercepted it, and after this experience Henry Raymond retired from war reporting and returned to where he belonged, in New York.

While Henry Raymond was a personal friend of Lincoln's—he was a leader in the campaign that reelected Lincoln, and he remained active in politics throughout his editorship of *The Times*, which he sometimes neglected as a result—*The Times'* coverage of the war was as objective as it could be, and some *Times* readers in the North accused it of being pro-South. *The Times'* controversial correspondent in Charleston, a spiritual sire of Herbert Matthews and Harrison Salisbury, was constantly berated in letters as a "secessionist" and Rebel propagandist, but this suddenly stopped when, after he had been caught making notes while watching the bombardment of Fort Sumter, he was arrested by the South as a Federal spy. He spent a day or two in jail, and then was released and told to take the next train northward, forfeiting his watch and wallet to the jailkeeper.

The *Times* building itself was threatened by a New York mob in the summer of 1863 during the draft riots, a time when angry young men protesting conscription burned houses, wrecked stores, and shot at policemen. Henry Raymond, among other publishers, denounced the protest and called for law and order, writing in *The Times:* "Were the conscription law to be abrogated tomorrow, the controlling inspiration of the mob would remain the same. It comes from sources independent of that law, or of any other—from malignant hate toward those in better circumstances, from a craving for plunder, from a love of commotion, from a barbarous spite against a different race, from a disposition to bolster up the failing fortunes of the southern rebels."

After Greeley's *Tribune* building had had its windows smashed, and might have been greatly damaged had not the police fought back the mob, Raymond supplied his staff with rifles and gave them permission to fire upon invaders. Raymond also obtained from the War Department, largely because of his friendship with Lincoln, two Gatling guns, which were mounted just inside *The Times'* business office under the supervision of a *Times* stockholder named Leonard Jerome, a grandfather of Winston Churchill. A third Gatling gun was installed on the roof of the five-story *Times* building, which occupied the triangle between Park Row and Nassau and Beekman Streets, near Greeley's building. But *The Times* was never approached.

After the war, *The Times'* popularity and prosperity went into temporary decline because Raymond was devoting too much time to politics—he had become a Republican Congressman, was chairman of the Republican National Committee—and also because his attitude, which opposed vindictive punishment of the South, offended the radical Republicans who had gained control of the party. But although some advertising was withdrawn and circulation fell for a while, Raymond's *Times* continued as before, calm, uncontentious, undramatic—it announced Lee's surrender with a single-column headline, as it did Lincoln's assassination, and except for its campaign against Boss Tweed and Tammany Hall, which occurred after Raymond's death and before Ochs's takeover, *The Times* did not involve itself with crusades.

Turner Catledge's grandfather, James Turner, returned after the war to the farm. It was a subsistence farm whose main purpose was to raise enough food to nourish the Turner family, a considerable undertaking since Turner and his wife would have fourteen children. The first-born was a daughter, Willie Anna Turner, Catledge's mother. Of all the women that Catledge would meet in his lifetime, none could approach the efficiency of his mother—she did everything with precision, remembered everything, reared her brothers and sisters and ran the home as her own mother could not have done had she tried, which she didn't, being pregnant most of the time, or recovering from pregnancy, or being too conditioned to life's raw realities in the shambled South to expect any miracle of comfort or order under her own roof. And so the daughter, Willie Anna, a plain Bible-reading young woman, kindly but stern, took over the home and the children. She did not seem to resent this task, recognizing it as a necessity, but as she became older and learned to master other people's affairs more and more, she discovered that they had become almost totally reliant on her, a burden she found overwhelming and annoying at times, but mainly she loved it and came to need it.

When her brothers and sisters were old enough to marry and have children of their own, Willie Anna helped in the rearing of *their* children, which they happily let her do. Willie Anna knew best, she did things *right*. Even after she had met and married Lee Catledge, a tall, slim, almost frail man with a long face, dark eyes, a drooping black moustache, a man four years younger than herself, she did not alter her routine very much. She had only two children of her own, her son and an older daughter, and she had time on her hands, energy to burn, and she seemed to enjoy most of all the large family reunions at the main farmhouse of her father, supervising the dinner while the old man sat back encircled by as many as forty grandchildren. He was a commanding figure, proud and vain, and what most impressed young Turner Catledge about his grandfather was how, with a minimum of effort, he got maximum results—with the slightest gesture, a soft word here, there, he could get other people to jump to his needs. He was Big Daddy, the grand progenitor, the boss—one of many bosses that Turner Catledge would observe during his career as a political reporter and editor, but his grandfather was the first and he left a lasting impression.

James Turner had done very well for himself and his family after the war. The immediate postwar years had been bad, with practically no money and a complete barter system, but as the South's economy revived toward the turn of the century, Turner's interests began to extend, with the help of his children, beyond the farm to the opening of small stores around Neshoba County. First there was a little hardware store and then a grocery store, both beginning as extensions of the farm; then a drugstore—and finally, a Ford agency. There were the seeds of Snopes in James Turner, and they produced degrees of vengeance and virtue in his offspring, but with his prodding most of them pushed forward, and if his prize daughter Willie Anna had her way, as he suspected she would, the next generation of Turners would do even better. Willie Anna's greatest hopes, of course, were with her son, Turner Catledge.

From his earliest years, the boy felt the pressure of his mother espousing the dignity of hard work, denouncing laziness and drinking, ballplaying and profanity. When the Sunday newspapers and comics arrived, Willie Anna would tuck them under her bed and not let the children see them until Monday, and she would not tolerate even the whistling of a secular tune in her home on Sunday. Lee Catledge, her husband, a brooding and sensitive man, never had much to say. He was an educated man, having been taught in a church school, and had been a teacher himself for a while, as well as a dabbler in local politics; but now he was working in one of Turner's many stores. His forebears had also been farmers, having come to America as Scotch-Irish immigrants and settling first in the Carolinas, later in Alabama, and then, before the war, in Mississippi. Lee Catledge's father had served in the Confederate Army but had not seen action, although five of his father's brothers had, and three had been killed. What was left of the family carried on at farming, but Lee Catledge, after his marriage to Willie Anna, became absorbed into the Turner clan, his gentility later providing a welcome and contrasting sense of soft sell behind the counter.

The destiny of young Turner Catledge, too, was to be fulfilled somehow in Turner trade, although nobody knew precisely where he should begin in 1922 after his graduation from Mississippi State College. There were really no good jobs in the Turner stores close to home, all being held by uncles, cousins, in-laws, and so it was decided that he should begin his business career in a wholesale hardware establishment in which the Turner family had a small interest in Memphis. In a way he was happy to be going to Memphis and to be escaping the claustrophobic feeling of the family. But when he thought more about it, he became angry and resentful. He felt that he was actually being forced outside the family circle because there was no place for him at home, and this shocked and disillusioned him. It was as if he had been deceived all these years by the warm-hearted family, his exemplary mother, and now, suddenly, as in some strange tribal rite, he was being sent away to test his skill at survival. He was frightened by the prospect, disbelieving; Memphis seemed so far away, as remote as Hong Kong—although it was actually a border city between Mississippi and Tennessee; still, Catledge had never contemplated living that far north, and he did not really fancy the hardware business either.

He did not precisely know what he wanted to do for a living. At college he had majored in science, had been bright in botany and zoology classes; he was possibly the only member of his family who knew the meaning of *entomology*. He was good in English, and was an excellent touch-typist, partly as a result of all the practice he had gotten from his part-time clerical job in the dean's office. He had held several jobs while attending college, his mother having made sure he would have no idle moments, and one of the summer jobs that he had held, and had most enjoyed, was an all-inclusive yet nondescript position on a little weekly handset newspaper named the *Neshoba Democrat*. He had done a bit of everything on that paper. He had solicited advertising, collected money over the counter for subscriptions, had gathered and written local-news items, helped out in the plant, learned to set type, and learned about the printers themselves, some of whom were Klansmen. It had been a marvelous job because it had never seemed like a job, with new and unexpected happenings every week. It was edited by a persuasive country editor called Peanuts Rand, who had liked Catledge very much, had admired his enthusiasm for hard work, his willingness to do any trivial task without sulking. And so while the Turner family was planning Catledge's career in hardware, Rand was thinking of keeping him in the newspaper business. Rand had just bought another country weekly in the northwestern corner of the state near the Tennessee and Arkansas borders along the Mississippi River, in a town called Tunica. Rand could use such an energetic handyman as Catledge up in Tunica, and when he proposed the job to the young man, Catledge accepted it immediately. He was now resigned to leaving home, and the last family favor that he would ask would be a ride to the railroad station—and the forlorn feeling of that day remained with him for a lifetime: being driven to the station on a quiet morning over bumpy dusty roads in the Model T Ford of Uncle Joe, his mother's brother, and then standing along the platform with Uncle Joe waiting for the whistle sound, and then being given a little pocket checkbook, a going-away present. "If you need any money," Uncle Joe said, "just write a check on me." It was meant in kindness, but it added to the gloom, the reality of the departure, and during the train ride up to Tunica Catledge felt the emptiness of a life left behind.

In Tunica, Mississippi, 1922, Catledge got along with people, liked what he was doing, liked the characters he met and wrote about. On the *Tunica Times* he did what he had done the year before on the *Neshoba Democrat* and would do a year later on the *Tupelo Journal*—he did a bit of everything, wrote news and ran errands, solicited advertising and set type, made mistakes and learned, made friends and kept them. To the country people of the town, Catledge seemed to be an engaging young man, earnest and modest. He gave the impression of efficiency without ever seeming to possess great ambition. Ambition, with its repugnant qualities of drive, grim determination, stepping out of line, stepping over older men to get to the top—any hint of this ambition that his mother had nurtured, that his father had lacked, would have been more a hindrance than a help to Catledge, particularly in the rural South. Here there was an observance of order; here one knew one's place and had respect for elders and preserved the past. A climber like Catledge, wishing to succeed quickly in the South in the early Nineteen-twenties, knew by heritage that it was unwise to seem superior, college-educated, or otherwise different from the plain homogeneous undereducated country people who were the majority. In the North, Catledge's contemporary opposites, the future tycoons from tenements, did not need such delicacy. In the North the rules were different, directness was appreciated, pushing was permitted, pushing was often *essential* if one were to compete in the overcrowded cities with their towering obstacles and tensions. And it might therefore have been assumed that the young men who had learned to live and survive in urban jungles would be more likely to achieve great power in New York than those quiet ambitious Southerners like Catledge who were moving slowly up through the placid back roads of the Deep South. But this assumption was not necessarily correct. For those who began in the South and got ahead and got along with country people, those who developed the flair for flattery and cajolery, affability and mock innocence that was standard in the South and was seen as "charm" in the North, those who understood the small-town Southerners' inbred inferiority and prickly pride, his suspicion of strangers and demands of loyalty, his poverty and resultant violence that was almost Sicilian in character—the young climber who took this rustic route northward during the Twenties and Thirties probably traveled a tougher course, faced more subtle challenges, made more personal adjustments, cultivated more disarming devices and weapons for success in New York than did his urban counterpart. If one could get along with country people in the South, one could get along with almost anybody. *And*, having mastered the art of apparent innocence, the Southerner ascended the executive ladders of New York with relative ease and without arousing great envy in others; on the contrary, his colleagues were disarmed by him, pleased by his triumph, amazed that such an unassuming individual of such "charm" could have gotten so far.

And so what worked in Mississippi worked as well in Manhattan, although the reverse was not so true. The impersonal pushing of the North was out of step with the South; Southerners could not easily accept it: the South was deep-rooted and fixed in its ways, as Federal lawmakers would later learn. The South set its own pace and style and stamped its people for a lifetime, and when Northerners went South to live, it stamped them, too. Northerners who settled in the South adopted the regional accent; Southerners who settled in the North did not.

So in Tunica, Catledge got along; and the country people that he met, and the small papers for which he worked in Mississippi as well as the larger papers that he later joined in Memphis, provided him with a repertoire of regional stories and oddities that would delight his companions and guests in future decades around Sardi's bar or "21" or in the backroom of some Southern Senator's office in Washington. The politicians to whom Catledge was most naturally drawn in Washington were those who shared his familiarity with the country South, who exemplified its style and had learned, as he had, how it could also work wonders far from home. In Washington, Catledge was friendly with, among others, Senators Pat Harrison of Mississippi, Carter Glass of Virginia, Thomas Heflin of Alabama, John Nance Garner of Texas, and James F. Byrnes of South Carolina. They confided in him, tipped him off to stories, drank with him—particularly Garner, who became Vice-President; and when Byrnes became Secretary of State, he offered Catledge an assistant secretaryship. Catledge turned it down, preferring the newspaperman's existence to the politician's, although in Catledge's case the two worlds were almost indistinguishable—Catledge behaved like a politician, talked like one, and no doubt would have made a great one had he ventured into a full-time political career. He remembered names, remembered old obligations, remembered old friends even as he made newer ones in more powerful places. By the time he had joined the Washington bureau of *The New York Times* in 1930, Catledge seemed to know people in every hamlet south of the capital—bootleggers, Baptist preachers, bellhops, used-car salesmen; country editors and judges; a Mississippi whore about whom Catledge had once written a flattering article for his paper's society page; a Memphis shoeshine boy named Willie Turner who had descended from slaves on James Turner's farm. In fact, Willie Turner had been named in honor of Catledge's mother, and when Catledge moved to Memphis he and Willie Turner would get together two or three times a week, and when Catledge's by-lines began to appear in the local newspapers—and later in the *Baltimore Sun* and *The New York Times*—his friend would clip them out of the various journals left behind each day by customers and he would paste them into a scrapbook that he kept under the shoe stand.

Catledge had ridden the rails into Memphis from Tupelo in 1923 and, luckily, he walked into the *Memphis Press* offices almost directly behind a newly appointed managing editor from Oklahoma City who was anxious to demonstrate his powers as a decision-maker. He hired Catledge on the spot. Later, when the newspaper had an economic setback, Catledge was laid off, giving him an opportunity to visit the *Memphis Commercial Appeal* and to walk directly into the office of its editor, a red-faced volatile Irishman named C. P. J. Mooney. As Catledge entered the room, Mooney was seated behind his desk rubbing his eyes with a hand that lacked a few fingers. Mooney listened to Catledge's spiel for a while, expressing particular pleasure at Catledge's being born in Mississippi, a state in which Mooney hoped to increase circulation. Then Mooney, rubbing his eyes again with the nub of his hand, interrupted Catledge and waved him out of the office, saying in a snappy tone that Catledge can hear even now: "Okay, okay, just walk down the hall, take a left, then take another left, and you'll see a red-headed Jew and tell him to put you to work."

Catledge followed the directions, and soon he was facing a ruddy, bushy-haired man named Sam Kahn, the city editor, and announcing with proper timidity that he had just been told by Mooney that he could join the reportorial staff.

"Mr. Mooney told you *what?*" Kahn responded incredulously, having previously been told that no new reporters would be hired.

"Mr. Mooney said you would give me a job," Catledge repeated.

"He told you *that?*"

"Yessuh."

"What were his *exact* words?" Kahn asked, still doubtful.

"He told me to walk down the hall, take a left, then take another left, and I'd see a red-headed Jew and to tell him to put me to work."

Kahn pondered for a moment, then said, "All right, you start at twenty-five dollars a week."

This was five dollars more than Catledge had been making at the *Memphis Press*, and, gratified, Catledge vowed that he would prove his worth to Mr. Kahn. Catledge's opportunity to do so arose a few days later when Mooney, who was writing an editorial about the boll weevil, suddenly appeared in the newsroom and asked in a loud voice to no one in particular: "Say, what do you call those fellows who study insects?" Nobody could answer, and Mooney glared contemptuously across the room, shaking his head. Then, to dramatize his disgust, he pointed to a particular staff member and repeated the question; and as one staff member failed to answer, Mooney quickly pointed to another, then another, then another, becoming angrier as he moved from person to person around the room, and getting dangerously close to where Sam Kahn was sitting. Catledge, watching from the other side, suspected that Kahn was no more brilliant than the others. So just as Mooney was about to point to Kahn, Catledge yelled out from the distance, "*Entomologist?*" Mooney swung around. He nodded, then left the room. Sam Kahn sighed in relief. The next week, Catledge received from Kahn a ten-dollar raise.

Catledge remained in Memphis until 1927, when his reporting was noticed by the then Secretary of Commerce Herbert Hoover, who recommended the young reporter to Adolph Ochs. After Hoover was elected President, and after Catledge had joined the *Baltimore Sun*, Hoover again asked Ochs about Catledge; and in the summer of 1929, at the age of twenty-eight, Turner Catledge became a *Times*man.

7

WHEN Catledge arrived at *The Times*, Adolph Ochs was seventy-one years old. He was now slightly deaf and distant, so rarely seen in the newsroom that each of his visits was an event, a time of quiet stirring and excitement, a turning of heads in unison following his every step along the aisle. He was a white-haired little man with somber blue eyes, a figure very erect but frail. Young *Times*men who had never seen him before were awed by the sight of him. There was something very visionary, almost spiritualistic about him, the way he looked and seemed to float through the building, saying nothing, and the way he appeared, disappeared, reappeared months later, giving just enough of a glimpse to reaffirm his existence. One day he was seen standing off to one side of *The Times*' cafeteria with a few elderly women, one of whom asked, "And these are all your people?" Ochs slowly gazed around the crowded dining room, a vast flock extending into the distance, and then he said softly and dramatically, and mostly to himself, *"Yes, these are my people."*

Ochs was not well during these final years. The left side of his face was falling, he looked like a man who had had a stroke, but his problem was more mental than physical—he was disconsolate, so deeply depressed at times that he did not read the newspaper for days. He spoke of turning *The Times* over to trustees, and thought regularly of death. He had two grand mausoleums built, one in Chattanooga, the other outside New York—to the very end, Ochs balanced his commitment.

His illness was referred to within the family as melancholia, but they could not understand the cause, it seeming so illogical and sad that he should be mournful now, in 1929, when his success was at its peak of recognition. He was being honored by university presidents, by statesmen, by the cities in which he had once worked as a printer's apprentice. Chattanooga had recently spent three days in celebrating him as its Citizen Emeritus, and Commander Byrd, whose explorations of Antarctica had been serialized in *The Times*, had just named glaciers and lakes after Ochs and his family. *The Times* now led the world's newspapers in advertising, and Ochs could afford to buy in White Plains, New York, a 57-acre estate with a white-columned mansion that had seventeen bathrooms. Ochs personified success, challenges faced and conquered, but now it all seemed lost on him; it would take his obituary to bring his story to life.

When he had bought *The Times* in 1896, it was losing $1,000 a day, had $300,000 in unpaid bills, and was given no hope of recovery. After Henry Jarvis Raymond's death in 1869, following a heart attack while in the apartment of a stage beauty named Rose Eytinge, *The Times* was taken over by Raymond's partner, George Jones. Jones brought credit to *The Times* by exposing the scandals of William Marcy Tweed's Tammany machine, but in 1881 when Jones deserted the Republican party, unwilling to support James G. Blaine for President, there was angry retaliation from many Republican advertisers and subscribers. *The Times'* annual profit dropped from the $188,000 it had earned prior to the paper's endorsement of Grover Cleveland, to $56,000; and by 1890 it was down to $15,000. But the political decision was not alone responsible for the decline. *The Times* was also poorly managed during these years, and things became worse after Jones' death in 1891. A syndicate headed by *The Times'* editor-in-chief, Charles R. Miller, took over the paper and eventually led it into bankruptcy. It was at this point that Adolph Ochs, thirty-eight years old, was able to acquire *The New York Times* for $75,000.

He had borrowed this sum from various bankers and others who had been impressed by his accomplishments in Chattanooga and his plans for New York, and also by the many letters of recommendation that Ochs had solicited from influential congressmen, railroad owners, ministers, editors, and also President Grover Cleveland, whom Ochs had once entertained in Chattanooga and with whom he had kept in touch. In a letter to the President, Ochs had explained:

> I am negotiating for a controlling interest in *The New York Times*, and have fair prospects of success. I write to respectfully ask that you address by return mail a letter to Mr. Spencer Trask, chairman of the New York Times Publishing Company, giving your opinion of my qualifications as a newspaper publisher, general personal character, and my views on public questions, judged by the course of *The Chattanooga Times*.
>
> In other words, say what you can of me as an honest, industrious, and capable newspaper publisher. I wish to assure you that the enterprise I contemplate is not too large for me. I am able to handle it financially and otherwise.

Within thirty-six hours, President Cleveland had replied to Ochs:

> In your management of *The Chattanooga Times* you have demonstrated such a faithful adherence to Democratic principles, and have so bravely supported the ideas and policies which tend to the safety of our country as well as our party, that I should be glad to see you in a larger sphere of usefulness. If your plans are carried out, and if through them you are transferred to metropolitan journalism, I wish you the greatest measure of success possible.

Ochs's $75,000 investment in *The New York Times* not only brought him that amount in bonds—it also immediately netted him 1,125 shares of stock, each

worth $100 because of the new company's inducement
plan that allowed fifteen shares of stock with the purchase of each $1,000 bond. Also, Ochs's arrangement
with the stockholders stipulated that if he could run
The Times without going into debt for three consecutive
years, he would receive an additional 3,876 shares of
stock, giving him a total of 5,001—or a majority of the
company's 10,000 shares. The 3,876 shares were held
for him in escrow, and it was then thought inconceivable that he would be in possession of them within
four years. But Ochs had very definite ideas on how to
resuscitate the paper and he wasted no time in imple-
menting them. Because of his experience in both the
editorial and mechanical sides of journalism, he knew
the newspaper business as few publishers ever do, and
he knew how to cut costs without cutting quality.

Before he had invested in *The Times* he had made a
study of New York, sometimes touring the city on a
bicycle he had rented in Central Park, and he felt certain
that there was a market for the type of newspaper he
had in mind. The most successful papers in New York,
selling for a penny, were Pulitzer's *World*, whose morning and evening editions had a total circulation of 600,-
000, and Hearst's *Journal*, whose two editions totaled
430,000. These two men featured a lively brand of reporting, muckraking, and pathos that Ochs deplored.
His paper, selling for three cents, would be competing
with the *Sun*, which Ochs thought well written but weak
in reporting, the *Herald*, more interested in higher society than anything else, and the *Tribune,* decidedly
Republican and reactionary. Ochs wanted his paper to
be impartial and complete, a journal that would appeal
to the businessman and, as he put it, "not soil the
breakfast linen." He wanted a paper that would "give
the news, all the news, in concise and attractive form,
in language that is parliamentary in good society, and
give it as early, if not earlier, than it can be learned
through any other reliable medium; to give the news
impartially, without fear or favor, regardless of any
party, sect, or interest involved."

He began by making *The Times* legible, purchasing

new type and utilizing his typographical talent and judgment. He quickly eliminated the installments of romantic fiction that Charles R. Miller had been buying and running in *The Times* in a desperate last attempt to lure readers; instead, Ochs demanded coverage of financial news, market reports, real-estate transactions, court proceedings, the official if dreary activities of government that other newspapers had long ignored. Ochs wanted a paper of record, and it was still *Times* policy in the Nineteen-sixties to note each day in the back of the paper, in tiny type, a record of every fire in New York, and it still is possible to read daily in *The Times* what the weather is like around the world, the names of visible satellites, the arrival time of mail ships, the air-pollution index, the texts of major speeches, the names of official visitors to the White House, the precise moment that the sun sets, the moon rises.

There were only two telephones in the *Times* building on Park Row when Ochs took charge, and he immediately made provisions for more; he also arranged for the purchase of more typewriters, over the protests of some *Times*men wishing to persist with pens. (Brooks Atkinson, however, whose exquisite penmanship was more legible than the typing of most other *Times*men, managed to write his theater reviews in longhand until his retirement in the early Nineteen-sixties.) Ochs's wife, Iphigene, a well-read woman who had written book reviews in Chattanooga, persuaded him to include a review section in *The New York Times*. But Ochs, who was not a literary man, urged that his review editors treat books as news and be courteous, if not restrained, in comment—Ochs was ever wary of offending. Except for his editorial page, which he could as easily have done without, he wanted few opinions in his paper. He adjusted to his book and theater critics, to be sure, and he did not tamper with their work, but it always pained him when a show was panned or a writer was condemned in *The Times*. And Ochs took an almost masochistic pleasure in printing the letters of readers who disagreed with *The Times*. The "Letters to the Editor" was not his innovation, but he gave it a lavish display, being shrewd enough to recognize its value in promoting good will for *The Times*, further proof of *Times* impartiality. His most flagrant act of promotion, however, was his sponsorship of a contest offering $100 to anyone who could write a ten-word motto to replace "All the News That's Fit to Print," his own slogan that had been scoffed at, laughed at, doubted, yet widely discussed by rival editors and various readers around New York. Twenty thousand suggestions were submitted, 150 of which were published in *The Times*. The winner, selected by a single judge, the editor of Century magazine, was "All the World's News, but Not a School for Scandal." But Ochs, after paying the $100 and being pleased by the publicity, decided that he liked his own slogan better, and so he retained it.

Three weeks after Ochs began, *The Times* printed its first illustrated Sunday magazine, a handsome supplement with halftone photographs that was immediately popular with readers. It featured such events as the opening of the opera season, the horse show, the good life in New York as well as occasional looks at royalty abroad, such as Queen Victoria's jubilee in June of 1897, to which Ochs devoted sixteen pages and a fifty-photograph layout of the spectacle.

And so Adolph Ochs, an inwardly spunky man, an outwardly formal man who called everybody "Mister" —he even addressed his clerks in this manner and insisted that *The Times* do likewise in its second reference to people in the news, a policy followed to this day in *The Times* except in the cases of criminals and athletes—Mister Ochs began to succeed in New York and his paper began to find an audience among the rising middle class in a city of three million. But then the Spanish-American War began, and Ochs faced a new problem.

In the months leading up to the war, Ochs's *Times* had opposed American involvement in Cuba and had urged caution on President McKinley. Now, however, with the sinking of the battleship *Maine*, *The Times* was suddenly out of concert with an incensed public and it was also being overwhelmed by the dramatic style in which other newspapers, principally Pulitzer's *World* and Hearst's *Journal*, were covering the war. Ochs did not yet have enough money to compete with Pulitzer and Hearst, who were dispatching boatloads of reporters, photographers, feature writers, and artists to obtain eyewitness accounts and sketches of the heroes and villains. *The Times'* coverage was limited to Associated Press dispatches and the mail correspondence of two *Times*men, and Ochs knew that if he wished to increase his circulation, indeed if he wished to maintain it, he had to think of something fast.

It was then that he decided to cut the price of *The Times* from three cents to one cent. His editors were appalled, warning that *The Times* was putting itself in the same class as the flamboyant penny journals. But Ochs insisted that *The Times* would maintain its dignity, adding that there were undoubtedly many respectable readers in the one-cent field who would switch to *The Times*, or read *The Times* in addition to other newspapers, if its price were lowered. Ochs perhaps also sensed the financial difficulties that Pulitzer and Hearst were having because of their extravagant and competitive coverage of the Spanish-American War. There had been rumors that both Pulitzer and Hearst were hopeful of reaching an agreement whereby both could go up to two cents. But when Ochs cut his price, Pulitzer and Hearst were forced to abandon any such plan. Had they gone up to two cents in spite of Ochs, he might have followed them, but perhaps he would not have gone up until he had cut deeply into the penny market. So Pulitzer and Hearst had to hold on, and they were forced to do so for twenty years, until the coverage of World War I proved so expensive that all three publishers were obliged to charge two cents. But by that time, Ochs's paper was preeminent.

In a single year, From September of 1898 to September of 1899, Ochs's one-cent edition had increased its daily average circulation from 25,726 to 76,260, and the advertising kept pace. Ochs's circulation was more than 100,000 in 1901, more than 200,000 in

1912, more than 300,000 in 1915. Ochs's staff, under its managing editor, Carr Van Anda—whom Ochs had hired away from the *Sun* in 1904—excelled in covering World War I as it had excelled in its coverage of aviation and polar exploration, finance and politics, prior to the war. *The Times* was the first American paper to publicize and patronize Guglielmo Marconi, and because of his wireless service, *The Times* obtained exclusive American rights to stories of naval battles off Port Arthur during the Russo-Japanese war of 1904.

Although *The Times*, along with most other papers, had ignored the Wright brothers' flight at Kitty Hawk, North Carolina, in 1903, Carr Van Anda from then on pursued stories about aviation with unremitting aggressiveness. When the *World* put up a $10,000 prize for an Albany–to–New York flight, Van Anda, confident that Glenn Curtiss would win it, hired a special train for *Times* reporters and instructed them to follow Curtiss' flight down along the Hudson River, which *The Times'* reporters did, and thus they reported Curtiss' flight more thoroughly than did the staff from the *World*. *The Times* itself sponsored many flights within the United States as well as becoming the patron of several explorers, the most notable being Commodore Robert E. Peary, discoverer of the North Pole in April of 1909, and Roald Amundsen, discoverer of the South Pole in December of 1911. *The Times'* edition of April 16, 1912, its front page completely devoted to its exclusive coverage of the sinking *Titanic*, was a high point in the personal career of Van Anda and it also added to the growing prestige of Ochs. His paper was now expanding so rapidly that in 1913 he had to vacate the Times Tower building, a thin 22-story trapezoid on Forty-second Street into which he had moved from Park Row in 1904, and to transfer most of his operation into a new building on Forty-third Street, which has since been enlarged and remains the paper's headquarters today.

Ochs had borrowed $2.5 million in completing his Tower, which was inspired by Giotto's campanile in Florence, and Ochs was a long way from repaying the loan when, in 1913, a victim of his growth, he had to buy new machinery and occupy the larger quarters; and his situation was further complicated by the fact that the Equitable Life Assurance Society, one of his creditors, was suddenly under investigation by a legislative committee. *The Times* covered this investigation thoroughly, many of its stories being written by a reporter named Percy Bullock. One day Bullock was visited at his desk by a little man wearing a Panama hat, and while Bullock paused long enough to answer the man's questions about the investigation, a newly hired editor, Frederick T. Birchall, irritated by the delay that Bullock's conversation was causing in the writing of the story, jumped up and quickly walked down the aisle to Bullock's desk and snapped, "Mr. Bullock, you may entertain your friend some other time. I want that insurance piece right away." Bullock, rising, said, "I'm sorry, Mr. Birchall." Then, nodding toward the man with the Panama hat, Bullock added, "Let me introduce you to Mr. Ochs." Birchall shook hands, but continued impatiently to Bullock, "Finish that story, laddie, get along with it." Ochs apologized to Birchall, explaining that he did not realize that the deadline was so close, and then Ochs quietly left the newsroom.

Ochs remained concerned, however, about his involvement with the insurance company and what the Hearst or Pulitzer papers might write should they discover that *The Times* was in debt to Equitable. Finally Ochs approached Marcellus Hartley Dodge, a member of the industrial family that had lent Ochs $100,000 in 1896, and Dodge now arranged for a loan of $300,000 that helped Ochs repay Equitable. As collateral, however, Ochs offered his majority of *Times* stock. This was kept for eleven years in Dodge's vault. In 1916, when Dodge needed money, Ochs repaid the loan. This transaction was kept secret until years after Ochs's death.

In the spring of 1916, Ochs was fifty-eight and he had been publisher of *The Times* for twenty years. The anniversary was marked by a small ceremony in his office in which he received an ornate leather album, hand-lettered and illuminated, medieval style, that contained tributes from the staff. Some of those who congratulated him on that day had worked on *The Times* even before he had bought it—Charles R. Miller, for example, the editor of the editorial page, a very large and stodgy man with a white Vandyke beard, and Edward August Dithmar, an old bulbous man who had joined *The Times* in 1877, two years after Miller, and liked to boast that he had read every issue of *The Times* from its very beginning in 1851. There were also Louis Wiley, Ochs's business manager, a small energetic flatterer who always told Ochs what Ochs wished to hear; Ben C. Franck, Och's corporation secretary, confidant, and cousin, who had been brought up from Chattanooga to help keep a family eye on the business; Henry Loewenthal, Ochs's financial editor, who had given Ochs the idea of publishing regularly a column of names, "Arrival of Buyers," which helped to establish *The Times* with retailers and advertisers of the garment industry; Frederick Craig Mortimer, a severely crippled man, a scholar and littérateur who each day selected a poem for *The Times'* editorial page and also wrote an anonymous essay, "Topics of The Times," which was continued for decades after his death by various contributors (including *Times* copyboys wishing to display their writing talent and earn $25 per column); but in the Nineteen-sixties, slowly and unobtrusively, John Oakes published fewer and fewer "Topics," and today Frederick Craig Mortimer's innovation has almost entirely disappeared from *The New York Times*.

The celebrants in Ochs's office in 1916 also included, of course, the managing editor, Carr Van Anda. Van Anda, like Charles R. Miller and a few other top aides, was a stockholder. Ochs was proud of Van Anda and recognized his genius, but Ochs was sometimes also fearful and resentful of Van Anda's power and fame, a fact that Ochs once confessed to a younger *Times*man whom he especially liked, not realizing that this person was then keeping a memoir of Ochs's private thoughts. For example, on July 7, 1915, at a large luncheon marking Miller's fortieth year on *The Times*, the memoir noted how Ochs, after standing to praise Miller, felt obliged to compliment Van Anda, who was also seated at the dais, calling Van Anda "the greatest news editor in the world"—the writer of the memoir adding: "And I knew all the time that Mr. Ochs is dissatisfied with the greatest news editor in the world and is planning to limit his authority in the organization by playing up another man against him, if another equal to the work and equal at the same time to the superhuman task of combating Van Anda can be found. I was intended perhaps to go in that direction, but I have gone more into the editorial region than into the news field. . . ."

The writer of this journal was named Garet Garrett. He was a brilliant, highly opinionated editor with a sense of humor and detachment, blue eyes, sharp features, and an elegant style in dress. At thirty-seven, Garrett was probably the youngest member of *The Times*' editorial council, and Ochs was impressed by his quick mind, which often challenged the thinking of older *Times* editors, and Ochs also liked the fact that Garrett was not so blindly pro-British as the others. Ochs was very sensitive in 1915 to rumors that *The Times* was partially controlled by British interests, that Lord Northcliffe of *The Times* of London could almost dictate Ochs's friendly policy toward England and its opposition to Germany. Actually, Ochs was neutral in 1915, as was most of the nation; he regarded the war as a European affair and did not want the United States to be drawn into it. When a *Times* reporter had interviewed Kaiser Wilhelm II in 1908 and had quoted the German leader as being contemptuous of Britain and predicting that Germany would someday go to war against Britain, Adolph Ochs, after consulting with President Theodore Roosevelt, decided not to publish the interview; it would undoubtedly inflame American opinion, and Ochs and Roosevelt both agreed that the impulsive Kaiser did not really mean all that he had said in the interview. Ochs did not want passion in his news columns. He wanted *The Times* to publish with objectivity both the British and German sides of the news. But some of his editors were emotionally incapable of this complete objectivity in 1915, and because Ochs was not always aware of this and because he was also reluctant at times to overrule such men as Van Anda, the treatment of the news was subtly slanted in Britain's favor. "*The Times* prints a very great deal of pro-German stuff and yet, the cumulative typographical effect of the paper is extremely anti-German," Garet Garrett wrote in his journal on June 29, 1915. "You can't prove it on any one day. It is the continuing effect that comes from having day after day unconsciously accepted the *Times* appraisal of news values—that is, reading that which is more displayed with greater interest and attention than that which is less displayed." One evening Garrett visited the newsroom and asked Van Anda's assistant, Frederick T. Birchall, a British citizen, if he realized what editorial power lay in the control of news display. "Yes, I know," Birchall said. "Let me control the headlines and I shall not care who controls the editorials."

Another subject that troubled Ochs at this time was the anti-Semitism that he personally began to feel through the hate mail that was reaching him in such volume that he finally decided to post a guard in the corridor leading to his office and also to install two plainclothesmen in the main lobby of the *Times* building. *The Times* was now being referred to in letters as a "Jewish newspaper," and one day in 1915 Ochs warned his city editor, Arthur Greaves, not to give too much space to the American Jewish Committee's call for a campaign to aid Jews in the war zones of Europe. "I don't approve of it," Ochs said. "They work to preserve the characteristics and traditions of the Jew, making him a man apart from other men, and then complain that he is treated differently from other men. I'm interested in the Jewish religion—I want to see that preserved—but that's as far as I want to go. There's Brandeis," Ochs continued. "He's become a professional Jew. A few years ago hardly anybody knew he was a Jew. He had never taken part in any Jewish movement. When President Wilson was forming a cabinet and somebody told him he ought to have one Jew on it, and suggested Brandeis for Attorney General, Wilson said, 'But he isn't a Jew.' And when Brandeis heard that, he apparently resolved to become Jewish."

The rising anti-Semitism in America in 1915 was also manifested in the dramatic and controversial murder case of a Jewish factory superintendent in Georgia named Leo M. Frank—a story which was given extensive coverage by *The Times*. Frank was accused of murdering a fourteen-year-old girl, a factory worker, in 1913 when she tried to obtain a balance due of $1.20 on her wages. But since the facts were in doubt, the governor of Georgia commuted Frank's death sentence to life in prison, arousing such hostility from mobs that the governor's own life was threatened and it was necessary for him to call out the militia for his protection. In July of 1915, Leo Frank was slashed by a fellow prisoner attempting to cut his throat, and when this failed to kill him, a mob broke into the prison a month later and captured Frank, driving him in an automobile for about one hundred miles to a spot near the factory girl's home, and there they hanged him from a tree. His death provoked a great counterprotest by Jewish groups and many others, all of which was reported by *The Times* in the same calm way that the newspaper had reported the events leading up to the mob's action, including a description of the anti-Jewish sentiment that was then rampant in Georgia. Ochs did not quibble with the facts or with his paper's duty to publish them, but they nonetheless filled him with a sense of conflict and gloom.

He had believed in Frank's innocence, although he gave his editors the feeling that he was not impressed with Frank's character. Ochs once said that Leo Frank was the sort of man who would feel cheated if denied the opportunity of making a speech from the scaffold. Ochs, as always, tried to see things from many angles, and he said that he could understand why many Georgians would be incensed by the handling of Frank's case—there was the great pouring in of money and publicity from outside the state; the decision of the governor, formerly a member of the Jewish firm that defended Frank, to commute the death sentence a day or two before leaving office; the fact that the legality of Frank's sentence had previously been confirmed by every court up to the United States Supreme Court. Ochs had hoped, however, that the anti-Jewish feeling was not as intense as it was reported to be in Georgia, a place he claimed as a Southerner to understand. But his judgment was abruptly shaken by the news of the lynching of Frank, and the fact that the leader of the mob was a brother of a man who was Ochs's personal friend.

Ochs was absent from the office for several days. Then he was back again and seemed in high spirits; but in May of 1916, Garrett's journal noted: "He ought to rest for a year. His nerves are very bad. Little problems upset him, yet he is unhappy if they are solved without his advice. Always he has insisted on touching everything with his own fingers, and now either the touch or the lack of it seems a kind of torment. I believe he begins to feel what all the rest of us feel, namely, that *The Times* is too big and unwieldy to respond to the touch of any man. . . ." Still, when Ochs was absent, Garrett was aware that something very vital seemed to be missing from the daily editorial conferences. "None of us values his mental processes highly, and yet, he has a way of seeing always the other side that stimulates discussion, statement and restatement, and leaves a better product altogether than is approached in his absence. Mr. Miller, when he presides, sees only one side of a thing, and smothers any effort to discuss the other. His mind is closed. It was a better mind than Mr. Ochs's, and still is, within the limits of its movement. But Mr. Ochs, for his lack of reasoned conviction, is all the more seeing. He can see right and wrong on both sides. He has a tolerance for human nature in the opponent."

In June of 1916, to Ochs's great surprise and regret, Garet Garrett resigned from *The Times*. Ochs called Garrett into his office and asked if the decision was irrevocable. Garrett replied that he had given his decision all the thought that it deserved, adding that none better than Ochs should understand the desire to help in the making of a thing—Garrett was going to the *Tribune*, a paper in the making; *The Times* was made. Thanks to Ochs's genius, Garrett said, *The Times* was so well and solidly made that there was almost nothing an individual could do to it. Garrett confessed his impatience to do things, and it was hard to get anything done on *The Times*—anything new.

"But you will not be as comfortable on the *Tribune* as here," Ochs said.

"I don't expect to be," Garrett said. "The trouble is that I am too comfortable here. The comfort is killing." Ochs seemed surprised and Garrett suddenly asked, "Why don't you buy the *Post*, and round out your career with an achievement in the way of a highbrow paper?"

"I'm glad to hear you say that," Ochs responded enthusiastically. "I've often thought of it. I could make a big success of the *Post*. Just the announcement that I had bought it would add a million dollars to its value. I know exactly what I should do with it. I'd use only the AP news, and bother no more about that end of it; but I'd spend a great deal of money on features of correspondence, articles on art and music and literature and politics. But tell me one thing—how would that help *The Times*?"

"It wouldn't help *The Times*," Garrett said, "but what of that?"

"It would divide my energies," he replied, "and in that way it would hurt *The Times*." Then, as if remembering what Garrett had said about *The Times* being made, Ochs added: "I've hardly begun here yet." That, Garrett thought, was Ochs's dream—that he had yet a great deal more to do to *The Times*; the fact was that Ochs was afraid to do anything more.

"You do not realize it," Garrett said, "but you yourself are limited in your own expression by the traditions of this great institution that your industry and genius have created."

Ochs refused to believe that. Instead he talked of

the great future of *The Times*, and of how futile the *Tribune's* competition would turn out to be.

Garet Garrett did well on the *Tribune* but, being more a writer than a journalist, he was happier after he had left the newspaper business and was writing books and also critical essays for the *Saturday Evening Post*, where he acquired a national reputation. He kept in touch with his friends on *The Times*, however, including Adolph Ochs, and in 1921, as Ochs celebrated his twenty-fifth anniversary as publisher, Garrett wrote in a letter:

> Dear Mr. Ochs:
> Twenty-five years ago you began with The Times. Twenty-four years ago you began with it. Ten years ago, five years ago, one year ago, yesterday, you began with it. That is what seems so wonderful to me. Each day you begin with The Times, and it is never finished. You do not say, "I have," but always, "We will." I remember once speaking to you of The Times as an institution; I wondered how it felt to have done it. You stared at me and said: "But I haven't begun yet."
> A perfect issue of The Times, if that were conceivable to your restless spirit, would give you but a moment's happiness. For perfection is of this instant; tomorrow is a new time, and tomorrow is where you live.

Ochs was momentarily cheered by Garrett's letter, it arriving at a time when he seemed almost incapable of contentment. He had reached the nadir of his depression late in 1918, two years after Garrett's resignation, and he had been only slightly better since then. If any single event was responsible for Ochs's condition it was probably the overwhelmingly negative reaction of readers to an editorial written by Charles R. Miller near the end of World War I. The Germans at that point were clearly being defeated in Europe, and the jubilant Van Anda, who was directing his correspondents like a general, plotting on his map each night their positions for viewing the next battle and Allied victory, telephoned both Ochs and Miller at their homes on Sunday, September 15, 1918, and announced, "This is the beginning of the end"—Austria had just proposed a nonbinding discussion of peace. Miller, responding to Van Anda's enthusiasm, wrote an editorial on the subject from his home and telephoned it into the office. Miller's editorial advocated consideration of the Austrian proposal for a "nonbinding" discussion of peace, adding: "Reason and humanity demand that the Austrian invitation be accepted. The case for conference is presented with extraordinary eloquence and force, a convincing argument is made for an exchange of views that may remove old and recent misunderstandings. . . . We cannot imagine that the invitation will be declined. . . . When we consider the deluge of blood that has been poured out in this war, the incalculable waste of treasure, the ruin it has wrought, the grief that wrings millions of hearts because of it, we must conclude that only the madness or the soulless depravity of someone of the belligerent powers could obstruct or defeat the purpose of the conference."

No *Times*man, not Miller nor Van Anda nor Ochs, could have anticipated the reaction that resulted from the editorial. Suddenly, several hundred telegrams, telephone calls, public statements, and letters from around the nation arrived at the *Times* building charging the paper with selling out to an enemy that should be forced to surrender unconditionally. The jingoists in America damned *The Times* for "running up the white flag," and the *Herald* began a circulation campaign under the slogan: "Read an American Paper." President Wilson was reportedly enraged by the editorial, and he demanded that his aides find out whether or not it had been cabled to Europe. It had. Within days the bitter reactions were coming into *The Times* from London and Paris, Rome and Belgium. In New York, the Union League Club, composed of many influential and powerful New Yorkers, men whose good will Ochs had sought above all others, scheduled a meeting to consider a public denunciation of *The Times*. Fortunately for the paper, tempers cooled within a week or so, and no public diatribe was issued, but this whole episode was shattering to Ochs. He felt that the entire institution was going under; all his work, his years of dedication to upright thinking and fairness, now, suddenly, was being demolished by a single editorial that he had not even read in advance of publication. Normally, Charles Miller's editorial would have been reread in galley form by either Miller or some other editorial editor, and perhaps also by Ochs. But since Miller had written it from his home in Great Neck, Long Island, and since Ochs was spending the weekend at his summer place in Lake George, New York, and since the other editorial editors who were on duty over the weekend thought there was nothing startling about Miller's words, the editorial was published without further consideration.

The next day, and for days afterwards, Ochs sat at his desk, stunned. Letters were piled high in front of him, telegrams and editorials from rival publishers were shown him, he could not believe that the editorial had provoked this violent response. Many of the letters attacked Ochs personally, as a Jew who was unpatriotic, as an internationalist with commitments abroad. Miller was also bewildered, and he quickly consulted the opinions of his friends outside *The Times;* one of them, President Charles Eliot of Harvard, agreed with Miller's editorial on the whole, though finding a few phrases ill-chosen. Ochs was urged by his editors to reveal somehow that he had not read the editorial beforehand, but he replied, "I could not do such a thing. I have always accepted public praise and public approval of the many great editorials Mr. Miller has written for *The Times*. When there is blame instead of praise I must share that, too."

Ochs did, however, arrange a private meeting with President Wilson's confidant, Colonel Edward M. House. He explained how the editorial was published, emphasizing how *The Times* had been consistently patriotic and pro-Ally throughout the war. House responded with understanding, and the issue was smoothed over, but at the same time Ochs was nauseated by his own manner in apologizing for *The Times* when he truthfully felt that there was nothing to apologize for; and when he returned to New York, he again spoke to his wife about retirement.

Now his daughter, Iphigene, was married, and immediately after the war his son-in-law, Sulzberger, and his favorite nephew, Julius Ochs Adler—his sister Ada's son, who had graduated from Princeton and had received many decorations for his courage as a combat officer in Europe—had joined *The Times*. Ochs had also brought into *The Times* as its "executive manager" an old friend named George McAneny, who had been president of the Board of Aldermen in New York. McAneny's duties were never precisely defined to the satisfaction of many editors, including Van Anda; officially McAneny was to concentrate on the newspaper's most costly item, its procurement of paper, which had been rationed during the war, but it soon became clear that McAneny was expanding his interests within *The Times*, was perhaps being used by Ochs to contain the others, and soon Van Anda had passed the word to his subordinates on the third floor that McAneny's questions were to be ignored. Ochs was aware of this, and very displeased, but he did nothing about it. McAneny would somehow have to overcome it by himself, Ochs confided to another friend, explaining that McAneny's primary role on the paper was to be that of a "kind of moral background," an individual who would not ever take over the paper— that power would remain within Ochs's family—but rather would be a corporate consultant and family adviser should something tragic occur.

In December of 1918, a year after Iphigene Ochs's marriage, Arthur Hays Sulzberger reported for work at *The Times*, still wearing his boots, spurs, and the rest of what was then the uniform of a second lieutenant in field artillery. Ochs sent Sulzberger down to see McAneny, and for the next year or so McAneny helped to guide Sulzberger through the New York plant as well as *The Times'* paper mill in the Bush Terminal building in Brooklyn. By 1921, it was obvious that Sulzberger had the capacity to learn the newspaper business, and George McAneny, who was making no profound impression on Van Anda and saw no real future for himself on *The Times,* resigned and later became chairman of the New York Transit Commission.

Whether it would be Arthur Hays Sulzberger or Julius Ochs Adler who would one day succeed Ochs at the top, however, was still an open question. Ochs himself was not sure which of the two would make the better publisher. They were very different—Sulzberger seemed more modest and sensitive, more cautious, an adherent of tradition; Adler, a broad-shouldered, chesty young man with a small brush moustache, was aggressive and direct. Ochs was proud of Adler, particularly of his war record and his image as a patriot, but there was some doubt as to Adler's adaptability or desire to fit into Ochs's scheme as a shrine keeper. Ochs finally decided to leave the matter of his succession up to his daughter and the two men themselves. He gave to each a single vote that would enable them to select his successor upon his death. As long as his daughter was happily married, the odds would be with Sulzberger 2 to 1.

In the interim, Ochs watched both men's performance, with Sulzberger's duties being primarily on the editorial side, Adler's on the business side. Iphigene, whom Ochs had reared as a Victorian lady, was to remain at home and produce grandchildren, which she did rather quickly. In December of 1918, thirteen months after her marriage, she had a daughter, Marian. Iphigene had a second daughter, Ruth, in 1921 on Ochs's birthday, March 12; then a third daughter, Judith, in 1923, and finally a son, Arthur Ochs Sulzberger, in 1926. Adler, who in 1922 married Barbara Stettheimer of San Francisco, had a son, Julius Ochs Adler, Jr., in 1924, and later two daughters, Barbara and Nancy, in 1928 and 1930. By the Nineteen-fifties, all of the Sulzberger and Adler children (with the exception of Judith Sulzberger, who became a doctor) were working in the family business; and by the Nineteen-sixties, the first member of the fourth generation was working for *The Times*, a nineteen-year-old reporter, Stephen Arthur Ochs Golden, Ruth Sulzberger's first son.

If it is true that a deeply depressed person is more likely to feel at odds with the world on holidays, sunny days, or periods of general contentment than he is on rainy days or times when the world seems dark, then there is possibly some explanation for Adolph Ochs's mysterious personality change in the final years of his life, in the early Nineteen-thirties, during the Great Depression. Ochs was suddenly a man of vitality again, an optimist. He was reading the paper each morning, writing memos, giving orders. Carr Van Anda was now in semiretirement, and Charles R. Miller was dead, meaning that Ochs had no other major egos to consider before responding to each impulse. He was now letting his white hair grow and he was combing it back along the sides of his head in imitation of George Washington, having been told by someone in Europe that he seemed to resemble the portraits of America's first President. Ochs had sold his house at 308 West Seventy-fifth Street—which had become overcrowded with the white marble busts of great artists and musicians, with trinkets from overseas trips, with endless photographs of the Ochs family and relatives, including pictures of his daughter, Iphigene, through every stage of her development—and he was now living with his wife and a retinue of servants and sometimes (at his insistence) with the entire Sulzberger family, in the White Plains columned mansion, with its great ballroom and sprawling lawns. For the first time in his life, Ochs was living in grandeur. From his paneled study he could peer through a big window and see part of his 57-acre estate, called Hillandale, which included a private lake and boat house, a gardener's cottage and green house, other small buildings and animal pens. He kept domestic pets as well as pigs, turkeys, and steer;

all the animals except the steer, which would be slaughtered, were given names. Mrs. Ochs, now a small plump cheerful pixie with long white hair, had a servant who did little else but cater to the dogs, and Mrs. Ochs herself occasionally gave parties for the pets, inviting her grandchildren and their friends, serving dog biscuits and hotdogs indiscriminately to all.

After the Lindbergh kidnapping, Ochs hired a guard to protect the estate against possible harm to the grandchildren, and at one point he insisted that they be taken to Europe for a while as a further precaution, and they were. Ochs was determined to preserve the Ochsian future, meanwhile enjoying what was left of the present. The Depression had little effect on him mentally, except that it seemed to make him feel better, or it possibly provided him with a new challenge, and it did not hurt him financially to any degree. After his one horrible experience with land speculation in Chattanooga more than forty years before, he had not invested in anything that was not concerned with his own business. He did cut his employees' salaries by 10 percent for a while in the Thirties, but this was a mere token of the austerity that existed elsewhere, and no *Times* employee was laid off either in Chattanooga or New York. He was nevertheless angered by the economic condition of the country, and he abandoned his lifelong Democratic conservatism to be come a liberal, endorsing Roosevelt before the 1932 election. At this time Ochs was also irritated when the Pulitzer family sold the *World* to Scripps-Howard. He did not want the various editions of the *World* for himself, but he had hoped that they would remain independent in one form or other. When he heard that the *Morning World* and Sunday edition were to be discontinued and that the *Evening World* was to be consolidated with Scripps-Howard's *Telegram,* Ochs cut short his vacation in Honolulu and returned as quickly as he could to New York, but not before the transaction had been completed. Ochs spent much of the next week telling his editors how the *World* might have been saved had *he* been in charge.

Och's vanity and optimism at this time, which in another man might have been seen as a sign of senility, was also evident at the racetrack. He would take groups of important people to the track at Saratoga, never betting on the favorite, nor did he ever permit his guests to lose a bet—Ochs paid for everybody's bets. He also picked everybody's horses. Before each race, after consulting with *The Times'* racing writer, a debonair young man named Bryan Field, Ochs would place a five-dollar bet to win on certain horses and then assign a horse to each of his guests. Should a guest object to the assigned horse because of its name, color, number, or for other reasons, Ochs would attempt to rearrange things. He wanted his guests to be happy. If a guest's horse won, the guest kept all the money. The guest could only win, never lose. Since the Saratoga track was known as a graveyard for favorites, there usually was a winner in Ochs's box after each race, and the Ochs party was invariably a happy, cheering crowd except for Mrs. Ochs, who did not like racing because the jockeys hit the horses.

One of Bryan Field's many jobs as *The Times'* racing expert was to assure Mrs. Ochs that the horses were not being cruelly treated. He explained repeatedly that the jockey's whips were only "poppers," a bat made so loosely and in such a way that it made a loud noise, *pop*, but it did not cut into the horse's flank. Mrs. Ochs remained unconvinced. Field's other tasks included the keeping of a record of each guest's horse, the buying of tickets before each race, and the collection of any winning money. It was a difficult and confusing job at times, particularly when the guests decided to switch horses after Ochs's initial assignment, but Field was consoled by the fact that he was becoming good friends with the big boss of *The New York Times,* an individual whom *The Times'* sports editor never saw.

On one Saturday afternoon at Saratoga, Ochs arrived with six guests and was seated in a box next to that of John D. Hertz of Chicago, the multimillionaire investor in films and banking, taxicabs and race horses. Field knew Hertz quite well, and Hertz was appreciative of Field's efforts a few years before in influencing William Woodward to send his champion, Gallant Fox, to race in Hertz's Arlington Park in Chicago. After Field had introduced Hertz to Ochs and had listened to their friendly conversation for a while, Hertz asked Ochs which horse he was betting in the next race. Ochs turned to Field, who had already placed the bets. Field knew that the next race, which featured two-year-old fillies, had such a large entry that some horses, Hertz's horse among them, had not been covered by any of Ochs's seven bets.

"Well," Hertz said, softly, "I think my horse has a chance here."

Ochs did not grasp the significance of Hertz's remark, but Bryan Field, who knew Hertz to be a very conservative man who rarely gave tips on his own horses, became excited. He whispered his feeling to Ochs, but the publisher was hesitant. Then one of the guests noticed that Hertz's horse was a 30-to-1 longshot, and Ochs, wishing to please the guest, turned to Bryan Field and told him to put five dollars on the Hertz filly.

Field ran up the aisle through the crowds toward the ticket window. It was seconds before the race was to begin. But before he could work his way to the window he heard the clang of the bell—the race had begun, and the bookmakers' slates snapped shut over their windows. Field headed slowly back toward the box, watching the horses galloping around the turn. As Field rejoined Ochs, the Hertz filly was breezing across the finish line ahead of the rest, and Ochs and his guests were applauding hilariously. At 30-to-1, the five-dollar bet had earned $150, and Ochs announced that since the bet had been an afterthought made in no particular person's name, the $150 would be divided equally among them.

John D. Hertz looked sharply at Field, sensing that something was not quite right, and he asked, "Did you get down?"

"Yes, sir," Field said cheerfully, as Ochs turned to listen for the answer.

After the excitement had subsided and the guests were seated again, Hertz, still sensing something disquieting in Field's manner, asked him what price he had gotten. Field quoted 30 to 1.

"You should have done better than that," Hertz said. "She drifted up in the betting and closed at 40 or 50 to 1."

Ochs missed this exchange, for which Field was thankful. But he was also upset by the idea that, despite his having to hand out $150 of his own money, Hertz did not think he had done well enough. And on the following Monday when things were quieter at the track, and Ochs was absent, Field approached Hertz. He explained that his horseplayer's pride was piqued by Hertz's insinuation that he had been a fool to take 30-to-1 odds when he might have gotten 40 to 1 or better; and then Field proceeded to tell Hertz the whole story. Hertz was very amused, and he said, finally, "Field, I'd have done the same thing. Mr. Ochs is a great man, and he likes you."

In February of 1933, in Palm Beach, Ochs and his wife celebrated their golden wedding anniversary, and a month later Ochs was seventy-five, and various newspapers contacted him and asked if he had any comments to make about himself or about the condition of the world as he saw it. Ochs decided to sit down and write a statement for the press, which he did in his own rather shaky handwriting, and it began:

Adolph S. Ochs, controlling owner and publisher of *The New York Times*, is seventy-five years old today. He was born at Cincinnati, Ohio, March 12, 1858. He is quietly celebrating the day here with Mrs. Ochs and his only child, Mrs. Arthur Hays Sulzberger, and her four children. . . .

Mr. Ochs is in good health, active and alert. He is in touch with the minutest details of *The Chattanooga Times* and of *The New York Times*, of which he has been the sole owner for thirty-seven years. He is also fully advised of the affairs of the Associated Press, of which for thirty-five years he has been a member of the Board of Directors, and Executive Committee member.

Mr. Ochs . . . expressed his confidence that the United States was still up to par and would so continue. He said we would emerge from the mess and confusion that the country was now in as we have on many other occasions when the pessimists had their day and were sure the country, and particularly our government, was doomed to destruction; that universal bankruptcy was certain.

Never in its history was the United States so rich, so strong, so powerful and with brighter prospects ahead than at present. We have barely scraped the soil of our opportunities, our ultimate resources, our industries, our inventive genius. We are, for the present, recovering from a wild debauch of frenzied finance, crazy speculation, and insensate greed. Everybody seemed to have lost the sense of responsibility of wealth, and a get-rich-quick epidemic swept the country, but I think the situation is now well understood and that we are sobering up and painfully getting our house in order. The tragic experience we are having will result in educating the people that care, caution, and conservatism are as necessary in economics as in physical health, and that the Ten Commandments and the Sermon on the Mount, cannot be ignored, nor forgotten. They should continue to be our guide to a philosophy of life. Spirituality and idealism, now so frightfully dormant, will be awakened for the peace and comfort of our children, and this will be full compensation for our tribulations.

Two years later, on the day before he died, Adolph Ochs was on a train bound for Chattanooga. He was accompanied by a nurse and by his sixteen-year-old granddaughter Marian, who six years later married Orvil Dryfoos. Ochs had insisted that he had business to attend to in Chattanooga, and he refused to let Sulzberger or Adler go in his place. The dogwoods would be flowering on Lookout Mountain, he said, and he wanted to see them again, and he also wanted to revisit some old familiar places, friends, and relatives.

In Chattanooga, Ochs spent the night in the big rambling brick house that he had bought in 1882 when he was the rising young publisher of the *Chattanooga Times*. Now the house was occupied by his sister, Mrs. Harry Adler, and her family. Many visitors called on Ochs during the afternoon and evening, invariably remarking on how well he looked. Early the next morning he walked through the *Chattanooga Times'* plant, shaking hands with the staff in the newsroom and the printers in the composing room. Ochs sat for a while with the newspaper's general manager, Adolph Shelby Ochs, son of his younger brother Milton, a few editors, and the nurse. There was jovial conversation around the table for a few moments, then the waiter brought menus, and the men studied them.

"What do you think you'll have, Adolph?" Milton asked. When his brother did not answer, Milton looked up from the menu and saw Adolph's color changing. Then he collapsed at the table, unconscious. He had had a cerebral hemorrhage. He never regained consciousness.

The death of Ochs on April 8, 1935, at seventy-seven, was marked by tributes from Franklin D. Roosevelt, among hundreds of other leaders, and the wires of the Associated Press were silenced for two minutes around the world. Every business office and factory in Chattanooga closed for a day, and New York City's flags were at half-mast. Iphigene and Arthur Sulzberger brought the body back to New York, and Ochs was buried on April 12 in Temple Israel Cemetery in Mount Hope, New York, not far from Hillandale.

8

ONE month after Ochs's death, Arthur Hays Sulzberger became the publisher of *The Times*. He was forty-four years old and he had been on the paper for eighteen years. On the day after his elevation he announced in *The Times* that he would never depart from the basic principles of Ochs, but privately he told his editors that there would be come changes in the paper within a year. The era of the patriarch was over.

Now organized labor, stronger than ever, was trying to recruit all *The Times*' reporters and copyreaders. Sulzberger objected to this, saying that while he did not oppose unionism he did not want his entire staff to be affiliated with any single group with a "smaller common denominator than its Americanism." He agreed to testify before the National Labor Relations Board, and, wishing to present his position effectively, he kept as a reminder in his vest pocket a small piece of paper on which he had written: "Keep calm, smile, don't be smart." He smiled throughout the four-day hearings, never agreeing to the closed-shop ambitions of the Newspaper Guild but never antagonizing the labor leaders. His gentle manner was an undeniable asset.

At *The Times*, Sulzberger was mildly aloof without seeming directorial. Some of his senior editors would never let him forget that he had been Ochs's son-in-law, but Sulzberger accepted this as graciously as he could, and a few of his speeches in public began: "Perhaps you wonder how to get to be the publisher of a great newspaper. Let me tell you my own system. Get up early, work hard—and marry the boss's daughter."

He liked to present this side of himself, the lightly humorous and mildly self-deprecating side that, while ingratiating, revealed very little. In his home he also behaved at times like an entertaining guest, telling funny stories and making puns and surprising the family with clever little gifts or gimmicks. One night after dinner a servant placed on the table a cake that Sulzberger said marked the date on which Iphigene had turned down his initial proposal of marriage. The icing on the cake read: "For A.H.S. Only." Sulzberger took a knife, sliced a piece for himself, and then passed the cake around the table. The rest of the cake was wooden.

On another occasion, after Sulzberger's children were fully grown and had neglected his request to contribute some personal anecdotes and remembrances to be included in a privately published book on the Sulzberger-Ochs family, Sulzberger decided to do the book alone. When finished, he presented to each family member a handsome leather-bound volume entitled "An Anthology of Humorous Tales in the Sulzberger-Ochs Clan"; it began: "With my children's assistance I have put together a collection of stories of both them and their children. As the years roll on you may find it amusing to glance over and recall the episodes." The rest of the book's pages were blank.

He rarely forgot a birthday or anniversary, and the cards that he sent usually contained one of his clever drawings or limericks. When he was absent from one of his children's graduations, which was often, he invariably wrote them tender letters. He sometimes seemed closest to his children when he was farthest away. He was a complex man whose inner tension was evidenced by the occasional rash on his face, by his long silences and the way he drank at night, although he nearly always held his liquor well. He was an extremely handsome man, courtly and sophisticated, the center of romantic gossip, but he was also a totally dedicated publisher under whom *The Times* prospered beyond Ochs's grandest dreams. But it would be part of Sulzberger's burden to live a life of secret victories, private triumphs in the name of Ochs. Neither man would have had it any other way. Even when expressing a personal opinion in a letter to be published in *The Times*, Arthur Hays Sulzberger preferred to sign it with a pseudonym, "A. Aitchess." He was relatively unknown outside the world of politics and journalism; he blended into the institution and worked through his senior executives, and yet he was keenly aware of the staff and was more human in his feelings toward them than was his more formal father-in-law. When a certain staff member died, Sulzberger sent a note of sympathy not only to the man's widow, but also to his mistress.

Sulzberger assumed command of *The Times* during a very delicate period in its growth. The paper was not only being challenged from within by the Newspaper Guild but it was also being condemned in public: by the Zionists because of the paper's policy toward Jews, by the Catholics because of Herbert Matthews' reporting from Spain, by the isolationists who charged that *The Times* was helping to push the nation into another world war. Every week, it seemed, there was a delegation representing one faction or other that visited the publisher's office or issued a statement denouncing *The Times*. "I am not used to being called a son-of-a-bitch," Sulzberger remarked to an editor after one unpleasant experience, "but I suppose I shall learn to like it."

Sulzberger's closest associate during these years was his chief editorial writer, Charles Merz, a tall, hefty, well-tailored man who wore a blue homburg, walked with the stride of a Prussian officer, and, partly because of a ruddy complexion that suggested high blood pressure, and partly because his small steel-rimmed glasses were so tightly drawn around his broad face and nose that his ears pressed forward, he seemed like a man about to explode. Actually Merz was an even-tempered, amiable gentleman. He had been educated at Yale, had served as a lieutenant in military intelligence during World War I, and he later wrote for *Harper's Weekly*,

Collier's, and the *New Republic*. One of his contributions to the latter, in 1920, was a two-part series co-authored by Walter Lippmann in which *The New York Times'* coverage of the Russian Revolution between March of 1917 and March of 1920 was severely criticized. Merz and Lippmann wrote that *The Times'* reporting day after day was so slanted against the Soviet revolutionaries, was so eager to present the facts that were most digestible to the United States and its allies, that *Times* readers were lulled into thinking that the Bolsheviks could not win. The facts favorable to the Bolsheviks were made to seem like propaganda; the unfavorable facts were presented as irrefutable truths. And one of the major conclusions of the Merz-Lippmann analysis of *The Times'* reporting was that:

> The news as a whole is dominated by the hopes of the men who composed the news organization. They began as passionate partisans in a great war in which their own country's future was at stake. Until the armistice they were interested in defeating Germany. They hoped until they could hope no longer that Russia would fight. When they saw she could not fight, they worked for intervention as part of the war against Germany. When the war with Germany was over, the intervention still existed. They found reasons then for continuing the intervention. The German Peril as the reason for intervention ceased with the armistice; the Red Peril almost immediately afterwards supplanted it. The Red Peril in turn gave place to rejoicing over the hopes of the White Generals. When these hopes died, the Red Peril reappeared. In the large, the news about Russia is a case of seeing not what was, but what men wished to see.

Charles Merz had worked closely with Lippmann on the New York *World*, and it was from Lippmann that he first heard about the secret negotiations concerning the sale of the *World;* and in 1931, a day before the *World* folded, Merz was hired by *The Times*, relieved that no *Times* editor had mentioned his criticism in the

New Republic, causing him to wonder if *The Times'*
editors had even read it.

Almost immediately, Merz and Sulzberger, who were
about the same age, were liberal politically, and had
much in common, became good friends. They went on
vacations together with their wives, spent weekends at
Hillandale. Merz at one moment would be discussing
Times policy with Sulzberger; a few moments later, he
would be helping Sulzberger to complete *The Times'*
crosswood puzzle, a hobby that Sulzberger got into the
paper only after Ochs's death.

Sulzberger's relationship with his other editors was
not nearly so personal as it was with Merz. The managing editor, Edwin James, who replaced Birchall in 1932,
was a bit too crusty for Sulzberger's taste although the
publisher did not find James intolerable. The Sunday
editor, Lester Markel, who had come from the *Tribune* in 1923, was despotic and self-important but he
was doing extremely well with the *Magazine* and the
"Review" section, and Sulzberger did not interfere. The
Washington bureau chief, Arthur Krock, did cause
Sulzberger considerable uneasiness, however, and there
were moments when Sulzberger could not believe that
he had been among Krock's enthusiastic admirers
shortly after Krock had come to *The Times* from the
World in 1927. It had been Sulzberger, in fact, who
had strongly supported Krock's ambitions to write a
political column from Washington in 1933 after Ochs
had expressed reluctance, fearful that such a column
would draw *The Times* into endless controversies with
very important people. It was bad enough by Ochs's
standards that *The Times* had an editorial page and
allowed its critics to express opinions on the arts and
entertainment; but the idea of permitting a correspondent to pass judgment on the President of the United
States and the Congress was, in Ochs's opinion, highly
injudicious. Ochs had proposed instead that Krock
write a kind of "letter" from Washington to an imaginary "Aunt Hattie," a suggestion that Krock had
thought was terrible, and Sulzberger had agreed and
finally prevailed upon Ochs to let Krock write the sort

of column that he wished. But now, a few years after Ochs's death, Sulzberger was beginning to appreciate Ochs's circumspection.

Even when Krock's prose was dignified and convoluted, which it most often was, there was an undercoating of acid between the lines, particularly when Krock was writing about the New Deal and Franklin Roosevelt. While Sulzberger himself did not greatly admire Roosevelt, and while *The Times'* editorials had condemned him for such maneuvers as attempting to pack the Supreme Court, *The Times'* opposition had never been so personal as Krock's, and Sulzberger could understand Roosevelt's bitterness and his tendency to refer to Krock in public as "Li'l' Arthur."

"Li'l' Arthur," Roosevelt said, delivering a typical parable to a press gathering that did not include Krock, "once made a trip to Paris and wanted to see the sights. He asked for a guard of honor and was given the President of the Republic and the Commander-in-Chief of the Army, for that is the way he likes to do things. By and by, they came to the Louvre Museum, and there they saw the Venus de Milo. 'Ah!' exclaimed Li'l' Arthur, 'what grace, what classic beauty, what form divine!' But—approaching nearer—'Alas, alas! She has halitosis!' "

Arthur Krock responded with satires in which Roosevelt was portrayed as a cunning "Professor" or "Br'er Fox," and Krock charged that Roosevelt was guilty of "more ruthlessness, intelligence, and subtlety in trying to suppress legitimate unfavorable comment than any other figure I have known." Krock, a conservative Southern Democrat, regarded the New Dealers as a menacing group who were destroying States' Rights, were using the Federal Treasury to perpetuate themselves in office, and were fostering legislation that could one day allow the country to succumb to a more virulent type of liberals, or "a species of fascists."

Among Krock's habitual targets within the Roosevelt circle was the Undersecretary of State, Sumner Welles, whose eventual resignation was partly the result of all the publicity that Krock gave to Welles's disagreements with the Secretary of State, Cordell Hull, who was Krock's friend. Another recipient of the Krock stiletto was Roosevelt's close adviser Harry Hopkins, about whom Krock once wrote: "Mr. Hopkins may, at times, have thought that something the President said or did was not perfect. If so, he suppressed the unworthy thought with ease."

Short of replacing Krock, there was little that Sulzberger could do except to hint that the columnist was going too far, a hint that Krock could and did ignore. Krock was one of the most powerful and best journalists in America. During his years as a political reporter he had established valuable news sources and he had produced countless exclusives for *The Times* throughout the Roosevelt era. In 1933, on a tip from Senator Robert F. Wagner of New York, Krock revealed the outline of Roosevelt's National Recovery Act, a decision to abandon the conservatism within the 1932 platform in favor of a vast public-works program. Roosevelt quickly denied knowledge of any such plan, and a few reporters printed refutation of Krock's story as a result, but not long afterwards the NRA was legislated by Congress at Roosevelt's request.

While Roosevelt's financial advisers were believed to be debating the question of whether to issue scrip for currency, Krock telephoned a high official to verify a report that the scrip plan had been canceled. "Yes," the official said, "that's good, isn't it? But don't you think it's wonderful about gold?" Krock was momentarily silent. Could this mean the abandonment of the gold standard?—Krock was afraid to ask, suspecting that any indication of surprise or ignorance on his part would merely call attention to his informant's unwitting disclosure. Krock hung up and called the most unwary man he knew in Washington, the Secretary of the Treasury, William H. Woodin, who was playing the piano in his hotel suite when Krock's call interrupted him. Casually, quickly, Krock asked, "When will the President announce that the United States has gone off the gold standard?"

"Saturday morning," Woodin replied unhesitatingly, and Krock's story dominated the next day's *Times*.

After Woodin had resigned because of ill health in 1934, Roosevelt appointed in his place an old friend, Henry Morgenthau, Jr., a man much disliked by Krock, and during the next decade Morgenthau would complain often to Sulzberger and others about the "intrigues" of Arthur Krock, being particularly offended by Krock's often-expressed opinion that Joseph P. Kennedy, Jesse Jones, or John W. Hanes would make ideal replacements for Morgenthau, and being embarrassed near the end of his career by Krock's premature exposure of the so-called Morgenthau Plan. Krock first learned of it after an important source had invited him for a drink of bourbon and then asked, "Do you know where Henry Morgenthau is?" Krock, admitting that he did not, was promptly told that it might be wise for him to find out. It developed that Morgenthau was at the Quebec Conference pressing his plan to transform postwar Germany into a wholly agricultural nation; also that this mission had received Presidential sanction and that Morgenthau had left for Quebec without notice to either the Secretary of State or the Secretary of War. It was such reporting as this, the recognition of Krock's great contacts, that made Sulzberger reluctant to intrude. As much as any *Times*man was irreplaceable anywhere, Krock was irreplaceable in Washington. He had gone there in January of 1932 for *The Times* as a favor to Ochs, having previously covered the capital for other newspapers and grown tired of the town, preferring to live in New York. But Richard V. Oulahan's unexpected death from pneumonia in December of 1931 left Ochs with no *Times*man very willing or able to take over the bureau, and so Krock accepted the job on his own terms, which amounted to almost complete autonomy. There are very few moments in a reporter's life when he has his publisher at a disadvantage, but this was one of them, and so Krock pressed his luck while he could, finding the experience strange and wonderful.

His previous relationships with publishers had invariably ended in his disappointment. At the *World,* where he had been assistant to the publisher, Ralph Pulitzer—who had once written: "Krock has a tongue as sharp as emery and a heart as soft as hominy"— Krock had imagined himself to be in a very favored position, but he was suddenly soured when Walter Lippmann was appointed editor of the *World,* and not long afterwards Krock joined *The New York Times.* A decade before, when Krock had been an editor on the *Louisville Courier-Journal* and *Times,* working for a while under the walrus moustache and sardonic nature of Colonel Henry Watterson (for whom Adolph Ochs had worked as a printer in Louisville in 1875), Krock's position was undercut after Robert W. Bingham, the future Ambassador to England, acquired the papers. When Bingham installed another editor over Krock, Krock quit and headed for New York. (Many years later, while Ambassador Bingham lay dying in a hospital, Krock reported exclusively in *The New York Times* that Joseph Kennedy would be the next Ambassador to England, infuriating President Roosevelt, who complained that Krock did not even have the courtesy to wait until Bingham was in the grave before announcing his successor.)

Nothing had come easily to krock in his professional or private life, and men of privilege, impressed by Krock's humor and his soft and stately manner, were often surprised by his depth of rancor. A plain-looking bespectacled man of five-feet-nine, with hazel-brown eyes and clear, almost pink complexion, Krock possessed no physical distinction until his full head of dark fine hair had turned a fluffy white during his senior years; then, honored three times by the Pulitzer Prize committee, Krock was known within press circles as a "pundit" and "dean." He did not consider the latter title especially flattering, it reminding him of the elders who dominated Washington journalism when he arrived in the capital in 1910—a "small group of pompous frauds," he wrote of them, "identifiable not only by their disinclination to do legwork, which was great, but in most cases by their attire. They habitually wore frock coats and silk hats, dropped big names in profusion, carried canes and largely made contacts with their single news source in the noble saloons of the period."

Arthur Krock might be accused of many things, but never of a "disinclination to do leg work." He had hustled throughout his working life, being equally diligent as a *Times* pundit as when he was a young reporter on horseback galloping to an assignment in his native Kentucky. He had been born in the southern part of the state, in the city of Glasgow, near the Tennessee border, on November 16, 1886. His father, an intelligent man who was frustrated in his work as a bookkeeper and wrote verse in his spare time, was Jewish; his mother, the daughter of a local dry-goods merchant, was part Jewish. When his father left home for Chicago, pursuing a dream that Krock could never envision, his mother moved in with her parents, and it was in their home that Arthur Krock was reared.

In 1904 he was sent to Princeton, but he had to drop out after one year, because of a lack of money, which deeply distressed him. He did receive a junior-college degree from the Lewis Institute in Chicago, and then he returned to Kentucky hoping to get a newspaper job in Louisville. As with many journals in those days, the Louisville papers had a "cub system" in which young men of no experience began without a salary for the honor of learning the craft, an honor that Krock could not afford; so he presented himself convincingly as a reporter of vast experience, and thus he was hired by the *Louisville Herald* at $15 a week.

Krock learned fast. Within a few years he was one of the busiest reporters in the state, covering all sorts of assignments—including a few back-country elections in Kentucky that were conducted with Hatfield-McCoy shotgun etiquette. One evening while assigned to the Breathitt County election, Krock was sitting with a few people in the home of the county attorney, who was on the wrong side politically, and a shotgun blast shattered the window and blew up a lamp. Everybody crouched down, and then Krock gallantly volunteered to escort the two women in the room across the Kentucky River bridge to the other side. Soon he was leading them across a trestle two hundred feet above the water, carrying in front of him a lantern that within seconds was shot to pieces by one of the sharpshooters standing under the bridge. Krock and the women crawled the rest of the way, and when they arrived he had an acute attack of appendicitis.

On another day, also in Breathitt County, Krock met a pretty girl along the road who smiled at him and, after a brief conversation, suggested that he walk her home. As he was doing so, he noticed a surly-looking man observing them from the other side of the road, and Krock asked the girl, "Who's that?"

"He's my beau," she said.

"What's wrong with him?"

"He don't like your walkin' with me."

Without hesitation, Krock abandoned the girl and approached her beau and said, "Listen, this is nothing. I have no intentions of any sort and I'm going back to town right now." And he did.

In 1911, when Krock was twenty-four, he married the daughter of a railroad official, and they had a son who later went into public relations. Krock's marriage was a happy one that lasted for twenty-seven years, ending with the death of his wife after a long illness in 1938. Krock then was introduced at a Washington party to a fashionable Chicago divorcée named Martha Granger Blair, a society columnist for the Washington *Times-Herald*. She had seen him before and had listed him in her column as one of Washington's "glamour boys." She had described him as a man who tries very hard to be charming to women and "thinks he has a deceptive charm, but hasn't." Although "he looks so fierce and takes everything so seriously," she wrote, he has "enticement."

They were married in 1939. They lived with her two children (one of whom later became a *Times* reporter) at a country home in Virginia surrounded by 296 acres and in a large apartment in Washington. Krock was earning more than $30,000 a year from *The Times,*

had been honored by foreign governments for his reporting, had received an honorary degree from Princeton, and had fulfilled most of his professional and
social ambitions. At home with his wife and step-
children, he was relaxed, warm, and informal. On returning from the bureau in the evening, if he and his
wife were not going out to dinner, he would make a
bourbon old-fashioned, puff his fine cigar, and read to
the family the column he had just written, an effort
that was rarely appreciated although they pretended
to follow every word.

In the office with his men, Krock was a paragon of
formality. He was *Mister* Krock even to reporters who
had known him for years.

"How long does a man have to work around here
before this 'Mister' business stops?" a *Times*man once
asked him.

"As long as you care to stay here," Krock replied.
"I'm sorry, that's the way I am."

Arthur Krock had much more in common with Ochs
than Sulzberger. Though Sulzberger was only five years
younger than Krock, Krock seemed part of the Ochs
era. Krock and Ochs were regally remote, politically
conservative; they were self-made men, confident and
vain and hardened by experiences that Sulzberger had
never had.

Finally Sulzberger came to accept Krock as part of
the Ochs legacy—not a painless inheritance, to be
sure, but Sulzberger had little choice. Krock knew every
important figure in Washington, was possibly more influential in the nation than the Secretary of State. If
Krock was made unhappy, he might quit and accept
one of the many offers of other publishers. Krock was
not so attached to Washington that he would not leave:
as Krock himself said, "I like Washington the way a
chemist likes his laboratory—in spite of its smell—
because it has the materials with which he must
work." Sulzberger did not want Krock to leave, not
having as yet a replacement of sufficient stature who
could get the news and run the bureau as Krock was

running it. There was no doubt in Sulzberger's mind that Krock had greatly improved the daily performance of the Washington bureau over what it had been under the previous bureau chief.

And so Sulzberger turned his attentions elsewhere, allowing Krock and the bureau more self-rule than *The Times* had ever permitted before and ever would again. When *The Times* endorsed Franklin D. Roosevelt for President in 1944, Krock wrote a column opposing Roosevelt, and the editors in New York did not change a word; this was part of Krock's understanding with Ochs. Conversely, when *The Times* had supported Wendell Willkie for the Presidency four years before, and the editor-in-chief of the *Chattanooga Times* had insisted on endorsing Roosevelt, Sulzberger had objected, insisting that the *Chattanooga Times'* editor and his associates either endorse Willkie or take six months' leave of absence *with* pay. They chose the latter, and thus the *Chattanooga Times* backed *The New York Times* in supporting Willkie in 1940. Sulzberger's reasoning was that since he and the other *Times* policy makers in New York were responsible for the editorial viewpoint of both papers, it was somehow improper to support a Republican in the North and a Democrat in the South, a stringency that Sulzberger did not apply in his dealings with Arthur Krock in Washington.

Turner Catledge worked under Krock for almost ten years. He actually joined the bureau two years before Krock took it over—Catledge had arrived in Washington in January of 1930, five months after he had been hired in New York, while the Washington bureau chief was Richard V. Oulahan—and Catledge could later see and feel, not always happily, the stylistic differences between these two men: Oulahan, a dignified gentleman who had run the bureau since 1912, had permitted his staff to cover Washington with a kind of roving detachment; Krock, after Oulahan's death, informed the staff that it would now function as a team, which meant taking orders.

Krock installed under himself a vice-chief, an ad-

ministrative assistant who was loyal and efficient and
not excessively ambitious or egotistical; his job, among
other things, was to coordinate the coverage of the
capital. Krock also did not want his reporters to vary
their assignments from day to day, or week to week;
instead he wanted each of them to concentrate on a
particular area of the government and to develop
sources and stories within that area—one reporter
might focus on the Pentagon, a second on the White
House, a third on the State Department, a fourth on
the Department of Labor, and so on until every
agency in the government had a *Times*man watching
over it.

In theory this system had obvious advantages. Reporters would become more knowledgeable and would
presumably write with more depth, would be less likely
to make mistakes, or to misinterpret, or to be duped
by government spokesmen. But there were also inherent
disadvantages in this system—reporters could become
too familiar with their subject, eventually assuming,
unconsciously, a familiarity on the reader's part that
did not exist; and reporters might also become victims
of what Walter Lippmann considered the bane of the
newspaper business, "cronyism," a camaraderie among
the press and government sources, resulting from their
close daily relationships, their personal trust in one
another and mutual reliance on professional cooperation, that eventually could—and often did—mean that
the reporter became spiritually a part of the government. Or if not a spiritual part, the reporter had at
least a proprietary interest in his section of the government, his daily by-line depending on his ability to get
information from sources in that section, and their cooperation was unlikely if he had written an unfavorable
story on the previous day. So it was in the best interest
of most reporters to have a positive approach to government news, and only the very best reporters, the
most independent and ambitious ones, would be un-
susceptible to cronyism.

While this did not present a problem during Krock's
years as the bureau chief, he being too vigilant and

skeptical of the government and too demagogic to permit any personality but his own to flavor the news, the regulation of the Washington bureau was less rigid after James Reston, a more patriotic and flexible man, took over in 1953. But even under Reston, cronyism was never too noticeable; and even if it had been, the editors in New York would have been reluctant to condemn it strongly. Reston, like Krock, was a man of rank and reliability who condoned little interference from New York. As Krock had built his empire under Ochs, so did Reston have a strong alliance with Sulzberger, and an even stronger one with Sulzberger's successor, Orvil Dryfoos. It was also true that when Reston assumed command of the bureau, the possible existence of cronyism would not have caused great concern or notice in the New York office because the United States government was still a popular and trusted institution, the "credibility gap" was years away —the triumphant spirit of World War II, the complaisance during the postwar prosperity, the faith in the nation's wisdom and righteousness was deeply infused in American thought, and this philosophy was not shattered by the Korean War or by the scandals in the Truman administration. It was not until Eisenhower's final years that many illusions about America began to fade.

The disillusionment was hastened by such factors as the shock of Soviet achievements in space, and by the United States' being caught in a lie during the U-2 incident, an opening round in the "credibility gap"; and by the Nineteen-sixties the national doubt had intensified into nationwide dissent, inspired primarily by a new generation of Americans untouched by old illusions. This generation was unwilling to support on moral grounds the United States military acts in Vietnam or its Civil Rights posture at home, and it was also motivated by hundreds of private reasons and human fears that found release in the larger voice against the government—flags and draft cards were burned, patriotism became the property of the nut fringe, and the old attitudes and terminology were twisted—"law and order" could really mean racism; "mother" and "peace" could be controversial words; the media manufactured dramatic events and colossal characters out of many small incidents and minor men. The government's word was to be accepted with suspicion, and *The Times*' editors in New York, influenced as much as anybody else by the new disenchantment and skepticism, began to prod the Washington bureau as never before to keep a watchful eye on the government, to expose its sins; and if the Washington bureau failed to do so, a few editors in New York, among them Harrison Salisbury, began to quietly suspect that the bureau was overly protective of its sources, was a victim of cronyism.

The bureau chief at this time, beginning in 1964, was Tom Wicker. Wicker had been on *The Times* only four years when Reston, wishing to devote more time to his writing and also a bit weary of office politics, vacated the bureau job after almost twelve years and installed in his place the thirty-eight-year-old Wicker, in whom Reston saw qualities that reminded him of himself. But what Wicker did not yet have in common with Reston—and Krock—was singular strength with the publisher's office, a personal bond that is built slowly during years of outstanding service on *The Times*. And so without a solid relationship with the owners of *The Times*, and not having had sufficient time to establish a national reputation as a journalist, Tom Wicker, from his very beginning as the bureau chief, was vulnerable in ways that Reston and Krock had never been.

Wicker's added disadvantage, that of inheriting the bureau when the government's honesty was widely doubted, required of his bureau an escalation of its right to question and challenge—and this at a time when Wicker lacked the power to direct his staff with anything approaching autonomy, and when *The Times* itself was undergoing vast internal changes and second-guessing, in part because of its sudden growth as a newspaper (a growth accelerated by the disappearance of the New York *Herald Tribune*), and also because of the expanding ambitions and philosophical differences of some important executives within *The Times*.

No matter what Tom Wicker's personal limitations might have been in the mid-Sixties, he seemed to be plagued also by several forces beyond his control—his dilemma seemed to be linked, in fact, with the larger problems of the government of the United States. As the Johnson administration had lost much of its stature and believability with the American people, so had Wicker's bureau lost much of its prestige and persuasiveness within the *Times* organization—the afflictions of the administration had infected the bureau, or so some New York editors thought, or *preferred* to think. For now they were trying to downgrade the bureau and to eliminate the last vestiges of its self-rule so that *The Times* could become *one* corporate body with all the power centered in the main office in New York. In this sense, it was the New York office that was moving on a parallel course with the government of the United States, a government of increasing federalization, of unprecedented power in the Presidency, of deteriorating States' Rights. And it was neither coincidental nor surprising that *The New York Times* as a whole would reflect, in miniature, the collective style of the government because the two institutions at the top are shaped by the same forces historically, socially, and economically—what happens to the government inevitably happens to *The Times*. Should the United States continue as a preeminent power, *The Times'* words will continue to carry weight in the world. Should the United States decline as an international influence, so will *The New York Times*—following in the wake of *The Times* of London, which today does not thunder across the sea as it did during the glorious days of the British Empire.

And yet despite the United States' incredible wealth and growth in the Nineteen-sixties, both the government and *The New York Times* were beset by internal conflicts, factionalism, executive scurrying—part of which had undoubtedly resulted from the sudden changes at the top following the premature death of a chief executive. Orvil Dryfoos, whose death occurred in 1963 some months before Kennedy's, had been *The Times'* publisher for only two years. His sudden departure, shaking as it did the executive order and alliances within the institution, added momentum to forces already in motion, and it led some older *Times*men to believe, with regret, that the paper had now completely severed its spiritual ties with the permissive patriarchy of Adolph Ochs. In Ochs's earlier days, when the United States government was an isolationist power with more lofty and independent ambassadors, *The Times* was characterized by bureau chiefs and correspondents who enjoyed a kind of ambassadorial status in the major cities of the world. But now in the mid-Sixties, the home office of *The Times*, like the White House, seemed bent on ruling by direct control. Through the marvels of instant communications, jet airplanes, and various computerized gadgets available to a modern oligarchy, the New York office was indeed capable of directing the movements and minds of its men around the globe with speed and without having to work through bureau chiefs. There was no longer a need for strong bureau chiefs. Now the job could be done by superclerks. An electronic edict from New York could flash almost instantly thousands of miles away on the desk of the superclerk, who could convey it to his *Times* colleagues, who, ideally, would quickly comply with New York's wishes.

And it was such an assumption as this, if not by such methods, that led some New York editors to believe, in the summer of 1966, that the Washington bureau would accept New York's conclusion that Tom Wicker should be replaced—perhaps by a *Times*man from the New York office. Wicker had held the job for two years. This was long enough, it was believed in New York, to prove the point that Wicker had not adequately inspired the staff to the kind of aggressive reporting that was desired in Washington. Not only was Harrison Salisbury of this opinion, but so were Clifton Daniel and A. M. Rosenthal, among others, and the same might be said of Turner Catledge; although Catledge seemed to be stalling for time, as if hoping to let the forces play out their aggressions before making his move.

If there was particular hesitancy on Catledge's part to push for Wicker's removal, it was perhaps understandable. Catledge had been part of the Washington bureau; he was the only New York editor who had ever worked in the bureau on a regular basis. He had been able to observe firsthand the power-building process of Arthur Krock during the Nineteen-thirties, knew the strengths and weaknesses of the Krock system, and had also benefited from it, had gotten the front-page by-lines that helped to establish his own reputation in the capital with the Congress and the President. Krock had regarded Catledge as the finest reporter on the staff, and in 1936 Krock had given Catledge the title of Chief Washington News Correspondent. But by 1941, it was obvious to Catledge that he could go no further. The bureau was really a one-man show. Catledge felt that his progress had stalled—he was hitting his head "against the bottom of Arthur Krock's chair," he described it to a friend—and so in the winter of 1941 Catledge quit *The New York Times*. He accepted what appeared to be a dream job, that of roving chief correspondent for the *Chicago Sun*, founded by Marshall Field III to compete with the *Chicago Tribune*. But Field's ambition was never fulfilled, and Catledge was never happy in Chicago. His "roving" job consisted mainly of covering the Rio Conference in 1942, and there was considerable discord among the management members of the paper. Even his later promotion to the position of editor-in-chief of the *Chicago Sun* did not elate him. He had never caught the mood of Chicago, never felt a part of it. He became acutely aware of this one day as he sat in a courtroom, representing the *Sun* in a lawsuit; as the lawyers mentioned various sections of Chicago, the names of particular streets, Catledge realized that he had never heard of them. After seventeen months in Chicago, he was still very much a stranger.

He also missed working for *The New York Times*.

There is a very agreeable sense of privilege about employment on *The Times* that can forever spoil an individual who identifies personally with corporate greatness and tradition. Catledge had grown accustomed to *The Times'* size and sway, the way it facilitated the opening of doors on almost every level of life. He let it be known that he wanted to come back, and in the spring of 1943 he was rehired by *The Times*. He was given the title of national correspondent, meaning that he could travel around the country reporting on politics and related subjects; his salary of $12,000 was not to be compared with the $26,500 he had been making in Chicago just before he left, but he did not quibble.

Returning to *The Times*, even after a relatively brief absence, Catledge was able to see the newspaper with more perspective. *The Times* had made many changes since Ochs's death—obvious changes such as the printing of fashion and food pages, which Ochs would never have allowed, as well as the increased use of photographs, the greatly improved Sunday *Magazine*, and the brighter daily reporting, particularly by such men as Meyer Berger of the New York staff, and James Reston, who in 1944 became the diplomatic correspondent of Krock's bureau, after having worked in London and as an assistant to Sulzberger. But *The New York Times* was also coasting a bit on its success, Catledge thought. It had now grown so enormously in the New York newsroom, mainly because of the hiring of many new editors and deskmen to handle the war news, that there was a vast depersonalization and coolness about the place. The paper lost a fine reporter, Robert Bird, to the New York *Herald Tribune*, and it would later take from the *Tribune* such men as Peter Kihss and Homer Bigart, but the New York editors seemed generally unconcerned over who came or went: *The Times* was unquestionably the best newspaper in sight, even though the *Tribune* in those days was a serious and interesting newspaper, and was no doubt a more congenial place for reporters wanting literary freedom. For straight reporting, however, and depth of coverage, *The Times* was incomparable. It was

especially clear during World War II, when *The Times'*
staff so outnumbered and outdistanced the *Tribune*'s,
despite the remarkable efforts of some *Tribune* reporters
who were as good as *The Times'* best, that the *Tribune*
could never again gain on *The Times* in circulation or
advertising.

The decision to increase *The Times'* staff and spare
no expense in covering the war was Arthur Hays Sulzberger's, and within that decision he revealed a business acumen that may rank as the wisest move he ever
made as publisher. Since the raw materials for producing a newspaper—paper, ink, metal—were rationed
during the war, the newspaper publishers around the
nation had to decide whether they would try to become
rich by filling their newspapers with more advertising,
which was then available in great abundance, or whether
they would resist the easy revenue and print more
news. Sulzberger chose the latter alternative with a
resoluteness that the *Tribune*'s owners did not try to
match, and as a result *The Times* conceded millions
during the war years, but produced a superior newspaper. Sulzberger also maintained the good will of his
advertisers, large and small, by permitting them to publish minimum-sized ads in *The Times:* a national advertiser who formerly might have purchased a full-page
ad in *The Times* was restricted to a quarter-page, and
a merchant seeking employees through the help-wanted
columns could not exceed two lines for each appeal.
But the additional space that *The Times* was able to
devote to war coverage instead of advertising was, in
the long run, a very profitable decision: *The Times*
lured many readers from the *Tribune*, and these readers
stayed with *The Times* after the war into the Nineteen-
fifties and Sixties, while the *Tribune*, which featured
columnists and sprightly makeup at the expense of
solid reporting, began to lose its circulation, and its
advertisers began to withdraw.

Sulzberger himself made trips to the European and
Pacific fronts during the war, and a few *Times* staff
members not normally associated with international
reporting went overseas to bolster the war coverage.

Brooks Atkinson temporarily left his job as drama critic to report from Burma, India, and China; he flew with Chennault's Flying Tigers on a bombing mission over Japanese targets, and he was the first journalist to report that General Joseph W. (Vinegar Joe) Stilwell, who was having arguments over policy with Chiang Kai-shek, was being called home.

Meyer Berger left his sidewalks-of-New York beat to report briefly from London, and as the war was ending he toured North Africa and Europe. Turner Catledge, too, visited the European battlefronts in 1943, writing articles about the activities of the American Red Cross. In the fall of 1944, while Catledge was scouting the political campaign in Fargo, North Dakota, he received a telegram from Sulzberger asking him if he would be interested in taking a trip with the publisher to inspect the Pacific front. Catledge wired back his acceptance, and in November they began their 27,000-mile flight with a stop at San Francisco. They checked into the Mark Hopkins Hotel, went almost immediately to the Top of the Mark for a few drinks before dinner. They were seated at a comfortable divan, and through the big windows that surrounded them they could see the panorama of the north side of the city, the neck of San Francisco Bay with the ships coming and going, and to the left, the Golden Gate Bridge.

They ordered a Scotch, then a second round. On the third round Sulzberger proposed that they be "doubles." Then they ordered two more "doubles" and continued to talk about everything—*The Times*, the San Francisco landscape, *The Times*, women, *The Times*, the strange workings of the Oriental mind. They ordered still another round of "doubles." When the waiter brought them, Sulzberger asked, "Are you sure these are doubles?" The waiter said, "Am I sure? You've drunk practically a bottle already."

They had a few more rounds and then they stood up to go to dinner. But before they left, Arthur Hays Sulzberger looked at Catledge, then extended his hand, saying, "Well, you pass."

Catledge asked what he meant, but Sulzberger

changed the subject. Then later, during dinner, Sulzberger recalled a trip that he had made to Russia the year before with Reston, mentioning how Reston's engaging companionship during the day was not so satisfactory at night. Reston was not one for night life and drinking, and it was Reston himself who had suggested that the publisher's traveling companion during this Pacific tour should be someone who could keep up with Sulzberger at night. And so, in San Francisco, Sulzberger had decided to put Catledge to the test, and Catledge had passed.

The nocturnal drinking and many discussions throughout their long trip gave Sulzberger the opportunity of knowing a great deal about Catledge; though the publisher did not reveal it at this time, he was considering Catledge for an executive position in the New York office, perhaps as the heir apparent to Edwin James as managing editor. Reston was also under consideration, but Reston was not anxious to leave Washington or to give up his reporting career. Sulzberger now also had a nephew on the staff, Cyrus L. Sulzberger—the son of Arthur Hays Sulzberger's brother, Leo—but C. L. Sulzberger was enamored of life as a foreign correspondent, and the publisher was content to let him remain overseas. Catledge also was uncertain about the choice of moving permanently to New York. He had a home, a wife, and two daughters in Washington, and there was always the possibility of his replacing Krock. But this might take years, and Catledge, now in his early forties, saw in the New York job a more immediate opportunity. There seemed to be no other *Times*man of his generation with a better chance of succeeding James. Catledge had had many years' experience as a reporter on several newspapers, and he had worked as an editor in Chicago. He was ambitious, and he knew that Sulzberger liked him. Catledge would have to work under Edwin James, who could be a difficult man, but James was at least a Southerner and Catledge was sure that he could get along with him.

And so Catledge accepted Sulzberger's proposal to

move to New York, and in January of 1945 Sulzberger named him an assistant managing editor. There
were other assistant managing editors, of course, but
all were older men, contemporaries of James, and when
Catledge's desk was placed in the spot nearest to
James's office, the newsroom observers were sufficiently
convinced that Catledge would be the next managing
editor. A few days after his arrival in New York, Catledge received a note from Krock that read: "Now
that you're my boss, won't you please call me Arthur?"

9

DURING the six years that Catledge worked under Edwin James
he was exceedingly careful, pro-
voking James's anger only once, and that was over
James's son, Michel.

Michel James was a very thin, sinewy young man
with sallow complexion and a lean, almost haunted
look relieved now and then by an impish smile or grin.
He dressed himself in narrow, rather bizarre clothes,
lived near Gramercy Park in lower Manhattan, with a
dog named Bidet, and frequented what were then considered the more far-out places in Greenwich Village.
Had he been a young man in the Nineteen-sixties instead of the Forties, he would probably have become
attracted to the hippies. But during the postwar years,
the avant-garde was not so formalized nor magnetic,
having no great unifying cause in dissent, and so what
passed for Bohemia in New York consisted mainly of
a few overly publicized old Village "characters," a
dozen deliberately dingy bars patronized by young
writers and painters, by homosexual choreographers
and designers, by not-very-radical student radicals
from N.Y.U. and postdebutantes having their first and
only affairs with Negroes—and there was also in this
milieu a large segment of nondescript individualists
who worked uptown, dressed with a casual flair, and
lived as impulsively as their imagination and income
would allow. Among this latter group was Michel
James.

He had been born in Paris during his father's days
there as a correspondent, and he was completely bi-

lingual, speaking English perhaps better than his brusque and colloquial father, and speaking French as well as his Parisian mother. When Edwin James brought his family, which included two daughters, to live in New York City, Michel was sent to Princeton, from which he graduated in 1941. During the war, Michel joined the American Air Force, becoming a bombardier on a B-17, and Edwin James was never more proud of his son than he was then. He kept a framed photograph of Michel in uniform in his office at *The Times*, and he instructed a *Times* war correspondent to keep him informed on Michel's activities in Europe. The correspondent's reports were generally favorable and uneventful until one day when James heard that Michel, due to an illness, had missed a bombing mission—and it was during that mission that his B-17 had been shot down and the entire crew was lost.

After the war, Michel worked briefly for the Associated Press and for *Time* magazine. Then in 1947 he was up for employment on *The New York Times*. He had been proposed by the paper's chief foreign correspondent, C. L. Sulzberger, who from his office in Paris, and from his position as the publisher's nephew, had attained virtual control over *The Times'* foreign staff—it had become his overseas annex, and now he wished to add to it the son of *The Times'* managing editor. And when Edwin James seemed amenable, Turner Catledge decided that he had better step in quickly and raise an objection. When he did, Edwin James became infuriated.

Catledge's reasoning was based on several factors. He felt that the hiring of a relatively inexperienced reporter who was the managing editor's son would put a burden not only on the son but also on *The Times'* other editors and on the paper as a whole. While Catledge recognized that nepotism knew no limits within *The New York Times*, and that Cyrus Sulzberger would be among the last to condemn the practice, Catledge believed that it should be curtailed whenever possible. Of course Catledge was privately suspicious of Sulzberger. If Sulzberger had Michel James under his wing in Europe as a kind of hostage, Sulzberger might carry even more weight with Edwin James, and there was no telling where that could lead. At the very least it might establish pro-Sulzberger policies that Catledge would inherit should he succeed James as the managing editor. Sulzberger, who was in his middle thirties, would be part of the organization for many years to come, and Catledge knew that if he were to achieve his ambition in unifying the paper, in breaking down the principalities and leveling the dukes and reestablishing the power in the managing editor's office, he had better act before the principalities became empires, as they had become in the cases of Markel's Sunday department and Krock's bureau in Washington.

Cyrus Sulzberger had already established himself as a man of great boldness and drive. He was a tall, stern-looking man with almost opaque grayish eyes behind glasses, and he invariably wore a frayed trench coat in all weather—he rather typified the trench-coat type of journalist, the sort who not only liked to cover wars and to hobnob with the mighty, but also liked to influence world policy and the men who dictated it. There were few dictators, kings, or sultans in postwar Europe and Asia that Sulzberger had not met and interviewed—and from whom he had not received, at his request, autographed photographs which he later had framed and hung in his Paris Office.

Sulzberger had joined *The Times* in 1939, after graduating from Harvard, and after working for five years as a free-lance journalist in Europe and as a reporter for the United Press in Washington and for the *Pittsburgh Press*. During his first three years at *The Times* he traveled more than 100,000 miles through thirty countries, reporting turmoil and intrigue in the Balkans and North Africa, Italy and Russia, the Near and Middle East. He was once arrested by the Gestapo in Yugoslavia on charges of espionage, and on another occasion he was denounced by one of Mussolini's aides as a "creeping tarantula, going from country to country, spreading poison."

But in the course of his travels, which would eventually lead him to a Pulitzer Prize, Sulzberger did manage to pause here and there to enjoy the pleasanter side of Europe and to indulge his fine taste in women and wine. His eye for women was obvious in his choice of secretaries, who were invariably pretty, and there was probably not a capital in Europe or Asia in which he was not acquainted with at least one woman who was either elegant, royal, or rich. Early in his career, while visiting Athens, he was introduced to a fascinating Greek woman who had connections to the royal family of Greece. He later kept in touch with her from Turkey via shortwave code, and a year later, in Lebanon, they were married.

While Turner Catledge could not fault Sulzberger's choice in women nor his industriousness as a reporter, he did question his judgment in wanting the managing editor's son to join the foreign staff. But Catledge was powerless to prevent it because the idea appealed to Edwin James. So in 1947 Michel James became a *Times*man, and, to nearly everyone's surprise, he had talent.

It was a writer's talent, to be sure, a feeling for words and a fluidity that was uncommon in a *Times* reporter. Michel James also had a sense of humor, seeing the world in his peculiar way—it was not the serious and solid planet recognizable to most *Times*men but it was rather an uncertain, shaky place overrun with idiots. This attitude occasionally was evident in his reporting, and because of this and because of his exploits overseas, Michel was soon to be regarded as a questionable asset to *The Times*. He ran up enormous and exotic expense accounts, once hiring a yak to transport him and his equipment to an assignment in northern Pakistan. He would sometimes be incommunicado for days, weeks, and then he might suddenly appear in Bonn or Paris with a pet monkey on his back. Michel James reported dramatically in *The Times* a full-fledged offensive by Algerian rebels that nobody else saw in quite that way, and when he returned to New York for a tour in the newsroom he could usually be counted upon to enliven the place by some word or deed. An excellent photographer of voluptuous nudes, his desk was regularly encircled by other reporters lusting over his pictures. Once he managed to have printed in *The Times'* annual "Neediest Cases" charity drive a one-dollar donation in the memory of a cranky old *Times*man who was still alive and working on the staff.

Such imagination as this was not destined to make Michel James an indispensable part of *The Times*, and years later he quietly resigned and left New York to settle in some small Western town, and he was not heard from again. As to whether his presence on the foreign staff was to increase C. L. Sulzberger's influence in the managing editor's office, it was never possible to tell. For in December of 1951, Edwin James died. And Arthur Hays Sulzberger's memo on the bulletin board of the newsroom read:

> To the Staff:
> When death takes a valued member of an organization, it is always a sad occasion. Such it was with the passing of Mr. Edwin James. But the institution must go on, and I have today appointed Turner Catledge to the post of Managing Editor of the Times. . . .

Causing as little commotion as possible, Catledge now began his campaign to centralize the News department, to bring friendly forces into his camp. He began by appointing two men to the rank of assistant managing editor, Robert E. Garst and Theodore M. Bernstein. Bernstein and Garst had filled vacancies caused by the resignation of Neil MacNeil, a large, proud man who had been on the paper for thirty-three years and had resented Catledge's plan for centralization, and David H. Joseph, who had been on *The Times* for forty-four years and had been given so little to do in recent years that he finally took the hint and approached Catledge one day. He walked into Catledge's office and said, "Do you know what I would do if I were in your place?"

When Catledge looked up almost listlessly, David

Joseph became suddenly more intense, repeating *"Do you know what I would do if I were in your place?"*

Catledge saw before him an elderly man, pale and partially bald and with deep sad eyes, trembling with an inner rage that was uncharacteristic of the man that Catledge had known for the past few years. Joseph had always seemed unemotional and methodical, too methodical by Catledge's standards, an office antique from the Ochs era that Catledge could have done without, but would not have disposed of, certainly not during his first year as *The Times'* managing editor. It would have been scandalous to attempt that. There were still many Ochs men on the staff, and it was said that during Ochs's days *The Times* had only one personnel director—God. When a *Times*man became old and feeble and almost incompetent he was not fired or forced into retirement; he was instead kept on the staff until God had disposed of him. Ochs himself had hired David Joseph, being impressed with Joseph's formality and shyness, and the fact that Joseph, like Ochs, had worked for the *Louisville Courier-Journal*.

"Are you a poet?" Ochs had asked, noting on Joseph's application form the fact that he had briefly taught English after graduation from Columbia and had earned a Phi Beta Kappa key.

Joseph seemed too embarrassed to answer, and Ochs was elated and touched by the applicant's apparent modesty, and Ochs announced, "Come to work Wednesday." That was Wednesday, October 21, 1908. And David H. Joseph proved to be a fine reporter, reliable and objective in the tradition of Ochs and Van Anda. In 1927, Joseph was appointed the city editor, and in 1948 he became an assistant managing editor under James. Now, four years later, Joseph stood glaring at Catledge, demanding an answer to a question that confused Catledge.

"All right," Catledge said finally, "what *would* you do if you were in my place?"

"I'll tell you," Joseph said, "but first let me be in your place."

Catledge looked at Joseph again, more perplexed

than before. But Joseph was obviously *not* kidding. He stood waiting for Catledge to stand up, walk to the front of the desk, and trade places, and there was such conviction in Joseph's trembling manner that Catledge obliged, moving to the front while Joseph took Catledge's place behind the desk.

"Now, if I were you," David Joseph said, gaining composure, "I'd ask for my resignation."

Catledge stood silently for a moment. Then he said, softly, "Well, Dave, you took the words right out of my mouth."

And so it was done—Joseph's retirement was official. It apparently had been so difficult for Joseph to sever his relationship with *The Times* after so many years that he had to stage an incident, a dramatic scene to accomplish what he could not otherwise bring himself to do. Catledge was moved by the gesture, and pleased by the result. He called the publisher's office and informed Sulzberger of Joseph's decision to retire. And in the next issue of the newspaper's house organ, *Times Talk,* there was a long and kindly article about Joseph's career, and a farewell party was arranged for him at the Essex House. It was attended by Iphigene and Arthur Hays Sulzberger, by Charles Merz, the editor of the editorial page, and by other senior *Times*men. Catledge delivered a few words of appreciation for Joseph's many years of service and then he presented to Joseph a gift from the staff, a wallet, and finally everyone stood and sang "Auld Lang Syne."

Turner Catledge was never so presumptuous or quixotic as to think that he himself could dominate *The New York Times'* News department. It now had become too large and unwieldy for that; and even if *The Times* were a coordinated force, which it was not, it would not respond most effectively to direct commands from a martinet. For all its size, *The Times* was a rather delicate and sensitive monstrosity. It had to be petted, cajoled, prodded gently. It was like an elephant, Catledge thought, a slow-moving, heavy creature that, if improperly led, could be made to look awfully foolish and could also make a fool of its leader. It was a serious animal. If it wished to dance in public, it had better dance well.

Still, *The Times* had to move along, to keep pace with a faster life in the Fifties. Now the newspaper industry had a serious new threat, television, and Catledge knew that the formula that had worked so well for Van Anda, Birchall, and James would require some adjusting. A newspaper could not compete with the speed of television in covering spot news, nor could it match television's dramatic presentation of a single news spectacle, such as a political convention or the coronation of a queen; but Catledge was confident that newspapers could bring readers more details and could explain the significance of these details more effectively than could television. Television reporters, with few exceptions, were really skimming the headlines, hitting the highlights of a few top stories. Newspaper reporters would now have to dig more deeply into more areas and to inform the public more thoroughly; they could no longer merely report all the facts, but they would often have to interpret the meaning behind these facts. The trick was to do this without editorializing. While there was a difference between interpreting and editorializing, Catledge knew that the line between the two was sometimes thin, and if *The Times* was to achieve the new goal and yet avoid making a mockery of Ochs's motto about objectivity, it had to have a more vigilant copydesk, more unchallenged authority in New York—and here again arose the problem of power. Who was to decide what and where? Catledge had privately decided that the bureau chiefs could no longer stand between his senior editors and the reporters around the nation and overseas, but he also knew that it would now be unwise to push too hard or too fast. It would take time to whittle down the chiefs. *Everything* took time on *The Times*, and occasionally Catledge might have to rely on help from God. Catledge would have to remain patient, cautious. Already there had been complaints from a few old-timers to Iphigene Sulzberger that "things aren't what they used to be," and "your dear father would never put up with what's going on around there now." And Cyrus L. Sulzberger, too, was aware of slight changes in New York, and periodically he would fly in from Europe, would stride across the newsroom into the bullpen carrying a satchel full of complaints from his men with copies of their stories that had allegedly been butchered in New York. Then Theodore Bernstein, Catledge's dean of grammar and enforcer of rules, would attempt to defend the editing, and once Bernstein threw up his hands and cried, "Dammit, Cy, what do you want, an *un*edited paper?" Cyrus Sulzberger indicated that this was not a bad idea.

There was a time, twenty and thirty years earlier, when the paper had been almost unedited. But in those days the cost of newspaper production and labor was not so high, and *The Times* could afford to be more lenient with its space allotment for news. It was then also common at *The Times* for some reporters to work on "space," meaning that they were paid on a measurement basis which, while it inspired some of them to cram more facts into their stories, also led to wordiness and padding in *Times* articles that persisted long after the space system was abandoned. But now, in the Fifties, it was imperative that *The Times* tighten its writing style. The paper could no longer financially afford to print lengthy stories about relatively minor news events. While the top executives did not wish to emphasize it, the paper was now actually printing fewer columns of news than it had been printing in the Nineteen-twenties and -thirties. And since the end of World War II, it also had greatly increased the volume of advertising to a point where it regularly carried more lines of advertising than lines of news; and it also was accepting the advertising of certain budget-boasting smaller department stores that *The Times* had once been too haughty to accept. The executives justified the increased advertising on the grounds that *The Times* *had* to make more money to meet the rising costs of producing a newspaper and paying higher salaries to a staff that had nearly doubled in size since Catledge

had become a *Times*man in 1929. The only way that
The Times could both cover the news and pay its bills
was to get its reporters to say more in less space, as the
tabloid men from the New York *Daily News* had been
doing so well for years. But on a newspaper where things
moved slowly, this was not easily achieved. Older *Times*
reporters, who for decades had worked in a system
that had condoned long leads and pedestrian writing if
all the important facts were in each story—"I want
it *all,*" Ochs had said—could not be expected to adjust
happily to a shorter, snappier style. Of course, Bernstein's deskmen could rewrite the stories, but this
would alienate the reportorial staff and would place
excecessive authority in the hands of copyreaders—and
Bernstein himself. Catledge did not want that. Bernstein was an aspiring man who, with the slightest encouragement, would take over the newsroom. Bernstein
did know more about newspaper editing and the English language than any other man on the staff—certainly
more than Turner Catledge—and he was never hesitant
about flaunting his knowledge. While editing Winston
Churchill's memoirs for *The Times*, Bernstein wrote
to Sir Winston suggesting places where the writing
might be improved or cut out entirely. Churchill,
annoyed, replied that he was then "fully engaged" in
other matters and requested that Bernstein publish the
memoirs as written, which was eventually done.

But Catledge was wise to keep things in delicate
balance between the forces of Bernstein and the reportorial staff. Not all the reporters were in need of editing;
indeed, there were some reporters with smooth and
graceful styles that would probably be stifled under
the heavy hand of a domineering desk, which usually
contained its quota of frustrated writers and peda-
gogues; and Catledge was also mindful of the fact that
The New York Times was an immensely successful
enterprise, and that any changes that were introduced
or permitted by him might adversely affect the winning combination.

Quite apart from what he might think of Cyrus Sulzberger's position as an overseas viceroy, Sulzberger

was a first-rate reporter; and the foreign staff, too, while having its intractable members, was probably as good as or better than any staff ever assembled overseas by *The Times*. Many of the correspondents were linguists and distinguished authors; a few were scholars, and nearly all of them had spent years as world travelers and had witnessed the war in Europe or Asia. And now, as Catledge cautiously assumed the duties of managing editor, the foreign staff was moving knowledgeably around the world reporting the political and economic trends of the postwar era and the eruption of new hostilities. Sulzberger and Anne O'Hare McCormick were in London analyzing the British elections, and other stories from England were being written by Clifton Daniel, Tania Long, and Benjamin Welles, son of the former Undersecretary of State. Raymond Daniell, chief of the London bureau, was in Glasgow traveling with Churchill. In Paris, a Rhodes scholar from Georgia, Thomas Jefferson Hamilton, was preparing to cover the meeting of the United Nations General Assembly, being assisted by an alert young reporter named Abe Rosenthal. Also in Paris was the chief of the regular six-man bureau—Harold Callender, who had been on *The Times* since 1924, having traveled with Franco's forces in the Spanish war and having worked in Germany before the World War and in Norway until the Germans entered Narvik. In Rome, the bureau chief was Arnaldo Cortesi (whose father had previously worked for the AP in Rome, having allegedly used as character references the King of Italy and the Pope); Arnaldo followed his father into journalism after being trained as an engineer—and one day at *The Times'* office in Rome, after it had been announced that half a million people had jammed St. Peter's Square, Arnaldo Cortesi went down to calculate the surface of the entire piazza to the last square inch, determining finally that the half-million figure was slightly exaggerated.

In Teheran, Michael Clark was filing a story about the silent oil wells at Abadan, and Albion Ross was in Cairo writing about the British-Egyptian crisis. Sydney

Gruson was in Tel Aviv describing the latest Middle East dispute, and Camille Cianfarra was with the United States Sixth Fleet in the Mediterranean. In Athens was the venerable A. C. Sedgwick, whose wife was an intimate of the Queen and was also an aunt of C. L. Sulzberger's wife, a convenient arrangement all around. In Karachi, which was part of the so-called "prickly-heat beat," Robert Trumbull was analyzing events following the assassination of Pakistan's premier. Tillman Durdin was in Djakarta covering Indonesia's campaign against the Communists. Henry R. Lieberman, who had previously traveled through most of China by every conceivable conveyance from a goatskin raft to a wooden Tsinghai saddle, was now China-watching in Hong Kong. Lindesay Parrott, a boisterous little man who had gone to Princeton and later became the villain in a romantic novel written by his former wife, was now the bureau chief in Tokyo, reporting the Korean truce negotiations together with another *Times*man, Greg MacGregor, who had first visited the Orient as a Marine at Guadalcanal. In Korea with the troops were Murray Schumach and George Barrett, being invaded periodically by *Times*men from Markel's Sunday department and Krock's Washington bureau. Harrison Salisbury was in Moscow reporting the Cold War, while the reactions to it in Belgrade were being recorded by M. S. Handler, in Berlin by Farnsworth Fowle, in Bonn by Drew Middleton and Jack Raymond, in Geneva by Michael Hoffman, in Stockholm by George Axelsson, in Dublin by Hugh Smith, in Vienna by John MacCormac, at The Hague by Daniel Schorr, in Madrid by Sam Pope Brewer, and from General Eisenhower's headquarters at SHAPE by Edward A. Morrow. *The Times* also had Foster Hailey reporting from Buenos Aires, R. Hart Phillips from Havana, Crede Calhoun from Panama, Ford Wilkins from Manila —and there were several other *Times* correspondents and stringers stretched from the sub-Sahara to Reykjavík; and if Catledge wished to find fault with them, or with the way the foreign staff was run, he could—and would—but not now. He would concentrate on the foreign staff after he had had an opportunity to visit the overseas bureaus, but now he would remain at home and try to get his own office in order and see if anything could be done to improve the performance of the many men and women who worked in the New York newsroom.

The New York staff, the largest of all the departmental news staffs of *The Times*, was undoubtedly the most tradition-bound and also the most uncoordinated. Each morning hundreds of people would file into the newsroom and would either seat themselves behind vast rows of desks like parishioners at church, or they would disappear in the distance behind some pillar or interior wall, some dark nook or glass-enclosed maze on the doors of which was printed "Science" or "Real Estate" or "Drama" or "Sports" or "Society"—and even when Catledge stood outside his own office gazing around the newsroom through his binoculars he could never see at a single sweep everybody on his staff nor did he precisely know what they were all doing there. For this information, he would have to consult his various and sundry subeditors, and sometimes he wondered what *they* were all doing there. Sometimes it seemed that the brigades of *Times* employees posted throughout the third floor were not really all working for *The Times* but were rather occupying positions from which to run a mail-order business, or to write magazine articles or novels, or to use the telephones to supervise a trucking business (indeed, one man did exactly this from his desk in *The Times'* morgue), or to use the phones to place bets with a bookmaker—although Edwin James's bookmaker, who was employed as a news clerk near the bullpen, was still very much in operation.

The newsroom was in many ways like New York City itself—vast, varied, overpopulated, confusing, and characterized by a heterogeneous assortment of skilled workers, geniuses, oddballs, and drones. When a great disaster occurred in New York City—such as when an airplane hit the Empire State Building, or when New York's electrical power failed, or when, a few hours away, two ocean liners, the *Andrea Doria* and the

Stockholm, collided at sea, killing several passengers, including *Times* correspondent Camille Cianfarra— *The Times'* city editor had merely to pick up his loudspeaker to summon dozens of men and dispatch them to the scene. In the course of such coverage, *Times*men often met other *Times*men for the first time. While these individual *Times*men were perhaps not as dynamic or hard-working as some reporters from other newspapers, *The Times* always overwhelmed the opposition by sheer numbers—it had more men to dredge up more facts, and then these facts were funneled into the newsroom, were sorted by clerks, were scrutinized by echelons of editors, then were passed down into the hands of a few superb rewrite men with fast fingers and well-organized minds. The newsroom remained generally quiet during the coverage of cataclysms, and when there was no momentous news event to preoccupy the staff, the men in the newsroom seemed to totter between total inertia and vague distant distractions. It would take years for Catledge to fathom the mysteries of the place, and to know all the people who worked there—the baseball writers who rarely appeared in the office, the ballet critic who fluttered through at night, the old white-haired scrivener of chess tournaments who wore a heavy overcoat in summer, the music critic who never wore an overcoat even in snowstorms, the chief copyreader on the obituary desk who never removed his hat in the office, the happy clerk in the telegraph room who during his off hours was an undertaker, the quiet clerk in the telegraph room who, unknown to *The Times*, was employed by the CIA.

The newsroom was many things to many people; and seemed at times to be operated, as one visiting correspondent observed, somewhat along the lines of a Paris café. In the late afternoon, he noted, the reporters at their desks would lean back in their chairs, sip coffee, read the newspapers, and watch other people walking back and forth in front of them. There was often a card game at one of the desks, always a conventional gathering at another desk, and there was also a late-afternoon tranquillity about the place that induced sleep. Some of the men and women who were having love affairs would, after the senior editors had disappeared into the 4 p.m. news conference, slip away to one of the hotels in the Times Square area, having only to remember to place an occasional precautionary call to a friend in the newsroom and to return before six-twenty, for that was when the city editor would stroll along the aisles giving his traditional "good-night" to individuals on the early shift. There was one reporter named Albert J. Gordon who had once left for home at the end of the day without a "good-night"; later reached by phone he was told that the editor wished to discuss with him a most important matter—*now*, and in person. Gordon lived at an inconvenient distance from the office, and it was also then raining heavily, but he reappeared in the newsroom as soon as he could. There, wet and sullen, he stood for a few seconds in front of the city editor's desk until the editor looked up and said, almost with a smile, "Good-night, Mr. Gordon."

The city editor and his assistant editors also followed tradition when they assigned stories to the staff each morning; the best local stories were given to the front-row veterans, and the younger reporters near the back usually ended up with such stories as a watermain break in Yorkville or a small fire in Flushing, or were sent to Watertown, New York, to cover the training activities of the Seventy-seventh Division, General Julius Ochs Adler's old outfit, a traditional "must" on the assignment sheet. Younger reporters who wrote with style were never completely trusted by the city editor and his associates, the assumption being that "writers" would compromise the facts in the interest of better literature. Such writers therefore were usually assigned to cover the weather or parades or the Bronx Zoo and the circus—where, if the quotes were brightened a bit, there was a reasonably good chance that the clowns and animals would not complain in letters to the publisher.

There was a traditional manner, too, in the way the New York editors planned the coverage of those news events that occurred on an annual basis, such things as the opening of the opera season, the Easter parade, the governor's budget message, the horse show, the debutante parties at the Plaza, the lighting of the Christmas tree in Rockefeller Center—any particular occasion that had been successfully and uncontroversially covered and printed in *The Times* last year and the year before, and the year before *that*, could be (and usually *would* be) covered in the same way this year. The layout would be identical, with the same size photographs and poses and an almost identical headline and lead as had appeared in *The Times* a year ago; and often the same reporter was assigned every year to the same story. Except for the alteration in the date and certain names, the reporter's story written last year could have sufficed for this year and next.

While Turner Catledge did not wish to tamper with tradition at *The Times*, he did think that some New York editors went to the extreme, although it was understandable that the newsroom would be the hub of habit within *The Times:* it had been so long under the personal scrutiny of senior editors who were Ochs fundamentalists, who had been indoctrinated by Van Anda's Swiss Guard, that the subordinate editors who worked in the newsroom found it easier to follow a safe formula than to try anything new. Even Arthur Hays Sulzberger, with all his modernism and willingness to make concessions to a changing world, was nevertheless drawn back occasionally to the methods of the past. When President Franklin D. Roosevelt died, Sulzberger sent for the old *Times* files to see how Lincoln's death had been handled in 1865 by *The Times'* original publisher, Henry J. Raymond, and Sulzberger noted the black mourning borders that separated each column of type of the front page. Then Sulzberger sent for a copy of *The Times* on the day of Adolph Ochs's death announcement in 1935, observing the black borders that framed the picture of Ochs at the top of page one; and Sulzberger finally decided to make the Ochs page a model for *The Times'* front page in 1945 that announced President Roosevelt's death. Like Ochs, Roosevelt was displayed with a black-bordered four-column picture in the center of page one, near the top.

While such direct supervision of *The Times'* makeup was uncharacteristic of the way that Sulzberger normally functioned as publisher, he did pay particular attention to typography and photographs, and this may explain in part his sudden indignation—and the rather drastic results to his picture editor—on the day that *The Times* published a photograph of Marilyn Monroe kissing Joe DiMaggio.

The picture editor was a tall, casual, easy-going Southerner named John Randolph. Randolph was a personal friend of Turner Catledge, having worked under Catledge on the *Chicago Sun* as picture editor, and he had also worked with Catledge on the *Baltimore Sun*. In 1949, when Catledge began to have influence under James, he helped to get Randolph onto *The Times* as a copyreader. And in 1952, a year after Catledge became the managing editor, he made Randolph the picture editor, thinking that it would be a very pleasant job for a very pleasant man, and thinking, too, that John Randolph—who had demonstrated a lively style as a caption writer in Chicago and had also shown talent as a free-lance writer for *Collier's* and *Esquire* and for magazines devoted to hunting and fishing, which were Randolph's passionate hobbies—would enliven the captions and headlines that accompanied photographs in *The Times*.

While Randolph had no talent or ambition as an administrator, he did enjoy working with the deskmen and photographers on *The Times'* picture desk, he did supply some spark to caption writing, and he certainly did enjoy the extra money that his job as picture editor had brought him. During Randolph's long career as an itinerant newsman, he had never saved money, nor could he ever drive himself to earning more until he was absolutely broke. Hunting, fishing, and gambling at cards were always more enticing than writing articles for magazines, and the only reason he wrote his first article for *Esquire* in 1937, on the training of bird dogs, was to pay for the birth of his daughter.

Randolph was then married to a former schoolteacher whom he had met one night at a house party in Vermont. She was the daughter of a moderately prosperous New England farmer and sheep breeder, and when she was introduced to Randolph he was unshaven and hungover and claiming to be a newspaperman from Washington, D.C., who had come up to Vermont looking for Dillinger. When her parents finally met Randolph, they were very skeptical. He had no land or money, and his credentials were unimpressive. Born in Louisiana to a roving country newsman, Randolph had spent one year at the University of Alabama, another at George Washington University, and had played a little semiprofessional football, which accounted for his broken nose. He had shifted from newspaper to newspaper in and around Washington, D.C., where he occasionally also drove a taxicab. In Washington he was known as the only cab driver who read Shakespeare on the job, sometimes turning down a fare if he was particularly engrossed.

But when the courtship between Randolph and the schoolteacher continued through the mail after he had returned to Washington, her parents finally began to accept him, and her father was particularly impressed with the graceful letter that Randolph had written requesting consent to the marriage.

With the coming of World War II, after Randolph had worked on various copydesks and had done public-relations work for the Roney-Plaza Hotel in Miami, he applied to the Office of War Information, was trained as a linguist, and was sent to China. His job there was to furnish propaganda that would be published in pamphlets and be distributed in the hope of encouraging wider Chinese participation in the fight against Japan. But the program was largely a fiasco because, as Randolph later explained to his wife, the Chinese generals, in addition to being very corrupt, were reluctant to engage their troops in battle because to do so would result in a loss of men and hence of status, power, and—

most important—supplies that could be sold on the black market for large sums of money.

After the war, and through his fortunate friendship with Turner Catledge, Randolph came to *The New York Times*, but he never really liked living in New York City nor in its suburbs. The suburbs, while not the city, were not the country either—and so, soon Randolph had moved his wife and children to Colrain, Massachusetts, and he took the train up there on weekends: he preferred two days in the country and five alone in New York City to seven in the suburbs. He spent his evenings in New York playing cards in the newsroom, a nightly game that *The Times'* executives tolerated because it kept many extra men in the office long after their "good-night"—and thus they were readily available should a big story break.

The marriage of Marilyn Monroe and Joe DiMaggio in January of 1954 was not momentous news to *The Times,* but it *was* news, and a brief account of the ceremony was scheduled for page 21, and it was also decided to use a photograph of the couple. Randolph had several pictures to choose from, but they all seemed essentially the same: the couple, just married, standing in a posed embrace for the San Francisco photographers along the sidewalk outside of City Hall.

So, Randolph routinely picked one picture from out of the pile, marked it for a two-column cut, and put it aside to be submitted later to the bullpen, which passes on all photographs before they are sent up to the Engraving department. The picture showed Marilyn Monroe with her head back and her mouth slightly open, and DiMaggio with his lips puckered and his eyes closed. There seemed nothing particularly vulgar or exceptional about the picture—at least Randolph did not think so, nor did Theodore Bernstein and the other bullpen editors who later passed on it.

The next morning, John Randolph was no less surprised than dozens of other *Times*men to hear that the picture in *The Times* had caused a "great flap" in the publisher's office, and that Randolph was no longer *The*

Times' picture editor. Randolph at first could not believe it. He could not believe, nor could the other *Times*men, that Miss Monroe's open-mouthed French kiss would so offend the sensitivities of Arthur Hays Sulzberger, or Iphigene Sulzberger, or whoever may have registered an objection in the publisher's office. Of course, it was true that there was an incredible double standard where sex was concerned at *The Times;* that is, while sex has been the traditional excess of so many of the paper's most prominent reporters, editors, executives, and shrine keepers—"Drink is the bane of the *Herald Tribune,"* one old saying went, "sex is the curse of *The Times"*—it was equally true that the personal habits of *Times*men rarely if ever tainted the purity of the paper itself, which remains comparatively Victorian. Young *Times* reporters writing about sex education or birth control or deviates are forewarned about being "too clinical," and *Times* editors have been known to have the genitals of dogs airbrushed out of photographs before printing them, and to have cloaked the cleavage of some buxom opera sopranos. But on the other hand, the Monroe photograph was not "cheesecake"—she was wearing an unrevealing black dress— and she and DiMaggio *were* married and it did not seem inappropriate to publish a mildly passionate wedding-day kiss in Mr. Ochs's newspaper. Or so Randolph thought.

In any event, he was out as the picture editor. He was not embittered nor angered by Sulzberger's decision, which was relayed to him by Catledge—just surprised. Catledge seemed deeply embarrassed by the whole incident. He asked Randolph more than once if he had sent to the bullpen *other* pictures of the DiMaggio-Monroe wedding; if Randolph had, then the choice would have been the bullpen's, and Catledge might have been able to spread the blame around and permit his friend to remain as the picture editor. But Randolph answered that he had submitted only the one picture that had appeared in the paper. He was willing to quietly accept the entire blame, and he did.

Catledge assured Randolph that his salary would not

be cut—he would merely be transferred as a copy-reader to the national-news desk on the other side of the newsroom, and there was in Catledge's manner the hint that Randolph, who had played the game well, would somehow be taken care of after things had cooled off.

Two years later Catledge heard that there was to be an opening in the Sports department—the writer of the "Wood, Field, and Stream" column, who had held the job for nineteen years, had resigned to accept an important management job at a big resort in the Bahamas, and Catledge thought that Randolph might like to take over the column—which carried with it a large expense account and the freedom to travel around the country to hunt and fish and to write about it for *The Times*. Randolph was delighted by the offer, and if there was ever a *Times*man who was ideally suited for a particular assignment, Randolph was suited for this one—and his column became immediately one of the most readable features in the paper. It was not so much his knowledge of the outdoors or his expertise as a fisherman or hunter that brought distinction to his writing; it was almost the opposite. Randolph was neither a lucky fisherman nor a great one. While he was a good shot, he was not superb. He was like a million other men who hunt and fish merely because they enjoy the act of doing so, and particularly enjoy escaping from a clamorous city and wandering through the woods or relaxing on a boat; and a typical Randolph column began:

> The only trouble with this story is that it is not a lie. That is too bad, because it could raise perceptibly the sorry level of fishing lies, which, taking them by and large, are paltry things.
>
> It is the only department in which fishing has not progressed. Research carried out by seven doctors of philosophy for four years and endorsed by three bishops has proved that no really good fishing lie has been written since Moby Dick. . . .

It was generally conceded within *The Times'* news-room that John Randolph had the softest job on the paper. He was the only *Times*man who got paid for playing. His columns appeared from warm sunny places during winter, from cool lakes during summer. On the longer, more interesting trips he usually took his wife, not only because he liked her company, but also because without her he was nearly helpless. The simplest gadget, whether it was a can opener or a lighter, baffled him and sometimes infuriated him. He was endlessly absentminded, leaving almost every hat he ever owned, and a few overcoats, on trains. He burned cigarette holes in most of his suits, never filled in check stubs, and once sat fishing while his tackle box floated out past his feet and sank.

He was a terrible driver with little judgment, and he needed a valet-chauffeur and personal manager, which was his wife. He loved to complain about "TV jolly boys," hated all commercials, yet he would sit mesmerized before one and then complain loudly when it was over to his wife: "Jean, don't buy that." A political cynic, he thought that all politicians were corrupt in one way or another. He was impatient with theories and intellectual "preciousness," but he was awed by academic honors and pursuits (an Oxford don was the most fascinating creature he could think of), and he was hurt and disappointed when his very intelligent daughter, Belden, when elected to Phi Beta Kappa, failed to buy the key.

Randolph could not name five good contemporary novelists or dramatists, but he was entranced by Shakespeare, Cervantes, Gibbon, and Twain. His own column in *The Times* had among its readers many literary figures, one being the novelist Vance Bourjaily, who wrote in one of his books that it was through reading Randolph in *The Times* "that I first realized that it is possible to write of hunting with wit and gentleness, in a spirit of equal love for the creatures hunted and for the follies of those of us who hunt them." Randolph neither knew nor cared what was happening in contemporary music, but he loved opera, Verdi in particular; he always said that he wanted the "Triumphal March" from *Aïda* played at his funeral. It wasn't.

He died of lung cancer in 1961 at a hospital in Massachusetts. He had written the column in *The Times* for five years, and soon another *Times*man filled Randolph's space on the sports page. Randolph spent the last several weeks of his life sitting in a hospital bed, being kept alive on oxygen and miracle drugs until there remained only the husk of the man. He drifted through dope vaguely from consciousness to semiconsciousness. Speaking left him exhausted; listening, only less so. And so he said little and waited with his family and friends in the hospital, but at one point before he died he looked toward the corner and said to his daughter: "Belden, get me my fishing rod."

She had to say that it was not there. He looked a little confused and closed his eyes, seemingly exhausted. Then his hands moved for maybe thirty seconds, not in the random way that the deeply drugged move their hands, but with some direction which at first his daughter did not understand. Then the pattern of his motions made it obvious. He was fly casting.

10

FOR several thousand Americans, their first and only interior glimpse of the *Times* building was provided on a Sunday afternoon in the spring of 1954 when a CBS camera crew from *Omnibus* was admitted to the newsroom to do a live telecast of *Times*men working on the next day's edition. It was, like most *Omnibus* shows, a dignified and erudite presentation, enhanced as always by the soft British voice of Alistair Cooke. While the cameras moved around the newsroom focusing on the bent heads of copyreaders and the furrowed brows of reporters tapping typewriters, Alistair Cooke described the scene in hushed, almost reverential tones that Adolph Ochs would have approved of and appreciated. Cooke's commentary revealed something of the size of the staff, the enormous effort and expense that is required to publish the paper each day, and then he moved across the newsroom to speak with a handsome, gray-haired man who stood leaning, arms folded, against a desk near the bullpen —Arthur Hays Sulzberger, who had come into the office on this Sunday to participate in the show.

Sulzberger spoke warmly of the staff, conveying great pride in them and modesty about himself, and he also gave his views on the role of a free and responsible press in a democracy. Then the cameras moved upstairs to observe a large, broad-shouldered, serious man seated behind his desk—Charles Merz, reading from an editorial that he had just written for tomorrow's *Times*. The cameras later caught the mood and clatter of the composing room on the fourth floor—

the ink-stained printers wearing aprons and picking, pecking, pounding with rubber mallets upon iron tables of type; the silent men who sat straight-spined behind large linotype machines, lightly gliding their fingers over the keyboards amid a tinkling tune of words on paper turning to metal. The cameras also moved into the managing editor's office during a conference, where, at the head of the table, relaxed and avuncular, sat Catledge. On his right was Theodore Bernstein; on his left, Robert Garst. Across from him, at the opposite end of the table, was the city editor, Frank S. Adams, flanked by the foreign-news editor, Emanuel Freedman, and the national-news editor, Raymond O'Neill. Along the sides of the table sat other editors, including the picture editor, John Radosta, who had replaced John Randolph after the DiMaggio-Monroe incident.

Although a few editors were made mildly self-conscious by the presence of cameras and microphones, they generally conducted themselves with remarkable poise, and they apparently proved to be of great interest to the television audience. Seconds after the show had ended, the telephone switchboard at *The Times* began to light up with hundreds of congratulatory calls from readers around the nation, some of them old retired *Times*men who said that the show had made them very nostalgic. There were also several telegrams of praise from *Times* correspondents who had watched the show from their bureaus in major American cities— Richard Johnston wired in from Chicago, Seth King from Des Moines, Gladwin Hill from Los Angeles, Lawrence Davies from San Francisco, as did several others, including Reston from Washington, whose telegram to Catledge read: "You all did fine. Guy just called up and said he wanted to subscribe to *The Times*. Sounded as if he'd never heard about it till today.

It was an altogether satisfying day at *The Times*, one of handshaking and fraternal harmony that confirmed, if only briefly, the picture of unity that had been presented on the television screen. And this picture no doubt reflected positively on the *Times*men themselves, reminding them of the grandeur of the institution and of their meaningful contributions to its purpose, which was something that they had not given much thought to during the past year—a most unhappy year at *The Times*. Three months before the *Omnibus* show, there had been a photoengravers' strike that had been supported by most of *The Times'* news staff, and as a result *The New York Times* failed to publish for the first time in its history. The strike, though it lasted less than two weeks, disrupted not only the publication of the newspaper, but it also inspired deep personal dissension among certain members of the staff: those reporters and copyreaders who crossed the picket line outside the *Times* building had incurred the animosity of the vast majority that had not. And even after the strike had been settled, the strikebreakers within the newsroom were quietly ostracized by *Times*men who now looked to the labor leaders for guidance, not to the spirit of Ochs.

The paper had grown beyond the pale of paternalism, or so it seemed to many on the staff who were aware of top management's desire for a more efficiently run operation—and if this were the case, then the staff members would become more self-protective and practical, more committed to unionism and less romantic about *The Times*. This new attitude was soon apparent in the casual way that certain reporters began to submit overtime slips to the city editor whenever they had worked a half-hour or so beyond their normal quitting time. In the old days, *Times*men would have been too embarrassed to do this, thinking it an honor and pleasure to occasionally work overtime for a newspaper that usually demanded so little of them and had a traditional policy of early good-nights. But the old thinking was fading fast in the newsroom, and while *Omnibus* briefly reminded *Times*men of what the paper represented to the nation, and while this had its salubrious playback in the newsroom for a while, it did not last for very long. Three months after the show, Meyer Berger, the most honored and admired reporter on the New York staff, told a few editors that he was thinking of quitting *The Times*.

They could not believe it. Berger had been a *Times*-man since 1928, and except for one year at *The New Yorker* between 1937 and 1938, he had been the star of the staff, a tall, thin, shy, gentle man with a long nose and soft inquiring dark eyes who sat in the front row and talked to the copyboys, clerks, and reporters who usually stood around his desk; he would regale them with humorous stories, would advise them on the *Magazine* pieces or "Topics of The Times" they were trying to write, and he would listen patiently while they spoke of personal problems. And then, as his deadline approached, he would turn to his typewriter and, within a half-hour, he would produce a dramatic 1,000-word article about a gangland murder that he had covered earlier in the day, or a poignant sidewalk scene that he had observed while coming to work; or he might produce a prose poem to New York:

> New York's voice speaks mystery. . . . It has a soft, weird music, a symphony of wind at high altitudes, of muted traffic in endless serpentine twisting over city hills and grades, of jet hiss and propeller thrum, of the hoarse call of tugs on many waters, of great liners standing in from the broad sea. . . .

There had practically been a work stoppage in the newsroom in 1932 when Berger's stories on the Al Capone tax trial in Chicago began to arrive, page by page, on the telegraph machines: copyboys would grab the pages, reading them as they slowly walked to the copydesk; then the copyreaders would read and reread every word of the courtroom drama and the dialogue of Al Capone; finally the editors would take their turn, being as absorbed as the others before sending the story up to the printers on the floor above.

When Berger wrote similar pieces about the tax trial of Dutch Schultz, even Schultz read them with grudging admiration, although he was offended that Berger had quoted one source as saying that Schultz was a "pushover for a blonde." When the gangster next saw Berger, he called him over and complained about that line.

"But it's the truth, isn't it?" Berger asked.

"Yes," Schultz said, "but what kind of language is that to use in *The New York Times*?"

In 1947, when the first American war dead, in 6,248 coffins, were transported by ship from Europe into New York harbor, Berger produced a journalistic classic—as he did in 1949 when a war veteran named Howard Unruh went berserk in the streets of Camden, New Jersey, and with a pistol shot thirteen people before surrendering to the police. Berger had spent six hours retracing Unruh's footsteps, had interviewed fifty people who had seen parts of the rampage, and then he sat down and reconstructed the whole scene in a 4,000-word article in two and one-half hours:

> . . . Men and women dodged into open shops, the women shrill with panic, men hoarse with fear. No one could quite understand for a time what had been loosed in the block.
>
> Unruh first walked into John Pilarchik's shoe repair shop near the north end of his own side of the street. The cobbler, a 27-year-old man who lives in Pennsauken Township, looked up openmouthed as Unruh came to within a yard of him. The cobbler started up from his bench but went down with a bullet in his stomach. A little boy who was in the shop ran behind the counter and crouched there in terror. Unruh walked out into the sunlit street . . .

Meyer Berger won the Pulitzer Prize for that story, and he sent the $1,000 prize money to Unruh's mother. Berger then spent most of the next two years researching and writing the official history of *The Times*, which in 1951 was marking its hundredth anniversary. This was perhaps the most difficult assignment of his life, not because the task was so formidable for his great reporting talent, but because as the "official" book on *The Times* it had to be approved by various members of the Ochs, Sulzberger, and Adler families, as well as by some senior executives, and it seemed virtually impossible to please them all. There were many deletions and revisions on the book, and when it was published in 1951, and in spite of its critical and commercial success, Berger confessed to a few friends that he sometimes wished his name were not on the book's cover.

And now, in the summer of 1954, after having written his "About New York" column in *The Times* for more than a year, he was again depressed by a few negative reactions to it that he had received from the publisher's office and from an editor in the newsroom. Finally the editor himself felt compelled to record Berger's statements about quitting and to send copies of the memo to other editors and also to the publisher's office:

July 8, 1954—

This is a memorandum on a conversation I had with Mike Berger this afternoon at his instance. He apparently was disturbed at recent evidences of some dissatisfaction with his column which were capped by the criticism I made of the piece he had written for last Monday. . . . He is, of course, very sensitive to criticism and seems to have a feeling that although the column is well liked by readers, it is not well thought of inside the office. I told Mike that he should pay less attention—as I do—to comments within the building than to the reactions that the promotion department reports, which have been uniformly favorable. . . .

Turning to specific comments that have been made about the columns, he referred to a suggestion, which he attributed to the Publisher, that the column should be more topical. He said he did not think that the Publisher realized the difficulty involved in trying to write on top of the news and still keep ahead of the game on future columns. I replied that I thought only some of the columns need be topical, perhaps one out of four, and again offered him the use of a leg-man to help him if he thought it advisable. He again did not seem to like this idea. He mentioned also "tear-jerker" columns, which he thought the Publisher was interested in. He said that while those were all right the mail he receives indicates that what people are most interested in is material about old New York. Again, I told him I thought it was a question of changing pace from time to time. . . .

July 9, 1954—
    Today I understand that he is still in a rather depressed frame of mind and is still talking about the idea of quitting. . . .

Berger did not quit. He continued with his column through July and August, then he took a month's vacation. He returned, somewhat refreshed, but later he again began to complain about the number of changes that he had been ordered to make in his column, and of instances where his column had been killed entirely, requiring that he insert another in its place. He continued to write the column, but said that he did not really like it. He would have preferred to be what he had always been—a reporter.

In the fall of 1954, with the death of Anne O'Hare McCormick, Cyrus Sulzberger took over her three-times-a-week column on the editorial page. This was a full-time job and it meant that Sulzberger could no longer devote time to influencing the foreign staff, for which Catledge was thankful, and Catledge was also pleased to announce within the office that the title "chief foreign correspondent," which Sulzberger had held for ten years, would forthwith be terminated. It was also Catledge's present hope that his foreign-news editor in New York, Emanuel R. Freedman, would become established as the one and only channel through which foreign correspondents should deal with the paper. But some of the correspondents continued either through habit or design to write to Cyrus Sulzberger, or to the managing editor's office, or to the publisher himself. A principal offender was a correspondent in the Far East named Greg MacGregor, who one day received a cable: "CANNOT UNDERSTAND WHY YOU CONTINUALLY BY-PASSING THIS DESK STOP PLEASE EXPLAIN STOP FREEDMAN."

MacGregor was confused by the cable, and when he met up with a friend, Keyes Beech of the *Chicago Daily News*, who had recently visited New York, MacGregor asked if he had ever heard of anyone named Freedman on *The Times*.

"He's your boss, you goddamned fool," Beech said. "He's the foreign editor."

After a bit of research, MacGregor discovered that Freedman had been the foreign editor since 1948. MacGregor tried to reply to Freedman's cable as diplomatically as he could but he suspected that this misunderstanding would not easily be rectified, and, in retrospect, he was sure that he had been right.

Although MacGregor had for years sent photographs to Markel's Sunday department from the Far East—such photographs as battle scenes in Korea, or activities in Formosa, or pictures from other places where he was working as a reporter—MacGregor received a letter from Freedman one day that said, in effect, "Do not forget that your paycheck comes from the third floor." The Sunday department is on the eighth floor. So MacGregor stopped sending pictures to the Sunday department. But while in New York on home leave in 1955, MacGregor was seen by Markel in the *Times* building and was asked why he had ceased to submit pictures. MacGregor said that there was a reason, but that he would rather not discuss it. Markel quickly assured him that anything said would remain confidential, and he pressed for the explanation. After MacGregor had given it, Markel remained silent for a moment, then looking at MacGregor, he asked, "Do you think you're working for Manny Freedman or for *The New York Times*?"

MacGregor replied that he felt exactly the same way, but he asked that Markel look at the situation realistically—he had *already* had a few misunderstandings with Freedman, and he did not want to risk having another one. Markel reassured MacGregor that there would be no problem, adding that he would be having lunch with Freedman in a day or two, that he would broach the matter very discreetly, and that he was confident that MacGregor's expert photography would again be available to the Sunday *Magazine* and the "Review" section.

When MacGregor next saw Freedman a few days later, he looked very dour. Freedman waved him over, saying, "Ah, about that letter you got—I think that you have misunderstood. Or maybe I did not put it just right. I just meant that you should never sacrifice time from your regular news coverage to go out and shoot pictures for the *Magazine*. But of course, we're all working for the same paper."

As Freedman, his eyes looking down at his desk, continued to mumble and shuffle papers, MacGregor interrupted to express the hope that there were no hard feelings. Absolutely not, Freedman said, no hard feelings—but MacGregor did not really think that Freedman sounded as if he meant it. (MacGregor later learned from a friend in the newsroom that Markel had taken the issue up with Sulzberger before mentioning it to Freedman.)

A week later, MacGregor visited the Washington bureau, it being the practice then, as now, for foreign correspondents on home leave to spend time working or observing others at work in the major news departments within the *Times* building, and also to visit the bureau in Washington briefly. The Washington bureau chief was now James Reston, and in the course of a pleasant conversation Reston suggested that MacGregor spend about a month in the capital to get the feel of America again after being away so long in the Orient. MacGregor thought that this was a fine idea, and when Freedman called a few days later to ask when MacGregor would be leaving for Singapore, MacGregor informed him of Reston's plan, to which Freedman asked, "Who is running the foreign desk, Scotty or me?" MacGregor relayed this to Reston, who later called Arthur Hays Sulzberger and also Freedman. Reston then told MacGregor, "Everything's okay, just carry on."

MacGregor remained in Washington for the next three weeks, during which time Reston had lined up a number of appointments for him with government officials, and MacGregor felt that his time in Washington had been both enjoyable and profitable. After arriving in Singapore, MacGregor made out his expense account to cover his home leave, including the per diem charges for his stay in Washington, and mailed it to Freedman. Weeks later, MacGregor received a letter informing him that his Washington expenses had not been allowed. This item represented between $400 and $500. MacGregor wisely decided not to press the issue at this time, but rather to wait until he was again in New York to discuss it personally with Catledge. This he did in 1960, and he was finally reimbursed, although his relations with the foreign desk had now deteriorated beyond repair. After a few years in the newsroom as a general-assignment reporter and a rewrite man on the late-night shift, MacGregor resigned from *The Times* to become editor of an English-language publication that specializes in the coverage of South American affairs.

As soon as Catledge was free to do so, he began making trips abroad and spending time with foreign correspondents, and he frequently was amazed at how well they lived, the number of servants they had, the size of their homes.

In Mexico he visited the young bureau chief, Sydney Gruson, who explained at the outset, "Okay, Turner, while you're here we can go off each morning and see people, and I'll make phone calls, and I'll pretend that this is the way I really work here. Or," Gruson said, eyes lighting up, "we can do what I really do here. I own five race horses, I see them run two or three times a week, and I play golf three or four times a week. And, well, how do you want to do it, Turner?"

"Don't be silly," Catledge said, "we'll do it the way you always do it."

During the next week they had a magnificent time. They went to several parties, they bet on Gruson's horses, losing every time, and went to the bullfights, where Gruson had arranged for a bull to be dedicated in honor of Catledge.

Ten days later, after Catledge had returned to New York, Gruson received word that his Mexican assignment was over. He was to report back to the New York office, and some months later he was reassigned to Prague—with Catledge maintaining that his Mexico trip had nothing to do with it.

Sydney Gruson did extremely well during his assignment in Eastern Europe, and his coverage of the anti-Stalinist revolt in Poland was so outstanding that he was nominated for a Pulitzer Prize. He did not get it, but he did receive from Clifton Daniel, who by then was an assistant to Catledge, a short note in May of 1957:

> Dear Syd:
>   This is a letter of non-congratulation. The Pulitzer Prizes were announced today. You should have had one. I'm sorry you didn't get it.
>
> Sincerely,
> ECD

Sydney Gruson folded this note and tucked it into his wallet, and he carried it with him for the next nine years.

A year after his trip to Mexico, Catledge visited London and was told by the London bureau chief, Drew Middleton, about a bright young man named Sander Vanocur that Middleton wanted to hire for his bureau. Vanocur was then working for the *Manchester Guardian*, and, though still in his mid-twenties, he had already demonstrated talent not only as a reporter but also as a gracious and likable individual who moved easily through the British social and diplomatic scene, and Middleton was convinced that Vanocur would be an asset to *The Times* in London. Catledge, who was now insisting that all hiring be done in New York, said that he would be happy to consider Vanocur's application when the young man was next in the United States. A few months later, during the winter of 1955, Sander Vanocur appeared in Catledge's office.

He was tall, husky, dark-haired, and rather handsome, and he wore a finely tailored suit and brown suede British shoes. Catledge was impressed. Vanocur had, on his own initiative, already gone to Washington to see Reston, having had the appointment arranged by Eric Sevareid, who had known Vanocur when the latter was a stringer for CBS. Reston had liked Vanocur, and so did Catledge; and so did Catledge's special assistant on personnel selection, a former news editor named Richard D. Burritt—who was regarded by irreverent staff members as the office psychiatrist.

Richard Burritt was not really a psychiatrist—this position being held by a licensed practitioner who spent one day a week in the *Times*' Medical department on the thirteenth floor—but Burritt's technique while interviewing an applicant, his tendency to ask personal questions and then to lean back and quietly listen, observing reactions, nodding, analyzing tendencies, nodding, noting the way in which the applicant had knotted his necktie, the width of his lapels—all this, and more, had earned for Richard D. Burritt the title of *Times* "shrink," which he carried with an aura of either notoriety or esteem, depending largely on who was describing him. If Burritt was being described by an individual who had failed Burritt's imaginary psycho-trial, who had been turned away for not being "*Times* material," or who had been hired by Burritt as a copyboy but had never been promoted beyond that, then Richard D. Burritt was seen as a crazed contemptible corporate clod. But if described by an individual whom Burritt had favored and who had subsequently risen from copyboy to clerk, from clerk to reporter, then Burritt was characterized as a sensitive sage, a perceptive appraiser of men, an executive of rare flexibility. Burritt *was* more flexible than his critics would ever concede, a fact that was demonstrated when Bur-

ritt—who preferred hiring as copyboys tweedy graduates of Ivy League colleges who swore by *The Times,*
who would eagerly accept employment in the *Times*
building even as window washers—was approached
one day by a skinny, six-foot five-inch pimply young
army sergeant in uniform. Yet there was something
about the applicant that intrigued Burritt, and, together
with another *Times* personnel expert, Burritt proceeded to interrogate him. Everything was fine until
Burritt asked the applicant to name the college from
which he had graduated.

"I did not attend college, sir," he said.

Burritt shook his head sadly, explaining that all copyboys on *The Times* had to be college graduates, adding
that there were copyboys employed at that very moment who had Master's degrees and Ph.D.'s.

Suddenly and dramatically, the tall sergeant rose to
his feet and announced, "Gentlemen, I regard the
essence of education to be the enlightenment of the
mind by the introduction of ideas!" As the two *Times*
personnel experts looked at him in startled silence, he
continued, "It is true that I am not a college graduate,
but I am literate and articulate and I *dwell* in the realm
of ideas."

"Yes," Burritt interrupted, "we can see that you do,
but you could not live in New York on a copyboy's
salary of $27 a week."

"Leave that to me," he said, and he displayed such
self-assurance that Burritt decided to hire him. Within
a few years he had risen from copyboy to clerk, then
to reporter, and soon he was one of the best reporters
on the paper—McCandlish Phillips.

In the case of Sander Vanocur, the situation was different. He was hired not as a copyboy but as a reporter,
which in many ways was a great advantage over
the way that McCandlish Phillips began on *The Times.*
The copyboy's life consisted of filling paste pots, fetch-
ing galley proofs, walking across the street to obtain
coffee for the copyreaders and rewrite men, and also
a quart of ale for the superintendent of copyboys, a

white-haired stout ruddy man named Steve Moran, whose nightly consumption of ale is one of the unheralded legends of *The New York Times*. After Steve Moran had gone off duty, the copyboys came under the supervision of a tiny tyrannical man named Sam Solovitz who, at four feet eleven inches, resembled an aging jockey, which is what he claimed to be to any woman he met in a Times Square bar. Working under Steve Moran during the late afternoons, or under Sam Solovitz during the evenings, was no bargain in either case, and as a result many copyboys became so obsessed with a determination to escape their plight that they *wrote*; they wrote more than Proust; they stayed all night in the newsroom and borrowed a reporter's typewriter and wrote a "Topics of The Times," or a piece for *The Times'* travel section, or an article for the Sunday *Magazine*, or *anything* that they could get into print and send to Richard Burritt as an example of the "initiative" that he always said was the hallmark of great *Times* reporters. And this is how dozens of copyboys got onto the reportorial staff.

But for a young reporter already on the staff, like Sander Vanocur, the display of "initiative" could be a handicap. Or at least it was during the Nineteen-fifties when the city editor and his subordinate editors, traditionalists all, often misinterpreted initiative in young men as a sign of insubordination or gall or a desire to take stories away from older, more deserving *Times* reporters—particularly on those many days when there were not enough stories to go around. The young reporter was supposed to sit at his desk near the back of the newsroom and await his turn. Sometimes an assistant city editor would wander back and ask him to rewrite a three-paragraph publicity release, or sometimes the reporter would hear his name bellowed over the newsroom microphone, meaning that he was either to report to the city desk for some minor assignment outside the office ("Mr. Vanocur—city desk, please"), or that he should remain at his desk to answer an in-coming call from a funeral home ("Mr. Vanocur —obit, please"). Unlike the copyboys, who at least were kept busy during their working hours, the young reporters would sit and wait.

Occasionally, they would be assigned to substitute for, or to work under, a veteran district reporter in the "East Side shack" or the "West Side shack"—which were two apartments within two buildings near the two major police precincts in mid-Manhattan, the first on East Fifty-first Street, the other on West Fifty-fourth Street; or they might be assigned to the shack in Brooklyn or the one in downtown Manhattan across the street from the headquarters of the New York City Police Department. This assignment consisted mainly of looking out the window at the police precinct to see if there was any "activity," or listening to the Fire Department's bell-code apparatus that was installed within the reporter's shack and periodically clanged out bongs in a special rhythm and frequency that revealed the precise location of the fire that had just been reported somewhere in New York City. All veteran district reporters knew the firemen's bell-code by heart, and they could tell within a second of hearing the bongs how large the fire was, where the fire was located, and whether or not it was worth covering—a decision that was influenced both by the size of the fire and by the progress of the card game that was going on among the reporters from all the newspapers that assigned men full time to shack duty. The shacks were actually like men's clubs, and the reporters who were full-time district men (i.e., reporters who spent their entire working day in a particular shack until a four-alarm fire, or a gangland killing, or a riot demanded that they temporarily leave it and gather the necessary information and *telephone* it into a rewrite man in the newsroom before returning to the shack and the card game: the district men themselves did not write stories) —these reporters liked the life in the shack: it was like a cozy retreat from the wife and the city editor; it was an ideal spot for an older newspaperman who liked to play cards and did not mind the incessant bonging of bells.

But for a younger reporter, life in a shack could be

sheer misery. He could neither sleep nor read novels nor concentrate on his own free-lance writing because of the bells. And it was also very boring to spend hours looking out the window watching the front door of the police precinct—*The Times* did not publish that much crime news anyway. And so the young reporter soon joined the older men from the *Journal-American*, or the *World-Telegram* or the *Herald Tribune*, in a card game, leaving most of the work to be done by the tabloid men from the *Daily News* and the *Mirror,* which featured crime and which usually had reporters who had relatives either on the police force or in the Mafia. Vanocur had neither.

Following his tour of the shacks and after a session as a *Times* correspondent in Queens, Sander Vanocur returned to the newsroom and took his turn on night rewrite. The rewrite bank was a rather caste-conscious place at *The Times* during the Nineteen-fifties. The city editor, Frank S. Adams, who had been a first-rate rewrite man himself during his earlier reporting days, took great interest in the nocturnal performance of the rewrite bank, which consisted of about seven men clustered within three tight rows of desks near the front of the newsroom facing the city editor's desk. The very best late-breaking stories went to the man who sat in the first row on the aisle—he was known as the "dean" of rewrite, and he was unquestionably the most trustworthy and imperturbable under deadline pressure. His name was George Barrett. The other rewrite men in the front row got good stories *if* they occurred when Mr. Barrett was out to dinner, which he had each night at nine o'clock after two J&B's-with-water in Gough's Chop House across the street from the *Times* building, or at Downey's on Eighth Avenue—where he could always be reached should something *really* big occur.

The reporters in the second row were a mixture of old reliables, men who were capable of writing but tired of running, and a few maturing reporters in their final polishing stage prior to becoming foreign correspondents. In the Fifties, this latter group included

Tad Szulc, Bernard Kalb, and Wayne Phillips (no
relation to McCandlish Phillips)—and these three were
very fast and lively and they reflected the spirit that
the city editor wanted to see on his rewrite bank, and
he did not complain when they hung a sign on one of
the pillars overlooking their desks that read: "Greatest
Bank in the World—Human Interest Compounded
Nightly." These three men also played jokes regularly
on the copyboys, and sometimes—using one of the
telephones in the back of the newsroom—they would
phone in a fake story to one of the older unsuspecting
rewrite men, imitating the voice of one of the district
reporters from the shacks, or perhaps the breathless
correspondent that *The Times* had in Riverhead, Long
Island—J. Harry Brown. J. Harry Brown had a very
distinctive telephone style—rapid-fire, repeating every
phrase: "Hello, Hello. This is J. Harry Brown, J. Harry
Brown, in Riverhead, Riverhead, Long Island."

Early one morning in Damascus, Syria, where Wayne
Phillips was then assigned following his triumphant
tour on rewrite, he was suddenly startled from his slumber by a telephone call in his hotel room that began:
"*Hello. Hello. This is J. Harry Brown, J. Harry Brown,
in Riverhead, Riverhead, Long Island.*" Wayne Phillips
had been drinking arrack in an Oriental cabaret until
dawn, and the familiar staccato of J. Harry Brown
brought him bolt upright in bed—until the caller finally
identified himself as Bernard Kalb, Phillips' former
colleague on rewrite, who was being dispatched by
The Times to Djakarta, and whose plane had briefly
stopped at the Damascus airport. Phillips, overjoyed
to hear Kalb, quickly dressed, rushed down through
the hotel lobby, jumped into a taxicab, and roared off
to the airport, where he found Kalb in the terminal.
They had coffee and reminisced until Kalb's plane was
ready for takeoff. On Phillips' way back to the hotel he
encountered along the road a convoy of troops in
trucks and tanks, security guards, road checks, dust,
and confusion. "What's going on," Phillips yelled to
his driver," "an invasion?" The driver stopped to inquire, and then he said to Phillips, "That's what *they*

want to know. From the way you took off for the airport they thought an attack had started."

Sander Vanocur worked on rewrite, but a great story never occurred while Mr. Barrett was out to dinner, or while most of the other rewrite men were busy or away from their desks or gone for the night—which had been Wayne Phillips' good fortune while on rewrite a year before when the poet Maxwell Bodenheim was discovered murdered in a dingy furnished room on the fringes of the Bowery; and which had happened to another young rewrite man, Max Frankel, a year later, in 1956, when after midnight there was the radio flash on the *Andrea Doria—Stockholm* collision at sea. Frankel, who was twenty-six, did a superb job of organizing the facts and writing the story clearly and swiftly, and at 2:34 a.m. the press machines began to roll with Frankel's front-page story and by-line under an across-the-page headline: "*Andrea Doria* and *Stockholm* Collide; 1,134 Passengers Abandon Italian Ship in Fog at Sea." The next day, *The Times'* top reporters, Meyer Berger, Milton Bracker, Peter Kihss, and others took over the story—but Frankel had been the newsroom hero of the night, and later that year, shortly after the outbreak of the Hungarian revolution, he was sent to Vienna to help in *The Times'* coverage of the revolution and the refugees streaming out of the country. Frankel's foreign assignment was listed as "temporary," but he never returned to the New York newsroom. After Vienna he served as a vacation replacement in Belgrade for one month, and then he was assigned to *The Times'* Moscow bureau, where his major assignments included Khrushchev's rise, Zhukov's fall, and the discovery of a young American pianist—Van Cliburn.

Vanocur wrote good stories for *The Times* while on night rewrite and while on general assignments during the day, and he received by-lines; but none of the stories that he wrote in the newsroom between 1955 and 1956 were sufficiently dramatic to be splashed across the front page and gain the attention that might have propelled him toward the overseas assignment that he had hoped for. Catledge seemed to have forgotten all about him, and the only personal attention that he received from an influential editor was brief and meaningless: it occurred late one afternoon when Clifton Daniel, on his way to the men's room, noticed Vanocur sitting behind his desk wearing one of his British suits, and with his brown suede British shoes propped up on the typewriter. Daniel stopped in the aisle, and from a distance of about twenty feet he focused on the shoes and the cut of the suit, recognizing them immediately as British-made—and, though Daniel said nothing, his mood suddenly seemed to drift and fade, perhaps back to some glorious yesteryear in his favorite city, London, and to fleeting recollections of that most adventurous time of his life. . . . Then Daniel stiffened a bit, looked away from Vanocur's shoes, and continued on his way to the men's room.

Not long after that, Sander Vanocur, impatient with the pace of *The Times*, resigned and became a television reporter for NBC, and within a few years he was recognized as one of the very best in the nation.

The years 1955 and 1956 were hardly ideal times for young reporters to be getting a start in the newsroom. Not only was the New York staff so tradition-bound that it would take Catledge several years to make an appreciable dent in its hardened habits, but *The Times'* top management—including Catledge—were very distracted and disturbed in 1955 and 1956 by the intrusive tactics of a Senate subcommittee that was investigating communism in the press and seemed determined to concentrate on the former Communists who were on the payroll of *The New York Times*.

The Senate investigation began in the summer of 1955 with one CBS correspondent's admission that he had been a Communist spy, and it widened in December of 1955 when, before the start of secret hearings in New York, thirty-five subpoenas were issued—twenty-six of them to past or present employees of *The*

Times. In January of 1956, before the start of public hearings in Washington, eighteen subpoenas were delivered—nine of them to *Times* employees, and two to individuals who had recently left *The Times*.

In the history of the paper, there were few months more dismal than December, 1955, and January, 1956. When *The Times* had been scrutinized on other occasions, it could either ignore the issue or easily justify its position, but now it was not so invulnerable. The dynamics of McCarthyism were still pervasive in the land, and *The Times* did have among its reporters and copyreaders, and among its workers in the mechanical departments and other sections within its total employment of 4,000, a number of men who in the past had been members of the Communist party in America. Some had joined the party as students in the Nineteen-thirties, and had quit after a year or two. Some had been party members while working for other newspapers, and had resigned long before joining *The Times*. Others had been party members as recently as a few years ago, although all claimed to be nonmembers at this time. There was supposedly one copyreader, however, who had quit the party before joining *The Times*, then he had rejoined the party—and one afternoon, after subpoenas had arrived in Catledge's office, Catledge walked out into the newsroom to have a word with this copyreader, and discovered him editing a *Times* dispatch from Moscow.

It was a strange, awkward, embarrassing time for the paper, one of suspicion and conflict, anger and compassion. There were *Times* staff members, political conservatives and superpatriots, who now deeply resented those who had been exposed as one-time party members, and as a result some personal friendships and even office courtesies were abruptly ended. There were other staff members who, while they privately abhorred McCarthyism, and while they deeply regretted the exposure of their colleagues, nonetheless were now a bit more cautious and remote in the newsroom when in the company of those who had been named. There were just as many—or more—*Times*men who did not cease being friends with the eight or ten employees on the third floor, or the various others throughout the building, who had been cited by the committee; if anything, friendships may have strengthened at this time, fortified by a determination to remain unintimidated by the witch-hunting tactics of a few subcommittee investigators, whose true purpose was being questioned by *The Times'* top management, and whose methods had already revealed signs of carelessness. One day an investigator entered Catledge's office with a subpoena for one "Willard Shelton." Catledge shook his head, replying that *The Times* had no one by that name (although, to himself, Catledge remembered a Willard Shelton he had known on the *Chicago Sun*). Then the investigator, momentarily confused, asked, "Well, do you have *anybody* named Shelton on your staff?" Catledge said that there was a Robert Shelton—and then, to Catledge's utter amazement, he saw the investigator erase *Willard* and write in *Robert* on the subpoena.

The investigation was in some ways a sham, there seemed little doubt of that; and yet *The Times* could not obstruct the investigative process. And while *The Times'* top executives and editors tried to remain calm and objective, assigning uncontroversial reporters each day to cover the subcommittee's hearings fully and accurately—which was done—the internal repercussions were also felt whenever one of the exposed *Times*men would enter the newsroom and take his place at a copydesk or behind a typewriter. There would be a slight rustle of unnatural movement around him—a forced conviviality on the part of some colleagues, or a brief halt in conversation, or an expression of sympathy, or a conscious avoidance of any mention of the fact that *The Times'* most recent edition had carried the testimony and a photograph of the *Times*-man who had just walked into the newsroom. In one way or another, the entire staff was touched by the inquiry, and the men who had been singled out felt the pressure from many directions. Two veteran reporters who had been listed, and who had appeared before the subcommittee, now went days without an assignment from the city desk. One reporter who had worked in the Washington bureau since 1947, and had covered many stories from the press table in the Senate chamber, was released by Reston and was sent to New York, where, for the next two years, he sat in the last row of the rewrite bank doing what was essentially a clerical job—assembling the daily news summary and index. Eventually, his penance paid, he regained his place as a by-line reporter—though never again in Washington—and he was also denied, years later in New York, a chief correspondent's job for which he was qualified; and he was never completely forgiven by another former Communist in the newsroom for revealing to the FBI the names of party members who had worked on a Long Island newspaper between 1937 and 1939.

On the highest levels of *The Times*—in the offices of Arthur Hays Sulzberger and Orvil Dryfoos, Charles Merz and John Oakes, Turner Catledge and James Reston, and others—there was considerable wrestling with the angels: How could *The Times* remain consistent with Ochs's traditional patriotism and yet not overreact to the investigators and possibly violate the principles of individual civil liberties and freedoms that *The Times* had so clearly espoused for years on its editorial page? There was little doubt among top management that the Senate Internal Security Subcommittee's investigation, headed by Senator James O. Eastland of Mississippi, had singled out *The New York Times* precisely because of the vigor of its opposition to many of the things for which Senator Eastland (and his colleague, Senator William E. Jenner of Indiana, and the subcommittee's counsel, Julien G. Sourwine of Nevada) stood—that is, because *The Times* had condemned segregation in Southern schools, had challenged the abusive methods employed by various Congressional committees, had denounced McCarthyism, had attacked the restrictions of the McCarran Immigration Act; because it had criticized a security system which concealed the accuser from his victim, and because it had insisted that the true spirit of American democracy demanded a scrupulous respect for the rights of even the lowliest individual.

On the other hand, Sulzberger recognized that the press was not sacrosanct, and was as properly subject to Congressional inquiry as any other institution in American life. Sulzberger himself, in his public speeches and statements within the office, said that he was a prejudiced witness for the capitalist system, and that he did not want a single Communist on his payroll, insisting that all employees who had been called by the subcommittee should cooperate, and that he hoped they would not plead the Fifth Amendment. The first two *Times* reporters who had been subpoenaed admitted that they had been members of the Communist party for a short time but had quit in the Nineteen-thirties when they saw that they had made a mistake. But the next witness, a copyreader, refused to reveal his past political background, and when he appeared before the subcommittee, he invoked the protection of the Fifth Amendment. Sulzberger fired him.

His dismissal shocked some of the more liberal members of the staff, and it also brought a letter of protest from the American Civil Liberties Union on the grounds that invoking the Fifth Amendment is a Constitutional right and should not be in and of itself grounds for dismissal. *The Times* published the letter on its editorial page with Sulzberger's reply:

. . . I agree with you wholeheartedly that, particularly when freedoms are under attack, it is vitally important that Constitutional rights be upheld. These include not only the rights guaranteed by the Fifth Amendment, but also the freedom of expression, which, as you point out, is the core of the First Amendment. It seems to me, however, that you have overlooked important consequences of this in your discussion.

. . . Our willingness to trust our associates brings with it a corresponding duty on the part of those who are trusted. They owe candor to their colleagues and equal candor to the public. Those whose business it is to edit and report the news have greater responsibilities than those who follow the ordinary walks of life. . . .

. . . Like any other citizen, a newspaper man has the undoubted right to assert his Constitutional privilege not to incriminate himself. But invocation of the Fifth Amendment places upon him a heavy burden of proof of his fitness to continue to hold a place of trust on the news or editorial staff of this newspaper. And it lays upon the newspaper an obligation to consider whether in view of all the facts, including the stand he has taken, he still is qualified to hold his position. Nowhere is it written that a person claiming protection against self-incrimination should be continued in these sensitive departments where trust and confidence are the tools of a good workman.

This letter was praised in some quarters, denounced in others, and it was very unsatisfactory to a few of the very liberal editorial writers such as John Oakes, who objected to Sulzberger's position against the Fifth Amendment. But Sulzberger persisted in his thinking, and in late November of 1955, as more *Times*men revealed their intentions to not cooperate fully, Sulzberger and Dryfoos had a draft of a statement written to justify the dismissal of future *Times*men who invoked the Fifth Amendment: The draft, dated November 22, 1955, was a form press release that began:

————was dismissed from the news (Sunday news) department of *The New York Times* because, while working in such a sensitive position, he failed fully to disclose his past association with the Communist Party to a duly constituted committee of the United States Senate. By invoking the Fifth Amendment, Mr.———— exercised a Constitutional right. He failed, however, in our judgment, to give sufficient consideration to the specific obligation resting upon newspapers by reason of the guarantees under the First Amendment. A community

which is assured a free press is entitled to a frank
press. In this instance frankness was not forthcoming.

When John Oakes received a copy of this statement
for his opinion, he scribbled across the top of it a
sentence to Orvil Dryfoos—"Orv: I don't think this is
at all adequate. JBO." Oakes, though a member of the
Editorial Board, was years away from replacing Charles
Merz as the editor of the editorial page; still, Oakes
had written most of the anti-McCarthyism editorials
for *The Times*, and he was never hesitant about expressing his views to Merz, or to Dryfoos, who was
then a vice-president, or to the publisher himself, Sulzberger. On January 2, 1956, Oakes wrote Sulzberger:

Dear Arthur:
　　Since our conversation a few weeks ago re *Times*
policy on Fifth Amendment cases, I've been doing a good deal more thinking on the subject. I
still don't see how we can take a position automatically firing Fifth Amendment people and at
the same time remain consistent with our own editorial view as expressed as recently as this spring.
　　What to me is much more serious, I don't see
how we can do this and avoid the charge that we
have knuckled under to the Eastlands. That is
what really worries me most of all.
　　I am very much concerned that anything we write
in the future on basic civil liberties and Bill of
Rights problems will be weighed against our own
actions and statements in this critical situation.
Therefore, much as I favor making public our
views about the committee and its investigation, I
urge that we do not irrevocably commit ourselves
on any Fifth Amendment position. If we handle
each case on its merits, and if we make no declarations of Fifth Amendment policies, I think we will
be in an infinitely stronger position and will save
ourselves much future embarrassment.
　　　　　　　　　　　　　　　　　　　　　　JBO

Turner Catledge was personally acquainted with Mississippi's Senator James O. Eastland. They were not close friends, but Catledge had known of the Eastland family from his boyhood days in Mississippi, and Senator Eastland's father, Woods Eastland, had been the district attorney in Catledge's district, and Catledge had regarded Woods Eastland in those days as a kind of hero. During a brief period when Turner Catledge thought that he might wish to become a lawyer, and when he wanted to conjure up an impressive figure that he might emulate, he invariably thought of Woods Eastland. While James O. Eastland had never stirred Catledge's fancy in quite that way, Catledge was sure that he could go down to Washington during the investigation and have a warm, personal chat with the Senator and perhaps discover what it was that Eastland hoped to achieve by giving so much attention to *The Times*, and to cooperate in any way that he could.

Catledge arrived in Eastland's office on a Sunday afternoon, and the Senator was affable and smiling, and he took Catledge's hand and said, with sincerity, "*Hell*, Turner, I'm not trying to get *The Times*."

"Well, what are you after then?" Catledge asked.

"Well," Senator Eastland said, shrugging his shoulders, "nothing, really."

And there was very little else that Eastland would add —it turned out to be a rambling, smiling, unproductive afternoon for Catledge, with Eastland indicating that he did not know what was going on, and that it was the subcommittee's counsel, Julien G. Sourwine, who was spearheading the investigation. But when James Reston later interviewed Sourwine while writing a piece for *The Times*—describing the counsel as "squat, soft-spoken"—Sourwine insisted that he had never done anything without the permission of Senator Eastland, and certainly had never issued any subpoenas without authorization. Catledge did not really know what to think after concluding his talk with Eastland, except to remind himself that the Eastlands were planter types from the Delta, and in Mississippi it was said by some Mississippians that Delta people were a most peculiar breed—they were property people, shifty as the seasonal cycles they lived by, social people who did not want to be caught treading on anyone's toes, oblique people who talked one way, acted another, and were hard to know—or so it was said.

Those who knew Catledge during this period thought that *he* was becoming hard to know. He was often remote and vague. He had been separated from his wife in 1948 and was spending a good deal of time in Sardi's bar, so much in fact that his picture was soon hanging on the wall and his name was on the menu ("Veal Cutlet Catledge"); and now, in 1955, he revealed to his friends a deeper sense of frustration and failure, and once he told them that he thought he might be replaced as the managing editor.

If Arthur Hays Sulzberger had ever given consideration to this, he kept it to himself. The only obvious change in Sulzberger's attitude now seemed to be his decision to harden *The Times'* position with regards to the Eastland subcommittee, and to take a somewhat softer line on the Fifth Amendment—although a second *Times* copyreader had since been fired, and an assistant to the Sunday "Book Review" editor had resigned under pressure, after seeking protection under that amendment.

But the opinion of John Oakes as expressed in his earlier memo to Sulzberger—". . . If we handle each case on its merits, and if we make no declarations of Fifth Amendment policies . . ."—seemed to have influenced Sulzberger, Dryfoos, and Merz. And in a long editorial in *The Times* in January of 1956, Merz wrote:

> . . . In the case of those employees who have testified to some Communist association in the past, or who have pleaded the Fifth Amendment for reasons of their own, it will be our policy to judge each case on its own merits, in the light of each individual's responsibilities in our organization and of the degree to which his relations with this newspaper entitle him to possess our confidence.

Then, with an emotion that does not often penetrate *The Times*, Charles Merz ended his editorial with a paragraph that Sulzberger particularly approved of:

> We cannot speak unequivocally for the long future. But we can have faith. And our faith is strong that long after Senator Eastland and his present subcommittee are forgotten, long after segregation has lost its final battle in the South, long after all that was known as McCarthyism is a dim, unwelcome memory, long after the last Congressional committee has learned that it cannot tamper successfully with a free press, *The New York Times* will still be speaking for the men who make it, and only for the men who make it, and speaking, without fear or favor, the truth as it sees it.

11

IN the spring of 1957, in a trip that would produce both a journalistic coup and a wonderful excuse for being away from the office, Turner Catledge went to Russia. He had no idea beforehand that Nikita Khrushchev would grant him an exclusive interview, but the Soviet Union was still following its so-called peace offensive—"Party-Going in Moscow is New Party Line," read a recent headline—and so Catledge, reacting instinctively, sent cablegrams to Khrushchev and Bulganin, to Zhukov, Molotov, Gromyko, and others and on the evening of April 28, he boarded a plane in New York for Copenhagen, then switched to a Russian plane, and landed the next day in Moscow. He was met at the airport by *The Times*' bureau chief, William Jorden, who told him that a big reception, given by the Japanese Ambassador in honor of the Emperor's birthday, was being held in a Moscow hotel. So they went—and it was there that Catledge met Khrushchev.

Catledge saw Khrushchev standing in a large, crowded room, a jovial, smiling porcine man encircled by Japanese diplomats and journalists. Catledge also noticed in another part of the room the stocky figure of Nikolai Bulganin, president of the Soviet Council of Ministers, standing near several long tables on top of which were dirty plates, empty and overturned bottles, used glasses, and rumpled linen from what had obviously been a grand feast. Bulganin was also surrounded by people, but it was a smaller crowd than Khrushchev's, although Bulganin too was smiling, bowing to the Japanese, and behaving no differently, Catledge thought, than a Kentucky colonel at an after-Derby party.

Catledge's bureau man, Jorden, who spoke Russian and a bit of Japanese, led him toward Bulganin's circle and made the introductions. Bulganin bowed low, extended his hand, and welcomed Catledge to the Soviet Union. After a few more pleasantries, Bulganin proposed a toast. He turned around looking for a bottle, but the liquor had run out. Then an aide came running with another bottle of vodka, and Bulganin and Catledge raised glasses to mutual happiness and health. At that moment, Khrushchev appeared, bouncy and red-faced, and Bulganin introduced him to Catledge. This led to another toast. Catledge did not make his bid for the interview at this time, but it was a propitious beginning, and it was followed later in the week by more of the same. At one party, a Soviet official toasted Catledge by saying, "Here's best to *The New York Times*," adding, "Of course, what *I* think is best for *The New York Times* and what *you* think is best for *The New York Times* are greatly different. But here's to the difference."

After watching the May Day parade, and after sightseeing trips to Kiev and Leningrad, Catledge was informed that his request for an interview had been accepted by Khrushchev, who asked that Catledge appear at the Kremlin on Friday afternoon, May 10. Catledge went to bed early the night before. He already had a list of questions that he had previously prepared with the help of Salisbury and Daniel in New York, and Jorden in Moscow. Catledge arrived at the Kremlin at the appointed hour with Jorden and a press official from the Soviet Foreign Ministry. As they were ushered into Khrushchev's office, Khrushchev bounced up from behind his desk, extended his pudgy little hand, and led Catledge to a long wooden table, seating Catledge in a chair next to himself.

Catledge, through an interpreter who sat at the head of the table, began by saying that he had not come to Russia to argue about anything, but rather to obtain Khrushchev's views and to pass them along to readers of *The Times*. Catledge explained that he was in charge of the "factual" side of *The Times*, and had nothing to do with the "editorial" side, a distinction that Khrushchev could not understand, and he indicated somehow that it was a crazy way to run a newspaper. But he motioned for Catledge to proceed with the questions, and the interview lasted for two hours. It was characterized by a friendly tone toward the United States, a hope for coexistence, a reminder of Soviet strength; it was a reaffirmation of Khrushchev's demonstrated anti-Stalinism, which, through *The Times*, he was conveying directly to the capitalists on Wall Street and the politicians in Washington.

As the interview continued, Khrushchev seemed to warm up even more, gesticulating freely, giving long answers; and while Catledge waited for the translation, he lapsed into reflections. Catledge tried to remind himself of the importance of the occasion—to impress upon himself that he was at this moment sitting at the very center of the international Communist conspiracy, in the presence of the chief engineer of the apparatus, a powerful little man who could influence the preservation of peace or the destruction of the world. Catledge could convince himself of this intellectually. He accepted this as a fact. But he simply could not *feel* it. Perhaps it was the lack of distance. This face-to-face meeting with communism's number one man left nothing to imaginary free play, journalistic interpretation, televised hallucination, the whole gambit of informational gadgetry that could produce games of panic— that *did* during the McCarthy days cause national suspicion; that did during the bomb scare chase optimists into fallout shelters and others out of cities; that did during the Eastland hearings agitate the equilibrium of *The Times* itself. But in the Kremlin, where Catledge could hear Khrushchev's breathing, could see his blue eyes and ruddy face and neck and workman's hands—and know that, with proper attire, Khrushchev could fit that Saturday-afternoon scene in the courthouse square of some Mississippi town—here the menacing specter of Communist aggression that

Catledge had been hearing about for years did not alert him, fascinate him, pacify or move him in any way— he could feel nothing, he had hit an emotional dead-spot; and months later, he would still be trying to ana-lyze this lack of reaction.

As the interview ended, Khrushchev stood, shaking Catledge's hand again and wishing him well. Khrush-chev said he would like to continue the interview, but that he now had to go out to meet the Mongolian delegation. He did mention the possibility of visiting the United States, but added, with a chuckle, that he could not come as a tourist without being fingerprinted, and he did not like that. Catledge quickly pulled out his Defense Department Accreditation Card to show *his* fingerprints on the back of it, explaining that no one in America took offense at being fingerprinted for such documents.

"Then you must be a criminal," Khrushchev said with a laugh. Then Khrushchev walked with Catledge and Jorden and the Soviet press aide through the outer office into the main corridor, and there he left them, tipping his little hat as he waddled away, saying, "Off to see the Mongolians."

While visiting other *Times* bureaus on his way back to New York, Catledge was quickly reunited with the reality of his own regime. One *Times* correspondent, an old friend, reminded Catledge of a promised raise in salary, a substantial raise, and Catledge said that he had not forgotten it. But the correspondent, suspecting perhaps that it would be a long time before he would again have the managing editor's undivided attention, pressed the issue—and, after a few more drinks with Catledge, the conversation became very direct and per-sonal, with the correspondent charging that Catledge, his old friend, had greatly disappointed and failed him. Then a rather unexpected thing happened, one that might have been triggered by Catledge's travel fatigue or the liquor or other inexplicable factors—but tears now came into Catledge's eyes, and there was a sudden release of open emotion, honesty, hostility, the admission of frustrations that he had felt in New York. The reason that the raise had not come through, Catledge said, was that the budget had been frozen by the publisher's office. It seemingly was not Sulzberger's decision so much as it was that of Orvil Dryfoos, who, at forty-four, had become president of The New York Times Company. Sulzberger was still the publisher, but he had not been feeling well this year, having some of the symptoms of the series of strokes that would follow; and, at sixty-five, he had decided to delegate more authority to his son-in-law and successor.

The Times was still making an annual profit—in fact, the company had been in the black each year since Ochs had bought it. But the rising cost of newspaper production, and the recession in 1957, had cut into The Times' profits, which were never as large as outsiders generally presumed, since the Sulzberger family had followed Ochs's policy of reinvesting most of the profit back into the business. It had become one of the corporate jokes within The Times that most of the money earned did not come from publishing the greatest newspaper in the world but from the 42 percent interest that Ochs had bought in 1926 in a paper-making mill in Canada—The Times made more money producing paper without words than paper with words. The Spruce Falls Power & Paper Co., Ltd., of Toronto, which supplied two-thirds of The Times' paper, had accounted for about 53 percent of the New York Times Company's total profit in recent years. The rest of the company's earnings came largely from advertising, although in 1957 this income had decreased, largely because of the recession, which caused a 24 percent loss in revenue from the help-wanted ads. Between 1956 and 1957, there was a $624,245 drop in profits, which meant that The New York Times' net income after taxes had been only $1,426,814—an amount that The Times' correspondent overseas could not accept as justification for withholding his raise, but Catledge was powerless to do anything about it now.

While Catledge's relationship with Dryfoos was cordial, it was not to be compared with the friendship en-

joyed by Reston, or by a vice-president of *The Times*
named Amory H. Bradford. Bradford was a lean, lanky
New Englander, the son of a Congregational minister
and a graduate of the Yale Law School, former intelligence officer who had married Carol Warburg Roth-
schild—an altogether formidable man. When Amory
Bradford addressed the other executives on the fourteenth floor, he seemed to know everything that was
going on within the building, seemed to have even the
most infinitesimal facts at his fingertips, and Dryfoos
was pleased to have such a man on his staff.

Catledge did have a fine relationship with Arthur
Hays Sulzberger's son, Arthur Ochs Sulzberger—
known as "Punch"—but Punch Sulzberger had little
power, and if he had any ability or promise, he had so
far concealed it. He had a reputation within the office
as a playboy, and Dryfoos would often complain that
Punch did not even *read The Times*. At thirty-one,
Punch Sulzberger held the title of assistant treasurer,
although nobody in the newsroom knew precisely what
he did. They knew only that he had done badly in the
schools he had attended, had joined the Marines, had
been married and divorced, and that he was an amiable
young man who often ended up in Catledge's back
office late in the afternoon, after the news conference,
when Catledge was mixing drinks for some of his
Times cronies.

But Catledge himself seemed at loose ends now, and
he had been out of the office so much that many staff
members assumed that Theodore Bernstein was running the department—although this assumption required adjusting later in 1957 when Catledge promoted Clifton Daniel to the rank of assistant to the
managing editor, a position from which Daniel could
peruse the daily practices and prerogatives of Bernstein.

After Catledge had returned from Russia, he was off
again to San Francisco to attend a convention of the
American Society of Newspaper Editors. It would turn
out to be a fortunate trip. One editor at the convention introduced Catledge to a fine-looking, dark-haired
woman from New Orleans who appealed to Catledge

very much, and when he returned to New York he seemed more refreshed and decisive than he had been in a long time.

One of the first items on his schedule was to hire a new food editor; the woman who had held the job for years had just resigned because her husband's business required that he be transferred out of New York, and the applicant for her job that Catledge was to see on this day was a man—a somewhat shy, blushing man with a round, smiling face and rosy cheeks who, upon entering Catledge's office, introduced himself as Craig Claiborne.

The idea of a man holding the food editor's job had never occurred to Catledge, because, in addition to making the rounds of restaurants and writing knowledgeably about them, it was also important that *The Times'* food editor be able to cook well, to compile recipes, and to feel comfortable while working within a circle of lady journalists in the Women's-news department on the ninth floor.

"Where did you go to school, son?" Catledge began, after Claiborne had sat down.

"Mississippi State, suh," Claiborne said.

Catledge nodded approvingly. Then he asked, "Where did you live down there?"

"Polecat Alley," Claiborne said, referring to a somewhat rundown row of student quarters on the campus.

Catledge smiled.

"So did I."

When Catledge asked if Claiborne felt qualified for the job on *The Times*, Claiborne said that he did. He had, after leaving Mississippi State, obtained a journalism degree from the University of Missouri; and in 1953, after his release from the Navy, he had graduated from the Swiss Hotelkeepers Association in Lausanne, which some gourmets consider to be the best cooking school in the world—although Claiborne *did* admit that *The Times'* food editor's job was an awesome assignment, one that no cooking school could entirely prepare him for. He also said that he had heard that Mr. Markel already had someone in mind for the job.

Catledge reddened in anger.

"*I* do the hiring and firing around here, son," he said.

Then, calm again, Catledge asked Claiborne to tell more about himself, and Craig Claiborne, relaxing as Catledge seemed to relax, proceeded to tell something of his personal life, although not too much, for there were parts of it that made him uneasy, even petulant at times, emotions that he usually concealed nicely behind his smiling friendly face.

His mother had run a boardinghouse in the small Mississippi town of Indianola, and she was a fantastic cook. There had been an article in *Liberty* magazine years ago about her cooking, and even after he had returned from school in Lausanne he still made use of the manuscript cookbook that she had once given him. She had been born Mary Kathleen Craig in Alabama, a veritable Southern belle when she was younger. But though her family was prosperous, there had been drinking problems bordering on alcoholism not only among her kin but also among some of their friends— and as a result, she would never allow whiskey in her own home except at Christmas time, when she made eggnog heavily spiked with bourbon, and she was not above soaking bourbon into the fruitcake. Craig Claiborne remembered that in order to get the bourbon, his mother would give money to one of the boarders and ask that a bottle be obtained from the bootleggers. Like many good Mississippians, she condoned bootlegging but loathed whiskey.

She had married a man fifteen years her senior whom she always referred to as *Mister* Claiborne—even, Craig suspected, in bed. Mister Claiborne was a quiet man, an accountant by trade who might have done better as a minister. He never missed the Methodist church services on Sunday mornings, or the prayer meetings on Wednesday evenings. As a boy he had gone to tent meetings with other zealously religious members of the Claiborne clan across the border in Tennessee,

where he had been born, and he had a sister who had
served as a missionary in China and had known Henry
Luce when he was a boy. Until her dying day she believed that Luce was the founder and editor of *McCall's*.

Mister Claiborne's failure to make money was the
main reason that his big rambling white house eventually took in boarders; but he seemed not to notice
them, nor was he distracted or influenced by their
habits. He read his Bible, and milked the cows each
morning, raised chickens and grew vegetables that
were served at the table, and he never drank anything
stronger than Coca-Cola, which he called "dope," and
the only time he was heard to say "damn" was when
the pickup truck that he was driving collided with
another car. Though the boarders tried often to entice
him into a game of cards on Sunday afternoons, he always smiled softly and shook his head. Then one Sunday, someone opened the door to his upstairs bedroom
—and there he was, playing solitaire.

Young Craig Claiborne learned whatever he learned
about the facts of life from Negro nurses. His mother,
when she was not cooking or otherwise supervising the
house, was usually playing bridge. At Indianola High
School, he was shy and unathletic, and the football
coach—who was also the mathematics instructor—
called him "sissy" in front of the class, and even now
Craig Claiborne cannot cope with arithmetic. During
World War II he enlisted in the Navy, then reenlisted
during the Korean War, finding in this shifting existence a marvelous escape from the sense of suffocation
that he felt in the house dominated by his mother,
whom he alternately adored and despised, and with
whom he would ultimately compete—and surpass.

He can remember precisely the moment when he
felt the culinary calling. It was in 1949, while he was a
passenger aboard the *Ile de France*, about to see Paris
for the first time, and at dinner he was served fillet of
turbot princesse—turbot with a white-wine-and-mush-
room sauce—and, as he later described it to a friend, it

was a little like getting religion, or more exactly, it was the *dépucelage* of a palate.

Previously he had done much of his own cooking, but now he had savored cooking as an art, and he began to contemplate a career that would somehow combine cooking and writing and earning a living. It was with this in mind that he went to Lausanne in 1953, and he graduated eighth in a class of sixty. Settling in New York, he tried to get a job on *Gourmet* magazine. When there were no openings at first, he took an interim job as a bartender and continued to call *Gourmet* until there was an opening as a receptionist; he accepted this, and eventually worked up to an editorial position. He had meanwhile met the woman who was *The Times'* food editor, having called her one day shortly after returning from Lausanne suggesting that a story be written about himself: "How would you like to interview a young Mississippian who's just graduated from the best cooking school in the world?" She wrote the story, and the two became friends. Thus he knew in advance about her plans to resign in 1957, and at her suggestion he applied to *The Times*; and one morning he was called to appear in the office of Turner Catledge. It was a perfect time for Claiborne to apply. Catledge had not had an easy or uncomplicated decision to make in a long time, and the appearance of a young man from Mississippi wanting to become the food editor appealed to Catledge's fancy. And when Claiborne mentioned that Markel had someone else in mind for the job, that cinched it—"*I* do the hiring and firing around here, son"—and Claiborne was hired.

It was a decision that Catledge did not regret. Within a remarkably short time, Craig Claiborne became one of the best-known by-lines on the paper and possibly the most-feared customer of restaurants in New York. Unlike his predecessor, whose reportorial eye reflected more the viewpoint of a market browser and home-maker than a critic, Claiborne placed great emphasis on restaurant criticism, eating all of his meals out, including breakfast, and he began publishing in *The Times* a restaurant-rating system—four stars for superb, no stars for heartburn. Soon, the headwaiters of dozens of restaurants were on the alert for his visit. A few had obtained from mysterious sources small photographs of him, which they posted behind the cash register or in the kitchen. But even with a photograph Claiborne is not easily picked out of a crowd, having no distinguishing facial characteristics, and being neither tall nor short, thin nor fat. He also never makes a reservation in his own name, either appearing without a reservation or using the name of his guest. He prefers dining with at least one other person, and sometimes two or three; this allows him to sample a wide variety of dishes. He will often order for everybody at his table a different dish, and he will taste a bit off each plate. He *never* finishes a single dish, and as a result he keeps his weight to where he wants it. Each morning before leaving his apartment in Greenwich Village or his home in East Hampton, he weighs himself, usually registering exactly 150 pounds. Each evening he weighs 160 pounds. He can tell during the day from what he is eating how much he is weighing at that moment, and he can also predict what effect, if any, it will have on his skin coloring (which occasionally breaks out into a rash in the line of duty), and on his digestive system. Though rarely dyspeptic, he always carries in his pocket, in a small black enamel box, several digestive pills. So far he has never been poisoned.

If the food in a restaurant that he is visiting for the first time is especially good or bad, he will most likely return and dine again before writing his critique, hoping to determine whether the chef had previously been lucky or unlucky. While sampling the food, Claiborne is also attentive to the decor of the restaurant, the table arrangement and sound (he hates Muzak), the efficiency of the waiters, their speed at emptying ash trays, and their general appearance. There are restaurateurs who consider Claiborne a jinx: as soon as he arrives, it seems, something awful happens. The air-conditioning may fail, or a tray of dishes may crash to the floor, or an argument may erupt between an intoxicated diner and a rude waiter because of the restaurant's policy against credit cards. Claiborne himself has had bread rolls bounced on his head and shoulders, has had silverware knocked out of his hands, has been doused with ice water and hot soup. He accepts all this with resignation and good humor—as the stars recede in his mind —and even when trying to digest an indigestible mouthful, he attempts to repress his reaction, although a look of mild pique creases his face occasionally as he softly complains to his guest: "There is *margarine* in the hollandaise."

His favorite restaurants (four stars) are both French —La Grenouille and La Caravelle, whose prices are no object because he is on an expense account. Even when he is displeased with a restaurant, however, he is not—like *The Times'* drama and film critics—capable of mayhem. At the very worst, Claiborne may chastise an otherwise commendable New York restaurant because "the tables are too close for total comfort, a recent bottle of Valpolicella was too tart for pleasure, and the restaurant's ventilation leaves something to be desired" (one star); or, in the case of a restaurant that he visited in Washington, D.C., he complimented the "exuberant smile and enthusiasm" of the owner-chef and then wrote that "the decor is gauche modern, with starburst chandeliers and sparsely covered walls, and the quality of the cooking is uneven, ranging as it has on occasion from an excellent rack of lamb to a small plate of overcooked asparagus with tasteless hollandaise and an ordinary preparation of duck à l'orange" (no stars). In addition to writing his reviews and feature stories, Claiborne also edits the recipes and does his share of food testing in the office with the newspaper's home economist and the second-string restaurant critic, who refers to herself as "the Craig Claiborne of the depressed areas." Claiborne had also found time to edit a number of cookbooks. One of them, *The New York Times Cookbook*, has sold more than 200,000 copies. But he is extremely modest about his success, attributing much of it to the fact that he is published in *The New York Times* and has little competition from other daily connoisseurs—cribbling a line, he comments on his fame: "It is not that I am the ultimate in my profession but it may be that I am the only one."

Turner Catledge's desire for a more tightly edited *Times*—a fast-reading newspaper that would report more fully and interpret more trenchantly than television—could not be fulfilled without the aid and guidance of Theodore Bernstein. *And*, if Catledge allowed Bernstein the necessary freedom to achieve the desired goals, it was inevitable, sooner or later, that Bernstein would incur the displeasure of one of the remaining independent dukes, who was used to working unchallenged—the Sunday editor, Lester Markel.

This began to happen when, shortly after Catledge had made Bernstein an assistant managing editor, Bernstein proceeded to appraise in his interoffice periodical, *Winners & Sinners*, not only the work of the daily staff, but also the efforts of Markel's Sunday department. Markel did not appreciate this. If judgments were to be made on the Sunday department, Markel would make them himself.

It was not strictly a jurisdictional issue with Markel, although that was a factor—Markel was becoming uneasy about the whole new trend of thinking on the third floor: the advocacy of interpretative reporting (which had long been the specialty of Markel's "Week in Review" section); the introduction of such daily "background" features as the "Man in the News" profile, the news analyses, the in-depth articles (which had been a function of the Sunday *Magazine* and the "Review"). And there were Bernstein's various and prissy rules about writing and copyreading that, while perhaps applicable to the regular staff, were not so suitable for the Sunday department as Markel wished to run it. One of Theodore Bernstein's principles that Markel questioned was that, in the interest of clarity and comprehension, a single sentence in *The Times* should usually not contain more than one idea. After this suggestion appeared in *Winners & Sinners*, Markel dictated a memo:

> Mr. Bernstein:
> I have read with great interest your special edition on the short sentence—
> Or rather—
> I have read your edition of Winners & Sinners. It is a special edition. It interests me. No end.

Markel then had working on his Sunday *Magazine* an urbane and exacting writer named Gilbert Millstein, whose dazzling style was a conspicuous contradiction of nearly every one of Bernstein's principles. While Bernstein preferred short leads, Millstein wrote long ones; while Bernstein stressed simplicity, Millstein epitomized complexity; while Bernstein wanted one-idea-per-sentence, Millstein often crammed in a half-dozen. And almost every week, it seemed, Lester Markel would publish a Gilbert Millstein article in the *Magazine* or drama section that not only emphasized the individuality of the writer but also emphasized the separate editing standards of the Sunday department; a typical Millstein lead began:

> It is an impressive tribute to the rationale of modern industry that while it took the theatre something like 2,500 years, give or take a century, to produce the image of the playwright, fining him down here, shading him there, ripening him quietly, like a chunk of Stilton, television has eliminated all such waste motion, briskly packaging a race of dramatists in a decade and even endowing them with readily indentifiable caste marks.

Or:

> One of the most highly developed and gratifying forms of riding to the hounds of culture (up the hills of status, down the dales of acceptance as, in full cry, they bay at the heels of the Philistines)

is attendance at the opening of an art show, a phenomenon so far removed from its original function, the exhibition of paintings for sale, as to be, like the vermiform appendix, vestigial.

Lester Markel saw himself as one of the great editors of his time; or, now that Harold Ross of *The New Yorker* was dead, perhaps *the* great editor. Markel had joined *The Times* before its peak period of accelerated growth, and he had expanded his Sunday department as the paper itself had expanded, both forces riding the crest of a rising American economy that would produce after World War II a larger, better-educated, more concerned, more prosperous, more acquisitive society—a portion of which would find *The Times* indispensable, particularly on Sundays, when there was more time to spend with it.

The appeal of the Sunday *Times* was due to several factors, some of which Markel had little or nothing to do with—the tremendous volume of advertising, for example, that the aggressive army of admen under Monroe Green brought in and which was read as avidly as was the news; ads for cars, mink coats, motorboats, houses to buy, apartments to rent, secretaries to hire, dresses from Bonwit's, dresses from Bergdorf's, dresses from Gimbel's—no matter what condition the world was in, no matter how many soldiers had just been ambushed, nor who had just been assassinated, nor who was rioting or starving to death, pretty dresses danced next to the gray columns of news in *The Times* every Sunday of every month of every year.

The Sunday *Times* was prosperous, too, because the newspaper's circulation staff placed it in every major city in the nation, and because the promotion men proclaimed it on billboards, in booklets, in schools, spoonfeeding it to the future affluent society; and it was also successful because the main news section of the Sunday edition, produced under Catledge's aegis on the third floor, carried more news items than did competing journals—more football scores, more engagement announcements, more dispatches from more cities around the world.

But what really made the Sunday *Times* unique were those features that were completely controlled by Lester Markel—the Sunday *Magazine*, the "Week in Review," the "Book Review," the drama section, the travel section; the pages on art, television, music, dance; the garden page, the do-it-yourself page, the various special sections on fashion or home furnishings or children's books or high-fidelity recordings. Markel inspired many of the ideas for these sections, wrote headlines, scrutinized picture layouts, read every word that his staff or his contributors had written; edited every line before it was set into type. Markel was an indefatigable, driving man who terrorized many members of his staff; and yet, if a person had never seen him before, or was unaware of his reputation, Markel would appear to be a rather unstriking, plaintive individual. He had an angular face that suggested no special vitality; wavy gray-black hair combed tightly back from his high forehead, and soft, timidly inquiring eyes behind steel-rimmed glasses. His voice was not strong; it was, in fact, almost high-pitched, wavering and imploring when he spoke normally. But since he so rarely spoke normally in the office, the Markel voice that a stranger might overhear in the lobby of a theater or at a cocktail party was not the voice that was most familiar to *Times* employees in the Sunday department. With them, Markel was more often shrieking with anger. And since he never seemed stationary, but was always moving determinedly about the office in restless pursuit of something or someone, or was frowning at a photograph that had just been shown him, or was dissatisfied with the article that he had just read or the answer that he had just received—since Markel's physique was so overwhelmed by his emotions, his staff did not know so much how he looked as how he felt, and how he was making *them* feel. The tension within the Sunday department was such, many *Times*men said, that they could sense it even as they rode in an elevator passing by the eighth floor, a claim that was accepted as an exaggeration by almost every-one except those who worked on the eighth floor.

Upon leaving the elevator on the eighth floor and entering the Sunday department, one passed the receptionist, a convivial red-faced gentleman: to his left was a door leading into the Sunday "Book Review"; to his right was a dim corridor that led past the door of Markel's office, and past the office doors of two senior editors—Daniel Schwarz, a tall man with a fixed smile, and Lewis Bergman, a sensitive man of inner turmoil. At the end of the corridor, in a very large room that extended the length of the building, and contained sixty or seventy desks arranged in rows or at right angles, sat most of Markel's staff, usually in various states of distraction or concentration—typing, reading, talking, or staring into space; writing, rewriting; editing, re-editing. Since the *Magazine* deadline was Monday, the "Book Review" Wednesday, the drama section Thursday, the "Week in Review" Saturday, there was an uneven distribution of daily pressure within the department: while the *Magazine* people were working furiously with last-minute changes on articles or layouts, the "Week in Review" people were sitting casually on the other side of the room reading newspapers, their deadline being days away. But when Markel, who checked everything and was *always* under deadline pressure, walked into the room, he would immediately transmit an intensity that everyone could feel. He had merely to enter, to stand in the aisle and look around for a few moments, and it was like a hot blazing sun curling caterpillars, legs tucking inward, bodies slowly bending —it was, as Gilbert Millstein might write, an ordeal by fire, an apocalyptic experience.

Many members of the Sunday staff were deep in analysis, and it was their involvement with the psychological, their acute awareness of themselves and their work, their love-hate relationship with Lester Markel—"Markel," one of them said, "is our great Jewish father-figure, and we are his sons, and he has a way of convincing us that we are always failing him"— that distinguished the Sunday staff from the larger, more impersonal staff that worked in the newsroom on the third floor. Also, the two staffs looked different.

While nearly all the reporters and copyreaders were conventionally dressed, very *bourgeois* in their button-down shirts and ties and suits of unexceptional styling, the Sunday-department employees seemed to express themselves in their clothes—they wore gloomy dark sweaters and black cuffless trousers, brightly colored shirts and black knit ties, loose tweed jackets with patched elbows, casual shoes bought from a creative cobbler in the Village; and there was somehow suggested in all this, and in their manner, the detached air of the *artiste*, the intellectual rebel, the actor, the writer, the whole cultural scene that the Sunday staff covered, cared about, was really a part of—indeed, men had been on the staff when they were writing plays (Harvey Breit), poetry (Harvey Shapiro), novels (Herbert Mitgang)—and two men who had quit Markel's staff had written novels with characters modeled after Markel himself. Neither book was very flattering, although one had been written out of spite by an editor who resigned after his boyfriend had been fired by Markel.

The women in the Sunday department were not beautiful but they did seem better-read and better-educated than the females on the third floor, more interesting in a neurotic way, and altogether different from one another. One woman on Markel's staff was very assertive; it was said that she had "something" on Markel and, as a result, he rarely yelled at her. Another woman, a mysterious type with a small, painted mouth and bobbed hair, sat quietly in a corner all day reading, very quiet, very still, very distant—a snapshot pose from the Café du Dôme in the Twenties.

It was the general consensus on the eighth floor that the news reporters on the third floor, with some exceptions, were artless writers who lacked the organizational ability and reportorial depth to produce *Magazine* articles, and as a result a large percentage of the regular contributors to the Sunday *Magazine* were outsiders, free-lance writers and authors, or politicians and statesmen whose views Markel shared, or whose friendship he was cultivating: in either case, though the politicians and statesmen often required the help of a "ghost" on the Sunday staff, their articles were printed. But the reporters on the third floor who submitted *Magazine* articles received no such assistance or consideration, and those who had difficulty writing the way that Markel wanted them to write, or who would not conform to his viewpoint or approach on a particular subject, either grew to resent him or to merely refuse to accept future assignments from him.

In 1957 Markel was paying only $300 for a full-length *Magazine* article, and the money was not worth the aggravation of his criticism or his continual requests for revision. Meyer Berger refused for years to write for Markel. So did Brooks Atkinson. One reporter, Robert Plumb, who did accept an assignment, had it returned to him five times for rewriting. Finally, Plumb gave up—and, taking a pair of scissors, he cut his article into small strips, tucked them into an envelope, labeled it "The Robert Plumb Do-It-Yourself Kit," and sent it back to Markel.

Markel was disappointed by this and similar reactions to his demanding nature. He could not understand why some writers would object to rewriting—after all, he thought, it was for their *own* good as well as the *Magazine's*. His role, as he saw it, was that of a taskmaster, and they were to meet his standards. If they would follow the outline that he gave to them before beginning to write the article, an outline that set forth the thesis and the points to be covered, there would be little difficulty; but too often, he felt, they did as they pleased, ignored his outline, and then blamed *him* for being too rigid, too systematic. He was systematic, he conceded, but he saw this as a necessity, and he was no less demanding with his gardener at home than he was with his makeup editors at the office. To see one seed sown out of line was intolerable for Markel He was offended by an overdone piece of toast, a misplaced memo, a slow-moving cab driver, a busy phone when he wanted to reach someone. He demanded aisle seats near the front of all Broadway openings, and refused to wait in line to see a new film, and consequently attended only previews. When there were no reserved seats for the preview of Marilyn Monroe's *Let's Make Love*, Twentieth Century-Fox allegedly assigned two office boys to occupy a pair of seats in the Paramount loge from 5 p.m. until the time of Markel's scheduled arrival at eight-thirty.

Lester Markel was the son of a Lower East Side banker named Jacob Markel, *another* systematic man who was accustomed to being fawned upon in the world that he knew. Jacob Markel, whose father had been a banker in Germany, founded the Markel Brothers Bank at 93 Canal Street, in downtown Manhattan. There he hung a portrait of himself on the wall, sat back and considered the appeals of those who approached him for loans, many of these men being Middle European Jewish shopkeepers and peddlers who wished to send their sons to college or to purchase steamship tickets to bring their families to the United States.

Lester Markel, the first of Jacob's three sons, was born in a house on Madison Avenue at Ninety-fifth Street. But later Jacob felt that the boys should get out of the city and live in the "country"—which meant the Bronx. This borough still had many farms and pleasant woodlands in 1906, when the Markel family moved to 165th Street in the Morrisania section; but the Bronx was also in the early stages of a real-estate boom, a great uptown movement that included an influx of Jews into areas that had been largely German and Irish. It was here, at the age of twelve, that Lester Markel began to experience deeply the anti-Semitic insults of other boys, and sometimes they would chase him and throw rocks at him. Jacob Markel saw no reason to move. He seemed almost insensitive to his son's harassment, being remote from it all day in his bank downtown, and perhaps being resigned to such conditions as part of a young Jewish boy's education.

As a young man growing up, Lester was humorless and shy. He attended Townsend Harris High School, where he was very studious, and then went on to City College and the Columbia School of Journalism. He had begun to write articles at eighteen for a small newspaper in the Bronx, and he discovered journalism to be suited to his temperament—being inquisitive but diffident, he now had an excuse for approaching strangers and seeking answers to his questions.

He met Iphigene Ochs on the campus at Columbia, but he did not attempt to get a job on *The Times* after graduating from Columbia in 1914. He was only nineteen and required experience. He began first with the Bronx *Home News,* then he switched to the *Evening Post*, and finally got a reporting job on the *New York Tribune*, where he would remain for nine years. On the *Tribune* he met Garet Garrett, an editor who had worked on *The Times* and had known Ochs well. Markel also became acquainted with Franklin P. Adams, Marc Connelly, Robert Benchley, George S. Kaufman, and many others who would go on to better things; and when Adams switched to the *World*, he urged Herbert Bayard Swope to hire Markel. Markel had done a bit of everything on the *Tribune*—reporting, rewrite, copyreading; he had been successively the city editor, night editor, and, at the age of twenty-seven, assistant managing editor. Swope was impressed, and he sent for Markel, and he seemed eager to hire him until he asked: "How much do you make?"

"Ten thousand," Markel said.

"That's a lot of money," Swope said, shaking his head—to which Markel asked, "How much do *you* make?"

But two years later, in 1923, Adolph Ochs learned of Markel, and he invited him to spend the weekend in Atlantic City, where the publisher was relaxing with his wife, his daughter, and Sulzberger. Shortly after Markel arrived, Ochs took him on a two-hour ride in a rolling chair along the boardwalk. He questioned and evaluated the young man, and he liked most of Markel's ideas for improving the Sunday edition of *The*

Times, although Ochs was somewhat wary of Markel's plan for a special supplement that would interpret the week's news. Ochs thought that this would foster excessive opinion in the paper, and would also be repetitious of what had already appeared, and it was not until 1935, a few months before Ochs's death, that Markel and Sulzberger were able to launch the "Week in Review" section, which would later earn a special Pulitzer Prize citation.

It was said that Markel hit his full stride as an editor with the publication of the "Review" section, which had finally provided him with the proper format for news interpretation: the daily *Times* told readers *what* had happened, and Markel's "Review" told readers *why* it had happened. The *Magazine,* too, kept pace with the news, with no article appearing without a "news peg": if there was to be an article about a Broadway stage star, that star had to be appearing in a show that was either about to open, or was somehow in the news; if there was to be an article about a certain politician, or city, or country, they also had to be in the news. If there was a formula about Markel's system, that was it—news interpreted, news explained, newsworthy personalities revealed. When Markel joined *The Times* in 1923, the Sunday edition's circulation was 546,497 and the daily's was 337,427; when Markel completed his twenty-fifth year on *The Times* in 1948, and had expanded his staff from five to fifty-five, the Sunday circulation was 1,106,153 and the daily's was 539,158.

In marking his twenty-fifth anniversary, a party was held in his honor on the eighth floor, and a few members of the staff presented to him a mock version of a "Review" devoted entirely to his own career. The reporting was very detailed, perhaps *too* detailed: it dealt with Markel's mannerisms, his daily routine, his "system"—it told of his rising at 6 a.m., reading the morning papers, including the *Daily Worker,* and then taking a ten-minute sunlamp treatment while listening to the newscast from a portable radio perched on his stomach. While taking a shower, he kept a pad and pencil on a special hook within reach should an idea occur to him—he also kept next to his bed a pad that lit up when the pencil was withdrawn so that he could jot down ideas in the middle of the night—and the general tone of the profile was that Lester Markel was a restless machine who on weekends "relaxes intensely" and fiddled endlessly with his television set until he got a perfect image, then switched to another channel.

Markel saw little humor in this profile, and he was displeased to learn later that several copies of the mock "Review" were in circulation around the building. There was also one copy in his personal folder in *The Times'* morgue on the third floor, but there was also attached to it a memo written by Markel's editor in charge of the "Week in Review":

NOTICE—NOTICE—NOTICE

The material on the attached proof is *not* available for public distribution. The article was prepared for limited circulation. It is *not* to be considered as research material. It is not to be shown to any outsiders seeking information about Mr. Markel without the specific permission of Mr. Markel. And if such permission is obtained then each specific bit of information must be rechecked before it can be used.

J. Desmond
Sunday dept.

While no part of the Sunday department was exempt from the pressure of Markel's presence, the editor of the Sunday "Book Review," Francis Brown, probably felt it less than did the other Sunday editors. This condition existed because Markel considered himself a newspaperman, not a *littérateur*, and therefore he did not try to influence the "Book Review," except when he had a special interest in a certain book. Another reason for the relatively good fortune of the "Book Review" was Francis Brown himself—he knew how to handle Markel, had a way of humoring him, patronizing him without going too far, chiding him softly with a benign little smile: "Oh now *really*, Lester, you can't be serious!"

Francis Brown was a tweedy, stocky, gray-haired man with an impressive leonine face and the leisurely, mildly condescending manner of the academician that he was. He had taught at Dartmouth and Columbia, he had a Ph.D., and he was a friend of Orvil Dryfoos, another Dartmouth alumnus. Brown had come to *The Times* in 1930 at the personal request of Adolph Ochs's brother, George Ochs-Oakes, who, at sixty-eight, was taking courses at Columbia University toward a Ph.D. He had met Brown while the latter was teaching in the Columbia history department. The two men became friendly, and Brown later accepted the offer to become an associate editor of *Current History*, a monthly auxiliary publication of *The Times* that Ochs-Oakes edited on the tenth floor of the *Times* building.

In 1936, five years after Ochs-Oakes's death and a year after Ochs's death, Sulzberger sold *Current History*, and Francis Brown moved to the Sunday department, where he became one of the important men on Markel's newly formed "Week in Review." But in 1945, Brown resigned to accept a lucrative offer from *Time*. Markel regretted Brown's leaving, and, after a few "Book Review" editors had left because they could not tolerate Markel, Francis Brown was offered the editorship of the "Book Review," which he accepted in 1949. Markel did not want to lose Brown a second time, and so this contributed to their *modus vivendi*.

Brown's staff consisted of about twenty subordinates who helped him plan and edit the "Book Review." Since only 2,500 of the 7,500 books sent each year to *The Times* by book publishers would be reviewed, it was a tight selective process from the start. Books by "name" writers would be reviewed, of course, as would books by new authors who had somehow received pre-publication attention—either through serialization in magazines, or through the testimonials of other literary figures, or through the promotional skill of the publisher or the author, provided that the publisher or author was not regarded as merely a huckster or a hack and had not made enemies of influential people within *The Times*. As was often the case within *The Times*, "influence" was not necessarily the exclusive prerogative of top editors. Sometimes a clerk, on a busy day, could add a decisive little push that would determine whether or not a single piece of incoming mail—be it a book, a news feature, a photograph, a press release, or any of a hundred other items in the daily deluge—was taken from the pile and brought to the attention of the proper editor, or was ignored until it was too late. (Smart press agents who were especially anxious that a certain press release not be ignored by *The Times* would sometimes send a copy directly to Sulzberger's office: they knew that Sulzberger himself would never see it, but they hoped that one of Sulzberger's secretaries, in redirecting the release to the proper editor, might attach an "F.Y.I." slip bearing Sulzberger's initials; an editor receiving a press release with an "AHS" sticker was unlikely to ignore it.)

Once a book had been selected for review, the next step was to designate a reviewer. There were hundreds of men and women around the nation—authors, educators, politicians, editors and journalists, critics from magazines and quarterlies—who reviewed books for *The Times* because of the prestige attached to it, and because, in the cases of some, they hoped that as regular *Times* reviewers they might receive the same courtesy that *The Times* almost always extended to its own staff members whenever they had published a book. Books by *Times*men were rarely panned and were nearly always given generous, if not extensive, treatment in both the daily edition and the Sunday "Book Review." This was not necessarily the result of pressure on the part of anyone, it just happened that way, it was more or less a tradition—just as it had long been the practice that when a *Times*man died, he received a longer obituary in the paper than he would have received had he not worked for *The Times*. Adolph Ochs had been a great believer in fine obituaries for *Times*-

men. Ochs had been awed by grand funerals, and when a senior *Times* editor died Ochs had wanted his executives to attend the funeral as a group, and then to accompany the body with a procession of carriages past the *Times* building; and Ochs had wanted to see all the other *Times* workers lined along the sidewalk with their hats off in tribute. Since Ochs had not appreciated harsh criticism of any sort in his newspaper, he did not expect to see the literary efforts of *Times*men condemned *in The Times*. This Ochsian expectation became traditional, and it was extended, too, to Ochs's friends, to friends of *The Times*. (After Orvil Dryfoos had been named a trustee of Dartmouth College, there had appeared in *The Times* a complimentary "Man in the News" on Dartmouth's president, John Sloan Dickey. James Reston had complained about this to Sulzberger, saying that it might seem that *The Times* was "buttering up" a friend. Sulzberger saw Reston's point, and he regretted that the story about Dryfoos' trusteeship and the profile on Dickey had appeared within such a short time. It had just happened that way.)

The friends of *The Times* who wrote regularly for the Sunday "Book Review" were reviewers who greatly admired the paper, stood by its principles, and shared its traditional respect for the established order and solid middle-class values. While they regarded John O'Hara as a puerile writer and often dismissed his work, and were not overly impressed with Hemingway, they generally tried to find something favorable to say in each review. If they wrote reviews that were too derogatory there was always the possibility that the books would be deemed unworthy of the space, and thus the reviews might not be published—except in cases where the review dealt with such writers as O'Hara, that denigrator of the middle class. (In partial retaliation for *Times* criticism O'Hara was believed to have established a tradition of his own: he insisted that his publisher, Random House, schedule the publication of his books on Thanksgiving Days, a time readers had little to do except read the paper, and the one day the reviews of Orville Prescott, the daily *Times'* rather prudish book critic, did not appear.

Adolph Ochs had wanted books to be presented "as news," to be treated in *The Times* as other news items were treated; he did not want his reviews to become a precious literary forum for intellectuals and critics who were determined to display their erudition or superiority without telling *Times* readers what the books were about. While some of Ochs's concepts were changed after his death, they changed slowly, and much remained unchanged as Francis Brown settled into the editorship of the "Book Review." Most of the Sunday reviewers wrote as Ochs would have wished—they rarely seemed impassioned or scathing, their language was quiet and discreet. They were obviously respected members of their communities: professors from Princeton and Smith, lady novelists in Westchester, liberal editors from the South, venerable retired scholars in the Southwest; they were experts on Japanese art, the Civil War, anthropologists and social commentators, biographers of presidents. They were friends of *The Times*. When an anthology that Markel had edited arrived on Francis Brown's desk, Brown selected a reviewer—and, when the review came in, it was favorable, very favorable. And this intramural delicacy between *The Times* and its reviewers went on for years, and Brown seemed to have one of the easier executive jobs on the paper. In spite of the hiring of a few new young editors with mildly radical ideas, the "Book Review" still covered books "as news"—and while it tolerated occasional diversions, the reviewers would feel the unseen hand of Markel responding instinctively to the ghost of Ochs if the review went too far. This was the experience of a new young reviewer named John Simon, a man with a reputation for being brilliant and tough as a film critic for *The New Leader* and drama critic for *The Hudson Review*. He had been approached by one of Francis Brown's subordinate editors, Eliot Fremont-Smith, to review two books on the theater, one by John Mason Brown, the other by Walter Kerr.

Simon was very pleased, it being his first opportunity to appear in *The Times*, and within a few weeks his review was completed and sent in. Simon had been very critical of both books, and in summarizing the flaws in the book by the *Herald Tribune's* critic, Walter Kerr, John Simon added:

> All this would be less disturbing if Mr. Kerr were not the best of today's daily reviewers: the only one whose collected articles can actually be read through and whose daily views can provide some guidance. But must we accept the one-eyed king?

When Lester Markel read this paragraph, he decided that it would have to be rewritten or eliminated. Markel was not going to permit Simon's left-handed compliment of the *Herald Tribune's* Walter Kerr to dismiss *The New York Times'* theater reviewers in such a cavalier fashion. This was embarrassing for those caught in the middle—Francis Brown and Fremont-Smith. Privately, they saw nothing wrong in publishing Simon's review exactly as written, but Markel was unyielding—it would have to be changed. When Simon was told this he refused to change a word, even though he was also told that the elimination of the single paragraph would not destroy the validity of the review, and there was also the hint that the Simon review was being considered for the lead position in the Sunday "Book Review," or, in any case, near the front of the section.

Unappeased, John Simon replied that if the review were not printed as written that he would like to have it returned, and would try to sell it elsewhere. Simon was upset, and there was always the chance that Simon's displeasure would be relayed by him to other young new critics outside *The Times* as an example of censorship—a situation that Francis Brown hoped to avoid.

Weeks passed, nothing happened. Telephone calls and notes between Simon and *The Times'* "Book Review" did not produce a happy compromise on either side. Then finally *The Times did* run Simon's entire review—not on the cover or near the front, as he had been told, but in the back of the "Book Review," displayed as inconspicuously as possible. And later, when John Simon's own book, *Acid Test*, was published, *The Times'* Sunday "Book Review" did not review it.

12

LONG before Catledge knew exactly what to do, he knew that something radical had to be done about the lethargy of the New York staff. But when Theodore Bernstein suggested that Catledge replace the city editor with A. M. Rosenthal, who was then, in 1962, *The Times'* correspondent in Tokyo, Catledge vacillated. Rosenthal, who was thirty-nine, had no experience as an editor, had not lived in New York in nearly a decade, and might be intimidated by the enormous task of running the New York staff and trying to change it. Catledge also debated the logic of removing from the reportorial staff a by-line that *Times* readers looked for (stories "by A. M. Rosenthal" from Tokyo, and before that from Poland and India, had possessed a special style, a warmth and readability and sensitivity to the nuances of politics and people. Rosenthal had won a Pulitzer Prize after his expulsion in 1959 from Poland, where, in the government's opinion, he had "probed too deeply" into its internal affairs. One of the *Magazine* pieces that Rosenthal had written in Poland for Markel—an article based on a visit to Auschwitz, the Nazi concentration camp in which millions had died in gas chambers during World War II— became a journalistic classic:

And so there is no news to report from Auschwitz. There is merely the compulsion to write something about it, a compulsion that grows out of a restless feeling that to have visited Ausch-

witz and then turned away without having said or
written anything would be a most grievous act of
discourtesy to those who died there. . . .

If Rosenthal were to be made the city editor his reporting days would be over. Rosenthal would have to
devote all of his time and energy to solving the problems of the newsroom, and there was a chance that
he would be unwilling to do this. The finest reporters,
with few exceptions, were hungry for public recognition
and acclaim, and they would not quickly trade this
for the extra money and anonymous power of executive
life. And yet there was a point of no return. After a reporter had won all the prizes, had been everywhere,
had covered every imaginable type of story, he began
to recognize a repetition about his work—the situations and places seemed the same, the shortcuts were
learned, there were no new challenges. If a reporter
could obtain a column, of course, as Reston had, then
journalism could still be interesting. But if the individual was destined to remain a reporter for twenty or
twenty-five years, it could lead to stagnation and frustration, which would exist until he quit newspaper work
and tried something else—or, if he had an opportunity
to become an editor, he might find that stimulating.
Catledge had never missed reporting and by-lines after
he had become an editor. The same had been true of
Clifton Daniel. Maybe Rosenthal, too, could be won
over. There was little chance of Rosenthal's getting a
column as long as C. L. Sulzberger was writing one
on foreign affairs for *The Times*. Perhaps, at thirty-
nine, Rosenthal had gone as far as he could go with his
writing. But if Rosenthal had the desire and talent to
become a great editor, if he could somehow inspire
a sluggish staff in New York and transfer his technique
to other reporters, then Rosenthal's loss as a writer
would be well worth it to *The Times*. Whether it would
be worth it to Rosenthal was another question. But
Catledge, as he thought more about it, was becoming
intrigued with the idea of Rosenthal in the newsroom,
and Catledge decided that during his forthcoming trip

to the Orient he would spend time with Rosenthal, would sense his mood and see if he was tired of writing and living overseas and would like to come home and try something new.

In Tokyo, Rosenthal was having the time of his life. He was living with his wife and sons in a tatami-floored house with servants. He was enchanted with the Japanese people, their efficiency and industriousness, their vibrancy and verve in a racy, gaudy city of joyous confusion. Protected by the American military, the Japanese concentrated on their industrial expansion and prosperity, and they were endlessly fascinating to write about. The Japanese women were delightful and intelligent, and the men seemed to Rosenthal to be ever on the make—making money, making love, dancing, singing, enjoying themselves without a sense of sorrow. This is what most appealed to Rosenthal about the Japanese—he did not feel sorry for them. They were enjoying their prosperity, they knew how to live, they moved noisily through the night and woke up guiltlessly each day, and Rosenthal was soon influenced by their spirit. In Poland, Rosenthal had felt gloom, repression, and suspicion—as he wrote in *The Times*: "In Poland there is a strange daily sensation of seeing and hearing things that look and sound ordinary, but have a startling twist to them, like bullets coming out of a child's popgun." In India, where he had worked between 1954 and 1958, it had been different, and in many ways worse. Surrounded by street sights of unbelievable poverty, Rosenthal felt a nagging discomfort and guilt. He had not quite been prepared for what he found in India, even though he had been warned in advance by Krishna Menon at the United Nations one day, a tense day in which Rosenthal had provoked Menon's anger by nodding casually while the Indian diplomat was discussing poverty—"*Don't nod your head at me like that, young man! You don't know what kind of poverty I am talking about!*"

Menon had been right. Nothing that Rosenthal had known before could be compared with India, although

Rosenthal as a boy in America had lived in poverty and had experienced inadequate medical care as a charity patient, had suffered the premature death of his father and four of his five sisters due to accidents or incurable illnesses or inferior care, and he had been reared with the thought that the essence of life was the absence of pain. His mistrust of doctors was deep and perhaps permanent.

As a teen-ager he walked on crutches or with a cane, victimized by osteomyelitis that had forced him to drop out of school for two years. The hospital to which he had been assigned in New York was a squalid, ill-equipped place where the patients were all but ignored, sometimes being treated by an intern—the "doctor of record" rarely appeared—and sometimes being unable to reach either a nurse or an orderly. One operation on Rosenthal's legs had been done in the wrong place, and during his recovery he was told that he would never walk again. Fortunately, one of his sisters had written to the Mayo Clinic, which accepted him as a charity patient, and successfully used sulfa drugs that eventually restored his mobility. The Mayo Clinic became his boyhood symbol of humanity in America, and he was able to return to school, although he would never be an active participant in sports. Shy, skinny, and intense, he became a reader of books, a young man of quiet determination.

Reared in the Bronx, he was the only son of a house painter, Harry Rosenthal, who had been born in Byelorussia. Harry Rosenthal's real surname was Shipiatski; he had permanently borrowed "Rosenthal" from a maternal uncle whom he had visited in London after he had left Byelorussia and was en route to Canada. He was a rugged, very physical man with muscles that bulged from his shoulders, and when he arrived in Ontario, in the late Eighteen-nineties, he took a job laying railroad tracks. Later he worked on one of the early utopian farms, leading a wild and semipoetic existence that he elaborately described in letters home to his father, a somewhat rakish rabbi, letters that so excited his younger brothers that they, too, soon left

Byelorussia for Canada, as did a girl friend whom Harry Rosenthal later married.

After leaving the utopian farm, where the utopianism had eventually bred inefficiency and tedium, Rosenthal became a fur trapper and trader in the Hudson Bay area, and of all the things that he did, he enjoyed this the most. With a sled and a team of huskies, he wandered far and wide, becoming enthralled with the open air and sense of freedom that he felt, and he hoped that someday his son, Abraham Michael Rosenthal—who was born in 1922 in Sault Sainte Marie, Ontario—would work in the outdoors, perhaps as a forester, which he considered the ultimate of aspirations. But before the boy was old enough to work, the family had moved from Canada. The Depression was on, the fur business was in decline. After several trips back and forth across the Canadian border, Harry Rosenthal settled his family permanently in the Bronx and went to work as a house painter. He had done this on previous occasions and had disliked it. He disliked it now even more, and he came to hate New York, to wish that he were back in the open land and rustic freedom of Canada. One day while painting, he fell from a scaffold. As a result of his injuries, he later died.

Abe Rosenthal attended elementary and high schools in the Bronx. The death of his father had been preceded a year before by the death of one of his older sisters, of pneumonia; then, while young Rosenthal was a student at City College, a second sister died of cancer that had been misdiagnosed. A third sister died during postnatal care after a hospital had released her; and finally, several years later, a fourth sister died of cancer. Abe Rosenthal remembered the addresses of every apartment that he had lived in since leaving Canada, remembered how the apartments became smaller and smaller as there was less money and more death.

At City College, Rosenthal worked on the campus newspaper. He did not plan to become a journalist, having nothing so precise in mind. But he did well on the paper, and when the student who was the CCNY correspondent for the *Herald Tribune* was drafted by the Army, Rosenthal took over that position. Primarily because of the draft, there was a rapid turnover among students holding these campus correspondents' jobs for metropolitan newspapers, but Rosenthal, who was 4-F because of his illness, was not affected. When *The Times'* correspondent left, Rosenthal quit the *Tribune* for *The Times*, which paid a few dollars more—twelve dollars a week—and on a winter afternoon in 1943, Rosenthal, nervous and awed, entered *The Times'* newsroom for the first time. He walked up the aisle and sat at an empty desk near the back, removing from his coat pocket some notes pertaining to campus activities. But he was so petrified that he could not begin to use the typewriter; he merely sat upright and stared around the big room at all the people who seemed quietly preoccupied and distant. Then he was startled by the soft voice of a stranger behind him, a lean and homely-looking man wearing glasses, asking, "What's your name?"

"Abe Rosenthal."

"What do you do?" the man asked pleasantly.

"I'm the City College correspondent."

"Do you need paper to type on?"

"Yes."

"Do you know where we keep the paper around here?"

"No."

"It's over there in that box," the man said, and then he proceeded to walk down the aisle, to grab a batch of paper, and to place it on Rosenthal's desk.

"Do you know how to slug a story?"

"No," Rosenthal said.

The man showed Rosenthal where his name should go, at the upper left-hand corner, with a single word to describe the subject of the story.

"Do you know what you do after you finish your story?"

"No," Rosenthal said.

"You give it to that copyboy standing over there."

Rosenthal nodded.

"By the way," the man said, "my name is Mike
Berger."

"Thank you, Mr. Berger."

"Mike," the man said.

As was the practice with other campus correspondents,
copyboys, and clerks who hoped to one day become
Times reporters, Abe Rosenthal attended a church
service each Sunday morning so that he could write a
brief account of the sermon for the Monday edition of
The Times. Sometimes these stories by Rosenthal and
about eight others would fill more than a half-page of
The Times with pithy exhortations and homilies that
hardly anyone read except the preachers who delivered
them, and the young aspiring journalists who reported
them. While these stories, each of which rarely ex-
ceeded five or six paragraphs in length, never carried
by-lines, their authorship was known to *The Times'*
religious-news editor, who made the assignments, and
who was alert for any signs of irreverence that the
church coverage might reveal.

Many of the men and women who later became
Times reporters broke into print initially by covering
Sunday sermons. They were paid about three dollars
per story, and this amount was to include the cost of
transportation to and from the church, and also any
donation that they might feel compelled to drop into a
collection basket. The tradition was to deposit a quarter
in the first collection, and to dodge the second.

While the competent coverage of a Sunday sermon
was just one of many preliminary tests confronting
an aspiring *Times*man, and was not in itself regarded
as singularly significant as the writing of a "Topics of
The Times" or a short editorial—which paid respec-
tively $25 and $15—it was also true that the *incompetent* coverage of a sermon was very significant. If
a young man could not reliably cover a church sermon,
the editors reasoned, he could probably not reliably
cover anything—which was sometimes the case. The
misspelling of a pastor's name, the misquoting of the
sermon, or the misinterpretation of the message were

all irredeemable sins. There was one *Times* copyboy who, hoping to cover a sermon without attending the church service—thus avoiding the collection plate—arrived at the church a half-hour early, walked to the rectory door on the side of the building, and rang the bell, planning to ask the pastor for an advance text of the sermon. But the bell that was rung was not the doorbell; it was the fire alarm. And its sudden clangor interrupted a Sunday school class, sending children scurrying into the street; and it provoked a pastoral protest that started the young *Times*man's career in reverse.

Such indignation as this was never caused by Rosenthal's coverage. He was diligent and cautious, determined to let no incident stall his progression to the reportorial staff. After he had done several outstanding articles about campus life at City College and dozens of impeccable sermons, and after seeing that his work during his first year as a correspondent was hardly ever changed by the copydesk, Rosenthal summoned the courage one day to approach the city editor and ask about his promotion to the staff. Rosenthal's inquiry had been prompted by his awareness that a girl who had been the Columbia College correspondent was in possession of a reporter's press card, a fact that he discovered inadvertently after her handbag had fallen open to the floor. Rosenthal's competitive spirit was stirred by the sight of her press card, and he sat silently at his desk for a while watching the city editor's every move, waiting for the perfect moment to approach, being both timid and aroused. Then, as the city editor, David H. Joseph, stood and was putting on his coat and was about to leave the newsroom, Rosenthal sprung from his chair, rushed down the aisle toward Joseph, and unhesitatingly asked the question: when would he be promoted? David Joseph's reaction was neither one of shock, surprise, nor even great interest. It was as if the question were too trifling to justify Joseph's delay in getting home to dinner. "You want to go on the staff," Joseph said, casually, "okay —you can go on the staff." Joseph then buttoned his coat, turned, and left the room, leaving Rosenthal frozen in a state of disbelief and ecstasy.

At twenty-one, he was a *Times*man, and one of the first things that he did was to quit college. He had only four credits to go for a degree, but he now felt so totally involved with *The Times* that his relationship with City College seemed an intrusion. Years later, after Rosenthal had established himself as perhaps the brightest young man on the New York staff, he was cited as a distinguished alumnus of City College, and one of the deans requested that he address the student body. When Rosenthal explained that he had never graduated, the dean said that a degree could be arranged if Rosenthal would submit a paper. But Rosenthal never found the time to write it, being so busy covering daily news from the United Nations, and so finally the dean asked Rosenthal to submit one of his magazine articles, which Rosenthal did—a *Collier's* magazine piece about the United Nations—and, with that, he received his degree.

At this time, in 1950, Rosenthal's by-line from the U.N. was regularly on page one. He had begun writing about United Nations activities in 1946 when Turner Catledge, wanting to see a feature story written about the New York City life of a U.N. delegate, presented the idea to the city editor, and Rosenthal drew the assignment. The subject of the feature was to be Andrei Gromyko of the Soviet Union, and Rosenthal trailed Gromyko for an entire day, jumping into taxicabs to follow Gromyko's limousine no matter where it went. Luckily for Rosenthal's story, Gromyko—who seemed unaware that Rosenthal was following him— took a sightseeing tour during the afternoon, encircling most of Manhattan while Rosenthal pursued him in a cab and charted the entire excursion, observing where Gromyko stopped his limousine and what New York sites seemed to attract him. Rosenthal's story, a well-written descriptive account, delighted Catledge. It was given a big play in *The Times*, complete with a map that Bernstein had ordered to show exactly where Gromyko had traveled, and this article led to Rosenthal's being assigned to *The Times'* bureau at the United Nations.

The United Nations then, early in 1946, was meeting in temporary quarters on the campus of Hunter College in the Bronx, a subway stop from where Rosenthal was then living with his mother. It was an ideal assignment—*The Times* gave almost unlimited space to the daily activities of the U.N., meaning that there was adequate room for feature articles and pictures as well as news stories and texts, and Rosenthal was fortunate, too, in having the freewheeling, informal William H. Lawrence as his bureau chief. Lawrence allowed Rosenthal to handle many of the lead stories and also to write impressionistic pieces about this rather bizarre Bronx scene of flapping flags and Brooks suits, wide Communist trousers, and silk Hindu saris. The United Nations populace seemed much more united on the Bronx campus, and later at Lake Success on Long Island, than it would seem after it had moved in 1951 into its present headquarters, the glass skyscraper and smooth complex along the East River in Manhattan. The skyscraper would bring verticality to the U.N., would divide it into a thousand tiny compartments, would section off these people who had come to New York from all sections of the world seeking unity. But in the Bronx and Long Island, before the Manhattan structures were opened, the U.N. was horizontally spread through several smaller buildings, and the delegates, their aides, and the press were forced to do a great deal of walking from place to place—and there was much more mingling and meeting along the paths, streets, and steps, and the U.N. seemed to Rosenthal to be a spontaneous and convivial place. The Security Council in 1946 even held some of its sessions in a Bronx gymnasium, and *The Times'* bureau in those days was set up in what had been a hair-drying room for girls. It was here that Rosenthal first met James Reston.

Rosenthal was then twenty-four, and Reston, at thirty-seven, was the most admired and envied member of the staff. Reston seemed to Rosenthal to have everything—success, fame, and he radiated health; he walked with the bouncing step of a winner, slightly forward and on his toes. He had good complexion, even teeth, a full head of dark hair—a college athlete who had remained in shape, a onetime golfer now playing for higher stakes. It was said that during the previous year, in 1945, Reston had persuaded the powerful Senator Arthur Vandenburg to influence the Republican party away from its isolationist policy. In the same year, Reston had distinguished himself while covering the United Nations conference in San Francisco, and in 1944 he had won his first Pulitzer for his reporting of the Dumbarton Oaks conference, which established the foundation for the United Nations. It was before that conference in Georgetown—attended by the United States, Britain, Russia, and Nationalist China—that Reston had quietly obtained the position papers of the Allied powers, and during the meetings he was able to dip into his file and to write knowledgeably about the private sessions. Not only were Reston's journalistic rivals upset by his series of exclusives, but many diplomats were dismayed. The Russians suspected that the Americans had leaked the information to Reston, while the Americans believed that he had gotten the data from a friend in the British Embassy. After a note of caution had been sent to the British, and after the F.B.I. had begun to investigate, the British Ambassador, Lord Halifax, refused to see Reston even though the two were friends and the British had leaked nothing. Lord Halifax explained to Reston: "I'm not going to keep your friendship at the price of losing that of the American Secretary of State." Reston's source had actually been from within the Chinese delegation, which had been displeased with the political arrangements at the conference, and was therefore willing to cooperate with *The Times*—confirming one of Reston's lessons to journalists: "You should always look around for the guys who are unhappy."

Rosenthal spent eight years covering United Nations activities. He wrote hundreds of articles about the great issues and debates, the power blocs and vetoes, the walkouts and reconciliations; he wrote about Trygve Lie and Gromyko, Anthony Eden and Bernard Baruch, the pageantry and "little people" at the U.N.—the linguistic shoeshine stand, the barber who knew the hair styles of all nations—and he wrote about a delegate from India whom he particularly admired, Sir Benegal Rau. Then one day Sir Benegal lied to him. It was in response to a very delicate question, the sort of lie that every top diplomat in the world has undoubtedly told at one time or other in the name of national security. But for young Rosenthal it was a new and disillusioning experience—the distinguished and genteel Sir Benegal, lying like any political ward heeler in the Bronx—and Rosenthal bitterly approached him and told him what he thought. The Indian delegate was indeed sorry and somewhat touched, and he tried to explain, "But, Abe, it was in the best interest of my country to lie to you."

"Yes," Rosenthal replied, sharply, "and it is in the best interest of my newspaper not to ask you questions again." Then Rosenthal continued, "Why didn't you at least answer my question with a 'No comment'?"

"Because," Sir Benegal said, "you would have then known it was the truth."

Sir Benegal was undoubtedly right about that. But Rosenthal would never again be so trusting of a news source, although his friendship with Sir Benegal was soon restored, and from then on, when Sir Benegal did not wish to reply, he merely answered, "No comment."

Eight years of covering the United Nations was too long a period for one assignment; but for some unaccountable reason, though he often tried, Rosenthal was not able to obtain a transfer to a *Times* bureau overseas. It was as if someone were keeping him off the overseas staff, although he could imagine no reason for this, and it did not bother him during his early years because there was great variety and excitement at the United Nations. Sometimes after a full day of listening to foreign languages and accents, and seeing the various costumes and reporting the speeches and debates concerning distant discord, Rosenthal felt that he was indeed overseas in Cyprus or Rhodesia or Pakistan—or India, where he especially wished to be. India then had an interesting delegation at the U.N., not only Sir Benegal but many others, and Rosenthal was drawn to them from the beginning, and he became increasingly infatuated with their history and culture, their social style and religion, their political relationships with Pakistan and Nepal—in fact, the very names of the cities in that part of the world conjured up for Rosenthal the sound of bells and exotic sights. *Bangalore. Bombay. Calcutta. Katmandu. Ootacamund. Travancore. The Khyber Pass.* When Rosenthal finally became *The Times'* correspondent in India in 1954, ten years after he had been promoted to the staff, he would on one occasion travel more than 1,500 miles just to file a story that would have the dateline: *At the Khyber Pass.* And years after doing that—after he had left India and had enlarged his reputation in Poland—Rosenthal would finally discover why it had taken him so long to become a foreign correspondent; and the disclosure would shock him.

He learned of it while traveling by car toward Geneva in 1959 with Sydney Gruson and C. L. Sulzberger, who were all good friends by then, and they were enjoying one another's company and the scenery while on the way to cover a foreign ministers' conference in Geneva. The conversation was animated and often interrupted by Rosenthal's demands that Gruson not drive so fast. And then, rather suddenly and out of context, Cyrus Sulzberger switched the subject to a serious reflection of an incident that had involved Rosenthal in Paris in 1948. Rosenthal had gone to Paris during that year as part of *The Times'* U.N. staff to help cover a United Nations General Assembly session. One afternoon, returning to his hotel room, Rosenthal had noticed that a twenty-dollar traveler's check had been removed from his bureau drawer. He had angrily reported this to the concierge, hinting that if it were not returned he would deduct that amount from his bill. The concierge, equally angry, had telephoned *The Times*' Paris office and had reported young Rosenthal's assertiveness to Cyrus Sulzberger.

Sulzberger had not forgotten this, and now, in 1959, driving with his two colleagues to Geneva, he seemed to want to relieve from his mind one aspect that was bothersome, and finally he did: he admitted to Rosenthal that Rosenthal had been kept on the U.N. staff in New York all those years because he, Sulzberger, had wanted it that way. He explained that Rosenthal in those early days in Paris had seemed the sort who would cause problems abroad. Sulzberger conceded, casually, that his judgment had been harsh and obviously wrong, and now he merely wished to tell his friend Rosenthal the aftermath of that hotel incident in 1948.

As Rosenthal listened he could feel the tension building within him, recalling quietly the many years of waiting in New York to get an overseas assignment, and thinking, too, that if Cyrus Sulzberger's influence as an overseas duke had been continued through the Nineteen-fifties, he might never have gotten to be a correspondent. And the recollection of this silly little impulsive moment in a French hotel, and the realization of the consequences, caused Rosenthal to feel such a whirling sensation of both nausea and fury that he could barely, just barely, contain himself until they had reached Geneva.

Turner Catledge arrived in Tokyo in the spring of 1962 and sought Rosenthal's reaction to the proposal that he quit reporting and take over the New York staff. Rosenthal was flattered and, without committing himself, he expressed interest. He imagined himself as the city editor of *The Times*, a catalytic agent between the news, the staff, the spirit of New York; a much-involved man who would know the New York politicians and businessmen, the artists and writers; a man who would stimulate and inspire reporters on the most important newspaper in the most vital city in the world. Yes, he told Catledge, the idea had appeal.

Even the fact that he had not lived in New York

City in years might be an advantage—he would see the city with fresh perspective, would not be influenced by the traditional methods of the newsroom. Rosenthal recognized that reporters in New York were restricted in ways that foreign correspondents were not—most New York reporters were either specialists or were told what to cover each day by the city desk; foreign correspondents generally selected their own subjects when not involved in covering a big story—and yet Rosenthal thought that the New York reporters placed unnecessary restrictions on themselves, and tried to justify their own lack of initiative and imagination by blaming the "system." Perhaps Rosenthal could change this negative attitude, and could get the reporters to explore New York as foreign correspondents explore cities abroad. Rosenthal believed that what people were doing and thinking in Manhattan—or, alas, the Bronx—was as interesting as what people were doing and thinking in Rangoon or Accra. It would not be a simple matter to change the "system" in the newsroom, or the staff's attitude toward it, but it would be a challenge to try to do so, and Rosenthal seemed optimistic to Catledge, and Catledge was hopeful.

During their hours together Catledge was impressed with all of Rosenthal's ideas except one, and that was Rosenthal's view that if he became the New York editor he would wish to not only control the various general-assignment reporters and specialists in the newsroom but would also want jurisdiction over the critics and cultural-news reporters that had recently been established as a separate unit behind a wall to the west of the newsroom on the third floor. This section was mockingly referred to within the newsroom as "the culture gulch," and its residents included such people as the theater critic Howard Taubman, the music critic Harold Schonberg, the art critic John Canaday, the television critic Jack Gould, the movie critic Bosley Crowther, and such reporters as Sam Zolotow, Richard Shepard, Louis Calta, and dozens of others. For years these staff members had been under the aegis of the city desk; but early in 1962, Turner Catledge, in an effort to break up the vast New York bureaucracy as well as to improve cultural reporting, removed them from the city desk's jurisdiction and put them under a subordinate editor who was answerable to the managing editor. Now Rosenthal was suggesting that if he were put in charge of the New York staff, he hoped that he would also be in charge of "the culture gulch." The cultural and ethnic and political life of New York were all part of the integrated coverage that he envisioned, and to remove the cultural personnel from the scope of the New York editor, Rosenthal believed, would diminish the significance and possibilities of the job that he was being asked to contemplate. Rosenthal knew that his viewpoint sounded like empire building. However, when it came to empires, he told Catledge, he was perfectly happy to remain in Tokyo and run the bureau that consisted of one reporter—himself. But if he were expected to take a big job in New York, then he would expect to be given the necessary tools and the scope to accomplish his aims in that job.

What Rosenthal was not revealing to Catledge at this time was his reluctance to give up writing—or more specifically, his secret ambition to write a column someday for the editorial page. Reston and Krock were writing columns from Washington; Cyrus Sulzberger was writing the column from Europe; and Rosenthal had already discussed with John Oakes, informally and unofficially, the idea of writing a column entitled "Asia." But if Rosenthal were to become the New York editor, his dreams of writing a column would be over.

Catledge left Rosenthal in Tokyo without offering the New York job and without Rosenthal's assurance that he would accept it if it were offered. Catledge planned to go on to Taiwan, Hong Kong, Manila, Saigon, Singapore, Bangkok, and then Delhi. He asked Rosenthal to give more thought to the New York job and asked that he rejoin him in Delhi so that they could discuss it further.

. . .

Weeks later, Rosenthal flew to Delhi and suggested, tentatively, that he would give the New York job a try. Catledge was delighted, and it was obvious that the job was his. While Rosenthal did not insist on having the cultural staff under his control at the outset (he could press that later), he did reveal his secret ambition of becoming a columnist, an admission that Catledge accepted with an expression of pain and disgust. Catledge hated columns, referring to them as the "malignancy" of the newspaper business. He preferred a newspaper with just news, well-written and properly interpreted news—and no columns that permitted reporters to sound off on days when they often had nothing to say, and were wasting valuable space. If Rosenthal would pour his whole heart and identity into the editor's job, Catledge said, selling it hard now, Rosenthal each day would have not just *one* byline—he'd have *forty* by-lines, *fifty* by-lines: each story by one of Rosenthal's men would represent part of him, *Rosenthal*, and the gratification each night, the challenge each morning, would be something Rosenthal could never imagine until he had experienced it. Catledge concluded the talk by emphasizing how eagerly he awaited Rosenthal's completing the Tokyo tour and beginning his new career in New York.

Later, before Catledge had left for New York, he discussed other things with Rosenthal—among them the fact that there would be a new column in *The Times* after all—one by Reston's colleague in Washington, Russell Baker. Catledge tried not to look too deeply into Rosenthal's face when he said this, but he knew that, had he hurled a bucket of cow dung into it, Rosenthal's expression would have been about the same.

Back in New York, Catledge occupied himself with a new venture—*The Times*' Western edition. This edition, which was to begin publishing in Los Angeles on October 1, 1962, represented *The Times*' most ambitious attempt to become the first truly national general newspaper in the United States. Most of the larger newspapers along the West Coast were insubstantial, it was believed in New York, and after years of contemplation *The New York Times* now had the confidence and the electronic equipment to invade California journalism in a big way. Its major weapons would be high-speed transmission machines that would carry stories already edited in New York into the Los Angeles newsroom at the rate of 1,000 words a minute. In Los Angeles, a team of ninety *Times*men—executives and technicians, advertising and circulation crews —would put the paper together and would distribute it up and down the Coast. Within a few months, the Western edition would attract 100,000 new readers to *The Times*, or so it was hoped by *The Times'* forty-eight-year-old publisher, Orvil Dryfoos.

This would be Dryfoos' first major undertaking since he had succeeded Arthur Hays Sulzberger in the spring of 1961. Dryfoos was not a driving executive. He was patient and reserved, a broad-shouldered, somewhat stocky man with a strong friendly face and bushy eyebrows. He had been hesitant about joining *The Times* after his marriage to Marian Sulzberger in July of 1941. He had been doing well on Wall Street, had bought a seat on the New York Stock Exchange. Anyone who ascends at *The Times* through marriage must anticipate, along with the sense of grandeur and soaring integrity, an occasional feeling of clipped wings and emasculation—it was the son-in-law syndrome in the House of Ochs. Marriage could not be easy with Ochs's heirs of that generation—the grandchildren who had played at Hillandale and had been loved and spoiled and made rich by Ochs. Dryfoos wanted to marry Marian Sulzberger but he was not sure whether he wanted all that went with the marriage—the commitment to *The Times*, the iron sweetness of Iphigene Sulzberger, the cautious curator's eye of Arthur Hays Sulzberger, the whole cast of in-laws and institutional duennas and will-watchers.

Dryfoos managed to resist *The Times* for six months; and it was not until he had been married and on *The Times* almost eight years that he finally decided to sell his seat on the Exchange. By then he was Sulzberger's assistant, and, consciously or unconsciously, he had adopted Sulzberger's style—or, more likely, they were innately similar in style. They were reliable men, quietly firm, the properly reared New York sons of prosperous German-Jewish families in the textile trade; they had both gone from the Horace Mann School to the Ivy League, where both had been good students and fine swimmers, tasteful in their dress and graceful in manner. After Dryfoos had joined *The Times*, it was obvious that he would fit easily into the Sulzberger pattern. Dryfoos was handsome (Sulzberger could barely have tolerated a son-in-law who was not handsome—particularly in the case of his beautiful daughter, Marian), and Dryfoos was neither boisterous, aggressive, nor immodest. Once, when asked to list the factors that determined his career, Dryfoos wrote: "Marriage to the daughter of the publisher of *The New York Times*." Sulzberger liked him; and, like Sulzberger, Dryfoos was dedicated to expanding Ochs's paper without distorting its fiber. As Sulzberger had extended *The Times'* word across the Atlantic with the publication of a European edition in 1949, so now did Dryfoos hope to spread it westward to the Pacific. The surveys and tests prior to 1962 all had been encouraging, and Dryfoos was optimistic that *The Times'* Western edition would become a crowning achievement. He called it Project Westward Ho.

Dryfoos' chief executive on the fourteenth floor during the planning of the Western edition was Amory Howe Bradford, *The Times'* vice-president and general manager. Bradford had joined the paper in 1947 as an assistant to Sulzberger, having been introduced to the publisher by Iphigene Sulzberger, who had learned of Bradford's qualifications from Bradford's in-laws, the Rothschilds. Bradford was a tall, blondish, wavy-haired man with an air of self-assurance that could be offensive to some but impressive to others. Dryfoos was impressed with him, as the Sulzberger family had been from the beginning. There was nothing tentative about Bradford; he seemed to be on top of everything. Prior to joining *The Times*, he had practiced law in New York with Davis Polk Wardwell Sunderland & Kiendl. Before that he had worked within the State Department in Washington, to which he had gone shortly after his discharge as a captain in military intelligence, having entered the Army as a private in 1943. A graduate of Yale and Phillips Academy at Andover, Bradford's rise on *The Times* had been quick: secretary of the corporation in 1954; membership on the board in 1955; business manager in 1957; general manager in 1960. He was also a kind of house Protestant in *The Times'* hierarchy, one who could represent the paper very well in those tight social circles where Jewish executives might not feel entirely welcome.

Though his dealings within *The Times* were on the highest corporate level, he was occasionally seen on the third floor entering or leaving Catledge's office. He seemed so tall that his head would graze the portal, but it never did, nor did he slouch in the way of some tall men: Amory Bradford's exits and entrances were always perfect, he walking very erect while puffing his pipe, very impressive in a dark pin-striped suit. One day a young man entered the newsroom with a similar walk: it was Bradford's son, a very tall Choate student who entered Theodore Bernstein's office to complain about a particular story in *The Times*. There had been a somewhat condescending reference to Choate in a feature story written by one of the *Times'* sportswriters, and young Bradford wished to know why Choate had been described in that manner. Bernstein, who could offer no explanation, had the sportswriter summoned by the city desk's microphone. Within a few moments the sportswriter appeared, looking up as the spindly teen-ager in a tweed jacket stepped forward and was introduced and asked his question. The sportswriter quickly replied that there had been no disrespect toward Choate intended. Silence ensued. Bernstein smiled reassuringly at Bradford, and then thanked the sportswriter, who returned to his desk. Young Bradford's right to question was already taken for granted.

Nobody in the newsroom wanted to be in conflict with anyone named Bradford during these years at *The Times,* and this included Turner Catledge. One day after Catledge had received from a subordinate editor an estimate of what the news budget should be regarding the Western edition, Catledge accompanied the editor up to Amory Bradford's office for an approval of the figures. The editor had seemed uneasy about showing the figures to Bradford, but Catledge had said, "Look, if this is what you absolutely think we'll need, then let's go up and get it." After Bradford had studied the budget sheet, however, he shook his head and said that it could be reduced by $25,000. Catledge said that he had seen the figures, had checked them, and thought that the figures were about right.

Bradford suddenly lost his temper.

"I'm very busy," he snapped, and he would not discuss the matter further.

Catledge turned and left Bradford's office.

"Well," the editor said in the corridor, walking with Catledge toward the elevator, "what do I do now?"

Catledge's face was red with anger and humiliation, and he glared at the editor, saying, *"Do what he says!"*

Dryfoos' delegate to supervise the Western edition directly was not Amory Bradford but another executive who was on a slightly lower management level on the fourteenth floor. His name was Andrew Fisher, and, unlike Bradford, he had no reputation on the third floor —neither bad nor good; he was virtually unknown to all but a few, and those few who knew him said he was virtually indefinable. This was not meant with derision —they honestly could not comprehend him. Having never known a newspaper executive such as Andrew Fisher before, and therefore lacking standards of comparison, they were forced to fasten onto one of Fisher's obvious delights, his fascination with computers, and to try to reveal him in vague scientific

terms. He was a futuristic figure, they hinted, a por-
tender of a species of space-age administrators who
might one day convert the *Times* building into a fourteen-story robot. Within this facetiousness, however,
there was a serious and growing concern among older
*Times*men about the modern trends of the paper—the
tendency toward impersonal efficiency; the reliance on
costly computers instead of experienced political reporters for election-night prediction; the electronic
printers that would be used in the Western edition.
And emerging somehow as a symbol of all this, de-
servedly or undeservedly, was Andrew Fisher, about
whom they knew so little even though he had been on
The Times for fifteen years. He had worked most of
that time in areas remote from the newsroom. He had
begun in 1947, at the age of twenty-seven—after graduating from the Harvard business school and Amherst,
and after rising from private to captain in the Army—
in *The Times*' business department under Julius Ochs
Adler. He had been involved with the problems of labor
in a modern technology, and with corporate projects
of the distant future. During the Nineteen-fifties, Fisher
spent considerable time in the paper's newly constructed plant on the West Side of Manhattan behind
Lincoln Center—a plant in which some printing was
done but which presumably was built as the foundation
for the skyscraper headquarters of *The Times* in the
twenty-first century *if* the Forty-second Street area ever
succumbs to the total decadence that has long been
predicted by resident clergymen and social reformers.

In 1960 Andrew Fisher became the assistant to
Amory Bradford, who since the death of General Adler
in 1955 had become increasingly powerful on the fourteenth floor. Fisher and Bradford were compatible
although very dissimilar. Bradford was a man of emotion and decisiveness, while Fisher was an individual
of quiet control, and yet he was also friendly and approachable. He had the wholesome all-American looks
of a preserved astronaut—a lean strong face, blue
eyes, neatly trimmed graying hair, and, when he
smiled, a perfect set of white teeth. A native of Rich-

mond, the only son of a Virginia woman who proudly ponders her ancestral link with George Washington, Andrew Fisher speaks the language of the new technology—he mentions the "optimum way of doing things" and the "fright quotient" of certain people, and he expresses enthusiasm over the paper's "press replacement program" and its "information retrieval" and its "pricing philosophy." While some traditionalists on *The Times* see Fisher as part of a depersonalization process, Fisher sees himself as a preserver of *Times* tradition: if the Ochsian foundation is to be carried into the twenty-first century, *The Times* must keep pace with the changing world, must adjust and expand—and when discussing this expansion Fisher speaks of "satellite plants."

And so the vision of Andrew Fisher, projected through electric eyes and wireless circuits, was about to focus upon the California coast in the fall of 1962 —Project Westward Ho. It represented a tremendous investment in money and risk in reputation, but Dryfoos and Bradford and the Sulzbergers had endorsed the plan, and that is what mattered.

As for Turner Catledge in 1962, he was trying to preserve the present. He was getting along with Orvil Dryfoos well enough, although he found the new publisher quite distant at times, and Catledge was aware that when Dryfoos had important matters to discuss, it was Reston who was often consulted. Iphigene Sulzberger considered Reston a member of the family, an imaginary son-in-law, and Dryfoos would go to almost any length to keep Reston happy. When the very talented Russell Baker was becoming bored with reporting and was seriously thinking of quitting *The Times* to become a columnist on the *Baltimore Sun*, Reston refused to hear of it; he contacted Dryfoos, who invited Baker to New York and began to offer him a series of important overseas assignments. He offered him the bureau in Rome. When the London bureau was suggested, Baker was interested—but Clifton Daniel informed Dryfoos that the London bureau had been promised to Sydney Gruson, who was then in Bonn. Finally it became the issue of a column on *The Times'* editorial page, which John Oakes did not want. But Dryfoos prevailed upon Oakes to give Baker a chance as a columnist, occupying the space that had for a half-century been reserved for "Topics of The Times." Reluctantly, Oakes acquiesced, and Russell Baker's Column, beginning in 1962, was called "Observer." When it first appeared, however, it did not carry Baker's by-line at the top. Instead, Oakes put Baker's name at the bottom, in small type, where its removal would be as inconspicuous as possible should Baker fail or should Oakes otherwise wish to alternate him with various contributors. But after several months of high-quality writing and satire by Baker, Oakes finally accorded him the full recognition as a columnist and moved his name to the top.

Unlike Reston, Catledge could not, or would not, become so personally engaged in the singular affairs of individual staff members. Reston, with his smaller force in Washington, could be the *paterfamilias*, the champion of individualism, but Catledge's problems were too large, the men under him too numerous, for him to devote himself to the cause of an individual unless that individual were part of a larger plan that Catledge was trying to master. He was still trying to centralize the power in New York, and now, in the fall of 1962, he issued an announcement that was intended to disfranchise the last outposts of dukedoms in *Times* bureaus abroad. He decided to rotate three bureau chiefs who had become established in European capitals: Drew Middleton would be moved from London to Paris: Robert Doty from Paris to Rome; and Sydney Gruson from Bonn to London.

Drew Middleton was unhappy about the announcement. He had been the London bureau chief for nine years; he was an Anglophile, a club man, and within newspaper circles he was known as "Sir Drew." He had worked in Russia, Germany, and elsewhere, but London was his spiritual home, he having gone there as a young American correspondent in 1939—a twenty-five-year-old sportswriter for the Associated Press who, like Reston, would make the transition from covering the heroics of sports to the heroics of war. Middleton's front-line dispatches during World War II had not only won press awards but also a decoration from the British government. Partly through his friendship with Arthur Hays Sulzberger, whose favorite city was also London, Middleton had managed to return there as the bureau chief in 1953, edging out Clifton Daniel, who had wanted the London job but had been sent instead to Bonn. Now Middleton was being ordered to Paris—a pleasant assignment for most correspondents, but Middleton was neither fluent in French nor fond of Frenchmen. He would go, of course, but not happily.

Robert C. Doty, who was being transferred after five years in Paris to Rome, would *not* go. This was immediately apparent in a series of sizzling cables between himself and New York that had become the talk of the newsroom. Doty, a superior man who wrote very well, *too* well to remain contentedly and endlessly a reporter, refused to go to Rome as a replacement for one of the aging dukes—the sixty-seven-year-old Arnaldo Cortesi, who, against *his* will, was being retired. Doty's reasons were personal. He had been on *The Times* since 1950, and years before taking over the Paris bureau he had worked as a reporter in North Africa, the Middle East, and France, willingly and tirelessly chasing the headlines between Cairo and Damascus, Baghdad and Teheran, Syria and Libya and Somaliland. Catledge could now fire Doty for refusing Rome, or he could wonder how anybody could refuse Rome, or he could make life miserable for Doty on *The Times*. But no matter what Catledge did, it was obvious that he was not going to get Doty into Rome at this time. So Catledge recalled him and assigned him to the New York staff, sending Milton Bracker to Rome to replace Cortesi.

The third man involved in the bureau-chief switch, Sydney Gruson, was pleased to be going to London, for which Catledge was grateful. This assignment would reunite Gruson with the city where he, like so many of his colleagues, had begun as a correspondent. He had first gone to London in 1943 for the Canadian Press—a Dublin-born frisky young reporter who had gotten into a fist fight with a superior one night at a party that resulted the next day in his resignation from the Canadian Press. Gruson then approached his friend on *The Times*, Clifton Daniel, whom he had met while Daniel was working for the Associated Press, which had its London office on the same floor as the Canadian Press in the Reuters Building; Daniel spoke to *The Times'* bureau chief, and in June of 1944 Gruson joined the London bureau at $75 a week.

Now, in 1962, earning five times that amount, and knowing that he would earn more, Gruson anticipated his return to a city that suited his sophisticated taste far more than had Bonn during the last four years. Gruson was one who not only liked to cover the world —he liked to live in it, to enjoy it, to luxuriate whenever possible in fashionable places with fashionable people. But this attitude of apparent frivolity, the legend of his race horses in Mexico, his penchant for good wine, his reply to the lady who had inquired about his secret ambition ("I'd like to become the Perfect Weekend Guest"), had obscured the fact that Gruson was a first-rate reporter, and that he also had another ambition. Gruson in 1962 wanted very much to become a United States citizen. A special bill had been introduced in the House by Francis Walter and in the Senate by Kenneth Keating to waive Gruson's residential requirements, the effect of which would have been to enable him to be sworn in as a citizen immediately after the bill had passed. But the bill was being blocked. He did not know who was blocking it, but he had certain suspicions—thoughts that he kept largely to himself because to express them might leave him open to charges of paranoiac grandeur. But he sometimes truly believed that the bill was being blocked on orders from President Kennedy himself.

This would seem absurd only to those who underestimated Kennedy's interest in the press, and the lengths that he would sometimes go to demonstrate his displeasure with certain critical journalists; and there was good reason to believe in 1962 that President Kennedy was very displeased with Gruson's reporting from Bonn. In the spring of 1961, after Gruson had described the new Administration's policy toward Germany as undiplomatic—defining the policy as an attempt not to become too dependent on Chancellor Konrad Adenauer and the Germans, and adding that this policy might have serious repercussions in Germany if it succeeded—Kennedy became infuriated, complaining to another correspondent in Washington that he could "not understand a Jew being a spokesman for the Germans." There were other stories, too, that disconcerted the President, and when Robert F. Kennedy, visiting Paris, had been introduced to *The Times* Robert Doty, Kennedy was overheard to remark, "I hope he's not like that bastard Gruson."

And so when the White House press secretary, Pierre Salinger, was in Bonn, and when Gruson and the other American correspondents were invited by a United States Embassy official to join Salinger for drinks, Gruson refused, revealing to his host his suspicions about the Kennedys' role in withholding his citizenship—half doubting it as he admitted it, yet reassuring himself that the Kennedy people were indeed capable of doing such a thing.

On the evening of Salinger's arrival, Gruson received a call at home from a friend in the Embassy saying that Salinger wanted to come to Gruson's home and discuss the matter; which he did. Salinger ridiculed the notion that President Kennedy had done anything to delay the bill's passage, but he promised to discuss it with the President when he telephoned him the following day. Salinger did this at great length, according to what Gruson heard later from his friends in the Embassy, and soon the matter was receiving close attention in Washington from Kennedy's aides. They discovered that the bill was not being blocked by anyone influenced by the White House but possibly by forces under Senator James O. Eastland, the Mississippian who had shown interest in *The Times* during the subcommittee investigation of communism and the press in 1955 and 1956. To draw any relationship between Eastland's feud with *The Times* in the Fifties and Eastland-Gruson in 1962 would be pure conjecture Nor could it be proven that Eastland had the slightest interest in slowing down the Gruson bill—or even knew who Gruson was. But in any event, the Gruson bill was soon pried loose, and, in September of 1962, it quickly passed both Houses, and Sydney Gruson became a citizen.

13

Oh—
You—
Can—

Slant the news,
Twist our views,
Warp the facts,
Give us the ax—

But—
If—
You—

Stand tall in Georgetown,
Stand tall in Georgetown,
Stand tall in Georgetown,

You're—
All—
RIGHT!

THE scene from an Allen Drury novel about the press in Washington, *Capable of Honor*, describes a skit at the annual Gridiron Club show in which a chorus line of journalists, jovially and satirically, remind themselves of their duty to *stand tall in Georgetown*—i.e., to play ball with the Administration, to not rock the boat, to report the news in a way that will maintain their own social acceptance within the fashionable section of the capital . . . "Got to stand tall in Georgetown!" announces a reporter, explaining why he praises Robert Kennedy, vilifies Nixon, sanctifies Stevenson, denounces Goldwater . . . "Better watch out," another reporter warns a colleague whose recent writings did not advance the proliberal line, "or you won't stand tall in Georgetown!"

Drury's portrait of Washington as a city of compromise and cronyism, a portrait that began in 1959 with the publication of his best-selling *Advise and Consent,* bears little resemblance to the Washington that is presented each day in newspapers. But as *Time* wrote of *Advise and Consent:* "It covers enough truth to make some Washington newsmen squirm." The book characterizes members of the Washington press corps, largely composed of liberal Democrats—Drury is more conservative—as slanting the news in favor of liberal politicians and viewpoints. Drury elaborates on the theme of partiality in *Capable of Honor*, his third novel, recounting how a generation of young reporters from all over the nation arrive in Washington "fired with an idealistic vision, supported and held by the determination to tell America the truth honestly and fearlessly regardless of whom it might help or hinder"—but then: "Almost without their knowing it they soon began to write, not for the country, but for each other. They began to report and interpret events, not according to the rigid standards of honesty upon which the great majority of them had been reared in their pre-Washington days, but according to what might or might not be acceptable in the acidly easygoing wisecracks of the Press Club bar and the parties at which they entertained one another." As surely as Washington's seductive glamour corrupts some politicians, Drury concluded, so does it corrupt some members of the press even though the process is hardly conscious and seldom sinister.

Drury was a member of *The Times'* Washington bureau when he wrote *Advise and Consent*, and while the politically conservative Arthur Krock liked it, the moderately liberal James Reston did not. Reston thought that Drury's picture of the press was unfair. Reston did not tell this to Drury personally, but he did relate it to a news magazine, which piqued Drury. For Allen Drury, like the newsmen in his novels, desired the approval of his colleagues, particularly such illustrious ones as Reston, and his failure to get it from Reston was disappointing and frustrating. Each morning Reston would walk into the office with a smile and good-morning for everyone, but with no reference to Drury about the novel that was the talk of Washington, a big best seller in the making. Drury was a tall, dark-haired bachelor, a bit shy and remote; he had been a political reporter on the Washington *Evening Star* before joining *The Times*; he had in fact been the first reporter that Reston had hired after the latter had become the bureau chief in 1953. Drury was assigned by Reston to cover Capitol Hill, principally the Senate, but within a few years Drury felt the restrictions and limitations of such reporting. Coverage of the Senate offered no outlet for his creative talent, and the injection of any style in his reportage was invariably eliminated by the deskmen in New York.

While Catledge and other senior editors in New York trumpeted the call for brighter writing, they often did not really seem to want it when they got it; or they did not know how to get it into the paper when they got it. The decisive power lay with the deskmen, the copy-readers—finally it was *they* who decided what was bright, what was not, what was fit to print. Since most copyreaders were not known for their sense of humor—nor was their thankless job likely to produce one, nor to sustain one if they ever possessed one—the reporter attempting to inject brightness into his reporting of a Senate session was combating great odds, even if what had happened in the Senate might have justified a lighter treatment. *The Times* traditionally covered the Senate with drab restraint. It was as if *The Times*, despite Catledge's pronouncements, really wanted to be boring about the Senate and other official government bodies. *The Times* was awed by what was official. It was easier, safer, to report accurate boring accounts of government activity than accurate interesting accounts. And so in *The Times* the Senate was a body of stone, a stagnant stream of statistics and measures—not a vibrant congregation of human mannerisms and conceits, drives and ambitions, that somehow responded to the vibrations of the nation. The Senators themselves, and the *cognoscenti* in Washington, were not displeased with *The Times'* reporting, for they were among the few who could read between the lines and fill in the blanks; but average readers hardly ever got a full and penetrating picture, and therefore had little idea of what the Senate was really like until they themselves had visited it, and then they were often amazed at how vital it seemed. But in *The Times,* if there was a descriptive paragraph or two about the interior of the Senate, the mood, the atmosphere, it was usually buried near the bottom of the story, and was carried over into an inside page. A reader had to scan a thousand words to reach the few revealing lines. This was not true of *Times* reporting on the *un*official phases of American life—business, industry, fashion, sports, the arts—about these *The Times* could be expressive, clear, and critical—it seemed so much easier for a *Times*man to write honestly and frankly about Arthur Miller than about Senator Wayne Morse.

Of course, reporters like Allen Drury could always fight harder with the copydesk, if the deskmen were the actual repressors of readability—indeed, some *Times* reporters fought constantly with the desk, challenging each change, but this was not as easily done in Washington as in New York. A New York reporter working in the newsroom at night might see an early galley proof of his story, might learn the name of the offending copyreader and argue with him in a corner of the newsroom after the first edition had gone to press, possibly persuading the copyreader to restore a choice phrase for the second edition. But the Washington reporter did not see *The Times* until the following morning. Any complaint that he made was after the fact, and it was also quite formal—it had to be channeled through Reston, who might relay it to Dryfoos or Catledge, and then it would filter down through Daniel or Bernstein to the national-news editor, to the assistant national-news editor, to the head of the national copydesk, finally to the copyreader. It was unwise to berate copyreaders for tampering with a reporter's prose style unless the editing had distorted the facts or the meaning of the story. *The New York Times* was not a writers' colony, after all, and confrontations with copyreaders might disrupt their morale and diligence, might eventually lead to a permissiveness on their part, or a fear of making changes, that could eventually allow careless or tasteless writing to appear in *The Times*. The copyreaders were the enforcers of discipline, Ochsian disciples who upheld traditional standards, and they should not be undermined. Since "bright" writing was subjected to the copyreaders definition of what was bright, the reporter could only do his best and *not* read his story after it had appeared in *The Times*, as some reporters did; or he could fight constantly with the desk, as other reporters did; or he could do what Allen Drury did—give *The Times* what it seemed to want, and preserve his energy and talent for his outside writing.

Each day Drury would cover the Senate, would write accurately if uninspiredly, would file his story through the bureau to New York, and then promptly leave the office and work on a novel that portrayed the Senate, the Presidency, the Washington press and society with an insight that had never appeared under his by-line in *The Times*. Shortly after *Advise and Consent* had been completed for Doubleday & Company, it became a *Reader's Digest* condensed book, then a Book-of-the-Month Club selection. Arthur Krock, Russell Baker, and Mary McGrory of the Washington *Evening Star* wrote approving blurbs for the book, and Drury was being congratulated and discussed all over town—but still no word from Reston. Drury knew that Reston had little interest in novels, reading mostly nonfiction books that were useful to him as a journalist—"The Nineteenth Century was the era of the novelist, the Twentieth Centruy is the era of the journalist," was Reston's convenient assessment—and yet Reston was an individual of awareness, and Drury could not believe that Reston had not heard of *Advise and Consent*. Finally, unable to resist, Drury virtually demanded recognition. He approached Reston's secretary one day and remarked that everyone seemed to know about the book except Scotty Reston.

The next evening, Reston, passed by Drury's desk, and in a couple of terse but amiable sentences he congratulated Drury. He said that he had not realized that Drury had been working on such a project. When Drury reminded him that he had mentioned it two years before, when he had begun to write seriously, Reston replied, "I hadn't realized that was what you meant," adding that he thought the whole thing was great—and then, smiling, Reston was on his way, walking in that inimitable glittering manner.

Drury watched him and thought about him and his impression of Reston then, and years later, remained essentially the same: Reston, the supreme reporter and excellent writer, was also a major ego, a very self-centered, not deliberately cruel but fiercely competitive individual, even when he was indisputably on top. He did many kindnesses for people, Drury conceded, but generally as the grand seigneur. Reston's ego and competitive spirit were such that he simply could not take such competition from an underling, particularly when the underling not only dared the gods but succeeded and was going into orbit.

Drury resigned from *The Times* in 1959, not long after *Advise and Consent*, which would win a Pulitzer, became the number one best seller. One of the last articles that he wrote for the paper, and one of his best, was an article for the house organ, *Times Talk*, in which he revealed that in spite of his success, the copydesk and top management still seemed unimpressed by him. "It keeps you humble," he wrote, adding, "My friends on the copydesk are the same old lovable, ham-handed, insufferable hatchetmen they always were." The most gratifying result of his book, he said, was the invitation that he received from his fellow reporters to address them at the National Press Club, and the standing ovation that he received afterwards.

Later, at the annual Women's Press Club Congressional Night at the Statler Hotel, while Drury was standing and talking to Secretary of the Interior Stewart Udall and Mrs. Udall, Reston and his wife, Sally, came along, and Udall called out, "Here's one of your boys."

Reston grinned at Drury and said, "I'm one of his."

So we do not dislike one another, Drury thought, and he was very pleased.

Drury's Washington was not Reston's Washington, nor Lippmann's nor Buchwald's nor Gore Vidal's Washington—but the vulnerability of the politicians in Drury's world of fiction, and the partiality and self-protectiveness and self-aggrandizement of the Washington press, formed a tableau of the capital that a few *Times*men in New York believed to be quite realistic. It was not that the New York editors wished to portray an unflattering picture of Washington in *The Times*, but they were interested in a sharper, deeper sense of the city than they were getting. And as usual, they suspected that one reason they were not getting it was that the Washington bureau was overly protective of its sources. This complaint, which was nearly as old as the *Times* building, was first presented formally in 1916 when one New York editor, representing the opinion of others, wrote a lengthy memo to Ochs charging that Richard Oulahan, Krock's predecessor, was being "used" by the Woodrow Wilson administration, and was regularly writing propaganda. It was then suggested that Oulahan make weekly trips to New York so that he might dine with the editors and receive the benefit of their wisdom. But Ochs, who did not then regard a pro-Wilson policy as a vice, particularly since *The Times* had recently been accused of being pro-German, refused to interfere with Oulahan, and this attitude prevailed until Oulahan's death. Then Krock was sent from New York to Washington, and as one problem was solved another took its place—the problem of Krock himself. Now, in 1962, Krock's successor, Reston, after nearly a decade as the bureau chief, was beginning to sense a revival of old pressure from New

York, much of it coming from an editor who had just been named to run the national-news desk—Harrison Salisbury.

The national-news editor handles not only the stories that are sent in from Washington, but also those from *Times*men in other bureaus around the nation—Philadelphia and Boston, Chicago and Detroit, Kansas City and Houston; the men in the Deep South covering the Civil Rights movement; the men on the West Coast —Gladwin Hill in Los Angeles, Lawrence Davies in San Francisco. Salisbury had been appointed by Catledge, with strong support from Clifton Daniel, to bolster the national coverage; Salisbury had very definite ideas on how to achieve this, and he did not care if he became very unpopular in the process. Salisbury was not an office politician. He was sharp and direct, a tall man with a long stride, a lean catlike face with quick eyes and a little moustache that seemed somehow to be working for him. He had a sense of humor, but it was subtle, so subtle that few perceived it. This did not bother him. His primary concern was to improve the national reporting. He wanted more imagination, more mobility and drive from his correspondents, more jet journalism and less waiting for events to occur in their own backyards; and if his regional correspondents did not respond to his wishes, he would invade their territory with eager young journalists borrowed from the New York staff. Salisbury had made dozens of recent trips around the country as a lecturer and reporter, and he knew what news was there, what new trends and reactions were changing America, and he wanted his correspondents to report these fully and to write them well. To guarantee that the writing would not be disjointed by the copyreaders, Salisbury hovered over them, overruled them when necessary, and was unconcerned about the sensitivities of the deskmen's demagogue, Theodore Bernstein.

Salisbury also had definite feelings about Washington; he had worked there for the United Press, and he had also worked in *The Times*' bureau during the summers of 1955 and 1956, covering the State Department. Reston had suggested that he might remain in Washington, but Salisbury, very much his own man, was not interested. Reston and he would soon be at loggerheads, he thought, and after completing his summer tour in Washington he returned to New York and worked on special assignments. When Catledge offered him the job of education editor, Salisbury saw it as too limiting; but when he was offered the national-news editorship in 1962, he accepted it.

Soon Reston's men began to feel Salisbury's presence and to resent it. They were unaccustomed to such scrutiny and they complained to Reston, who interceded. But Salisbury was not easily discouraged. Every few days, it seemed, he would pepper the bureau with more memos, calls, tips on some new government plan or conspiracy, and if the bureau did not produce the story that he believed was there, he was dissatisfied. It was implied somehow that they had not checked with enough people; or they were buying all that was told them; or there "had to be more to it" than that. Some members of the bureau were astounded by Salisbury's suspicious nature, and they attributed it to his years in Russia during the dark days of Stalin. Other bureau men resented Salisbury's comparing them unfavorably with certain Washington reporters on the *Herald Tribune,* or the *Washington Post,* or the *Wall Street Journal.* The lively reporting that he seemed to like in the *Herald Tribune*, they said, merely represented a desperate last attempt by a dying newspaper to call attention to itself, and they were surprised by his decision to publish President Kennedy's s.o.b. remark in *The Times* during the Administration's confrontation with the steel industry in April of 1962. Wallace Carroll, Reston's deputy, had written in his story that President Kennedy had been enraged at the steelmen's decision to raise prices across the board and had spoken unflatteringly of them, but Carroll did not attribute to Kennedy the direct quotation that would later appear in his story ("My father always told me that all businessmen were sons of bitches but I never believed it till now!"); it was Salisbury who identified these words as the President's, getting the information from sources whom he trusted. Salisbury then called Carroll and asked him to write an insertion that would include this quotation. Carroll objected, saying that *he* had not heard the President use such language. When Salisbury persisted, Carroll snapped back, "The hell with it—you write it in yourself!"

If Reston had not been so busy at this time writing his column and running his bureau, fortifying its future with such younger men as Wicker and Baker, Max Frankel and Anthony Lewis; and if Reston's time and interests were not also involved with keeping up with the nation, the world, and his own family, which included three sons whom he rarely saw enough of, Reston could have devoted his entire career to fighting the editors in New York. Reston had more worthy ambitions than that. Salisbury's intrusions could be annoying, but Reston recognized Salisbury as a good newsman whose instincts were often right if his personal approach was often wrong; and if things became intolerable Reston could always go to the publisher. Dryfoos, in fact, had recently discussed the possibility of Reston's coming to New York at some future date to serve as "Editor" of *The Times,* which was a title that did not now exist, but from Dryfoos' vague description it would seem to give Reston more power than the managing editor. Reston, however, made it clear that he preferred living in Washington, and under no circumstances would Reston want to relinquish his column. For the column was both Reston's joy and his special base of power within the organization. Because of the column, and what he had done with it, Reston had become a national figure, a confidant of presidents, an individual that other publishers would quickly hire away from *The Times* if they could. If he gave up the column, he would not carry the weight that he did with world leaders, and soon his position within the paper would be less than it had been—he would be more identified with his *Times* title, less with his own name, and there was no advantage to that.

And so as long as he had his column and had such valuable subordinates as Wallace Carroll to relieve him of many administrative burdens, Reston was resigned to an attitude of give-and-take with New York (with the ageless Arthur Krock muttering in the background that when *he* was bureau chief he took nothing from New York). Reston was now approaching his middle fifties; he had books to write, sons to think about, little time for bickering with fellow editors. He had achieved his goals and, more important, he was a happy man.

The Sulzberger family was proud to call him their own—and never more proud than in December of 1962, when during a New York newspaper strike, Reston read his Sunday column on television, communicating to millions his affection for *The Times* and his sadness that it was now being struck by the labor unions.

> Reading *The Times* is a life career, like raising a family—and almost as difficult. But I've become accustomed to its peculiar ways and can't break the habit. It is a community service, like plumbing.
> This is the season of peace, and somehow—I don't know why—peace seems to have a better chance in *The Times*. Everybody else seems to be shouting at us and giving the human race six weeks to get out. But *The Times* is always saying that there was trouble in the Sixteenth Century too. . . .
> Without newspapers, the procedures of life change. Tired men, sick of the human race after a long, gabby day at the office, cannot escape into the life story of Y. A. Tittle or the political perils of Harold Macmillan, but must go on talking to strangers all the way to Westport.
> It's bad enough on the public, but think of a reporter. I've been fielding *The Times* on my front stoop every morning for 25 years and it's cold and lonely out there now. Besides, how do I know what I think if I can't read what I write?

The strike, which began on December 8 in 1962, lasted for 114 days. It affected not only *The Times* but also the *Daily News*, the *Journal-American*, the *World-Telegram and Sun*; and also three other New York dailies and two on Long Island that had *not* been struck by the printers' union but whose owners, as a sign of ownership solidarity, had either suspended or curtailed the publication of their papers. The strike, coming in the middle of the big pre-Christmas advertising campaigns, deprived the publishers of millions of dollars, thus weakening some publications to a point of no return—indeed, the *Mirror* would fold not long after the strike had ended; and within a few years, the merged edition of the *Herald Tribune*, the *World-Telegram and Sun,* and the *Journal-American* would also disappear after another strike. During the 1962–63 strike it had been predicted by Bertram A. Powers, president of the printers union, that the number of New York dailies would eventually dwindle to three, and he was right. Only *The Times* and two tabloids, the morning *News* and the evening *Post*, would remain in a city that in 1900 had sixteen dailies, and that in 1930 had a dozen.

The disappearance of newspapers in New York is attributed to many causes, and is interpreted differently by the spokesmen of management or labor; but from either view it is a history of failure, of mismanagement, miscalculation, and mistrust. The publishers were beset by the rising costs of newspaper production, by the higher wage demands of workers and the intrusion of television for the advertising dollar, and they scrambled and experimented to keep pace with economic trends and a changing society, often taking wrong turns and going astray. The workers feared the new automatic machinery that the publishers saw as tools of survival; despite the vague promises and euphemisms of the new technologists, the workers knew that automation would ultimately destroy their craft and their security, and so they drove harder bargains—too hard, the publishers thought, but publishers thought as publishers, as profiteers, not as philanthropists. The publishers lived off Fifth Avenue or in other fashionable neighborhoods, and they had weekend homes; while they championed the cause of equality, they sent their children to private schools and dwelled behind tall fences and doormen. The publishers made many speeches about freedom of the press, but they said "no comment" to reporters covering strike negotiations and often barred the press from their business meetings. In any economic crisis, the publishers of various editorial opinions would stand as rich men always stood, together.

The workers were different. They were unnoticed men with soiled fingers whose work was recognized only when they had made a mistake, had dropped a line of type, had hit the wrong key. They lived in small row houses or apartments in what remained of ethnic neighborhoods, and they worried not about China or the Common Market but about encroaching slums, and their small investments, and the neighborhood school. If they worried about distant wars it was because their sons would be among the first to go. Their loyalty was not to their newspaper but to their union, within which they practiced a basic nepotism similar to the publishers'; but otherwise they had next to nothing in common with a publisher.

During a long strike, publishers could seek and receive the support of the President of the United States— politicians being always anxious to do favors for publishers; but the workers looked only to their union, and in 1962 their attention was focused on a hardened realist named Bertram A. Powers. At forty-one, Powers was head of the New York printers' union. He was a tall man with a sharp angular face, blondish hair fading into white, a man of singular vision and no gift for small talk. He had left high school after two years and become a printer, and he recognized unionism as a necessity; if employers had been fair with their employees, if they had not exploited them, there would never have been unions, Powers thought. But generosity had not been the employers' traditional trait, and Powers knew from his own experience as a printer that publishers made few concessions voluntarily. Even such printers' functions as washing their hands and urinating were provided for within a contract—in fact, one of the items in the 1962 discussions with the publishers was the printers' willingness to surrender fifteen minutes a day of "toilet time" so that their work week could be reduced from thirty-six and one-quarter hours to thirty-five hours. But the publishers resisted on the assumption that the printers would indulge in toilet time whether or not it was contractually sanctioned, adding that a reduction of the work week would drive up production costs.

There were many other points of disagreement between Powers and the publishers. Powers wanted more money for his printers, more than the current wage of $141; he wanted an increase in paid sick leave from one day a year to five; higher employer contributions to the union's pension and welfare funds; a share in the money saved by the publishers' installation of automatic equipment. These and other things that Powers wanted were not always specifically spelled out—he wanted the publishers to propose, the union to decide—and he also wanted something that was not in the contract. Identity. It was not strictly a personal identity that he sought, although this would be the charge of many who opposed him; it was rather an identity for his union, which for many years had remained in the background during the biennial negotiations between the publishers and the other unions—the photoengravers' union, which had inspired the strike in 1953; the stereotypers' union, the pressmen's union, the deliverers' union, the electricians and mailers and the whole cast of other workers necessary to large daily newspapers. The printers' union had gone along with the others, and it had especially gone along with the New York Newspaper Guild, the union that represents reporters and copyreaders, clerks and copyboys, elevator operators and cleaning ladies and cafeteria cooks and anyone else not affiliated with one of the nine craft unions. When the Guild had called a strike against the *New York World-Telegram* in 1951, the strike had succeeded because the craft unions had supported it; and since then the Guild had assumed a kind of leadership among the unions that it had not previously enjoyed. Every two years, before its contract expired on October 31, the Guild's representatives would confer with the publishers; and after they had come to terms it was assumed that these terms would be acceptable to the craft unions, whose contract expiration date always occurred on December 7. Bertram A. Powers now wanted an end to these assumptions and procedures.

Instead of the Guild being in the position to set the standards by virtue of its earlier expiration date, Powers wanted all union contracts to expire on the same date—hopefully the Guild's date of October 31, so that the craft unions could confront the publishers before the big pre-Christmas advertising bonanza, a time when publishers would be most anxious to avert a strike. Powers' union, founded more than a century ago, had not called a strike since 1883—except for a "voluntary vacation" in 1919 in the hope of achieving a forty-four-hour week. But this protest, staged in defiance of the International Typographical Union, had failed. And while the more aggressively led unions had made impressive gains during the century, the printers' had not kept pace, and it would never catch up by continuing to accept four-or five-dollar-a-year salary increases, and the assorted fringe benefits, that might be acceptable to other unions whose base pay was higher.

What the printers also needed, Powers believed, was a stronger sense of their own identity. A newspaper could be produced without reporters and copyreaders—the executives, the bureaus, and the wire services could fill the word gap—but a newspaper could not be produced without printers; at least not at this time. Of course if the automatic typesetting machines, which responded like player pianos to perforated strips of paper tape, were allowed to multiply, they could eventually lead to the eradication of printers, and of the union and of Powers himself—a harrowing thought for Powers, if not for all the publishers.

Some publishers, emotional and bitter, came to hate Powers during the strike. They saw Powers as a ruthless threat to their survival in journalism. Of the New York dailies, only *The Times* and the *News* were consistent money makers; the others survived on subsidies from newspaper chains or from individual owners whose wealth was derived from outside sources. While the Publishers Association had assured the union that no regular employees would lose their jobs through automation, the publishers nevertheless wanted to immediately begin using the automated machines to set all the Wall Street listings and related stock charts on their financial pages. The machines would receive the tape containing this information from the Associated Press or United Press International. But the unions balked, insisting that a share of the savings made possible through the use of tape should go into a special fund for printers' retraining, or for their early retirement or other supplemental unemployment benefits. The publishers objected, aware that publishers in other large cities had received union approval for the increased use of tape without having to set up special funds for printers. And so a stalemate resulted, attitudes hardened on both sides, and in 1962, a few weeks before Christmas, the strike began.

Picket lines of printers paraded back and forth in front of the offices of *The Times*, the *News*, the *Journal American*, and the *World-Telegram and Sun*. The owners of the city papers not being struck—the *Post*, the *Mirror,* the *Herald Tribune*—stopped their own presses and locked their doors, Suddenly, the reading habits of millions of New Yorkers were changed. Some New Yorkers, their routines interrupted, would learn to live without newspapers and would never return as regular readers. They watched more television, or read news magazines more thoroughly, or books, discovering that New York seemed a more normal and placid place without the daily barrage of blazing headlines from Hearst, the rumored gangland shootings in the *News*, the threatening international strife in *The Times*.

Other New Yorkers, hooked on the daily habit, read *The Times'* Western edition that their friends in California mailed to them; or they bought the out-of-town papers now stacked on newsstands—the *Philadelphia Inquirer,* the *Christian Science Monitor*—or they read the *Wall Street Journal,* or *Women's Wear Daily,* or one of the slim special strike editions being produced and edited by groups of journalists, including some from *The Times.* For these and other *Times*men, the strike did not inspire the inner conflict and regret that had characterized the strike of 1953; that past strike had been a new and disturbing experience, one that had prevented *The Times* from publishing for the first time in its history, and while most *Times*men felt compelled to respect the picket lines they had also felt a sense of abandonment and betrayal of *The Times.*

Now, however, the personal bond was not so strong. *The Times* had seemed to become a much less personal place in recent years, more coolly corporate as it had grown larger and more important, and veteran *Times*men were at peace with themselves as they watched the picket lines. Some younger *Times*men even felt a sense of adventure and freedom during the 1962–63 strike, particularly during its earlier stages: their daily lives now did not revolve so directly around *The Times,* they had time to think more about themselves, to re-evaluate their present circumstances, to contemplate the future. They could see that life went on without *The Times,* the world went on without *The Times,* and as the newspaper strike continued they gained in self-confidence and awareness; they explored new areas of the city at a slower pace, they saw new people, thought new thoughts, dressed more casually, acted more impulsively, sensed what it would be like not to be a *Times*man—no privileged treatment from politicians, no free tickets from press agents, no guarantee that a telephone call would be returned from an important person; no sense of responsibility to these important people, no restrictions when writing a *Times* story, no feeling of personal restraint and caution in public dealings or private involvements—they saw two sides of their life during the strike, the one side more privileged and somehow neutralized, the second less assured but perhaps more fulfilling— they weighed these two worlds, and they waited. They drew unemployment checks and union benefits, or they found temporary jobs on television, or in government, or in public-relations firms, or on magazines, often earning as much as or more than they had on *The Times*. One *Times* reporter, Philip Benjamin, completed his first novel during the strike—*Quick Before It Melts*, featuring Antarctica, where he had been on assignment for *The Times*—and this humorous novel, published in 1963, was sold to Hollywood for $50,000.

Nearly all the strikers, the craft unions as well as the newsmen, adjusted to the prolonged strike without great financial strain. The average printer, backed by union funds and state unemployment insurance, was earning about twenty dollars less than he would have earned had he been working. If the strike hurt anyone financially it was the newspaper owners— and also those outsiders whose businesses were influenced by newspapers: the proprietors of stores that relied on local advertising, the producers of Broadway shows, the buyers and sellers of real estate, the investors, the speculators, the publicists. The strike was disheartening to an artist making a debut, to a debutante just engaged, to a stenographer seeking a job, to an owner of a missing pet or a lost diamond, to the maker of a speech—although political orators who were not assured of television coverage generally withheld their words. The strike, however, had no consequential effect on world economics or politics, and it did not last long enough to revive the art of secret diplomacy nor to deflate the art of trial balloons. New Yorkers wishing to remain informed did so—although, without *The Times*, not so thoroughly—by reading what was available, and by tuning into the expanded coverage on radio and television. While the absence of

The Times deprived electronic journalism of its greatest news guide, the media responded admirably to the challenge, and NBC's Channel 4 in New York also presented a series of Sunday-afternoon telecasts featuring *Times*men who had not struck the paper and who read or commented on the news that might have appeared in the Sunday *Times* had there been one. Clifton Daniel was the star of the show, his suave and understated manner reminding some viewers of the British actor Leslie Howard; but all the *Times*men presented the news and themselves commendably—Berstein and Salisbury, Reston and Oakes, Bosley Crowther and Charlotte Curtis; James Roach, the sports editor, and Craig Claiborne, the food editor, and dozens of others. Perhaps only Claiborne seemed petrified by the camera, his hands trembling and the dishes clattering as he demonstrated his cooking, but he turned this nervousness to his own advantage with the home audience when, as he prepared to pour the sauce, he said: "And you take a shaky gravy boat . . ."

As the strike continued into its sixth week, and as the Secretary of Labor and even President Kennedy were unable to influence a settlement, or even to get serious negotiations under way, James Reston became indignant. Reston, together with his bureau in Washington, the bureaus around the nation and overseas, and a small force of executives and nonunion employees in the New York office, had now perhaps felt the strike more strongly than the strikers themselves. The nonstrikers were getting paid for doing very little, and were feeling uneasy about it, and Reston was especially aware of the anguish that the strike was causing the Sulzbergers and Orvil Dryfoos. On January 12, 1963, Reston wrote a column for *The Times*' Western and International editions, and its news service to seventy-two out-of-town papers, that attacked Bertram Powers and the printers' union, advocating that the publishers print their New York papers in nonunion shops if necessary and distribute the editions through the mail. Reston's column read in part:

The President of the United States cannot censor the New York papers. The Congress of the United States is specifically forbidden in the first article of the Bill of Rights to abridge their freedom, but Bert Powers, the boss of the New York Printers, can not only censor them but shut them down.

What is "free" about a press that can be muzzled on the whim of a single citizen? . . .

So the flow of information in the nation's largest city is left to the play of sheer power, and the power struggle is wildly uneven. For the union is using all its power to stop publication and the owners are not using all their power to publish.

This may be an acceptable situation in a meat factory or a steel mill, but newspapers are not pork chops or iron fences. Unless everybody from Jefferson to Mencken and Gerald Johnson has been kidding us, our job is to print the news and raise hell, with the kind permission of Bert Powers if possible but without it if necessary.

I know this view is not shared by all publishers, but reporters are part of this profession too, and if, failing to make an honorable peace, we acquiesce in the proposition that news is a dispensable commodity like soap, then we shall be treated like soap peddlers and deserve it.

This column was killed by *The Times*. It did not appear in the Western or International edition of *The Times*, and a cancellation notice was sent to the out-of-town papers subscribing to the news service. The decision was ultimately Orvil Dryfoos'. When Dryfoos saw Reston's column, there seemed a faint sign of hope around the bargaining table, an illusory sign that quickly faded. But Dryfoos was taking no chances. Reston was disappointed but powerless on this occasion to influence Dryfoos. Dryfoos was still Reston's very close friend and admirer, but more than that Dryfoos was a publisher. He did not wish to affront Bertram Powers, the villain of Reston's piece, and possibly cause more discord between labor and management.

Nevertheless, the strike went on. And ten weeks later, with the strike still on, Reston's unpublished column appeared in the *New Republic,* with a rejoinder from Murray Kempton. Though admiring Reston's spirit, and critical of *The Times'* decision to censor Reston, Kempton did not agree with the general thesis of Reston's article. "We read here about devils and holy men as we used, to Reston's discomfort, to read about them in the speeches of Secretary Dulles," Kempton wrote. Reston's anger, Kempton thought, was not aroused so much by the printers' strike against newspapers as by the printers' striking against *The Times.* "He is not so much a man of the left or right as he is a man of *The Times,*" Kempton wrote, wishing that Reston were less cavalier about strikes in such places as steel mills and meat factories. "If a strike at a meat factory throws 20,000 persons out of work," Kempton wrote, "theirs is a private interest which deserves to be a public concern." The striking printers, Kempton concluded, were men who were out to affirm their pride as trade unionists if not as craftsmen—"They have a notion of society's debt to them as inflated as Reston's and my own notion of journalists' contribution to society."

As the strike extended through the winter, Dryfoos seemed frustrated and weary. Though he had just turned fifty and was considered a healthy man, Dryfoos had had rheumatic heart disease as a younger man, a discovery that he made when he was rejected for military service in World War II. Now, as publisher, he tried to influence a fair and conciliatory settlement, and during a crucial moment when the negotiations seemed about to break up in angry recriminations, Dryfoos persuaded the chief negotiators to resume talks and submerge their hostility. Much of the hostility had been directed at Dryfoos' own colleague and adviser, Amory H. Bradford, *The Times'* general manager, who had been nominated by the Publishers Association before the strike to serve as its chief spokesman with the union. The publishers were aware of

Bradford's imperiousness but they admired his independence and assurance, and they believed that they had in Bradford a formidable emissary to protect their interests against the ambitions of the union. What they did not anticipate was the unionists' reaction to Bradford. If there was one man who was utterly incapable of affecting the "regular guy" manner that executives so often try to project during their talks with union leaders, it was Amory Howe Bradford. When Bradford mingled with unionists, it was like the rigid proctor of a proper boys' school mingling with slum children. Bradford's smile was reminiscent of the way the Duke of Edinburgh used to smile at native chieftains while touring the African colonies: a downward-tilting, royal-eyed, bonny look into the distance. No matter what Bradford did or said in the company of the unionists, it seemed somehow wrong. His towering height was wrong; his lean blondish New England handsomeness was wrong, and so were his pipe and his dark double-breasted Foreign Office suit. It was also no advantage that his opposite number across the bargaining table was Bertram Powers, a tenacious up-from-the-ranks American-Irishman with unpleasant memories of Harvard students romping with detachment through his Boston neighborhood. That Bradford was a Yale man made little difference to Powers. At the slightest sign of conceit on Bradford's part, Powers would stiffen. And as the continuing strike put Bradford under great pressure from the newspaper owners, from the business community, and from politicians and peacemakers in New York and Washington, Bradford's manner became increasingly chilly and arrogant. Not only did Powers and other unionists feel this, but it extended also to New York's Mayor Robert F. Wagner, who had held several conferences in behalf of the strike; to Theodore W. Kheel, an impartial strike mediator; and to Dorothy Schiff, publisher of the *New York Post*. As the strike approached its third month Mrs. Schiff became so exasperated that she quit the Publishers Association and resumed publication. She felt that New Yorkers should have at least one local paper to read, and so far there seemed little hope of a settlement. Dozens of meetings, some of them lasting until dawn, had produced few concessions on either side, only more bitterness. Bertram Powers was particularly embittered by the personal attack made upon him by President Kennedy during a televised news conference. Kennedy, reading a statement that favored the publishers, accused Powers of holding out for unreasonable demands and he urged that the dispute be put up to a third party for settlement. "It is clear," President Kennedy said, "in the case of the New York newspaper strike that the local of the International Typographical Union and its president, Bertram Powers, insofar as anyone can understand his position, are attempting to impose a settlement which could shut down several newspapers in New York and throw thousands out of work."

If Amory Bradford had said that, it would not have agitated Powers, but to hear such words from the President—a Boston Irishman for whom Powers had rung doorbells during the 1960 campaign, a revered figure that Powers had not associated with the Harvard boys of his Boston past—was a shattering experience for Powers. And not only Powers—the union was equally resentful, disturbed, and surprised by Kennedy's criticism.

Two days after the Kennedy statement, Powers was approached by a Washington publisher who was a friend of the President's—Philip L. Graham, the president and chief executive officer of the *Washington Post* and *Newsweek*: Graham had heard that *Time* was preparing a cover story on Powers, and, contemplating the same thing, he invited Powers to his New York hotel for a private conference, and the two men talked for six hours. Powers felt comfortable with Graham, and the Washington publisher would not have guessed that Powers' formal education had ceased after the tenth grade. Powers was socially poised and articulate, having gained considerable self-confidence during the strike, becoming accustomed to articulating his views in the daily spotlight of television cameras while encircled by crowds of people. He had gone to numbers of fine restaurants with important peacemakers during the strike, and he had come to understand with more intimacy the symbols of success. He had seen how the headwaiters at "21" welcomed the well-publicized and handsome strike mediator Theodore Kheel, and he had become familiar with the interior of City Hall and with the mayor's residence at Gracie Mansion, and with the people who came and went there. Powers had also gotten a closer view of how publishers live, how casually they traveled back and forth to Europe, how they sometimes took *two* vacations during the winter, in Florida or Nassau or Bermuda— even during a newspaper strike. The top national labor leaders, too, enjoyed the good life—at the very top, labor was not much different from management; finally there was little to choose between these men after they had achieved power, and were invited to the same political banquets, and sat elbow-to-elbow along the dais; and soon—at least among the younger labor leaders—they were going to the same tailor, were having their fingernails buffed by the same sensual manicurist, were probably thinking the same improper thoughts.

All this had not suddenly occurred to Powers during the newspaper strike—he had been a vice-president in his union for eight years before becoming its president in 1961, and his marriage to a schoolteacher had also helped to smooth some of his rougher edges and heighten his awareness. But his experience during the 1962–63 strike was new and dramatic; he now understood as never before the importance of the media as an instrument to power. And so when he received a call from Philip Graham requesting a talk at Graham's suite in the Carlyle Hotel, Powers wasted little time in getting there, knowing immediately its location. It was on Madison Avenue and Seventy-sixth Street, and it had been regularly publicized in newspapers because it was where Harry Truman always stayed and Kennedy frequently stayed.

Graham was impressed with Powers' frankness and

conviction, and at the conclusion of their discussion Graham telephoned President Kennedy in Palm Beach and, with Powers still in the room, praised Powers to the President and denounced the New York publishers. When Kennedy learned that Powers was present, he asked Graham to call later, which he did. As a result of the next call, during which Graham expressed interest in becoming an intermediary between the New York publishers and the unions, Kennedy endorsed the idea. But when the New York publishers learned of it, they refused to consider it. If Graham entered the New York negotiations, they said, they would walk out.

In the relative quiet of *The Times*' newsroom, Theodore Bernstein decided that when the strike was finally settled, *The Times* should attempt to explain to its readers why there had been a strike in the first place, why it had lasted so long, and what had gone on behind the negotiating scenes day after day. Bernstein consulted with *The Times*' labor specialist, A. H. Raskin, and the project was outlined. It was an unusual assignment. It would mean that Raskin would not only be analyzing the demands and stubbornness of the unions and their leaders, but he would also be required to balance it with the implacability of the Publishers Association, including its spokesman, *The Times*' own Amory Bradford. In the history of *The Times* this seemed unprecedented, a word that Bernstein had banned from the paper on the theory that nothing was unprecedented; but if Raskin did write a critical account of *The Times*' vice-president, and if *The Times* published it, it would be a most unusual happening.

When Raskin began his research he discovered, to his utter lack of amazement, that newspaper executives were like big businessmen anywhere—equally quick at dodging reporters when the news was not so pleasant. When Raskin tried to reach Bradford at his office and left messages with his secretary, the calls were not returned. If Bradford was in his office on the fourteenth floor, and was not occupied elsewhere with the negotiation, *The Times* might have been witness to the bizarre scene of a working *Times* reporter banging on the locked door of a reluctant *Times* executive.

When Raskin's story did appear in *The Times*, on April 1, 1963, a day after the employees had finally returned to work, Bradford was very upset by it. The one-hundred-fourteen-day strike had ended, Raskin wrote, with Powers achieving breakthroughs on three of his key issues. Powers was guaranteed a thirty-five-hour week (in return for relinquishing the fifteen minutes of daily toilet time). He achieved the common expiration date on union contracts with the publishers —not before the big pre-Christmas advertising campaign, as he had hoped, but before the pre-Easter advertising, which was almost as good. And Powers also managed to limit the use of automatic equipment by one-third of what the publishers had wanted, with a joint committee formed to analyze what money had been saved and how much of it should go to the union. The salary increase, totaling $12.63 a week per man over a two-year period, was roughly $2.50 more than would have been earned had there been no strike.

Mayor Wagner of New York, and Theodore Kheel, the mediator, were favorably portrayed in Raskin's article as the packagers of the acceptable settlement, but Powers and Bradford and most of the other personalities were seen as considerably less than heroic. Powers was said by Raskin's sources to be "honest, clean, democratic—and impossible"; "cold, ambitious and utterly incapable of setting any realistic priorities for himself," although Powers was conceded to be "the ablest and most forward-looking" of the graphic arts union leaders. Amory Bradford was credited with a keen mind and articulateness, but Raskin also reported that Bradford had brought "an attitude of such icy disdain into the conference rooms that the mediator often felt he ought to ask the hotel to send up more heat." Raskin also characterized Bradford as an "aloof" man who operated on a "short fuse" and who called the mayor's strike methods "foolish" and had become "sick and tired of the whole proceedings." Mayor Wagner was quoted as saying that the forces of management and labor had conducted the strike with equal incompetence, adding " 'both sides deserve each other.' "

When Raskin finished writing his story, it was read by Bernstein and then by Catledge. After Catledge had finished it, he immediately called Dryfoos and asked him to look at it. Dryfoos said he would read it when it appeared in *The Times*. Catledge urged him to read it prior to publication. So Dryfoos took the story with him to Central Park, where he could read it alone near the lake, and Catledge remained in the office uncertain of Dryfoos' reaction and whether the story would ever be published in *The Times*. Although Dryfoos had recently killed the Reston column, Dryfoos' overall record was quite commendable in permitting to be published in *The Times* stories that most publishers would eliminate. Dryfoos had not vetoed anti-cigarette editorials although they had cost *The Times* thousands of dollars in cigarette advertising. Dryfoos had not objected when *The Times'* television critic, Jack Gould, during the greatly publicized television quiz show scandals, wrote a column informing readers that newspapermen were "not entirely qualified to don the mantle of unsullied virtue." One common vice, Gould wrote, was the "junket"—whereby a business concern pays all the travel and living expenses of a journalist who covers an event of direct interest to the company, such as the opening of a new hotel in the Caribbean, or the filming of a movie in Europe or Mexico. Gould also mentioned the tradition of "Christmas loot" in newspaper offices, the deluge of gifts to the press from private companies. While Gould did not single out any particular newspaper, *The Times* was always high on the seasonal list: indeed, *The Times'* reception room during Christmas week was stacked with newly arrived bright packages—cases of liquor, baskets of fruit, silver serving sets, movie cameras, and other tokens of affection from various New York promoters and merchants.

With a knowing smile, Dryfoos reminded Gould that he was "opening a can of worms" with the story, but Dryfoos seemed pleased to publish it, and almost immediately there was posted on the bulletin board in the newsroom a request that *Times*men hitherto return all gift packages, a policy that did little to enhance Gould's popularity within the office.

Now after reading Raskin's article, Orvil Dryfoos returned it to Catledge's office. Dryfoos whistled softly and raised his eyebrows, but he told Catledge to print it. Dryfoos could anticipate the reaction it would have with his colleague, Bradford, but Dryfoos felt that *The Times* had no choice but to publish it. Raskin's reputation for accuracy and judgment was unquestioned, and so the piece was relayed to the composing room on the fourth floor, where the printers read it with interest, and when Amory Bradford saw it he became enraged. He urged Dryfoos to reconsider, but the publisher said he could not. And so, on April 1, it appeared, taking two full pages in *The Times*; and soon it was celebrated around the country—and in a piece in *The New Yorker* by A. J. Liebling—as a remarkable example of independent journalism. President Kennedy, discussing it later in a conversation with a *Times*man in Washington, said that if he had been Dryfoos, he would probably not have published it.

This represented one of Dryfoos' final decisions as a *Times* publisher. He left the office almost immediately afterward for a short vacation in Puerto Rico. He was very tired and he looked it. But his vacation in Puerto Rico was interrupted by illness and he entered a hospital near San Juan; then he was flown back to New York and he went directly from the airport to the Harkness Pavilion of the Columbia Presbyterian Medical Center. That is where he died on May 25 of a heart ailment, at the age of fifty.

The death of Orvil Dryfoos was followed by messages of condolence from leaders around the nation and world—President Kennedy and U Thant; Dean Rusk and Adlai Stevenson; Jean Monnet of France, Adolfo López Mateos of Mexico, Jaja Wachuku of Nigeria, dozens of congressmen, governors, publishers, hundreds of friends. His funeral at Temple Emanu-El on Fifth

Avenue was attended by two thousand mourners, and the eulogy, delivered by James Reston, began:

> The death of Orvil Dryfoos was blamed on "heart failure" but that obviously could not have been the reason. Orv Dryfoos' heart never failed him or anybody else—ask the reporters on *The Times*. It was steady as the stars—ask anybody in this company of friends. It was faithful as the tides—ask his beloved wife and family. No matter what the doctors say, they cannot blame his heart.

Reston then recounted Dryfoos' qualities as a publisher, his ability to make sound decisions under pressure—such as in the newsroom on election night in 1960 when Dryfoos was the first man to "sense that we had gone out on a limb for Kennedy too early and insisted that we reconsider. And again in 1961," Reston continued, "when we were on the point of reporting a premature invasion of Cuba, his courteous questions and wise judgment held us back."

This last point seemed to carry just the slightest sting for a few New York editors assembled in the temple—*they* had planned to play up the Bay of Pigs invasion, but Dryfoos, agreeing with Reston, had ordered the story toned down.

In addition to the Sulzberger and Dryfoos families, and the political dignitaries, the assemblage in the temple included most of the top executives and editors—Markel and Krock, Catledge and Oakes, Daniel and Salisbury, and many editors from past decades: Charles Merz, former editorial-page editor; Neil MacNeil, an assistant managing editor who had worked under Van Anda, Birchall, and James; David H. Joseph, a retired city editor who had been hired personally by Ochs. Amory Bradford also attended the funeral service but he did not sit among the many executives near the front. He sat several rows back, and Harrison Salisbury, who has an eye for such things, immediately foresaw Bradford's resignation.

After Dryfoos was buried in a grave near the mausoleum in which Adolph and Mrs. Ochs are buried, on a knoll looking west over the Saw Mill River in Westchester County, there followed weeks of intense guessing in the newsroom as to who the next publisher would be. Arthur Hays Sulzberger, who was seventy-two and restricted to a wheel chair because of his heart condition, was not capable of resuming command even briefly. His only son, Arthur Ochs (Punch) Sulzberger, thirty-seven years old, had little executive experience. Since Dryfoos had appeared to be in good health until the strike, it was assumed by the Sulzbergers that Dryfoos would be the paper's chief executive through the Nineteen-seventies, and there had meanwhile been no sense of urgency about developing a successor.

Now *The Times* was in the awkward position of having no family member of experience to step in as Dryfoos had stepped in for Sulzberger, or as Sulzberger had for Ochs. The selection of another son-in-law to replace Dryfoos was not possible: Richard N. Cohen, the second husband of Dr. Judith Sulzberger Cohen, the youngest of the three Sulzberger girls, was a successful insurance man; and while he served on *The Times'* board of directors he had little interest in journalism as a career. The other son-in-law, Ben Hale Golden, husband of the Sulzbergers' second daughter, Ruth, did have newspaper experience—he was publisher of the *Chattanooga Times;* but their marriage was going badly, and there would later be a divorce. Mrs. Golden, however, was herself mentioned in the newsroom as a possibility in New York. She was an extremely intelligent woman who wrote gracefully and had an executive background with the *Chattanooga Times*. There was also talk of John Oakes becoming the publisher, or of the publisher's duties being shared somehow by two individuals—a family member might serve as an overseer of the business side of *The Times*, while the news side would be under an editor with close personal ties to the family. An obvious choice would be James Reston, who was a particular favorite of Iphigene Sulzberger's.

Iphigene Sulzberger was now seventy-one, but she was as alert as ever. She was active on the board of directors—which included, in addition to the Sulzberger family, such nonfamily members as Bradford; Eugene R. Black, former head of the World Bank; and Paul Van Anda, son of Carr Van Anda. But of the directors, Iphigene Sulzberger seemed undoubtedly the most influential, especially now that her husband was in such poor health. She controlled about two-thirds of the voting stock of *The Times*. Upon her death, her father's fortune would be divided within the family, but she was now very much alive, and while *The Times*' official statements would continue to be made in the name of Arthur Hays Sulzberger, the firm hand of Iphigene Sulzberger would be helping to form each word.

On June 20, a little more than three weeks after Dryfoos' death, a statement from the office of Arthur Hays Sulzberger announced that his son, Arthur Ochs Sulzberger, would be the publisher of *The Times*. The new publisher, at thirty-seven, was the youngest chief executive that the paper had ever had. His grandfather, Adolph Ochs, had been five months past his thirty-eighth birthday when he took over *The Times* in August of 1896.

"It can be truly said," Arthur Hays Sulzberger stated, "that *The Times* is a family enterprise."

14

THE new publisher was a friendly, unostentatious, young man who had curly, dark hair, smoked a pipe, wore Paul Stuart suits, and always said hello to whoever was in the elevator. If he bore any physical resemblance to his distinguished-looking father, it was not obvious to those in the newsroom: he seemed more an Ochs than a Sulzberger. He had his mother's dark penetrating eyes, and he had Adolph Ochs's large-lobed ears that turned up at the bottom. He was of average height, square-shouldered and solidly built, yet lean enough to fit into the Marine Corps uniform that he had worn more than a decade ago, and his hair was sufficiently close-cropped to pass almost any military inspection. There was no regimental quality about him, however, not even a trace of rigidity, and in this sense he was unlike the publishers who had preceded him. Adolph Ochs had been a model of formality, a starched figure most comfortable at a distance, a self-made man of Victorian presence who rarely lowered his guard in public. While Arthur Hays Sulzberger and Orvil Dryfoos were more mellow and genteel, they were nearly always pressured by the tight strings of the title that they had acquired through marriage. Punch Sulzberger was different—he had been *born* to the title, he had grown up within *The Times,* had skipped through its corridors as a child. He was never awed by the great editors that he met there, for they had always smiled at him, seemed happy to see him, treated him like a little prince in a palace, and he developed early in life a sunny, amiable disposition.

He had been born in New York City on February 5, 1926. His parents had then been married for nine years, had had three daughters, and it seemed likely that they might never present the sixty-seven-year-old Ochs with a male heir. Whether or not Ochs was panicked by this possibility was hard to tell. Ochs had been enchanted in 1918 by the birth of his first granddaughter, Marian (the future Mrs. Dryfoos). She had arrived during Ochs's period of melancholia, which had deepened as *The Times* had become embroiled in controversies during World War I (the worst of which occurred in September of 1918 with the publication of the famous pro-Austria editorial that provoked charges of unpatriotism against *The Times*); but the birth of Marian on December 31, 1918, was seen by Ochs as an auspicious end to a gloomy year.

The Sulzbergers were then living in Ochs's large, darkly ornate house at 308 West Seventy-fifth Street, and upon his return from the office in the evening Ochs would invariably slip into the baby's nursery with his arms filled with new toys. The sounds of the baby thrilled him, the frills of the nursery contrasting cheerfully with the dim decor and statuary that cluttered the house; with only one child of his own, two having died, Ochs could not be casual about a birth in his family.

When a second granddaughter, Ruth, was born three years later on Ochs's own birthday, March 12, it was another extraordinary occasion, and Ochs's ritual of toys were continued, although the Sulzbergers were now occupying another residence nearby. With the birth of a third daughter, Judith, in December, 1923, the Sulzbergers had moved across Central Park into a five-story whitestone building at 5 East Eightieth Street, off Fifth Avenue. But Ochs was still a habitual visitor, and his presence was so pervasive, his affection so boundless, his possessiveness of his daughter, Iphigene, so natural, that Arthur Hays Sulzberger sometimes felt a bit out of place. Ochs was the man of the house no matter which house he was in; while his generosity was enormous, it often made the recipient feel a sense of obligation, a response that Ochs did not exactly discourage. Some of Ochs's relatives in Chattanooga and elsewhere also had had this feeling and had quietly resented it. Iphigene was aware of this, but she was too romantic about her father to concern herself unduly about the sensitivities of his beneficiaries; although, in her husband's case, she tried to make the best of the situation. When her son was born in 1926, and after Ochs had gleefully announced that the boy would be spoiled rotten, she decided that his middle name would *not* be Ochs. He would instead be named Arthur Hays Sulzberger, Jr. Six months later, however, her husband persuaded her to alter it to Arthur Ochs Sulzberger—a noble gesture that Ochs appreciated.

The Sulzberger children and many of their cousins spent the summer months at Ochs's home in Lake George, New York, and after he had sold his New York town house and had bought Hillandale, the entire family would often gather there and live in the mansion. It was a fantastic setting for children growing up—the endless rooms to romp through, the private lake, the tennis court, the sprawling lawns, the animals, the procession of distinguished visitors: Franklin D. Roosevelt, Charles Lindbergh, Richard Byrd, Herbert Lehman, David Lilienthal, various musicians and artists, and also Madeleine Carroll, who was one of Arthur Hays Sulzberger's favorite film actresses. (Madeleine Carroll's fourth husband, incidentally, Andrew Heiskell, the *Time* executive, would in 1965 marry Sulzberger's daughter and Dryfoos' widow, Marian.) Of the three Sulzberger girls, Marian was often referred to by family friends as "the beautiful one," while the second daughter, Ruth (who would become publisher of the *Chattanooga Times* after her divorce from Ben Golden), was called "the brilliant one"; and the third girl, Judith (who would become a medical doctor), was "the interesting one" and also very individualistic. Her strict French governess could not easily intimidate her, and Judith was quite frank and outspoken even as a child. One night before being put to bed in the Sulzberger home on East Eightieth Street, her parents had promised that their dinner guest, Admiral Byrd, would later come up to say good-night to her. When Admiral Byrd did appear and was introduced, the little girl, confused and obviously disappointed, turned to her parents and exclaimed, "*Byrd!*—I thought you said *Lindbergh!*" Admiral Byrd tried to seem amused.

Judith and Punch were inseparable as children, and this closeness continued through the years. Since Judith was called "Judy" at home, Arthur Hays Sulzberger began calling his son "Punch," and the nickname was still with him when he became *The Times'* publisher. As a youth, he had little interest in newspapers, except in the comics, which he read assiduously. Since he was not permitted to play with toy soldiers or guns as a boy —his father was a leading advocate of gun legislation —he would spend considerable time in other children's homes playing with their toys. He was very adept at Chinese checkers, occasionally beating such opponents as Wendell Willkie and other Presidential aspirants who visited Hillandale, and he was also skillful at hobbies or games that required manual dexterity, having received special tutoring from a manual arts instructor who lived near Hillandale. He set up his own train set in the ballroom at Hillandale, enticing as playmates the young men who had come to take out his older sisters. He liked to build tables, to tinker with gadgets, to disassemble machinery, and one day while playing with a little Westchester girl Punch explained to her the mysteries of birth in simple, mechanical terms: the male inserts his organ into the female, Punch said, and then the baby inside grabs hold of it and is pulled out.

Once in school, however, Punch Sulzberger's theories and special talents were of little use, and being unaccustomed to hard discipline, he did poorly. His sister Ruth, in a light recollection of her brother's problems, once wrote in the newspaper's *Times Talk:*

Nearly every school in the vicinity of New York was graced with Punch's presence at one time or another. They were all delighted to have him, but wanted him as something other than a spectator. One after another confessed that though they found him charming, they were not "getting through" to him. One school kept him rather longer than the others. It turned out that the Headmaster's wife was a sculptress and thought Punch had such a beautiful head that she was using him as a model. Since he did not afford anyone the opportunity to judge what was inside his head, it was gratifying that the outside at least was admired.

He, too, was amusing in later life when recalling his school days at Browning or Lawrence Smith or Loomis, or his tutoring at Morningside. But on rare occasions, though he tried to conceal it with his laughter and his casual manner, there was a hint of deep hurt at the dark memory of his father's displeasure. "They sent me to St. Bernard's, then based on the English school system, and I rebelled," he once said. "I was a natural left-hander, but I was made to write with my right. And the result even now is that I do a lot of flipping —instead of writing '197' I'll reverse it to '179' . . . anyway, I was at St. Bernard's for maybe five or six years, and I still get those letters addressed 'Old Boy.'" Then, lips hardening, he added quietly, "I never gave them a penny."

In 1943, at the age of seventeen, Sulzberger left The Loomis School in Windsor, Connecticut, and applied to the Marine Corps. His parents were not happy about it, but they gave their consent. While awaiting his call, he worked as a "screw and bolt" man in *The Times'* telephoto department, displaying his great tinkerer's enthusiasm, and then in January of 1944 he was inducted into the Marines and was trained to become a radioman. His drill instructor at Parris Island was a tough corporal named Rossides who achieved in a few weeks what a generation of educators and the *Times* family had failed to do in twelve years—Punch Sulzberger reacted immediately to orders, he kept up with his class, and he actually enjoyed the rugged life. He also enjoyed being away from home, which had provided a liberal and loving atmosphere but also much second-guessing from parents and elders: in the Marines the commands were loud and clear, and there was no doubt as to who was the boss. Sulzberger's family connections carried no weight with Rossides, nor was Rossides swayed by Sulzberger's boyish charm and idle promises, deceptions that had sometimes worked in private school. Decades later, when Sulzberger was *The Times'* publisher, he would remember Corporal Rossides with gratitude and affection.

During the war, Sulzberger was sent to the Philippines, serving through the campaigns at Leyte and Luzon, and later he was transferred to Japan. He acted as a naval interceptor operator and also as a jeep driver at MacArthur's headquarters. He was promoted to corporal, and then in the spring of 1946—on April 1, which he thought was a very appropriate date—he was released from the service and was returned to New York. One of the first things that he did was to take a high school equivalency examination so that he might qualify for college. After receiving a passing grade— "and armed with the fact that my old man was on the board at Columbia"—he entered Columbia and did very well, occasionally making the dean's list. While a student, he married a very pretty young woman, Barbara Grant, who lived near Hillandale and had also worked as a *Times* office girl on the fourteenth floor. Married in July of 1948, they would have a son, Arthur Ochs Sulzberger, Jr., and a daughter, Karen Alden.

Punch Sulzberger received his Bachelor of Arts degree from Columbia in 1951, and then he joined *The Times* as a cub reporter in the newsroom, where he quickly made what was considered a horrible mistake. Assigned to a banquet with instructions to report what was said there, Sulzberger unfortunately was away from his table and in the men's room when it was announced that a substitute speaker would deliver the text instead of the scheduled speaker, who was unavoidably absent. Sulzberger returned in time to hear the speech, quoting from it in the short article that he wrote for the next morning's *Times*, but he did not realize that the scheduled speaker was absent. When *The Times* was informed of the error, and was obliged to print a correction, the city editor, Robert Garst, sent for Sulzberger and lectured him in a stern grim manner worthy of Rossides.

During the Korean War, Sulzberger's unit was recalled. After he had earned a commission and had attended the Armed Forces Information School at Fort Slocum, New York, Sulzberger served in Korea as an assistant public information officer with the First Marine Division. He returned to the United States to work in the office of the legislative assistant to the commandant in Washington, and later in 1952 he was released with the rank of first lieutenant and he resumed his newspaper training.

He was now twenty-six, considerably more mature and poised, well liked around the newsroom, eager to learn about journalism. And he would learn a good deal during the next few years, but he would never become a top reporter, lacking qualities that are essential and rarely cultivated by such men as himself, the properly reared sons of the rich. Prying into other people's affairs, chasing after information, waiting outside the doors of private meetings for official statements is no life for the scion of a newspaper-owning family. It is undignified, too alien to a refined upbringing. The son of a newspaper owner may indulge in reporting for a while, regarding it as part of his management training, a brief fling with romanticism, but he is not naturally drawn to it.

The reportorial ranks are dominated by men from the lower middle class. It is they who possess the drive, patience, and persistence to succeed as reporters; to them reporting is a vehicle to a better life. In one generation, if their by-lines become well known, they may rise from the simplicity and obscurity of their childhood existence to the inner circles of the exclusive. They may gain influence with the President, friendship with the Rockefellers, a frontrow seat in the arenas of social and political power. From these positions they might not only witness, but influence, the events of their time—as did Reston, the son of poor Scottish immigrants; as did Krock and Catledge, Daniel and Wicker, the sons of the rural South; as did A. M. Rosenthal and dozens of other Jewish Americans whose forebears escaped the ghettos of Europe.

Not only on *The Times*, but on other newspapers, the news staff were largely populated by products of the lower middle class—by liberal Jews and less liberal Irish Catholics from the North, by progressive Protestants from the South and Midwest; and, not unexpectedly, by relatively few Italo-Americans. The immigrants from Italy took longer to become familiar with the English language and its literature, as did other ethnic groups to whom the English language was difficult; they did not produce many newspaper reporters, except in the category of nonwriting "legmen" or district men in the police "shacks." Negroes were only tokenly represented in the newsroom for a number of reasons—they lacked the education or incentive, the encouragement or opportunity, or some combination of all these. On *The Times'* staff, there was often only one Negro reporter, rarely more than two. Conversely, nearly every one of *The Times'* elevator operators was a Negro, smiling plantation types in uniform, a hiring practice that had begun with Ochs, who was a conventional Southerner on the issue of race.

The fact that most newspaper reporters descended from lower-middle-class whites did not mean a total absence of the sons of the wealthy and privileged; but few of them became outstanding reporters. The job seemed almost antipathetic to their nature. They found newspaper reporting interesting, as did John F. Kennedy, but not for very long. If they did not crave bylines to satisfy their need for a name, having already a family name that guaranteed special considerations, then there was little inclination toward a reporting career except if they liked the irregular life or regarded journalism as an important public service or an instrument for social reform. But the rich could perhaps more adequately satisfy their social conscience and encourage change by buying a newspaper and controlling the editorials—or by entering political life and becoming a reform candidate or a financial supporter of such candidates. But as reporters their privileged past was no asset, and few of them could compete favorably with the hungrier newsmen with more keenly developed instincts—a critical eye, a cynicism and skepticism based on firsthand experience, a total commitment to their craft because it was all that they had. The best reporters, even when not on assignment, were always working. In the middle of a crowd they felt apart, detached observers, outsiders. They remained subconsciously alert for the overheard quote, the usable line, the odd fact or happening that might make a story. They reacted immediately to events in ways that Punch Sulzberger and Orvil Dryfoos—who had also worked briefly as a *Times* reporter early in his career—would not.

In 1955, Punch Sulzberger, after a year on the *Milwaukee Journal*, was back on *The Times* and working as a reporter in the Paris bureau. One day in June of 1955 he was attending the automobile race at Le Mans. He was not assigned to cover it, nor was any *Times*man—it was not then the practice of *The Times* to send staff reporters to many European sports events. Suddenly, one of the drivers lost control of his car. The vehicle jumped the road, went spinning through the air, and plowed into a section of spectators. Eighty-three persons were killed. Sulzberger saw the accident and was horrified by the sight. But it never occurred to him to call *The Times*.

Sulzberger was returned to the New York office later that year to become an assistant to his father. He was now separated from his wife, Barbara, and he was spending considerable time in the company of Turner Catledge, who was also separated, and with other Catledge cronies who were either having marital difficulties or were so happily married that they could take liberties with their wives, staying out drinking in Sardi's bar or in Catledge's little "club" behind his office on the third floor. Catledge's circle of *Times*men during these years included Joseph Alduino, *The Times'* controller, and Irvin Taubkin from promotion, both of whom had marriage problems; and also Nat Goldstein, the circulation manager, whose tolerant wife never counted on his appearances at home. Catledge also enjoyed the company of several actors whom he had met around Sardi's—Robert Preston, David Wayne, and Martin Gabel.

Catledge had a very paternal way with young Sulzberger without ever being condescending. He gave advice willingly, but Sulzberger made his own decisions. And this warm relationship would continue through most of the next decade, although their drinking pattern would be altered considerably after they had met the women who would become their second wives. Catledge met Mrs. Abby Ray Izard, a widow, at an editor's convention in 1957, and Punch Sulzberger met a striking brunette divorcée, Carol Fox Fuhrman at a New York dinner party in 1956.

The party was in the home of Orvil Dryfoos' brother Hugh, on Park Avenue. Hugh Dryfoos had first noticed Mrs. Fuhrman at a beach club in suburban New York. She was sitting in the sand with her parents and her young daughter when Dryfoos, a friendly, untimid man, approached her, introduced himself, and engaged her in conversation. Dryfoos' blond wife, Joan, was then sleeping on the beach, although she would wake up in time to join her husband and receive from him an introduction to the brunette.

Later in New York—after Punch Sulzberger had said that he would be attending the Dryfoos' dinner party without a date—Joan Dryfoos decided to invite Carol Fuhrman. Sulzberger and Mrs. Fuhrman got along quite well, and he drove her home that night. Weeks later, Sulzberger invited the Dryfoos' to a restaurant, and they were surprised and pleased to see that he had brought Carol Fuhrman—and Joan Dryfoos also noticed that Carol was wearing a gold friendship ring. She commented on it, but received only a blushing evasive reply—very different from the reaction of Punch Sulzberger's estranged wife, Barbara, when *she* would learn of the ring. It was not that Barbara Sulzberger objected to her husband's dating other women, for she had dated other men, and they were about to be divorced: but she *did* object to receiving the bill for the ring, sent to her by a prominent Fifth Avenue jeweler and listed as one "gold wedding band." It turned out to be a mistake on the store's part, however, not a sample of Sulzberger humor. And after the initial reaction and embarrassment had subsided, there were no further complications—the divorce proceedings continued, and in December of 1956 Carol Fox Fuhrman and Punch Sulzberger were married.

The new Mrs. Sulzberger objected to the nickname "Punch," preferring to call him Arthur. "Punch" was a reminder of a troubled boyhood that was part of the past, and she hoped that he would be seen for what he was to her—a sensitive and quick-thinking young man with commendable qualities that had long been obscured by his more obvious easy manner and his old image. There were some *Times* executives, like Catledge and a few others, who also felt that Sulzberger was capable of major responsibilities on *The Times* if given a chance, but until 1963 that chance did not come. Orvil Dryfoos was running the paper and was assisted by Amory Bradford; neither was very impressed with Sulzberger and both thought that it might be better if he learned the newspaper business elsewhere. As a minor executive, he had little to say or do on the fourteenth floor. He sometimes attended the four o'clock news conference and was often seen around the third floor, a clean-cut, dark-eyed young man puffing a pipe, smiling, then looking up at the walls in the newsroom inspecting the paint, or scrutinizing the air-conditioning ducts, appearing to be endlessly fascinated by the mechanical system and machinery around the building. He knew a great deal about automation and the new equipment being used in *The Times'* West Coast and European editions. His opinions on news coverage, however, were rarely solicited or expressed, and he was often ignored by some top *Times*-men. Even James Reston, when he would come flying in to New York from Washington, would, after a quick handshake and hello, breeze past Sulzberger into the office of the publisher, Orvil Dryfoos. Dryfoos was a vigorous man not yet fifty, the man who was expected to direct the paper through the next two decades. Sulzberger was in his thirties, and he seemed younger. When Amory Bradford would preside at meetings on the fourteenth floor, Sulzberger would sit back quietly and listen like a schoolboy. Sulzberger was awed by Bradford, confused and dazzled as the vice-president stood before the other executives and quickly ticked off facts and figures that everybody in the room seemed to understand except himself. While they nodded knowingly at Bradford, Sulzberger tried to conceal his ignorance with his impassiveness, but inwardly he was embarrassed. Only after he had become the publisher did he learn that the other executives had been no less confused than he.

The death of Dryfoos and the elevation of Sulzberger brought sudden changes to *The Times*, and one of the first announcements was the resignation of Amory Bradford. Bradford submitted his public resignation with the amenities that are traditional in such documents, and it was replied to in a statement from the office of the chairman of the board, Arthur Hays Sulzberger, that read: "Amory Bradford has been a valuable source of strength and leadership in our organization. We are sorry he has decided to resign. He will be greatly missed."

Later that year, Bradford was appointed assistant general business manager of the Scripps-Howard newspapers. He would remain at Scripps-Howard for a year and a half, but he would not be happy there, and in 1965 he would resign and move to Aspen, Colorado. While cleaning out his desk at Scripps-Howard, he would discover a copy of A. H. Raskin's strike story that had appeared in *The Times*. Bradford had never read the story completely through. Now, seated at the open-drawered desk that he was vacating, he would pick up the two-year-old newspaper article and begin to read, and be reminded of the fretful months of the negotiations between 1962 and 1963, the frustration and anger, the additional heat provided by the television coverage, the whole cast of characters from the White House on down. The strike had altered the careers and destiny of so many people. The printers' leader, Bertram Powers, had gotten the recognition that he sought. Some New York newspapers would become so financially weak that they would never recover. The strike had possibly hastened the death of Dryfoos, and it certainly had not helped Bradford's own newspaper career, and he conceded that it might have also influenced the course of his marriage, which ended in divorce. Both he and his former wife would remarry. He would marry a California widow who was an artist and conservationist, and he would work as a consultant to the Department of Commerce, heading an experimental program in Oakland aimed at solving problems of minority unemployment.

After Bradford had finished reading A. H. Raskin's *Times* article on the strike of 1962–63, he was rather sorry that he had been too pressured during the negotiations to cooperate more with Raskin. Even so, though the article was critical of him, Bradford thought that Raskin's reporting was very well done.

Bradford's place on *The Times* was taken by Harding F. Bancroft, an extremely proper, soft-spoken, and handsome man of fifty-three—a descendant of Richard Bancroft, Archbishop of Canterbury (1604–1610). Bancroft had attended the Harvard Law School after graduation from Williams College, practicing law in New York for five years. After service as a naval officer during World War II, Bancroft worked in the State

Department in 1945, meeting and becoming friends with Amory Bradford. In 1951, Bancroft had been appointed by President Truman as the United States deputy representative to the United Nations Collective Measures Committee, and in 1953 he began a three-year assignment in Geneva as legal adviser of the International Labor Office. Bancroft became associate counsel and assistant secretary of *The Times* in 1956, and secretary in 1957; and with Bradford's departure, Harding Bancroft was named *The Times'* vice-president, moving into Bradford's office on the fourteenth floor.

The chain of command under Bancroft, as Punch Sulzberger took over *The Times*, included many corporate administrators who had been there for years, had their names printed atop the editorial page every day, yet were practically unknown outside the *Times* building—in fact, with few exceptions, these executives were unknown to most *Times* reporters and subordinate editors *in* the building. Monroe Green, the head of advertising, was an exception because his office was on the second floor, and he was often seen there by employees who were collecting their weekly paychecks at the cashier's window, which was not far from Green's office. But Francis A. Cox, *The Times'* secretary-treasurer, who had been on the paper since 1951, was recognizable to very few *Times* employees. Each day Cox came and went at *The Times*, a quiet former CPA with a softly pleasant undistinguished face, and of the more than five thousand *Times* employees perhaps a few dozen knew who he was. Andrew Fisher, Sulzberger's newly appointed business manager for production, was known in certain mechanical areas but not generally in the *Times* building; although this was beginning to change with his appointment to head *The Times'* Western edition, an assignment that brought him into contact with a number of editors and his photograph into the pages of the paper's house organ, *Times Talk*.

Another key administrator on the new publisher's

executive staff was a smallish, bow-tied, dark, very capable man named Ivan Veit. Veit was in charge of *Times* promotion, personnel and industrial relations, and also radio station WQXR. He joined *The Times* on his twentieth birthday in 1928, having graduated from Columbia, whre he earned the Phi Beta Kappa key that always dangled from his vest. Veit was born in the upstate hamlet of Hornell, New York, as was *The Times'* former business manager, Louis Wiley, a close friend of Adolph Ochs's; and it was through meeting Wiley during one of Wiley's hometown visits that Ivan Veit was invited to apply for a job at *The Times*. Veit's first assignment on the paper in 1928 was that of a classified-ad taker, at eighteen dollars a week, but he moved up through the system quickly. One reason for his swift ascent was his compatibility with Wiley's brother, a large cauliflowered wrestler named Max Wiley. Louis Wiley was rather embarrassed by the sight of his burly brother, who toured as a wrestler at county fairs, and who visited *The Times* whenever he was in the vicinity of New York. When Max Wiley would appear, Louis Wiley would employ his young protégé Ivan Veit to get Max out of the office *fast*—to take Max to the movies, to the Bronx Zoo, to Coney Island, *anywhere*, so long as it was far from *The Times*. Veit managed to do this with such esprit and speed that Louis Wiley was ever grateful, and Veit's early career was off to a good start. He became the promotion chief of *The Times* in 1934, and not long after World War II his department grew to a staff of eighty and a budget of more than a million a year. This staff included copywriters, artists, researchers, statisticians, production men; and they worked on newspaper and magazine advertisements, radio and television spot announcements, window displays, book fairs, suburban and subway posters—and one of the most successful subway campaigns, stressing the influence of classified advertising in *The Times*, featured the smiling faces of people announcing, "I Got My Job Through *The New York Times*." (This campaign was parodied by rightwing political groups, who often waved posters in parades that quoted the slogan under the smiling bearded face of Fidel Castro.)

Although it was stated in *The Times* on the day of Punch Sulzberger's take-over that no executive changes were planned other than the promotions of Harding Bancroft and Andrew Fisher—Catledge was to continue as managing editor, Lester Markel as Sunday editor, Oakes as editorial-page editor—there would shortly transpire a series of changes more dramatic than any in *Times* history. Punch Sulzberger, who had previously revealed so little of his inner character, who had done almost nothing that he did not *have* to do, now suddenly began to demonstrate an initiative and decisiveness that was surprising and startling.

The first thing that he did, in January of 1964, was to fold *The Times'* Western edition. It had been operating for only sixteen months, but it had failed to attract sufficient advertising and it was losing tremendous amounts of money when the home office could least afford it. The 114-day newspaper strike had cut deeply into *The Times'* financial reserves, and while Mrs. Arthur Hays Sulzberger was one of the wealthiest women in America—*Fortune* magazine would claim in 1968 that she was worth between $150 million and $200 million—Punch Sulzberger did not like losing thousands of dollars each week in supporting a force of ninety men in California and the costly electronic equipment that relayed the news from the *Times* building on Forty-third Street to the regional headquarters in Los Angeles. While the prepublication surveys had indicated that Pacific Coast readers wanted a regional edition of *The Times*, a paper that they could buy each morning on the newsstands in Los Angeles, San Francisco, San Diego, and dozens of other Western cities, Sulzberger felt that the circulation figures had not fulfilled that promise, and he did not believe that things would get much better. When the edition had begun in October of 1962, its circulation had been 120,000, but it had dropped to 87,000 in March of 1963, and to 71,000 in June of 1963. Equally discouraging was the fact that this circulation was spread over thirteen Western states—too widespread a readership to appeal to an advertiser in Los Angeles. The owner of a specialty shop in Beverly Hills saw no advantage in buying an ad in *The Times*' Western Edition if its readers were thinly sprinkled from the Mexican border up the California coast to Seattle and back to the Rocky Mountains and the desert of Las Vegas. Another problem was that the Western edition was not tailored for Westerners. It had been almost assumed by Dryfoos and his advisers in New York that *The Times*' success formula on the East Coast would work equally well on the West Coast. So the Western edition was really a thin version of the New York edition, featuring a heavy diet of foreign and national news, the mood of distant jungles and capitals, but lacking the fashion advertising that women like to read, lacking the "feel" and the news of the region west of the Rockies. It was a newspaper run by remote control—the very method that had been mocked by Arthur Hays Sulzberger and James Reston after they had been to Moscow in 1943 and had visited the offices of *Pravda*, where they were astonished to discover that while *Pravda*'s printing facilities were on the premises, the news came over wires from government offices elsewhere. "The 'reporters' were technicians," Reston would recall in one of his books more than twenty years later, "processing what officials elsewhere decided should go in the paper." This is exactly what *The Times* tried to do in 1962—its California staff members were mostly "technicians": electronic experts, admen, circulation crews, only a minimum of copyreaders and editors, and no special staff of Western reporters. Consequently *The Times* could not compete in advertising or local reporting with the suddenly aroused *Los Angeles Times*. If *The New York Times* did nothing else in California, it helped to make the *Los Angeles Times* into a better newspaper. The latter not only launched its own news service in partnership with the *Washington Post,* but it sharpened its coverage around the nation and overseas and especially at home. When the riots occurred in the Watts section of Los Angeles in the summer of 1965, the *Los Angeles Times* sent dozens of reporters and photographers in to cover the incidents and the aftermath, a performance that would win the 1966 Pulitzer for general local reporting.

Sulzberger's decision to close down the Western edition greatly disappointed some *Times*men who were affiliated with the project. They believed that sixteen months had not provided them with enough time to properly test the edition and make adjustments. Other *Times*men wondered aloud about how the failure would affect *The Times'* image. "You can't close down the edition, Punch," one said, "we must save face."

"We're loaded with face," Sulzberger replied quickly. "It's a bad paper. Let's get rid of it."

So in late January of 1964, Sulzberger made the announcement, and the California contingent was disbanded. Some people remained with the *Times* organization, others found jobs elsewhere. No *Times*man was more disheartened than Andrew Fisher. Though the Western project had been Dryfoos' "baby," Dryfoos was now gone, and so was Bradford, and the executive most closely associated with the regional edition was Fisher. When Fisher returned to New York he wondered if he would now be gradually eased out. He knew that to some older *Times*men he symbolized the new technology that had long stirred their doubts and suspicions. Furthermore, the technology had failed in California; the scientific surveys had misjudged the people, and *The Times* had lost a big battle because of faulty intelligence; and if a scapegoat was to be sought it would most likely be Andrew Fisher. As he reestablished himself on the fourteenth floor, sitting in his office adorned by a two-faced clock simultaneously ticking the time of California and New York, and as he moved through the corridors of the building and rode the elevators that had now become automated, Fisher sensed that it was difficult for some executives to look him straight in the eye. A delicate distance was being maintained, he thought, and he asked himself more than once, *Why don't they fire me? Why are they keeping me here?*

With Punch Sulzberger, however, Fisher did not feel this way, and the discovery was wonderful and reassuring. Sulzberger seemed no different than before, no less friendly, no less confiding than when Fisher had been promoted to head the production department seven months previously on the occasion of Sulzberger's own elevation to publisher. Fisher and Sulzberger had gotten along very well when Dryfoos was alive. Fisher had been the only executive close to Sulzberger's age on the fourteenth floor, and they quickly discovered that they had much in common. They were both informal and frank, yet possessing a military passion for orderliness, a respect for charts, training aids, systemization, and brevity in the arrangement of details; they were both enamored of the gadgets and tools of science, and they believed that when certain tools proved inadequate for a job, that these tools should be unsentimentally replaced by newer, better tools. And it was precisely this clear and practical reasoning that had caused Fisher to wonder after the California fiasco if he might be finished at *The Times*. If not finished in the sense of being fired, then insofar as his future career was concerned. As a tool of the institution he had in a sense failed; and yet this was apparently not the value judgment that Punch Sulzberger had placed on the West Coast venture.

There had been a major mistake, it was true, but no one individual or group was to blame, nor did Sulzberger's manner indicate that he was greatly distressed or discouraged by the failure. Failure was nothing new to Punch Sulzberger. While he could not now casually condone it, not with the stakes so high, he also did not believe in overreacting to it. The West Coast reversal represented to him a single setback in a large forward-moving operation. He saw no reason to become suddenly defensive, or to shy away from experimenting with the modern techniques that might help run *The Times* more effectively and economically in the future.

On the contrary, Sulzberger now more than ever wanted to experiment with modern systems and to learn more about them; his newspaper could not merely follow the formulas of his father or grandfather. *The Times* would have to preserve what was inviolable in its tradition, yet adjust to changing trends and new tools. *The Times* had to make more money than was the custom, Sulzberger believed: the economics of newspaper ownership was never more precarious than at present—the recent newspaper strike had shown how vulnerable some New York newspapers were to the whims of labor, how quickly old institutions can decline and crumble. While *The Times* had had the cash reserves to withstand strikes, a greater income was essential not only to meet the rising costs of production and higher salaries, but also for the paper to remain unpanicked during future labor threats. One way to make more money was to sell more newspapers and to charge higher advertising rates, to diversify and to gamble on such expansionistic ventures as the Western edition and to try something else if these failed; another way was to operate *The Times* more economically—*not* by skimping on the news coverage or the hiring of top talent, but rather by modernizing the plant, by retiring aging veterans (God could no longer be *The Times'* personnel director), and by cutting down on the employment of more bookkeepers and clerks to handle the mounting paperwork. *The Times* would have to accept the computer. The computer was still a rather controversial subject at *The Times*, but now in Sulzberger's first year as publisher he began to prepare the institution for its introduction. *Times*men would have to overcome their aversions and romantic notions about the newspaper business: while it was true that *The Times* was the most influential paper in the nation, it could not relax, because there were other papers outside New York that were advancing fast. The *Washington Post* and the *Wall Street Journal* were better than ever, matching and occasionally beating *The Times* in the coverage of politics and economics. And the *Los Angeles Times* while still primarily a regional paper with limited influence around the nation, had a daily circulation in excess of eight hundred thousand. It was about to overtake the second-place *Chicago Tribune*, and it was clearly topped only by the tabloid New York *Daily News*, whose two-million weekday circulation was more than double that of any other metropolitan newspaper in the nation. The *Wall Street Journal*, being in a specialists' market, was often not classified with general newspapers; but its four regional editions each day gave it a total national circulation of more than eight hundred thousand.) Among the other big-city dailies, *The New York Times* ranked number seven in 1964, averaging a weekday sale of about six hundred and fifty thousand, although this figure would suddenly climb as other New York newspapers went bankrupt in the wake of labor difficulties; and *The Times* within a few years would exceed eight hundred thousand and surpass the *Philadelphia Bulletin*, the *Detroit News*, the *Los Angeles Herald-Examiner*, and even the *Chicago Tribune*. But it would still follow the second-place *Los Angeles Times*. While circulation figures are not necessarily indicative of the economic strength of a newspaper (the *New York Mirror*, for example, folded in 1963 with a daily circulation of more than nine hundred thousand), there was no question of *The Los Angeles Times*' wealth. For nearly a decade the *Los Angeles Times* had led the nation's dailies in advertising linage, and if it had great ambitions east of the Rockies it could now afford to gamble on them, being backed by the Chandler family's Times-Mirror Company, which had diversified and profited tremendously in recent years with the purchase of several new companies publishing everything from telephone books and Bibles to aeronautical charts for pilots. The *Los Angeles Times*' newspaper plant was a model of modernism. As the only major daily without unions, being militantly antilabor during much of its history, the *Los Angeles Times* had been free to automate as it wished—to have computers to make up the payroll, to set type, to analyze circulation trends, to pinpoint people who owed money for ads. *The New*

York Times, centered in a tight city of organized labor and rooted in different traditions, could not compete electronically with the *Los Angeles Times* even if it wished to do so, but Sulzberger wanted to modernize as much as prudently possible, and he began by arranging for the rental—at eight thousand dollars a month—of a Honeywell H.200 computer to do the accounting paperwork of twenty-five employees. While the employees were being retrained to do other work, the computer would be moved into a white-walled windowless room, dehumidified and dust free, on the seventh floor of the *Times* building. The room, twenty-five feet by thirty-two feet, was to be off limits to all *Times* employees except those who worked in conjunction with or fed the computer. The computer was under the supervision of a newly appointed systems manager at *The Times*, a former New York University professor from Georgia named Carl Osteen. Osteen and the computer were both answerable to Andrew Fisher.

In another move to modernize *The New York Times*, to centralize its executive authority and eliminate the last of the ancient "dukedoms," Punch Sulzberger decided that as of September, 1964, Turner Catledge would be appointed to the newly created title of "executive editor." This title would give Catledge unquestioned authority over Lester Markel's Sunday department, over Reston's bureau in Washington, and over all *Times*men in the newsroom and in the bureaus around the nation and overseas. Catledge had been envisioning this arrangement for nearly twenty years. Now he had it. He would not have had it if Orvil Dryfoos had lived, or if other events had not prematurely occurred, or if Punch Sulzberger had not been a part of Catledge's little backroom "club"—but such dialecticism was of minor significance at this point: Turner Catledge, at the age of sixty-three, slightly overweight, ailing with the gout, a large, tall, flaccid man with a round, red face, slack jaw, quick darting dark eyes that missed almost nothing, a soft and courtly manner that had long defied description, preventing most people in the newsroom from knowing exactly whether he was a corporate genius or a lucky bumbler—Catledge was now to become so eminent in *The Times'* News department that Arthur Krock in Washington would remark with an inflated sigh: "I hesitate to breathe his name."

Catledge would be serving as a kind of regent to young Sulzberger. Sulzberger had much to learn about the News department, and he wanted to have at his side the one man who knew it all. Catledge's vast experience made him the obvious choice, although even Catledge could make only a highly educated guess about what was going on under him, for the department was now too large, too spread out and mobile to be kept constantly in check even by computers. The News department consisted of almost 20 percent of *The Times'* total employment of more than five thousand—about one thousand people who in various ways helped to write and edit the daily and Sunday editions of *The Times.* Not counting the senior editors in New York or the foreign correspondents, or the secretaries in bureaus, or the stringers, or chauffeurs; not counting *The Times'* national correspondents around the United States and in Washington; not counting the women's-news staff on the ninth floor of the *Times* building, or the supporting casts on other floors, but counting only the news personnel on the *third* floor, there were about two hundred staffers under the New York editor, fifty-nine under the financial-news editor, fifty-two under the sports editor, forty under the cultural-news editor, twenty-five under the picture editor.

The entire News department at home and abroad—including copyboys, clerks, copyreaders, foreign correspondents, subeditors senior editors—would run up an annual operating bill of approximately $11 million to the Sulzberger family. The cost of publishing *The New York Times* each year—the cost of paper, ink, machinery, the delivery trucks, trains, planes, the salaries and expenses of *Times*men everywhere, and the taxes—would be more than $134 million. If the projected earnings were accurate, if there were no long strikes or unforeseen liabilities or recessions, *The*

Times would realize from its advertising revenue, its circulation sale, and smaller incidentals, between $136 million and $137 million. Thus the profit from owning what is regarded as the greatest newspaper in the world would not be enormous—a bit more than $2.6 million.

To increase that profit Sulzberger did not want to jeopardize tradition or the uniqueness of *The Times'* coverage. A *Times* editor should never give a second thought to tossing out an ad in making room for an important late-breaking story. *The Times* should continue to publish long texts of speeches that few people read, as well as such historical documents as the Warren Commission's *Report* on the assassination of President Kennedy, which would fill forty-eight pages of a *Times* edition in September of 1964. And so Sulzberger believed that the advertising rates should go up, and so did Andrew Fisher and Ivan Veit; but the advertising manager, Monroe Green, felt differently. A rate increase might cause a decline in advertising linage, which was Green's special source of pride, his batting average, and he was reluctant to change the rules under which his department had dominated all other New York newspapers in advertising linage for many years. In 1964, Green's department had recorded 67.7 million lines of advertising, bringing $100 million into *The Times'* treasury; the *New York Herald Tribune* had printed only 18.5 million lines at lower rates, and Green saw no reason to tamper with this kind of success. Green also felt a bit uneasy about young Sulzberger. When Arthur Hays Sulzberger had been the publisher, Green's judgment had rarely been questioned, but now Green felt changes in the wind; he felt somehow threatened by Fisher's closeness to the new publisher. There had been rumors that Punch Sulzberger someday hoped to bring Green's Advertising department, Veit's Promotion-Circulation department, and Fisher's Production department under one head, as the news divisions were about to be consolidated under Turner Catledge. It was said that Sulzberger liked the chain-of-command management style of the Marine Corps, a single line of authority from top to bottom. Whether this could work at *The New York Times* remained to be seen, although Green had little doubt that Sulzberger would attempt it. Sulzberger had already revealed his inclination with his decision to unify the daily and Sunday news staffs under one editor; and Sulzberger's official statement, when it was finally announced on September 1, 1964, gave insight perhaps into his general approach to running *The Times*. In naming Catledge to supervise the entire news operation, the daily as well as Sunday sections, Sulzberger added: "I feel that we are recognizing the current trends in our operations and their future course."

The elevation of Turner Catledge was reported in *The Times* on the first page of the second section, on September 2, 1964. The article was accompanied by photographs of Catledge and five other editors who would be affected by the move—Markel, Daniel, and Reston, Tom Wicker, and Daniel Schwarz. But the wordage of the article was couched in such corporate vagueness, was so lacking in the *interpretation* that *The Times* now deemed essential to modern reporting, that it is doubtful whether any outsider understood the full significance of the story. If there had been an executive reorganization in the television industry or the State Department, or if there had been a bureaucratic shuffle in Romania, then *The Times* would have opened up its columns to clear reportage, interpretative analyses and editorials, cold facts interspersed with speculation ("According to informed sources . . ."); but no newspaper, including *The Times*, is very informative about its own executive maneuvers. And so there was no hint of the behind-the-scenes jockeying, the tension and despair, that had occurred within the *Times* organization during the weeks prior to Sulzberger's public decision to end the dukedoms and to centralize the news flow under Catledge. The article in *The Times* made it seem that the principal figures were all being calmly, cheerfully moved up to greater challenges within the institution. The four-column headline over the article and photographs read: "Catledge Named Executive

Editor of *Times*," and the smaller headlines banked
underneath: "Markel, Reston Raised to Associate
Editors—Schwarz Sunday Chief; Daniel Managing Editor—Wicker Will Direct Washington Bureau." And
the article began, routinely: "Six major changes in editorial assignments for *The New York Times* were
announced yesterday by Arthur Ochs Sulzberger, publisher."

When Lester Markel first learned of Sulzberger's plan,
he was furious. Markel was seventy years old. He had
built the Sunday *Times* into an American institution, a
five-pound package thick with advertising and with a
circulation that was climbing slowly but steadily toward
1.5 million. Now Markel saw his whole life's career
being undermined by what he considered the negative
trends of the paper—not only by Catledge's collectivist
ambitions that were being fulfilled by Sulzberger; not
only by the theories and innovations of such third-
floor editors as Theodore Bernstein, who had introduced the "Man in the News" profile, and other daily
background features that had intruded somewhat into
Markel's former prerogatives—but Lester Markel was
now equally concerned with what he sensed as a tendency to change *The New York Times* from a "good
gray lady" into a swinging operation with circulation
trucks boasting: "Without It, You're Not with It." *The
Times* had achieved uniqueness, Markel believed, not
from being *with it* in an ultramodern superficial sense,
but rather by remaining always a bit *above* it. This
did not mean that *The Times* had failed to cover trends
—Ochs's *Times* had, in fact, led the way in covering the
great scientific discoveries, the preludes to wars, the
major questions and debates of every decade—but
Ochs's *Times* had not been swayed by popular fads
and froth; it had remained remote, a little stodgy and
stiff, a manner that Ochs had fancied. Even when *The
Times* had stooped to report the great murders or
scandals of the Nineteen-twenties or Thirties, it did so
with a tone of Victorian restraint. As late as 1942,
The Times was referring to Frank Costello, the racke-

teer, as a "sportsman." And in the Twenties, when
Markel had asked Ochs why *The Times* was devoting
as much space as the *Daily News* to the scandalous
Hall-Mills case—a still-unsolved murder in which Reverend Hall and his choir mistress, Mrs. Mills, were
discovered slain under a crabapple tree in New Jersey
—Ochs had replied: "When the *Daily News* prints it,
it is sex; when *we* print it, it is sociology."

Now, in 1964, despite his vigorous health and his
even more vigorous protests, Markel was being replaced as the Sunday editor. Markel was aware of his
unflattering reputation, but he had been hired by Ochs
forty-one years ago to do a job, and he had done it;
and he attributed much of his personal reputation to
embittered writers who had failed to meet his test—
and there were some who admired Markel, such as the
deskman in the Sunday department who said: "The
trouble with Markel is that he's always right." Marilyn
Monroe, with whom Markel had occasionally dined—
and whom he had once escorted through the *Times*
building—had considered him charming and brilliant,
and there were others who sensed a tenderness and
great vulnerability beneath Markel's terrorizing exterior.
Markel had been absolutely shattered when he had not
been invited to Brooks Atkinson's testimonial party
at Sardi's. It had been a grand affair attended by the
top names on Broadway and by every major executive
on *The Times*. But Mrs. Atkinson, in reviewing the
guest list in advance, had eliminated Markel from the
group. This had quickly become the talk of the *Times*
building, and when Orvil Dryfoos had arrived at Sardi's,
the first thing he had asked was, "Is Markel here?"
When told that he was not, Dryfoos, shaking his head,
had exclaimed, "Boy, I'm going to catch hell tomorrow."

But Punch Sulzberger possessed none of the traditional timidity toward Markel. While appreciative of
Markel's enormous contributions, and respectful in
his approach, Sulzberger nevertheless insisted, in a face-
to-face meeting with Markel, that Markel relinquish
the Sunday editorship to Daniel Schwarz, a judicious

and well-liked man who had been Markel's assistant since 1939. Schwarz would now be answerable to Catledge. Markel would move up to the fourteenth floor as an "associate editor," would get his name printed on the editorial page masthead each day, and would work in the newly established department of public affairs, which was concerned with "the advancement of a better-informed public." Markel would continue to serve as the host on his educational-television news show, being regularly joined by Tom Wicker and Max Frankel, and he would also deal broadly with *The Times'* expanding ventures in adult education, radio, and books. Of course, all the prose padding and euphemisms in the world would not belie the fact that Markel was being kicked upstairs, an event that inspired no great protest on the eighth floor. And yet in this inglorious time of his life, Markel somehow revealed a strength of character that was admirable. Instead of wallowing in self-pity, or walking out in a huff, or being destroyed with humiliation, Markel—after an initial outburst of anger—accepted the inevitable and proceeded to move up to his new office on the fourteenth floor. There he worked energetically in the months ahead, and eventually he expanded his assignment in scope and importance. Within a few years he would take on such newer responsibilities as the chairmanship of *The Times'* "Committee of the Future," which Markel, adapting to space-age jargon, would call "COMFUT"; this committee, whose membership included other executives and research assistants, was to ascertain what effect social changes and technological advances would have on newspapers in general, and *The Times* in particular, in the coming decades. The committee would try to perceive what human habits will prevail, how nonworking hours will be utilized in the Nineteen-seventies and Nineteen-eighties, and how *The Times* can best meet the challenges of this new scene. Some of the Markel committee's research would be done in an office within *The Times*, while much of it would be farmed out to scientific-research organizations.

And so Markel's energies would continue to propel,

although the fragility of his ego would be shown by the fact that he rarely set foot in the Sunday department after Sulzberger had removed him. If Markel had spent time browsing through his old domain on the eighth floor, he would have passed, across the hall from his former office, a rather formally furnished Spanish-style room with a refectory table, wooden chairs, and an iron chandelier. On the wall was a portrait of Lester Markel, unsmiling. The room, which has no important function in the department, is most often empty and very quiet. It is sometimes referred to as Markel's "chapel."

When the preliminary word of Sulzberger's reorganization plan first reached the Washington bureau, the reporters and other staffmen were shocked, but not surprised. They conveyed the impression that nothing from New York, no matter how preposterous, would surprise them. For two years now, or ever since Salisbury's promotion to national editor in 1962, and since Clifton Daniel's ascendancy as the assistant managing editor under Catledge, the Washington bureau had felt the bombardment of second-guessing from the New York office. If it was not Daniel claiming that the *Washington Post* or the *Wall Street Journal* had published something that *The Times* had not, then it was Harrison Salisbury on the telephone relaying his story ideas, his suspicions, and questions: Was there any Murchison money behind that Lyndon Johnson deal? What was Abe Fortas *really* up to? Was it true, as rumored, that the State Department would finally recognize Mongolia? Getting recognition for Mongolia seemed to be one of Salisbury's pet campaigns, perhaps because he thought that Mongolia would make an ideal "listening post" for China-watchers—or perhaps Salisbury was just fond of Mongolians. In any case, Salisbury had promoted Mongolian recognition in one of his books, and he was regularly hearing "rumors" of Mongolian recognition in Washington. Washington bureaumen claimed that they had queried the State Department so often about this that soon, out of boredom or harassment, the State Department *would* recognize Mongolia.

With the death of Orvil Dryfoos, the balance had shifted from Washington to New York, and one of the first results of this shift was the resignation of Reston's number two man, Wallace Carroll. Carroll claimed to have "seen the writing on the wall" in the summer of 1963, shortly after Sulzberger's appointment as publisher, and so Carroll decided to leave *The Times* and become the editor-publisher of the Winston-Salem *Journal* and *Sentinel*. Carroll had been on *The Times* since 1955, had run the bureau under Reston with efficiency and composure, and when Dryfoos had been alive he had thought of Carroll as a possible successor to Markel. But Carroll quickly saw that he had nothing to look forward to but increased pressure from New York, and he could not be dissuaded from quitting. Catledge, who had liked Carroll, offered him the Rome bureau, or any other bureau that was open, if he would change his mind. Reston had volunteered to turn over the Washington bureau to Carroll, devoting himself entirely to the column. Carroll was appreciative, but his decision was irrevocable; he sensed what life would be like under Daniel as the managing editor, and Salisbury as Daniel's deputy, and so he accepted the position in Winston-Salem, where he had once worked, and he was happy to be going back.

Unknown to nearly everyone during this period, Reston was contemplating his own resignation. He had been deeply disappointed that no member of the Sulzberger family had consulted him during those weeks after Dryfoos' death and before Punch Sulzberger's appointment as the publisher. This was odd, considering how close Reston had always been to the family. But in retrospect, it was also revealing. Reston, at least for the present, was out of the inner circle. Reston had delivered the Orvil Dryfoos eulogy at the funeral, and then had returned to Washington as the Sulzbergers and the directors had gathered in secret session to select the successor. There had been rumors of Reston's playing a key role in New York, but nobody had approached him, and this had disturbed and confused him. If he had been offered the executive editor's job, he might have turned it down; and yet he would have appreciated the opportunity of considering the job. Now he did not know exactly where he stood. He was outranked by Catledge, that was clear. When Dryfoos was alive, Reston had been *officially* under Catledge, but in actuality he was not. Reston had immense pride, and he could not accept the situation as it now stood, and he seriously considered accepting the impressive offer extended him by his close friend Katharine Graham, president of The Washington Post Company. In a position at the *Post*, Reston would not only continue as a syndicated columnist but he would also have a hand at guiding her newspaper as well as the company's other publication, *Newsweek*. Reston would receive enough money and stock benefits to guarantee that he and his family would be quite rich, and he no doubt could lure to the *Washington Post* a few of the very best young *Times*men. So during the summer he gave serious thought to quitting, and discussed it with such friends as Walter Lippmann. In the end, however, Reston decided to remain at *The Times*.

There was no newspaper like *The Times*, no other medium that each day reached the people that Reston wanted to reach with his words and thoughts. Reston could get along without *The Times,* and vice versa, but that was of minor importance. By staying with *The Times*, and concentrating on his column, he was more influential with American policy makers, with the power brokers of the nation and the leaders abroad, than he would be if he quit at triple the money. Reston believed that *The Times alone* had the audience that moved America. The President of the United States read it every morning, and so did the Congress, and so did seventy embassies in Washington, including the Russians. More than half the college presidents in the United States read *The Times,* and more than 2,000 copies were sold each day at Harvard, more than 1,000 at Yale, 700 at Chicago, 350 at Berkeley. These were the people that Reston wished to influence—the Establishment of today, the Establishment of tomorrow: he was the Establishment columnist, and he could be that only on *The Times*.

Reston also loved the paper. He had once told Carroll that he would sooner divorce his wife than quit *The Times*. This was, of course, not even close to the truth—Reston had debated quitting *The Times* in 1953, until Krock had stepped down as bureau chief; but there was no doubt that Reston was a *Times*-man in the old sense, a man emotionally committed to the institution as a way of life, a religion, a cult, and it would not be possible for him to quit as easily as Wallace Carroll had done. Reston had joined *The Times* in 1939, had grown with it, had used it, had been used by it—they had been a wonderful combination, and Reston, at fifty-four, still had a considerable way to go. And so he decided to remain on *The Times* and see what was ahead for himself and for it. Young Sulzberger was now feeling his oats. The paper was in a strange state of transition. Arthur Hays Sulzberger was too ill to influence it, being confined to a wheel chair, and being so stricken with heart attacks that he was now a thin, drawn figure, very different from his handsome photographs and his large portrait in the *Times* building. Iphigene Sulzberger had the financial power but she also had a son, only one son, and he was now the publisher, the hope of the future. She could not, *would* not interfere at this point. Punch Sulzberger had spent much of his lifetime being second-guessed by people who knew better or thought they knew better, but these days were gone, as were most of these people. All that Reston could do was to try to understand the Sulzberger that he had never known, to perhaps build a working relationship that would deepen with time into a warm friendship. And so Reston flew to New York and spent amiable hours with Sulzberger during the summer of 1964, shortly before the announcement about Catledge was to become final. Reston made one last attempt to get Sulzberger to reconsider, talking to Sulzberger in the concerned, public-spirited way that Reston spoke with presidents and senators, suggesting that the youthful publisher might be wise to surround himself not with older men but rather with the bright young men of his own generation—such men as Tom Wicker, Max Frankel, or Anthony Lewis. Sulzberger listened, but he was not now responsive to the idea of altering his plan. Catledge was to be the boss of the News department, indisputably responsible for the whole news section—everything except the editorial page, which would remain under Sulzberger's cousin, John Oakes. Reston could not, under these conditions, continue to serve as the bureau chief. And so at his own request, Reston asked to be relieved of his title and to select his successor. Reston would become, like Markel, an "associate editor," and would continue to occupy an office in the Washington bureau from which he would write his column. Sulzberger did not want to lose Reston, and he was relieved and delighted that Reston would remain, and he was agreeable to Reston's selecting his own successor. Reston chose Tom Wicker. Sulzberger did not know Wicker well, but he admired his reporting. Reston knew Wicker very well, not only as a reporter but as an individual. Wicker was the sort of man, Reston believed, who could be driving down a country road during a political campaign, could jump over a fence and learn what a farmer was really thinking, and could then go back to town, change into a tuxedo, and be equally at home at an embassy party. Such an individual, of course, was not unlike Reston himself.

And so in the summer of 1964, Sulzberger endorsed Wicker as the next Washington bureau chief, not fully anticipating the effect that it would have on the New York editors, who now would be unable to select a man of their own choosing to solve what they considered the problems of Washington coverage, the cronyism, the lack of imagination and drive. And there would also be two *Times*men in Washington who would not be elated by the selection of Wicker, one of these being Max Frankel.

Frankel had nothing personal against Wicker, but Frankel, who had been almost a child prodigy on *The Times*, now felt that the quick pace of his earlier development had stalled; and his failure to become the bureau chief, at the age of thirty-four, did little to relieve his anxiety. He had become a *Times* reporter at twenty-one, in the summer of 1951, between his junior and senior years at Columbia. He had begun writing for *The Times* as a Columbia campus correspondent in 1949. Those were the Eisenhower years at Columbia, and it had been a very important assignment for a young correspondent; and Frankel had made the most of the opportunity. He was an alert young man, politically oriented and curious, rather stocky, bespectacled, round-faced, fast-stepping—one to whom the drama of World War II had not been learned out of a history text, but had rather been felt personally by himself and his family.

Max Frankel had been born in Gera, Germany, now in the East Zone, and had lived near Leipzig for eight years until his family was expelled in a mass roundup of Jews of remotely Polish ancestry. Driven to the German-Polish border by the Gestapo, the Frankels were finally admitted to temporary residence in Cracow, Poland. In 1939 he returned with his mother to Germany to try to arrange for emigration to the United States. His father, remaining in Poland, soon was fleeing the Nazi armies and was later taken into custody by Soviet authorities, who tried him as a German spy and gave him a choice between Soviet citizenship and a fifteen-year sentence of hard labor in Siberia. Jacob Frankel chose the latter, vaguely hoping to someday rejoin his wife and son, who had meanwhile obtained from the Gestapo an exit permit and had sailed from Holland for the United States, arriving in Hoboken, New Jersey, in the winter of 1940.

They settled in the Washington Heights section of New York, not far from the George Washington Bridge, in an area of refugees sometimes called the "Fourth Reich." There Frankel attended public schools, studying hard, and after the war his father, released from prison, left the Soviet Union and rejoined the family, later opening a small dry-goods store in West Harlem. Frankel graduated in 1948 from the High School of Music and Art in New York, where he had edited the school newspaper; then he worked six months for the United World Federalists as an Addressograph machine operator, and then, winning a New York State scholarship, he enrolled at Columbia. His rise from campus correspondent and editor-in-chief of the *Columbia Daily Spectator* to *The New York Times'* staff was rapid, as was his elevation to a prominent place on the staff. After an impressive tour as a rewriteman in the newsroom, following two years' service in the United States Army, Frankel became a *Times* correspondent in Vienna, then Belgrade, then Moscow. In 1961, after ten years of extensive and varied experience, Frankel joined Reston's bureau. In the next two years he covered the State Department, the White House, occasionally the Pentagon, the CIA, the Congressional committees and foreign embassies. When Reston decided to relinquish his bureau job, Frankel was ready for something other than just straight reporting.

Two days after Wicker's appointment as bureau chief, Max Frankel resigned. In a long and emotional letter to Punch Sulzberger, Frankel announced that he was joining *The Reporter*, where he hoped to have the freedom to write on national as well as international subjects, official as well as human affairs; to travel freely, to deliver lectures, to teach occasionally, to appear on television, to see if he could make the grade as a writer, not merely a reporter; to write with a subjectivity that in *The Times'* news columns is forbidden. Frankel wanted to become more his own man, he suggested to Sulzberger. But then, after he had sent the letter, Frankel had a rather sudden change of mind. *The Times* loomed larger, the outside world seemed less enticing, he could not break the knot. Finally, and with considerable embarrassment, Frankel sent a telegram to

The Reporter's editor, Max Ascoli, stating that he had withdrawn his resignation from *The Times*—he simply could not leave.

The second *Times* reporter in Washington who had hoped to succeed Reston was a cool, lean, well-scrubbed-looking, intense, and brilliant young man named Anthony Lewis. At thirty-seven, Lewis was three years older than Frankel, and he was Frankel's opposite in many ways. Whereas Frankel could be emotional, Lewis seemed tightly contained at all times, incredibly controlled, his orderly mind concentrating only on those things that were relevant now, at this second, and he was careful not to overstate his case or overstep his boundaries. His handwriting was an exquisite example of perfect letter formation, neatness, clarity of communication. His eyes were brightly alert, and his hairline, receding beyond an already high forehead, made him appear almost tonsured. His voice was soft, sometimes warm and friendly, and with just an edge of tension when things displeased him. He had been born in New York, had attended Horace Mann School, a private school, and then had gone to Harvard, graduating in 1948. Even now, sixteen years later, he somewhat symbolized in appearance, if not in fact, the Ivy League style of that postwar period—conservative, Brooksbred, conditioned to blending, accentuating the symbols of similarity, toning down any natural eccentricities or temptations. Only those who knew him well, or with whom he was sufficiently impressed and thus responsive, sensed the interesting man beneath—the connoisseur of opera, the serious man married to a tall, blithe student of modern dance, the superb mimic of W. C. Fields, the charming dinner guest. Few reporters in *The Times'* bureau knew this side of him. They knew mainly the perfectionist, the purposeful, hard-working reporter who had won a Pulitzer in 1955 for a series of articles on the Federal loyalty-security program, while working for the *Washington Daily News*. Lewis had won a second Pulitzer in 1963 for his reporting on the Supreme Court. It had been Reston's idea, encouraged by Justice Felix Frankfurter, to have a *Times*man specialize in the coverage of law. Lewis drew the assignment, returning to Harvard for a year on a Nieman Fellowship to study law. And Justice Frankfurter later said of Lewis's Supreme Court coverage: "There are not two members of the Court itself who could get the gist of each decision so accurately in so few words." In 1964 Lewis published an important book concerning a landmark decision of the Supreme Court—*Gideon's Trumpet*, which was excerpted in *The New Yorker*.

And yet if Reston had selected Lewis as his replacement, there were *Times*men in Washington who said they would resign. He was too coolly ambitious and driven, they believed, lacking the easy congeniality of a Reston or a Wicker. In New York, some editors felt that Lewis, who had also specialized in covering the Justice Department, had become overly enamored of the Attorney General, Robert F. Kennedy, developing a friendship that was possibly a flaw in Lewis's objectivity. Reston was aware of all this, and while he was proud of Lewis and liked him personally, he thought that Wicker would be more suitable as the head of the bureau than either Frankel or Lewis.

Anthony Lewis was deeply disappointed by Reston's decision. And when Lewis had the opportunity to become the London bureau chief, he took it. He replaced Sydney Gruson, who was returning to New York as the foreign editor, replacing in turn Emanuel R. Freedman, who was becoming an assistant managing editor, joining Theodore Bernstein and Robert Garst. Harrison Salisbury, who had vacated his national-news editor's job to an energetic Atlanta-born reporter named Claude Sitton, was also moving up to become an assistant managing editor under the newly appointed managing editor, Clifton Daniel.

During all this shifting, and before turning the Washington bureau over to Tom Wicker, James Reston had arranged one other detail with Punch Sulzberger that seemed very inconsequential at the time, but as events would transpire in the years ahead, it would perhaps rank as a marvelously astute move, one that would reveal something of the Restonian mind—its awareness of corporate whimsy, its knowledge of how executive wives can sometimes build the bridges that can more tightly bind their husbands. Reston, knowing that Sulzberger and his wife, Carol, would be going on a trip to Europe after the November election, planted the idea with Sulzberger of inviting Wicker and Wicker's wife, Neva, to accompany them. This would be an ideal opportunity for Sulzberger to get to know more intimately his new bureau chief, and Sulzberger agreed. These executive trips could be disastrous, Reston knew—the constant companionship could magnify personality differences, or result in hours of boredom in the middle of the Atlantic, or there was always the chance that the wives would not get along. Or such trips could produce harmonious results, bringing a young publisher and a young journalist closer as men, ultimately producing perhaps the kind of friendship that had begun in the Forties when Reston had taken trips with Arthur Hays Sulzberger—and it is possible that Turner Catledge would have never become managing editor in 1951 if he had not proven to be such a compatible drinking companion for Arthur Hays Sulzberger in 1944 during their Pacific junket. So the executive trip was a gamble—a source of envy to those executives who had been left at home, but perhaps a great boon to the executive who accompanied the boss: in any case, Reston thought that it was a chance worth taking, for Wicker would have to emerge as a major figure on the paper if the bureau were not to be completely swallowed up by New York. Reston was also confident that Wicker and Sulzberger would get along. They were both the same age, were both very informal, and they both were married to pretty young brunettes. Neva Wicker was a delicate and appealing North Carolina girl who knew when *not* to talk. Carol Sulzberger sensed simplicity and sincerity in people and admired it, and she had only briefly met Neva Wicker, and had barely known Tom Wicker.

So it was arranged—a month's trip to Europe in November of 1964, just Punch and Carol Sulzberger, Tom and Neva Wicker. And, as Reston had imagined, Punch Sulzberger got along well with Wicker—and their wives got along very well.

15

SEATED behind his big desk in the middle of the newsroom, Rosenthal momentarily looked up from the stories that he was reading and gazed around the room at the distant rows of desks, the reporters typing, talking among themselves, sometimes looking at him in a way he suspected was hostile—*they must despise me*, he thought, being both irritated and saddened by the possibility, *they must really hate my guts*.

It was the winter of 1965. A. M. Rosenthal, who had given up his career as a foreign correspondent during the summer of 1963 to take over the local staff, had incorporated many of the changes that Catledge and Bernstein had hoped for, improving the paper no doubt; but he had also hurt in the process many older *Times*men whom he had liked personally and who had been kindly toward him when he was a cub reporter in this same room twenty years before. The changes in the Sixties were necessary, Rosenthal believed. The seniority system was outmoded, younger reporters who wrote concisely and well had to be favored over older men who could not. *The Times* could no longer afford to print long dull columns of news about municipal officialdom merely because *The Times* was the "paper of record." The emphasis was shifting to sharper writing, faster reading, saying more in less space, saving time for readers, saving money for management—covering all the important news, but not in the stolid way that had long been tolerated. It would be a painful adjustment for some older *Times*men who had been trained under the more leisurely pace of the past, when there had been twice as much room in the paper for local coverage, but now the economics of the business demanded tighter control over men and space. Both Catledge and Bernstein had agreed years ago that the New York staff had become tradition-bound—it was a barnacle-encrusted example of Parkinson's Law, Bernstein had thought; an old elephant, Catledge had thought, a great big package of habit.

So Rosenthal had come to New York, and within a remarkably short time he had begun to make a name for himself as an editor. The city hospitals, whose inadequate care he had experienced first-hand as a charity patient during his boyhood, were now scrutinized by *The Times* as never before. Rosenthal directed a young investigative reporter named Martin Tolchin to explore hospital life and to write about the decrepit conditions, the substandard care given to poor patients, the general medical mismanagement—and these articles inspired legislative investigations and some reforms, and also brought journalistic honors to Tolchin and *The Times*. Rosenthal assigned other reporters to write in depth about the New York public school system—how the whites were abandoning it to the blacks; the new euphemisms of Park Avenue liberals and Queens racists; and he also sent *Times*men into the ethnic neighborhoods, including his own old neighborhood in the Bronx, to describe the atmosphere, to listen to the complaints and hopes, and to write "talk" pieces, or series of articles, about the city that had changed so radically during the years that he had been abroad. Rosenthal was now seeing New York as a foreign city, his fresh eye stimulated by sights and sounds that other New Yorkers might not notice. It seemed to Rosenthal that homosexuals were more obvious on city streets than when he had last worked in New York, and this led to a superb article that was, by old *Times* standards, quite revolutionary. Rosenthal also assigned reporters to write about the increasing number of interracial marriages in New York, the increasing opulence of bookmakers and loan sharks, and finally to write about the remarkable case of a young woman who, screaming for help, was murdered one night in a quiet neighborhood while thirty-eight people heard her calls, and did nothing. This story, reprinted and commented upon around the nation, led Rosenthal to explore more thoroughly the subject of apathy in the city, the attitude of New Yorkers who, either through fear of becoming physically or legally involved in a crime that they had witnessed, elected to pretend that they had not seen it. Rosenthal wrote a magazine piece in the Sunday *Times* on this subject, later expanding it into a short book, and for more than a year he featured stories that re-echoed the incident—an overwhelming public apathy interspersed occasionally by a courageous citizen who became "involved"—and this became almost a private Rosenthal campaign. The news stories that he published were not editorial in tone, but their frequent appearance in *The Times* conveyed his "message," the need to become involved, and it emphasized more than ever that the New York coverage was changing under Rosenthal.

Rosenthal wanted to touch the nerve of New York. He wanted his staff to scratch beneath the surface and reveal something of the complexity and conflict of the city. He wanted the stories to be accurate and complete, but also interesting, and some older *Times*men, losing out to younger men who were more enthusiastic and imaginative, became resentful and helped to spread the word that the new policy was to "fake" stories and overdramatize events. When Rosenthal would assign "project" stories that would perhaps require three or four days' research and would make greater demands on a reporter's ability to organize the facts and weave them with transition, there was the sullen reaction from some older men that the paper was becoming a "magazine."

Rosenthal was aware of the disenchantment in the newsroom, and he was deeply upset by it. He was, like the city he was examining, filled with conflict and complexity: he was aggressive and sentimental, driving and tender; he had been eager to shake up the staff, to break the eggs necessary for the omelet, but he had not wanted to lose the sense of popularity and affectionate

welcome that he had felt years before whenever he had
entered the newsroom during home leave, becoming encircled by smiling familiar faces and handshakes and
calls of "Hello, Abe!" Rosenthal had then been the
skinny hometown hero who had done so well overseas,
an inspiration to copyboys and other young men starting up from the bottom, a source of pride to older men
who recalled his early reporting days under the rigid
editorship of Robert Garst.

Now things were different. The sensitivity that had
contributed to Rosenthal's greatness as a reporter was
contributing to his misery as an editor. It had not de-
terred him from his ambitions—he had exercised full
authority, had made quick tough decisions; but inwardly he had known the effect that it was having, not
only on others but on himself. One of the difficult aspects
of the New York job was that he had to see the faces of
those that he was demoralizing. If a once-privileged
senior reporter had to be downgraded in some way,
had to be removed from his regular assignment, or had
to have his stories regularly rewritten or reduced in
length, it was Rosenthal who had to become personally
involved, sooner or later, in a face-to-face confrontation
with that *Times*man. Rosenthal could not, like the foreign-news editor or the national-news editor, commu-
nicate with his reporters via cable or telephone. Not
surprisingly, a few veteran *Times*men resigned during
Rosenthal's early years as an editor, and Rosenthal
was partly pleased and relieved—they could not write
well enough, they had lacked enthusiasm—and yet
he felt remorseful, guilty, for they had served *The Times*
loyally and adequately for many years.

When one younger reporter, Robert Daley, who did
write well, announced his plans to quit *The Times* in
1965 and devote himself to fiction and magazine pieces,
Rosenthal had been greatly disappointed. Daley was the
sort who could thrive under the new system in the newsroom, Rosenthal believed, and he had liked several of
the pieces that Daley had produced since returning to
the local staff after years in Europe as a sports correspondent. It had often been said around the office,

though never ruefully, that Robert Daley was a better sportswriter than his father, Arthur Daley, who had been on the paper since 1926 and had won a Pulitzer as *The Times'* sports columnist. But Robert Daley possessed none of his father's attachment to *The Times*, and he was determined to quit, believing that he could go further as a writer, and make more money, by leaving *The Times*. So he became Rosenthal's first unwelcome defector. Rosenthal said good-bye to Daley in the newsroom, wishing him luck. Then after Daley had left, Rosenthal turned and walked into the men's room with tears in his eyes.

An individual who was discussed and debated almost as much as Rosenthal during these years was Rosenthal's hand-picked assistant, a lanky creative tower of tension named Arthur Gelb. Gelb and Rosenthal were about the same age, and they had known one another intimately for years. They had corresponded regularly while Rosenthal had worked abroad and Gelb had risen from local reporting to an editorship in the Cultural-News department. On the occasion of Rosenthal's winning the Pulitzer in 1960, Gelb wrote a humorous article in *Times Talk* about Rosenthal that the latter had not immediately appreciated. It had portrayed Rosenthal as a master of one-upmanship, a sharp-witted egotist who, upon receiving the Pulitzer, had written Gelb: "A little small, but the thought was there." The article went on to quote another Rosenthal letter: "About Poland. I don't know. I don't know. The natives here are rather insolent and don't speak English. The curry stinks but the herring is excellent. We have a nice house. Small men in small cars follow me around. We have a lovely collie named Jack or Jock or something like that. He adores me. Our cook quit. I saw Stevenson. He knew my middle initial, the test for all candidates for the presidency."

In some ways the article had told as much about Gelb as it did about Rosenthal; as when Gelb concluded:

I have tangled with Abe quite a few times, as I rather enjoy being One-Up myself, but I can recall only two instances when I came out ahead. In one, I had to resort to physical violence (always an unanswerable argument, since I'm bigger than he is; I only use that technique on him when he truly infuriates me—for example, by disagreeing with me about something) and, in the other, I admit I had to have my wife's help to win.

The time I had to knock him down was because he didn't understand the ending of a J. D. Salinger story in *The New Yorker*, and he kept giving me his cockeyed version and insisting he was right; I sat on his chest until he admitted *I* was right. He knows better than to contradict me on literary matters, now.

The other time was when I had to show him, once and for all, that it's just silly to be stubborn about some things. My wife and I dropped up to see Abe and his wife, Ann—a doll, if ever there was one—rather late one evening, and we picked up a little poundcake and brought it with us to have with coffee, but we decided to drink Scotch instead of coffee, and Abe said we had to take the poundcake home with us. We refused. As we were getting into the elevator to leave, Abe thrust the box with the poundcake at us, but, quick as a wink, and just as the door was closing, I hurled the package back at him. The Rosenthals lived on the second floor, and the elevator was pretty slow. When we reached the lobby, the doorman handed us the package, which Abe had run down the stairs with. Did you ever hear of anyone so stubborn? We had to take it, of course, but as soon as we got home, we called for a Western Union messenger and had it sent right back to the Rosenthals. (The 40-cent poundcake now had about three dollars invested in it, but it was the moral issue that was at stake.) We didn't hear anything for the next day or two, but then slices of it began arriving in the mail, and within the next few weeks, whenever a mutual friend of Abe's and mine, like Bernie Kalb or Hal Faber, came over to our house, he brought us a slice, too, with Abe's greetings.

Well, it kept going back and forth like that for a while, and then one day, when the Rosenthals were at our house for dinner, my wife sneakily slit open his overcoat lining and sewed in the cake —reduced, by now, to a handful of crumbs. I called him up when he got home, and told him he had the cake. He admitted that we had outdone him in ingenuity, and he gave up. . . .

Rosenthal and Gelb worked closely and well together, and they drove the New York staff as never before. The reporters sometimes referred to the new team as Rosencrantz and Guildenstern. While they were both serious and creative editors, they provided an electric, almost show-biz snap and tension to the newsroom, much of it the result of the restless Gelb's unending flow of ideas. It seemed that every five minutes he would propose a new idea for a story to Rosenthal, who would respond with delight—or a look of nausea. Each morning just off the train from Westchester, Gelb's tall, thin, dark bespectacled figure would come breezing into the newsroom with pockets packed with ideas—twenty ideas, thirty ideas: people to interview, tips to check, angles to investigate, grand "projects" that might take weeks to complete. Some of these ideas were brilliant, most had merit, a few were wild, all meant work, lots of work. So the less-ambitious *Times*-men, whenever they saw Gelb getting up from his desk and about to look around, would pick up their telephones, or would walk to the dictionaries located behind posts.

Inevitably, most of Gelb's ideas went to the eager younger men, and he employed an almost hypnotic manner in communicating his ideas to them. He would whisper. First he would put an arm around a young man, would walk him down the aisle, and then would whisper, very confidentially, hand over mouth, into the young man's ear—the inference being that this particular idea was so great that Gelb did not want to risk its being overheard by other reporters who would surely become envious. Finally, before the reporter would leave the room to embark on the assignment, Gelb would whisper again, "And remember, *there's a great deal of interest in this story.*" There was the barest hint that this idea might be Rosenthal's, or maybe even Daniel's or Catledge's, and the young reporter had better do his best. Then, after the reporter had gone, Gelb would have his arm around another reporter, and again there would be the parting whisper, "And remember, *there's a great deal of interest in this story.*"

Rosenthal and Gelb would later read the stories as they came in, page by page, and would check to see that the touches and angles that they had requested were there. Then they would try to assure that the story was not overedited by a copyreader; on occasion, in order to prevent the cutting of a certain paragraph or phrase, Rosenthal would carry the appeal to Bernstein himself. When Rosenthal was particularly pleased with the way a story had been done, the reporter would receive a congratulatory memo, and Rosenthal also pressured Daniel and Catledge into quickly producing big raises for certain of his favorites. One of his young stars was R. W. Apple, Jr., whose popularity with older *Times*men was hardly enhanced by the rumor that, after a few months on Rosenthal's staff, he was making $350 a week.

If so, he was earning it. An indefatigable young man with a round smiling face and a crew cut, the look of a slightly overweight West Point cadet, Apple was very gung-ho; he never stopped running, the perspiration showing through his shirt by 2 p.m., and he never dismissed one of Gelb's ideas without giving it a try. The result was that Apple got more good stories into the paper than anybody on Rosenthal's staff. This is not what bothered his older colleagues so much, for they soon recognized his ability to get a story and write it; what really unsettled them was Apple's incredible enthusiasm for *everything* he had been assigned to cover—a Board of Estimate hearing, a talk by the tax commissioner, a repetition of political speeches—and Apple's insistence, once he had returned, on telling everybody in the newsroom about what he had seen or heard, or what had happened to him while on the story. Once, returning from the Democratic National Convention in 1964, Apple burst into the newsroom to report that Ethel Kennedy had sneaked up and pinched his behind on the boardwalk in Atlantic City. Later, sent to Vietnam to work with two other *Times-*men, Charles Mohr and Neil Sheehan, Apple reported back that while pinned down under enemy fire, a bullet had slit open the back of his trousers. When he returned to New York briefly on home leave he revealed that he had actually killed a few Vietcong, to which one of his skeptical colleagues replied, "Women and children, I presume."

Perhaps Rosenthal's most dramatic story as editor of the New York staff occurred during the winter of 1965. It began with a letter from a friend who worked in a Jewish agency. The letter from Rosenthal's friend claimed that a New Yorker named Daniel Burros, who had two days before been identified in *The Times* as the New York head of the Ku Klux Klan and also a member of the American Nazi Party, was Jewish. The *Times* article had not mentioned this last fact, having no knowledge of Daniel Burros' religious background, a secret well kept by Burros as he had traveled around the country with his fellow Nazi "troopers" advocating hatred and death to Jews everywhere.

Rosenthal stood up at his desk as he read the letter. He was fascinated, excited. He considered his friend to be a very reliable man, and yet Rosenthal's excitement was mixed with disbelief, a skepticism that always grips an ambitious journalist whenever he is handed a story that seems too good to be true, too shockingly odd and marvelous; he desperately wants the facts to finally fit the fantastic story that is already forming in his mind, building within him, expanding, he can almost start writing it, but he must suddenly stop and wonder with cool detachment whether the facts are accurate: Rosenthal looked around the newsroom for the right reporter to handle this story. He wanted a reporter of unquestionable reliability—a patient researcher and subtle writer. Two things had to be answered: first, was Daniel Burros indeed Jewish, and if so, how and why did a Jewish boy become a Nazi? This assignment might take days to complete, and would require following many small leads that might be unproductive; the ringing of strangers' doorbells, the waiting on street corners in the hope of locating Burros' friends or parents, who would most likely be uncooperative. There should also be attempts made at contacting Burros' former teachers, his friends from his days in the United States Army, his rabbi. (According to the letter, Burros had been bar mitzvahed.)

Burros had no telephone, his address was uncertain. His parents, who possibly had no knowledge of his Nazi activities, lived in the Richmond Hill section of Queens, in New York City. Burros was twenty-eight, was said to be stocky, blond, blue-eyed—"a knowledgeable and virulent Nazi" who was out of jail pending appeal on a two-year term for rioting and possessing a switchblade knife. Burros might become violent after he had learned of *The Times'* interets in publicizing his secret. The story would undoubtedly ruin his career as a leader on the far right fringe. For this reason Rosenthal wanted a reporter who was a perceptive and skilled interviewer, a reporter who also had empathy for the people he was interviewing. This was not to be a crime story for an aggressive police reporter, or an odd tale for a clever feature writer; Rosenthal believed it would be a complex personal portrait of a Jewish boy's self-hate, and it would have to be written with care and compassion.

Continuing to look around the newsroom, Rosenthal focused on a tall, skinny, pale reporter seated in the first row behind the rewrite bank. His name was McCandlish Phillips. At thirty-seven, Phillips' black hair, slicked down and precisely parted, was graying at the temples; he wore a dark blue suit, white shirt, and blue tie, and, as usual, there was a Bible on his desk near his typewriter. Rosenthal knew, as everybody in the newsroom knew, that McCandlish Phillips was an evangelical Christian who, when not working on a story, sometimes sat reading his Bible or praying. On Phillips' days off, or at night, he regularly preached in churches, or in private prayer meetings, or sometimes at a sidewalk pulpit near his apartment at 116th Street and Broadway. Once seen, he was hard to forget. He stood six-feet five-inches, and he spoke eloquently in a high-pitched voice that was filled with conviction but was never overbearing. He did not preach in the rasping, flailing Damned-Shall-Perish style of those barely literate philosophers who gathered each night in *Times Square*. Phillips was a man of quiet dignity and learning. He had a sense of humor, but more than that, he had a tranquil manner, a serenity that was based on his absolute faith in God and his belief that, come what may, it was God's will.

In the newsroom Phillips never preached to his fellow reporters, although he was always approachable and even eager to discuss with them, if they wished, the teachings of the Bible or any other subject, including the sins of copyreaders. When one of Phillips' stories had been butchered, Phillips did not immediately attribute it to the will of God, but rather to the dumbheadedness of deskmen, and he was never reluctant to complain—although he always did so with a certain decorum and never with profanity. He was well liked and admired by the staff, and he was often referred to as "Long John"—John was his first name; nobody called him "McCandlish," his middle name, except those many readers who knew him through his by-line. Stories *by McCandlish Phillips* were invariably distinguished by their fine use of language, their slightly archaic, almost biblical precision and conciseness, often their humor, and always the author's compassion for his subject.

When Rosenthal approached Phillips' desk, he tried to convey his enthusiasm for the story without overdoing it.

"Look," Rosenthal said, pulling up a chair next to

Phillips and handing him the letter, "here's the head of the K.K.K. for New York, and he's a Jew. Let's take a look at it. Get hold of this guy and see if you can find what makes a Jewish kid from Queens grow up to be a Nazi. It could make a terrific story."

Phillips was interested. Not only was it an unusual story, but it confirmed for Phillips a premonition that he had had earlier in the week about working on this day. He had planned to take a four-day weekend, having accumulated many days owed because of overtime work; but while praying at home he had felt the Lord, clearly and unmistakably, telling him not to take the four-day weekend. And so on this Friday morning, October 22, 1965, Phillips was at his desk.

After Rosenthal had relayed everything that he knew about Daniel Burros, Phillips, assisted by two younger reporters, began to pursue the leads. There was information to be gotten from the police, who in recent years had arrested Burros at Nazi rallies; from the Anti-Defamation League, which had a confidential file on Burros; from the schools that Burros had attended and the places where he had worked. In Washington, the House Committee on Un-American Activities was aware of Burros; it had included him in a list of "prominent Klansmen," and it knew that Burros had attended a meeting of the United Klans of America in North Carolina during August of 1965. Phillips also had found, in *The Times'* morgue, the names of a few members of local Nazi or racist groups who might know something about Burros.

He compiled a list of people and places to check, divided it with the two other reporters, and later in the afternoon Phillips, accompanied by a photographer named Carl Gossett, set out for a neighborhood in Queens where he believed he might find Burros.

The address was of an apartment over a shop on Lefferts Boulevard, but when Phillips inquired he was told by the shopkeeper that no one named Burros lived in the apartment upstairs. A few youngsters standing nearby, however, recognized the name and pointed to a brick apartment house a few blocks away.

There, within a small vestibule, among four name plates on an old brass mailbox, Phillips saw "Burros." He rang the bell; no answer. He rang the other bells; none answered. Noticing a traffic cop outside, Phillips walked over and asked if he knew anyone named Burros. The policeman said that he did, an elderly man who had just left the apartment house about an hour ago, and would probably return soon. The policeman did not know if the man had a son. Phillips and Gossett waited. As people passed the building, Phillips, leaning low to be heard, courteously asked if they knew Daniel Burros. A few of them did, and they proceeded to describe him. He was somewhat stocky, short, and wore glasses. He was blond. They did not know exactly what he did for a living, but he was in and out of the neighborhood at odd hours. He was an only son, a very good boy, never destructive. His mother worked as a sales clerk in a department store; his father, ill, usually remained at home. Nobody in the neighborhood, Phillips realized, seemed to know about Daniel Burros' political activities.

The afternoon passed; it grew dark and began to rain. Gossett had no chance of getting a photograph of Burros into the next day's *Times* at this late hour, and so after telephoning the picture desk he was told to leave. He loaned Phillips the raincoat that he always carried in his car trunk, then drove home. Phillips waited alone for the return of the elder Burros, or perhaps of Daniel Burros himself.

Phillips felt a bit queasy as he stood in the entrance of the building under a globe light that was broken. It was an old, rundown two-story yellow brick building that was divided into four apartments. The Burros family occupied one of the apartments on the second floor. The neighborhood was like dozens of other neighborhoods in Queens that spread low and unglamorously beyond the skyline of Manhattan. Its inhabitants were predominantly lower-middle-class whites who had escaped their old neighborhoods of ethnic distinctiveness in Brooklyn, the Bronx, or lower Manhattan, and had created, in such places as this, settlements of sameness. Travelers could pass through most sections of Queens hundreds of times—en route to the airports, or to Shea Stadium, or to the beaches beyond—and discover no reason for stopping except the traffic lights. Some of the houses were extremely well kept and had tidy lawns, and trees; but there was no more sense of the country or the suburbs here than there was of the city. Across the street from the Burros apartment there was a bar with a neon sign; a supermarket was half a block away; a U.S. Army recruiting poster, swinging in the wind, stood close to the curb near a bus stop.

But it was the anticipation of meeting Daniel Burros, and not the neighborhood, that accounted for Phillips' slight feeling of uneasiness. Neighborhoods, be they elegant or shabby, had little effect on Phillips. Material objects did not interest him. He had never spent money on luxury items or on entertainment. What was left after paying for the necessities of New York, he gave away—to his church, to his mother—who had been separated from his father, a traveling salesman, years before his father's death—or to his younger sister. McCandlish Phillips had never married, and solitude did not often bother him because he felt the omnipresence of the Lord, and because he also had spent most of his adolescence moving from town to town, school to school, making friends and then being forced to leave them.

After he had graduated from high school, and after taking the advice of one elderly editor who assured him that college was a waste of time, Phillips accepted a $20-a-week job on a weekly sports publication in Boston. Later he became a general-assignment reporter for a small newspaper chain in Brookline, and it was there that he met a man who would alter the course of his life.

The man, a devout Christian, worked in the advertising department. One day he asked Phillips if he might like to accompany him and his wife to church on some Sunday morning. Phillips accepted and he was soon pleased that he had. It seemed obvious to Phillips that the words of the minister from the pulpit were carrying right into the lives of the people. There was a clearness of countenance about them, a directness of manner, a certain warmth that seemed much more than mere sociability; it seemed genuine.

Phillips accepted the man's offer to return, and did so for the next nine Sundays. On Phillips' tenth visit, after the sermon had ended, the minister asked that all heads be bowed, all eyes closed. "You have heard the words that have been spoken this morning," the minister said, "you have heard that Jesus Christ died for your sins, and that he is ready to come into your life and to govern your life. . . ." Then the minister asked if there was anyone in the congregation who acknowledged himself as a sinner, and who recognized the need of Christ as his Savior—would those persons please raise their hands? It was not a thought process with Phillips. All he knew was that he wanted to raise his hand, and he did.

He was drafted into the Army shortly after his conversion as a "born-again" Christian, being stationed for the next two years at Fort Holabird, Maryland. He rose to the rank of sergeant, and although he sometimes thought about his future he mainly felt that it was in the hands of Christ. Before his release from the Army, hours before he was to leave Fort Holabird, Phillips felt a great sense of adventure—he did not know exactly where he would go when he walked through the military gate for the last time, He thought that he might end up in Alaska, or Hawaii, or wherever the Lord would lead him to do what was to be done. When Phillips received no sign, he bought a train ticket to Boston, but he never got there. He got off at New York, checked into a hotel in Times Square, and prayed. The next morning he bought *The Times* and the *Herald Tribune*. In the middle of one of *The Times'* classified advertising pages there was a half-inch notice: "Editorial trainee wanted. Apply NYTimes Personnel."

Phillips got on his knees and prayed, then walked toward the *Times* building. . . .

McCandlish Phillips had been standing outside the Burros apartment building for more than an hour when he noticed an elderly man, starting to walk slowly up the path. It was almost too dark and misty to see the man's face, but he was stocky and slow-footed, and, as he got closer, Phillips could observe a bulbous nose, pale pouted cheeks, sad eyes. He wore a thick coat slightly frayed.

"Mr. Burros?" Phillips asked.

The man looked up, but his vacant expression hardly changed as he answered, "Yes."

"I need to reach Dan," Phillips said.

"Who are you?"

Phillips gave only his name. Mr. Burros remained silent and waited for a fuller explanation.

"I'm with *The New York Times*," Phillips added, finally. "We have a story about Dan, and I need to talk to him."

Quickly, Mr. Burros turned away.

"I got nothing to say," he said, pushing the door open, then closing it. Phillips remained in the doorway, watching the thick-necked elderly man, about seventy years old, slowly climbing the steps to the second floor. Phillips had no story for the next day's edition, and because of the damp chill of the evening, and because he also did not wish to encounter Daniel Burros at this time, a reaction that he did not pause to analyze, he decided to walk to the bar across the street and to call *The Times*. Rosenthal had left, but an assistant editor told Phillips to come back to the office. Before doing so, Phillips wrote a note to Daniel Burros and returned to the apartment to leave it for him. He then left the building for the subway station, and the long ride back to Manhattan.

Daniel Burros did not respond to Phillips' note, nor to a followup telegram, although Phillips later learned that Burros had received and read both. Phillips meanwhile continued to dig into Burros' past, assisted by the two younger *Times*men. They interviewed dozens of people who had known Burros, had gone to school with him, had employed him, or had arrested him; and slowly the bizarre sketch of young Burros began to materialize.

Burros had been born in the Bronx in March of 1937 to parents who had married late in life—his mother had been thirty-four, his father forty-two, both descendants of Russian Jewish immigrants. Daniel Burros' father, the tired man that Phillips had briefly met, had joined the Navy before World War I when he was about sixteen, and after one enlistment he had transferred to the Army, serving with a division that had pursued Pancho Villa. During World War I, in France, Burros had received a throat wound that would forever impair his speech. In civilian life he became a machinist, but his health was bad, and when Phillips had met him he was not working, living mainly on his government pension and on whatever income his wife earned as a saleswoman in a department store in Jamaica, Queens.

Esther Burros was devoutly religious, and when she produced, at thirty-five, her only child, she became extremely loving and protective. Even when Daniel Burros was in the sixth grade, Mrs. Burros would often walk him to school and return to take him home afterward, although the school was only a half-block from the Burros apartment. Daniel Burros had gone through the bar mitzvah ceremony, he later confided to a friend, because he had been "pressured" into it at home, but Burros had seemed to enjoy a warm relationship with the rabbi until the rabbi, offered a larger congregation on Long Island, had accepted it because he had needed more money for his family. Daniel Burros had appeared to be disappointed by the rabbi's decision, but the boy continued to do well in school, and had registered an I.Q. of 154, which labeled him a "gifted child." His grades in high school continued to be outstanding, but warped signs of confusion and rebellion began to appear. He took pride in his blue eyes and blond hair, and began to represent himself as a German-American, not as a Jew. With his friends, those who did not know that he had attended Hebrew school, he argued often that the German leaders had been misunderstood during World War II. He seemed awed by the top German generals, and was resentful of those fellow students who disagreed with his opinions. One day, after an argument with a Jewish student had led to swinging fists, Burros blurted out bitterly: "Jew bastard!"

Burros was somewhat influenced in high school by his history teacher, an Irish-Catholic McCarthyite, who helped to crystallize some of the right-wing philosophy that Burros was espousing. Burros' poorest school grades were in Hebrew, which he had flunked, while his grades in German had been excellent. He finished high school with a four-year average of 87, which would have qualified him for a scholarship to college, but he had not been interested, explaining to one friend that college was for "Jew boys" trying to dodge the draft. Burros wanted to become a soldier, and in 1955 he had enlisted in the United States Army paratroopers, serving with the 101st Airborne Division and the 187th Airborne Combat team. He made seventeen parachute jumps, and was among the troops sent to Little Rock, Arkansas, under Major General Edwin A. Walker, to control the disturbances caused by the school integration program. Burros' letters to friends revealed that he had been appalled by the sight of white soldiers "protecting niggers," and that he believed that the nation was becoming a left-wing police state.

Though he had wanted to achieve status as a brave soldier, Burros' companions in the service were more amused than impressed by him. He looked almost comic in uniform. He had lost his flabbiness and was broad-chested and thick-armed, but he nonetheless was very short and seemed to be weighed down by the parachute pack, the large round helmet, and boots. His snappy salute was *too* snappy. He was a mockery of militarism. They laughed at him, and on more than one occasion he tried to commit suicide. Sent to an Army psychiatrist, Burros was diagnosed as an emotionally immature individual overwhelmed by childish fantasy. In 1958 he was discharged.

He had worked for a year and a half in the Queens Public Library as an office-machine operator, but by 1960 he had quit and become active in the American Nazi party, commanded by George Lincoln Rockwell. He found a $300-a-month job in Washington as a multilith operator with the United States Chamber of Commerce, but his main activities were centered in Rockwell's barracks in Arlington, Virginia, where he lived and established himself as perhaps the most militant of anti-Semites. There he had drawn pictures of gas chambers, hoping to amuse the other troopers. He also displayed a little green-wrapped bar of soap that was labeled: "Made from the finest Jewish fat." Burros had been an active public demonstrator with the Nazis, once picketing the Chamber of Commerce building where he worked. He was fired, and he was later arrested and fined $100 for pasting swastikas in an elevator at the B'nai B'rith building in Washington. He was convicted on three other occasions during the summer of 1960 for using profane language and for fighting with spectators at street rallies.

Not long after this Burros quit Rockwell's followers and went to New York hoping to strengthen a local Nazi contingent. But he failed. The New York Nazis were so poor that they could not even afford uniforms, a fact that had greatly disappointed him. When a racist friend obtained an invitation for Burros to join the Klan, Burros accepted with pleasure, becoming the recipient of a white gown and hood. His enthusiasm was obvious, his energy boundless, and soon he was appointed the Grand Dragon of New York, presiding over dozens of members, and coming to the attention of the police and government authorities that specialize in the infiltration of political fringe groups. One day Burros' parents were visited by a government agent who later discovered that the family was Jewish. The agent did not intend to expose Daniel Burros' secret at that time, partly out of sympathy for the parents, who had been suffering in silent shame ever since their son had been arrested with Rockwell's men. The agent also knew that to expose Burros would be to eliminate from the racist movement a possible informer.

So that is where matters stood until, on October 22, 1965, Rosenthal received the letter from his friend about Burros' background. And on October 29, exactly one week after McCandlish Phillips' first visit to the Burros apartment, Phillips decided to go back and try again. He set his alarm for 5:15 a.m., and took the subway from upper Broadway to Queens via Brooklyn, thinking that he would arrive outside the Burros apartment before anyone had gotten up. He planned to post himself outside the door, all day if necessary, in the hope of meeting Burros.

The subway ride was frustratingly slow. It was almost 8 a.m. when Phillips finally arrived, walking down the long flight of steps from the elevated platform. As Phillips turned onto Lefferts Boulevard, the very instant he made the turn, he caught a quick glimpse of Daniel Burros walking into a barber shop. The timing was unbelievable. If Phillips had arrived at that spot two seconds later, he would have missed Burros— would have walked past the barber shop to the Burros apartment with no assurance that Burros would have returned until nighttime, if then. Phillips had never seen Daniel Burros before, but he knew him from photographs. There was no doubt about the identity.

When Burros came out of the barber shop, his hair cut short to trooper length, Phillips stepped forward and introduced himself. Burros recognized the name immediately from the note and telegram.

"I need to talk to you," Phillips said.

"Okay," said Burros.

Burros did not seem sinister. He was civil, almost pleasant. He explained that he could not grant a formal interview, but was willing to sit down for a few minutes and confirm some facts that Phillips had. They walked a few blocks to a small luncheonette dimmed by the shadows of the elevated platform. They occupied a booth near the door and sat facing one another. Phillips ordered scrambled eggs, Burros a Coke. A waitress placed napkins, knives, and forks in front of both of them. Phillips was not able to get a good close look at Burros' face because the latter, who seemed embarrassed, kept his eyes downward, or focused on a corner of the table, occasionally flashing a direct glance at Phillips, but when again looking down or away. Burros did not know exactly what Phillips wanted.

Phillips, very gently and courteously, began to reveal what he knew of Burros' military career as a paratrooper, and his later activities with Rockwell's followers and the Ku Klux Klan. The facts and minute details, the obvious time and effort that had been involved in the research, greatly impressed Burros, who more than once exclaimed, almost with pleasure, "Gee, *fantastic.*" Burros was not embarrassed by this side of his life, nor was it a secret. It had been in the newspapers in abbreviated form, and Burros was of course aware that the Congressional committee and the police had a file on him. And as Phillips, extemporaneously and uncondemningly, continued to recount Burros' past, Burros began to relax, seemed to enjoy it; and instead of merely confirming facts, Burros proceeded to elaborate on them. He pulled from his pocket his Klan identification card and showed it to Phillips. He also displayed a small picture of himself wearing a white hood. He spoke at length about his days with Rockwell, his experience with the United States paratroopers in Little Rock, and his fears that Little Rock had signaled the beginning of a left-wing takeover of the nation, which Burros was dedicated to stopping. He fondly recalled his McCarthyite history teacher in high school, and he admitted that he had communicated through the mail with right-wing groups in Germany. He revealed his contempt for the Jews, adding that if the "purge" came to the United States it would be more viciously prosecuted in the "wild" atmosphere of America than it had been in the "civilized and highly cultured" society of Germany more than twenty years ago. Burros looked at his watch a few times during the interview, saying that he wanted to catch a bus for Pennsylvania, but he seemed content to remain with this very tall stranger who knew so much about him, and with whom he felt free to expound upon his theories. Phillips was a good listener. He seemed to understand the fervor and dedication of the committed individual.

Finally, Phillips decided to raise the question that had been on his mind since their talk had begun. There was nothing else that Phillips needed from this interview except some clue into the essential paradox of Burros' life.

"There's one thing about you that just does not fit into the picture," Phillips began, slowly, casually, "and I can't figure it out." Daniel Burros glanced at his watch. He said rather urgently that he had to catch the 1 p.m. bus for Pennsylvania. "Your parents were married by the Reverend Bernard Kallenberg in a Jewish ceremony in the Bronx," Phillips said. He waited for the reaction.

Burros seemed to deteriorate physically before Phillips' eyes. There was a visible sign of inner collapse, the blue eyes growing distant, cold, the round stock figure seeming to sag and sink under the weight of a stunning blow. Then Burros leaned across the table at Phillips, looked directly into his eyes, and asked, "Are you going to print that?"

Phillips said that it was not in his power to withhold it—the fact of the marriage was a public record in the Bronx Supreme Court House.

"If you publish that," Burros said, quietly tense, "I will be ruined. All my friends, all my associations, everything I've lived for for the last seven years will be gone. . . ." Then he added, in a voice regaining composure, "If you publish that I'll come and get you and I'll *kill* you."

Now Phillips felt a sense of panic rising within him. He was aware that he was trapped in a booth, his long legs almost pinioned between the table top and supporting metal, and the luncheonette itself seemed to be shrouded in blackness, it did not look like the place he had entered. Burros' threat had not been shouted, but it was rather more ferocious in its even-toned intensity.

Phillips heard Burros repeating the threat, adding that Phillips would die *before* leaving the luncheonette. Phillips, knowing what he did about Burros' past, knowing how desperately the latter had tried to conceal the secret, believed Burros to be quite capable of fulfilling his threat here and now. He felt Burros' eyes upon him, heard him say that he had a vial of acid under his coat. He saw Burros put a hand inside his coat, waiting for Phillips' reply to the question—was he going to publish the fact? Phillips, praying *Lord help me*, did not really believe that Burros had a vial of acid inside. It seemed unlikely that a man would carry such an item into a barbershop at 8 a.m. But Phillips *did* see the knife and fork at Burros' fingertips. He had to say something immediately. He did not want to lie, but he wanted to say something that would divert Burros from his threat. Phillips, trying to appear unintimidated, told Burros that he would not print the fact until he had talked to Burros one more time. This seemed to lessen the tension, slightly. But again there was the warning, "If you publish that, I'll come and get you and I'll kill you. I don't care what happens to me. I'll be ruined. This is all I've got to live for."

Phillips told Burros to call him that evening, and then he took out a dollar and placed it on the check. "Let's go outside," Phillips said, and he was relieved when Burros stood up and quietly followed. Outside Phillips could at least duck or run. He had his story; now he wanted to get away. Phillips was a man of the Lord, but he had been a journalist this morning, totally journalistic. He believed that it was the Lord's will that he write this tory, recalling how one week before he had received a signal from the Lord urging that he not take the four-day weekend. It did not occur to Phillips now, nor had it occurred to him at any time during the past week, to forget the story and permit a desperate and demented young man to preserve his fantasy. Phillips considered himself a journalist by the will of the Lord. The judgments were sometimes harsh, but they were nonetheless as the Lord wished.

Still Phillips felt a need to reach this small, miserable

man who stood next to him outside the luncheonette. "I'm through talking to you as reporter to subject," he said. "The interview is over. Now I want to talk to you as one human being to another." They began to walk slowly through the shadows under the train platform, and Phillips was not aware of anyone else on the streets, nor of any noise. Burros said that he felt trapped by what Phillips might print, but Phillips replied, "No, you're trapped by who you are, by everything you've got mixed into." Quoting from the New Testament, Phillips continued, " 'If any man be in Christ he is a new creature; old things are passed away, behold all things are become new.' "

Burros looked up at him.

"You're trying to con me."

Phillips said that he was not. "What you have to do to break the grip fascism has on you is to call upon the name of Jesus Christ," Phillips said. "If you do that, He will take care of the rest."

As he reached the entrance of the elevated platform, Phillips shook hands with Burros. Burros turned toward his home.

When Phillips had arrived in the newsroom, there was a message that Burros had called. Phillips called back, and Burros said that he wanted to trade some other story for the one about his Jewish origin. Phillips said he could not do that. When Burros called later in the afternoon, there was despair and anger in his tone.

"I know I can't stop that story," he said, "but I'm going to go out in a blaze of glory." Without specifying when or how, he suggested that he was going to shoot up the *Times* building.

Phillips described this threat and the earlier ones in a memo to Gelb, who was in charge while Rosenthal was attending a conference out of town. Gelb notified Clifton Daniel, and he also called the New York Police and *The Times'* security guards. Photographs of Burros were reproduced and distributed to the security force. After Phillips had finished writing the story, a twenty-four-hour bodyguard was ordered for him, and he was driven home that night by detectives. The editors wanted him to leave town for a few days, but he said that he wanted to be close to his church.

On Sunday morning, October 31, after one of the paper's legmen had obtained a record of Burros' bar mitzvah—the proof that Gelb wanted before releasing the story for publication—*The Times* featured the article on page one. Daniel Burros was in Reading, Pennsylvania, on that morning, spending the weekend with other Klansmen who had been told by their leaders to remain inconspicuous while the "heat" was on from the Federal investigators. Burros had mentioned his interview with *The Times*, but his friends did not know the full extent of his concern until after he had purchased a *Times* at the newsstand and had returned with it. Then his friends heard him groan "Oh, my God," and then he was upstairs yelling and breaking the furniture with karate kicks and chops—and finally, before anyone could stop him, he had taken a gun and put one bullet in his heart and another in his head.

During the next week, *The Times* received letters from readers who denounced the paper for "invading the privacy" of Burros. Others questioned the wisdom of exposing an obviously sick person; even some staff members in the newsroom felt that *The Times* in this instance had gone too far. Burros had not been a major public figure, they reasoned, but merely an oddball, and they interpreted the story as another example of the overly dramatic journalism that was being condoned at *The Times*.

Other reporters and readers, however, disagreed. They believed that *The Times* had performed a public service in focusing attention on a potentially dangerous fanatic—the sort who would attempt to assassinate a President or other world leaders. Burros had relinquished his right to privacy, they said, when he had become a political activist.

A. M. Rosenthal was upset by the consequences and criticism of the story, and the first thing that he did after hearing the news was to call his friend from the Jewish agency who had supplied the tip on Burros. They spoke for a long time, both expressing sorrow at having been instrumental in the death of another human being, but both agreed that Daniel Burros had been pointing a gun at his own head for years, and that it was merely a matter of time before some individual or event would trip the trigger.

When Arthur Gelb had received the news, he was immediately concerned over how it would affect Phillips, and Gelb spoke very gently and slowly over the phone. Phillips was saddened, for he had regarded Burros as a man inextricably trapped in a web of evil; but Phillips had no doubt of *The Times*' rectitude in publishing the story. On the eve of Burros' suicide, Phillips had been at home reading the Third Psalm, which he thought appropriate in the case of Burros (". . . *there is no help for him in God* . . ."), and after Gelb had telephoned, Phillips had suggested that Gelb also read the psalm.

"What I think we've seen here, Arthur," Phillips said, "is the God of Israel acting in judgment."

16

WHEN Abe Rosenthal first read *The Times* on this June day in 1966 he did not notice the item; it was on page 30, and it was printed in agate type deep within a long list that announced the names of City College students who had received awards: and yet there it was:

> BRETT AWARD to the student who has worked hardest under a great handicap—Jake Barnes.

To anyone who has read Ernest Hemingway's *The Sun Also Rises*, the references were clear: Lady Brett and the sexually impotent man who loves her, Jake Barnes. In *The Times!*

Rosenthal's deskmen, who had edited and checked the story the night before, had obviously overlooked the item too, and perhaps it would have gone completely unnoticed by Rosenthal if he had not just received a telephone call from a *Newsweek* staff member who had asked about it, thinking it very imaginative and funny. But Rosenthal saw no humor in it. He was, in fact, infuriated, and was not assuaged by the fact that on the same page, spreading across the top, there was a story from Princeton with a five-column headline that read: "Goheen Tells Princeton Class a Sense of Humor Is Needed."

If the young *Times* correspondent who had been assigned to cover the City College story, and to compile the list of awards, had been guilty of deliberately inserting false information into *The Times*, there was no recourse, Rosenthal thought, but to fire him. Many years ago, A. J. Liebling, then employed as a copyreader in *The Times'* sports department, had done something like this: instead of listing the correct name of the basketball referee in the agate box score, as was required, Liebling—who always experienced difficulty in getting the reporters to remember to get the referee's name— would merely write, in place of the name, the Italian word *ignoto*—"unknown." Mr. *Ignoto* would some- times be listed in *The Times* as the referee of two or three or even four basketball games a night, in various cities—far too energetic and rambling a referee to go undiscovered indefinitely. When the prank became known, Liebling was fired, and he went on to use his imagination more wisely on *The New Yorker*.

The difficulty in the City College incident was that the correspondent who *might* have been guilty—Rosen- thal had not yet called him—was Clyde Haberman, one of Rosenthal's favorites, a young man of twenty- one who reminded Rosenthal very much of himself. Haberman was skinny and driving, as Rosenthal had been twenty years ago when *he* was the City College correspondent for *The Times*, and Haberman had quickly demonstrated an ability to sense a story, then to write it well. In the eight months he had been the City College correspondent, Clyde Haberman had produced more than sixty pieces, a remarkable achievement for an individual whose beat was limited to one campus. Haberman had made one slip, in an article about col- lege tuition, but he had otherwise been reliable, had seemed very dedicated to journalism, and he had im- pressed Rosenthal as an excellent candidate for the reportorial staff of *The Times*.

Rosenthal hoped that Haberman had not inserted the "Brett Award." There was no chance of supporting a young man in this situation as Rosenthal had supported another man two years before, a Negro named Junius Griffin, who had written a front-page piece for *The Times* about the existence of a "Blood Brother" gang in Har- lem, a militant band of men who were trained in karate and would soon invade white Manhattan if conditions in the ghetto were not quickly improved. The Blood Brother story was immediately picked up by the networks and other newspapers, spreading minor panic in some quarters, provoking angry denials elsewhere, including in Harlem, where the story was challenged as an exaggeration and even an outright hoax. Rosenthal had checked into the story, and had claimed that his reporter was not writing fiction. But *The Times* was nonetheless doubted and criticized in other newspapers and periodicals—an opportunity they never miss when they think *The Times* has overstepped its traditional caution. They could find no such organization, and even in *The Times'* newsroom there were older staffmen who smiled cynically, saying that this sort of thing was bound to happen when inexperienced reporters were given wider range, and when the New York staff felt the pressure of having to make a fine showing each day in the paper. Some reporters began to refer to the Blood Brother story as Rosenthal's Bay of Pigs.

Clyde Haberman was in bed when Rosenthal called his home in the Bronx. Haberman had been awakened fifteen minutes before by a call from the City College publicity department saying that it had been receiving inquiries about the "Brett Award." It was then, and only then, that Haberman remembered that he had forgotten to move the humorous award, as he had intended, or as he had perhaps intended, from the long list before turning it into the desk the afternoon before. He remembered how bored and drowsy he had then been in the newsroom, having spent hours behind the typewriter copying the interminable list of names and awards that were to be presented at the college's commencement ceremony two nights hence—hundreds of names and awards whose publication in *The Times* was a waste of space, he thought, was an annoyance to his eyesight, was giving him a headache—he could understand that *The Times*, a paper of record, would devote space to a Congressional roll call, or would print long texts of speeches . . . but to fill *three columns* with City College student awards seemed absolutely prepos-

terous to Haberman; and the more he typed, the more
frustrated he became . . .

the RICHARD MOBY AWARD for excellence in
community relations—Eugene Scharmann;
the THEODORE LESKES MEMORIAL AWARD
to the student who has demonstrated unusual
promise in the field of civil liberties and civil
rights—Phyllis Cooper;
the BENJAMIN LUBETSKY MEMORIAL
SCHOLARSHIP to the deserving student of
engineering—Arnon Rieger;
the NEHEMIAH GITELSON MEDAL to the student who best exemplifies in his undergraduate
career the spirit of the search for truth—Gregory
Chaitin;
the . . .
BRETT AWARD to the student who has worked
hardest under a great handicap—Jake Barnes.

It had just popped into Haberman's head, his fingers
reproduced it quickly on paper, he had laughed, he
had thought it very funny, he had decided to take it
out, *not* to take it out, he continued to type . . . and
later he had become busy with something else, forgetting
about Barnes and Lady Brett as he had turned the story,
and the long list, into the desk. And it had taken the
morning phone calls to remind him, first from the City
College press agent, and then from Rosenthal.

"Clyde," Rosenthal began softly, "did you see the City
College prize list this morning?"
"Yes."
"Did you see a Brett Award?"
"Yes."
"How did that get there?"
"I, uh, guess I put it in," Clyde Haberman said
timidly, "in a moment of silliness."
"You did," Rosenthal said slowly, his voice getting
hard. "Well, that moment finished you in newspapers."
Haberman could not believe the words. He was

stunned. *Finished with newspapers,* Haberman thought, *he must be kidding! It isn't possible over an inane thing like this!*

Haberman got dressed, having been told by Rosenthal to appear in the newsroom immediately, but even as he rode the subway to Times Square, Haberman could not believe that he was finished at *The Times.* Haberman had sensed that Rosenthal was an extremely sensitive man, a feeling that Haberman had first gotten from reading Rosenthal's classic on the Nazi concentration camp at Auschwitz. It was so revealingly sentimental, Haberman had thought, reading the piece a second time, that he wondered how Rosenthal could have exposed such tender emotion. Now in the subway Haberman thought that Rosenthal was merely upset by the joke in *The Times;* Haberman knew him well enough to sense that Rosenthal regarded a joke on *The Times* to be a joke on him. Yet he was confident, once the lack of malicious intent had been explained, that the mistake would pass and be forgotten.

It was noon when Haberman entered the newsroom. Nearly everybody was out to lunch. He walked up to the big desk where Rosenthal sits, and he addressed a broad-shouldered gray-haired clerk named Charles Bevilacqua, who had been there for years.

"Is Mr. Rosenthal in?" Haberman asked.

"Out to lunch," Bevilacqua said.

Haberman walked away, but Bevilacqua called after him harshly, "You'd better stick around. He wants to talk to you."

Haberman wanted to whirl around and say, *No kidding, you idiot, why didn't somebody tell me?* but being in no position to act offensively, he retreated meekly into the newsroom's rows and rows of empty desks, occupied only by the obituary writer, Alden Whitman, a reporter, Bernard Weinraub, and a young man on try-out, Steve Conn, a friend of Haberman's.

"Hey, Clyde," Conn said, laughing, "did you see that Brett Award in the paper today?"

Haberman said he had. Then he admitted writing

it, and Conn smacked a hand gently against his forehead and groaned; "Oh, *God*."

Haberman took a seat in the middle of the newsroom to await Rosenthal's return. He focused on the silver microphone up ahead—a most intimidating gadget, he always thought, for most young men on the paper: they feared, after having turned in their story, the sight of an editor picking up the microphone and booming out their names, paging them to the New York editor's desk to explain their ambiguities or errors. Just from the sound from the microphone, Haberman knew, a young reporter could usually tell the mood of the editor: if the editor paged the reporter in a snappy, peremptory tone—*Mr. Haberman!* very quick—it meant that there was only a small question, one that the editor wished to discuss hastily so he could get on to other matters elsewhere. But if the editor languished on the sound of a young man's name—*M r H a b e r m a n*—then the editor's patience was thin, and the matter was very serious indeed.

Twenty-five minutes later Haberman saw Rosenthal walk into the room, then stride toward his desk. Haberman lowered his head as he heard the microphone being picked up. It was the voice of Charles Bevilacqua, a low sad note of finality, *M r H a b e r m a n.*

Haberman got up and began the long walk up the aisle, passing the rows of empty desks, thinking suddenly of a course he had taken under Paddy Chayefsky in screenplay-writing, and wishing he had a camera panning the room to capture permanently the starkness of the scene.

He saw Rosenthal standing before him. "Sit down," Rosenthal said. Then, as he sat, Haberman heard Rosenthal begin, "You will never be able to write for this newspaper again."

Haberman now accepted the reality of it, and yet made one final attempt at reminding Rosenthal of the work he had done from City College, the many exclusives and features, and Rosenthal cut him off: "Yes, and that's why you acted like a fool—I had backed you, and written memos about you, and you could have been on staff in a year or two. . . . You made me look like a jackass. You made *The Times* look like a jackass . . ."

There was silence. Then, his voice softening and becoming sad, Rosenthal explained that the most inviolate thing *The Times* had was its news columns: people should be able to believe every word, and there would never be tolerance for tampering. Further, Rosenthal said, if Haberman were pardoned, the discipline of the entire staff, the younger men and the established reporters, would suffer—any one of them could err and then say, "Well, Haberman got away with it."

There was a pause, and in this time Rosenthal's voice shifted to yet another mood—optimism for Haberman, not on *The Times* but somewhere else. Haberman had talent, Rosenthal said, and now it was a question of accepting the fact that it was all over with the Gray Lady and moving on determinedly to make the grade somewhere else.

Rosenthal talked with him for another five minutes, warmly and enthusiastically; then the two men stood up, and shook hands. Haberman walked back, shaken, to a desk to type out his resignation. Rosenthal had given him the option of doing this so that he would not have officially been fired. Rosenthal had discussed this point an hour before with Clifton Daniel, and also with Emanuel Freedman, an assistant managing editor, and Richard D. Burritt, the personnel specialist, and they all agreed to accept the resignation as soon as Haberman could type it out.

Having done so, and after handing it in, Haberman was aware that other people in the newsroom were now watching him; he felt a strange sensation of being in a warm spotlight. He did not linger. He quickly collected some papers in a manila folder, tucked it under his arm and walked out of the newsroom and through the lobby toward the elevators. He stood there momentarily, then heard his name being called by Arthur Gelb, who had come running, saying, "Clyde, wait."

Haberman had never particularly liked Gelb, having been influenced by the Old Guard's view; but now Gelb

was deeply concerned about Haberman, and he reassured the young man that the world was not over,
that there were brighter days ahead. Haberman
thanked him and was very moved by Gelb's concern.

Then Haberman rode the elevator down to the first
floor, not pausing as he passed the stern statue of
Adolph Ochs in the lobby, nor stopping to talk with the
few friends he met coming through the revolving door.
He would return to City College for his final session in
the fall, and then after graduation worry about what
would happen next. He might work briefly for another
newspaper, and then he would probably have to serve
for two years in the Army.

The next day there was a "correction" in *The
Times,* only a single paragraph. Yet it reaffirmed that
there were a few things that had not changed in the
slightest at *The Times.* The paragraph, written by
Clifton Daniel, read:

> In Wednesday's issue, *The New York Times* pub-
> lished a list of prizes and awards presented at the
> City College commencement. Included was a
> "Brett Award." There is no such award. It was
> put in as a reporter's prank. *The Times* regrets the
> publication of this fictitious item.

Despite the occasional tension and shifting, the revitali-
zation that Catledge had wanted in the newsroom was
being supplied by Rosenthal and Gelb, and one result
of all the chasing, writing, and rewriting was the disappearance of the late-afternoon card game. Another
was the traditional "good-night," inasmuch as Rosenthal did not care when his reporters came and went,
so long as they got the story. A third result was that
the national and foreign staffs, once so superior to New
York's, were now beginning to feel intensified pressure
and competition for space on page one. On some
mornings, *The Times'* front page would carry five or
six stories that had been produced by the New York
staff, while the national and foreign staffs would each
have three or four. During the early evenings, after

the stories had been turned in and were being edited or set in type, Rosenthal and Gelb would wait for the layout sheets that would show which stories had been selected by the bullpen for page one, and if there were five or more by the New York staff, Rosenthal and Gelb would leave the office in a triumphant mood. Once when Rosenthal had left the office before seeing the layouts, he telephoned a subordinate editor and was told that five stories had made it. But moments after Rosenthal had hung up, the subordinate editor received a revised layout showing that two New York stories had been replaced by late-breaking stories from out of town. The editor, upset, walked over to the bullpen carrying the revised layout and said, "Look, I already told Abe we had *five* stories on page one."

"Well," one bullpen editor replied casually, "you now have three."

"Yes," the New York man said quickly, "and what's Abe going to say about *that?*"

"You mean Abe is going to get mad at *you?*"

"Well," the New York man said tentatively, "you know Abe."

Perhaps no editor in the newsroom felt the pressure of the New York desk more than Claude Sitton, the forty-year-old national-news editor. It was unlike anything he had known during his grueling years as a reporter, a period during which he had been away from home about twenty days a month, working sometimes twenty hours a day while traveling through his native South covering the Civil Rights movement. He had then aroused the contempt of the Klan and other racists with his reporting, had braved the dogs and harassment of Chief "Bull" Connor in Birmingham, had once been thrown out of a store in Mississippi by one of Catledge's kin. As a reward for his work, and with Catledge's blessing, Sitton had been brought back to New York in 1964 and made the national-news editor, succeeding Harrison Salisbury, who had been promoted to assistant managing editor.

But the emergence of Rosenthal and Gelb, and the

shadow of Salisbury, had introduced Sitton to challenges that were occasionally more aggravating than
any open animosity he had felt in the rural South. He
had known that it would not be easy as Salisbury's successor. Salisbury had been enormously energetic—an
individual of great prestige and persuasion. But Sitton
had not fully anticipated the interoffice competitiveness
that went with the job, the barely perceptible but nonetheless real and constant crosscurrent of tension that
seemed to exist between the desk that Salisbury had
just vacated to Sitton, and the one occupied by Rosenthal across the room. It was as if Salisbury, despite his
elevation, was still anxious that his old bailiwick, the
national staff, not fall behind the fast pace being set by
Rosenthal, and Sitton was immediately caught in the
middle. There seemed little doubt that Salisbury was
not Rosenthal's favorite person, and the driving personalities that they both possessed often enabled them
to see things only one way, their own way; and the divergent backgrounds from which they came, the totality of their experiences at home and abroad, their
egos and ambitions, the way they saw the world, seemed
destined to keep them apart both socially and philosoph-
ically—Rosenthal, the son of a Jewish immigrant from
Russia, the correspondent who had been banished
from Communist Poland, was more nationalistically
American and reverential toward its American institutions than was the more sophisticated Salisbury, an almost stoical Midwesterner who had lived through the
worst years in Stalin's Russia, and had descended from
a family of individualists who had settled in America
more than three hundred years ago and had lived under
a variety of political saviors and scoundrels that were
often indistinguishable. When Harrison Salisbury, cool,
overtly direct, seemingly unselfconscious, would approach the New York desk with an idea or an opinion,
Rosenthal seemed almost to bristle. Salisbury appeared
to be unaware of the effect that he was having on the
sensitive Rosenthal, and he would be surprised, or would
claim to be surprised, when hearing that Rosenthal had

gone to Clifton Daniel to settle issues that Salisbury had not even known were issues.

When Claude Sitton became the national-news editor in 1964, he began to experience incidents similar to those that had arisen between Salisbury and Rosenthal during Salisbury's last year on the national desk—differences that were not always due to personalities but were the result of honest disagreements over whether certain stories should be handled by the New York desk or the national desk. While stories from overseas uncontestably fell under the jurisdiction of the foreign desk, the jurisdictional boundaries between the national desk, which included the Washington bureau, and the New York desk often overlapped. The Kennedys, for example, were considered the property of the national desk, but when the Kennedys, after the Presidential assassination, divided their time between New York and Washington, and established residences in New York, the question of which desk was responsible for which Kennedy story was often debatable.

In 1965 the New York desk blocked an attempt by *The Times'* national political correspondent, David S. Broder, stationed in Washington, to cover President Johnson's speech in Princeton, New Jersey, because Princeton was part of the New York desk's territory. In possible retaliation, the national desk refused to let the New York reporter who had covered Johnson's speech make a trip to Hot Springs, Arkansas, to report on the National Young Republican board's action on the New Jersey Rat Fink case. Instead, David Broder was ordered to Arkansas by Sitton. Broder wrote his story from there and filed it with the New York desk, and it was killed after one edition. Broder felt the rivalry of the desks in a number of his assignments and he also felt restricted by *The Times'* bureaucracy; and in August of 1966 he resigned from *The Times* to join the *Washington Post*. At Clifton Daniel's request, he wrote a memo listing his grievances against and impressions of *The Times*, and his view of its political coverage and the situation in the Washington bureau. Broder's typed memo, single-spaced, ran

nearly eight pages. In it he described elaborately, sometimes scathingly, the frustration of dealing with the
New York office. The morale in Washington, he wrote,
was very low, and he chafed repeatedly at the editorship of Claude Sitton and at the general tendency in
New York to overplay news stories with big names and
to underplay trend stories or stories of a more analyti-
cal character:

> For example, *The Times* front-paged my story
> about the Eisenhower-Reagan meeting, though
> nothing of significance happened there, but it gave
> routine, inside-page treatment to my carefully-
> documented, ground-breaking report that Nixon,
> far from lacking a political base, had already lined
> up almost solid support from the South for his
> 1968 candidacy. . . .
> In general, it was my impression that *Times*
> editors had a certain few stimuli to which they re-
> acted in a political story: Instances of extremism,
> either of the New Left or the Radical Right;
> political action by Southern (but not northern)
> Negroes; Kennedy stories of any variety. These
> may be the grist of political talk at New York cock-
> tail parties, but, as you know, they do not begin
> to embrace the variety of concerns that really ani-
> mate national politics.
> . . . Bureaucratic frustrations. I hesitate to bore
> you with these, but they are so much a part of
> the difficulty of covering a beat for *The Times* that
> they cannot be ignored. Every reporter has his own
> set of horror tales; the only thing distinctive about
> this particular beat is that frequently you're out
> somewhere alone on a story, and when you get
> raped in New York, your cries of anguish can never
> be heard. Examples: You file a "dope story" from
> Washington, telling how Romney is under heavy
> pressure from Congressional Republicans not to
> blackball Bob Griffin for the Senate nomination
> for a second successive time, and you tell how
> Romney's impending decision on the matter bears
> on his presidential prospects. The national editor

[Sitton] reads it and says it's "too speculative, let's wait until he decides." When he decides, you're off on another story, and all that appears in *The Times* is a two-paragraph stringer item, devoid of any of the necessary background. . . .

You're leaving California two days after the primary to fly cross-country to your next assignment in Boston. In early morning, from the L.A. airport, you phone the national editor to tell him you have a California story you want to write, if it's OK with him and the L.A. bureau. He says fine. You write the story on the plane and as soon as you land in Boston, you phone the L.A. bureau to check a couple details; the aide on duty there says nothing to indicate any conflict in plans, so you dictate the story from the Boston airport to New York. When you reach your hotel an hour later, you call in to the national desk to see if there are any problems, and you are told your story is being held out because L.A. has decided to file a Q-header [news-analysis piece] and there isn't room for both. You protest but are overruled. Inexplicably, the next day's paper contains neither the Q-header nor your story. Your story finally runs two days later and the Q-header never shows up. . . .

David Broder was one of many Washington reporters who had become disenchanted with Claude Sitton, expecting him to stand up to the bullpen and the other senior editors as Abe Rosenthal was doing, demonstrating the stubborn partisanship that had enabled the New York staff to make its strong showing. But Sitton seemed to have neither Rosenthal's *chutzpa* nor his editorial leverage. As the national-news editor, Sitton presided over a dozen regional bureaus around the nation as well as the national copydesk in New York that edited both the regional stories and those filed from Tom Wicker's bureau in Washington. When Wicker's men became angered by the editing or cutting of the copyreaders, or by the imputations from Salisbury or Daniel that a certain Washington story had been inadequately covered, they usually channeled their explanations or objections through Claude Sitton, but they did not often feel that he was sufficiently sympathetic; or if he was sympathetic, he seemed powerless to avert the continued second-guessing that emanated from Daniel's office, or from the desk of Harrison Salisbury, or from the bullpen. In the old days when the Washington bureau had such ranking figures as Arthur Krock or Reston to do its bidding, it had been accustomed to getting quick results, and usually favorable results; but now in 1966 it felt mainly frustrated, and it believed that Sitton was partly to blame, and Washington reporters sometimes wondered aloud over what had become of the raw nerve and toughness that had once characterized Sitton's stand against Bull Connor and the Klan.

Sitton was aware of his image in Washington and of the Broder memo, and he considered both to be unjustified. Sitton was, after all, answerable to Salisbury and Daniel, and if they were displeased with Wicker and the bureau, which they were, there was little that Sitton could do about it. One of the complaints against Sitton in Broder's memo was that, as the national political correspondent, he, Broder, had been refused the necessary freedom to do a proper job: it was Broder's contention that the national political correspondent should have the right to visit any state where he (and the national-news editor) thought there was a political story of national significance, and that the correspondent should be in charge of that political coverage unchallenged by the regional bureau chief in that state. But such free-floating reportage was rare on *The Times*, being limited to such men as Reston and Salisbury, and if it were permitted in the cases of less-established correspondents, it could be dispiriting to those bureaumen permanently located in those regions. Nevertheless when Broder quit and joined the *Washington Post*, it was not taken lightly in New York by Daniel, which was one reason why Daniel had asked for the memo. It was not often that a political correspondent on *The New York Times* quit to become a political correspondent on another newspaper. The fact that that other paper was the *Washington Post*, the major competitor of *The Times* in the capital, added to the significance of Broder's resignation, and he quickly became a kind of martyr in Wicker's bureau, a symbol of its frustrations with the New York office. Xerox copies of Broder's memo were bootlegged out of the bureau and were distributed through the mail to *Times*men in Paris and other foreign posts. Sitton, not knowing how much importance Daniel had attached to the memo, was feeling increased pressure from many sides. He was being doubted in Washington, was feeling the daily squeeze of the New York desk, was being pressed from above and within himself to meet challenges that were rather unfocused. He wanted to be fair both to the regional correspondents and to the staff in Washington, but felt sometimes that there were prima donnas in Washington who were incurably spoiled by the privileges of the past. He tried to live with their criticism, however, to work long hours in New York and to react quickly to any incident or angle that might produce stories for the national desk. He allowed his bureau chief in the Southwest, Martin Waldron, to spend several weeks investigating the increased land holdings of President Lyndon Johnson, recording the fact that as President Johnson had purchased new land in Texas, the state highway improvements were never far behind. Sitton also kept an alert eye on the daily activities of the Civil Rights movement in the South, his old beat, and he put particular pressure on a reporter who had succeeded him, Roy Reed. After James Meredith had been shot in Mississippi, and a wire service photograph of his prone body on the road was received in New York, Sitton grabbed the photo and scanned its edges, asking, *"Where's Roy Reed?"*

In the spring of 1966, a novelist and biographer named William Manchester had completed a 380,000-word book on the assassination of President John F. Kennedy. It would be called *The Death of a President*, and would be published by Harper & Row. The Kennedy family had first approached Theodore White and Walter Lord to write the book, but both were unavailable— the book was to be an "authorized version," and the Kennedy family would have prepublication approval of the manuscript. Manchester, however, agreed to the Kennedy conditions, and no great difficulty had been anticipated by either side. The Kennedys regarded Manchester as a friend—he had in 1962 published a pro-Kennedy book, *Portrait of a President*, that *The Times'* book reviewer had described as "adoring"—and after being approached in 1964 by Pierre Salinger, in behalf of Mrs. Kennedy, to consider writing a book about the assassination, Manchester felt that it was both an honor and an obligation to history to do so. This was to be *the* book on the Dallas tragedy. It would be done with the utmost in accuracy and good taste, it was hoped, and would negate attempts by other authors to produce books about the assassination that might be crassly commercial or inaccurate.

So William Manchester, with humility and dedication, accepted the assignment in 1964. During the next twenty-one months, sometimes working fifteen hours a day, he interviewed hundreds of people who had known President Kennedy, had worked for his administration in Washington, or had been involved in some way with the fatal day in Dallas. Manchester had also taped two interviews with Mrs. Kennedy, during which she had revealed intimate and poignant details about her last hours with her husband, and her first hours as his widow. Manchester had also received close cooperation from other family members and friends, had received access to personal letters and other memorabilia. The book was to be edited by Harper & Row's executive vice-president, Evan Thomas, who had edited John Kennedy's *Profiles in Courage*. Harper & Row had published Robert Kennedy's *The Enemy Within*, also edited by Evan Thomas, as well as other books by such Kennedy associates as Theodore Sorensen. Thus the publishing house, the editor, and the writer had seemed ideally suited for the production of a historical work that would be pleasing to the Kennedy family, and the first indication that this was not exactly the case was learned by Claude Sitton during the early winter of 1966. He had heard rumors from some of his sources in government, and had also read an item in a tabloid-sized monthly trade paper called *Books*, that Mrs. John F. Kennedy had requested the cancellation of the Manchester book.

> As *Books*/October went to press, it was exclusively learned that Mrs. John F. Kennedy had requested Harper & Row to *cancel* publication of William Manchester's official and candid account of her husband's assassination, "The Death of a President." Mrs. Kennedy has been quoted as having said, "If I decide the book should never be published—then Mr. Manchester will be reimbursed for his time." Reimbursement talks have begun.
>
> Top-level meetings have been held at Harper's to determine its response to Mrs. Kennedy's request. Should Harper's elect to ignore Mrs. Kennedy's request—the moral issue of censorship, $3,000,000 in international book and magazine sales, and future relations with the Kennedy family are at stake . . .

The "candid" details that Mrs. Kennedy found objectionable dominated the news and gossip channels for the next two months. The details were leaked to the press each day from both Kennedy partisans and the forces rallied behind Manchester—each side sought the sympathy of public opinion in its attempt to ban the book as an invasion of privacy, or to publish it as a testimony to truth. The book, it was said, contained scenes of the Kennedys' last night together in Texas; Mrs. Kennedy's thoughts following her husband's death; how she had wrestled with a nurse at Parkland Hospital, how she had placed her wedding ring on the late President's finger. The book also was said to describe tensions on the flight from Dallas to Washington, the bitterness between the Kennedy and Johnson factions on board; how Johnson occupied Kennedy's quarters, how Johnson's aides, while shocked and saddened by the assassination, could barely conceal their pleasure over Johnson's takeover; and how the loyal Kennedy aides, namely Kenneth P. O'Donnell, had literally blocked Johnson's exit from the plane at the Washington airport, preventing the new President from descending with Jacqueline Kennedy and the other close Kennedy mourners.

These details, and many more, were leaked to the press by individuals who had read, or who claimed to have read, Xerox copies of the Manchester manuscript —individuals employed in the publishing house, or within the magazine that had purchased the book's serialization, or the literary agency, the book club, the law firms, the friends of friends—these people collectively became the press's "spokesmen," and for weeks their revelations and opinions dominated the news. Prior to the Manchester controversy, there had been front-page articles in *The Times* and other metropolitan dailies about a dispute in Washington between Senator Robert Kennedy and J. Edgar Hoover that *Time* magazine had described as the "Battle of the Bugs": Hoover had charged that Kennedy, while he was the United States Attorney General, had known that the F.B.I. was using bugging devices to invade the privacy of private domains and conversations; Kennedy denied the charge. It seemed that a larger story might emerge, festered by the old hostilities of these two men. But then the Manchester-Jacqueline Kennedy affair suddenly mushroomed—and the Hoover-Kennedy story faded.

The New York Times' first major story about Jacqueline Kennedy's objections had been reported by one of Rosenthal's men, responding to reports already published in other newspapers; it had occurred during a weekend, while Claude Sitton was off, but Sitton immediately asserted that this story was a national-desk assignment, and it was. To Rosenthal's displeasure, Sitton took it over on the second day. Sitton now had an episode that could produce front-page stories for weeks—and it did.

Normally, the national-news editor did not have direct control over a single reporter in the newsroom; all the newsroom reporters were under Rosenthal. Sitton's closest reportorial subject, geographically, was in the Philadelphia bureau. So if Claude Sitton wished to assign a newsroom reporter to an out-of-town assignment that was perhaps more quickly or easily reached from New York than from a regional bureau, or if Sitton wished to use a newsroom reporter on a New York story that was deemed to be of national political significance, as was the Kennedy-Manchester issue, then Sitton had to approach Rosenthal and ask for the loan of a reporter. Sitton would naturally desire the services of one of Rosenthal's best men, such as Homer Bigart, but whether or not he got Bigart might depend on how Rosenthal felt toward Sitton on that particular day. If Rosenthal was feeling kindly, and if Homer Bigart himself liked the assignment and wanted to work on it, Sitton might get Bigart. But if Rosenthal was piqued, he might claim that all the top reporters were occupied on other stories and assign Sitton the reporter he was most anxious to get out of sight.

When the Kennedy-Manchester story broke, however, Sitton was very lucky. He happened to have working in the newsroom, on temporary duty, his Philadelphia bureauman, an individual named John Corry. Corry had been part of a team of *Times*men assigned to travel around the country, including Dallas, to check the findings of the Warren Commission's *Report*. When Sitton took charge of the Manchester coverage, Corry was sitting quietly in the newsroom reviewing his Warren Commission notes—but there proved to be nothing very newsworthy in this venture, and so Corry was reassigned to the Manchester affair, a story that would influence Corry's future career on *The Times*.

John Corry was a clean-cut, outwardly bland but pleasant man of average height and build, hazel eyes and light brown hair, neat but not fastidious. At thirty-four he was happily married, the father of two girls. Although he did not inspire confidence, he did not discourage it, and as seen by Sitton he was entirely reliable, solid, possessing keen powers of observation balanced by good judgment—Corry was not the sort who, wishing to call attention to himself, would overdramatize a story or distort it with clever or conspicuous phrases. But simmering within Corry, unknown to Sitton, was a deep dissatisfaction with the image that people like Sitton had of him. What Corry really wanted out of life, precisely, he was reluctant to admit, conceding that his ambition was possibly inconsistent with his character and probably beyond his reach. Corry wanted fame. Not *great* fame, just a touch, enough to lend a bit of flicker to his name, a few nods of recognition around New York—enough to justify the secret little outbursts of absurdity and wildness that he knew were within him, awaiting the slightest excuse to erupt. Usually, he suppressed the urge.

As a boy in Brooklyn, Corry had planned to become a minister. His father had been a bank clerk, rigid and predictable, an Irish Protestant antipathetic to most Irish Catholics, a man whose suit-and-tie to work each day were his mark of elevation in this lower-middle-class neighborhood. John Corry hated the place, the repressed existence within tight rows of apartment houses with fire escapes in front; he was happy to be off to Hope College in Michigan, run by the Dutch Reformed Church, and he lived in a boarding house with other students. One night after a house party, drunk and wearing only his Jockey shorts, Corry crawled down the steps into the bedroom of the landlady, through her room as she became hysterical, into the hall, out the front door, and into the cool night air. He spent the next three years at Hope College on probation.

In the Army, where he conveyed an impression of high discipline, he was trained for the Military Police. But one day, harassed by a young lieutenant, Corry became wildly insubordinate and was court-martialed.

Later he received an honorable discharge. He returned to New York in 1956 and found a job as a copyboy in the *Times'* Sports department, and soon he was promoted to agate-clerk, his concern being the tiny type of baseball batting averages and team standings. Within a few years he was made a copyreader, editing stories about the great outdoors—but he could barely stand it. He was transferred in 1961 to another long desk in the newsroom, the national desk, which was more interesting for him, although he really wanted to become a reporter, to get outside the office and see the city. On his own initiative he began writing stories for the daily *Times* and the Sunday *Times' Magazine* that displayed an uncommon perception, and in 1966, ten years after joining *The Times*, he became a reporter. In October of that year, he was assigned to Philadelphia.

When Claude Sitton approached Corry with the Manchester assignment, he did not want it. There had been so many books about the Kennedys since the assassination, so much merchandising of the myth, that Corry did not want to be part of any more of it. Corry had greatly admired John Kennedy and had voted for him, but he also felt sympathy for William Manchester. During Corry's visit to Dallas earlier in the year on the Warren Commission assignment, he had been cursed and threatened one evening by a mob, and he could imagine how difficult Manchester's research in that city must have been, and he could understand Manchester's anxiety now that his book, his years of sweat and total commitment, was being threatened with sudden suppression. A writer rarely pleased the people he was writing about if he tried to write with honesty—Corry knew this already from personal experience. On two recent occasions he had sent *Magazine* articles in advance to the persons being profiled, and in both cases they had tried to change what he had written. One of the men, Algernon Black, had carried his case to an executive on *The Times*. He did not get very far, but it was nonetheless unpleasant for Corry. The other man, the novelist Ralph Ellison, thinking Corry's article hinted at Uncle Tom-ism, suggested that this might be grounds for a law suit. Ellison did not sue; in fact, he later wrote Corry a complimentary note about the piece. But Corry vowed that he would never make that mistake again. And yet had he been faced with Manchester's decision, with the stakes so high and opportunities so great, he honestly did not know how he might have reacted. Perhaps he also would have consented to write the authorized account of the most dramatic event of his lifetime. Every word he wrote for *The Times*, after all, was authorized.

But Corry's instinct was to shy away from this assignment and let some other *Times* reporter take it. It was a fine opportunity to move with the Kennedy crowd, to bask in the limelight, to get some feel of fame, Corry admitted, but his ultrasensitive side urged him not to take it. Claude Sitton, however, seemed to exude such Gelb-like enthusiasm for the story, such confidence in Corry, that Corry found himself reacting. *There was a great deal of interest in this story*, Sitton said, hinting that someone high up, perhaps Daniel, was personally involved in the coverage—and if Daniel *were* fascinated by this story, Corry knew that the space would be almost unlimited. It was the kind of story that almost every editor, and particularly Daniel, would be intrigued by, for it combined the elements of history and tragedy with high fashion. Corry deliberated momentarily, and then he told Sitton, yes, he would be glad to take on the assignment.

In the beginning it was exhilarating; he sensed the vast machinery of *The Times* moving and reaching across the world grasping for the truth. From the *Times'* bureau in Madrid, a cable was sent to Corry stating that Mrs. Kennedy had called *Look* magazine's Gardner Cowles during the summer imploring him to revise the serialization plans. From Washington, Reston had called Corry with a tip about a Kennedy pep rally in New York, adding that Senator Robert Kennedy was not really concerned about the book—it was largely Mrs. Kennedy's doing, inspired by her horror of the death of

Camelot, the killing of the myth. Corry later recognized these phrases in Reston's column; Reston had apparently been trying out his column in advance on Corry, and Corry hoped that he had responded properly. Corry had also received tips and memos from other *Times*men around the nation, and he was constantly impressed at how smoothly the enormous organization seemed to be closing in on a single story—dozens of men all contributing to one reporter's work.

Hoping to get an exclusive interview with Manchester before the other newspapers got to him, Claude Sitton arranged for Corry to board a cutter one day at 4:30 a.m. and ride it out to meet the *Queen Mary*, which was bringing the writer back to New York from England, where he had sought escape from the clamor; but now he was forced home by the rumors of Mrs. Kennedy's legal threats. Corry had been up until 3 a.m., unable to sleep, and his usual nervous stomach was worse than ever. Corry arrived at the ship and found Manchester; but he refused to be interviewed, saying that he could not talk until after the difficulties were settled. Corry, feeling too sick to argue, returned to the *Times* office happy that he had only a small story to write about Manchester's arrival. But then, without knowing exactly why, he telephoned Evan Thomas, Manchester's editor at Harper & Row, and boldly said that he had heard from an "unimpeachable source" that Mrs. Kennedy was threatening to sue them over the Manchester book. There really was no "unimpeachable source"—Corry was only guessing. But with sudden astonishment, Thomas asked how Corry knew, the legal papers had *just* been served!

John Corry's story was on page one that night, and he felt like a small hero as he walked into the newsroom the next day. The other reporters congratulated him, and asked Corry how he managed to get the exclusive. Corry tried to look knowing. Claude Sitton came by, smiled, and repeated that *The Times* was "going all out" on this one, and offered Corry more help. "What do you need—money, more reporters?" Sitton asked. "How about hiring a helicopter?" Sitton smiled again, but Corry felt that had he requested it, *The Times* might have given him a helicopter.

Later that morning, Sitton told him that the Kennedy people were planning a press briefing, and he gave Corry a telephone number that turned out to be Senator Kennedy's New York apartment. Corry called the number, identified himself, there was a pause; then Richard Goodwin, a thirty-five-year-old former Kennedy speech writer, came on the phone and told Corry that the briefing would be in Mrs. Kennedy's office at 3:30 p.m. but, if Corry wished, he might drop over to Senator Kennedy's apartment earlier for a private session.

When Corry arrived at the address, a towering new glass skyscraper at Forty-ninth Street and United Nations Plaza, a doorman greeted him deferentially but firmly, asking if he could help. "The Senator's apartment," Corry said. "Oh, yes," the doorman said, seeming to sense who Corry was, and he made a motion to a uniformed guard behind the revolving doors of the lobby. The guard, smiling, led Corry to the elevator. Corry was impressed that the doorman had not called ahead, which he imagined a lesser doorman would have done; Corry had passed some little test. He brooded about this in the elevator.

The housekeeper led Corry into a large room with big windows all around, some paintings on the walls, pictures of President Kennedy and other Kennedys on the shelves, a curiously unlived-in atmosphere. There were two white telephones with maybe six buttons on each, and several men were seated or standing at one end of the room. Richard Goodwin stepped forward, dark, big eyes, bad skin, looking like a hungover Italian journalist. He introduced Corry to Burke Marshall, a slightly-built forty-four-year-old lawyer wearing glasses, the chief spokesman for the Kennedy family; John Seigenthaler, thirty-nine, a rugged-looking Nashville newspaperman credited with helping Robert Kennedy dig up the evidence to convict James Hoffa; and Frank Mankiewicz, a somewhat stocky balding man of forty-two who was Kennedy's press secretary, and a nephew of the Hollywood producer.

Corry began by asking Burke Marshall if he would help *The Times* get a look at the autopsy photos on President Kennedy, Marshall having represented the family when the photographs were turned over to the Federal archives. But Marshall refused and quickly shifted the subject to the Manchester book, going through the whole chronology—when the manuscript had been finished, who had read it, what Mrs. Kennedy's objections were. John Corry listened, nodded, and took notes. But every once in a while he kept reminding himself, *I am being told exactly what they want to tell me.* But this was fair enough, he thought, and he found himself liking Kennedy for having such smart men around. None of Corry's questions, even those he thought provocative, seemed to disturb the composure or patience of Marshall or Goodwin, nor to cause them to give the impression that the Kennedys were ever at a disadvantage. When Corry asked, "Won't the book strain political relations between Senator Kennedy and President Johnson?" one of them said, softly and off the record, "Bob comes off very well in the book" and its publication would only help him.

Burke Marshall's briefing was over within an hour, and then Goodwin explained that they were going to hold a strategy session and he hoped Corry would not mind going over to Mrs. Kennedy's office alone while they huddled in the car. Corry graciously agreed. No matter how often he had reminded himself to keep his emotional distance, he could not help admiring their informality, their disarming way of letting him in on their little behind-the-scenes planning. *It's not me, it's The Times they're catering to,* Corry corrected himself. *These people wouldn't spit in my eye if I wasn't on The Times.* He had to be careful with them, stick to the facts. Make one mistake in any of these stories, and these men will go right over your head, over Sitton's head, and complain to Sulzberger himself. Still, Corry had felt very comfortable in the presence of these four

Kennedy men. They had made his job easier, and he felt very relaxed around them. Perhaps it was Goodwin's bad complexion, he thought, or the fact that Burke Marshall speaks in a squeaky voice and looks like a clerk. Or that Seigenthaler was wearing a checked shirt and a crummy-looking tie, or that Frank Mankiewicz was a chain-smoker. John Corry, now up to three packs a day, could not help noticing how Mankiewicz had nearly kept pace puff by puff.

Fifteen minutes later Corry was in Mrs. Kennedy's office on the fourteenth floor of a building on Park Avenue. The room was crowded with newsmen, and against a wall were four gray steel cabinets with twenty boxes of envelopes on top, and on the floor were cardboard cartons, one of which, in ink, was labeled "Tributes for Library." A small color photograph on the wall showed Mrs. Kennedy in the foreground, the President in the background. Mrs. Kennedy was not present at this gathering, but Corry noticed in the crowd Mrs. Kennedy's secretary, Pamela Turnure, wearing a ratty cardigan, her hair limp, no makeup. Corry distrusted her instantly. Irrationally but instantly.

A moment later Burke Marshall walked in with Goodwin, Seigenthaler, and Mankiewicz. Marshall, presiding, immediately began to brief the press on the Manchester book. He presented the facts in exactly the order that Corry had heard them an hour before. Corry smiled. It now occurred to him that he had served as a dress rehearsal for this briefing. He was almost sure that, on their way to Mrs. Kennedy's office, they had evaluated his knowledge of the controversy, observed his reaction to what they told him, and had gained from his questions a better idea of what questions they might now expect from the other newsmen. And it had worked. Corry's questions were now being repeated by the other newsmen, and the Kennedy men answered with ease.

For the next week or so, life went very well for John Corry. His stories were on the front page nearly

every day, and Sitton seemed pleased. Late one afternoon in the newsroom when Corry let it be known that
he was due at a black-tie dinner party that night, and
had been unable to get away from the typewriter long
enough to go out and buy a suitable pair of shoes and
a cummerbund, Sitton offered to send a copyboy out
to shop for Corry. But another editor, hearing that
Corry wore size 9½ shoes, volunteered to lend Corry
his shoes and cummerbund, and a copyboy was dispatched to get them.

Corry had not yet gotten to Manchester, but he had
gotten a close look at Jacqueline Kennedy during the
past week. Having learned that she would appear at 1
p.m. in the law offices of Sullivan & Cromwell, 48 Wall
Street, Corry arrived one hour early and waitied along
the sidewalk with a second *Times* reporter and a photographer. At 1:15 p.m. a new blue Oldsmobile cruised
down the street—in it were Mrs. Kennedy, her lawyer
Simon H. Rifkind, and Richard Goodwin. The car
slowed down, but then Goodwin spotted Corry, and it
sped away. Corry told the other *Times* reporter to run
after it and see if they got into the building through a
side or rear entrance. A few minutes later, the Oldsmobile came around again. This time it stopped, and Mrs.
Kennedy stepped out, followed by Rifkind and Goodwin. The *Times* photographer began snapping pictures
of the three of them entering the building, and Goodwin glared at Corry. The look was so expressive that
The Times used that photograph on page one the
next morning, and it was picked up by both *Newsweek*
and *Time* and used again. The three of them marched
past Corry through the revolving doors into the building, the wrong building. Corry had been standing in
front of Number 50 Wall Street, not Number 48, and
he watched the three of them in the lobby staring up
at the directory on the wall while a cleaning man with a
mop stood nearby, gazing at Jacqueline Kennedy, his
mouth open. A moment later Rifkind came spinning
through the door, squinted up at the building number,
then went back in again, and then came out this time

with Mrs. Kennedy on his arm. Goodwin followed. Goodwin looked at Corry and smiled, weakly.

Corry, after they had disappeared into the law offices, returned to the *Times* building, leaving the other reporter to patrol the sidewalk and get any comment that might be made after the session in the law office. The story that Corry wrote that day was typically objective and made no reference to their entering the wrong building at first, nor to the startled expression of the cleaning man with the mop. Corry was tempted at times to slip these little absurdities into his stories, but he doubted that they would get past the copydesk.

For no particular reason, and without his awareness at first, things began to go wrong for John Corry in early January, 1967. It he had to pinpoint a date of decline, he could not, nor could he logically analyze what was happening. It was just a vague feeling within him that things were not as good as they had been. The compliments were not coming, and he sensed that some *Times* editors felt that they had overplayed the story, and now wanted to jump off this merry-go-round that they had helped create but could not because the other newspapers and media kept it going day after day. Corry suspected that he was tired of writing about this subject, *Times* editors were tired of printing it, the Kennedys and Manchester were tired of reading it, and everybody was a little tired of one another. He did not know. But the second-guessing within the newsroom, he was sure, was increasing.

On the Friday before, January 6, *Look* magazine had sent over six advance copies of its issue containing the first installment of the Manchester book, and the *Times'* editors sent one copy to Tom Wicker in Washington, who was to read it for political revelations; one copy to Gene Roberts in Atlanta, who was to read it for any data on the assassination; and gave one copy to Corry, who was to do the general wrap-up story containing all other details. The *Look* release date was 6 p.m., Monday, January 9. But during the weekend the *Chicago Daily News* broke the release, and sud-

denly on Saturday before noon John Corry was called
and told to come quickly to the office and do his story
for the Sunday edition. Since Roberts in Atlanta had
not yet seen his copy, Corry was told to include any
assassination angle in his story. Sitton then telephoned
from his home in Westchester and told a deskman to
have Corry also include items of political significance,
but another editor in the bullpen later countermanded
this. Then Clifton Daniel, who was hardly ever seen in
the *Times* building on a Saturday, appeared. He withdrew to his office and sent out word that he wanted to
read Corry's story page by page as it came out of the
typewriter. After Corry had written a few pages he received word that Daniel wanted something in the story,
high up, on how the *Chicago Daily News* broke the release date. Daniel left shortly afterward, but later telephoned an editor in the bullpen with the reminder that
Times readers would wish to know what, exactly, had
been revised by *Look* in its first installment, and he also
wanted to know if anything had been taken out of
Look's first installment and moved into later installments.

As these and other questions were relayed down to
Corry, who was writing against an early deadline, he
began to fret. Replying to one of Daniel's questions,
Corry quickly typed out an insert: "It was not known
if anything had been taken out of *Look*'s first installment and moved into later installments." But other re-
quests for new inserts kept arriving—it was as if Daniel's
mere presence had made the editors more literal-minded
than usual. After Corry had written that *Look*'s first
installment "tells of laxity in the Secret Service," there
was a discussion among four editors, three from the national desk and one from the bullpen, on Corry's use
of "tells." Was that the right word? Corry was too distracted to care. And he was also disturbed by something
else. He had gotten a telephone call from William Manchester a few moments ago, a complete surprise after
weeks of unsuccessful effort, and the conversation had
left Corry very nervous and confused. Manchester had
apparently called in response to a telegram or note

from Daniel, requesting that he cooperate with *The Times*, but what confused Corry was Manchester's friendly informality over the phone—he called Corry "John"—and Manchester's conditions under which he would agree to be interviewed.

"Do you take shorthand, John?" Manchester had asked.

"No."

"Do you take notes rapidly?"

"Average."

"You ought to use a tape recorder, John. I have all these letters, memos, documentation . . ."

And then Manchester said something that left Corry completely stunned: he suggested that Corry tape their interview with a recorder, and then he, *Manchester*, would edit it!

"I'd want any tape to begin with the words 'This tape is the property of William Manchester, and will not be re-recorded or transcribed' . . ."

Incredible, Corry thought, *incredible, mad, wild—* here is Manchester, the persecuted writer and victim of Kennedy censorship, trying to do the same thing to *me* that they were trying to do to him!

There was a pause on the phone. And Manchester seemed to sense the irony too.

"This would in no way be censorship," he said quickly. "It would just be to see if the names, dates, that kind of thing, were accurate . . ."

"I d-d-don't know," Corry said, looking at the clock, his deadline getting closer.

"It's not censorship," Manchester repeated.

"I just . . . it's not *Times* policy to do that," Corry said finally. Corry wanted to get off the phone, fast. He did not want to antagonize Manchester and ruin a possible future interview, but Corry could not commit himself to what Manchester was suggesting. Corry would never be that naive again, not after his experiences with Ralph Ellison and Algernon Black.

"Would *The Times* let you come down to the Caribbean for a couple of days?" Manchester asked.

"I don't think so," Corry said, contemplating the

scene of his isolation on some island, with Manchester peeking over his shoulder as he wrote.

After a few more minutes of halting conversation, Manchester mercifully hung up.

The next morning, as the telephone rang in Corry's apartment on West End Avenue in Manhattan, Corry decided not to answer it. He was tired. His wife and children had chicken pox. He was disillusioned—this whole experience was distorting so many wonderful illusions he had once had about fame and power, and he had stayed up drinking the night before, hoping it would calm his nerves and allow him to sleep. It had not. Now the phone was ringing and he was sure it was the office. It was probably Sitton calling, Corry thought, and he let it ring four, five times. Then he picked it up. It was Sitton.

Claude Sitton, born on a Georgia farm, was accustomed to rising at dawn, and when he became a newspaperman he continued to live farmer's hours: now he was enthusiastically telling Corry, who was groggy and unhappy, that there was some action in progress at the State Supreme Court—a Manchester-Kennedy settlement seemed near.

Corry rolled out of bed and took the subway to lower Manhattan. At the courthouse he was told that things had been delayed, and returning uptown to the newsroom Corry learned that Manchester and Cass Canfield, the head of Harper & Row, would read statements that afternoon at the Overseas Press Club. They had apparently reached an out-of-court settlement with the Kennedys.

At the press club, dozens of reporters and photographers were gathered around Manchester as he prepared to read his statement. Corry slipped in close and said quietly, "Hello, I'm John Corry."

"Oh, *yes*," Manchester said, smiling. Then, holding Corry's arm, he leaned forward and added quietly "Get to me later."

Maybe he would grant the interview, Corry thought: Sitton would be very pleased.

After the statement, which conceded the settlement, Manchester refused to answer questions about the Kennedys or his book. Then, flanked by his lawyers and agent, he headed for the elevator. Once outside, Corry, assuming the air of one of Manchester's lawyers, walked near Manchester along Fortieth Street toward Madison Avenue. He entered an elevator with Manchester at the Harold Matson Company, literary agents for the book, where he was told to wait briefly in an outer room. After ten minutes, Manchester returned and agreed to meet with Corry for an exclusive interview on the following evening, in Middletown, Connecticut, where Manchester lived. Corry thought of little else during the next twenty-four hours.

The next morning, Tuesday, January 17, the telephone rang in Corry's apartment. Sitton. He said that *The Times* was thinking of using a long roundup story by Corry, a "takeout," in the Friday edition. The "takeout" would run approximately four thousand words, taking up a full page in *The Times;* it would summarize everything that had so far transpired in the Kennedy-Manchester case. Corry, knowing the work involved in doing such a long piece, said he could not possibly do it for the Friday edition. The takeout also did not excite Corry's interest now because he was looking ahead to the exclusive interview he had been promised by Manchester on this evening in Connecticut. Sitton was interested in the Manchester interview, too, but there seemed to be some confusion in Sitton's voice—it was as if the editors above Sitton, perhaps Daniel, were having second thoughts about some phase of the coverage. Later, Sitton telephoned Corry a second time, telling Corry to proceed with the Manchester interview, and not to worry about the takeout for Friday's edition. But, Sitton added, he hoped that Corry would finish the takeout by late Friday afternoon so that the editors could read it during the weekend. Corry sulked. He repeated that he could not do all the necessary work in so short a time—he had to be in Connecticut with Manchester on this evening, Tuesday; on Wednesday he had to organize his notes and write the interview; on Thursday, in preparation for writing the takeout, he had to check back with all the principals involved in the dispute during the last several weeks—the Kennedy people, the Harper & Row spokesmen, the lawyers, the agents, the *Look* editors, the people who could evaluate the political repercussions at home and abroad—he could not *possibly* finish the takeout by Friday afternoon. "John," Sitton interrupted softly, trying to conceal the pressure that he was apparently feeling from above, "John, you're working for a daily newspaper, not a magazine." Corry continued to sulk, then hung up. He got out of bed and took the subway downtown. Soon he was riding a big Trailways bus upstate to Middletown, Connecticut.

The interview with Manchester had gone fantastically well. Corry had had dinner with Manchester on Tuesday night, had talked afterwards at Manchester's home, receiving from Manchester stacks of documents and letters to use as he wished—no conditions had been set about preediting what Corry elected to quote, and Corry did not dare bring up the question. Manchester had seemed delighted by the opportunity to finally open up to a *Times*man, to present his side of the story after the weeks of restraint imposed on him by his lawyers. Corry spent the night at a motel in Connecticut, had breakfast with Manchester the following morning, taked with Manchester through the afternoon. Corry had a great interview, he knew, and he contemplated the reaction it would get when published in *The Times*. As Corry sat in the Trailways bus bound for New York City that night, he was very tired but very happy. He had done his job, had gotten an exclusive interview with the most-talked-about writer in the world. At 2 a.m. Thursday, instead of going directly home after getting off the bus, Corry walked across Eighth Avenue to the *Times* building. There were only a few rewrite men and copyreaders on duty then. Corry sat at a typewriter in the front row and prepared to leave a memo for Sitton describing the extraordinary interview. Corry pecked at the machine but seemed to miss the keys. It was as if he were drunk, although he had not had a drink all day. It was possibly the combination of fatigue, tension, excitement. He finally managed to type a single paragraph telling Sitton that he was back in town, had gotten the exclusive, and would telephone him later in the day after he had gotten some rest.

Later in the day, Corry telephoned Sitton, and Sitton told him that *The Times* did not want the Manchester interview. The words did not get through to John Corry. Sitton repeated them, gently. There was now "resistance" in the office, he explained, to doing so much more on this Manchester-Kennedy thing. One big round-up story, the takeout, should cover everything nicely, Sitton said. No need for Corry to write a separate interview with Manchester; he could weave some of the Manchester interview into the takeout, which was now due *after* the weekend. Corry was despondent. He mentioned that *Newsweek* magazine was on Manchester's trail and would probably publish their interview with Manchester in the next issue. Corry *had* heard that *Newsweek* was after Manchester but he had never thought of mentioning it until now. This tactic is common among reporters—whenever an editor is reluctant to run a story, they counter with the threat that another publication is onto it, and this usually frightens the editor into running the story right away. Sitton was onto this trick, of course, having probably used it himself many times when he was a reporter. And yet, there was the possibility that Corry was telling the truth, and so Sitton said he would discuss it with Clifton Daniel at lunch.

Corry called back after lunch. Sitton said that Daniel was still opposed to the idea of the interview. Corry quickly got dressed, appeared in the newsroom, and pleaded his cause in person—but unsuccessfully. *The Times* just wanted the takeout, Sitton repeated, adding that Corry would have to give equal space to the views of all the principals—there must be balance. Corry walked back to his desk. He thought of turning in his resignation. He had talked to his wife about it earlier in the week, and she agreed that this story was taking its toll and perhaps he should quit *The Times*.

On Sunday afternoon, January 22, Corry was at home organizing his research to write a first draft of the takeout. He had had several interviews during the last few days, and he was very tired. The phone rang shortly before 5:30 p.m.—it was the office. An editor on the national desk was on the line now asking Corry to please come into the office right away. They needed him to write a story for the first edition of Monday's paper. An advance copy of *Newsweek* had arrived, the editor said, and it carried an exclusive interview with Manchester, and would Corry now cover *The Times* with a story?

Corry wanted to cry. He held the telephone away from his mouth for a moment, then rested his forehead against the butt end of the speaker, tapping it lightly against his skull.

"Go to hell," Corry said quietly. He hung up. Then Corry called Sitton at home. Sitton called Daniel. Sitton then called Corry. At 6:30 p.m. Corry was in the newsroom at his typewriter scrambling through stacks of notes trying to carve out a story based on his earlier interview with Manchester. It was all very disorganized, imprecisely recollected in his mind, and Corry was forced to spend valuable time separating his Manchester notes from all the other notes he had collected during the week. Later Sitton appeared in the office. A six-column hole had been opened up in the paper by the bullpen. Corry was told that after his first-edition story was completed, he could then write more expansively for the second edition—that would be the takeout. Corry said that he could not do it. There must have been something in his manner at that moment; nobody argued with him.

He wrote a first-edition story of a column and a half, about 1,100 words, and then Sitton told him that a "hard" lead was needed for the second-edition story. Sitton suggested something that had appeared near the bottom of Corry's first-edition story—Senator Kennedy's telling Manchester to "shred and emasculate" the manuscript so that *Look* could not print it. Corry began his second-edition story with this in the lead, but later an editor in the bullpen came over to ask Corry if "shred" meant that Senator Kennedy had wanted Manchester to literally tear the manuscript to pieces. Corry, numb, said no it did not mean that.

He continued typing, completing a two-and-one-half column story, about two thousand words, in time for the second edition. It quoted Manchester, related the author's sadness that a controversy had arisen through a misunderstanding—it was a case of too many people becoming involved, of emotions gone rampant— but Corry could not properly convey all that he had hoped in this story. The story was out of focus, badly organized, awful, he thought. And the next morning when he reread the story on page one, Corry was *sure* that it was awful. But this did not really upset him. He was so tired, beaten, it was all so laughable in a way, that he got out of bed on Monday relieved that the nightmare was over, and, by rote, continued his research on the takeout. He had an interview with Evan Thomas at Harper & Row; Thomas sat with his lawyer, Nancy Wechsler, on one side, and his publicity man, Stuart Harris, on the other. Corry heard Thomas say, "I'm deeply distressed by all that's happened," and then Thomas turned to his lawyer and asked, "It is all right if I say that, Nancy?" Corry wrote this in his notes, thought it was funny, but did not smile.

He returned to the office that afternoon. Sitton came over, put an arm around Corry, and suggested that Corry write a follow story on the Manchester interview. Corry said he did not know how to do it. The next day, Tuesday, Corry was asked to do a short piece about the Kennedy dispute with *Look*. Corry tried, but could not get past the third page. Corry's first lead was returned, not "hard" enough. His second lead was rejected, so was his third. Sitton spoke to Daniel. It was decided to hold off and give Corry another day on the story. The next day, Wednesday, Corry appeared and began the story with the first lead that had been rejected the day before. He had kept a carbon and copied it word for word. It got through.

Then Corry resumed work on his takeout. At the end of the week, he had finished it. It had grown to six columns in length, and he finished it on Friday, determined to stay out of the office the rest of the weekend and let the editors do whatever they wanted with it. Corry went home. On Saturday, the phone rang. It was the office with many questions on his takeout, and he was asked to return and to help answer them. When he arrived, he saw that there were between thirty and forty questions to be replied to: Claude Sitton had written some questions on the margin of the piece, and Clifton Daniel had answered some of the questions himself just below. Eerie, Corry thought—here are two top editors writing notes to themselves on the margin of *my* story. Here was Sitton's handwriting in the margin asking, "Why did *Life* get two copies of the manuscript?" and below it Daniel had written, "Because one of their editors was sick and wanted to read it at home." On another spot Sitton asked, "Why did Kennedy call Harding?" and Daniel answered below, "Because Harding is the general counsel."

On Sunday afternoon, Corry was asked to come into the office again. Daniel had requested that the galley proofs be sent to his home. He had a few more questions. So did Sitton. On Monday, the takeout appeared in *The Times*. Corry read it. Deadly dull, Corry thought, shaking his head, deadly, deadly dull.

Corry thought that he had to get away, now, far away. He conveyed this to Sitton, who gave Corry five weeks off. Corry had meanwhile received a call from a book publisher, Putnam, asking Corry to write a book about Manchester's book. Corry was intrigued, although he was quite literally sick of the story. He had kept a little diary of sorts during the past several weeks, a therapeutic dodge to release some of the venom that *The Times* would never print. Yes, Corry finally said, he would be glad to do the book. He saw it as an opportunity to write something that he had so far been

unable to write, and which might say something about
America in the Sixties, its fascination with glamour
and trivia, its vulgar commercialism, its hypocrisy. So
he signed a contract with Putnam, and left word with
his wife that he would be unavailable for the next five
weeks. He moved to another apartment within the same
building on West End Avenue, an apartment temporarily vacated by a couple visiting Corpus Christi,
and Corry began his book. He flipped through his
diary and his stacks of notes accumulated during the
long assignment. He reread his comments, his day-by-
day experiences. Here was a copy of Seigenthaler's
telegram to Turner Catledge complaining about one of
Corry's stories, and here were memos on telephone
talks that he had had with Richard Goodwin and assorted lawyers, with friends of friends and political tipsters with axes to grind. Here was a comment he had
made about Mrs. John F. Kennedy, doubting that she
really wanted privacy, but rather enjoyed playing at it
—liked appearing in the smart ski resorts, on yachts
in the Mediterranean, titillating the *papparazzi*. The
press was as much to blame, Corry conceded, including *The Times*; the press built her up, *we* built her up,
and so did the fashion magazines photographing her
in every mood, and peddling pillbox hats and bouffant
hairdos through the advertising—everybody had a piece
of the action, it was a very big business, and I am now
part of it. This book he was beginning, he agreed, was
part of the whole scheme. Okay, Corry thought, so
how do I begin?

At first he planned to begin the book in the form of
an open letter to his younger daughter, Janet, not yet
one year old. Many years from now she might like to
know about the ridiculous fuss made over this episode
—but on second thought, Corry did not really want to
get his daughter involved, did not want to begin the book
"Dear Janet." It was an invasion of her privacy, he
thought, and as he thought this he was amused. Yes,
here I am, part of possibly the biggest invasion of privacy of all time; I am taking advantage of it, making
money off Jacqueline Kennedy, parlaying Manchester's

misery into a book of my own; but when *my* privacy is concerned, or that of my daughter, I behave as badly as the others. I am no better, Corry conceded; but who said I was better? he asked. So he tore up his first page, put another piece of paper into his typewriter, and began his book again.

John Corry's book, *The Manchester Affair*, would not become the big best seller that Manchester's own book was destined to be, but Corry would receive respectful reviews, would make some money, and would derive professional satisfaction from seeing his work between hard covers. After finishing the manuscript, Corry thought that he had gotten the whole journalistic nightmare out of his system, and he returned to *The Times*. But the thought of resuming his career in the Philadelphia bureau filled him with gloom. He also discovered that he was no longer enthusiastic about newspaper reporting. He seemed stricken with inertia, confusion, conflicting values. He did not know precisely what was wrong; he merely felt that he was changed from what he had been.

He confessed this sense of confusion to Sitton, and Sitton was very concerned. Soon Corry was in Clifton Daniel's office, seated across the desk from the managing editor, and Daniel also seemed troubled and sympathetic.

"What would you like to do on *The New York Times?*" Daniel asked, as if Corry had his pick of any job.

"Well," Corry said, thinking about it, "nothing, really."

"What does that mean?" Daniel asked.

"Well," Corry said, "I . . . I can go back to the copy-desk."

Daniel looked at him, curiously. Then Daniel, trying to relate to Corry, recalled his own despondency during his assignment in Russia in 1954, his last tour as a foreign correspondent before returning home and meeting Margaret Truman; Daniel remembered his loneliness as a forty-year-old bachelor in Moscow, how fatigued he had become from overwork, how ill he had been from an ulcer . . . and Daniel wondered if Corry might also be physically ill. Before Corry could reply, Daniel was saying that he wanted Corry to go up to the thirteenth floor and visit *The Times'* Dr. Goldstein— Daniel himself picked up the phone, making the appointment. Corry, thanking Daniel, left the office and took the elevator to the medical department. Dr. Goldstein was waiting for him, smiling, reassuring, saying to Corry, "I'd like you to meet our Dr. Hess."

"Who?" Corry asked.

"He'll talk to you," Dr. Goldstein said, guiding Corry softly towards another office, and it suddenly occurred to Corry that Dr. Hess must the *The Times'* psychiatrist.

"Is Dr. Hess a *psychiatrist?*" Corry asked, in a voice rising with suspicion, but Dr. Goldstein seemed not to hear the question—he merely said, comfortingly, "Dr. Hess is a wonderful man . . . some of our top executives see Dr. Hess. . . ."

After seeing Dr. Hess, John Corry was apparently discovered to be in working order. He returned to the newsroom, but he felt no better than before. He continued to resist the Philadelphia bureau, and it was eventually agreed that he could remain in New York, working once again as a deskman. For the next several months Corry worked quietly in the newsroom, writing on rare occasions—one notable exception being a long profile on Cardinal Spellman for *Harper's* magazine. Then one day, John Corry's feeling of indecisiveness left him as inexplicably as it had come—suddenly he wanted to write long pieces of more depth and emotion than he thought was permissible on a newspaper. When he received a contract to write for *Harper's*, Corry thought that this might be the challenge and the change that he had been seeking; and so deciding to find out, he summoned the courage and he resigned from *The Times*.

17

AS the *Times'* managing editor, Clifton Daniel is often invited to deliver speeches around the nation, and whenever his schedule permits, he accepts with pleasure—he enjoys appearing at banquets as a featured guest, likes traveling first-class by jet, is soothed by the tidiness of terminals, the well-dressed people, the muted sounds of women's heels and soft music; he relishes the two drinks before dinner served by winsome stewardesses who appeal to him not only because of their good grooming and precise tailoring, their pleasant smiles and desire to please, but also because of their almost ritualistic movements as they bend to serve, so graceful and controlled. They are America's geisha girls, he once thought, flying back to New York after a speech in the Midwest, and then he remembered, almost wistfully, that he had never known an airline stewardess. A few of them had once lived above his apartment in London years ago, and he used to hear them at night, but he had never gotten to know them.

The speeches that Daniel makes around the country, usually concerning the role of a free press, are intoned in his style of cool elegance, and are followed by questions from the audience. People are very curious about *The Times*, and many of them get from hearing and seeing Daniel a confirmation of their own ideas about the paper, its calm posture and pride in appearance, the respect for its tradition and the certainty of its virtue. They get from Daniel the image the institution has of itself, which is not necessarily all the reality beneath the surface. For there are other sides to *The Times*, other speeches made by *Times*men gathered at a Forty-third Street bar, or *Times*men talking to themselves in bed at night that reveal the frustration in working for a place so large, so solvent and sure—a fact factory where the workers realize the too-apparent truth: they are replaceable. The paper can get along without any of them. The executives like to deny it, and nobody likes to talk about it, but it is true. And this truth evokes both sadness and bitterness in many who deeply love the paper, who had romanticized and personalized it, thought of it as some great gray goddess with whom they were having an affair—forgetting that no matter who they are, nor how well they have performed, they will soon be too old for her. She is ageless and they must yield to newer, younger men.

Sometimes they are replaced as casually as light bulbs in a great movie marquee—changed automatically, though luminous as ever, once they reach a certain age; and this act was not going unnoticed by *Times*men still on the scene. During the mid-Sixties they lamented the automatic retirement, while still in fine health, of Brooks Atkinson, the theater critic, and William L. ("Atomic Bill") Laurence, the science writer; and the baseball writer, John Drebinger, who at his farewell party announced, trying to seem cheerful after a few drinks, "Well, if I'd known retirement was so great, I'd have done it long ago," to which an executive responded, coolly, "Well, then, why did you give us so much trouble, John?"

Automation, together with the process of depersonalization, was a complex problem shared by big businesses around the nation, and yet at *The Times* there was a lingering notion that *The Times* was not a business, but a calling, and expressions of mockery greeted the half-dozen machines that were rolled into the newsroom before election night to do what the late Leo Egan and Jim Hagerty, Sr., used to do so well, predict the outcome; and there was contempt among the workers in the composing room for the technological gadgets that did everything better than men—except strike. There was irreverence in the newsroom for those items promoting communication without contact—the memos, the silver microphone; and there was perhaps also a realization among the top executives that *The New York Times*, which had long taken pride in being "in touch," had now become so large that it did not really know what was going on under its own roof. Thus it was that Punch Sulzberger, reaffirming his faith in new techniques while striving to preserve something of the old *Times* spirit, announced that a team of trained psychologists would be engaged by *The Times* to interview a "scientifically selected random sample" of *Times* employees in an effort "to determine how, in this large and varied organization, it can establish greater rapport with the men and women who work for it."

This move was considered absurd by some editors, while others, including Clifton Daniel, wondered what impact the employees' complaints against such men as himself might have with the publisher. Daniel did not know exactly where he stood with Punch Sulzberger, or, for that matter, with the Sulzberger family. Daniel had been *Catledge's* choice as the managing editor during the great shuffle in 1964, following Dryfoos' untimely death. Sulzberger had endorsed Catledge's nomination of Daniel as the managing editor, but Sulzberger's concurrence did not necessarily signify personal approval of Daniel—nor was Daniel's formal British manner likely to charm the informal young publisher, it being in fact reminiscent of the stiff Tory tutors who had once horrified Sulzberger as a schoolboy at St. Bernard's. Further, there was the personality of Daniel's wife. Ten years of marriage, the birth of four children, and her husband's position on *The Times* had in no way diminished Margaret Truman Daniel's singular concept of herself as an American princess, and she was not the sort who would ever indulge in small corporate games as a *Times*man's wife—paying court to the Sulzbergers, ingratiating herself with Ochsian heiresses, or tempering her strong opinions when in the company of those gently spoken women. Daniel, to be sure, was a model of correctness with everyone —with his employers as with his wife. He had sought to impress Iphigene Sulzberger with his attentiveness and courtesy, and hoped that he had. Recently he had begun a speech with her favorite ancedote about *The Times* being the product of "cathedral builders, not stonecutters." But Daniel could not really know what the family thought of him privately, having never gotten close enough socially to perceive his status, and he had so far been unable to establish a direct working relationship with the publisher because Catledge was in the way. This was no doubt the most unfortunate aspect of Daniel's managing-editorship—his benefactor, Catledge, after vacating the managing editor's office, had not retired or severed his connections with the News department. Instead, while occupying a new third-floor office unseen from the newsroom, and acquiring the vague new title of "executive editor," Catledge had proceeded to pull the strings from behind Clifton Daniel. Catledge could do this because he—and he alone —had the friendship, the confidence, and the ear of the young publisher. In addition, Catledge's and Sulzberger's wives had become fast friends, and the couples had solidified their relationship by spending weekends together out of the city, and by taking trips together to Europe.

There were times when Daniel felt that Catledge was sufficiently satisfied with the way things were going, or was sufficiently uninterested, to allow Daniel free rein. During such periods Daniel felt a pleasant identity with the photographs of the men on the wall—Van Anda and Birchall, James and Catledge. He felt confidence in himself as an executive, satisfaction in the reporters or critics whom he had hired, reassurance in the style in which *The Times* was covering the world. While Daniel often gave the impression of vaingloriousness and was unquestionably proud of his title, he also saw himself as an instrument of the institution, a good soldier, a loyal subject, and there was not a man in the building who was less likely to betray a corporate secret than Clifton Daniel. Catledge had recognized this quality of organizational loyalty in Daniel many years ago. He had seen it in Daniel's performance as the number two man in the London bureau, had observed it at closer range during the years that Daniel had been a subordinate editor in the newsroom, after his return from Moscow, and in 1964 it had influenced Catledge's nomination of Daniel as his successor—although the promotion was of questionable significance as long as Catledge continued to hover in the background. Ostensibly, Catledge's presence was essential to *The Times* during this transitional period caused by Dryfoos' death—the inexperienced Sulzberger preferred an old trusted adviser like Catledge to be close at hand—but Daniel did not know how long the sixty-five-year-old Catledge would remain, nor what would happen after Catledge had retired. Perhaps the title of "executive editor" would be retired with him and "managing editor" would again be preeminent on the third floor. Or perhaps Daniel would become the executive editor. Or there was always the grim possibility that another individual closer to Sulzberger would be moved in over Daniel. Daniel could only hope that this would not happen. During his twenty-two years on *The Times*, Daniel had played by the rules, had never stepped out of line or gone over Catledge's head. He had sulked on occasion, as in 1953 when hearing that Drew Middleton had been appointed the London bureau chief instead of himself, but Daniel had submitted finally to the wishes of *The Times*. He had conceded that *The Times*' purpose was more important than an individual's preference—he liked to think of *The Times* as functioning somewhat along the lines of the English monarchy: despite its variety of weak or great rulers, the monarchy had perpetuated itself from century to century, maintaining its formality and tradition and its predictable line of succession.

As a *Times*man, Daniel had respected this system. It had brought him compensation and an identity with greatness, and it would hopefully continue to do so unless the system was abruptly altered by the young publisher. This prospect had not concerned Daniel during Sulzberger's first two years at the top—Sulzberger had then seemed to be gently and effectively guided by Turner Catledge. But during the late summer of 1966, and into the fall and winter, things had occurred within the organization that had made Daniel wonder. Decisions that had seemed imminent were suddenly changed; there seemed to be a subtle shifting of attitude, of pondering and postponing from Catledge's back office. It was as if Catledge's regentship was now being counterbalanced by the weight of an emerging figure from above.

The plan to hire a team of psychologists under the auspices of an independent research firm—Daniel Yankelovich, Inc., of 575 Madison Avenue—to sample the thinking of *Times* employees seemed rather injudicious. Not only was it an open admission that all was not well within, but it seemed contrary to *Times* policy to permit outsiders to probe into the paper's internal affairs, and it also suggested a lack of confidence in the paper's own editors to analyze the situation and deal with it. There were other things, too, that had begun to concern Daniel. There was the continuing prospect that his chief aide, Harrison Salisbury, might be transferred out of the News department. And there was the unexpected survival of Tom Wicker as the Washington bureau chief after Wicker had been told by Catledge during the summer that he would have to relinquish the bureau if he wanted to take over Arthur Krock's column upon Krock's retirement, at the age of seventy-eight, on October 1, 1966. Wicker had agreed, saying that if forced to choose between running the bureau and writing the column, he would take the column. But then somehow, after becoming a columnist, Wicker had also managed to hold onto his title as bureau chief.

But what had most directly and personally perturbed Clifton Daniel during the late summer of 1966 was the abrupt dismissal, on orders relayed by Catledge, of the theater critic, Stanley Kauffmann, whom Daniel had hired eight months before and whose work he admired. Kauffmann had come to *The Times* from the *New Republic*, where he had been the film critic, but he had also had a background in the theater: he had been trained for the theater through four years of college, had spent ten years in a repertory company devoted to classics, had written and published plays, had directed in summer theaters and elsewhere, and between 1963 and 1966 he had been the drama critic of the educational television station in New York, Channel 13. Before being hired, Kauffmann had been invited by Daniel and Salisbury to the *Times* building for conversations about the so-called "cultural explosion" in America, the affluent society's fling with the arts, and how *The Times* had responded to this by forming, in 1962, a Cultural-News department with a staff of forty to examine, report, and appraise the cultural scene. It had worked out quite well, Daniel and Salisbury conceded, but they were not entirely satisfied with some of their critics' intellectual capacity or writing style, which was too often couched in generalities and glib journalese. When they sought Kauffmann's own opinion of *The Times'* cultural coverage, he said frankly that it seemed like a "cultural dump," adding that it was also the opinion of the intellectual community, as he knew it, that *The Times'* critics were held in very low esteem. He excepted *The Times'* critic on architecture, Ada Louise Huxtable; its dance critic, Clive Barnes; and one of its art critics, Hilton Kramer.

Kauffmann could not have made three more appropriate exceptions when condemning the critics—Daniel and Salisbury were also admirers of the work of Mrs. Huxtable, and they had been active in the hiring of Hilton Kramer and Clive Barnes. In the case of Kramer, whose criticism had appeared in *The New Leader, Commentary*, and *The New York Review of Books,* Harrison Salisbury had seemed more knowledgeable than Daniel about Kramer's work—although before Kramer had been hired officially, he had talked not only with Daniel and Salisbury, but also with Emanuel R. Freedman, an assistant managing editor; Joseph G. Herzberg, the cultural-news director; Seymour Peck, the editor of the arts and leisure section; Daniel Schwarz, the Sunday editor; and Turner Catledge. Clive Barnes had gone through pretty much the same ritual, although his employment by *The Times* had been entirely Daniel's idea. Daniel, who had become an appreciator of ballet during his years in London and his friendship with Dame Margot Fonteyn—about whom he wrote his final *Magazine* piece in 1956 before settling down as a *Times* editor—had read and enjoyed Clive Barnes's dance reviews in the London *Times* and the *Daily Express*, and thus began a series of transoceanic phone calls from Daniel to Barnes that led, in 1965, to Barnes's leaving London to join *The New York Times*.

After Daniel's and Salisbury's consultations with Kauffmann, and after Kauffmann had made the rounds and made his recommendations on how *The Times* might improve its cultural coverage, he was offered the position of drama critic, replacing Howard Taubman, a former music critic who had succeeded Brooks Atkinson in the drama chair after the latter had begun writing a critic-at-large column. But with Atkinson's retirement, Howard Taubman was assigned to write critic-at-large pieces on cultural affairs, although not as a regular columnist, and Kauffmann was to move into Taubman's spot. It was agreed that Kauffmann would have the job for a minimum of a year and a half, but as one executive put it, the hope was that "this will be for life."

Kauffmann's career as a *Times*man had begun on January 1, 1966, and except for minor complaints about his polysyllabicisms and elliptical references, he had received only praise from the editors. But as one who took his critic's job very seriously, perhaps too seriously, Kauffmann was soon making enemies among a number of Broadway producers, performers, and backers. In several letters to the publisher's office, and in visits to certain of the publisher's representatives, they complained that Kauffmann did not seem to like anything, and there was the indication that even when he did, he could not write a selling review. Although this was not really true, a few *Times* executives privately felt that Kauffmann was a bit too ponderous and professorial about the theater: he seemed mainly interested in analyzing the play, examining its weaknesses and strengths, and did not create sufficient excitement in his reviews, a sense of anticipation and pleasure that many ticket buyers associate with the theater.

In fairness to Kauffmann, he had problems that no other critic had on *The Times*, that of being second-guessed behind his back by numbers of *Times* executives who regularly attend Broadway shows, who socialize with producers and investors, in Sardi's and around New York, who have an emotional interest in, and a conviction about the theater that they do not have about films or ballet, art, television, or architecture. Kauffmann was also unfortunate in joining *The Times* during its transitional period when no editor knew precisely which way the new publisher and the top executives were leaning, and there was also the problem of the power inherent in the drama job itself. Unlike the movie critic, whose influence on the box office is mitigated by the fact that a film may be opening in fifty different cities simultaneously, the theater critic's comments are directed at one stage in New York, and bombardment by *The Times* can possibly destroy a play's chances of survival on Broadway as well as its touring opportunities elsewhere—unless the production is endowed with a large advance sale, or a superstar with great appeal, or with several fine reviews in other publications, particularly from Walter Kerr in the *Hearld Tribune* and from the news magazines and *The New Yorker*. After the departure of Brooks Atkinson, whose eminence and seniority as a drama critic had made him invulnerable to counter-criticism from *Times* editors or Broadway people, *The Times*' top executives had thought of Kenneth Tynan

as a replacement, having respected his judgment and
literary style in *The New Yorker*, and seeing him as a
kind of witty, skillful surgeon who could cut without
killing. The drama job on *The Times*, the executives
generally agreed, was potentially a blunt and dangerous
instrument in improper hands—*The Times* was fearful
of the power invested in that one employee, and it was
felt that Tynan might concurrently fulfill the need of
serious criticism, responsibility to the theater, and entertainment to *Times* readers. But Tynan himself admitted that he could not produce his kind of review in
the little more than one hour that was available to a
critic on a morning newspaper; and Tynan was also
anxious to be getting back to London.

When Stanley Kauffmann had been approached by
The Times, he had raised the same point—there simply was not sufficient time between the end of the play
and the paper's deadline to write a considered review,
and as a result of this discussion, Clifton Daniel had arranged for Kauffmann to attend plays during their final
preview before opening night—the assumption being
that if a play was not then in shape it could not be sig-
nificantly improved within twenty-four hours, and it
would also permit the critic to give more time and
thought to the words that carried such weight with
ticket buyers. Daniel had hoped that the critics on
other newspapers would follow this practice, but they
did not, and one reviewer described *The Times'* plan
as a confession of Kauffmann's journalistic inability to
meet a deadline. When Kauffmann's reviews began to
appear, the producers mounted their protest; but at
first neither Catledge, Sulzberger, nor anyone else on
the paper seemed unduly concerned. *Times* executives
are accustomed to a certain amount of criticism of their
critics: Howard Taubman had been condemned regularly around Sardi's as a weak replacement for Brooks
Atkinson; and even Atkinson had been denounced by
producers on many occasions, and one of *his* predecessors, Alexander Woollcott, had even been barred from
a theater after an unfavorable review. This had oc-

curred in 1915 after Woollcott had described a particular Shubert brothers' comedy as "not vastly amusing" and "quite tedious"; and the Shuberts had retaliated by sending a set of tickets to their next production to Carr Van Anda, with a note suggesting that *The Times* assign another critic to review it, adding that if Woollcott presented the tickets they would not be honored. When Adolph Ochs learned of this, he instructed Woollcott to buy his own ticket. Woollcott did, but when he arrived at the theater door he was blocked by a doorman and Jacob Shubert himself.

Ochs immediately sought an injunction in court and he eliminated from *The Times* all of the Shuberts' advertising. The controversy became the talk of Broadway, was publicized around the nation, and was not settled in court for months. Although Ochs's injunction was ultimately overruled—an appellate division contended that while a theater owner could not bar a patron because of color, creed, or class distinction, he could do so for certain private reasons—the Shuberts, wishing to resume advertising in *The Times*, finally conceded *The Times*' right to select its own reviewers, and the bitterness ended with the Shuberts sending Woollcott a box of cigars at Christmas.

Ochs had made his point—outsiders were not going to tell *The Times* how to run its business—but this did not mean that Ochs was not personally offended on occasions when reading a snide or excessively negative review in his newspaper. Ochs's philosophy was that of a booster, particularly insofar as business or community affairs were concerned; and since the Broadway theater was one of the major attractions of New York, he hoped that his critics would not fail to appreciate and applaud fine efforts whenever possible. In his final will, completed three months before his death, Ochs urged that his editorial page continue to be "more than fair and courteous to those who may sincerely differ with its views," and he expected the same from his critics. At the same time, he expected them to uphold standards, and he rarely interfered with the publication of a review once it had been written. In Brooks Atkinson's long career as the drama critic, which had begun in 1925, he could remember only one occasion when Ochs had personally approached him and asked, after reading an advance copy of a review, that a word be changed. This occurred after Ochs had attended the opening of one of S. L. (Roxy) Rothafel's theaters in Rockfeller Center, an extravagant spectacle that Atkinson criticized for its gaudiness. Ochs, dressed in formal clothes, had walked back to Atkinson's desk later that evening and asked to read the review, and when he did Atkinson could see a look of pain beginning to crease Ochs's face. Ochs was a friend and admirer of Roxy, a remarkable show-business entrepreneur and the son of an immigrant German shoemaker—Ochs admired any successful man who had come up the hard way, and he could anticipate how distraught Roxy would be upon reading this review. Ochs said nothing for a few moments. Then very softly and timidly, the white-haired publisher pointed to a line in the review and he asked, "Mr. Atkinson, would you mind changing this one word?" Atkinson looked at the word and thought that its removal did not alter the meaning of the sentence in any way; it was such a minor change that Atkinson soon forgot what the word was: but he changed it, and then Adolph Ochs thanked him, said good-night, and left.

Ochs's successor, while equally reluctant to interfere with their critics, nevertheless have shared Ochs's booster philosophy toward the community, and when in 1966 the paper's critics panned the opening of the new $45.7 million Metropolitan Opera House in Lincoln Center, Punch Sulzberger was appalled. The opening featured Samuel Barber's *Antony and Cleopatra*, which *The Times'* music critic, Harold Schonberg, found "vulgar" and "exhibitionistic"; the ballet within the opera was not satisfactory to Clive Barnes; the art on the walls was unexciting to John Canaday; the architecture was "sterile" to Ada Louise Huxtable; and the 3,800 first-nighters, which included Mrs. Lyn-

don Johnson, John D. Rockefeller 3d, and Mayor John
Lindsay, were characterized by Charlotte Curtis vari-
ously as "overachievers," "nabobs," "moguls," and a
"mob." When Punch Sulzberger had finished reading
the views of these five *Times* writers in the paper, he exclaimed, "My *God*, couldn't they find *anything* good to
write about?" He expressed his feelings to a few executives, but there was no hint of restraining the critics.
If he wished to temper a critic's tone, or was otherwise
dissatisfied, he would not lecture the critic—he would
remove him. And that is what Sulzberger had done during the previous month, in August of 1966, in the case
of Stanley Kauffmann. Clifton Daniel had learned of
Punch Sulzberger's plan gradually: first Daniel had
heard from Catledge that the critic Walter Kerr, whose
Herald Tribune had just merged with the *Journal-
American* and the *World-Telegram* after a long strike,
and who had not joined the new *World Journal Tribune*, was being considered for employment by *The
Times*. Daniel was told to tell Kauffmann, who was on
vacation in Connecticut, of the discussions that *The
Times* had been having with Kerr. (Kerr was then in
Austria participating in the Salzburg Seminar in American Studies.) But before Daniel could arrange to meet
with Kauffmann, in fact on the very day that Kauffmann was scheduled to appear in Daniel's office, Catledge told Daniel that Walter Kerr had just accepted
The Times' offer.

When Kauffmann walked into Daniel's office, the managing editor was obviously shaken, blushing from embarrassment—Kauffmann had never before seen a
man more acutely embarrassed, and Kauffmann began
to feel sorry for *him*. Daniel said what he had to say
as briefly as he could—Walter Kerr, having been offered the critic's job, had just accepted it; and now,
Daniel continued quickly, the next step was to find
something else that Kauffmann might do on *The Times*.
Daniel said that he would give thought to this over the
weekend, hoping that Kauffmann would do the same.
Kauffmann, seated across the desk, a soft-spoken man

with gray, wavy hair, very dignified and controlled, had not reacted angrily; he was upset, but on this occasion he was Daniel's superior at keeping up appearances. He was not even privately disappointed in Daniel, realizing that Daniel had had nothing to do with this decision, a fact that was perhaps almost as disconcerting to Daniel as the decision itself. Kauffmann was also not entirely surprised by the news. He had imagined that something was wrong when Daniel had requested Kauffmann's appearance during his vacation.

Daniel proposed that they meet again on the following Monday outside the office, perhaps in the evening, to continue their discussions about Kauffmann's future on *The Times*. Later Kauffmann received a telephone call from Daniel's office saying that the managing editor could not get away for the Monday night meeting, and asked that Kauffmann come into the office. When Kauffmann arrived, wishing to relieve both Daniel and himself of continued embarrassment, Kauffmann said that he had been unable to think of anything that he could do—or would wish to do—on *The Times*; instead he proposed that *The Times* fulfill its contractual obligations to him, and that he leave the paper. Daniel nodded in agreement, and on his desk he had Kauffmann's file from the auditing department ready and waiting.

Stanley Kauffmann returned to his desk, planning to spend the rest of the day getting his private affairs and correspondence in order, and then he received word that Catledge wished to speak with him. In the executive editor's office, Kauffmann heard Catledge explain that the decision to replace him had been part of a "consensus," and with a certain awkwardness Catledge added: "I was part of that consensus." Whether the consensus had also included the publisher's advisers who operate outside the News department—Harding Bancroft, the executive vice-president; Ivan Veit and Andrew Fisher, the two vice-presidents from promotion and production—Kauffmann did not know, nor did he care. Strangely, or perhaps not so strangely, Kauffmann had felt no vindictiveness toward anyone as he left Catledge's office. He did not now think of the paper in human terms, but rather as an impersonal institution. As an institution it had behaved badly, he thought; it had promised that his tenure would last for a minimum of a year and a half, and it had ended after eight months. He was quite certain that he would never again enter the *Times* building.

After leaving the paper, he regained his position as the drama critic for Channel 13 and returned to the *New Republic* as a literary critic and cultural commentator. He soon lost touch with most of his acquaintances on *The Times*, although after his pieces had begun to appear in the *New Republic* he received a complimentary note from Clifton Daniel. He also received one day at home a rather odd letter from Daniel Yankelovich, Inc., the research organization that *The Times* had hired to conduct its scientific survey on employee morale. The Yankelovich correspondence, which included forms to be filled out, informed Kauffmann that he had been among the 150 *Times*men chosen to give confidential opinions on *The Times* and its executives. Kauffmann was amused by this obviously unintended final note of irony. He was seriously tempted to fill out the forms and tell what he *really* thought. But this impulse soon passed, and Kauffmann never replied.

Tom Wicker's position had also been threatened in the summer of 1966, and his survival as the Washington bureau chief was a strange reversal on New York's part that Wicker was content to accept without further explanation. To dare to inquire into the causes of his good fortune might jinx its continuance, although he had heard that Punch Sulzberger himself had altered the New York editors' plan that would have removed Wicker as the bureau chief while giving him a Washington column after Krock's retirement. Now Wicker had a column *and* the bureau, and he often wondered if the controversial Broder memorandum might have helped his cause in some way.

David Broder's lengthy criticism, written shortly before Broder had resigned from *The Times* in August of 1966 to join the *Washington Post*, had not only attacked Claude Sitton and the bullpen, indeed the whole New York bureaucracy, but it had cited the low morale in Wicker's bureau that was the result of New York pressure, a condition that Sulzberger was perhaps not fully aware of. He had quickly become more aware of it, however, after Wicker had personally placed the Broder memo in Sulzberger's hands while the two men were riding a train together between Washington and New York. Wicker had brought up the subject rather casually, "What did you think of that Broder memo, Punch?" Sulzberger had looked at Wicker quizzically. He had obviously never heard of it. Apparently Daniel or Catledge had not relayed it to the publisher. Wicker, smiling, told Sulzberger, "I *just* happen to have a copy with me"—and he pulled it out and handed it to Sulzberger.

The publisher's interest seemed stirred as he scanned it, and he undoubtedly might have wondered why Daniel or Catledge had never mentioned it to him, although it certainly was not in their own interest to do so. It appeared that Sulzberger might personally look into the matter of Washington's morale more deeply, but Wicker was not counting on it. Wicker's optimism had reached a low point between 1965 and 1966, a period during which he had constantly been criticized by the New York editors for his handling of the bureau. Their habitual complaint was that he was not producing enough front-page exclusives out of Washington—Rosenthal *was* in New York—and Wicker's executive career seemed to hang in the balance. It sometimes also seemed, however, that Tom Wicker's competence or incompetence in Washington was really a side issue to something deeper, more complex—it was as if he had become the symbolic figure in a psychodrama that other men yelled at, a focal point upon which *Times* editors could concentrate their personal grievances and professional differences. Wicker himself was incidental to the cause, he was a tall, ruddy, hefty, ambitious, shrewd, almost folksy Southerner whose presence in Washington had provoked so much emotion and reaction among the other editors that they had inadvertently revealed more about themselves than they had about him. Wicker was a product of events, an individual whose career had been advanced by the reporting of the John Kennedy assassination and by the death of Dryfoos, the latter shifting as it did the balance of power within the newsroom away from Reston to Catledge, prompting Reston to vacate his bureau to his hand-picked successor, Wicker, and to withdraw mainly into his column on the editorial page, over which Catledge had no jurisdiction. Wicker's appointment had been very acceptable in 1964 to the new publisher, Punch Sulzberger, who was eager to keep Reston on *The Times*; although the elevation of Wicker had hardly been pleasing to Clifton Daniel when Daniel had learned of it. It meant that Daniel—whose promotion to managing editor had been procured by Catledge while Reston was advancing Wicker—had been deprived of any role in the selection of his chief subordinate in Washington. In the two years that followed, Daniel had tried to limit his criticism of Wicker to the coverage of news, but Wicker could nonetheless sense an undercurrent of personal coolness, and Wicker could understand it. Wicker was *Reston's* boy, a reminder of Reston's lingering influence; and there was perhaps another factor that was of no small annoyance to the class-conscious Clifton Daniel: Wicker, like Daniel, was from North Carolina, and Wicker knew where Zebulon was.

Salisbury's quarrel with Wicker was much more political than personal. Salisbury had become increasingly suspicious in 1966 of the Johnson administration's self-righteous and optimistic attitude toward the war in Vietnam and American issues at home—the government machinery in Washington had seemingly become a manufacturer of illusion, and Salisbury believed that Wicker's bureau had been derelict in its duty to probe and expose. It was not that Wicker himself was naive; since taking over Krock's column, Wicker's writing had reflected a growing concern in the capital over the way things were going, but Salisbury was less interested in Wicker's perceptions as a columnist than he was in Wicker's ability to push his staff toward a more aggressive brand of investigative reporting. Salisbury felt that Wicker could not do justice to both jobs, could not write a column *and* direct the bureau, and A. M. Rosenthal had agreed with Salisbury in this instance, it being one of the few things that Rosenthal and Salisbury *could* agree upon.

But Rosenthal had not been very vocal in his criticism of Wicker during the summer and winter of 1966, even though Wicker, a contemporary of Rosenthal's, was the only man in sight who seemed to pose a threat to Rosenthal's dream of one day becoming the top executive in the newsroom. This was all the more reason for Rosenthal to restrain himself, not to behave ungraciously or impulsively when it appeared that he was soon to be promoted to an assistant managing-editorship. Rosenthal's image as a driving editor of the New York staff had done him no harm with higher management when he had taken over the staff in 1963, for it was then generally conceded that drastic action was necessary; but now, more than three years later, when Rosenthal seemed destined for a higher office, he was wise to refrain from any display of partisanship or derogation. If the older editors wished to indulge in it, that was their prerogative; but Rosenthal had more at stake. He had given up his writing career to become an editor, had forsaken the by-line and public acclaim—which neither Reston, Salisbury, nor Wicker had done —and Rosenthal's goal was to eventually run the entire department. At forty-four he could look forward to fulfilling his ambition, if he did not foolishly incur the displeasure of his superiors in the years ahead. Within a decade or much less, nearly all the senior editors currently running the paper would be gone. Catledge was sixty-five, and within a few years he would probably retire in the South with his pretty wife and write his memoirs, as Krock was now doing. Reston was fifty-seven, and he had often indicated that he preferred living in Washington to living in New York. Clifton Daniel was fifty-four, and, without Catledge, his position on the paper would undoubtedly be weakened, unless he could establish a better rapport with Punch Sulzberger. Failing to achieve that, and if the Democratic party remained in power, Daniel might pursue—with a bit of help from his father-in-law—an ambassadorship. The four assistant managing editors—Bernstein and Garst, Freedman and Salisbury—were all pushing sixty, or were beyond it. Of the younger editors coming up, there was Claude Sitton, the national-news editor, who had had his troubles; and Sydney Gruson, the foreign-news editor, an epicurean who was about to accept a more prepossessing assignment in Paris, where he would take over *The Times'* International edition, which Sulzberger hoped would catch up with the stronger Paris *Herald Tribune*, now jointly owned by John Hay Whitney and the *Washington Post*. Drew Middleton had been interested in replacing Gruson as the foreign-news editor, but Daniel had not helped him to get the job, endorsing instead a forty-four-year-old correspondent named Seymour Topping, a very efficient, very loyal organizational type who, like Daniel, had come up from the AP, had headed *The Times'* bureaus in Moscow and Bonn, and had married well—the daughter of the Canadian diplomat Chester Ronning.

And so of the whole caravan of characters passing through the great timeless tundra of *The Times* in the second half of the twentieth century, none at this point seemed in a more advantageous spot than A. M. Rosenthal, and nothing would be less providential of him than to display signs of impatience or impiety, or to join in the chorus of dissent against Tom Wicker. Wicker was being criticized enough by other New York editors, and such criticism might have already been carried too far, having achieved for Wicker perhaps increased sympathy from Punch Sulzberger, and having perhaps given Sulzberger the idea that Salisbury, the troubleshooter, might more valuably serve *The Times* in another department—namely the Book Division, where the newsroom rumors had divined him, with Rosenthal moving up into Salisbury's spot. Or it could have been that Catledge and Sulzberger, after deciding that Wicker *should* devote himself entirely to the column, could not find a suitable substitute who could take over the bureau without further demoralizing the Washington staff. Harrison Salisbury, who might have performed remarkably well in Washington, would perhaps also inspire mutiny. Max Frankel, a popular member of the bureau, was unacceptable in New York. Frankel had been described as "too emotional," the executives having not forgotten his long letter of resignation in 1964. James Reston meanwhile continued to defend Wicker, believing that New York, while charging Wicker with a lack of administrative initiative, usually failed to explain what specific big stories Wicker was missing; the criticism seemed too often vague and unconstructive to Reston, and he was not appeased when he was reminded that during *his* younger days in Washington, he had come up with numerous exclusives. Washington was a very different city in those days, Reston replied—World War II had recently ended, it was a world of emerging nations, news was more easily gotten. But now Washington was pretty much a one-man town, *Johnsonville*, and if Wicker were the sort who was merely interested in protecting his own flank from New York's attack, Reston continued, Wicker could have focused each day on President Johnson's movements and moods, the ruffles and flurries, and remained unconcerned with a more balanced, objective coverage of the capital.

Wicker himself had been deeply upset during this period not only by his own inner frustration but by the effect that it was having on his staff. The bureau, until Broder's resignation had seemed to lend veracity to its complaints with New York, had considered itself voiceless, unrepresented, or misrepresented in the *Times*

hierarchy. Reston had seemed to be building a stronger
relationship with Sulzberger, as the publisher himself
was becoming more independent, but Reston did not
wish to intercede too often or too quickly for Wicker.
Wicker was the bureau chief, the hope for the future,
and Reston preferred biding his time in the background
while Wicker attempted to deal with the bureau's problems, to build his own relationship with the Sulzberger
family, and to build up confidence in himself. Hearing
from Reston, as Wicker had in July of 1966, that New
York had decided to retain him as the bureau chief,
had been encouraging news for a while, but the pressure from New York had not subsided. Two weeks
after Broder had quit, it seemed that another *Times*man,
a man admired and respected, was destined to resign.
This reporter, who had been covering the Senate ethics
committee's investigation of Senator Thomas Dodd of
Connecticut, had become so repulsed by the bullpen's
frumpishness and haggling that he demanded that
Wicker take him off the assignment. In a memo to
Wicker the following day, the reporter wrote:

> I am sorry about having exploded yesterday, be-
> cause you have enough troubles without my add-
> ing to them. I am staying out today to try to
> straighten out in my mind what I think I should
> do.
>   Let me begin with the treatment of the Dodd
> story, and then move on to what—it seems to me
> —it illustrates.
>   As you know, I resisted the pressure from New
> York, after the first Pearson-Anderson stories ap-
> peared, to duplicate their stuff. My position was
> that when the case reached the courts, or when
> the committee set to work on the documents,
> then we should go into it. I did not wish to repeat
> the allegations without having any evidence of our
> own, or supplied by hearings.
>   The first trouble we ran into was that mandatory
> kill of the Dodd-Klein relationship, on the ground
> that it was "potentially libelous." This, after the

allegations had been repeated in the plaintiff's complaint. It took three weeks to get New York straightened out on this.

Now the bullpen holds up the story on Sunday night on the ground that we seemed to be "persecuting" Dodd.

First, I do not believe that the bullpen would have taken that attitude if the *Washington Post* had the story fronted. It would have had a message down demanding that we duplicate it. . . .

In any event I should like to drop the story and have no responsibility for it for the reason set forth below:

This Dodd story illustrates, in a small way but vividly, what seems to me the basic problem in our relations with the editors in New York, but particularly with those in the bullpen. This is that they do not have confidence in those employed to report the news, nor respect for the reporters' judgment.

Let me give some instances that leap to mind on what were extremely important developments:

1. On the Cuban white paper in 1961, the insistence of the bullpen that the lead be based on an insignificant point, with the result that a totally wrong impression of the paper was given and that we were a laughing stock at the White House and the State Department.

2. On the Vietnam white paper, the mandatory kill on Finney's first story, which accurately reflected the substance of the paper, and the substitution of a lead based on what Dean Rusk told Catledge.

3. On the Mansfield report last January, the refusal to devote a separate story to the report when the release was broken by the Paris Herald Tribune and the insistence that the report be inserted in a rather pro forma story on Dirksen. (We never did run that report, unlike the Post and the Star.)

4. On Bobby Kennedy's first long statement on Vietnam, the resistance of Sitton to the importance of the story, overcome only after long argument

about whether the clips would not show that Kennedy had said the same thing before.

We can make mistakes down here, and when we do, we should be hauled up short. But what takes the sap out of a reporter who is doing his level best to make the Washington report worthy of his idea of The Times is that all-too-apparent lack of confidence. . . .

18

THE anticipation of Harrison Salisbury's departure from the newsroom was based strictly on rumor, to be sure, but even rumors have a kind of special validity within *The New York Times*. One reason is that seated around the newsroom much of the day are some of the most inquisitive men in the world, reporters and deskmen who can observe a series of seemingly insignificant details—an overheard word here, a gesture there, a minor change in pattern—and piece them together into a revealing conclusion. They also have ample time to devote to this since the staff is large, and there are always some people sitting around minding other people's business. Another factor is that nearly everything of interest either occurs, or is contemplated, in this one big open newsroom or in the adjoining smaller room, Daniel's office, meaning that anyone making an inordinate number of entrances or exists through Daniel's door—including Daniel, en route to Catledge's back office—will not escape attention.

During the winter of 1966, as the rumors of Salisbury's being "kicked upstairs" became even more persistent, Harrison Salisbury sat calmly at his desk against the south wall of the newsroom composing a letter to a Communist friend who might be able to help him obtain a visa for North Vietnam. This story intrigued Salisbury—the scene in North Vietnam, a big story unreported so far by any American journalist because none could get visas. The story from South Vietnam, on the other hand, was somewhat stale with repetition, Saigon having become the capital of journalistic overkill, a stage for many American actresses and politicians wishing to blend their sincere concern with maximum personal publicity, and the television reporting from there was becoming surrealistic: a young commentator, microphone in hand, stands in the jungle describing the war drama while a helicopter hovers overhead, rifles crackle, and a platoon of Marines march past the television screen but do not look into the camera. But North Vietnam had yet to be invaded by the circus of American communications, and in his long career Salisbury had proved to be a master at slipping into places that had been forbidden.

He did this by keeping up unceasing barrages of cables, calls, and letters to hundreds of influential people around the nation and the world—diplomats, dictators, bankers, propagandists—appealing to their vanity, urging their help, timing his own moves occasionally to coincide with moments when these people might also think it beneficial to have stories published in *The Times*. In 1957 Salisbury managed to get into Romania and Bulgaria, two countries which had barred *Times* correspondents since 1950, and he also was admitted to Albania, where no American correspondent had been since the end of World War II. (Salisbury later sent a Christmas card to one Albanian who had been very helpful during his visit, and that man has been neither seen nor heard from since.) In 1959 Salisbury was permitted into Mongolia, where only one other American newsman had been since before World War II, and in that year he also got back into Russia, which had barred him during the previous five years because of a series he had written on Russia for *The Times* in 1954, winning a Pulitzer Prize. He regained his admission to Russia when, as Anastas Mikoyan toured the United States in 1959, Salisbury followed him and wrote stories that so pleased Mikoyan that he produced a new visa, being unaware of the controversy caused by Salisbury's previous articles. Later, after Salisbury had got to Russia and was at a reception one night talking to Mikoyan, a voice from across the room suddenly called out, "Mr. Mikoyan, beware!

You don't know to whom you are talking. That man has written slanderous things about the Soviet Union." Salisbury turned in surprise, as did Mikoyan. It was one of the Soviet foreign office men who deal with the press. The man came closer and repeated the remark. There was an awkward silence. Then Mikoyan said quietly that he knew who Salisbury was, adding that Salisbury's reporting during his trip to America had been very objective.

Salisbury had been trying to get into North Vietnam for nearly two years. In the summer of 1966 he had even traveled around the periphery of China in a personal appeal, hoping to get down into Hanoi or up into Peking, but at every point he had been rejected. In August he had returned to New York, resuming his duties as an assistant managing editor, but continuing his private campaign with cablegrams and letters to anyone he thought might have influence in North Vietnam. When he learned that the North Vietnamese people had made a martyr of an American, Norman Morrison, who in 1965 had burned himself to death in front of the Pentagon while protesting American policy in Vietnam, Salisbury quickly got in touch with Morrison's widow and asked that she write a letter to the North Vietnamese authorities in his behalf. She did. Months passed. Salisbury heard nothing.

In November of 1966 Salisbury became fifty-eight years old. He had been aware of the talk about him in the newsroom, and he had known of Catledge's feelings that Abe Rosenthal should be moved up to gain experience as an assistant managing editor and Daniel's possible successor in the future. But what was not yet known around the newsroom was that Salisbury had no intention of yielding his position without gaining another one that would justify his considerable talents. He was *not* going to be kicked upstairs. If higher management considered him an ideal choice to head *The Times*' expanded Book Division, then Salisbury had grandiose plans for that department. He had privately discussed the project on occasion with Catledge, Sulzberger, and

Ivan Veit. Salisbury saw worthwhile opportunities for
The Times in the book business, and if he became
affiliated with it he expected' virtual autonomy, being
answerable to the publisher, of course, but not necessarily to Sulzberger's high-echelon advisers. When there
was reluctance on the part of Sulzberger, Catledge, and
Veit to Salisbury's approach, Salisbury decided that he
would remain where he was. He was a tenacious man.
He had spent much of his career writing about Russian purges and plots, power politics and executive intrigue, the ups and downs of commissars, and he was
a master at bureaucratic gamesmanship. He was also
supremely confident in himself. He had prevailed during long years of loneliness, had struggled as a writer,
had successfully written fiction and nonfiction, was a
respected journalist, lecturer, and linguist—he would
never starve. He was a loyal *Times* executive but not
a supplicant, not the sort who could be quietly eased
out and made to accept a high position in limbo, being
pacified by the faith and conviction that it would all be
handled gracefully in the press release: "making full
use of his broad experience" and "wider vistas" and so
forth. If Catledge thought that Salisbury was so easily
disposed of, Catledge had something to learn, although
the executive editor was not unlike many *Times*men in
his lack of insight into Salisbury. Even when Salisbury
was being warm, friendly, and open, which he was
capable of being, he seemed to be functioning on more
than one level; no matter where he was, part of Salisbury remained remote and unreachable.

Harrison Salisbury came by his independence naturally:
he was born within a tight, close family that lived in a
large, well-kept Victorian house that stood rather conspicuously in the middle of a slum in Minneapolis. The
impoverished people who surrounded the Salisbury
home in the early 1900's were Orthodox Jews who
had escaped military conscription in Russia; they had
migrated first into Canada, later moving in large masses
down into north-eastern Minneapolis, causing the usual
panic and quick property sales in the neighborhood,

and soon only the Salisburys were left with these strange striving people who denounced an authority thousands of miles away

Salisbury's father, an insular man, was not disturbed by the change in the neighborhood's character since he generally avoided all neighbors regardless of their origin. His interest centered only on his family and the house itself, which had been owned by *his* father, a physician, a distinguished member of this old American family of freethinkers. The first Salisburys had come from England in 1640 as craftsmen and farmers, and many had fought against the Indians in King Philip's wars in New England. By the early 1800's, Salisburys had moved into Buffalo, and one of them kept a detailed journal of the War of 1812, observing in person some of the sea battles on Lake Erie. A brother of this man had begun a print shop and bookstore in Buffalo, and founded a newspaper, the Buffalo *Gazette*, and had a son, Guy Salisbury, who was a fine editor but a heavy drinker, and one day in 1869 he fell into Buffalo Creek and drowned.

Around this time, one Amasa Salisbury traveled along the Great Lakes and moved into Wisconsin, and had one son whom he named after President Harrison —Augustus Harrison Salisbury. This son fought in the Civil War, later became a doctor and distinguished citizen in Minneapolis, and it was in honor of him that his grandson, the journalist on *The Times*, was named.

As a boy, Harrison Salisbury was extremely shy. Surrounded in his neighborhood by Orthodox Jews and their children, he was an outsider from the start. And yet in having such friends, in over-hearing their references to life in Russia and sensing their conflict with remote rulers and issues, he became prematurely curious about geography and politics. At this time, too, there was living in the Salisbury home an old white-bearded man, a great-uncle who had fought in the Civil War and been imprisoned at Andersonville; he had been released in such poor health that he never recovered nor married, and so he lived in this big house with Salisbury's mother and father, an aunt and uncle, and young Salisbury and his sister, and each evening before dinner the old man would take the children, a youngster on each arm of his chair, and read aloud the Minneapolis *Journal*'s latest dispatches from the battlefronts of World War I.

Salisbury devoured them. He placed large maps on the floor and pointed to the places. At the age of ten he had written his own history of the Great War, beginning "All Europe was astire . . ." In class he was a precocious student, graduating from grade school at twelve, from high school at sixteen. Being two years younger than his classmates kept him outside the contemporary circle, and nearly all of the Jewish friends he had grown up with had been forced to drop out of school and take jobs. So Salisbury spent more time reading, his home being lined with books, and writing poetry and essays, one of the latter on Alexander Hamilton, winning Salisbury a prize from a local historical society. He joined the Boy Scouts and earned enough merit badges to become an Eagle, and he particularly liked the long hikes and camping out all night; at first he could not sleep without a pillow, but he trained himself and then he could not sleep with a pillow, it being one of many little comforts he learned to avoid.

Though his father was an atheist, his grandfather, Dr. Salisbury, had been a leader in the Minneapolis Universalist Church, now merged with the Unitarians, and this church, which Harrison Salisbury attended, partly influenced his political philosophy. The Universalists were opposed to strict dogma, advocating instead a broad and liberal attitude, urging that its members not fail to look at things also from the other man's point of view. This was healthy, harmless advice for a young man growing up, but when that man continued to reflect some of it twenty-five years later as a newspaper correspondent in Russia during the Cold War and the McCarthy era, he inevitably became controversial.

It seemed unlikely from the start that Salisbury could have become anything but a journalist. He had those qualities that so many journalists have. He was very

shy, very curious, and journalism was the perfect vehicle for overcoming the first and satisfying the second.
At the University of Minnesota, Salisbury became editor of the campus newspaper and, coming out of his
shell a bit, became the center of what was then called
the Great Nicotine War. After the university's president
had issued an ultimatum banning the smoking of cigarettes in the vestibule of the library, Salisbury dispatched his reporters to test the law, to smoke and
see what would happen. He then sent other reporters
to record the dialogue that would invariably ensue
between the janitor of the library and the smoking students being evicted; and Salisbury himself later personally appeared on the scene. These confrontations, of
course, provided lively stories for Salisbury's newspaper; but, to his surprise, caused his sudden suspension
from the university in 1930. This event, which even
made page one of *The New York Times*, inspired student demonstrations around the campus, though the
suspension of Salisbury was not lifted for several
months. But the United Press bureau in St. Paul,
Minnesota, which had covered the story, offered him a
job during the interim—his first step in professional
journalism.

Salisbury worked for the United Press for nearly
twenty years, moving from St. Paul to Chicago, from
Washington to New York to London to Cairo to Moscow, a hundred cities in between, moving so quickly to
the clamor of new disasters and datelines and deadlines
that his own life sometimes ceased to exist—he became
an action addict, blurring the reality of his own personal problems while blending into the restless, competitive world of the agency man. There simply was no
time to think about anything but the news, to get it
and write it, and write it *fast*, and this was particularly
true at the United Press during Salisbury's earlier days.
The United Press had neither the manpower nor money
to compete on equal terms with the larger, richer Associated Press, and so to offset the odds the UP men
had to travel more and type faster, and there appeared
within the United Press, and the still smaller Interna-

tional News Service, an almost special breed of journalists: aggressive young men willing to be underpaid and overworked for the experience and adventure; they were the low-budget boys who came tearing into town, who shot from the hip and caught the next plane out, and among this group Harrison Salisbury was a star.

He loved the long hours, possessing phenomenal energy, and he loved the excitement and tactics. He was in Chicago during the days of gangland killings, wrote stories about Al Capone, and covered his tax trial. One day at the United Press bureau one of Salisbury's reporter friends, a man who had a pipeline into the mob, received a tip that the mayor of Chicago, Tony Cermak, would be shot. Appreciative of the help, the UP bureau quickly planned the coverage, arranging for telephone lines to be kept open and selecting a code word to flash the news. It never occurred to any of them to notify the mayor or the police. When the event did not materialize, however, the reporter who had been tipped off became confused; and his confusion turned to anger when Mayor Cermak, traveling with President Roosevelt, was shot in Miami. "Those bastards double-crossed me," the reporter said, insisting that Cermak and not Roosevelt had been the target.

Salisbury got married in 1933 to a girl he had met in Chicago a year or so before, and he would regard it as one of the unfortunate decisions of his life. But he was part of the busy Washington bureau a year later, working most of the night, and by 1942 he was off to cover the war from London, leaving his wife and son in New York. The departure from his son, who was three years old, was difficult for Salisbury, but he had been anxious to get overseas for years, to be part of a historic event that would be the high point of so many reporters' lives, and so he went. And he can remember very vividly, even now, the sharp small details of England then—the decor of his room in the Park Lane Hotel, the clatter of rooftop shingles as the planes roared low, the rustle of people moving very close to him in the night on the dark streets of London's blackout—London would never seem more beautiful to him than during those dangerous, glamorous nights of the blackout. Some friends he made then would remain friends for years, among them Daniel of the AP and Walter Cronkite of the UP; and Salisbury also met a marvelous young woman, a Red Cross worker, who would reappear in the United States after the war to complicate his already complicated personal life.

In 1944, following a short tour in North Africa, Salisbury was sent to the UP bureau in Moscow, and he began reporting the Russian army's destruction of the retreating Germans, the recapturing of Russian villages and towns, and in May of 1944 he reported the bloody scene on the Black Sea off Sevastopol in which 25,000 Germans were trapped, waiting in vain for evacuation ships:

> You couldn't walk more than a yard or two in any direction without stepping on a body . . . along the shore were remnants of small rafts the Germans had attempted to use for escape. Thousands of papers swirled in the dust—passports, military documents, letters, playing cards . . . Russian salvage crews swarmed over the battlefield like ants, sorting usable parts from wrecked ME-109 and FW-190 planes, trucks and tanks. The city of Sevastopol itself is rubble. In a ninety-minute drive through the streets I saw only five buildings which appeared habitable. Mayor Vassely Yetrimov estimated that 10,000 civilians remain from the prewar population of 100,000. I saw only thirty . . .

After the war Harrison Salisbury returned to New York, to his wife, and to a new job as foreign-news editor of the United Press. The war had been his escape, he admitted that, and now he hoped to adjust to life at home. The birth of his second son in 1947 brought a new closeness between his wife and him, but it did so only temporarily. He was tense much of the time, and the woman he had known in London appeared in New York. He wanted to quit the United Press and work for *The New York Times*, but there were no openings, and he would not accept the editorships available to him at *The Reporter* magazine or *Time*. The indecisiveness of his private life, the frustrations of his professional life; the end of the war, the end of the marriage, the general wretchedness of his daily existence drove him to a point where he could not work at all. He was a victim of what he believed was anxiety neurosis. One day he entered the Payne Whitney Psychiatric Clinic.

Many years later some of his friends would point to this period as the nadir of his life, expressing admiration at his ability to rebound and to continue to rebound when things seemed to be going against him still later in his life. But Salisbury always dismissed such interpretations as melodramatic. Exaggerations. The logic of people wishing to arrive at too-easy conclusions. He saw his life not as one of ups and downs, but as a slow, steady progression. His time of tension was not a breakdown, he asserted, but a wonderful opportunity for reevaluation and reexamination, the kind of thing that every man can use periodically in his lifetime. It would surprise him, during those later years after he had risen within *The Times*, to be told that some people feared him or disliked him or considered him conspiratorial. Such opinions would not greatly concern him, merely surprise him, for he was confident that they were unfounded. If he was disliked by others because he was so sure of himself—well, he *was* sure of himself. Some *Times*men were a little pleased in 1960 when his racial reporting from Alabama became part of a big libel suit, thinking this might teach him a lesson But *The Times* won the case on appeal. A young *Times* reporter was shocked when Salisbury suspected CIA men in very respectable circles, but the young man thought differently after the CIA's activities were exposed, being featured most tellingly in *Ramparts* magazine. Salisbury was not surprised in 1964 when

Clifton Daniel made him an assistant managing editor ("I'd have been surprised if he hadn't"). Few things caught Salisbury admittedly unaware; he conceded few weaknesses and dismissed as melodramatic the little insights other people claimed to have into his character. It seemed impossible to hurt his feelings, or to catch him in a revealing moment of self-doubt. He seemed always busy, always preoccupied with his work at *The Times*, yet occasionally he suggested his skill at quiet observation: "I like the way you walk, and the way your eyes move around the room," he once told a young reporter he knew only slightly. But nobody at *The Times* claimed to know him well, and so they were left with their unverified versions. Or with what little they could learn about him from his work, but this was difficult. As Salisbury himself wrote in 1961 in *The Northern Palmyra Affair*, his novel in a Russian setting that now could be anywhere:

> So seldom was anyone what he appeared on the surface. Nor for that matter even what he seemed to be at the first level below the surface. No, indeed. Everyone these days played a triple role or a quadruple role. If a man said something the possibilities were almost infinite. What he said might be true. This was the rarest possibility. . . .

Harrison Salisbury was hired by *The Times* in January of 1949, after persistent visits to the office of the managing editor, Edwin James. Salisbury was assigned immediately to Moscow. Had Salisbury not succeeded, after equal perseverance, in getting a visa from the Russians, he would not have gotten onto *The Times*, for the Moscow bureau, unstaffed for eighteen months, was the only job open. *The Times*' last regular correspondent there, Drew Middleton, who had written with relative unrestraint, had been denied reentry in 1947, and the newspaper frequently had difficulty in covering Russia. Its coverage of the Russian Revolution at first overlooked, then underestimated, the impact of Lenin. Its correspondent in the Twenties and

Thirties, Walter Duranty, had become, in the opinion of *Times* editors, an apologist for Stalin. The *Times*-man in Russia from 1941 to 1943 turned up later writing for the London and New York editions of the Communist *Daily Worker*. Before Salisbury had been sent to Moscow, *The Times* had conducted an investigation of his past activities, political and personal, and the bullpen had been alerted by the publisher to keep a "sharp eye" on his reporting. Even so, Salisbury soon became controversial; his dispatches reflected what many readers considered excessive sympathy for the Soviet Union, and there was the hint within journalistic circles, particularly from the right wing, that the only reason the Russians had granted Salisbury a visa was because he was politically naive. This was not true; but these were years of passionate opinion, not of measured restraint; it was McCarthyism in America, the worst days of the Cold War, and Moscow had become a city of suspicion and dark plots. There was conflict between Mao and Stalin; Tito had broken away; a new state secrets act had been imposed which was so strict that it could be interpreted as preventing a Russian telephone operator from giving the correct time to a foreigner. For Salisbury in Russia these were days of denial and loneliness, a time when he came to suspect that his every move was watched, his every story censored, when nearly every young Russian woman who caught his eye was later questioned by the secret police. One day word was received in the newsroom that Salisbury's life was in danger—the Soviet secret police, believing him to be a CIA agent, were about to torture him, bring him up for a spy trial, and dispose of him. When Salisbury had not been heard from for several days, a reporter on the New York staff, Will Lissner, wrote the advance obituary of Harrison Salisbury.

Salisbury's reputation with American readers might not have been so controversial if *The Times'* editors had made it clear that the articles that they were printing under Salisbury's by-line had previously been censored by the Russians. On several occasions, Salisbury had written the editors requesting that the notation *Passed by Censor* be inserted over his dispatches, but this was never done, and so he was regularly attacked in the letters-to-the-editor columns and in American magazines as being soft on Communism. Salisbury was not quite sure why there was reluctance on the part of *The Times'* management to the use of Passed by Censor, but he wondered if it was because Jewish censorship in Israel then was equally harsh, and that some *Times* editors or the owners did not wish to antagonize the powerful Zionist groups in America by putting a censorship tag on their stories. But this might have been called preposterous reasoning by his superiors on *The Times*, and Salisbury decided that it was better left unsaid. And besides, censorship existed then in one form or another from Egypt to the Dominican Republic, and how could *The Times* accurately label all those varying degrees of censorship on its dispatches? *The Times* did occasionally express regret in its editorials for the "distorted or incomplete report from Russia, through no fault of our correspondent." This helped Salisbury to a degree, but not to the degree of offsetting the sting that came on those days when *The Times* would run, next to one of Salisbury's censored-soft pieces, a highly critical piece on Russia by *The Times'* resident Soviet expert, Harry Schwartz.

A former Soviet-affairs analyst for the OSS and State Department, later a professor at Syracuse University, Harry Schwartz had been denounced by the Russians as a "capitalist intelligence agent." He had started writing for *The Times* about Russia from Syracuse in 1947, the year that the Russians had denied Drew Middleton's reentry; by 1951 Schwartz had moved down to New York as a full-time staff writer for *The Times*, producing his stories in an office on the tenth floor that was stacked with Communist newspapers, magazines, and pamphlets. The way that Schwartz wrote about Russia 4,600 miles from Moscow, and the way that Salisbury could write about Russia from Red Square, resulted, of course, in Salisbury's seeming to be a Red propagandist, and resulted eventually in a private little Cold War between these two *Times*men.

Salisbury became furious when he had heard that Harry Schwartz, attending the *New Republic*'s forum on the Soviet Union, indicated that Salisbury was being "taken in" by the Russians or was "trying to get in good with them." The charge was investigated in New York. After an examination of the transcript of Schwartz's remarks, the editors could find no such statements, and Salisbury was advised to pay no attention to such rumors, merely to continue his fine work under the obvious handicaps. Still, the Salisbury-Schwartz relations remained cool, as many of Salisbury's dispatches were discarded in New York in favor of the uncensored pieces that Schwartz produced after analyzing the latest Communist journals and consulting his Soviet sources in Washington and elsewhere. (Years later, after Salisbury had returned to New York, he reviewed in *The Times* a book by Harry Schwartz. Schwartz was not pleased.)

In 1954, after more than five years in Moscow, and after Clifton Daniel had volunteered to replace him there, Harrison Salisbury returned home. He was forty-five, he had gotten a divorce after years of separation, and he hoped that he could adjust to a quiet and productive life in New York City. It is never easy for a foreign correspondent of *The Times* to return to the home office, no matter how severe his life might have seemed abroad. There are compensations with those hardships. One is not surrounded by so many editors, so much interoffice pettiness when one is thousands of miles away. While the foreign correspondent is occasionally aroused from his sleep at 4 a.m. by anxious editors from New York requesting an insert in a story to match information published in another newspaper, he nevertheless enjoys long stretches of freedom, writing and moving about as he wishes. All this stops when the correspondent returns, as Salisbury did in 1954, to the home office. The correspondent is first assigned

to a desk within one of the many rows; he no longer
has a secretary, as he probably did overseas; and now
instead of a chauffeur he will travel by subway. Seated
around him in the newsroom are many ambitious young
men and also some tired old correspondents who have
been everywhere and will never go again. Their only
sign of having been abroad is the suits they wear, somewhat threadbare now, but obviously made by foreign
tailors. These old correspondents sometimes also continue to wear their hair long, in the style of their last
European city, but they no longer write many stories
for *The Times* that appear on page one. These go to
the young spry men shooting for the big overseas assignments.

When Salisbury returned, at forty-five, he was considered neither old nor young. His reputation was too
formidable for him to be seated in the middle or rear
of the room, surrounded by the *carnivore* or the older
men, and so he was put on the aisle in the first row,
next to *The Times'* top frontline reporters. Peter Kihss
and Russell Porter and, later, Homer Bigart. But Salisbury was operating under an added disadvantage. His
final assignment for the foreign desk, a series of articles
on Russia that he had written shortly after arriving
back in New York (and that would win for him the
Pulitzer in 1955), made Salisbury suddenly quite famous as a correspondent. His photograph appeared in
The Times' promotional ads, circulation soared, and
people around town were talking about him. Yet some
editors on the New York desk, for whom Salisbury had
never worked, were skeptical of his talent, and so they
indulged in a procedure that no longer persists at *The
Times* but was then quite common: they would level
Salisbury a bit, bring him down to earth. The first assignment they handed Salisbury upon starting as a member of the New York staff was about trash and garbage.
This was a recurring assignment, Salisbury discovered,
being revived almost every time that Iphigene Sulzberger had returned from Europe—a trip during
which she usually observed that the streets of London,

or Paris, or wherever she had been, seemed cleaner than those in New York. Her gently phrased, delicate memos containing her observations might then come bouncing out of the managing editor's office to an assistant managing editor, then to the city editor, and finally to an assistant editor who would look around the room for a reporter. None of the editors was offended by this chore: the Sulzberger family, after all, owned the paper and were far less intrusive than the publishers of other newspapers; and only in infinitesimal ways might the Sulzberger taste be felt, such as *The Times'* radio station, WQRX, not playing Mozart too often because Arthur Hays Sulzberger did not like him—and then, of course, there was Mrs. Sulzberger's interest in such things as parks and in a cleaner New York. The reporters assigned such stories usually dispensed with them in less than an hour: a quick phone call to the New York City Sanitation Department would get either a shocked denial from the commissioner, or perhaps his sudden announcement of an antilitter drive in New York. This story could be done in six paragraphs, and would land near the bottom of page 41 of tomorrow's *Times*, and that would be it until Mrs. Sulzberger's next trip.

When Salisbury, in 1954, got this assignment he did not know what to think at first. But he suspected that this was a subtle little plot to cool him off, and his reaction was sudden: he would turn this into the biggest trash-and-garbage story in the history of *The Times*. And he did.

He spent weeks digging up facts about trash and garbage, discovering that on certain days 16,402 tons of trash were collected in New York, that this collection is handled by 9,675 city cleaners, that the amount is almost four and one-half pounds of rubbish for each person in New York, or almost one-and-a-third tons for each sanitation worker, there being one trash collector for every 835 New York inhabitants. Salisbury wrote thousands of words on this subject, it became a three-part series that started on page one, and it began:

No city in the world comes within ten million dollars of spending what it costs New York each year to keep clean. And no great city of the world, with the possible exception of a few in Asia, has a greater reputation for dirt, disorder, filth and litter. Why?

When Clifton Daniel returned from Moscow to the newsroom in 1955, and began his gradual rise as an executive, life became more pleasant for Salisbury as a reporter, and, beginning in 1962, as an editor. Salisbury's personal life also began to improve around this time with a courtship that would lead, in April of 1964, to his second marriage. His new wife was a lovely divorcée who had been reared in Boston, and had worked as a Powers model. He had met her through friends in Salisbury, Connecticut, and she had accompanied him during the summer of 1966 on his trip to Asia, that he hoped would lead into Peking or Hanoi. In anticipation of succeeding, Salisbury and his wife, Charlotte, had had their passports cleared beforehand in Washington for travel into China, or North Vietnam, or North Korea, a fact that some people in Washington would in time regret, but not at this juncture, for the Salisburys had been unable to visit any of those places. In August of 1966, Salisbury returned to New York thinking there was little hope, but he continued to send messages to Hanoi advising the authorities of his continued interest in reporting events from within North Vietnam. He got no response. In November, Salisbury cabled Hanoi suggesting that if there were a truce at Christmastime this might make an appropriate moment for a trip into North Vietnam. No response.

The Times' editorial page had been critical of the war in Vietnam for years, and the dispatches from *Times* reporters on the scene had repeatedly angered or embarrassed President Johnson and President Kennedy, the latter once even suggesting to Punch Sulzberger that the paper replace its man in Vietnam, David Hal-

berstam. *The Times* refused, and Halberstam's reporting won a Pulitzer in 1964.

This did not mean, however, that there was not dis-
harmony within the *Times* building on the subject of
Vietnam. There existed, in fact, a wide variety of hawks
and doves—there were hawks in the News department,
in the Advertising department, and in the Advertising
Acceptability department (which refused, for "legal
reasons," a protest ad from a group of artists, writers,
and editors, including a *Times* editor on the Sunday
Magazine, Gerald Walker, who had organized the protest that advocated nonpayment of a portion of the Federal income tax). And there was a preponderance of
doves among the younger reporters, the copyreaders,
and particularly the copyboys and campus correspondents. One young man, hoping to employ the influence of the bullpen in the peace movement, scrawled
in red indelible ink on the walls of the private elevator
that carries the bullpen editors up to the composing
room each night to make up page one: "Mr. Bernstein, Please Stop the War!"

Punch Sulzberger, a Marine veteran of Korea, had
sanctioned *The Times*' antiwar editorial policy on Vietnam, but this policy more approximately reflected the
strong dovish attitude of Sulzberger's cousin, John
Oakes. The *Times* editor most appalled by Oakes's
viewpoint was the tall, lean, gray-haired Hanson W.
Baldwin, the paper's military specialist since 1937, and
an individual who in 1960 could barely conceal his displeasure over the failure of the captured U-2 pilot,
Gary Powers, to kill himself after being shot down by
the Russians. (". . . why did the pilot survive? This is a
question that only Mr. Powers can answer," Baldwin
wrote in *The Times*, "and he may spend the rest of his
life trying to answer it satisfactorily. . . .")

Lined up behind Oakes or Baldwin, or taking positions between the two extremes, were other editors
and editorial writers whose views on Vietnam occasionally fluctuated, being more emotional on some days
than on other days; and one result was that *The Times*'

tone on Vietnam was never entirely predictable. There was even an example in November of 1966 when an editorial on Vietnam changed its tone between the first and second editions. In the first edition, the lead editorial, commenting on the absurdity of a Christmas truce in Vietnam that lasted only for a few hours, began:

> Kill and maim as many as you can up to 6 o'clock in the morning of December 24 and start killing again on the morning of December 26. Do your damnedest until 6 a.m. December 31 and again after January 1, 1967, when it will be all right to slay, to bomb, to burn, to destroy crops and houses and the works of man until 6 o'clock on the morning of December 24, 1967.
> "Glory to God in the highest, and on earth peace, good will toward men . . ."

When Punch Sulzberger received his *Times* early edition at home that night and read the editorial, which had been written by Herbert L. Matthews, he called Oakes at home and said that he felt it should be killed. Sulzberger felt that the editorial was too emotional. Oakes, who had been off that day, it being Sunday— his place being taken by his deputy, A. H. Raskin, the former labor specialist—read the editorial, agreed that it was too emotional, but thought that killing it would be too obvious. Oakes convinced Sulzberger that it should be merely toned down, and Oakes did the editing himself in time for the second edition that night, eliminating Herbert Matthews' opening paragraph and starting the editorial with Matthews' second paragraph:

> By all means, let there be peace in Vietnam for a few hours or a few days over Christmas and the New Year. It is not much, but it is that much better than uninterrupted war . . .

The emotional version drew a great number of approving letters from readers around the country, while the second version received a few; but hardly anyone outside the *Times* organization noticed these changes that morning, the meshing of minds, the soul-searching, the treatment of touchy subjects being matters that usually stay within the walls of the *Times* building—usually, but not always. For within a month of the Matthews editorial there would be edited within the *Times* building a story so big and controversial that it would cause conflict and reappraisal not only among *Times* editors but through the nation and the world.

The hint of something unusual began in Washington on December 14, 1966, when, after Hanoi radio broadcasts charged for the second straight day that American planes had bombed residential areas of North Vietnam's capital, the United States admitted for the first time that it had raided military targets in Hanoi; and reporters in Washington now wondered if these raids had also killed civilians.

The next morning a cable from Hanoi arrived at the *Times* building for Harrison Salisbury. The newly appointed foreign-news editor, Seymour Topping, received it first, read it, and walked over to Salisbury's desk, asking, "Does this say what I think it does?"

Salisbury studied it. "Yes," he said finally, the language of the cable not being entirely clear. "I think it does."

"You're in," Topping said.

Salisbury's visa into North Vietnam was awaiting him in Paris. To make sure he was interpreting it correctly, Salisbury sent a return cable asking the North Vietnamese for a confirmation of this message; the next day the confirmation was received. He was to fly to Paris to pick up his visa, then fly on the International Control Commission plane into Hanoi.

Salisbury's older son, the one who had been three years old when Salisbury had gone off to London in 1942, was going to be married in New York at the end of December. Salisbury telephoned his son now and told him he would be unable to attend the wedding, that he would be out of the country. But he did not say where or why, and the young man did not ask.

· · ·

Salisbury's departure was a well-kept secret. Daniel, Topping, and Catledge knew of it, of course, but they discussed it with no one—not even John Oakes, who was later piqued by their failure to keep him informed. The reporters and copyreaders in the newsroom soon became aware of Salisbury's absence from his desk, but they imagined that he was on one of his out-of-town speaking tours—in Siberia, perhaps, for they now thought of Salisbury as a man doomed to some exiled spot within the executive suite of *The New York Times*. In a matter of days, the rumor went, Rosenthal's elevation to assistant managing editor, and Salisbury's departure from the newsroom, would be announced.

Harrison Salisbury's stories from North Vietnam began to appear in *The Times* during the last week of December, and they landed like bombs on Washington. In his first, after inspecting the damage in Hanoi and talking to the people, Salisbury reported:

> Contrary to the impression given by United States communiqués, on-the-spot inspection indicates that American bombing has been inflicting considerable civilian casualties in Hanoi and its environs for some time past. . . . It is fair to say that, based on evidence of their own eyes, Hanoi residents do not find much credibility in United States bombing communiqués . . .

Two days later, in describing the devastation done to the North Vietnamese city of Namdinh, Salisbury wrote:

> Whatever the explanation, one can see that United States planes are dropping an enormous weight of explosives on purely civilian targets. Whatever else there may be or might have been in Namdinh, it is the civilians who have taken the punishment.

Now in Washington, for the first time, American officials conceded to the press that American pilots had accidentally struck civilian areas in North Vietnam while attempting to bomb military targets. And a quiet bitterness and even an open hostility began to develop between some government officials and *Times*men in the Washington bureau.

"Here come the men from the Hanoi *Times*," said one official to two *Times* reporters from Wicker's bureau, one of whom liked Salisbury no more than the government spokesman. Secretary of State Dean Rusk, in a television appearance at the CBS studio, became aggressive with another Washington bureauman after the show; drinking his third Scotch, Rusk looked hard into the *Times*man's eyes and asked, "Why don't you tell your editors to ask Mr. Salisbury to go down and visit the North Vietnamese in *South* Vietnam?"

A few nights before, as Punch Sulzberger slept in his apartment on Fifth Avenue, he was awakened by a telephone call from Washington. It was Secretary Rusk. It was around 10 p.m., and though not fully awake, Sulzberger thought he heard Dean Rusk saying apologetically, "I hope I haven't taken you away from the dinner table."

Sulzberger, forty-one years old, was too embarrassed to admit that he had gone to bed so early. But he was alert enough to know that Rusk was surely calling about Salisbury.

"What were his instructions?" Rusk asked Sulzberger.

"He had no instructions," Sulzberger said.

"When is he coming out?"

"I guess I'll have to amend that, sir—he did have instructions to stay as long as he could with the proviso that he not become the resident correspondent of *The Times* in Hanoi."

"Is Mr. Salisbury asking the right questions?"

"I hope so," Sulzberger said.

There was no hardness in Rusk's voice—none of the tension that Sulzberger remembered of his talk with John Kennedy when the President wished to have *The Times* replaced Halberstam in Vietnam. After Rusk had hung up, Sulzberger called Clifton Daniel and asked him to call the Secretary of State back and get from him any questions that Rusk might wish to have Salisbury ask the North Vietnamese. Daniel did, but Rusk had no questions.

Other people had questions, however, many of them, and they reechoed much of the old criticism of Harrison Salisbury as a newspaperman—he was politically naive, he was being taken in by the Communists, he did not properly attribute his sources in North Vietnam. The *Washington Post* charged that Salisbury's casualty figures in the Namdinh raid were identical to those given in Communist propaganda pamphlets—to which Clifton Daniel replied in a statement, "It was apparent in Mr. Salisbury's first dispatch—and he so stated in a subsequent dispatch—that the casualty figures came from North Vietnamese officials. Where else would he get such figures in Hanoi?"

Within *The Times*, too, there was criticism of Salisbury's reporting, particularly from Hanson Baldwin, who was overhead muttering unpleasantries about Salisbury through the halls. Other *Times*men sincerely believed that Salisbury's lack of exactness in identifying his sources in his early dispatches had needlessly dragged *The Times* into another controversy. Still others, partisans of the desk wars in the newsroom, found new excuses for attacking Salisbury, with one *Times*man saying, "If Hanoi keeps Salisbury, we'll stop the bombing."

But Walter Lippmann wrote:

> Mr. Salisbury's offense, we are being told, is that in reporting the war as seen from Hanoi, he has made himself a tool of enemy propaganda. We must remember that in time of war what is said on the enemy's side of the front is always propaganda, and what is said on our side of the front is truth and righteousness, the cause of humanity and a crusade for peace. Is it necessary for us at the height of our power to stoop to such self-deceiving nonsense?

Harrison Salisbury returned to the United States in January, 1967, tired but exhilarated, ducking platoons of photographers and reporters at the San Francisco airport to take a different route to his plane to New York; and then, later in the morning, his taxicab pulled up outside the *Times* building, he hopped out, and walked through the marble-floored lobby toward the open door of an elevator. The first *Times*man he saw in the elevator was Hanson Baldwin. Salisbury greeted Baldwin with a wide grin. Baldwin nodded stiffly.

At the third floor, Salisbury stepped out and entered the newsroom. Had he been riding a chariot behind three white horses, his entrance would not have been more conspicuous. *The Times'* editors behind their desks stood. They walked over to shake his hand. His stories had gotten a fantastic reaction around the nation and the world, and the criticism of his reporting, so very trivial in view of the achievement, was now forgotten within *The Times*. Although it would take historians to evaluate the impact of Salisbury's reporting on the peace movement in America in 1967, the growing disenchantment with the Johnson administration, and the general public's disbelief and disillusionment with the men who were running the government, the Salisbury stories were considered by *The Times'* editors to be worthy of a Pulitzer, and thus he was nominated.

He would not, however, receive the prize for international reporting in 1967. While the Pulitzer jury had recommended him to the Pulitzer advisory board, the latter would reject the recommendation in a six-to-five vote, a decision that would be widely protested in editorials around the nation, but to no avail. Harrison Salisbury's stories, as Senator Mike Mansfield of Montana later conceded, had provoked a "sort of vendetta," or as a past president of the American Society of Newspaper Editors said, Salisbury failed to get the prize because he had "embarrassed the hawks in and out of the United States Government," and the hawkish members of the Pulitzer advisory board had gotten even. But Salisbury himself, after the disappointing announcement had been made, said that he did not care so much about the dissenting votes of the advisory board; he was more gratified by the vote of confidence that he had received from his fellow editors on *The Times*.

As Salisbury had arrived in the newsroom on that January day from North Vietnam, there was hanging on the bulletin board a memo to the staff from Clifton Daniel. It read:

> The rumors are true.
> A. M. Rosenthal is being promoted to assistant managing editor . . .

What was not said, however, was that Salisbury was *not* being kicked upstairs. He would also ramain an assistant managing editor. Rosenthal would assume many duties as Daniel's deputy, and Salisbury would be answerable to Daniel for special stories: he had a dream assignment, one in which he would have the rank to travel and write as he wished. He would begin by planning the coverage of the fiftieth anniversary of the Bolshevik revolution, an assignment that would take him back to Russia for a few weeks. He would continue to write his books, his articles, his speeches. Salisbury's victory abroad, it seemed, had fortified his position at home.

And so on the day following his arrival home, Salisbury began a series of guest appearances and speeches around the country—he stood before a large crowd of journalism students and others in a crowded auditorium at Columbia University. Salisbury stood very tall in front, looking around the room through his sturdy steel-rimmed glasses for a moment waiting for the audience to settle itself before beginning his speech. Seated in the back was a twenty-year-old boy that Salisbury knew, a student with very long blondish hair that fell over his ears. The hair was too long, but Salisbury knew that the boy would not cut it. He had worked as a *Times* copyboy the summer before in Punch Sulzberger's office, Salisbury knew, and *Sulzberger* had dropped hints, but the boy had reappeared each day with the long blond hair over his ears. The boy was Salisbury's younger son, Stephen.

Stephen listened quietly with the rest, now, as his father spoke about the adventure behind the enemy lines in North Vietnam. After Salisbury had finished, there was great applause. Then the students raised their hands to ask many, many questions about Vietnam, and China, and Russia.

Then one student, not Stephen but another young man with very long hair, stood and asked Harrison Salisbury if he did not find it irritating sometimes to be criticized so much. Salisbury shook his head.

Then, pausing just a moment, Salisbury added, "I have a little distrust for a newspaperman who gets too many bouquets. He must be missing part of the story."

19

THERE was room for only four assistant managing editors in the News department, and since Salisbury was being retained, one of three others would have to be transferred or retired to accommodate Rosenthal's promotion. The man selected was Robert Garst, and not unexpectedly, he responded with indignation. Garst was a quietly proud Virginian, lean and aloof, a man who since 1952 had sat against the south wall as an assistant managing editor observing, with feelings of mild discomfort, the trends of *The Times*. He had joined the paper as a copyreader in 1925, a period that he and a few of his contemporaries considered the golden age of *The Times*—Van Anda had then been the managing editor, Birchall had been Van Anda's chief assistant; there had been numbers of truly dedicated reporters, such men as Russell Owen, Joseph Shaplen, and the renowned Alva Johnston; and there had been Ochs himself.

A decade later, with Edwin James, a fellow Virginian, in charge of the newsroom, Garst had begun his rise through the desk system: he became a slotman on the New York desk, then a night city editor in 1938, then the city editor in 1948. With the death of James in 1951 and Catledge's succession, Garst began to feel inauspicious changes. Catledge's folksy manner was not Garst's idea of Southern charm, and Garst was affronted by the backroom political style of the managing editor, and also by the little clique in the bullpen that had been assembled by Garst's onetime friend and colleague on the Columbia journalism faculty, Theodore

Bernstein. Although Catledge had promoted both Garst and Bernstein to assistant managing-editorships in 1952, it was immediately obvious to Garst that Catledge favored Bernstein, and Garst was relegated to the lesser roles—the housekeeping chores of the managing editor's office: the equipment and supplies, the staff expense accounts, the personnel problems, the liaison duties with other departments within the building. On weekends, or when Catledge was out of town, Garst was in charge of the staff, but otherwise he functioned as Catledge's left arm; and when Clifton Daniel arrived on the scene, Garst felt even more removed from the vibrations of the newsroom.

With Daniel's promotion to managing editor in 1964, and Salisbury's rise as Daniel's chief assistant, Robert Garst was asked by Daniel one day to vacate his desk, which was close to the managing editor's door, to Harrison Salisbury, and to occupy a desk that was farther away, closer to the bullpen. Garst obliged, after directing a few cutting remarks at Daniel; and when Daniel asked Garst two years later to vacate the newsroom entirely to make room for Rosenthal, Garst was even more caustic. Unlike Daniel, Garst said what he thought, which was one reason why Garst had never been entirely popular with his fellow executives. But he nonetheless again complied with Daniel's instructions, occupying an office within Catledge's interior complex, and accepting the title of "special assistant to the executive editor," with the understanding that in March of 1967 he would retire from *The Times*.

Thus Daniel, seeking the appearance of orderliness and harmony, drafted a long executive memorandum as the new year began, outlining the different duties of Rosenthal and Salisbury, as well as restating Bernstein's position as the bullpen head and Emanuel Freedman's responsibilities in such areas as the recruitment of talent, labor relations, salary administration, and the travel and living allowances of *Times*men overseas; and Daniel also acknowledged that Arthur Gelb was succeeding Rosenthal as the New York editor, and that Garst was joining Catledge's office. Daniel added:

I shouldn't conclude this memorandum without saying that I have had the pleasure of working with a wonderful team of editors ever since I came to the New York office in 1955. The changes now being made in the lineup—inevitable as times goes on—conform to the great New York Times tradition. I am sure they will enable us to carry on with renewed vigor and strength of purpose. They do not represent a changing of the guard, but a changing of generations.

Daniel also affixed to the bulletin board a memo to the staff that noted Gelb's appointment and Garst's departure:

. . . Mr. Garst leaves the newsroom with the professional respect and warm personal regard of the entire department, which he served so loyally for 41 years.

Garst spent the next two months seated in an office doing very little. His responsibilities were to supervise the expanding *Times* News Service, which during 1966 had added forty-seven clients, and which was now wiring daily reportage, columns, and features to 155 newspapers in the nation and to eighty-eight overseas. But the News Service was very adequately directed by subordinate editors, and there was nothing in the work that Garst found challenging.

At the end of February, Garst arrived at *The Times* on a Saturday, which was a normal working day for him, and which was usually a very quiet day within the office. Only a minimum of reporters and editors were working since much of the Sunday edition—the *Magazine*, the real-estate section, the drama section—was already printed and distributed to newsstands, and since most of the business centers in New York and the government agencies in Washington were closed for the weekend. Except for the Sports department, which always had a busy schedule on weekends, the newsroom was characterized by small clusters of reporters sitting around and talking across rows of empty desks, or standing around a television set in the Sports department watching a game, the audio being low so as not to distract the copyreaders. The upper floors of the building were largely abandoned and dark, and there was about *The Times* a rather strange, hollow atmosphere.

Late in the afternoon, unobserved within his office in Catledge's interior suite, Garst began to clean out his desk. He stuffed a stack of personal papers and letters into manila envelopes, and he composed a note of good-bye to the secretary in the News Service and another to *The Times'* chief copyboy, the white-haired, stout Steven Moran, who had joined the paper in 1917. After depositing these into an out basket, and putting on his gray tweed overcoat, Garst took the elevator down, carrying the manila envelopes under his arm, and nodding as he passed the guards who are always conspicuous in the lobby on weekends. Then he pushed through the revolving door of the *Times* building for the last time. Outside, feeling no regret, Garst waved to a taxicab.

During the next week, it occurred to the other executives that Garst was gone for good, and he began receiving notes and letters from Catledge, Bernstein, Salisbury, and others. But Garst did not reply. When he received a call from Punch Sulzberger's office inviting him to an executive luncheon, which he suspected would turn into a farewell ceremony with forced smiles for a photograph to be printed in *Times Talk*, he declined the invitation, saying that he was otherwise occupied.

Punch Sulzberger was certainly aware of the awkward position he occupied as the deporter of men that his grandfather had employed, and he was also cognizant of the decline in staff morale. The Yankelovich report, when it was completed, told Sulzberger nothing that he had not previously suspected—"it just rubbed our noses in it," he explained one day, after reviewing it; and he had already embarked on programs that he hoped would improve personnel relations, and might also resurrect, with the help of modern techniques, some spirit of the past.

During the early winter of 1967, each *Times* employee received a handsomely designed blue cardboard kit that contained a letter from the publisher, a pamphlet itemizing employee benefits and health plans, facilities and services, and there was also included a brief history of the paper by Meyer Berger, a reporter whose death in 1959 had inspired perhaps the last surge of sentimentality and shared emotion to be felt through the building.

When Berger had been alive, everybody on *The Times*—printers, clerks, telephone operators, cafeteria cooks—knew him and admired him, and when he died suddenly of a heart attack at sixty, it seemed to mark the end of something quite special on *The Times*, and it evoked memorable reactions from the staff. A veteran journalist, assigned to write Berger's obituary, found it very difficult to do; and numbers of staff members, including copyreaders, cursed the bullpen for not putting the obituary on page one; and a woman put a rose in a glass of water and placed it on Berger's desk in the front row, the rose remaining there days after it had withered. Nobody wanted to remove Berger's name from the office mailbox, and the printers kept Berger's by-line set in type, ready and waiting.

Now, in 1967, Berger's by-line reappeared in the kit, on the cover of a twenty-page supplement that was a condensation of the paper's history written by Berger in 1951: the words described *The Times'* modest beginning under Henry J. Raymond, its coverage of the Civil War and the Tweed ring; its bankruptcy and its eventual revival under Ochs; its exclusive coverage of the Russo-Japanese naval battles, the expeditions of Peary and Amundsen, the *Titanic* and Lindbergh; its expanding influence from World War I into the space age. Punch Sulzberger's accompanying letter explained that while the primary purpose of the informational kit was for the enlightment of new employees, he felt that older *Times*men might also find it interest-

ing; it was all part of a new method of introducing
Timesmen to The Times, Sulzberger explained, adding,
"The truth is, we had been somewhat casual about it."

In another move to remain in touch with its past,
The Times encouraged the occasional publication of
articles in the daily paper by retired Timesmen; and
soon Brooks Atkinson's by-line reappeared over an
essay on nature, and there was a piece on the sports
page by the retired racing-car specialist Frank M.
Blunk; a political appraisal by Arthur Krock, who had
continued after his retirement to occupy his desk in
the Washington bureau. Krock's stepson, a very per-
sonable Times correspondent in London, W. Granger
Blair, was brought to New York to serve management
as its interoffice public-relations adviser and liaison
man with the staff, and Sulzberger also sought to improve morale by sharing the wealth more generously
with higher salaries to employees and with stock options
and other benefits to ranking editors and executives.
The New York Times Company's stock splits in 1964
and 1966 helped to make relatively rich men of such
executives as Catledge and Reston, Ivan Veit and Monroe Green; and numbers of editors and executives on
a lower level were earning between $45,000 and
$65,000 a year; critics were in a $20,000 to $30,000
class; and the very top reporters were receiving between $350 and $500 a week. The key editors and
executives also had access to a new status symbol that
had caught Sulzberger's fancy for gadgets: a small jet
airplane that could transport them to Florida on
weekends, or to various business visits around the nation. The plane's number, painted in black across the
rudder, was N 1851 T (1851 being the year that The
Times was founded).

Punch Sulzberger was now spending more money
than ever, but he was also making more. With the dis-
continuance of the Herald Tribune and the strike
against the newly merged World Journal Tribune,
which lasted from April 24 to September 12, 1966, The
Times' daily circulation climbed to more than 875,000,
an increase of about 100,000, and its advertising rates

were raised 8 percent. The Times Company's consolidated net earnings for 1966 set a company record —a net profit of more than $9 million ($4.28 per share) as compared with a net profit in 1965 of more than $5 million ($2.25 per share). With the closing down of the *World Journal Tribune* in May of 1967, *The Times'* daily circulation went over 900,000 and its advertising rates were raised another 9 percent. Monroe Green was not very happy about this, but Green, sixty-two, the advertising director since 1946, was on his way out. Sulzberger wanted higher rates, being unconcerned about advertisers' reactions or a possible temporary decline in advertising linage; Sulzberger also wanted to consolidate the Advertising, the Production, and the Circulation departments under a younger man, Andrew Fisher, forty-seven, an apostle of the computer. Since Sulzberger could not satisfactorily achieve this as long as Green remained—Green being accustomed to running his department with autonomy —Sulzberger planned to announce Green's retirement, with regret, at the end of 1967. Green, sated with stock and a large retirement, would go quietly and agreeably.

The Times' slim overseas edition, whose printing operation had in recent years been transferred from Amsterdam to Paris, had been losing money during most of its eighteen-year history—a total estimated to be $10 million since Arthur Hays Sulzberger had launched it in 1949; but it was nevertheless assumed by most editors in New York that Punch Sulzberger would continue to absorb the losses. They reasoned that he was sentimentally committed to the edition because his father had started it, and they also believed that the International edition of *The Times* was a prestige item of promotional value, and was not, like the *Times* defunct Western edition, a venture that was supposed to be self-supporting.

Their lack of insight into the young publisher became quickly apparent in the spring of 1967 when he announced that he was folding the International edi-

tion Although it had made gains during the year under
the editorship of Sydney Gruson, having increased its
circulation from 40,000 to 47,000 and having achieved
a 20 percent increase in advertising, it was still losing
more than $1.5 million annually. It also had failed to
overtake the solidly established Paris *Herald Tribune,*
which had been in Europe for seventy-nine years, and
which recently had been strengthened by its partnership with the *Washington Post.* The Paris *Herald Tribune*'s circulation was 60,000 and it was a more readable and sprightly paper than *The Times* for Americans
abroad. So, unable to beat the *Tribune* in Europe,
Sulzberger decided to join it. By merging his edition
with his rivals', he attained a one-third interest in the
new operation, which was expected to approach a circulation of between 75,000 and 100,000. Hoping to
appeal to a wide readership, it would publish James
Reston, Russell Baker, and other *Times* columnists
along with Walter Lippmann and Art Buchwald and
the reporting of the *Los Angeles Times—Washington
Post* News Service as well as *The New York Times'*
News Service. The new combination would continue,
however, to feature the *Tribune*'s name on its masthead and would be supervised by a *Tribune* editor.

Sydney Gruson remained only during the transition
period; then he returned to *The New York Times'*
staff as a roving correspondent, assisting in the coverage
of the Arab-Israeli war, and within a year he would
resign from *The Times* to become the associate publisher of the Long Island newspaper *Newsday.* Although Punch Sulzberger would attempt to dissuade
Gruson, sending his jet up from Florida to New York
to bring Gruson down for poolside reflections, there
was not really an important executive position open to
Gruson at this time. And although Sulzberger also regretted the loss of his International edition, he did not
fret about it for very long, having more important concerns in the home office, where he wished to build up
great cash reserves to be able to respond to the many
new challenges he saw around him.

Among other things, Sulzberger was pondering the

possibility of starting an afternoon newspaper in New York, which, with the disappearance of the *World Journal Tribune,* had only one afternoon daily—the *New York Post.* At certain moments Sulzberger felt that New York City both needed and would support a second afternoon paper; at other moments he was not so sure, his romanticism and desire for public service being balanced by the fact that the short-lived *World Journal Tribune* had cost its owners about $17 million. And the issue was not merely financial—it was also a question of how the New York Times Company's involvement with a second newspaper, perhaps a newly named, sophisticated journal featuring entertainment, the arts, political essays, and social commentary, would influence the reputation and character of the morning newspaper. Could Sulzberger, Catledge, or Bernstein insist on reportorial restraint in the morning and then relax the rules in the afternoon? If the new paper was to be completely divorced from the tone and strictures of the morning *Times,* if the new editors were to be given autonomy, would it not reintroduce the old problem of dukedoms within the organization? And there was finally the question of whether Punch Sulzberger had sufficient time to devote to a second newspaper, a situation similar to one that Adolph Ochs had faced a half-century ago when he had contemplated buying an afternoon paper in New York, the *Evening Post.* Ochs had eventually discarded the idea, believing that owning the *Post* would have divided his energies. And yet Ochs, a conservative man, had often underestimated his own capacity and the growth of his company: after completing the Times Tower building on Forty-second Street in 1904 (now the Allied Chemical building), he had been forced to vacate it nine years later because his paper had outgrown it. Thus he built *The Times'* present headquarters on Forty-third Street, which Arthur Hays Sulzberger had subsequently expanded with wings and an annex.

Now in 1967 this, too, was becoming inadequate for the rapidly growing *Times,* whose roster of employees had increased in about two years from 5,307 to 6,354,

and whose lack of storage space for the rolls of newsprint had required the renting of space in the adjoining
Paramount building's basement, to be followed by renting of additional space on the Paramount's upper
floors for more editorial room. *The Times'* West Side
plant, built in 1959 and used mainly for supplement-
ary printing of the Sunday edition—which in 1967 had
a circulation of 1,600,000 and was averaging 558 pages
per issue, varying in seasonal weight between four
and seven pounds—had become so overcrowded that
its lobby was scheduled to be eliminated and its 27-foot
lobby ceiling was to be lowered by about twelve feet.
The Times under Sulzberger was suddenly becoming a
very fat, rich operation, having $21 million in cash at
the end of 1966, and diversifying and expanding in
1966–67 as never before in its history. Sulzberger paid
$500,000 for a 51 percent interest in the Teaching
Systems Corporation of Boston, which specialized in
programmed learning material for schools and industry;
and Sulzberger also bought, for an unannounced sum,
the Microfilming Corporation of America, in Haw-
thorne, New Jersey, to supply the demands of the more
than two thousand libraries, colleges, and businesses
that subscribe to *The Times'* microfilm edition. *The
Times* started a tabloid-sized weekly paper in very
large type for people with poor sight, and it also introduced a tabloid version of *The Times* for school and
college students. It licensed Parker Brothers of Boston
to use historical front pages of *The Times* in jigsaw
puzzles, and it also began selling facsimiles of its
famous front pages as novelty gifts. *The Times'* Book
Division, in collaboration with outside publishing
houses, had produced more than fifty books between
1963 and 1967, ranging in subject from cooking to
communism, and *The Times* also gained the serialization rights to the book by Svetlana Alliluyeva, Stalin's
daughter, after she had defected from the Soviet Union.

The transaction with Mrs. Alliluyeva, completed in
April of 1967, demonstrated once again *The Times'*
revered position within the Establishment, its role as a
responsible spokesman for the system, and it also re-

vealed something of the interesting personal relationships that link top *Times*men with other influential
figures within the circles of government, communications, law, and literature—it was almost a little club
that emerged during the odyssey that brought Mrs.
Alliluyeva safely to Democracy; they all seemed to
know one another, and they worked smoothly together
with a tacit understanding of the rules by which they
would be of service to Stalin's daughter and to themselves.

Mrs. Alliluyeva's lawyer and literary representative,
a onetime general in the Pentagon named Edward S.
Greenbaum, was an old and dear friend of Arthur Hays
Sulzberger, and he had been the Sulzberger family
lawyer for more than forty years, a fact that *The Times*
somehow neglected to mention in its "Man in the
News" profile on Greenbaum on the day of Mrs.
Alliluyeva's arrival in the United States. Mrs. Alliluyeva's other chief comforter during her escape was
the former American Ambassador to the Soviet Union,
George F. Kennan, a friend of *The Times* and a neigh-
bor of Greenbaum in Princeton, New Jersey. Greenbaum not only arranged for *The Times*' serialization,
but he also arranged for the book to be published by
Harper & Row, another client of his law firm (Greenbaum, Wolff & Ernst), which had fought Harper's
battle during the previous year's Kennedy suit against
William Manchester's book. Mrs. Alliluyeva's editor at
Harper & Row, Evan Thomas (son of the famed Socialist Norman Thomas), had been William Manchester's editor, John F. Kennedy's editor, Robert Kennedy's and Theodore Sorensen's editor, as well as the
editor of Harper books written by Harrison Salisbury,
John Oakes, Tom Wicker, C. L. Sulzberger, and other
*Times*men.

The magazine rights to Svetlana Alliluyeva's book
went to *Life*, whose board chairman, Andrew Heiskell,
was married to Punch Sulzberger's sister, Marian, the
widow of Orvil Dryfoos. The inside story of Mrs. Alliluyeva's escape was written for *The Times* by Harrison Salisbury, who had gotten most of his information

from his friend, former Ambassador Kennan; but Salisbury had kept his by-line off the story because he did not wish to offend his sources in the Soviet Union at a time when he was traveling regularly through Russia, which was celebrating the fiftieth anniversary of its revolution. The translator of Mrs. Alliluyeva's book was Priscilla Johnson McMillan, a quietly wealthy, well-connected woman who had worked in the Senate office of John F. Kennedy, had met Punch Sulzberger and Clifton Daniel overseas, had known both Svetlana and Lee Harvey Oswald in Russia during her days there as a correspondent, and after the assassination was helping the assassin's widow, Marina Oswald, write a book for Harper & Row.

A magazine piece by Svetlana Alliluyeva that appeared a few months before her book, and had been inspired by her reading of Boris Pasternak's *Dr. Zhivago*, was printed in the *Atlantic Monthly*, whose publisher had published former Ambassador Kennan, and whose editor-in-chief, Robert Manning, had most recently worked in the State Department and knew all the right people in politics and journalism. In an issue of *Book Week* in April of 1967, Manning had written a very favorable review of James Reston's book *The Artillery of the Press*, and a month later Reston wrote a very favorable review in *The Times* on page one about Mrs. Alliluyeva's article in the *Atlantic Monthly*.

When Mrs. Alliluyeva's book, entitled *Twenty Letters to a Friend*, was distributed by Harper & Row in the fall of 1967, *The Times*' Sunday "Book Review" editor, Francis Brown, searching for an appropriate reviewer, selected Olga Carlisle, an American of distinguished Russian ancestry—she was the granddaughter of the playwright and short-story writer Leonid Andreyev, and her parents had been friends of Pasternak. Mrs. Carlisle's review was very favorable, and it was positioned on page one. *The Times*' daily book critic, Eliot Fremont-Smith, a keen student of office affairs—he had praised Reston's *Artillery of the Press* as "one of the important documents of our time"—

was profoundly moved by the Svetlana book, calling it "the rarest of events."

And so it had all worked out very well—Punch Sulzberger dwelled in the center of a rather tidy world. He had paid an estimated $250,000 for the serialization rights to the memoirs, had helped to launch Mrs. Alliluyeva's best seller, had pleased his many clients in *The Times'* News Service, and had somewhat restored *The Times* into the good graces of those patriots in the nation who had been offended by Salisbury's reporting from Hanoi, and by Oakes's aggressive dovishness on the editorial page. It was one of the remarkable qualities of *The Times* that it could be, almost simultaneously, so many things to so many people—it was a deep-rooted flexible tree that moved from left to right, right to left, making its quiet adjustments as it dropped its tired old leaves and rebloomed through a century of seasons.

In the winter of 1967, Herbert L. Matthews sat rather forlornly in Room 1048 along a corridor of editorial writers on the tenth floor. Nothing would please him less than to be described as forlorn, a man doing penance in an ivory tower because he had embarrassed *The Times* years ago in Cuba. Matthews was vain and valorous; at sixty-seven he was thin, tall, only slightly less energetic, and no less alert, than when he had first joined the paper in 1922, beginning a career that would find him in Peking in 1929 observing a triumphant Chiang Kai-shek; in Addis Ababa in 1936 riding with an invading Italian army; in Perpignan in 1939 writing his last dispatch from the Spanish Civil War; in Italy and India and North Africa during World War II, in London after the war, and in the Cuban hills in 1957 interviewing a bearded revolutionary that most people thought was dead.

Because of these articles about Castro and subsequent ones about Cuba, *The Times* would eventually be charged with Communizing that island, and many editors in the newsroom would become chary of Matthews. In 1963, as a member of John Oakes's Editorial department, Matthews revisited Cuba and Castro, and upon his return to New York he offered to write articles for the News department, but his offer was refused. In 1966, again representing the Editorial Board, Matthews reacquainted himself with Castro and Cuba. No other *Times*man could get into Cuba in 1966, and Matthews had amassed twenty-five thousand words of notes, but the News department again declined his offer to write for it; consequently, *The Times* went through the year with no information from Cuba from a member of the staff.

When readers wrote letters to *The Times* inquiring about Matthews' status, they received replies from Clifton Daniel's office explaining that Matthews was no longer writing for the News department because he was no longer, strictly speaking, a newsman, but rather a member of the Editorial Board, implying that editorial writers did not write for the News department. This was not true. Harry Schwartz, Murray Rossant, and numbers of other editorialists wrote frequently for the News department, and so had Matthews in years past. Now, however, he was a sensitive issue. While his by-line appeared from time to time over an essay or article on the editorial page, or perhaps in the Sunday edition, it rarely appeared more than once every few months. During 1966 it appeared a total of six times. But as an anonymous editorial-writer he was extremely productive. He wrote about Latin American affairs (being sometimes critical of Castro), about the Middle East and Vietnam, and other subjects that John Oakes thought worthy of comment. Oakes was very respectful of Matthews' talent and was fond of him personally, and he had never forgotten his first sight of Matthews in Paris forty years ago: Oakes, a schoolboy visiting the Paris bureau, saw Matthews walk in wearing a gray fedora, beige gloves and matching spats, and carrying a malacca walking stick.

The next time Oakes saw him was two decades later, in 1949, when both were writing editorials on the tenth floor under Charles Merz. Matthews was then a favorite son of the institution, enjoying a warm relationship with the owners of *The Times;* Iphigene Sulzberger was the godmother to Matthews' only son. But now, in 1967, after forty-five years, he was preparing to leave *The Times*, planning to devote himself to his books and to his belief that history will finally absolve him. Even now he believed that Castro was not a Communist when the revolution began, and in Matthews' final article on the editorial page—the last of four by-line reminiscences on the four continents that had been his beat—he wrote:

> For the United States, Fidel Castro and the Cuban Revolution brought Latin America to life after a long period of indifference and neglect. When Cuba's *Jefe Máximo* and his Government turned Communist and later almost brought on a nuclear war, somebody had to be blamed. I was.
>
> The influence of journalism on history is a fascinating and controversial subject which has engendered much nonsense. I would not deny that as I sat with Fidel Castro, his brother Raul, Ché Guevara and others up in the Sierra Maestra on the chilly morning of Feb. 17, 1957, Clio, the muse of history, touched me with her wand—or whatever she uses. The resulting publicity in The Times gave Castro and his guerrilla band a nation-wide and even a worldwide fame that, chronologically, was the start of the most fantastic career of any leader in the whole course of Latin America's independent history.
>
> However, Cuba was "ripe for revolution," as Arthur Schlesinger Jr. wrote for a State Department white paper. Fidel Castro was the man of destiny and nothing was going to stop him in the long run. . . .
>
> Looking back over the kaleidoscopic changes in the world during these 45 years and passing in review the men and women who made the history of our times is a process that leaves some pride, some humility—and a sense of helplessness. There is, at least, a residue of satisfaction in thinking that one did not always go the way of the crowd.

> A newspaperman walks with the great of many lands, but he must go his own way—right to the end of the road.

Herbert Matthews' kind of man, an individualist inspired by a touch of idealism and self-absorption, was out of style on *The Times* in 1967. The new foreign-news editor, Seymour Topping, did not want super-egos on his staff, nor did Clifton Daniel. Both Topping and Daniel preferred correspondents such as they themselves had been—dispassionate men, reliable, cool. Topping now had Daniel's permission to call home immediately any correspondent who was not functioning in accordance with New York's directives. With swift modern communications and jet airplanes at his disposal, Topping could move his men around the globe like pawns; he did not need nor would he tolerate the old system that had produced such figures as Drew Middleton in London, Harold Callender in Paris, A. C. Sedgwick in Athens, Arnaldo Cortesi in Rome, and Thomas J. Hamilton at the United Nations; and had permitted wide latitude to such roving correspondents as Herbert Matthews.

Under the new system, Topping functioned as a one-man control tower, and it was significant that in 1967 the only dominant correspondents were, like Topping, *former* correspondents who had become editors—Daniel, Salisbury, Rosenthal. Not surprisingly, the overseas expertise was emanating from Forty-third Street. The overseas bureau chiefs had lost their traditional stature, and it also more difficult in 1967 for a correspondent to get a story into *The Times*. Except for the staff in Vietnam, whose stories had top priority, the rest of the staff around the world had been instructed by Topping not to file dispatches each day unless absolutely necessary and to concentrate on "wrap-up" stories that condensed the events of several days. Space was limited, and there was no longer sufficient room for a daily spread of relatively minor government news from fifteen or twenty capitals. Even the Moscow bureau, whose stories had been so prominently played in *The*

Times when the bureau chief had been Topping or Daniel or Salisbury, was now of secondary importance to Saigon's and to the fact that Washington had emerged as the supreme capital of the Western world insofar as *The Times* was concerned. What Harold Wilson or de Gaulle or Aleksei Kosygin was thinking was not at this juncture so important as what Lyndon Johnson was doing or not doing. The big story was not in the major foreign capitals but at home—the American crisis over Vietnam and the Negro; the challenge to authority on the campus and in the street. And so unless a correspondent was in Vietnam—or in the Middle East during a periodic assault; or was, like Henry Tanner, in Paris during a student uprising, or, like Lloyd Garrison, in Biafra during a siege of starvation—unless the correspondent was encircled by death, destruction, or revolution of some sort, he might as well return to the United States, where there was enough tension and violence for everyone.

Perhaps the first *Times*man to rebel against the tighter controls abroad and to recognize the more dramatic opportunities at home was thirty-three-year-old David Halberstam, a tall, dark, low-pressured but very aware journalist who had graduated from Harvard, had worked for a small country paper in Mississippi, and had then moved up to the *Nashville Tennessean,* also writing pieces for *The Reporter.* A few of these magazine pieces were read by Reston, who in 1960 hired him for *The Times'* Washington bureau. Halberstam was moderately happy in Washington, but his true reportorial talent was not fulfilled until he had gone to the Congo in 1961 to cover the fighting there. He worked best when free to follow his own instincts, to pursue his own ideas without the guidance or resistance of an editor. More than any other *Times*man of his generation, Halberstam was in the best tradition of Matthews and Salisbury—to borrow one of Salisbury's self-descriptive phrases, Halberstam had "rats in the stomach." He was a driven, totally involved reporter who was unencumbered by conventionalism or the official version of events, and, like Matthews and Salisbury, he was destined to become controversial, particularly after arriving in Vietnam in 1962.

Halberstam's coverage of the war conveyed little of the optimism that the South Vietnamese leaders and their American "advisers" insistently proclaimed. As Halberstam saw it, the allied contingent was neither making friends, influencing people, nor winning the war in Vietnam. He was not the only reporter who felt this way—there were, among others, Neil Sheehan of the UPI and Malcolm Browne, of the AP, both of whom would later join *The Times*—but Halberstam, whose reporting appeared consistently on page one of *The Times*, became the most conspicuous *bête noire* of the American State Department and the White House. Those skeptical of Halberstam's reports began accusing him of exaggerations, and even some *Times* editors were privately worried during 1963 that the paper once again might be charged with abetting communism. The foreign desk questioned him with sharply worded cables, to which Halberstam responded even more sharply. After the overthrow of the Diem regime, and following the murder of her husband and her brother-in-law, Madame Nhu announced, "Halberstam should be barbecued, and I would be glad to supply the fluid and the match."

While Halberstam's winning a Pulitzer in 1964 quieted much of the professional rankling, he continued to have his personality differences with members of the foreign desk. He had gone too far, too fast; and they missed few opportunities to question his judgment. Halberstam resented many of their cabled queries, and he also became angered when a promised raise was inexplicably held up.

During his next assignment, in Warsaw, he met and married a Polish actress, Elzbieta Tchizevska, further complicating his relationship with the foreign desk: it was now feared that he would write softly about the Communist regime to avoid expulsion from Poland and separation from his wife. Halberstam did the opposite, writing several critical articles about the economic life of the people and of anti-Semitism in Poland, and in

December of 1965 he was expelled on charges of
"slander." When there seemed only mild concern in
New York over his personal welfare, in fact, when he
had heard that a few editors thought that he had
caused his own expulsion by his abrasiveness, Halberstam became even more embittered.

His next assignment was in Paris, where his wife
later joined him, but the stories in Paris bored him,
and there seemed no other foreign assignment with
the reportorial challenge that existed in the United
States. The glamorous era of the foreign correspondent
seemed over, at least for him, and he spent much of his
time in the Paris bureau writing a novel and occasionally
composing a letter to friends in New York that revealed
his frustrations under the present system:

> I am working more for myself than for Punch
> Sulzberger, but if its okay with him its okay with
> me. My attitude right now is pleasantly cavalier:
> the more faced with the prospect of leaving The
> Times, the more convinced I am that in the long
> run it is better for me, that I don't need their
> security, and that I can swim and swim well. . . .
> I have written Abe Rosenthal that I want to return
> to New York, and I hope he can do something
> about it (the correspondence with Daniel has all
> been very pleasant and non-explosive). About
> Daniel: he is I think the epitome of another genera-
> tion and particularly of the other generation on The
> Times, the generation that calls you Mister. He
> believes that this is the best of all possible worlds
> in the best of all possible professions—that there-
> fore it is an honor for you to work for The Times,
> really your privilege, and that it is your honor to
> talk with him, since he is its working embodi-
> ment. . . .
> We had a week with Charlotte Curtis, who is
> now one of the most powerful men on the paper,
> since Daniel values her opinions on everything and
> reads mostly her section (Jesus, in the middle of
> the collections we got a cable from him wanting to
> know *why* purple was the color this year, or some

crap like that). Charlotte and I talked rather endlessly about the future: she kept telling me that
newspaper writing was the only way to write and I
kept insisting that if you stay with it you hit a
point of no return, your talent levels out and
eventually diminishes, and that you retire without
even knowing it. I kept telling her that The Times
simply is not in a position to let me write what I
want to write and that as for magazine writing, if
it comes to that, I will work for a magazine I like
and not one I don't even read, The Times's own
weakly. She suggested I go to Bangkok and I said
fuck Bangkok. Bright, tough little broad. . . .

Halberstam later returned to New York, but even
under Rosenthal he could not gain the freedom to write
and travel around the country as he wished, and as a
result he resigned in 1967 to join the staff of *Harper's*.
The resignation of a young Pulitzer Prize winner was
unsettling to some editors, and Halberstam's departure
may have made conditions more flexible for other correspondents returning to New York. One of them,
J. Anthony Lukas, who had gone to Harvard with
Halberstam and had followed him into the Congo, was
rather gingerly treated upon his return, receiving top
assignments commensurate with his talent. In October
of 1967, Lukas was assigned to delve into the background of an eighteen-year-old girl from Greenwich,
Connecticut, who had been found murdered in New
York City with a hippie boyfriend in a boiler room
in the East Village. The idea for the assignment had
come from Rosenthal, who had a friend who knew
the slain girl's father, but the writing and approach to
the story were uniquely constructed by Anthony
Lukas.

After interviewing the girl's parents in their thirty-
room house in Greenwich, and after hearing her described as a wholesome, well-adjusted product of a
privileged suburban upbringing, Lukas shifted his attention to Greenwich Village, where he spoke with her
hippie friends. They described her life in a dingy hotel,

said that she lived with a number of young men, supported them on marijuana and LSD, and had herself been "freaked out on Methedrine." Lukas' portrait presented the two conflicting views of the girl, a story that *The Times* featured on page one and to which it devoted a full page inside. Even more unusual was the trouble that was taken in the layout of the story: the part dealing with the girl's parents in Connecticut, their opinions and insight into her character, was set in regular type; the version of her as presented by her companions in Greenwich Village was set in italics. *The Times* had rarely in the past made such an artful presentation of a story within its regular news columns, and there was perhaps no feature all year that was more talked about by *Times* readers, particularly those with young daughters living in fashionable suburbs. The article, entitled "The Two Worlds of Linda Fitzpatrick," would win a Pulitzer.

Lukas' Prize was the thirty-fifth Pulitzer won by *The Times*, and it was the first won by a member of the New York staff since Meyer Berger had won it in 1950 for his story about the war veteran who had gone berserk in Camden, New Jersey, and shot thirteen people. The award to Lukas was particularly gratifying to Rosenthal and Gelb, who had been trying to win a Pulitzer for the New York staff since 1963, and had thought that they had previously qualified with such efforts as McCandlish Phillips' profile on the Jewish Nazi, and the article about the thirty-eight people in Queens who had done nothing while a screaming girl was being murdered.

As an assistant managing editor, Rosenthal was now a step removed from the New York staff, but he and Gelb, continuing their close personal friendship, were still a team, consulting during and after working hours on story ideas and approaches to news. Since the cultural staff had recently been reunited with the New York staff, and had been made answerable to the New York editor, complying with Rosenthal's view, there was no endeavor in the city that was off limits to

Gelb's reporters. They could explore the world of the Broadway actor, the Bronx politician, or the Bowery derelict, having only to clear their assignment in advance with one man, Arthur Gelb. Gelb had achieved great scope as an editor and, according to predictions in the newsroom, if Gelb and Rosenthal continued in the future as they had in the past, did not overplay their hand, they would be running the entire News department within a few years. So far Gelb had demonstrated sound judgment as the New York editor, and Rosenthal had worked smoothly with the three other assistant managing editors, including Salisbury. Salisbury's and Rosenthal's duties were divided in such a way as to avoid conflict—Salisbury worked on special assignments for Daniel, helped Emanuel Freedman with recruiting, and assisted in the editing of special sections and supplements; Rosenthal was involved with the more routine day-to-day assignments of the staff at home and abroad, and when Daniel was absent Rosenthal took the managing editor's place at the four o'clock conference. Salisbury was not offended by this: Salisbury did not really care who sat where in the newsroom, just as long as his own independence was not restrained.

Theodore Bernstein, however, did become a bit upset one day after Rosenthal, with Daniel's approval if not encouragement, entered the bullpen to watch Bernstein and the subordinate editors performing their early-evening ritual of making up page one. Bernstein was extremely protective of this prerogative, and he did not want Rosenthal, whose executive potential he had recognized years ago, to now be placed in the position of a star pupil scrutinizing the teacher. When Bernstein confronted Daniel with this, Daniel assured him that there had been no change in policy—Rosenthal had just been observing, but the bullpen would continue to select for the managing editor which stories were worthy of page one. So Bernstein was placated, and he was otherwise generally satisfied with the way things were going in 1967. The same could be said of Salisbury and Rosenthal, Daniel and Catledge. The tension of recent months, the personnel changes and the difficult departure of senior *Times*men, was now fading from the scene and conscience of the institution. Only in Washington did there remain the massive problem of morale and coordination, the problem of Tom Wicker, a tenacious and symbolic standard bearer of one bureau's independence from New York. Supporting Wicker was the redoubtable Reston, and standing in the background, a hoary figure of yesteryear, retired but unretiring, was Arthur Krock.

At eighty, Krock had lost none of his tartness, and he missed few opportunities to express his opinion of the editors in New York. In November of 1967, after the resignation of Defense Secretary Robert McNamara was followed by rumors that McNamara had been eased out of office by a cunning President, Krock remarked in the bureau with a knowing smile, "Well, that's the way it is with large organizations."

James Reston, who was never entirely enamored of Krock's acerbic wit, saw no solution in a hardened cynical attitude toward the editors in New York, although he was no less concerned than Krock by New York's tireless attempt to run the Washington bureau by remote control. Reston, however, preferred at this time to remain a bit above the battle, to mark time and observe the trends. He had done considerable thinking during the last two years about the direction of journalism in general, and *The Times* in particular; he had delivered lectures on journalism at universities and before the Council on Foreign Relations, the latter series forming the basis of Reston's book *The Artillery of the Press*, published in 1967 by Harper & Row. There were moments when Reston felt that the discord within *The Times* was a rather healthy thing—like many great and enduring institutions, *The Times* was undergoing a period of self-analysis, experimentation, seeking to determine whether the techniques of the past were adequate for the future. While Reston was personally protective of the bureau, he was striving to see the Washington–New York issue in more practical and philosophical terms, was attempting to elevate and associate the struggle within *The Times* with something greater, more historically universal and less Byzantine.

Perhaps part of the problem, he thought, was that the world was changing faster than people were able to change themselves, and the leaders in government and the press were being guided by theories and assumptions that had once worked but were now outmoded. *The Times'* editors in New York, and editors everywhere, were possibly in a state of confusion or reappraisal over what news was really important in the Sixties, and how it should be presented. In the era of television, should newspaper editions print less hard news and more interpretation, or vice versa? Should the modern reporter be given more freedom and the editor less, or the reverse? Reston sometimes wondered, during moments that he regarded as slightly heretical, if the world was not becoming too complex and serious a place to be left to the reporting of newspapermen. The United States had been a world leader for two generations during which it had produced a large base of brain power in the universities, the foundations, big business, and other centers—a force comprising numbers of individuals who were as well informed on international and domestic affairs as anyone in the world. And yet, Reston thought, and said in his lectures, they were not sharing with other Americans a great deal of what they knew. Some were, to be sure, and these individuals were in the vanguard of what Reston saw as a new class of public servant, a group operating within the "triangle" of the university-foundation life, the communications media, and the government. They were roving writers, educators, government officials—McGeorge Bundy and Arthur Schlesinger, Jr., John Kenneth Galbraith and Theodore Sorensen, Richard Goodwin and Douglas Cater. But these were only a few of many, and Reston also felt that it was not enough that such men as these wrote occasionally for *The New York Times'* Sunday *Magazine*—he believed that their analysis of current developments should be in the daily paper, perhaps on a special page next to the editorial page.

This idea was considered meritorious in New York, was seen as something that *The Times* might incorporate into its future format if the space could be found, but the suggestion did not address itself to the more immediate issue of the aggressive reporting that New York seemed to want and claimed that it was not getting from the Washington bureau. *The Times* did not need essayists or more columnists, the New York editors felt, but it did need reporters who, untouched by cronyism, would probe into the activities of government more deeply and revealingly. These reporters should not violate the national security, but they should know the difference between the national security and the national interest. Theodore Bernstein had often said that when matters of national security arise in a war situation, or a near-war situation, there is not the slightest question about what course the press should follow; editors cannot have the information or specialized knowledge that would allow them to dispute an official determination that the country's safety might be jeopardized. But matters of national interest, Bernstein believed, were different: they may well be political issues, and one man's opinion of what is in the nation's interest may be as good as another's. The press had to keep in mind that the President himself plays different roles on different occasions, Bernstein had said; sometimes he is the Constitutional Commander-in-Chief, sometimes he is the country's political leader. The press had to draw the line between the national security and the national interest, and then to act appropriately, Bernstein had said, and it should not be swayed by outside judgments, including those of the President himself.

In principle, Reston agreed. It was in the application of these principles that differences arose, that sentiment and ego came into play, that the lifetime's experience of each editor produced a variegated vision. Reston saw New York as tradition-bound despite its many changes. It was a vast cumbersome operation that was often archaic in its attitude toward news. The bullpen reflected the values of Bernstein fundamental-

ists, desk dons who had risen through, or become influenced by, the desk maze and the value judgments
that were formulated during World War II. These
men had become conditioned to responding to happenings, particularly if they were dramatic, rather than
to the causes of happenings. The deskmen too often
regarded the causes as speculative, and therefore not
hard news enough for page one or top priority treatment within the paper.

The Times was allowing considerable space for food
recipes and society parties, and it was also devoting
about 40 percent of the daily space allotment to business and financial information, at the expense of some
space that might be more wisely devoted to exploring
what Reston considered the affairs of the mind—the
world's *thinking*, not merely its deeds, for here was
where the rebellions, revolutions, and wars began.
But the entire American press, not only *The Times*
was predisposed to minimizing the conflict of ideas in
favor of the conflict in the streets, Reston stated in a
lecture, without relating the second to the first. Reporters raced from crisis to crisis, like firemen, and
then left when the blaze went out. Newspapers had
sent hundreds of correspondents to Vietnam after the
big war had begun, and the front pages were filled
each day with their reports, simultaneously crowding
out news reports from the rest of the world; but sufficient numbers of correspondents had not been sent into
such inflammatory areas *before* the holocaust, when
reporting might have alerted corrective political action.
In Cuba the crumbling of the Batista government had
made headlines, but the social inequality and unrest
under previous regimes had been inadequately displayed in the press, Reston thought, although the exact
solution to these journalistic shortcomings was not
entirely clear even to Reston.

This seemed obvious to anyone who read his speeches
carefully. While they were lucidly written and raised
the most important questions, they did not have the
most important answers. In some instances there seemed
to be no answers, certainly none that Reston could

completely accept and also remain consistent with his own sense of responsibility to the United States government's best interests at home and abroad. This was the dilemma of James Reston. He recognized idealism but he was ultimately influenced, as were the statesmen that he so carefully wrote about, by the realities of Washington. Reston could insist, as he did in one of his lectures, that a better-informed American public was more essential than ever before, adding that the rising power of the United States in world affairs, the unprecedented power in the Presidency, demanded not a more compliant press but one that was more critical and less nationalistic. And yet Reston himself had not exemplified this spirit during his many years in Washington, feeling at times that it was obligatory to conceal from the public certain controversial truths that might have shattered whatever illusion of honesty was left in Washington in the Sixties. He had not only encouraged *The Times'* restraint during the Bay of Pigs coverage but he had secretly known for a year that the United States was flying high-altitude planes (the U-2) over Russia from a base in Pakistan, and until one was shot down *The Times* had not reported the information. It was a proper decision, Reston was sure, for it was in the national interest to protect American intelligence operations. The CIA was essential to the preservation of democracy, he believed, although he would phrase it more delicately. Since this was not an ideal world, there were occasions when Reston and *The Times* would have to be an accomplice to a White House lie. It was complicated, Reston might admit, and was no doubt unacceptable to student idealists picketing a dean's office. But since neither Washington nor Moscow nor Peking was being ruled by holy men, moral accommodations had to be made. The public had a right to know—up to a point. A premature publication of the movement of American ships and men to intercept the Soviet ships bringing missiles to Havana in the second Cuban crisis of 1962, Reston said in one of his lectures, could easily have interfered with what proved to be a spectacularly successful exercise of American power and diplomacy.

However, in the case of Vietnam, the Washington press corps learned too late of President Kennedy's decision—supported by Rusk and McNamara, and opposed by Undersecretary of State George W. Ball—to increase the American military "presence" in Vietnam from a few hundred "advisers" to a force of more than 15,000—the first big step in the American escalation. If the press had known of this meeting at the time, and had published stories about it, Reston guessed that all the headlines and leads would have highlighted the three key points: the decision to increase the American force to 15,000, the dispute among the Presidential advisers about escalation, and the fact that they were aware, according to Reston, that this move might result in a commitment of 300,000 Americans to Vietnam. Congressional clamor and national debate would have undoubtedly followed, and it might have resulted in a reversal of the decision and the saving of thousands of lives and of billions of dollars. Instead, the press in 1961 naively reported that the Kennedy administration was planning only a "modest" increase in American advisory help to South Vietnam, and in retrospect the government's conduct seemed to Reston like willful deception, and he also believed that the subsequent escalation was achieved almost by stealth. But he did not dwell on this subject during his lectures to the Council on Foreign Relations, and nobody knew precisely what he would have done had someone leaked to him the full facts of the Kennedy meeting. One could only presume, on the basis of Reston's philosophy as revealed in his work and conduct, that he would have kept the secret.

Reston was more sensitive to the awesome delicacy of White House decisions than any editor in New York. He wished to soften the sound of national alarm and to spare the President any unnecessary personal nagging. He thought that the press had been unfair with Lyndon Johnson during the summer of 1964 with its "silly" stories about Johnson's speeding along a Texas highway while drinking beer from a paper cup; and Reston, who had been sitting in Johnson's office when an aide had brought in a magazine's account of the incident, remembered how upset Johnson had become after reading it. Turning to Reston, Johnson had remarked, forlornly, that his one main ambition was to "unify the country," but he doubted whether he could do so because of the determination of some hostile elements of the press to portray him as "an irresponsible hick." Reston had tried to disagree, but Johnson would not be interrupted, wondering aloud whether the nation was "far enough away from Appomattox" for a Southern President to be able to unify the country. Reston conceded that Johnson had had problems with the press, but denied that it was antipathetic to Southerners, adding that there were enough real problems in the South without inventing new ones. Johnson had remained unconvinced. He had long felt that the Eastern liberal press establishment was incapable of total objectivity to such men as himself. Then he told Reston that the real question he had to decide, before the start of the 1964 convention, was not whether Robert F. Kennedy was a likely running mate but whether he, Lyndon Johnson, should agree to be nominated for President under circumstances where he did not think he had a chance of unifying the country. Reston had left the White House that day feeling both dejected and astonished.

It was not possible to live on the edge of power for more than two decades in Washington, as Reston had, and not to identify in some way with the President, to be affected by his conditions, troubled by his doubts. Although Reston had regularly left Washington and had traveled around the country, and back and forth to Europe, his views and sensitivities were pivoted around Washington. If Reston had not carried such weight with the Sulzberger family, he might have been removed from Washington years ago and been transferred to another city or capital, as other bureau chiefs had been rotated in the recent past on the assumption that they had become too cozy or familiar with the landscape and the leaders. But *The Times* traditionally had treated its bureau in Washington differently than it had those in other cities. The Washington bureau was the paper's principal embassy, and its chief was the Sulzbergers' ambassador to the White House. Ever since the days of Ochs, the ruling family had preferred that its Washington bureaumen be on familiar and friendly terms with those who occupied the seat of power in the capital, and this was at the heart of the New York editors' problem with Washington. Ochs, contrary to his slogans about independence, probably wanted cronyism to exist between his Washington chief and the leaders in the government. Ochs had not made a fortune out of the newspaper business by offending the mighty, crusading for reforms, espousing the causes of the have-nots against the haves. Ochs had refused to upbraid Oulahan, Krock's predecessor, despite complaints from the New York editors that Oulahan was adoring of President Wilson. While Krock had been considerably less adoring of Roosevelt, it also happened that Ochs and Arthur Hays Sulzberger had privately shared much of Krock's distaste for the President, who felt likewise about *The Times*. The paper's editorial page had been critical of every administration at one time or another, but the reporting out of Washington had invariably been sensitive to the system, and it was the reporting, the subtle shadings and emphasis, that made the greater impact with readers. And so while John Oakes's editorials condemned Lyndon Johnson's policies, and while such New York editors as Salisbury called for sharper reporting, the Ochsian heirs, having it both ways, maintained their traditional ties with the Establishment through such couriers as James Reston. Although the bureau had now lost its autonomy and although Reston was no longer its chief, he was still the Sulzbergers' main link to the capital, and no editor in New York had the power to transfer him or to change a word that he wrote. Reston's writing would have pleased Ochs, the family was sure, as it had pleased them. Hope sprang eternally from Reston, attracting Iphigene Sulzberger to his vision years ago. Now, during her son's apprenticeship at the

top, she had remained somewhat silent, and the elder
Sulzberger was regrettably inactive; but Reston continued to respond to *The Times* and the government in
his gentle fervent way, never forgetting, as Ochs had
not, his ultimate and similar obligations to both, and
not becoming overly distressed by the detours that
both now seemed to be taking. It was a period of dissent and change everywhere, within *The Times*, within
the nation, and as New York's editors would look dourly
at the government Reston would write spirited columns
on weekends from Fiery Run, Virginia, that would be
printed on Oakes's dovish editorial page, which was
adorned with an eagle. When *The Times* would publish a series of articles out of Washington revealing that
the government was selling more arms around the
world than any other nation, while government officials
were making speeches deploring the international arms
race, Reston would attempt to put things in perspective
by reminding readers that the Russians were selling
arms, too, and that it was in the "vital interest" of the
United States to maintain control of the Middle East
oil wells against possible aggression by Soviet-armed
Arabs. When one United States government dove had
leaked to the press the fact that American escalation of
the bombing of North Vietnam was imminent, Reston
became upset by the disclosure, and he wrote, "Public
discussion of the wisdom or stupidity of extending the
bombing to the populous areas of these two cities
[Hanoi and Haiphong] is fair enough, but public disclosure of the timing of operational military plans is
not."

Sometimes Reston thought that the influence of the
press was exaggerated; at other times he seemed not so
sure. It could not be denied that Herbert Matthews
had influenced Castro's career, that Halberstam had
caused ripples in South Vietnam and Salisbury in
North Vietnam. Television's dramatic films of the club-
bing of black marchers by Alabama state troopers in
Selma had suddenly aroused millions of Americans,
sending thousands of sympathizers into Selma in the
next few days to support the marchers, to inspire

THE KINGDOM AND THE POWER

new legislation, and to stir temporarily in America a national guilt and concern that would then fade as Stokely Carmichael, Rap Brown, and other racists, black and white, would dominate the news. Reston himself had on occasions during his career encouraged or inhibited political decisons by his words in *The Times;* and in the *Time* magazine cover story about him it was said that he sometimes planted one of his own ideas with government officials and, after being assured that it would be discussed, he wrote in *The Times* about the idea that was under consideration without hinting that he was its originator. There is nothing unusual about this in Washington, where some journalists have been known to write speeches for their favorite senators and to serve as unofficial advisers on policy, and where a large portion of the press corps's identity with the national interest had become so deep-rooted during and just after World War II, when Reston began his rise, that it is now often impossible to see a sharp line of demarcation between the role of the press and that of the government. In a capital where there were more journalists, about 1,400, than Congressmen, and where the columnists may remain in power for decades while the politicians come and go, there is an understandable desire on the part of politicians to cooperate with the press, to flatter and possibly confuse with confidence those journalists who are the most important or critical—but one result of close cooperation between the press and the government is that they often end up protecting the interests of one another, and not of the public that they presume to represent.

Reston saw the situation from various angles: he believed that the President had, perhaps, too much power, and that the press had to help counterbalance him; but Reston also believed that such criticism could also be excessive, as it might have been in the case of President Johnson, encouraging dissent throughout the nation, aiding the enemy. While Lippmann had argued that it was fallacious reasoning to consider that a divided public opinion would have any effect on the enemy, Reston thought that there was something to be said for both sides—for both the danger and the necessity of criticism. Reston, as Murray Kempton had once described him, was not so much a man of the left or right as he was a man of *The Times*.

Now in 1967 Reston saw himself locked in a debate with his colleagues in New York over the priorities and traditions of news coverage. Reston was urging more reportorial freedom, New York wanted tighter controls. New York's definition of *news* was often contrary to that of Reston and Wicker; Reston saw the world as revolving around Washington, while Catledge, Daniel, and the bullpen saw Washington in relationship to New York and the world. The place where the two factions in the debate might agree was that the modern newspaper could not stand still, but the proper course was questionable. Reston believed that the new role of the press was in the field of thoughtful explanation. *The Times* and other newspapers had already begun to rely more heavily on news analyses, articles that ran adjacent to news stories and interpreted controversial facts and statements, and counterbalanced them with the views of other authoritative spokesmen. Turner Catledge had been an early advocate of the news-analysis article, recognizing a need for modernizing Ochs's definition of objectivity, but Catledge later became disturbed, perhaps more so than Reston, by what he believed to be occasional abuses of this innovation. Catledge had not wanted the news analysis to become a reflection of a reporter's opinion, for opinions were to appear only on the editorial page and in the critics' columns. And so memos from New York warning reporters about opinions were sent to all the bureaus, which raised some doubts in a few reporters' minds about the sincerity of Catledge's previous exhortations about brighter writing.

In the Washington bureau, Tom Wicker pinned to the bulletin board one of Catledge's statements that included the comment that responsibility for maintaining *The Times*' traditional fairness "rests with the desks as well as with the reporters." This, one Washington reporter said, was a clever maneuver by the cagey Catledge to refuel the old antagonisms between reporters and copyreaders, keeping everybody off balance. But Reston had not felt that Catledge had a personal motive, preferring to believe that *The Times'* intramural differences were not really a reflection of personalities but were a genuine disagreement on principles.

Reston continued to think this way with regard to the New York editors through 1967, but in 1968 there would occur an incident that would suddenly disturb this conviction. That was when Reston would learn that New York had found the man to replace Wicker and to take over the Washington bureau.

20

JAMES Lloyd Greenfield, an agile and urbane dark-haired man of forty-three, cared a great deal about how he looked and about the impression he was making on each new person that he met. He remembered names, was always attentive, was often complimentary. His suits were well tailored and of excellent fabric, usually set off by a colorful shirt and a silk handkerchief sprouting from his breast pocket. He revealed a sense of humor through an easy Midwestern accent, and he reminded one somehow of the successful executives shown in the television commercials, the well-groomed youthful men being served martinis by blond stewardesses in the friendly skies of United; which is to say that there was nothing carelessly arranged about Jim Greenfield, that his taste was contemporary, that he symbolized the sort that large organizations were proud to display in public—men who did not quite get to the very top but who were often more presentable than those who did. Greenfield had worked hard to get to where he was, however, and the emphasis on his manner and appearance is not to demean his character but merely to suggest that he had cultivated what a more uncaring man, a presumptuous or ruthless man, might have been unlikely to cultivate. James Greenfield liked people, wanted to be liked in turn, and he was.

He had been born in Cleveland, the son of a job-printer and a former regular army sergeant, and his home life had been unhappy, particularly with regard to his father. Forced to shift for himself at an early age, working at fourteen in the office of the *Cleveland Press,* living with friends or relatives, Greenfield prematurely developed an adaptability to new people and places. He obtained a scholarship to Harvard, earning extra money by working in the university's news bureau. After his graduation in 1949 he joined the Voice of America, serving in New York and in the Far East. During the Korean War he became a correspondent for *Time,* remaining in the *Time* organization for ten years, moving from Tokyo to New Delhi, from London to Washington, acquiring a taste for the better life through a liberal expense account, meeting people around the world who would be his friends for years. One person whom he met in India, in 1955, was *The Times'* correspondent Abe Rosenthal. They were immediately companionable, and they sometimes traveled together on assignments through India and once into Ceylon.

When they were both transferred to bureaus in Europe—Greenfield to London, Rosenthal to Warsaw—they and their wives continued to remain in touch. In 1962, after Greenfield had spent a year in Washington as the chief diplomatic correspondent of the *Time-Life* bureau, he resigned to join the State Department as a public-affairs official. When Rosenthal visited Washington, he saw Greenfield; when Greenfield was in New York, he saw Rosenthal, and through Rosenthal he came to know Clifton Daniel, Arthur Gelb, and Punch and Carol Sulzberger.

James Greenfield left the State Department in 1965 to work with Pierre Salinger in Los Angeles as an executive with Continental Airlines, but this, he soon discovered, was not really what he wanted to do. He hoped to return to journalism, and during a business trip to New York, having lunch one day with Rosenthal at Sardi's, Rosenthal mentioned the possibility of Greenfield's joining *The Times.* When Greenfield expressed interest, Rosenthal discussed it with Daniel. In June of 1967, Greenfield came to New York as an assistant metropolitan editor under Arthur Gelb. Gelb had at least a half-dozen assistant editors on the local staff, and it was several days before a desk for Greenfield could be wedged into the tight fleet of gray metal that surrounded Gelb near the front of the room behind the silver microphone; but it was finally managed after the upanchoring and rearranging of a few other desks, and Greenfield's own graceful manner facilitated his entry. He did not appear to be jockeying for position among his peers, but rather he conversed with them and with the staff in a casual, pleasant way; and when he began to make suggestions, after a few weeks, he did so with delicacy and tact.

Rosenthal did not know specifically where Greenfield might best serve the paper, but he gradually came to regard him as perhaps the most imaginative subordinate editor in the newsroom, an idea man in ways quite different from Gelb. Gelb's ideas were largely attuned to the cultural or social life of New York City, while Greenfield's interests encompassed the nation and overseas; and not only those countries in which he had lived, but others to which he had been drawn by his journalist's curiosity. Greenfield was very well informed about the student protest movement in America, a problem that he had studied during his years in the State Department; after he had left Washington for the airlines job in Los Angeles, he had continued to remain intimately interested in the thinking on campuses and in such hippie centers as Haight-Ashbury, which he had personally visited. He knew about the latest fads, the philosophies, and the language of the young, and he was one of the first *Times* editors to perceive the hippie movement as national in scope, spreading from San Francisco to Madison Avenue, and he encouraged the wider coverage of teen-age preoccupations

Greenfield's personal knowledge of the inner workings of Washington was regarded as a significant asset by some senior editors in New York. He provided them with a check against Wicker's bureaumen. Greenfield had many contacts within the government and among those departed New Frontiersmen who hoped to regain power someday behind Senator Robert F. Kennedy; from these and other sources, Greenfield often received tips on matters that the Johnson loyalists were not anxious to discuss. If this information was not always substantial enough to produce major stories, it often added to the dimension or understanding of the news that was available. When the American ship *Pueblo* was captured by the North Koreans, Greenfield obtained information that described some of the drama and the scurrying on deck just before the ship's radio went silent and the crew was captured—the sort of detail that New York had long claimed it was not getting out of Washington. But at this time there was no plan to move Greenfield from his present position to Washington. Greenfield was to remain in New York for an indefinite period, and his first important assignment was to help in the production of the experimental afternoon newspaper that Punch Sulzberger had been contemplating ever since the disappearance of the *World Journal Tribune*.

Sulzberger was not the only publisher interested in the afternoon newspaper market in New York; the owners of the New York *Daily News* were also exploring the possibilities, as was the publisher of New York's Spanish-language *El Diario–La Prensa*, although these men, like Sulzberger, were extremely secretive about their projects. The only thing known about *The Times'* venture was that it would be six columns wide and would somewhat resemble the *Observer* in London. Rosenthal was put in charge of a twelve-man committee to supervise the first edition; he was assisted by a bullpen editor named Lawrence Hauck, by Arthur Gelb and James Greenfield, by numbers of other deskmen, makeup men, and reporters, all assembled in a temporary newsroom on the eleventh floor behind locked doors and windows that were covered to prevent outside peeping. There the plans were made for columns, features, and the entire news format, while outside the building representatives of the advertising and circulation departments conducted surveys to estimate the income such a newspaper might expect in New York.

After weeks of work and careful planning by Rosenthal, a dummy edition was laid out and was printed in the subbasement of the *Times* building at 5:30 one morning. Guards protected the stack of freshly printed forty-page papers from the random perusal or theft by outsiders. Then later in the day the papers were delivered to the office of the vice-president, Ivan Veit, where forty-five copies were numbered and distributed to a select list of executives through the building. A few days later all the copies were recalled, but one was missing. Tom Mullaney, editor of the Financial-Business department, had locked his copy in his desk drawer before leaving the building for the weekend; when he returned on Monday he discovered that his drawer had been jimmied; his copy was gone.

The response to the pilot paper, and to a second sample, was mixed—some executives liked it, some did not, some wavered and waited, others who had originally opposed the idea continued to oppose it, asserting that a second newspaper would adversely affect *The Times*. Sulzberger had initially been excited by the project, but the more he thought about it, the more reluctant he became. A second newspaper would require the creation of a philosophy that was different from *The Times'*, but was not inconsistent with it. There was also the problem of housing a second staff when *The Times* was having difficulty in fitting its present staff into the building, and there was the question of whether there was sufficient advertising revenue to support a new paper at a time when production and labor costs were higher than ever. Finally, there was doubt in Sulzberger's mind that he and the other top executives could divide their energies without jeopardizing *The Times*; and so he announced that he was suspending the afternoon operation. Since the other New York publishers had come to the same decision, the city was left for the time being with only one afternoon newspaper, the *New York Post*.

Rosenthal was very disappointed by Sulzberger's conclusion. Rosenthal had been very enthusiastic and optimistic about the new enterprise, and it had also represented his first major undertaking since he had become an assistant managing editor, and now he interpreted its rejection as a failure on his part. The other executives did not feel this way, at least did not express it; indeed, the afternoon editions had been so closely guarded that relatively few *Times*men were aware of Rosenthal's involvement and hopes. Nevertheless, he was upset—his smooth, quick climb had been interrupted, and Sulzberger's decision had hit him almost simultaneously with another aggravating bit of news. A book that he had coauthored with Gelb, a lengthy study of Daniel Burros, the Jewish Nazi who had committed suicide after reading McCandlish Phillips' article, had been unenthusiastically reviewed in certain periodicals, including *The Times'* own Sunday "Book Review." Almost as disconcerting as the review was *The Times'* choice of the reviewer—Nat Hentoff, a novelist and critic who had previously written disparagingly in the *Village Voice* about Rosenthal's editorship of the New York staff. The *Voice*, in fact, had sharpened its sights on *The Times* with Rosenthal's rise, or so it seemed to him, carping at such *Times* exclusives as the Harlem "Blood Brothers" story, and once printing in the *Voice* an anonymous article by a former *Times*man who blamed Rosenthal for the low morale in the newsroom and other changes for the worse.

Why the *Times* "Book Review" would send the Rosenthal-Gelb book, entitled *One More Victim*, to anyone on the *Voice* was both mystifying and infuriating to Rosenthal and Gelb, and they could not help but wonder if it had been done out of spite by some subordinate editor on the eighth floor with a malicious sense of humor. If such were the case, a book editor could rather easily fulfill his intentions: knowing his stable of reviewers, knowing their literary leanings and vanities and pet grievances, their tendencies when dealing with certain authors or subjects or political philosophies, the editor had merely to match a particular book with a particular reviewer to get an almost certain result. This game of literary crossbreeding for in-

vidious ends was not so possible on the lower levels of
the Sunday "Book Review" when Markel had been the
high potentate: in those days an effort had been made
to shepherd the books of important *Times*men, or
books by friends of *The Times*, into the hands of
genial reviewers. But now the *Times* "Book Review,"
no doubt tired of its bland old image under Markel and
also following the more rapier style of *The New York
Review of Books*, was trying to forge a sharper product.
John Simon, known as "Bad John Simon" in New
York cultural circles, was back writing for *The Times*,
his dispute with Markel a forgotten issue. *The Times*
had recently published a number of reviews that had
drawn protests from readers claiming that the critics'
well-known political positions and prejudices precluded
any chance of a fair review (e.g., Sidney Hook's review of Dr. Meyer Zeligs' *Friendship and Fratricide:
An Analysis of Whittaker Chambers and Alger Hiss*).
And *The Times* was also publishing critiques that
seemed more unjustifiedly venomous than any in the
past (e.g., Wilfrid Sheed's assault on William Styron's
The Confessions of Nat Turner).

With regard to the Rosenthal-Gelb book, the assignment to Hentoff had been made by a bright young
iconoclast who had recently joined the "Review"—a
man who read the *Voice* and who, in the absence of
Francis Brown, head of the department, had sent the
book to Hentoff with an awareness that the review
might produce a bit of flack. Although no sanctions
were levied against the impolitic editor, it was a fairly
good bet that, among the 6,354 employees of *The
Times*, his future was not now the brightest; nor
would his erudition and literary judgment henceforth
be considered so trustworthy as, for example, that of
Eliot Fremont-Smith, the daily critic, who had written
favorably about *One More Victim*.

Fremont-Smith, a neat and tweedy man of thirty-
eight, had come a long way from his own days as a
book critic for the *Village Voice*. A graduate of Anti-
och, with graduate work at Columbia and Yale, he had
started out on *The Times* in the Sunday "Book Review"

but had moved to the position of daily book critic in 1965, assuming the role of chief literary tastemaker that had been the function of Orville Prescott. It is remarkable on *The Times* how the title makes the man, and how the deprivation of that title suddenly does the opposite: Orville Prescott for years had been the terror of the book industry, an arbiter whose every approving nod could supposedly sell a thousand books; and yet when Prescott was replaced as the principal critic by Fremont-Smith, and although Prescott in semiretirement continued to review books in *The Times* and elsewhere, there was suddenly no longer fear nor felicity over the pronouncements of Prescott. However, Fremont-Smith, upon inheriting the mantle, soared to oracular heights; his words were reprinted in publishers' ads, he was the brahmin of Brentano's, the literary guide to ladies in Great Neck. Like his predecessor, he received more attention and earned more money from writing about other people's books than he probably could have from his own. Worse, he might never know if he could write his own. A critic spends his best years reading other men's words in quiet rooms, refining his own taste, making greater demands on his contemporaries, and most critics have neither the time, nor perhaps the nerve, to be tested themselves—their taste is possibly too good for their own good. The critic also knows that as a critic he has made enemies, and should he venture forth with a book of his own, they will be waiting in the wings to see that he gets his due.

So it is a rather vexatious life for the *Times* critic who writes well and who nurtures secret ambitions to gamble on his talent. His choice is to step down from his pedestal and risk being at the mercy of such men as he had been, or to try to play it safe within the House of Ochs, hoping that he will not be adversely affected by executive changes and will not lose touch with contemporary taste in literature, as it appeared that Prescott had done in his final years. Prescott had become a white-haired gentleman who fancied the traditional and who seemed offended by the literary outcroppings and droppings of the mid-Sixties, and this had hastened the appearance of his successor. Bright-eyed, sharp, *engagé*, an astute individual who knew better than to send a *Times*man's book to Nat Hentoff, Eliot Fremont-Smith was the sort of modern critic that Clifton Daniel wanted—a versatile journalist who could write an interesting and intelligent review, could carve with the best, and could parry and tiptoe when a situation seemed ticklish, as perhaps it was when the book by Svetlana Alliluyeva had been scheduled for review. Fremont-Smith had handled it well, not dismissing the work as a nonbook that had been trumpeted in the West for its propaganda value, but rather rhapsodizing the fact that Stalin's daughter was indeed alive and safely on American shores. In another column, reviewing *The News Media* by John Hohenberg, Fremont-Smith managed to work in the opinion that while criticism of the press was desirable, and while influential criticism was lacking, the particular brand of press coverage exhibited in the *Village Voice* was not the answer. The *Voice*, he wrote, "appears increasingly to have its own personal and political ax to grind, and is probably counter-influential"—a sentence that did him no harm with the front office.

As the emergence of Fremont-Smith had caused *Times* readers to forget Orville Prescott, so did the new theater critic, Clive Barnes, make readers forget Stanley Kauffmann and, to a degree, even Walter Kerr. Shortly after Kerr had replaced Kauffmann as the daily drama critic, and after the disappearance of the *World Journal Tribune*, there was great concern both on Broadway and within *The Times* about the excessive power of *The Times'* single critic; and it was Kerr who suggested that the paper have two drama critics—one who would review plays for the daily edition, the other who would write a roundup every week for the Sunday drama page. Kerr, wishing to take a longer view of the theater, volunteered for the Sunday assignment, and he was replaced on the daily beat by Clive Barnes, a short, bouncy Englishman of thirty-nine who, though primarily a dance critic for seventeen years, was very knowledgeable about the theater. Barnes was also sufficiently energetic to handle both ballet and drama criticism; he had insisted, in fact, that he be allowed to retain his position as a ballet critic, dance being his overwhelming passion, and he contemplated a schedule whereby he would attend most Broadway first nights and ballet second nights, altering the routine on occasions by attending, as Stanley Kauffmann had done, the final Broadway previews.

It was somehow hoped that the combination of Barnes and Kerr would split the power of the drama chair and provide readers with a divergent view of the theater. But the new arrangement did nothing of the sort—it merely shifted the daily spotlight away from Walter Kerr to Clive Barnes. Kerr's weekend reviews sometimes appeared a week or ten days after an opening, and they lacked the immediacy of Barnes' quick appraisals. No matter what Kerr wrote in his weekend column, the verdict was in, *The Times* had spoken. Another reason that the focus had shifted to Barnes was his more lively and lucid prose style. Since leaving the *Herald Tribune* for *The Times*, Kerr's style seemed to have lost some of its edge and vivacity; it was as if, in coming to *The Times*, he had been affected by the increased power, the awesome responsibility; the weight of the institution seemed to be pressing upon him. Clive Barnes, however, had not worked in the shadow of the *Times* building for years; had, in fact, known very little about *The New York Times* when it had first sought to hire him in London. Barnes had occasionally seen copies of the paper on London newsstands and in the offices of British publications, but what he had seen was the slim, unimpressive overseas edition, and he had not become aware of *The Times'* full influence until he arrived in New York.

Nevertheless, being a man who took neither himself nor his surroundings too seriously, Barnes continued to do what he had done before, which was to write about a great many things at great speed, pounding a typewriter with two tireless fingers, relying on his instinctive judgments. And this style had an instant freshness; his intellectuality seemed brilliantly dashed off and not intended to be ex cathedra. Barnes was witty and clever, and this helped him in his delicate task on *The Times:* instead of condemning a play in an exacting manner, as Kauffmann might have done, Barnes was capable of treading lightly, of adroitly conveying two things at once, of sometimes both praising and criticizing a production in a single sentence, thus preserving his own integrity and perhaps a bit of the box office. In reviewing the Broadway production of Joseph Heller's *We Bombed in New Haven*, Barnes wrote:

> If I was forced to a judgment I would call it a bad play any good playwright should be proud to have written, and any good audience fascinated to see.

In Barnes' appraisal of two of Harold Pinter's short plays, "Tea Party" and "The Basement," he wrote:

> To some extent—and please do not let me put you off from going, for these plays are exquisitely exciting—these are minor Pinter. But Pinter is one of the most important English-speaking playwrights since O'Neill, and minor Pinter is better than major almost anyone else.

There was also working in *The Times'* Cultural-News department at this time another critic who was gaining wide attention—a dark-eyed, dark-haired, determinedly dowdy young woman of twenty-nine named Renata Adler. Born in Milan of American parents, a graduate of Bryn Mawr, Miss Adler had attended the Sorbonne and had received a master's degree in comparative literature at Harvard. Prior to her joining *The Times* as its film critic in November of 1967, she had spent five years on the staff of *The New Yorker*, writing on a variety of subjects—the clamorous existence of New York disc jockeys, the Civil Rights march in Alabama, a New Left convention in Chicago; "Talk" pieces, and occasional reviews on films and books, the most memorable of which was a merciless vivisection of the work of novelist Herbert Gold. That Gold could have continued to be a productive writer after that review was an indication of rare resolve on his part; and that Miss Adler, who in person seems so disarmingly sympathetic and tentative, could have written the review was a revelation of another sort.

Miss Adler's work in *The New Yorker* had attracted the attention of Clifton Daniel, Harrison Salisbury, and other editors, but they had been unable to interest her in joining *The Times* until they had offered her the position of film critic, replacing Bosley Crowther, who had held the job for twenty-seven years. Crowther was still in fine health at sixty-three, but the editors believed that contemporary films required a more youthful observer, and thus Renata Adler was hired and Crowther was named a critic-emeritus. Emeritus is a gloomy word at *The Times*, and within a year he had retired from the paper to become an executive consultant for Columbia Pictures.

Miss Adler quickly became, as Crowther had been in his final months, a very controversial critic: Crowther's protest mail had largely concerned his failure to appreciate the symbolic significance of the casual mayhem in *Bonnie and Clyde*, while Miss Adler was regarded in the entertainment industry as priggish and passionless about films. According to *Variety*, she was happy with only two of the first twenty-seven films she reviewed (*Charlie Bubbles* and *The Two of Us*); she had reservations about such widely acclaimed productions as *The Graduate* and *In Cold Blood*, and one producer spent $6,000 for a full-page ad in *The Times* to question her taste after she had panned one of his films. The ad strongly implied that she did not really like films, a contention that she denied to a reporter from *Newsweek:* "I like movies and I like bad movies but that doesn't mean I have to say they're good."

The reaction to her criticism, however, seemed to upset her in the beginning, and when a free-lance writer sought her cooperation to do a personality profile on her for a magazine, she pleaded that the idea be postponed, explaining that she would probably be fired in the near future. But the editors at this point had no such intentions. While recognizing her considerable influence over moviegoers, particularly in the foreign or art-house market, she did not have, like Barnes, the power to make or break a production, and *The Times'* editors were also in agreement that Miss Adler wrote very well and entertainingly about subjects that often failed to entertain. In reviewing a United Artists release, *The Wicked Dreams of Paula Schultz*, in January of 1968, she wrote:

> Even if your idea of a good time is to watch a lot of middle-aged Germans, some of them very fat, all reddening, grimacing, perspiring, and falling over Elke Sommer, I think you ought to skip "The Wicked Dreams of Paula Schultz," because this first film of the year is so unrelievedly awful in such a number of uninteresting ways . . . [it] is a bit of bumbling, color pornography, a little nude film that lost its way on 42d Street and drifted on over to the Astor.

So Renata Adler passed her trial period at *The Times* and became the latest in a line of young journalists bringing sophistication to the news columns of *The Times*, fulfilling one of Daniel's aims as the managing editor.

As Clifton Daniel began his fourth year in that position, he could properly take pride not only in the more lively coverage of the arts, and, of course, society, but also in the better reportage emanating from other special departments. The decision to appoint Robert Lipsyte as a sports columnist, alternating with Arthur Daley, had brought a smooth literary touch to sports writing that had been missing in New York's morning newspapers since the disappearance of the *Herald Tribune* and Red Smith. Daniel had also played a role in *The Times'* better obituary writing, having assigned a dedicated specialist named Alden Whitman to the task. Fred M. Hechinger, installed as head of the Education-News department, had succeeded after other men in that position had not. Tom Mullaney had run the Financial-Business department admirably since the retirement of Jack Forrest a few years before; and the department that decides which wedding and engagement pictures will appear in *The Times* was under the capable jurisdiction of a status-conscious, unbribable man named Russell Edwards.

The foreign, national, and local staffs were clearly under the authority of New York, and Daniel seemed more self-assured now than he had in several months. The ungraceful dismissal of Kauffmann, a disturbing experience for Daniel, and been superseded by the success of Daniel's discovery, Clive Barnes.

Corporate life had seemed better for Daniel, in fact, since the triumphant return of his friend Salisbury from Hanoi in January of 1967; and while Daniel's relationship with Punch Sulzberger was not as warm as both men might have hoped, they had gotten along reasonably well through 1967, and with the arrival of 1968, Daniel was fairly certain of his place in the hierarchy. Catledge was still lingering in the background, but the executive editor had done considerable traveling of late, and one *Times* reporter who had visited New Orleans had brought back word that Catledge was building a home there. Perhaps Catledge was closer to retirement than most executives thought.

The only unresolved and pressing matter in the newsroom at this point was what to do about the Washington bureau chief. The 1968 political campaigns were already beginning to accelerate, and Wicker would be very busy with his column and often out of the capital; if there was ever a proper moment for Wicker to relinquish the bureau to another man with more time for administrative details, that moment was now. But, as in the past, there appeared to be no acceptable replacement for him. Daniel and most other New York executives, though not Rosenthal, were still resistant to Max Frankel, and no one else in Washington seemed qualified. In New York there had been hints dropped in Rosenthal's direction, but Rosenthal had not been anxious to vacate the executive mainstream for Washington, and Salisbury was probably still too controversial a subject in Washington to be able to function agreeably there. The same might be said of the chief London correspondent, Anthony Lewis, whom the Washington bureaumen remembered unsentimentally. If Lewis were given Wicker's title, it might result in the resignation of Frankel, among others; Frankel had done very well in covering the White House this year, and regardless of the reservations that Daniel, Catledge, and others had about Frankel's administrative capacities, they did not wish to lose Frankel's services as a reporter.

So the situation seemed almost unsolvable. Wicker, who possibly did not even want the job at this point, was stuck with it. He had to hold onto it as one must often seem to cherish an unwanted gift from a very important donor. Reston's vanity was involved, and Wicker was compelled to respect it until some graceful retreat or alternative could be arranged to Reston's satisfaction. It was obvious to nearly everyone, however, that Wicker was devoting most of his time and energy to the writing of his column, which had become an excellent addition to *The Times'* editorial page. Even the New York editors privately admitted this. Salisbury, in fact, had lately become a fervent fan of Wicker's writing, admiring the emotion and perception that Wicker regularly displayed in his reports of shifting moods within the capital and the nation.

And yet, strangely, Wicker was the only columnist who was not being featured by *The Times* in its promotional advertising. Russell Baker, C. L. Sulzberger, and Reston were regularly advertised by *The Times,* often with their photographs, and *The Times* did the same for such specialists as Craig Claiborne and Charlotte Curtis, and for its leading cultural critics. At first Wicker thought it was merely an oversight, although he had felt slighted on the very day that he had replaced Krock as a columnist. The *Times* story that announced

Krock's retirement had rightly recounted at great length the colorful career of the veteran *Times*man; it had failed to mention, however, that Wicker was Krock's successor. When for the next two years Wicker continued to be omitted from the house ads, it appeared that a Southern vendetta had indeed intruded upon the quiet carpets of *The Times*. Wicker's pride prevented him from pursuing the matter openly, but within himself he smoldered, and perhaps it was partly this, along with his many other frustrations as the bureau chief, that had driven him more deeply into his column, permitting the bureau to operate largely on its own momentum. He was not the bureau chief by New York's choice, but despite it, and he had survived primarily because New York had been unable to produce a substitute. It seemed, too, that the impasse might continue indefinitely. Then, suddenly, this situation changed. Wicker learned that New York had selected James Greenfield to replace him.

The idea had been Rosenthal's, and it had been endorsed gradually by Daniel, Catledge, and finally by Punch Sulzberger. Greenfield had had relatively little to do since the abandonment of plans for an afternoon edition, and Rosenthal was convinced that Greenfield could make a major contribution to the paper as its bureau chief in Washington. Greenfield still had important contacts in the government and on its fringe, people with whom he had worked during his years in the State Department, and he seemed to be in a very advantageous position both from the standpoint of getting the news and distinguishing it from the official obscurantism that government spokesmen so often emit. Rosenthal had long been impressed with Greenfield's sophistication and flare as a newsman, and, unlike Wicker, Greenfield would do no writing, devoting himself entirely to the running of the bureau. Greenfield's personality, a smooth blend of amiability and *politesse*, would also help to win the good will of the bureaumen, Rosenthal thought, overcoming what perhaps no other New York editor could overcome.

So the decision was final, and it was hoped in New York that it could be initiated without delay. But when Reston was informed, he suggested that any personnel changes in Washington be postponed until after the Presidential election. Reston wrote a long memorandum to this effect. When he received no reaction to it, he assumed that his recommendation was being followed in New York. But weeks later, shortly before Punch Sulzberger was scheduled to arrive in Washington to take Reston and Wicker to dinner, Reston learned that Sulzberger was still intent on installing Greenfield in Washington almost immediately. The New York editors saw no reason to wait until after the election, and Sulzberger had sided with them.

When Punch Sulzberger walked into the Washington bureau, on the day of his dinner date with Reston and Wicker, Reston was solemn and distant. Reston could not support the New York plan, and he told Sulzberger that he would not be joining the publisher for dinner; Sulzberger and Wicker should dine alone. Sulzberger was somewhat surprised by Reston's reaction, although he had sensed in advance the delicacy of the decision; that was why Sulzberger had come to Washington himself to present the plan officially, and had not sent Turner Catledge. Sulzberger also considered Wicker to be a close personal friend, and he thought that at a dinner meeting in Washington there would be less risk of a misunderstanding—it could be handled in the easy informal way that Sulzberger had often discussed business in the past with Wicker and Reston. Wicker had not fallen from grace in Sulzberger's eyes; instead Wicker would be free to do what he did best, and would be detached from the travail and trivia of office work. Sulzberger had previously been told by the New York editors that Wicker was quite willing, and possibly eager, to step down as the bureau chief, and Sulzberger had proceeded on the assumption that this was true.

But during Sulzberger's dinner with Wicker, he realized that this was not exactly so. Wicker was tense and obviously upset, agitated by the forces of his loyalty to the bureau, to Reston, to himself. Wicker felt bullied by New York's determination to replace him quickly with a bureaucrat of their own choosing; and his private suspicion was that Rosenthal, who probably saw Wicker as a future rival for the managing editor's chair, now wished to eliminate him from the running, simultaneously installing in Washington a less challenging and very indebted ally. Whether or not Wicker would ever be lured by such goals as the managing-editorship was inconsequential to his mood and rationale as he dined with Sulzberger. Wicker felt now that he was being pressed, pushed, and undercut—and he was angry.

After Sulzberger had said what he had come to say, assuring Wicker that Greenfield's appointment would make life easier for everyone, he flew back to New York on the following morning in his plane, being bumped and jostled during the journey by a storm which he thought he would never survive. After dining with Sulzberger, Wicker spent an uneasy evening, staying up all night in a fuming state of frustration and bitterness.

The next day Wicker telephoned Sulzberger and said that he was about to announce to the staff his resignation as bureau chief, but Sulzberger pleaded with him to delay it. There were other details that had to be completed first, Sulzberger said, adding that he had not yet had time to inform Anthony Lewis in London or Max Frankel. Wicker, aware of how quickly gossip travels in Washington and wishing to spare himself further humiliation, had hoped that his own announcement in Washington might imply that he had perhaps initiated the decision, or at least had been an agreeable part of it—he did not want it to appear to have been an ignominious, unconditional surrender to the editors in New York. But Sulzberger continued to urge that Wicker do nothing, and Wicker complied, although his discomfort was perceived and understood by his friends in the bureau, and soon Max Frankel and others were sharing Wicker's despair and were contemplating their own resignations.

James Greenfield was unsatisfactory to them not only because he was a New York appointee and his presence in the bureau would be an affront to Wicker and Reston, but because they truly considered him unqualified. He had been a *Times*man for only seven months, and before joining the paper, he had worked as an airline executive, a position obtained through his friendship with Pierre Salinger. He was seen by the bureau as a "Bobby Kennedy man," and it was felt that his political loyalties would, if he were put in charge of the bureau, cast doubt upon *The Times'* entire political coverage of Washington. They also recalled incidents in which Greenfield, working in the office of Undersecretary of State George W. Ball, had been less than candid with the press, and it was alleged that he had once tried to suppress information from a *Times* correspondent in the Congo and had then favored a reporter from *Time-Life* (Greenfield's former place of employment) on the same Congo assignment. A few bureaumen were opposed to Greenfield because they considered him a bit too suave, a name-dropper, an individual who seemed to be inordinately infatuated with the glamorous side of government life, what little there was of it. In short, they considered him unfit to represent *The Times* as its bureau chief in Washington.

And yet, despite this, his appointment was said to be imminent—and the word quickly spread through Washington. It circulated through the press corps and was discussed on the telephone by the disenchanted wives of *Times*men. Tom Wicker's wife, Neva, thought that the treatment of her husband was disgraceful, and she expressed her feelings in a telephone talk with Reston and in a later one from Carol Sulzberger. Through all this internal clamor the Washington bureau continued its task of covering the news without interruption; but there was an eerie aspect to the reporting, a strange similarity between the pressures being put on the bureau and the front-page stories that the bureau was writing during this first week of February, 1968: South Vietnam had just been unexpectedly assaulted—the

Vietcong had attacked twenty-six of the forty-four province capitals in South Vietnam, determined to overthrow, according to Hanoi radio, the "puppet" government and its American allies. Washington was shocked by the news, and Tom Wicker, reporting the reaction at the State Department, Capitol Hill, and the Pentagon, quoted senators who described the reports as "embarrassing" and "humiliating." But Max Frankel reported that the White House remained confident and resolute, with President Johnson vowing that "the enemy will fail again and again" because "we Americans will never yield." James Reston, as bewildered as most people were in Washington about the Vietcong offensive, devoted his column to speculating on Hanoi's strategy of terror; but days later—as the allies had counterattacked, sending jets streaking low over Saigon, Hué, and other cities in South Vietnam, tearing down what the allies had undertaken to defend—Reston's column pondered the dilemma of the allied decision, asking: "What is the end that justifies this slaughter? How will we save Vietnam if we destroy it in the battle?"

This question was not unlike one that Reston had been asking himself with regard to the editors in New York. Should he stage a counterattack that might block Greenfield's takeover but might also shake the entire *Times* hierarchy, causing a scandal that would damage the paper's image in the eyes of the public? Or should Reston accept the higher decision in the interest of corporate peace and harmony?

Reston waited for a few days; then he left for New York.

In the newsroom, James Greenfield had already accepted congratulations from some reporters who had heard about his appointment to Washington. At first Greenfield was reluctant to comment. The official announcement had yet to be released from Sulzberger's office, although Greenfield had heard that it was already written, and it was these few days' delay that had somewhat worried him. When he had revealed his doubts to Rosenthal, he was quickly reassured that there was no need to be concerned—the decision was final, the publisher had endorsed it, Greenfield would become the new chief of the Washington bureau.

Greenfield felt better, but he was still reluctant to talk about it at any length to those who questioned him in the newsroom, and he was amazed when the word spread quickly and he wondered why people seemed so interested—not only newsmen, but government people in Washington had asked their journalist friends about his appointment, right in the middle of the bad news from Vietnam, and Greenfield had just received a call from a young lady who worked for the "Press" section of *Newsweek*.

"We have information that you're to be the new bureau chief," she began, and Greenfield, laughing softly, replied, "Oh, news really gets around," adding: "Did you hear about it in New York?"

"No," she said, "from an excellent source in Washington."

"Well," he said, "I'm in the middle of the foreign desk right now, and there are people around here who don't know about it, and I can't talk very well here . . ."

"Well," she said, "can you tell me whether or not it's true?"

"Yes," he said, "it's true."

"When will it be announced?"

"Friday, I think," he said, meaning Friday, February 9.

"I heard it would be announced on Thursday."

"Oh," he said, "well, maybe your sources are better than mine."

The *Newsweek* reporter said that she would call him at noon on Thursday to arrange for an interview, and James Greenfield said that that would be fine.

On the fourteenth floor of the *Times* building ticks an old grandfather clock that had belonged to Ochs, and a bronze bust of Ochs stares across the wide corridor that one enters upon leaving the elevator. The ceilings are high, the dark wood is polished, and hanging from the walls are portraits of former homes of *The Times* and executives long dead. The receptionist is male, polite, soft-spoken; an individual with a long plain face and reddish hair who seems large and tall enough to redirect angry visitors from the street who occasionally intrude to complain about the state of the world, or about one of John Oakes's editorial indiscretions against some distant sultan. But otherwise the atmosphere on the fourteenth floor is very calm and orderly, and the executives' offices beyond the corridor are large, well-spaced, and quiet.

In the eastern wing, to the left from the elevators, are the offices of Harding Bancroft and Lester Markel; and beyond, the rarely occupied office of Arthur Hays Sulzberger. The seventy-seven-year-old chairman of the board, confined to a wheelchair, usually spends his days in his Fifth Avenue apartment that overlooks the reservoir: there he lives with his wife, his servants, and a pretty young nurse who attends to his needs, and with two frisky papillons that please him as they jump around and sometimes infuriate him when they bite into his favorite pieces of furniture, causing him to bang his cane. But he would never part with them: one of the things that he most remembers about his childhood was that he had not been permitted to have dogs.

In the other section of the fourteenth floor are the offices of the younger top executives—that of Andrew Fisher, who sits behind a modern curve-shaped desk; and at the end of the corridor is the office of the publisher, an elegant suite that is filled with antiques and rather resembles the parlor of the elder Sulzbergers' home—although, when Punch Sulzberger is present, he seems to dominate the large office with his informality. He often sits in his shirt sleeves behind the not very large antique table that serves as his desk, and he seems constantly in motion as he leans, reaches, stretches across the table toward the buttoned boxes and telephones that connect him with his business advisers, his editors, his pilot, or his secretaries across the corridor. The bookshelves around him are stocked with leather-bound volumes of enduring interest, but the books that he keeps close at hand concern the latest techniques of running a large corporation—books with such titles as *Management Grid* and *Management and Machiavelli*.

There is another office on the fourteenth floor, a comparatively small one, that is occupied by James Reston on those infrequent occasions when he is in town. On this cold, gray day in February, Reston had ostensibly flown up from Washington to attend a session of the Council on Foreign Relations, which meets at its headquarters on East Sixty-eighth Street, but the Council was far from Reston's thoughts as he sat in his office shortly after his arrival. He did not have an appointment with Punch Sulzberger, but Sulzberger soon learned of his presence, and the publisher proceeded to walk down the corridor in his typically casual way to greet Reston. Sulzberger immediately sensed Reston's mood, and the cause of his displeasure, but he nevertheless affected a lighthearted attitude, exclaiming to Reston as if surprised: "Boy, you're *really* upset by the Greenfield thing, aren't you?"

Reston's face told all. His skin was flushed, he seemed despondent, and when Reston spoke, his voice had the hard, distant, almost metallic timbre that characterizes his speech whenever he considers a situation to be very grave. A decision had apparently been reached, Reston said, in which "the younger men's blood would flow—not the older men's blood"—and then Reston added, quietly, "I'm with the younger men."

Sulzberger did not know exactly what this meant. The older men apparently referred to Catledge and Daniel; the younger men were Wicker, Frankel, and others in Washington: but did this mean that Reston, joining the younger bureaumen, intended to ally himself with a mass resignation? Or was Reston merely registering his feelings in a vague but dramatic manner?

Sulzberger did not like being placed in this situation. The publisher of *The New York Times* employs very high-priced executives to smooth out difficult details in advance, to leave nothing to doubt, and yet here Sulzberger found himself face-to-face with Reston and not knowing what would happen if he insisted that Greenfield be sent to Washington. As he stood there, watching Reston, and as the two men later moved into Sulzberger's suite, it seemed possible that nothing would happen; or perhaps half the bureau would quit and join the *Washington Post*, the *Wall Street Journal*, the *Los Angeles Times*. But Sulzberger was not so much perturbed by Reston as he was by Catledge and Daniel, and also with himself, for he had chosen to become personally involved when he had gone to Washington to speak with Wicker. Still, Sulzberger believed that Catledge and Daniel, the editors with final authority in the newsroom, should have been able to predict Reston's ultimate move, and they had not, and now Sulzberger, not wanting to trigger the outcome himself at this time, merely listened.

If Greenfield took charge as planned, Reston said, it would have the grinding, disintegrating effect of a buzz saw in Washington, and it would severely damage *The Times* both from within and from without. While Reston had nothing against Greenfield personally, he nonetheless saw Greenfield as an "outsider," and he asked Sulzberger to contemplate how it would look in the capital if *The Times* abruptly moved Greenfield in over the heads of such men as Wicker and Frankel—it would subject *The Times* to the charge that it did not trust the men that reported the activities of the government to run its own bureau. It would discourage the loyalty that New York sought from the bureaumen, and it would so damage *The Times*' reputation that the very best men on other newspapers, and the brightest students in the universities, would not aspire to work for *The Times*. Reston's discussion with Sulzberger shifted back and forth in mood and approach—at times he reasoned with Sulzberger, at other times he implored him, and he also dramatized the Greenfield episode as a battle of the generations: the old versus the young, and, as always in Reston's philosophy, there was the reminder that youth must be served.

When Reston left, Sulzberger found himself confronted by perhaps the most disturbing decision of his career. If he rejected Reston's appeal, he might lose Reston and those who worshiped Reston; but if he sided with him, then he would be reversing his own decision, and his own word would mean relatively little in the future. Sulzberger planned to spend the rest of the day and the evening thinking about it. Reston would be spending the night in a New York hotel, and they would meet again on the following day. Sulzberger had time to consult with a few executives who worked outside the News department—Harding Bancroft and such vice-presidents as Ivan Veit, whom he sometimes regarded as the publisher's confessor. And Sulzberger would consult, too, with his family—his wife, Carol; his sisters, Ruth, Marion, and Judith; and, of course, his mother, Iphigene.

Tom Wicker at this time was in New Hampshire writing about the forthcoming Presidential primary: Richard Nixon had just announced his candidacy for the Republican nomination and Robert Kennedy was yet unwilling to compete against President Johnson. Finishing his work in New Hampshire, Wicker flew to New York hoping to learn more about his own future. He had been very depressed since his dinner meeting with Sulzberger the week before, and Wicker had become embittered days later on hearing it rumored in Washington that he had been forced out as the bureau chief. If Sulzberger had not discouraged him from announcing his own resignation immediately after the decision had been made in New York, he would have been able to yield his position with a bit of grace and dignity; and from New Hampshire he had telephoned Sulzberger to protest the manner in which the Washington situation was being handled in New York. Sulzberger had listened with understanding, and then had asked Wicker to call Catledge and to repeat the complaint, which Wicker did, getting no great satisfaction. Now, a day later, Wicker was in New York.

It was noon as he arrived; the executives would all

be out to lunch, so Wicker decided to get something to eat himself before going to *The Times*. He walked into the Century Club, which is on Forty-third Street two blocks east of the *Times* building. He had recently been made a member of the Century, an exclusive men's club composed of many prominent authors and editors, historians, social critics, and editorialists; this was his first visit, and he felt awkward and very much alone as he entered.

In the lobby he was greeted by a porter-polite Negro wearing a white jacket, and then he ascended marble steps to find himself within oak-paneled rooms with high ceilings, and here and there men sat at tables speaking quietly over their preluncheon drinks, and in the library were other men in large soft leather chairs reading the *Wall Street Journal* or *The New York Times*. Wicker ordered one martini, then another, before proceeding to the floor above, where he discovered the dining area—a long communal table in one room with small tables nearby; and in other rooms were other tables occupied by quiet-spoken men forsworn to avoid all talk of business.

He felt the soft warm waves of martinis flowing within him as he ordered lunch, sitting at a table opposite an ancient little man who appeared to be ninety years old and who explained that he had once edited a magazine. While Wicker conversed hazily with the old gentleman, his gaze drifted around the room, and the rooms beyond—all the tables were occupied by strangers, with one exception. At one table, seated across from Eliot Fremont-Smith, was Harrison Salisbury.

Salisbury was a member of the Century, as were several ranking *Times*men, among them John Oakes, Clifton Daniel, and James Reston. Wicker was unaware of it during lunch but Reston was then also in the club, seated behind a partition with a former colleague from the Washington bureau, John Pomfret, presently a *Times* executive in labor relations.

When Reston and Pomfret stood to leave, they saw Wicker. They both seemed surprised and delighted to

find him there, and the three *Times*men soon became
engaged in rather intense conversation. Salisbury
watched them from across the room. His suspicion
was aroused, but he did not reveal this to Fremont-
Smith. Salisbury had wondered if the Greenfield appointment was going according to plan, but he had not
asked Daniel or Rosenthal about this during the past
week. He had, in fact, avoided any direct involvement,
not consciously but instinctively, with the plan to transfer Greenfield to Washington, for there seemed something not quite propitious about it, although Salisbury
himself could find no hard facts to support his notion.
His feeling was the result of his keen awareness of
office vibrations, and that his instinct was justified seemed
to be supported by the few days' delay in the announcement of Greenfield's appointment. Now, seeing Reston,
Wicker, and Pomfret with their heads together in the
Century's dining room, Salisbury's fine Kremlinolog-
ist's mind was whirling.

He left the club and walked back to the *Times* building. In the newsroom, the editors' expressions seemed
unchanged—Daniel and Rosenthal seemed composed,
and Greenfield appeared to be untroubled as he stood
speaking to a copyreader. At 4 p.m., Salisbury walked
with the other editors into Daniel's office for the daily
conference. Daniel presided as usual, and around him
sat Rosenthal, Bernstein, Topping, and the others. Behind Daniel, dressed in a blue pinstriped suit, seated
comfortably with his legs crossed, gently jiggling a polished black shoe, was Turner Catledge. If Reston and
Wicker had been in the newsroom, they would undoubtedly have been invited into the conference; but
neither man had been seen on the third floor, and Salisbury was perhaps the only *Times*man in the room who
knew that they were both now in New York.

The news on this Wednesday afternoon, February 7,
was no better nor worse than it had been for several
days—the war continued to go badly in Vietnam: So-
viet-made tanks were spearheading the North Vietnamese assault west of Khesanh, and Vietcong forces
were infiltrating Saigon. The Johnson administration

was still unable to induce the North Koreans to return
the captured *Pueblo* with her eighty-two surviving crew
members. In New Hampshire, Theodore Sorensen, acting in behalf of Kennedy, was reportedly trying to discourage any political movement to lure Kennedy into a
primary fight with President Johnson. Senator Eugene
McCarthy of Minnesota, the chief Democratic spokesman against the Vietnam war, was entered in the New
Hampshire primary and was being applauded on *The
Times'* editorial page, which had also condemned Robert Kennedy earlier in the week for neither supporting
McCarthy nor opposing Johnson. . . .

The conference had progressed in its normal manner for about twenty minutes when a secretary entered
the room with a message for Catledge. Catledge left
the room. It was not unusual for Catledge to be called
out to receive calls from the publisher's office, or from
very important individuals from the outside; but when
Catledge returned to his seat five minutes later, Salisbury detected a mild change in Catledge's expression.
It was not that Catledge had lost some of his composure; it was rather that he seemed *too* composed, *too*
casual, suggesting the look of a man trying desperately
to conceal his inner thoughts. When the conference
was over, the editors began to file out but Catledge remained, and asked that Rosenthal also remain; Catledge had something that he wished to discuss with
Rosenthal and Daniel. As Salisbury left the room he
was fairly certain that James Greenfield would not be
going to Washington.

"Gentlemen," Catledge said to Daniel and Rosenthal, after the others had left, "I have bad news. The
publisher has reversed his decision. . . ."

Daniel's white face paled even more, and he swallowed
hard. Rosenthal reddened. Both were momentarily
stunned. Then Rosenthal shouted angrily, "I'm calling
Punch!"

"Don't," Catledge said, softly, thinking that it would
do no good.

"I'm sorry, Turner, but I have to!" Rosenthal replied,

beyond control, walking quickly out of the room and grabbing a telephone at his own desk in the newsroom. But the publisher was unreachable: he was in conference, the secretary said, he could not be disturbed. Rosenthal hung up and turned back toward Catledge and Daniel. Both men were standing motionless in the middle of the big office, as silent and still as the photographs on the wall, two wax figures in a museum, the impact of Sulzberger's decision mounting in their minds. It was humiliating and unforgivable. It was unbelievable. They had been betrayed by the publisher, and now they did not know what to do. Were they expected to resign? *Should* they resign? If they remained, what power did they have? After decades of fidelity to *The Times*, after years of climbing the executive ladder and finally getting to the top, what did it mean? What was the point of being the executive editor or the managing editor if one could not replace the bureau chief in Washington?

It was all too disturbing to contemplate at this moment in Daniel's office, where only one thing was clear —Reston had won. What Reston had won was debatable, but he had undeniably won: New York had again failed in its attempt to control Washington. Sulzberger had permitted Catledge, Daniel, and Rosenthal to go out on a limb, and then Sulzberger had chopped them down. The big question was *why*? Even Catledge did not know the answer. The obvious guess was that Reston had somehow alarmed the publisher and alerted him to the fact that, particularly now, with the upcoming election, *The Times* needed a strong Washington bureau at its best, with the top reporters in high morale. There had been enough dissension on *The Times* within the last few years, and Sulzberger had perhaps felt that it was better at this point to let Reston have his way, although Catledge wondered what Sulzberger's reversal presaged for Daniel and Rosenthal. Catledge was near the end of the line—he had already told Sulzberger that he was contemplating his retirement— but Daniel and Rosenthal would have to deal now, and in the future, with a Reston whose influence with the publisher was clearly formidable. Whether Sulzberger's acquiescence represented solely his own change of mind, or whether the women of the family had played a decisive role, namely Iphigene with her fondness for Reston, was something to ponder at another time: now the important fact was that Reston had won, Wicker had survived, and Greenfield would not be going to Washington. And Greenfield did not yet know this. When this dawned on those standing in the office, Clifton Daniel volunteered to call Greenfield in and break the news, but Rosenthal insisted that he be the one to do it in another place. Greenfield was Rosenthal's friend, had come to the paper primarily because of Rosenthal; Catledge agreed, and Rosenthal walked out to the news-room, where Greenfield was smiling, accepting congratulations from members of the staff.

Rosenthal got Greenfield's attention and led him out of the newsroom into the third-floor lobby, then into one of two very small rooms near the receptionist's desk. These are windowless rooms, barely wider than a confessional, with tall ceilings and small chairs and a single desk no larger than a chess table. The rooms are sometimes used by subordinate editors when interviewing job applicants who are not quite ready for the rites within; or they are used by reporters when interviewing some of the wide-eyed people who arrive at *The Times*, unannounced, with incredible tales that are never fit to print; or they are used by staff members who do not have private offices and wish to speak confidentially. Rosenthal closed the door behind Greenfield, and the two men sat down. Then Rosenthal told him what had happened, and as he did he seemed about to cry.

Greenfield remembered his premonition, his own fear that it somehow would not work out. Even so, he was now shocked. If only Reston had been more explicit in advance, more demonstrably opposed to Wicker's removal, Greenfield thought, then this incredible office blunder could have been avoided. *If Reston had merely dropped a hint to George Ball*, Greenfield thought aloud, Greenfield would have been forewarned

and he would have refused to go to Washington. Greenfield had not sought the bureau job; when he had
joined *The Times* he had been promised an important
position, but nothing had been specified, and Greenfield had not been particularly eager about returning to
Washington, and certainly would not have gone if he
had known that Reston was unalterably opposed. But
Reston had been vague; and New York had perhaps not
really wanted to know Reston's true feelings on the issue, and had therefore skirted it—but now there had
been a head-on collision, and there was no saving face
in New York. Greenfield could see on Rosenthal's face
the depth of his demoralization, and Greenfield was
also overwhelmed with embarrassment.

"Abe," Greenfield said, finally, "do me a favor."

Rosenthal nodded.

"Abe, don't ever ask me to come into this place
again."

Rosenthal understood, and Greenfield resigned on
the spot.

Greenfield returned to the newsroom to get his things.
It was shortly before 5 p.m., the busiest hour of the
working day—the room was crowded with reporters,
deskmen, clerks; other staffmen were returning to their
desks after a coffee break in the cafeteria, or were returning more hurriedly from outside assignments.

One reporter saw Greenfield putting on his coat, and
called, "Hey, Jim, is it true you're going to Washington?"

Greenfield turned and tried to smile, but he could not.

"It *was* true," he replied, softly, "until a few minutes
ago. But there was flack from Washington, and so I'm
leaving. And I'm not coming back. . . ."

The reporter, sensing Greenfield's anxiety, did not
detain him with more questions. He shook hands with
Greenfield and watched him leave, and then the word
quickly began to spread throughout the newsroom. One
reporter tried to telephone a colleague in the Washington bureau for more details, but all the lines between
New York and the bureau were busy. Then a clerk

from one of the copydesks came back with the confirmed report—yes, he said, it was all true, Greenfield had just resigned; Reston had gotten Sulzberger to back down; Reston, Wicker, and Frankel had been spotted in the building earlier, presumably with their resignations ready.

Within a few hours it was on the early-evening radio and television news:

> NBC News in Washington reports that rumors spread through government circles today that former Deputy Secretary of State for Public Information James Greenfield was to be named chief of the Washington bureau of *The New York Times* . . . [but] Greenfield resigned his job as an assistant metropolitan editor at *The Times* today, according to *Times* managing editor Clifton Daniel. Daniel denied that a change had been contemplated in *The Times* Washington bureau. . . . Greenfield was not available for comment. . . .

Rosenthal sat at his desk with his eyes fixed on papers that he was not reading. He was aware of the talk in the room, the reporters circled around their desks. There was laughter among some of them when one reporter arrived and said, in a loud voice, "Hey, did you hear the latest?—the Washington boys just took over WQXR!" Rosenthal could not hear the jokes or comments, but he suspected the worst from a few reporters, those who had been against him since he had begun as an editor years before, and now they were no doubt repeating their old accusations—he was pushing too hard, too fast, and it was bound to catch up with him. As Rosenthal sat, he felt both an inner torture and an outward exposure to the rawness of ridicule—unlike Catledge and Daniel, who were now sheltered within their own offices, Rosenthal had no place to go but back to his desk in the newsroom, in full view of hundreds of staffmen. He felt that he was in a vast gray courtroom being judged simultaneously by several juries, being cross-examined, doubted, speculated upon, scorned; he felt as he had never felt before, the whole tide had abruptly shifted, everything was out of balance, the room had lost its perspective, the New York editorships seemed shattered. His goals destroyed, Rosenthal wondered where he stood. If Catledge had lost his influence with Sulzberger, if Reston was now the publisher's most trusted adviser, then Daniel and Rosenthal could be in a very awkward position: the line of succession might be shifted from New York to Washington, away from Daniel-Rosenthal to Wicker-Frankel or other Reston followers. Daniel would never succeed Catledge, Rosenthal might never become the managing editor. Since Rosenthal could not speak with Sulzberger, he had no idea whether he should leave or remain, and Catledge and Daniel were no doubt equally bewildered. Rosenthal did not want to stand up and walk to his locker to get his coat, a move requiring that he pass the reporters' desks and possibly look into their faces. Perhaps one of them would ask him a question, and he might reveal what he truly felt. Rosenthal could not hide his feelings as Daniel and Catledge could; he was transparent, incredibly honest—when he was happy, it glowed through every particle of his face; when he was miserable, his face floundered with despair or erupted with emotion. Now he felt gloom, guilt—his friend Greenfield had been an innocent victim of this mess, and he did not know what he could do to partially make amends. He would talk with Greenfield tonight. Rosenthal's closest friend, Arthur Gelb, was vacationing in the Caribbean, and there was no one in the newsroom at this time to whom he could turn, or would wish to turn. The other editors in the room had left, or were about to leave; only the bullpen editors seemed preoccupied with putting out the paper —a ninety-six-page edition dated Friday, February 9, 1968, *All the News That's Fit to Print*: Vol. CXVII. No. 40, 193 . . . 10 Cents . . . 56 *Marines Die in Battles in Tense Northern Sector . . . War-Ending Victory Seen As Aim of Enemy's Drive . . . Kennedy Asserts U.S. Cannot Win* . . . Rosenthal read through some of the cables and the carbons of local stories on his desk, but it was difficult to concentrate fully, and he imagined that the same was true of Catledge and Daniel. The great machinery of *The Times* was grinding out another edition, was moving ahead without them, was moving as great ships often move through the night with senior officers drifting in slumber—*we are three men sitting behind our desks in a state of confusion*, Rosenthal thought, his reporter's eye retaining some detachment; *we are in a state of mourning, like the old Hebrews. We are sitting shivah.*

The telephone rang on Rosenthal's desk. It was Reston calling from upstairs. He wanted to get together with Rosenthal and Wicker, at Wicker's suggestion, and Rosenthal proposed that they meet during the early evening at his apartment on Central Park West in the Eighties. It was a very spacious apartment with thick walls where they could have privacy; Rosenthal's wife was not feeling well but he would send out for Chinese food and perhaps it would be beneficial to bring their differences out into the open at once, before a hardness had set in.

But after Reston and Wicker had arrived, and after drinks had been served, it was obvious that this meeting was too charged with emotion and fury to serve any useful purpose. Reston had wanted Rosenthal to explain himself, and Rosenthal said exactly what was on his mind. He charged that Reston, who was presumably dedicated to preserving the paper's image, had now helped to tarnish that image, adding that while Reston himself would not give up his writing to edit the paper, Reston would not refrain from interfering with those who had devoted their energies solely to editing. Wicker, Rosenthal continued, was not equipped to write a column and run the bureau, and then Rosenthal, his voice rising, demanded to know why Wicker did not give up the bureau. Wicker objected to Rosenthal's tone and presumption, and he suspected Rosenthal of excessive ambition. Wicker had no designs on the managing editor's office, and had even implied as much in a note he had sent to Rosen-

thal the year before, pledging that he would do all that
he could to help Rosenthal achieve his ambition. But
now Rosenthal had gone too far, and Wicker was tired
of being the political football between New York and
Washington. After a few more caustic exchanges, Wicker
got up and left the apartment.

Reston remained until the early hours of the morning. During this time he and Rosenthal came to know
one another better than they had before, which was
not to say that the experience was one of harmony or
satisfaction. Each man argued from his own position,
believing it to be in the best interest of *The Times*, and
Reston resented Rosenthal's treatment of Wicker, and
he also thought that Rosenthal had been impetuous
during the whole Greenfield episode. Rosenthal felt
now that he was on trial with Reston, and he resented
being put in so defensive a position, and the situation
was far from resolved as Reston stood up to leave in
the middle of the night. After he did leave, Rosenthal
paced through the apartment in a state of anguished
monologue; and, at daybreak, unable to resist, he telephoned Reston's hotel, woke him up, and continued
the tense discussion. It was an outrageous thing to do,
and Rosenthal regretted doing it, but it was somehow
consistent with the bizarre events that had gripped the
upper echelon of *The Times* during the last several
hours—it had been a total nightmare for Rosenthal,
an executive theater of the absurd.

When he arrived at *The Times* later in the morning,
exhausted yet invigorated by the turmoil of the past
twenty-four hours, Rosenthal went directly up to the
fourteenth floor to keep an appointment he had with
Sulzberger. The publisher was expecting him, and when
Rosenthal had emerged from the elevator he saw Sulzberger coming toward him down the corridor with his
arms outstretched; and then, in the spirit of men who
had shared a sadness, they embraced and walked together into Sulzberger's office.

If Rosenthal had had any serious doubts about his
place on the paper, Sulzberger quickly dispelled them.
Sulzberger was personally relying on him, he said, to

help repair the damage done and to restore to *The Times* the harmony that had once prevailed. They had learned a good deal about *The Times* and about themselves during this experience, and Sulzberger thought that perhaps some good would come of it. The discord had at least been played out to the hilt, it had hit deep and low, and now there was nowhere to go but up. Sulzberger asked Rosenthal to spend the weekend at his country home for further discussions, and Rosenthal felt better. Returning to the newsroom, Rosenthal informed Daniel and Catledge of his weekend plans; he hoped that they also would attempt to reach an understanding with the publisher.

The next day, on page three of the *Washington Post*, under a headline that read: "A *New York Times* Coup That Was Almost Fit To Print," was the story. It reported the details of James Greenfield's departure and mentioned that there had been cheering in the Washington bureau after the announcement, with one bureauman having exclaimed: "We've won."

Rosenthal resented the story, as did most *Times* editors, including Reston and Wicker. There is a tacit understanding among most responsible newspapers that they not expose one another's internal difficulties—*The Times,* after all, had not focused on the *Post*'s executive machinations in past years—but the *Post* on this occasion had obviously not played by the rules, even though Reston had spoken on the telephone during the previous afternoon with his friend Katharine Graham, the president of the *Post*, and with her editor Benjamin Bradlee. But it had not suppressed the story, and now on the morning of February 9 it was in print, and *The Times*' editors suddenly had a fuller understanding of the meaning of the freedom of the press, and they knew, possibly for the first time, what it is like to be on the receiving end of reporting when the news is not favorable.

Despite the peace that Rosenthal had made with the publisher, the older editors still felt betrayed, and they ignored Sulzberger for several days. Catledge finally agreed to Sulzberger's earnest request that their years of friendship not be destroyed by this single incident, but Daniel continued to snub Sulzberger for almost two weeks; and when he finally did speak freely with him, late one day after the news conference, in the small room adjacent to his office, Daniel lost his composure and, in a shrill voice, lectured the publisher like a schoolboy. After that, it seemed unlikely that things could ever be entirely reconciled between Clifton Daniel and Punch Sulzberger.

The Times continued to publish as usual during the weeks ahead, although there were days when Catledge and Daniel seemed listless and utterly dejected. The embarrassing aspects of the Greenfield affair had received national exposure through such publications as *Time* and *Newsweek*, and there were rumors in the newsroom that Daniel was looking for another job and that Catledge was merely marking time until his retirement. But as disjointed as the executive situation was within the paper, the events of the outside world were worse, and this tended initially to have an almost positive effect on the editors—they were forced to submerge their own differences somewhat to concentrate on the sudden chaos in the nation. There was such flagrant disunity within the United States that Lyndon B. Johnson was driven to admit, on March 31, that he could not unify the country, and thus would not seek renomination for the Presidency.

The Vietnamese war continued to be a hopeless struggle, draining both the economy and the patience of citizens young and old, creating factions whose common trait seemed only to be hate and violence. In April, Martin Luther King was fatally shot by a sniper in Memphis, setting off riots in Chicago and Washington. In June, Robert F. Kennedy was assassinated in Los Angeles, where his bid for the Democratic nomination, begun three months before, had just peaked with his victory in the California primary. Between the two deaths, there had been clashes across the land between peace marchers and the police, with white racists calling for "law and order" and Negro racists calling for "black power"; and on the Columbia University campus in New York, in the most dramatic student protest of the year, five buildings were seized, classes were suspended, 720 demonstrators were arraigned, and the president of the university would resign during the summer. The Columbia protest had begun in April as students attempted to force the university to sever its ties with the Institute for Defense Analyses, a twelve-university consortium that performed military research for the government, and also to halt the construction of a nine-story gymnasium in Morningside Park that would form a kind of buffer between Harlem and the Columbia community—"gym crow" was the protest term for it.

But these issues were linked to larger breaches between students and administrators, were part of what was popularly being referred to as a worldwide "generation gap." Now there were student boycotts in Poland, organized protests in Czechoslovakia, surges of youthful idealism throughout Europe and Asia—while old men rushed to buy gold, seeking security and solidity against the unsteady standards of the Sixties. In America the large corporations, computerized, profit-minded, were producing new cars that were grated with flaws and worthless luxuries for a nation that had the best and worst of everything. As the corporations continued to make millions, young men died in Vietnam, and older young men like Punch Sulzberger seemed caught between the prismatic vision of the generation above and the one below. At forty-two, Sulzberger felt what other heads of institutions were now feeling: it was as if they had all been tuned into the same channel and were now all being jammed by the same static. On every level, authority was being challenged by the pressures for change, the prod of publicized protest; young people, though powerless themselves, had gained a fleeting influence through some mysterious combination of electronics and histrionics in a synthetic age—Mark Rudd, Danny the Red, Rap Brown; discothèque radicals and guitar-strumming nuns were the creations of a climate that had turned the heat on Johnson and de

Gaulle, on the international banker, the neighborhood schoolteacher, the cop on the beat. Even such a
fundamentalist institution as the Roman Catholic
Church was being forced into making concessions, being questioned about what had once been unquestioned.

Shortly after the riots had paralyzed Columbia, the
demonstrators turned their attention toward what they
considered another bastion of the enemy—*The New
York Times*. The Sulzberger family, products of Columbia education, had long been influential in the university's activities—like his father before him, Punch
Sulzberger was a trustee of Columbia, and he had supported the Columbia policies (including its military
research ties with the government) that the students
now found morally reprehensible. On May 2, eighty-
two young people assembled outside Punch Sulzberger's home at 1010 Fifth Avenue, demonstrated for
forty-five minutes, and chanted: "*New York Times—
print the truth!*" They charged that *The Times*' reporting of the Columbia protest had sided with the administration and had shown little understanding of the
students' position, and they also questioned the ethics
of a *Times* publisher who served as a trustee of a university that was regularly in his newspaper's headlines.
They saw this as a conflict of interest, but Sulzberger
denied the charge in a statement printed in the next
morning's *Times*, adding: "We do not believe that
executives of a newspaper need divorce themselves
from some service to the community." While he admitted that the editorials—which had condemned the
campus disorder under such titles as "Hoodlumism at
Columbia"—had reflected his opinion, he insisted that
the reporting had been objective. *The Times*, he said,
"had used its resources to provide full, accurate and
dispassionate coverage." But the students and their
supporters disagreed. The reporting, they believed, had
been neither fair nor dispassionate, and they were particularly incensed by one story that had appeared on
page one of *The Times* on May 1. It was a compas-
sionate article that featured the president of Columbia

University, Grayson Kirk. It described him as he stood in his large office that had been invaded by demonstrators—furniture was broken; the floor was littered with tin cans, half-eaten sandwiches, and dirty blankets —and Dr. Kirk, passing a hand over his face, was quoted as saying, "My God, how could human beings do a thing like this?" The story had been written by A. M. Rosenthal.

Rosenthal had given himself the assignment, appearing on the Columbia campus one evening, in response to an inner urge to experience again the fulfillment that he had felt as a reporter. He saw the Columbia story as a very tragic but significant event: a proud old institution of learning was being ravaged by young men that it was endowed to assist, and he wanted to know what had gone wrong, and why. But when he had informed Clifton Daniel of his plan to write about Columbia, the managing editor had objected. It had been understood that Rosenthal, on being made an editor, would retire from reporting, adhering to the policy and practice of both Catledge and Daniel. And until this time Rosenthal had complied. But now the power of authority had temporarily been weakened within the newsroom as elsewhere, and Rosenthal's more independent attitude was also possibly influenced by the recent triumph of Reston, who had never taken the vow of obscurity when *he* had become an editor and who had proven to be the most formidable man on the staff. When Rosenthal insisted that he wanted to write about Columbia, Daniel withdrew his objection. Daniel's eighty-three-year-old father had just died after a long illness, and he went immediately to Zebulon to be with his mother. Rosenthal was left in charge of the newsroom, free to do as he saw fit, and it was then that he wrote the story that described Columbia's tormented president, Grayson Kirk, walking in his disheveled office after having listened for hours to the sounds of police sirens, the smashing of glass, the students' chants of "Kirk must go":

He wandered about the room. It was almost empty of furniture. . . . He was still neat and dapper but his face was gray and he seemed to move and walk in a trance. So did almost everybody in the room. A policeman picked up a book on the floor and said: "The whole world is in these books; how could they do this to these books?" . . .

Dr. David Truman, vice president of the university, was there, too, exhaustion on his face. He wandered through the suite, back and forth from wrecked room to wrecked room and at one point he said, almost to himself, "Do you think they will know why we had to do this, to call in the police? Will they know what we went through before we decided?"

A police inspector strolled over to Dr. Kirk and silently showed him something he had just picked up from the floor that a student had left behind—a piece of iron pipe tied to a bit of rope . . .

The publication of Rosenthal's story enraged dozens of readers who saw Dr. Kirk as a villain of the uprising, a reactionary administrator whose ineptitude had fomented the discord, and whose tolerance of the university's involvement with government military research projects was an affront to the integrity of Columbia. Several angry letters were sent to *The Times*, and in the *Village Voice* there were articles by Nat Hentoff and Jack Newfield that criticized both Rosenthal's article and the paper's broader coverage. *The Times* was portrayed as a monstrous organ of the Establishment that, in attempting to whitewash its sister institution on Morningside Heights, had arranged the facts and conveyed a tone in much of its reporting that vilified the student demonstrators and had not given equal prominence to the causes of their dissatisfaction or to the brutality of the police. (Almost one hundred young people were reportedly injured in scuffles with the police, including a *Times* reporter whose head wound—from handcuffs being used as brass knuckles—required twelve stitches.)

Rosenthal was upset by the negative reaction to his article, and while he attributed much of it to critics from the New Left who would go to any length to fault *The Times*, he nevertheless wondered what had suddenly gone wrong within his life. After a prolonged period of success, recognition, and reward, it now seemed that everything he touched was ill-fated: the book that he had co-authored with Gelb had been condemned by the critics; the afternoon edition that he had edited had been discarded by Sulzberger; the attempt to place Greenfield in Washington had boomeranged; and now the first news article that he had written in years had become a *cause célèbre*. He did not know what he had done, or had not done, to deserve such reversals, but he was fairly certain of one thing—1968 was the worst year of his life.

It was also an unpleasant time for Mrs. Arthur Hays Sulzberger. She was soon to be seventy-six, and she had lately become deeply concerned with the future of *The Times*. In recent years there had been an extraordinary amount of criticism of *The Times* published in various periodicals and magazines—*Commentary* and *Encounter*, *The Saturday Evening Post*, *Esquire*, *The Public Interest*, among others—much of it concentrated on the paper's news coverage, some of it centered on the personalities of the men who help to run *The Times*. Following the publication of these critical articles, Clifton Daniel and his associate editors had carefully reread them to see if they could find any errors of fact or omission so that, should Catledge or a member of the Sulzberger family make inquiry, Daniel would be prepared to reply with a memo that might invalidate the criticism, and might also serve as a basis for a letter of correction to be sent to the offending magazine. Until 1968 Mrs. Sulzberger was convinced, as were nearly all the editors, that there had been little merit in the published criticism. The articles either made factual errors while accusing *The Times* of the same, or they gave the impression that *The Times'* editors were having grave personality differences and were engaged in an internal struggle. Mrs. Sulzberger believed this to be exaggerated, and she said so in one letter that she wrote to the author of one such magazine piece.

But now in 1968, following the Greenfield incident, she could no longer be so sure. She had also been disturbed recently by some stories that she had read in her own newspaper, stories that emphasized sex and suggested the younger generation's complete abandonment of the moral strictures of the past. One article that was particularly offensive to her appeared on the women's page: it described how young college women at New York City universities were living with young men in an atmosphere of sexual emancipation, and one coed who was cited but was not named was a sophomore at Barnard College, Mrs. Sulzberger's alma mater. The Barnard girl was reported to be living with a Columbia College junior in a $100-a-month apartment within walking distance of classes. The couple had lived together for two years, the article continued, and had once flown to Puerto Rico for an abortion. But now, having abandoned birth control pills, the couple was attempting to have children but was not necessarily ready for marriage, believing it "too serious a step."

Shortly after the *Times* article was printed, the Barnard authorities located the girl and sought to expel her because she had disregarded the dormitory regulations and had also lied in the process. But the coed asked for an open hearing, and this prompted student support within the adjoining campuses of Barnard and Columbia: they brandished signs and petitions in front of the Barnard College library, demanding a change in the student housing regulations, and these demonstrations and the debates that followed kept the story alive for months. *The Times* covered it fully, to Mrs. Sulzberger's increasing chagrin. It was as if the editors had just discovered sex, she thought, and one day she chided her son: "Why not put sex in perspective?" reminding him, "It went on in my day too."

But what most bothered her now was the seeming lack of direction that had gripped *The Times*; it was getting larger, fatter, richer, and yet it appeared to have lost some of its sense of mission. When she pondered this, her mood was not lighthearted and the question that she posed one day to her son was not meant to be answered easily or quickly. "*Where,*" she asked, "*are we going?*"

Punch Sulzberger spent the rest of the year trying to reply. His answers were in the form of documents that he composed, regarding them as part of his self-education, and he shared them with no outsiders. He sent the first document to his mother in the winter of 1968, and he continued to work on others throughout the year and into 1969. But within a few months of the Greenfield resignation, Sulzberger decided that an immediate and painful decision had to be made. The executive leadership in the News department had been shattered by the recent Washington–New York confrontation, and Sulzberger felt compelled to replace his old friend and adviser, Turner Catledge. Catledge had been one of the great figures of *The Times*, had taken over a sprawling mismanaged operation in 1951 and had coordinated it; but now, at the age of sixty-seven, Catledge's energies were not what they had been, and the scars from the February feud had not healed, and if the situation remained as it was, the morale of the entire staff might continue to deteriorate. Nobody in the newsroom seemed to know who the boss was; even the senior editors did not know which way to turn for a decision. Ochs had had similar problems a half-century ago, Iphigene informed her son, and Ochs had never permitted his personal concerns to impede the progress of the paper. *The Times* came first, and now Catledge had to be replaced by a man who could reunite the paper, perhaps restoring some of the Ochsian spirit of the past, and there was only one *Times*-man who could do this. James Reston.

At fifty-eight, Reston had been a *Times*man for nearly thirty years, and his stature was such that no other editor—not Daniel, Salisbury, Rosenthal, or Catledge —could question his right to the top job in the newsroom. Furthermore, by bringing Reston to New York, it would remove from Washington the one individual with the power to challenge the New York leadership; it was an ingenious plan that would centralize all the authority in the home office, would eliminate the last of the old dukedoms, and would also represent a triumph of sorts for Washington—their man had gained control of the newsroom, and the directives from New York would henceforth not seem so unsavory in Washington. Punch Sulzberger, his mother, and the rest of the family all agreed that the plan should be instituted as soon as possible, but the publisher, still sensitive to Catledge's feelings, was hesitant about revealing it at this time. So much had already happened in so short a time, and he would have preferred to wait awhile, although he knew that he should not. He did not want to risk losing Catledge, for he hoped that Catledge would remain as a director of The New York Times Company and a vice-president, devoting himself to the general problems of corporate policy and serving in his natural capacity as a kind of elder statesman and diplomat during the period of transition.

Sulzberger was contemplating this in his office one day in April when his friend Sydney Gruson, who had decided to leave *The Times* to become an associate publisher of *Newsday*, walked in for a brief chat. Gruson's new position at *Newsday* had already been announced, but he was not scheduled to begin until May, and Sulzberger, who felt very comfortable with Gruson, decided to discuss the Reston plan with him, adding that Reston had been consulted and had agreed to accept it. Gruson conceded that the move was a wise one, perhaps the only one that would accomplish Sulzberger's aims, although Gruson felt badly for Clifton Daniel. Gruson was one of the few men who had enjoyed a long and warm relationship with the managing editor; the latter had been instrumental in getting Gruson onto *The Times* in 1944 and had also supported Gruson's appointment to foreign editor in 1965. Daniel, who had been under Catledge for so long, would now be under Reston, and would never know the feeling of being completely in charge.

Later that day, Gruson was walking through the newsroom and he encountered Daniel, who was leaving his office. Daniel paused for a moment, and then invited Gruson into the office for a drink. After Daniel had fixed the drinks and sat down in the small room, he looked at Gruson and he appeared to be troubled and mildly confused. "Tell me," Daniel said finally, "what is going on around here?"

Gruson felt compelled to tell Daniel what he knew he should not. Sulzberger had spoken in confidence, and yet Gruson felt a strong sense of loyalty to Daniel, particularly now when things seemed to be uncertain, and so Gruson told Daniel what he had heard. Daniel turned pale and swallowed his drink. Then he stood and relayed the news to Catledge, who consulted with Sulzberger, and thus the elevation of Reston was confirmed.

Gruson was extremely embarrassed by what he had done on this Friday afternoon, and he quickly wrote a note of apology to Reston. On the following Monday, he revisited the publisher's office, and Sulzberger looked at him and swore in a loud voice, exclaiming, "Sydney, I didn't think you'd have the nerve to show your face in this place again!" But Sulzberger did not really seem upset. If anything, he seemed relieved; the word was out. He had since spoken at length with Catledge, and the latter would remain with the paper to help during the period ahead. It was possible that Sulzberger, subconsciously, had leaked the word through Gruson to the editors on the third floor. Among Gruson's many assets and charms, there was also an inability to keep secrets, and Sulzberger knew Gruson well enough to know this. So Gruson had really done Sulzberger a favor, and the publisher's fondness for Gruson was such that he wished he was not leaving to take the

Newsday job. Before Gruson left, the publisher informed the owners of *Newsday* that he would be making attempts to rehire Gruson; and within a year, he would. Gruson would return in 1969 as Sulzberger's special assistant.

Reston came to New York as the executive editor in the early summer of 1968, and within a very few months his presence had influenced the daily coverage of the news and had brought a new atmosphere of informality to the newsroom. Reston walked around the room in his shirt sleeves, introducing himself as "Scotty" to those *Times*men that he did not know, and his "office" was a desk in full view of everyone—it was actually Harrison Salisbury's desk, the latter having moved temporarily into the national-news editor's chair to replace Claude Sitton, who had resigned in May to become editorial director of the News and Observer Publishing Company in Raleigh, North Carolina. With Reston's arrival, the seat syndrome and much of the pomp and ritual of the newsroom was *passé*, and so was the four o'clock conference, which Reston thought was unessential. He did not abolish it, however; in deference to Daniel, who continued to preside at four o'clock, the meetings went on, although Reston himself did not attend, and soon other editors were regularly absent, sending subordinates. Reston held *his* conference at 11:30 each morning. It was held in Daniel's office and attended by Daniel and Rosenthal, Salisbury and Topping, Gelb and the new picture editor, John G. Morris, who had worked at Magnum and *Time-Life*. Daniel occupied his regular chair at the head of the table, but the focus of attention was entirely on Reston no matter where he chose to sit, and Reston's ease and geniality were pervasive—a stranger would never have guessed that there had recently been animosity and discord among editors at this table.

Reston had not come to New York as a conqueror but rather as a conciliator, and the editors now seemed to recognize the need for a *rapprochement*—for the

THE KINGDOM AND THE POWER

good of *The Times* and their own good as well. With a minimum of effort, Daniel was soon able to work under Reston as he had under Catledge, and Reston himself often visited Catledge's back office for advice and reassurance on subjects about which Catledge was better informed. Rosenthal and Salisbury seemed cordial, and it was Salisbury who suggested, at a meeting one morning, that Rosenthal write a column for the editorial page in July while Wicker was away on vacation; Reston endorsed the suggestion and Oakes concurred. Rosenthal had made his peace with Reston after their emotional scene following Greenfield's resignation; Rosenthal had called Reston in Washington a day later, saying that he did not want twenty years of friendship to be eradicated by the outbursts of a single evening, and Reston said that he felt the same way. Rosenthal did not exactly know what his future was under Reston in New York, but he quickly sensed the excitement and change that Reston's presence was bringing to *The Times*.

The 11:30 meetings, unlike the 4 p.m. recitals, were vibrant with new ideas and discussions about what should be covered and how. While Reston did not think that *The Times* should abandon its role as "the paper of record," he did want to reexamine the old definition of news, to eliminate much of the semi-official pronouncements and announcements that *The Times* had habitually honored, and to devote that space to a more reflective appraisal of daily events. Reston had once stated in a speech about journalists: "We are not covering the news of the mind as we should; we minimize the conflict of ideas and emphasize the conflict in the streets"—now he was in a position to change this, and hardly a day passed without *The Times'* carrying an interview with an important man of ideas: if it was not Justice Fortas commenting on modern youth and the law, it was Ben Shahn discussing his art, or S. J. Perelman lamenting the state of humor, or Jean Monnet reflecting on economic conditions in Europe. The difference in *The Times* was not so much the attention given to such individuals as these, who had often been in the headlines before; rather it was the elaborate display that the paper was now giving to what Reston had called "the news of the mind."

A very long interview with André Malraux, beginning on the first page of the second section, under a prominent headline and photograph, was continued in the back of the paper; in the days when the bullpen had decisive power, Bernstein would doubtless have not allowed such an interview or feature story to jump from that page (known within the office as the *second-front* to the back, insisting instead that second-front features be cut to fit entirely on that one page and to end above the index, a policy that discouraged long interviews. And it was no longer uncommon to find interviews with, or speeches by, such distinguished men as C. P. Snow, on page one.

Reston wanted *The Times* to report what the young people of the nation were thinking and saying, and one of his first instructions was that *The Times* print excerpts from the remarks being delivered by valedictorians to various graduating classes around the nation in 1968. If the valedictorians seemed no more in agreement on the national goals or solutions than the politicians or educators, it did not matter; Reston's point was to have "the conflict of ideas" reported as adequately as "the conflict in the streets," and he also wished to suggest through his newspaper that there was more to America in the Sixties than mere conflict. As a result of his editorship, numbers of stories were soon to appear that described the more tranquil mood of small-town America, the hamlets of central Pennsylvania, the flatlands of the West, and within the quietude of Ohio not far from where Reston had been reared— to such places *The Times* sent reporters and photographers to portray the silent majority, to record their frustrations and hopes, to ask them which man they preferred as their next President. Most of them, like Reston, were not very enthusiastic about either Hubert

H. Humphrey or Richard M. Nixon, and while they were worried about the war in Vietnam, they seemed equally concerned about the rising prices of food, the inabilities of television repairmen, and the violence of the noisy minorities at home. They did not feel, however, that America was as bad as the press made it out to be, and much of this attitude was reechoed in Reston's own columns, datelined "Washington," "Prague," "Moscow," during the summer and winter of 1968. While America could not boast of "law and order," this was perhaps all to the good, he suggested, for the alternatives might be totalitarianism, or the sort of suppression that the Soviet Union had just demonstrated in quelling liberal tendencies in Czechoslovakia. Reston wrote several pieces on this theme during the latter half of 1968, reminding readers that the United States, with all its flaws, was infinitely superior to lands overseas where there was "law and order" and little else.

The Nineteen-sixties might indeed prove to have been a glorious time in American history, Reston said in a speech at the University of North Carolina; Americans were not avoiding their problems, as the Soviets were, but instead were struggling with them openly—in the streets, on the campuses, in the courts—and he saw signs of great promise and hope for the new generation of Americans. Reston also found life in New York to be somewhat better than he had expected—the city was a fascinating study of daily recovery after daily turmoil, rhythmic in its discord, and he was enchanted by the everyday sights that most New Yorkers took for granted. From the windows of his skyscraper apartment near the United Nations, he and his wife were enthralled by the movement on the East River below —the endless tandem of tankers and tugs, yachts and submarines, seaplanes and freight-car floats, motorboats carrying commuters to Wall Street, Circle Line cruisers teeming with tourists, scows packed with garbage and being pursued by seagulls—it would make an excellent subject for a story, Reston told Gelb, and

Gelb quickly agreed and assigned a reporter to it, and within a few days a two-thousand-word article with photographs was lavishly spread across the second-front of *The Times*, "jumping" to the back.

As energetic as Reston was, it was soon apparent that he could not both write his thrice-weekly column and have sufficient time left for all the necessary executive chores; and so in November of 1968, in accordance with Punch Sulzberger's wishes, Reston announced the appointment of Rosenthal to the newly created position of associate managing editor, a title that placed Rosenthal over Bernstein, Salisbury, and Freedman, and invested in him full responsibility and authority for the running of the daily paper. Clifton Daniel, continuing as the managing editor, would be available to Rosenthal for higher consultation, but Daniel would be devoting himself more to relieving Reston of administrative details and to overseeing the non-news side of the daily operation. Daniel would also replace Lester Markel as the moderator of the National Educational Television network's news show; Markel, who would be seventy-five in January of 1969, was scheduled to retire from *The Times* and take charge of a project for the Twentieth Century Fund on the relationship between public opinion and public policy. And so, at forty-six, Rosenthal would be serving essentially as an untitled managing editor. He was answerable to Reston, and Daniel would not impose his will over Rosenthal's news judgment; Rosenthal would also be in a position of authority in the bullpen. When Theodore Bernstein had cited Rosenthal as a potential executive in 1962, and had prompted Catledge to make him the New York editor, Bernstein had no idea that Rosenthal's rise would be so rapid, would within six years put Rosenthal in a position to overrule the paper's renowned rule maker, Bernstein himself. But as Reston suggested in his statement while promoting Rosenthal in 1968, the moment had come "to bring along to the executive structure of *The Times* a new generation."

At the same time Reston achieved, as only Reston

could achieve, a smooth transferral of Wicker from the Washington bureau leadership to the position of associate editor. Wicker, forty-two, would now have his name printed each day on *The Times'* masthead on the editorial page, as would Rosenthal, but he would devote himself primarily to the writing of his column. Wicker would be replaced by Max Frankel, thirty-eight, although Frankel's bureau would be an adjunct of the New York office—the autonomous grandeur that had been created by Krock was now a thing of the past, if Krock himself was not. Remarkably, the eighty-one-year-old Arthur Krock was still a resilient fixture in the bureau; and he had just published a best-selling book, *Memoirs*, the contained, characteristically, a few barbs for the New York office. Krock charged *The Times* with "over-organization," a lack of patriarchal spirit, and excessive power and wealth, among other things, but the executives at *The Times* accepted the criticism as graciously as they could. They were reluctant to argue with Krock, having learned from experience that they probably could not win, and they also were now hopeful that the old differences would subside and a new era of understanding would begin. It had been a tumultuous year, 1968, but now it was over, ending on a final note of sadness that brought them together.

On the snowy, freezing Sunday afternoon of December 15, they gathered within a very large, ornate temple to mourn the death of Arthur Hays Sulzberger. He had died peacefully in his sleep three days before, at seventy-seven, living as long as Ochs. The memorial service for the chairman of the board, held at Temple Emanu-El on Fifth Avenue and Sixty-fifth Street, was attended by many of the nation's political and business leaders, and cables of condolences had been received from every part of the world. Among the more than one thousand mourners in the temple were New York's Governor Nelson A. Rockefeller, Mayor John V. Lindsay, Senator Jacob K. Javits, and also President-Elect Richard M. Nixon. The appearance of Nixon had been something of a surprise to most *Times*men in attendance, for the paper had not supported him for the Presidency and it had also recently become involved in a grudging dispute with him because of his running mate, Spiro T. Agnew. One month before the election, a *Times* editorial described Agnew as "utterly inadequate," and three weeks later John Oakes printed another editorial that dredged up old charges of conflict of interest that had been brought against Agnew prior to his election as the governor of Maryland in 1966. These charges, among others, had centered on Agnew's involvement in certain land-buying ventures and his affiliation with a bank that did business with the state; while they had made headlines, they had failed to establish evidence of illegality on Agnew's part, or even impropriety, and in 1966 *The Times* had endorsed Agnew in his gubernatorial race. But two years later, in an editorial urging the support of the Hubert Humphrey—Edmund Muskie Democratic ticket in the Presidential election, *The Times* reintroduced the old allegations about Agnew, concluding that "Mr. Agnew has demonstrated that he is not fit to stand one step away from the Presidency."

Nixon was incensed. In a CBS television interview, he cited it as "the lowest kind of gutter politics that a great newspaper could possibly engage in," adding, "A retraction will be demanded at *The Times* legally tomorrow." But John Oakes, instead of retracting it, reprinted the offensive editorial, thus generating a series of charges and countercharges between the newspaper and the Agnew campaign workers and lawyers. Agnew even took out a full-page ad in *The Times* to proclaim his innocence and to assert that the paper had made errors of fact yet refused to admit them; the headline of Agnew's ad read: "The truth hurts at Times."

But with Nixon's appearance at the Sulzberger service, it was obvious that the next President of the United States did not wish to continue his dispute with *The Times*, which had, after Nixon's election, immediately begun to build its bridges back to the White

House. Oakes had published editorials complimenting Nixon on his selection of Professor Henry A. Kissinger of Harvard as a Presidential assistant for national security, and Dr. Lee A. DuBridge as an adviser on science; and the announcement of Nixon's cabinet—together with the appointment of Daniel Patrick Moynihan to head the Council on Urban Affairs—was also greeted with enthusiasm in *The Times*—as Nixon himself was greeted when he walked into Temple Emanu-El with his Secret Service men to pay his respects to the Sulzberger family.

Turner Catledge shook Nixon's hand at the door, and with an arm over the President-Elect's shoulder, he escorted him up the aisle to a seat in the front not far from where the family was assembled—Iphigene Sulzberger, her son and her three daughters; members of the Adler branch, the Oakeses, and close family friends. In the pews to the right were such leaders as Bruce A. Gimbel, president of Gimbel Brothers, Inc.; Robert W. Sarnoff, president of the Radio Corporation of America; Eugene R. Black, Robert Moses, General Edward S. Greenbaum; David Rockefeller, Laurence S. Rockefeller, John D. Rockefeller 3d. The top men of *The Times* were there: Harding Bancroft and Andrew Fisher, Ivan Veit and Francis Cox; Clifton Daniel and Harrison Salisbury, Theodore Bernstein and Lester Markel and Daniel Schwarz. Among the many former *Times*men in the congregation were Brooks Atkinson, Charles Merz, and Bosley Crowther; and seated near A. M. Rosenthal was an individual who had worked briefly for *The Times*—James Greenfield.

Greenfield was now a news executive with the Westinghouse Broadcasting Company, having done very well since leaving *The Times* less than a year ago. He had also maintained close ties with many *Times*men, including Punch Sulzberger, with whom he planned to spend New Year's Eve. He had also visited with Tom Wicker in Washington shortly after the incident of last February, and there were no hard feelings between them. In October, with the announcement of Jacqueline

Kennedy's plans to marry Aristotle Onassis, Greenfield suddenly received numbers of calls from newspapers and networks seeking help in reaching Kennedy sources, most of whom Greenfield knew personally; among the callers was the Washington bureau of *The Times*, and Greenfield helped in every way that he could.

The service for Arthur Hays Sulzberger was a simple one, in accordance with the instructions that he had written five years ago for this occasion. He wanted no flowers, no elegant casket, no extravagant display of mourning—and no Mozart, a composer whose music offended Sulzberger's otherwise tolerant spirit. The service began with the singing of Schubert's musical arrangement of the Twenty-third Psalm, "The Lord Is My Shepherd." Then after Rabbi Nathan A. Perilman had recited three psalms, and after the choir had again sung, James Reston appeared in the bright light of the altar and climbed the pulpit that had been donated to the temple many years ago by Adolph Ochs. Reston was to deliver the eulogy, as he had done in 1963 for Dryfoos, and though his voice was solemn it seemed to convey a sense of history and continuity as it echoed through the towering heights of the great hall.

The passing of Sulzberger, Reston said, marked the end of the last member of the seventh generation of a remarkable family that had settled in America in 1695, before the country had gained independence. Sulzberger had inherited from his forebears a deeply serious strain, Reston said, a genuine modesty, a belief in service, and he had no fear of revision. Sulzberger was not a moralizer, Reston continued, but he was mortally afraid of abusing personal power, or the power of the paper; he thought of himself in terms of stewardship rather than of ownership, and he preserved the vanishing gift of actually listening to what other people were saying, and then thinking about it before answering. The result, Reston said, was that men went away from him feeling that they had been heard out to the end and that they were being treated fairly.

"If you have any doubt about the enduring quality

of his example and character," Reston said, looking up from the pulpit, his voice rising slightly, "all you have to do is look around. The new generation of this family is already in place, with another Arthur Sulzberger at its head, and he has carried *The Times* to even greater successes than ever before; and they are going to have to step lively, for the next generation is already knocking at the door.

"The test of great leadership," Reston concluded, "is whether it leaves behind a situation which common sense and hard work can deal with successfully. Reverence for the symbol and fearlessness of revision—all that we have and mean to defend—all that and Iphigene Ochs Sulzberger, and her children, and their children, who will learn the art in their time."

Author's Note

THIS book evolved out of an *Esquire* article on Clifton Daniel written during the summer of 1966. The idea for the article had come from *Esquire*'s editor Harold Hayes. After completing the article, and in spite of the fact that I had worked as a reporter on *The Times* for ten years, I began for the first time to see the paper in historical terms, to sense Daniel's relationship to others in the hierarchy, and it gradually began to occur to me that a story about *The Times* was no doubt as valid and dramatic as any *The Times* was reporting.

So the book was begun, and hundreds of interviews were conducted with *Times*men and former *Times*men during the next two and one-half years. Some talks were "off the record," but very few individuals refused to see me, and I was also granted interviews by the paper's executive and its owners, the Sulzberger family. Though my book was not to be submitted to *The Times* for prepublication approval or editing, I nonetheless received permission from many editors and staff members to make use of their personal files and to quote from their letters and memos. I received the loan of family albums, historical data, and other considerations from the publisher, Arthur Ochs Sulzberger, and his parents, sisters, and friends, in New York, Connecticut, and Chattanooga; and I also had access through John Oakes to the privately published memoir of George-Ochs-Oakes, which revealed something of the Ochs family philosophy. The authorized books commissioned by *The Times*—Elmer Davis' book in 1921, and Meyer Berger's in 1951—were very valuable insofar as the history of the newspaper was concerned, although a perhaps more vivid sense of the Ochs family is to be found in Doris Faber's book, *Printer's Devil to Publisher,* published by Julian Messner, Inc., in 1963. But for me the most interesting insights into Adolph Ochs himself were to be found in the private papers of a *Times*man named Garet Garrett, who knew Ochs and kept a kind of diary on Ochs and the editors in the early 1900's.

Garrett, who died in his seventies in 1954, owned a farmhouse on a river very close to the island resort of Ocean City, New Jersey, where I was born and reared. I remember as a boy seeing Garrett entering my father's store, a distinguished gentleman invariably wearing a dark blue hat, dark suit, and with long flowing white hair. He would sit sometimes for hours talking to my father about the state of the world or reminiscing about *The Times*, a subject that fascinated my father, who was one of three people in the town who read *The Times*, receiving it by mail each morning two days late.

After I had gone to work for *The Times* my father asked more than once if Garrett's name was ever mentioned there. I had to say no, never, and I wondered if the high esteem in which Garrett was held in my home as a journalist and raconteur was felt anywhere else on earth. Then after I had begun the *Times* book and was unable to understand enough about the style and character of Ochs from the interviews and reading that I had done up to then, I came upon a copy of *The American Scholar* during the summer of 1967 in which was printed part of Garet Garrett's journal about Ochs. It had been sent to *The American Scholar* by Richard C. Cornuelle, a writer and business consultant in New York who had also been a friend and admirer of Garrett. It was through Richard Cornuelle that I was able to read and profit from Garrett's entire diary.

Another valuable source of information were the *Times*men's own accounts of their experiences while on assignment for the paper—such as Tom Wicker's recollection of Dallas on the day that President Kennedy was assassinated, and McCandlish Phillips' description of his interview with the Jewish Klansman who later committed suicide after *The Times* published Phillips' piece. These and several other examples of personal reportage were printed in *Times Talk*, the newspaper's excellent house organ edited by Ruth Adler.

For the most part, however, the source material in this book came from personal interviews with *Times*men, or from my own observations during the many years that I worked in the newsroom (beginning in 1953 as a copyboy), or from what I had heard while gathered with other reporters listening to veteran *Times*men recalling the past, or from the long letters of reply from *Times*men answering my inquiries concerning certain anecdotes or incidents that are part of the office legend. Newspapermen write superb letters. Their letters are usually crammed with interesting detail and also a strong point of view, revealing not only what they had seen and heard with regard to certain situations, but also what they had personally felt and thought. These last two were of particular importance to me for the kind of book that I knew I wanted to write— a human history of an institution in transition, a book that would tell more about the men who report the news than the news they report, a factual story about several generations of *Times*men and the interplay within those generations, the internal scenes and confrontations and adjustments that are part of the vitality and growth of any enduring institution.

In pursuit of reporting this, I asked those I interviewed to describe not only the situations that they had witnessed or in which they had played a part—such as the events reported in Chapter 20—but also to tell me something of their own emotional reactions, what they felt and thought. The fact that I have been able to write in this book, as I often have, that so-and-so *felt* a particular way, or *thought* a certain thought, during the tense incidents that transpired within *The Times* during the Nineteen-sixties, is largely due to the co-operation of those *Times*men who were so candid and honest about themselves, and to whom I am indebted.

G. T.

February, 1969

Index